EC COMPETITION LAW HANDBOOK 2007/2008 EDITION

AUSTRALIA
Law Book Co.
Sydney

CANADA AND USA
Carswell
Toronto

HONG KONG
Sweet & Maxwell Asia

NEW ZEALAND
Brookers
Wellington

SINGAPORE AND MALAYSIA
Sweet & Maxwell Asia
Singapore and Kuala Lumpur

EC COMPETITION LAW HANDBOOK 2007/2008 EDITION

MARC VAN DER WOUDE
Professor, Erasmus University Rotterdam
Partner at Stibbe, Amsterdam/Brussels

CHRISTOPHER JONES
Head of Cabinet to Commissioner Andris Piebalgs,
European Energy Commissioner

Updated by

NICOLAS CHARBIT
Editor in Chief of Concurrence and e-Competitions

THOMAS CHELLINGSWORTH
Associate at Howrey LLP, Brussels

KYRIAKOS FOUNTOUKAKOS
Partner at Herbert Smith LLP
with the assistance of Ray Cahill
(senior associate at Herbert Smith LLP)

JOTTE MOULDER
Associate at Stibbe, Amsterdam

REIN WESSELING
Partner at Stibbe, Amsterdam

Preface to the First Edition
by GIANFRANCO ROCCA

LONDON
Sweet & Maxwell
2007

Published in 2007 by
Sweet & Maxwell Limited of
100 Avenue Road, London, NW3 3PF
(*http://www.sweetandmaxwell.co.uk*)
Typeset by J.P. Price, Chilcompton, Somerset
Printed and bound in Great Britain by
TJ International Ltd, Padstow, Cornwall

No natural forests were destroyed to make this product;
only farmed timber was used and re-planted.

A CIP catalogue record
for this book is available
from the British Library

ISBN 978–1–847–03241–6

Note: *The yellow star device is used in co-operation with the Office of Official Publications of the European Communities.*

This is not an official publication of the European Communities.

PREFACE TO THE FIRST EDITION

Council Regulation No. 17/62 forsees, inter alia, the possibility for undertakings to notify to the Commission their agreements and practices in order to obtain a negative clearance or an exemption. This Regulation has equally opened to natural or legal persons the right to file complaints regarding restrictive practices.

Corresponding to these rights and obligations is the requirement that the Commission examines the compatibility of these agreements and practices with European Competition Law and also undertakes the relevant procedures with a view to the termination of illegal practices.

At present, approximately 220 agreements are notified to the Commission each year. In addition to this, an ever-increasing number of proceedings which result from complaints or which are opened on the Commission's own initiative must be taken into account.

This represents a considerable workload when seen in the light of the fact that only 85 European civil servants work in the anti-trust section of the Commission. All this becomes even more significant if one compares the number of these "fonctionnaires"—competent for all the 12 Member States—to those in analogous national administrations, certain of which employ more than twice this number.

One of the main preoccupations of the Commission has always been to reconcile the need to take a position rapidly on notifications by undertakings with this very limited level of human resources. In this context, the Commission has striven, where possible, to make use of Regulations giving exemption by category and explanatory notices intended for the benefit of companies active on the European market. The adoption of such texts has the intention, insofar as possible, of reducing the number of agreements notified, whilst guaranteeing the legal security of undertakings participating in an agreement or concerted practice.

The work undertaken by the authors of this book, all fonctionnaires at the Directorate-General for Competition, may be interpreted as a confirmation of the wish of the Commission to facilitate as far as possible the application of European competition law, by permitting an easier access and a better comprehension of this law to those who wish to deepen their knowledge of this subject matter or must, through professional vocation, advise companies on matters being considered by Community authorities.

The effort accomplished by these fonctionnaires is all the more admirable in that it was accomplished in addition to the many daily tasks demanded of them. Their work involves the preparation of legal and administrative acts of the Commission in the sector of anti-trust.

I hope that the sense of public service that has led the authors to write this book may find its confirmation and justification in the practical usage that the reader makes of it.

Gianfranco ROCCA
Director at the Directorate-General
for Competition of the Commission of the
European Communities.

PREFACE TO THE EIGHTEENTH EDITION

The first edition of the EC Competition Law Handbook saw the light in 1990. Its 380 pages listed 311 Commission decisions and 169 judgments of the Court of Justice. This limited production seems an oasis of simplicity in comparison to the amount of materials covered by the latest editions of the Handbook. The bulk of those materials concern the output under rules that did not exist in 1989: the many decisions adopted by the Commission under the Merger Control Regulation and the often voluminous judgments of the Court of First Instance. In the meantime, the ESCS Treaty has ceased to exist.

In addition to these quantitative aspects, European competition law has also changed from a qualitative point of view. The notification system for the antitrust rules has disappeared. Firms must now assess themselves whether their conduct is caught by the prohibitions of Articles 81 and 82 EC. Moreover, the analytical approach of competition law has radically changed. The focus has shifted from restrictions on the freedom of commercial action to the market impact of commercial practices and mergers. It must be said, however, that this market oriented approach is not as new as most commentators tend to think. The Court of Justice already made this clear in its ruling of June 30, 1966 in *Société La Technique Minière vs Machinenbau Ulm.*

Assessing the impact of commercial conduct and concentrations on the functioning of market forces is not always a straightforward task. It is therefore not surprising that the role of economics has significantly increased in competition cases. This should be welcomed: competition law decisions and judgments should make economic sense. However, increased economic sophistication also has its downside. It may lead to Byzantine situations which no longer make sense for ordinary businessmen.

Another main difference in European competition law since the first edition of the Handbook is the role of national competition law. Following a trend of spontaneous harmonisation throughout the Union, all Member States now have competition authorities which closely work together with the Commission in the European Competition Network. This mechanism has its own dynamics. Leading decisions and precedents are not necessarily taken at European level. Increasingly, national authorities set precedents that may be leading for the whole Community. The decision of February 15, 2006 by the Italian authority in the *Trans Tunisian Pipeline Company* case offers an example of landmark case decided at national level. Gradually, European Competition Law is evolving into a body of rules and precedents determined by many players and institutions throughout the Union.

Proper access to the output of this wider system is therefore fundamental for competition law practitioners. The new edition of the Handbook seeks to address this issue by indexing and listing national cases in the Handbook. It relies to that effect on the input of a network of national commentators which are listed on page 180 of the book and on the participation of *e-Competitions,* a website service which was the first to offer regular updates and commentaries on national competition cases. The participation of *e-Competitions* implies that an English summary commentary and text of the national cases listed in the Handbook can be found on *www.concurrences.com*.

Obviously, disclosing the ever increasing output of European and national decisions and judgments is a huge and labour intensive task. The board of editors had to be increased considerably. It now includes a large number of enthusiasts which have closely worked together to produce the latest version of the Handbook. I would like to thank the editors for having achieved this result.

Finally, I would like to conclude with some personal observations. In times where the European ideal is seriously called into question by national politicians and the public alike, European Competition law and, hence, the Handbook offer a good example of how this ideal has already been achieved to a large extent. Antitrust lawyers and economists throughout the Union and beyond speak a common professional language and collectively contribute to make markets work so as to allow the consumer to prosper in peace.

Marc Van Der Woude
October 2007

EC COMPETITION LAW HANDBOOK—2007/2008 EDITION USER GUIDE

The Handbook is designed with the practitioner in mind. It is therefore organised so as to enable the swift identification of cases, legislation and other documents relevant to any question of EC competition law.

It is recommended that the user begin by reading the Table of Contents. This will give a good overview of the layout of the Handbook. The Handbook consists of four Books, divided by subject-matter. All the separate Books are essentially "case citators", but also include references to relevant legislation. **Book One** deals with the general behavioural competition rules; **Book Two** is concerned with Mergers and Acquisitions; **Book Three** collects key National Cases; **Book Four** deals with Coal and Steel.

Book One is divided into 11 Parts. For example, Book One, Part III, deals with Horizontal Agreements, whereas Book One, Part X, covers Procedure and Remedies.

Each Part is further subdivided into chapters covering particular types of agreement, practice or legal question, and should contain references to all legislation, documents and cases necessary for a practitioner's daily work. Thus, for example, Book One, Part III, Chapter 4, on research and development agreements contains a list of relevant cases under heading A, next under heading B a reference to Regulation 2659/2000, and then under headings C to E a "case citator" organised on an agreement-by-agreement and clause-by-clause basis.

Each case or judgment bears its *official case number* next to it, except for competition decisions where a *unique identifier* has been given.

So, for example:

— Commission Decisions pursuant to Article 81/82 EEC: "Microsoft 528"—528 being a conventional unique identifier linked to its corresponding Table 1.
— Judgment of the Court of First Instance: "SELEX T–309"—T–309 being the official number.
— Judgment of Court of Justice: "SGL Carbon C–328/05"—C–328/05 being the official number.
— Commission Cases reported in Annual Competition Report: "Sarabox 8th Comp. Rep. (paras 35–37)"—Reference to report and paragraph has always been given.

When an official case number is provided, users should be able to either move straight from the digest to an online search for the full text of the case/judgment or can consult the corresponding Tables to find its full reference.

The most important or interesting cases are marked with an asterisk.

Book Two is divided into five Chapters, each of which is further subdivided into headings. For example in Chapter 2, which covers questions of Jurisdiction, heading A deals with the concept of a concentration, heading B with the concept of Community dimension, and heading E with Article 9 referrals.

Each case or judgment bears its *official case number* next to it. Users should therefore be able to either move straight from the digest to an online search for the full text of the case/judgment or can consult the corresponding Tables to find its full reference.

The most important or interesting cases are marked with an asterisk.

Book Three is a new section of the Handbook and reports key National Decisions of almost all EC jurisdictions. National cases have been selected on the basis that they should be of relevance for a competition lawyer in another jurisdiction. The missing jurisdictions will be added in the future editions of the Handbook. This section follows the same general outline as Book I and Book II but, under the relevant subject headings, National Cases are presented with *unique identifiers* (e.g. for France: F1, F2, etc.). The cases may subsequently be traced by locating them in the corresponding Tables which give the relevant references to source them (including their web address).

Book Four is divided into four chapters and each case or judgment bears a *unique identifier* next to it, except for European court judgments, which uses its *official case number*. When an official case number is provided, users should be able to either move straight from the digest to an online search for the full text of the case/ judgment or in the case of unique identifiers, can consult the corresponding Tables to find its full reference.

The most important or interesting cases are marked with an asterisk.

For ease of reference, **Tables, Lists and Index** are collected at the back of the Handbook. Tables and Lists are comprehensive (see for example Table 1: Commission decisions, Table 3: CFI decisions, Table 4, ECJ judgments and Table 11: Fines). References are given to the Official Journal of the European Communities and the European Court Reports. Book Three slightly differs in that not all jurisdictions have the same standard of internet infrastructure available for accessing their key decisions and in some instances the cases reported have not been published on the internet. It may therefore take more time to trace the relevant decisions. The *e-Competitions* bulletin is in the process of commenting on all the cases that are included in this chapter. The text of most of these cases in their original languages with English summaries are available on the *e-Competitions* website *www.concurrences.com*.

e-Competitions is the first bulletin exclusively dedicated to the implementation of EU competition rules in the 27 Member States of the European Union. It is a twice-monthly electronic news bulletin and appears in English and on the internet only (*www.concurrences.com*). The bulletin exclusively deals with national competition laws.

e-Competitions is published by Transactive, a subsidiary of the Thomson/Sweet & Maxwell Group, in partnership with the Institute of Competition Law.

The 2007/2008 Handbook is up to date to April 30, 2007.

Note: A new edition of the EC Competition Law Handbook is published every year. This is the eighteenth edition of the Handbook.

TABLE OF CONTENTS

BOOK ONE: COMPETITION RULES

PART I

CONDITIONS FOR THE APPLICATION OF BOTH ARTICLES 81 AND 82

PART II

ARTICLE 81(1), (2) and (3)

PART III

HORIZONTAL AGREEMENTS

1. Cartels

5. Trade Associations

6. Trade Fair and Exhibition Agreements

PART IV

VERTICAL AGREEMENTS

PART V

INDUSTRIAL AND INTELLECTUAL PROPERTY AGREEMENTS

1. Technology Transfer Agreements

PART VI

JOINT VENTURES

4. Legislation

5. Operations/clauses typical of joint venture agreements

PART VII

ARTICLE 82

1. The Establishment of a Dominant Position

PART VIII

STATE INTERVENTION

PART IX

SECTORAL APPLICATION OF EC COMPETITION RULES

PART X

PROCEDURE AND REMEDIES

2. The Handling of a Case

4. National Jurisdictions and Authorities

PART XI

RELATIONS WITH OTHER AREAS OF LAW

BOOK TWO: MERGERS AND ACQUISITIONS

PART I

CONDITIONS FOR THE APPLICATION OF BOTH ARTICLES 81 AND 82

1. Undertakings

2. Effect on Trade between Member States

PART II

ARTICLE 81(1), (2) and (3)

PART III

HORIZONTAL AGREEMENTS

1. Cartels

5. Trade Associations

6. Trade Fair and Exhibition Agreements

PART IV

VERTICAL AGREEMENTS

1. Legislation

2. Distribution Agreements

7. Agreements Preventing Parallel Trade

PART V

INDUSTRIAL AND INTELLECTUAL PROPERTY AGREEMENTS

1. Technology Transfer Agreements

3. Copyright and Design Right Agreements

4. Breeders' Rights Licensing Agreements

PART VI

JOINT VENTURES

1. List of cases on joint venture agreements

2. Types of joint venture

PART VII

ARTICLE 82

1. The Establishment of a Dominant Position

2. Abuse of a Dominant Position

PART VIII

STATE INTERVENTION

1. Article 86

2. Application of Article 86

3. State Responsibility

PART IX

SECTORAL APPLICATION OF EC COMPETITION RULES

1. Agriculture

2. Transport

3. Financial Services

4. Sports

PART X

PROCEDURE AND REMEDIES

1. Procedural Legislation

3. Judicial Review

5. National Authorities and Courts

PART XI

RELATIONS WITH OTHER AREAS OF LAW

1. Legislation

2. Jurisdiction: Cases and References

BOOK FOUR: COAL AND STEEL

1. Restrictive Practices

TABLES

BOOK ONE

COMPETITION RULES

BOOK ONE—CONTENTS

USER GUIDE

Book One is divided into 11 Parts. For example, Book One, Part III, deals with Horizontal Agreements, whereas Book One, Part X, covers Procedure and Remedies.

Each Part is further subdivided into chapters covering particular types of agreement, practice or legal question, and should contain references to all legislation, documents and cases necessary for a practitioner's daily work. Thus, for example, Book One, Part III, Chapter 4, on research and development agreements contains a list of relevant cases under heading A, next under heading B a reference to Regulation 2659/2000, and then under headings C to E a "case citator" organised on an agreement-by-agreement and clause-by-clause basis.

Each case or judgment bears its *official case number* next to it, except for competition decisions where a *unique identifier* has been given. When an official case number is provided, users should be able to either move straight from the digest to an online search for the full text of the case/judgment or can consult the corresponding Tables to find its full reference.

The most important or interesting cases are marked with an asterisk.

BOOK ONE—CONTENTS

GUIDANCE

PART I

CONDITIONS FOR THE APPLICATION OF BOTH ARTICLES 81 AND 82

CHAPTER 1

UNDERTAKINGS

1. Concept of undertaking

World Cup Football 360 (paras 43–60)
UER 373 (para.45)
Stichting Kraanverhuur 382 (para.19)
Dutch Cranes 407a (ground 17)
Alpha Flight Services 432 (paras 49–55)
Italian Tobacco 433 (paras 21–22)
Eco Emballages 480 (para.70)
Mercedes Benz 490 (paras 123, 155–168)
German Bank charges 494 (para.171)
Christie's/Sotheby's 506 (para.185)
Methionine 504 (paras 235–237)
UEFA 519 (paras 105–106, 125–131)
Eurocontrol 532 (paras 21–30, 34)
CIK-FIA 533 (para.27)
Belgian Architects 535 (paras 36–44, 60–64)
Spanish Raw Tobacco 540 (para.564)
Choline Chloride 543 (para.168)
Bundesliga Broadcasting Rights 544 (para.21)
Dutch Bitumen 556 (paras 128, 189)
Dutch Brewers 559 (para.394)
CNSD T–513/93 (grounds 36–40)
HFB et al. T–9/99 (grounds 54–66, 83–88)
Minoan Lines T–66/99 (grounds 116–149)
Piau T–193/02 (grounds 69–72)
★DaimlerChrysler T–49e.s./02 (grounds 85–118)
Avebe T–314/01 (ground 78)
★GlaxoSmithKline T–168/01 (grounds 76–77, 87–88)
SELEX T–155/04
French Beef T–217/03 (grounds 49–55, 97–102)
★Höfner v Macrotron C–41/90
Poucet C–159/91
SAT v Eurocontrol C–364/92
French Insurance C–244/94
Dieglo Cali C–343/95
Job Centre C–55/96
Becu C–22/98 (grounds 25–31)
Brentjens C–115/97 (grounds 71–87)
Drijvende blokken C–219/97 (grounds 61–77)
Pavlov C–180/98 (grounds 72–82, 102–119)
Cisal di Batistello C–218/00 (grounds 31–46)
Wouters C–309/99 (grounds 46–49)
★AOK-Bundesverband C–264 e.a./01
Dansk Rørindustri C–189e.a./02P (grounds 112–115)
★FENIN 410 (grounds 25–26)

2. Natural persons

★AOIP/Beyrard 98
Reuter/BASF 107
RAI/Unitel 131
COAPI 402 (para.32)
Hydrotherm v Andreoli C–170/83 (ground 11)
Becu C–22/98 (grounds 25–31)

3. Change of corporate structure

Zinc Producer Group 217 (para.83)
★Polypropylene 247 (paras 99–101)
ARG/Unipart 278 (para.25)
PVC 305 (paras 41–42)
LdPE 306 (para.49)
Welded Steel Mesh 311 (para.194)
ARD 312 (para.38)
Carton Board 385 (paras 144–146)
Graphite Electrodes 482 (paras 117–123)
Vitamins 491 (paras 634–641)
Citric Acid 492 (paras 177–188)
Industrial Gasses 497 (paras 397–405)
Interbrew & Alken-Maes (para.331)
Zinc Phosphate 501 (paras 236–251)
Carbonless Paper 502 (paras 352–365)
Austrian Banks 503 (paras 473–481)
Methionine 504 (paras 233, 239, 248)
Organic Peroxides 524 (para.374)
Spanish Raw Tobacco 540 (paras 568, 585)
Needles 542 (para.289)

★ Indicates most important cases

[For the tables of case citations see Tables 1 to 4, 11 and 12 at the back of the book.]

Choline Chloride 543 (para.177)
AstraZeneca 545 (paras 885–895)
Italian Raw Tobacco 550 (paras 349–350)
Methacrylates 554 (paras 251–252)
Dutch Bitumen 556 (paras 193, 253, 270)
⋆Alloy Surcharge Readoption 557 (paras 112–134, 130–133)
⋆Gas Insulated Switchgear 558 (paras 337–339, 368–370)
⋆Enichem T–6/89 (grounds 235–242)
SCA Holding T–327/94 (ground 63)
Arbed T–175b, T–137/94 (ground 90)
NMH T–175j, T–134/94
PVC II T–305e.s./94 (grounds 978–992)
Stora Kopparbergs Bergslags II T–354/94 (grounds 60–70)
Cascades II T–308/94 (grounds 23, 55–64)
HFB et al. T–9/99 (grounds 101–117)
FETTCSA T–213/00 (ground 460)
JFE Engineering T–67e.s./00 (grounds 47–50)
Mannesmannröhren-Werke T–44/00 (grounds 254–255)
Specialty Graphite T–71e.s./03 (grounds 391–393)
Degussa T–279/02 (grounds 285, 288, 299–302)
Jungbunzlauer T—43/02 (grounds 122–133)
Avebe T–314/01
Austrian Banks T–259/02 (grounds 69–74, 324–336)
Zinc Producers C–29/83 (grounds 7, 9)
KNP BT C–248/98P (grounds 71–73)
Cascades C–279/98P (grounds 64–80)
Stora Kopparbergs Bergslags C–286/98 (grounds 31–39)
Aalborg C–204e.s./00P (grounds 354–359, 383)
ThyssenKrupp Stainless C–65/02P (grounds 81–88)

4. Collective responsibility of the group

Dyestuffs 27
Continental Can 46 (para.2)
Zoja/CSC-ICI 64
⋆Moët et Chandon (London) Ltd 172 (para.21)
Zinc Producer Group 217 (para.83)
Peroxide Products 218 (para.49)
Aluminium 228 (para.9)
British Plasterboard 299 (Articles 3–4)
Decca 304 (para.82)
PVC 305 (paras 45–46)
LdPE 306 (paras 49, 55)
World Cup Football 360 (paras 65–74)
Interbrew & Alken-Maes 500 (paras 295 & 331
Zinc Phosphate 501 (paras 236–251)
Carbonless Paper 502 (paras 353–365)
Austrian Banks 503 (paras 476–482)
Methionine 504 (paras 228–250)
Nintendo 505 (paras 354–361)
Methylglucamine 508 (paras 203–214)
Specialty Graphite 510 (paras 411–422)
Yamaha 517 (paras 182–184)
Georg/Ferrovie 521 (paras 73–81)
Organic Peroxides 524 (paras 375–390)
Topps 530 (paras 162–167)
Copper Tubes 538 (paras 544–579)
French Brewers 539 (para.79)
Spanish Raw Tobacco 540 (paras 371–400)
Needles 542 (paras 286–292)
Choline Chloride 543 (paras 171–176)
AstraZeneca 545 (paras 873–875, 888–889)
Italian Raw Tobacco 550 (paras 329–348)
European Cement Producers 548 (paras 73–75)
Methacrylates 554 (paras 246–250)
Dutch Bitumen 556 (paras 190–192, 199–203, 228, 237, 262–263)
Alloy Surcharge Readoption 557 (paras 125, 127)
Gas Insulated Switchgear 558 (paras 334–336, 354, 389–403, 415, 432–459)
Dutch Brewers 559 (paras 395–396, 401, 411, 418)
⋆Shell T–11/89 (grounds 311–312)
British Gypsum T–65/89 (grounds 148–154)
All Weather Sports T–38/92
Koninklijke KNP T–309/94 (grounds 45–50)
Metsä-Serla T–339/94 (grounds 41–59)
Unimetal T–175d, T–145/94 (grounds 597–602)
Siderurgica T–175h, T–156/94 (grounds 136–144)
HFB et al. T–9/99 (grounds 66, 83–88, 525–526)
Michelin T–203/01 (grounds 289–293)
Minoan Lines T–66/99 (ground 116)
Tokai Carbon T–236e.s./01 (ground 281)
Specialty Graphite T–71e.s./03 (grounds 58–61, 390)
DaimlerChrysler T–49e.s./02 (grounds 218–221)
Hoek Loos T–304/02 (grounds 117–122, 129)
Jungbunzlauer T–43/02 (grounds 122–133)
⋆Avebe T–314/01 (grounds 135–141, 145)
Akzo Nobel T–330/01 (grounds 81–89)
⋆Carbonless Paper T–109/02 (grounds 132–150)
⋆ICI C–48/69 (grounds 131–146)
Ciba-Geigy C–52/69 (grounds 43–45)

[For the tables of case citations see Tables 1 to 4, 11 and 12 at the back of the book.]

Sandoz C–53/69 (grounds 43–45)
Continental Can C–6/72 (grounds 15–16)
ICI & CSC C–6/73 (grounds 36–41)
AEG C–107/82 (grounds 49, 53)
Orkem C–374/87 (grounds 5–7)
Commission v Anic C–49/92P (grounds 139–145)
Stora Kopparbergs Bergslags C–286/98 (grounds 26–29)
Metsa Serla Oyj C–294/98P (grounds 32–37)
SCA Holding C–297/98 (grounds 23–30)
Aalborg 384 (grounds 354–359)
Dansk Rørindustri C–189e.a./02P (grounds 116–130)
ThyssenKrupp Stainless C–65/02P (grounds 66–69)

5. Intra-enterprise conspiracy doctrine

Christiani & Nielsen 21
★Kodak 29
BMW Belgium 126 (para.21)
Moët et Chandon (London) Ltd 172
Ijsselcentrale 335 (para.22–24)
Gosme/Martell 340 (para.30)
World Cup Football 360 (paras 65–74)
ZERA 374 (para.94)
HOV SVZ/MCN 381 (para.51)
German Bank charges 494 (para.171)
Zip fasteners 7th Comp. Rep. (paras 29–32)
Danish Fur Breeders T–66/89 (grounds 49–56)
Viho Europe T–102/92 (grounds 47–54)
Baustahlgewebe T–145/89 (grounds 74–82)
Tréfileurope T–141/89 (ground 129)
Consten & Grundig C–56/64
Italy v Council and Commission C–32/65
Beguélin v GL C–22/71 (grounds 7–9)
Centrafarm v Sterling Drug C–15/74 (para.41)
Centrafarm & De Peijper v Winthrop C–16/74 (paras 31–32)
BMW Belgium C–32/78 (paras 36–37)
Bodson v Pompes Funébres C–30/87 (grounds 19–21)
Ahmed Saeed v Zentrale C–66/86 (grounds 35–36)
★Viho C–73/95P
ThyssenKrupp Stainless C–65/02P (grounds 66–69)

6. Difference between undertakings and public bodies

Cane Sugar Supply Agreements 150 (paras 2, 20)
Aluminium 228 (para.9)
Magill 307 (para.19)
Spanish Courier Services 324 ARD 312
Ijsselcentrale 335 (para.21)
Eurocontrol 532 (paras 25–30)
Belgian Architects 535 (paras 41–43)
European Cement Producers 548 (paras 73–75)
Aéroports de Paris T–128/98 (grounds 75–82)
FENIN T–319/99 (ground 37)
★SELEX T–155/04
Sacchi C–155/73
★Italy C–41/83 (grounds 18–20)
Bodson v Pompes Funébres C–30/87 (ground 18)
★Höfner v Macrotron C–41/90 (grounds 21–23)
Poucet C–159/91
French Insurance C–244/94
Mauri C–250/03 (grounds 28–37)
Coname C–213/03 (grounds 12–13)

CHAPTER 2

EFFECT ON TRADE BETWEEN MEMBER STATES

A. GUIDELINES ON THE EFFECT OF TRADE CONCEPT CONTAINED IN ARTICLES 81 AND 82 OF THE TREATY [2004] O.J. C101/8

B. CASES ON DELIMITATION OF COMMUNITY COMPETENCE

★Grundig/Consten 5
Walt Wilhelm C–14/68 (para.3)
Delaval/Stork I 114 (para.3)
Woodpulp 227 (para.136)
SPO T–29/92 (ground 227)
LTM v MBU C–56/95
★Consten & Grundig C–56/64
Völk v Vervaecke C–5/69 (grounds 5–7)
Bilger v Jehle C–43/69 (grounds 5–6)
Hugin C–22/78 (ground 17)
Alsatel v Novasam C–247/86 (ground 11)

[For the tables of case citations see Tables 1 to 4, 11 and 12 at the back of the book.]

C. THE ASSESSMENT OF THE EFFECT ON TRADE

1. Direct, indirect, actual or potential effect

ServiceMaster 296 (para.23)
Scottish Nuclear 339 (para.31)
British Sugar II 434 (paras 155–157)
German Bank charges 494 (para.149)
Austrian Banks 503 (paras 439 & 456–459)
Christie's/Sotheby's 506 (paras 176–177)
Needles 542 (para.279)
Spanish Raw Tobacco 540 (paras 315–317, 333–336)
Italian Raw Tobacco 550 (paras 295–296)
Methacrylates 554 (paras 241–244)
Dutch Bitumen 556 (para.169)
Gas Insulated Switchgear 558 (paras 310–311)
Dutch Brewers 559 (paras 385–393)
RTE T–69/89 (grounds 76–78)
BBC T–70/89 (grounds 64–67)
Danish Fur Breeders T–66/89 (grounds 41–44)
British Gypsum T–65/89 (grounds 134–136)
SPO T–29/92 (ground 235)
Boël T–142/89 (grounds 100–101)
Société Métallurgique de Normandie T–147/89 (grounds 83–84)
Tréfilunion T–148/89 (grounds 98–105)
Société des Treillis et Panneaux Soudés T–151/89 (grounds 79–85)
VGB T–77/94 (139–146)
PVC II 467 T–305e.s./94 (grounds 753–755)
Atlantic Container Line T–395/94 (grounds 79–82)
Ke Kelit T–17/99 (ground 58)
JFE Engineering T–67e.s./00 (grounds 392–394)
Austrian Banks T–259/02 (grounds 162–166)
French Beef T–217/03 (grounds 63–68)
⋆LTM v MBU C–56/95
Völk v Vervaecke C–5/69 (grounds 5–7)
Bilger v Jehle C–43/69 (grounds 5–6)
Cadillon v Höss C–1/71 (ground 6)
Béguelin v GL C–22/71 (ground 18)
Suiker Unie C–40/73 (grounds 305–310, 530–553, 578–602)
Miller C–19/77 (grounds 8–10)
Hugin C–22/78 (ground 17)
Pioneer C–100/80 (ground 84)
AEG C–107/82 (ground 60)
Michelin C–322/81 (ground 104)
Höfner v Macrotron C–41/90 (grounds 32–33)
⋆Delimitis v Henninger Bräu C–234/89
Woodpulp C–89/85 (grounds 143–144)
Carlo Bagnasco C–215/96
Montecatini C–235/92P (grounds 168–170)
British Sugar C–359/01P (grounds 27 ff)
Italian Insurers 412 (grounds 38–51)
Asnef-Equifax 418 (grounds 34–44)
Dalmine 425 (grounds 89–91)

2. Structural arguments

2.1. Agreement may affect the structure of competition in the Common Market

Centraal Bureau voor de Rijwielhandel 118 (para.30)
Aluminium 228 (para.13)
⋆ENI/Montedison 256
Continental Can 46 (para.32)
ABG/Oil Companies 113
Michelin 165 (paras 51–52)
ECS/AKZO 242 (para.88)
Tetra Pak I 289 (para.48)
British Sugar 286 (para.79)
Organic Peroxides 524 (paras 362–366)
AstraZeneca 545 (paras 868–969)
⋆ICI & CSC C–6/73 (ground 33)
Stremsel C–61/80 (grounds 14–15)
United Brands C–27/76 (grounds 197–203)
Hoffmann-La Roche C–85/76 (grounds 124–127)
Greenwich v SACEM C–22/79 (grounds 11–13)
GVL C–7/82 (grounds 37–38)
Bodson v Pompes Funébres C–30/87 (grounds 22–25)
Glöckner C–475/99 (grounds 44–50)

2.2. Elimination of a competitor

ABG/Oil Companies 113
⋆ECS/AKZO 242 (para.88)
British Sugar 286 (para.79)
SABENA 295 (para.33)
United Brands C–27/76 (grounds 197–203)

2.3. Involvement of a transnational company

Delaval/Stork I 114 (para.8)
Flat Glass (Benelux) 216 (para.47)
Fire Insurance 220 (paras 30–32)
⋆Fatty Acids 254 (para.48)
Belgian Banking Association 261 (paras 38–43)
ABI 262 (paras 46, 52)
Yves Rocher 265 (para.55)
Continental/Michelin 290 (paras 19–20)

[For the tables of case citations see Tables 1 to 4, 11 and 12 at the back of the book.]

Flat Glass 300
Eirpage 344 (para.13)
Assurpol 346 (para.34)
Langnese Iglo T–7/93 (ground 122)
SSI C–240/82 (ground 49)
⋆Fire Insurance C–45/85 (grounds 48–49)
Bodson v Pompes Funébres C–30/87 (grounds 22–25)
Industrial 497 paras (370–374)

3. Cumulative effect of parallel agreements

3.1. Similar agreements concluded by the same and other companies

Breeders' rights; roses 236 (para.24)
Whitbread 439 (paras 106–118)
Vichy T–19/91 (ground 80)
Langnese Iglo T–7/93 (grounds 94–114, 129)
Schöller T–9/93 (grounds 71–88, 95–96)
⋆De Haecht v Wilkin I C–23/67
Bilger v Jehle C–43/69 (ground 5)
De Norre v Concordia C–47/76 (grounds 6–7)
Lancôme v Etos C–99/79
Delimitis v Henninger Bräu C–234/89

3.2. Similar agreements concluded by the same company

Nutrasweet 18th Comp. Rep. (para.50)
Béguelin v GL C–22/71 (grounds 13–18)
Dassonville C–8/74 (ground 13)
⋆Louis Erauw v La Hesbignonne C–27/87 (ground 18)
Neste C–214/99 (grounds 25–36)

4. Consideration of the agreement as a whole

Aluminium 228 (para.13)
Austrian Banks 503 (paras 443–448)
VGB T–77/94 (ground 126)
Austrian Banks T–259/02 (grounds 168–178)
⋆Windsurfing C–193/83 (grounds 96–97)
Louis Erauw v La Hesbignonne C–27/87 (ground 16)
PVC II 467, T–305e.s./94 (grounds 953–960)

5. Export bans, a per se rule?

WEA/Fillipacchi Music S.A. 68 (para.8)
Advocaat Zwarte Kip 79 Miller 108 (paras 5–6, 10–17)
Gerofabriek 111
⋆BMW Belgium 126 (para.23)
Arthur Bell & Sons Ltd 135
Teacher & Sons 136
Johnson & Johnson 160 (paras 35–36)
Moët et Chandon (London) Ltd 172 (para.13)
National Panasonic 186 (paras 55–56)
Polistil/Arbois 211 (paras 40–43, 50–51)
Bayer/Dental 327
Gosme/Martell 340 (para.36)
Newitt/Dunlop 351 (para.48)
⋆Needles 542 (paras 283–285)
Topps 530 (para.131)
Peugeot 549 (para.137)
⋆Parker Pen T–77/92 (grounds 37–40)
⋆Miller C–19/77 (grounds 7–15)
Woodpulp C–89/85 (ground 176)

6. Use of raw material for a product/service that is exported

Aluminium 228 (para.13)
ABI 262 (para.48)
Far Eastern Freight 399 (para.54)
Trans Atlantic 393A (paras 294–296)
Spanish Raw Tobacco 540 (paras 317, 334–336)
⋆BNIC v Clair C–123/83 (grounds 28–30)
Vlaamse Reisbureaus C–311/85
BNIC/Aubert C–136/86 (ground 18)
Woodpulp C–89/85 (ground 142)

7. Product/service cross-border in nature

German Bank charges 494 (para.156)
Christie's/Sotheby's 506 (para.180)

D. TYPES OF AGREEMENT THAT DO NOT NECESSARILY AFFECT TRADE BETWEEN MEMBER STATES

1. Minor importance: appreciability

See Notice on agreements of minor importance
SAFCO 48
Advocaat Zwarte Kip 79
Miller 108 (paras 12–15)
BMW Belgium 126 (para.23)
Natursteinplatten 159
Polistil/Arbois 211 (para.51)
Fire Insurance 220 (paras 33–36)
Breeders' rights; roses 236
⋆ABI 262 (paras 37–41)
Charles Jourdan 298 (para.35)
Vichy 334 (para.19)
⋆Eco System 344a (para.23)
Dutch Building Cartel 349 (paras 110–111)

[For the tables of case citations see Tables 1 to 4, 11 and 12 at the back of the book.]

Mars/Langnese 369 (paras 76–107)
Fujitsu AMD 395 (para.30)
Volkswagen 475 (paras 81–91)
Dunlop T–43/92 (grounds 39–46)
VGB T–77/94 (ground 139)
Ke Kelit T–17/99 (ground 58)
★Völk v Vervaecke C–5/69 (ground 7)
Cadillon v Höss 1/71 (grounds 8–9)
Papiers Peints C–73/74 (grounds 27–29)
★Miller C–19/77 (grounds 10, 15)
Hugin C–22/78 (grounds 15–26)
Salonia v Poidomani & Baglieri C–126/80 (ground 17)
AEG C–107/82 (ground 58)
Ciments et Bétons v Kerpen C–319/82 (ground 8)
Van der Har v Kaveka 110 (grounds 13–14)
Louis Erauw v La Hesbignonne C–27/87
Carlo Bagnasco C–215/96
Pavlov C–180/98 (grounds 94–97)
British Sugar C–359/01P (ground 31)

2. Trade with third states

2.1. Export to third states

DECA 6
Cobelaz 15
Cobelaz Cokes 16
CFA 18
★VVVF 22
SEIFA 23
Omega 33 (para.5)
Supexi 34
★The Distillers Company 123 (paras I.2.1, III.1.1(b))
Zinc 189
Cement 394 (paras 58, 60, 61, 63)
Organic Peroxides 524 (paras 265, 296)
Trans Atlantic 393A (paras 289–293)
Iqbal 21st Comp. Rep. (page 334).
Cement T–25/95 grounds (3868–3869)
★Greenwich v SACEM C–22/79 (grounds 11–13)
Zinc Producers C–29/83
Gøttrup-Klim v DLG C–250/92 (grounds 53–56)
★Javico/Yves Saint Laurent C–306/96

2.2. Import from third states

Grosfillex/Fillestorf I
Bendix/Mertens and Straet 3
Rieckerman 17
Kodak 29 (para.20)
Raymond/Nagoya 57
Frubo 80
Franco-Japanese Ball-Bearings 81
Aluminium 228 (para.13)
Siemens/Fanuc 246
BBC Brown Boveri 291 (para.22)
French African Shipping 353 (para.43)
Quantel 357 (para.41)
CEWAL 371 (paras 39–40, 92–96)
BT/MCI 387 (para.49)
TACA 441 (paras 386–396, 568–575)
Organic Peroxides 524 (paras 265, 296)
BEUC T–37/92 (ground 75)
CMB a.o./Commission T–24/93 (grounds 201–205)
JFE Engineering T–67e.s./00 (grounds 392–394)
★Frubo C–71/74 (grounds 33–39)
★EMI-CBS C–51/75 (grounds 25–29)
Tepea C–28/77 (grounds 47–48)

2.3 Trade between third states

Fujitsu AMD 395 (para.39)

3. Export boosters: increasing trade

Convention Faience 2
Grundig/Consten 5
Ceramic Tiles 35
★Floral 148 (para.II.3)
Milchfoerderungsfonds 221 (para.31)
Tréfileurope T–141/89 (ground 57)
★Consten & Grundig C–56/64
ANTIB C–272/85 (ground 30)
Asnef-Equifax 418 (ground 38)

4. National cartels

Cobelaz 15 (para.6)
Cobelaz Cokes 16
CFA 18
SEIFA 23
Supexie 34
Ceramic Tiles 35
VCH 47 (para.17)
Central Heating 60
Heaters and Boilers 72
Belgian Wallpaper 78
Fireplaces 90
Bronbemaling 95
Bomée-Stichting 97
Centraal Bureau voor de Rijwielhandel 118 (para.30)
CSV 134 (paras 73–80)
Fire Insurance 220 (paras 29–36)
★Roofing Felt 248 (paras 87–93)
Meldoc 253 (paras 70–73)
Flat Glass 300 (para.71)

Dutch Banking Association 310 (paras 58–60)
Eirpage 344 (para.13)
Assurpol 346 (para.33)
U.K. Tractors 347 (paras 57–58)
Dutch Building Cartel 349 (paras 102–113)
COAPI 402 (para.40)
Dutch Brewers 559 (para 385–393)
SPO T–29/92 (ground 229)
Austrian Banks T–259/02 (grounds 180–186)
★Cement Dealers C–8/72 (grounds 28–32)
★Papiers Peints C–73/74 (grounds 25–27)
FEDETAB C–209/78 (grounds 165–172)
Salonia v Poidomani & Baglieri C–126/80 (grounds 11–17)
Remia C–42/84 (grounds 22–24)
SSI C–240/82 (ground 46)
NSO C–260/82 (ground 58)
Belasco C–246/86 (grounds 33–37)
Carlo Bagnasco C–215/96

CHAPTER 3

WITHIN THE COMMON MARKET: EXTRA TERRITORIALITY

Rieckermann 17
VVVF 22 Dyestuffs 27
Raymond/Nagoya 57

A. CASES

Grosfillex/Fillestorf 1
Bendix/Mertens and Straet 3
Franco-Japanese Ball-Bearings 81
White Lead 142 (para.32)
Campari 130
Cast Iron & Steel Rolls 198 (para.66)
★Woodpulp 227 (paras 78–79)
Aluminium 228 (para.14)
Polypropylene 247 (para.95)
PVC 305 (para.40)
LdPE 306 (paras 47–48)
ANSAC 333a
Carton Board 385 (para.139)
Specialty Graphite 510 (paras 394–395)
Gas Insulated Switchgear 558 (paras 314–318)
1st Comp. Rep. (para.131)
2nd Comp. Rep. (paras 4–6, 17)
The Tripoli & Teheran Oil Agreements 2nd Comp. Rep. (para.61)
6th Comp. Rep. (paras 37–39)
11th Comp. Rep. (paras 34–42)
Gencor T–102/96 (grounds 90–94)
Béguelin v GVL C–22/71 (ground 11)
ICI C–48/69 (grounds 125–130)
Ciba-Geigy C–52/69 (grounds 10–12, 41–52)
Sandoz C–53/69 (grounds 10–12, 41–52)
Contintental Can 6/72 (ground 16)
Greenwich v SACEM C–22/79
Zinc Producers C–29/83
★Woodpulp C–89/85

B. NOTICE OF OCTOBER 21, 1972 ON IMPORTS FROM JAPAN [1972] O.J. C111/13

CHAPTER 4

DEFINITION OF RELEVANT MARKET

Commission Notice of December 9, 1997 on the Definition of Relevant Market for the Purposes of Community Competition Law [1997] O.J. C372/5

[For the tables of case citations see Tables 1 to 4, 11 and 12 at the back of the book.]

PART II

ARTICLE 81(1), (2) AND (3)

CHAPTER 1

AGREEMENTS

A. DEFINITION OF AGREEMENT

1.1. Understanding

Kodak 29 (paras 11–13)
Franco-Japanese Ball-Bearings 81
★Polypropylene 247 (paras 81–82)
Fisher-Price 275 (para.19)
PVC 305 (paras 29–31)
LdPE 306 (paras 37 -38)
HOV SVZ/MCN 381 (paras 46–109)
Carton Board 385 (para.126)
Cement 394 (paras 45, 46, 53)
Vitamins 491 (paras 554–564)
Citric Acid 492 (paras 137–148)
Industrial Gasses 497 (paras 318–330)
Christie's/Sotheby's 506 (paras 147–157)
Specialty Graphite 520 (paras 322–323, 337)
French Beef 513 (paras 121–123)
Organic Peroxides 524 (paras 297–306)
Copper Tubes 538 (para.436)
Spanish Raw Tobacco 540 (para.265)
Needles 542 (paras 234–235)
Choline Chloride 543 (paras 128–130)
Italian Raw Tobacco 550 (paras 228–229)
Methacrylates 554 (paras 204–214)
Dutch Bitumen 556 (paras 128–130)
Gas Insulated Switchgear 558 (paras 224–226)
Dutch Brewers 559 (paras 327–328, 335)
Rhône Poulenc T–1/89 (ground 120)
Petrofina T–2/89 (ground 211)
BASF T–4/89 (ground 238)
Enichem T–6/89 (ground 198)
Hercules T–7/89 (ground 256)
DSM T–8/89 (ground 227)
Hüls T–9/89 (ground 291)
Hoechst T–10/89 (ground 287)
Solvay T–12/89 (ground 252)
ICI T–13/89 (ground 253)
Montedipe T–14/89 (ground 230)
Linz T–15/89 (ground 301)
★Volkswagen II T–208/01
Specialty Graphite T–71e.s./03 (grounds 74 ff)
Luxembourg Brewers T–49e.s./02 (grounds 118–131)
Tepea C–28/77 (grounds 17–41)

1.2. Understanding may be tacit or express

FEDETAB 133 (para.78)
Belgian Banking Association 261 (para.36)
Bayer Dental 327 (para.9)
Solvay/CFK 331 (para.11)
Gosme/Martell 340 (para.43)
ZERA 374
Tretorn 401 (paras 20, 52–56, 68–70)
VW-Audi 429 (paras 121–129)
Specialty Graphite 510 (para.322)
Dunlop T–43/92 (grounds 54, 60–61)
Adalat T–41/96 (grounds 66–72 & 158–171)
Cement T–25/95 (grounds 3443–3444)
Marlines T–56/99 (ground 21)
★AEG C–107/82 (ground 38)
Sandoz C–277/87 (grounds 6–12)
★Adalat 408 (grounds 156–188)

2. Irrelevance of the form of the agreement

2.1. Written or oral

NCH 53 (para.7)
SCPA/Kali & Salz 70
Theal/Watts 110
National Panasonic 186 (paras 5, 43–47)
Tipp-Ex 269 (para.48)
Flat Glass 300 (para.62)
Solvay/CFK 331 (para.11)
Specialty Graphite 510 (para.322)
French Beef 513 (paras 121–123)
Italian Raw Tobacco 550 (para. 228)
★Tepea C–28/77 (grounds 17–41)
Tipp-Ex C–279/87 (ground 19)

2.2. Gentleman's agreement

★Quinine Cartel 24 (para.19)

[For the tables of case citations see Tables 1 to 4, 11 and 12 at the back of the book.]

Tréfileurope T–141/89 (grounds 95–96)
Gustave Boël T–142/89 (grounds 88–89)
Ferriere Nord T–143/89 (grounds 27–31)
Martinelli T–150/89 (ground 25)
ACF Chemiefarma C–41/69 (grounds 110–114)
Boehringer C–45/69 (grounds 27–29)

2.3. Meetings

Polypropylene 247 (paras 81–86)
Scottish Salmon Board 358 (para.19)
Carton Board 385 (para.126)
Cement 394 (paras 49, 53)
Carbonless Paper 502 (para.328)
Methionine 504 (para.212)
Specialty Graphite 510 (para.373)
Copper Tubes 538 (para.436)
Choline Chloride 543 (para.129)
Methacrylates 554 (para.214)
Dutch Bitumen 556 (para.137)
Dutch Brewers 559 (paras 336, 363–364)
Cement T–25/95 (grounds 1353, 1389, 3199)
Sigma Tecnologie T–28/99 (grounds 40–52)
LR AF 1998 T–23/99 (grounds 39, 147–159)
Ke Kelit T–17/99 (ground 38)
Brugg Rohrsysteme T–15/99 (grounds 36–39, 73)
Specialty Graphite T–71e.s./03 (grounds 65–66)
Degussa T–279/02 (grounds 128–129, 134–135)
Commission v Anic C–49/92P (grounds 72–88)
Sarrió C–219/98 (grounds 50–51)
Dansk Rørindustri C–189e.a./02P (grounds 142–150)
Acerinox C–57/02P (grounds 46–52)
Adriatica C–111/04P (grounds 48–53)

2.4. Unilateral conduct of a company in a contractual context

2.4.1. Sales conditions

⋆Kodak 29 (para.14)
Du Pont de Nemours Germany 71
Deutsche Philips 73
Gerofabriek 111 (para.II.a)
Arthur Bell & Sons Ltd 135
Teacher & Sons 136
⋆Johnson & Johnson 160 (para.28)
Moët et Chandon (London) Ltd 172 (para.10)
Sandoz 272 (para.49)
Fisher-Price 275 (para.49)
Bayer Dental 327
Opel Nederland 467
JCB 479 (paras 147–148)
Industrial Gasses 497 (para.351)
Topps 530 (paras 81–83)
Peugeot 549 (paras 89–91)
Volkswagen T–62/98 (ground 231)
Adalat T–41/96
GlaxoSmithKline T–168/01 (grounds 75–88)
Bayer C–2 & C–3/01P

2.4.2. Circular/recommendation/instruction

WEA/Filipacchi Music S.A. 68
BMW Belgium 126 (paras 3–5, 19–21)
FEDETAB 133 (paras 58–61, 94)
Ford Werke AG 199 (paras 21, 36)
⋆Konica 277 (para.36)
Eco System 344a (para.23)
Opel 467
Volkswagen 474 (paras 57–69)
Mercedes Benz 490 (paras 125–129)
Yamaha 517 (para.87)
Topps 530 (paras 81–83)
Peugeot 549 (paras 89–101)
Volkswagen T–62/98 (ground 231)
⋆Volkswagen II T–208/01
FEDETAB C–209/78 (grounds 85–89, 102)
Ford C–25/84 (grounds 20–21)
Volkswagen C–338/00P (grounds 60–67)
Bayer C–2 & C–3/01P
⋆Volkswagen 411

2.4.3. Refusal to sell in the framework of selective distribution agreements; termination or threat of termination of selective distribution agreements

Ford Werke-Interim Measures 182 (paras 11–15, 35–37)
Ford Werke AG 199 (paras 21–25, 36)
Peugot 250 (paras 38, 40)
Tipp-Ex 269 (para.49)
Opel 467
Topps 530 (paras 81–83)
Peugeot 549 (paras 96, 100)
Peugeot T–23/90
Volkswagen T–62/98 (ground 231)
Adalat T–41/96 (grounds 66–72 & 158–171)
GM & Opel Netherlands T–368/00 (grounds 79–88)
⋆AEG C–107/82 (ground 38)
Ford C–25/84 (grounds 20–21)
Tipp-Ex C–279/87 (grounds 18–24)
BMW C–70/93 (grounds 16–18)
Volkswagen C–338/00P (grounds 63–64)
⋆Bayer C–2 & C–3/01P

[For the tables of case citations see Tables 1 to 4, 11 and 12 at the back of the book.]

2.4.4. Unilateral measures implementing upstream agreement

Nintendo 505 (paras 297–304)

2.4.5. Monitoring mechanism

Peugeot 549 (para.96)
Adalat 383 (ground 83)

2.5. Court settlement

Nungesser C–258/78 (grounds 82–89)
Bayer v Süllhöffer C–65/86 (ground 15)

3. Relation between restriction of competition and agreement

3.1. Causation

IFTRA Aluminium 92
Flat Glass (Benelux) 216 (paras 40–42)
EATE Levy 231 (para.43)
⋆VBA 288 (para.108)

3.2. Agreement continues to produce its effects after termination of agreement

Quinine Cartel 24 (para.20)
Advocaat Zwarte Kip 79
Hercules T–7/89 (ground 257)
Solvay T–30/91 (grounds 71–73)
ICI T–36/91 (grounds 81–82)
SCA Holding T–327/94 (ground 95)
Ventouris T–59/99 (ground 182)
Sirena v Eda C–40/70 (ground 12)
⋆EMI-CBS I C–51/75 (ground 30)
AMP v Binon C–243/83 (ground 17)

4. Distinction between agreement and public authority decision

Pabst-Richerz BNIA 106 (paras II.1, IV)
AROW/BNIC 190 (paras 2–5, 48–57)
Aluminium 228 (para.10)
CNSD 375 (paras 42–44)
COAPI 402 (para.34)
EPI 444
French Beef 513 (paras 150–156)
Belgian Architects 535 (paras 46–49)
Asia Motor France T–7/92 (grounds 37–56)
Intertronic T–117/96
CNSD T–513/93 (grounds 53–74)
Weyl Beef T–197/97 (grounds 75–77)
Minoan Lines T–66/99 (grounds 176–197)
Strintzis Lines T–65/99 (grounds 119–140)
Ventouris T–59/99 (grounds 99–105)
Dresdner Bank T–330/01 (grounds 125, 129, 164)
GlaxoSmithKline T–168/01 (grounds 66–70, 108)
Duphar C–238/82 (ground 30)
⋆BNIC v Clair C–123/83 (grounds 17–22)
BNIC v Aubert 136/86 (ground 11)
Bodson v Pompes Funébres C–30/87 (ground 18)
Almelo v Ysselmij C–393/92 (ground 31)
Commission v Ladbroke C–359/95P (grounds 33, 34)
Arduino C–35/99 (grounds 34–43)
Fiammiferi 378
Mauri C–250/03 (grounds 28–37)
Cipolla v Fazari 420 (grounds 44–54)

5. Undertaking's liability for others' conduct in wider agreement

Nintendo 505 (para.287)
Specialty Graphite 510 (para.334)
Organic Peroxides 524 (paras 310–311, 320–322, 327–329)
Copper Tubes 538 (paras 446–448, 490, 496)
Needles 542 (paras 253–254)
Choline Chloride 543 (paras 147–148)
Italian Raw Tobacco 550 (paras 259–262, 267–268)
Methacrylates 554 (paras 220, 226–227)
Dutch Bitumen 556 (paras 139–141, 158, 353)
Gas Insulated Switchgear 558 (paras 266–267)
Dutch Brewers 559 (paras 347–348, 370)
Union Pigments T–62/02 (ground 87)
Austrian Banks T–259/02 (grounds 111–126, 189–194)
Carbonless Paper T–109/02 (grounds 207–209, 236, 422)

B. CONCERTED PRACTICE

1. Concept

1.1. Definition

Peroxide Products 218 (para.45)
Polypropylene 247 (paras 86–88)
Flat Glass 300 (para.63)
PVC 305 (para.33)
LdPE 306 (para.40)

[For the tables of case citations see Tables 1 to 4, 11 and 12 at the back of the book.]

Solvay/ICI 330 (paras 54–56)
Ferry Services 413 (paras 56–59)
British Sugar II 434
Interbrew & Alken-Maes 500 (paras 220–222)
Zinc Phosphate 501 (para.202)
Carbonless Paper 502 (para.318)
Austrian Banks 503 (para.415)
Christie's/Sotheby's 506 (paras 151–152)
Specialty Graphite 510 (paras 324–327)
Organic Peroxides 524 (paras 299–303)
Topps 530 (paras 84–88, 109)
Copper Tubes 538 (paras 438–440)
Spanish Raw Tobacco 540 (paras 267–269)
Needles 542 (paras 236–240)
Choline Chloride 543 (paras 131 ff)
Italian Raw Tobacco 550 (paras 230–232)
Methacrylates 554 (paras 206–209)
Dutch Bitumen 556 (paras 131–135)
Gas Insulated Switchgear 558 (paras 227–232)
Dutch Brewers 559 (paras 329–332, 336
Rhône Poulenc T–1/89 (grounds 121–124)
Petrofina T–2/89 (grounds 213–216)
BASF T–4/89 (grounds 240–242)
Enichem T–6/89 (grounds 199–262)
Hercules T–7/89 (grounds 250–261)
DSM T–8/89 (grounds 229–231)
Hüls T–9/89 (ground 293)
Hoechst T–10/89 (grounds 289–291)
Solvay T–12/89 (grounds 254–256)
ICI T–13/89 (grounds 255–257)
Montedipe T–14/89 (grounds 232–235)
Linz T–15/89 (grounds 303–306)
PVC II T–305e.s./94 (ground 725)
Cement T–25/95 (grounds 1852–1855, 1865, 3150)
FEG & TU T–5/00 (ground 287)
Degussa T–279/02 (grounds 132–136)
Westfalen Gassen T–303/02 (grounds 121, 132)
⋆ICI C–48/69 (ground 64)
BASF C–49/69 (ground 22)
Bayer C–51/69 (ground 25)
Ciba-Geigy C–52/69 (ground 26)
Sandoz C–53/69 (ground 26)
Francolor C–54/69 (ground 51)
Cassella C–55/69 (ground 30)
Hoechst C–56/69 (ground 30)
ACNA C–57/69 (ground 49)
⋆Suiker Unie C–40/73 (grounds 26–28, 148–155, 172–174)
Zuechner v Bayerische Vereinsbank C–172/80 (grounds 12–17, 21)
Zinc Producers C–29/83 (grounds 14–20)
Woodpulp C–89/85 (grounds 59–65)
John Deere C–7/95P (grounds 86–92)
Commission v Anic C–49/92P (grounds 115–126)
Hüls C–199/92 (grounds 158–166)
FEG 415 (ground 139)

1.2. Difference between concerted practice and agreement

Quinine Cartel 24 (para.20)
Pittsburgh Corning 63
⋆Polypropylene 247 (paras 86–87)
Flat Glass 300 (para.63)
PVC 305 (para.34)
LdPE 306 (para.41)
Carton Board 385 (paras 128–132)
Cement 394 (paras 45)
British Sugar II 434
Pre-Insulated Pipe Cartel 435
Graphite Electrode 482 (paras 98–104)
Interbrew & Alken-Maes 500 (paras 223–224)
Austrian Banks 503 (para.422)
Christie's/Sotheby's 506 (para.153)
Specialty Graphite 510 (paras 328–329)
Topps 530 (paras 91–93, 112–114, 119)
Spanish Raw Tobacco 540 (para.270)
Needles 542 (paras 241–242, 250–260)
Choline Chloride 543 (paras 135, 144–153)
Italian Raw Tobacco 550 (para.323)
Rhône Poulenc T–1/89 (grounds 118–128)
Petrofina T–2/89 (grounds 209–219)
BASF T–4/89 (grounds 236–246)
Enichem T–6/89 (grounds 196–206)
Hercules T–7/89 (grounds 254–269)
DSM T–8/89 (grounds 225–235)
Flat Glass T–68/89 (ground 330)
Hüls T–9/89 (grounds 297–299)
Hoechst T–10/89 (grounds 293–295)
Solvay T–12/89 (grounds 258–260)
ICI T–13/89 (grounds 259–261)
Montedipe T–14/89 (grounds 236–238)
Linz T–15/89 (grounds 307–309)
PVC II T–305e.s./94 (grounds 694–698, 715–726)
Cement T–25/95 (ground 1849)
HFB et al. T–9/99 (ground 231)
Commission v Anic C–49/92P (grounds 109–114, 131–132)
Aalborg C–204e.s./00P (grounds 258–261)

2. Evidence of a concerted practice

2.1. Similarity of behaviour

Dyestuffs 27
SCPA/Kali & Salz 70

Vegetable Parchment 129 (paras 55–59)
BP Kemi/DDSF 147 (paras 54–55)
Hasselblad 173 (paras 42–48)
SSI 181 (para.123)
Zinc 189
Woodpulp 227 (paras 82–83)
Flat Glass 300 (paras 63–64)
⋆ICI C–48/69 (ground 66)
BASF C–48/69
Bayer C–51/69
Ciba-Geigy C–52/69
Sandoz C–53/69
Francolor C–54/69
Cassella C–55/69
Hoechst C–56/69
ACNA C–57/69

2.2. Exchange of information

Cobelpa/VNP 115 (para.27)
⋆Vegetable Parchment 129 (paras 63–69)
White Lead 142 (paras 21–23)
BP Kemi/DDSF 147 (para.55)
Hasselblad 173 (paras 49–51)
Woodpulp 227 (paras 106–113)
Italian Raw Tobacco 550 (para.232)
HFB et al. T–9/99 (ground 216)

2.3. Meetings

Vegetable Parchment 129 (para.71)
Pioneer 152 (paras 51–57)
⋆Zinc Producer Group 217 (para.80)
Polypropylene 247 (paras 81–86)
Solvay/ICI 330 (paras 30–33)
British Midland 350 (paras 33–36)
Vitamins 491
Interbrew & Alken-Maes (paras 255 & 259)
Austrian Banks 503 (para.422)
Specialty Graphite 510 (para.373)
Dutch Bitumen 556 (para 137)
Dutch Brewers 559 (paras 336, 363–364)
Tréfileurope T–141/89 (grounds 58 and 85)
Gustave Boël T–142/89 (grounds 100–101)
Sotralentz T–149/89 (ground 53)
Buchmann T–295/94
BPB de Eendracht T–311/94
Moritz J. Weig T–317/94
Sarrió T–334/94
Enso-Gutzeit T–337/94
PVC II T–305e.s./94 (grounds 768–778)
Cement T–25/95 (ground 1849)
HFB et al. T–9/99 (grounds 216 & 223)
Sigma Tecnologie T–28/99 (grounds 40–52)
LR AF 1998 T–23/99 (grounds 39, 147–159)
Ke Kelit T–17/99 (ground 38)
Brugg Rohrsysteme T–15/99 (grounds 36–39, 73)
FEG & TU T–5/00 (ground 359)
Degussa T–279/02 (grounds 128–135)
Commission v Anic C–49/92P (grounds 72–88)

2.4. Difference between concerted practice and market behaviour resulting from the structure of the relevant market

⋆Dyestuffs 27
SSI 181 (para.123)
Zinc Producer Group 217 (paras 75–76)
Woodpulp 227 (paras 83–165)
Solvay/ICI 330 (para.44)
Baustahlgewebe T–145/89 (ground 107)
Sotralentz T–149/89 (grounds 63–71)
ICI T–36/91 (grounds 85–86, 92)
Eurofer T–175a, CS 33 (grounds 181–202)
Tate & Lyle T–202/98 (grounds 55–56)
⋆ICI C–48/69 (grounds 68–119)
BASF C–48/69
Bayer C–51/69
Ciba-Geigy C–52/69
Sandoz C–53/69
Francolor C–54/69
Cassella C–55/69
Hoechst C–56/69
ACNA C–57/69
⋆Zinc Producers C–29/83 (ground 20)
⋆Woodpulp C–89/85 (grounds 66–127)

C. DECISIONS OF ASSOCIATIONS OF UNDERTAKINGS

1. Association of undertakings

Ceramic Tiles 35
VCH 47 (para.15)
Fireplaces 90
BPICA I 116 (para.II.1)
AROW/BNIC 190 (para.52)
Milchfoerderungsfonds 221 (para.27)
⋆Roofing Felt 248 (para.75)
ABI 262 (para.32)
Hudson Bay 294 (para.8)
Assurpol 346 (para.26)
Railway Tickets 362 (paras 60–61)
Carton Board 385 (paras 173–175)
Cement 394 (para.44)
French Beef 513 (paras 109–117)
UEFA 519 (paras 106–108)
Organic Peroxides 524 (paras 312, 344–349)
Spanish Raw Tobacco 540 (para.264)
Europay T–39/92 (grounds 136–137)

[For the tables of case citations see Tables 1 to 4, 11 and 12 at the back of the book.]

Dutch Cranes T–18/86R
Cement T–25/95 (ground 1320)
French Beef T–217/03 (grounds 49–55)
FEDETAB C–209/78 (grounds 87–89)
Dutch Cranes C–268/96P(R)
Pavlov C–180/98 (grounds 83–89)
Wouters C–309/99 (grounds 50–64)

2. Decision

2.1. Definition of decision

EMO I 19
VVVF 22
ASPA 30 (para.14)
ASBL 31
Ceramic Tiles 35
VCH 47 (para.15)
GISA 67
Belgian Wallpaper 78
Bomée-Stichting 97
Pabst & Richerz/BNIA 106 (para.II.1)
Centraal Bureau voor de Rijwielhandel 118 (para.18)
FEDETAB 133 (paras 77–79)
AROW/BNIC 190 (para.49)
Nuovo/CEGAM 209 (para.13)
⋆Fire Insurance 220 (para.23)
Belgian Banking Association 261 (para.36)
Net Book Agreements 301 (paras 47–49)
Railway Tickets 362 (paras 62–69)
Jahrhundertvertrag 370 (para.26)
CNSD 375 (paras 42–44)
COAPI 402 (para.34)
Belgian Architects 535 (paras 97–99)
Eurofer T–136/94 (ground 116)
Cement T–25/95 (ground 1325)
FEG & TU T–5/00 (grounds 391–393)
Piau T–193/02 (grounds 73–75)
DaimlerChrysler T–49e.s./02 (ground 210)
French Beef T–217/03 (ground 89)
Papiers Peints C–73/74 (grounds 15–21)
FEDETAB C–209/78 (grounds 85–89)
NAVEWA C–96/82 (grounds 19–21)
⋆Fire Insurance C–45/85 (grounds 29–32)
Conte C–221/99 (grounds 20–23)
Wouters C–309/99 (grounds 66–71)

2.2. Agreements with associations of undertakings

Socemas 13
NAVEWA-ANSEAU 178 (paras 37–41)
SMM&T 201 (para.14)
VIFKA 251 (para.12)
Roofing Felt 248 (para.71)
International Dental Exhibition 274 (para.12)
APB 314 (para.33)
Cement 394 (para.44)
Organic Peroxides 524 (para.312)
Cement T–25/95 (grounds 1325)
⋆NAVEWA C–96/82 (grounds 19–21)

2.3. Agreements between associations of undertakings

Central Heating 60
FRUBO 80
⋆VBBB/VBVB 169 (paras 35–37)
NAVEWA-ANSEAU 178 (para.38)
EATE Levy 231 (para.40)
Dutch Building Cartel 349 (para.78)
Eurocheques; Helsinki 352 (paras 43–45)
French Beef 513 (paras 119–120)
Europay T–39/92 (grounds 76, 86)
French Beef T–217/03 (grounds 49–50)
Frubo C–71/74 (grounds 28–32)
BNIC v Clair C–123/83 (ground 20)
BNIC/Aubert C–136/86 (grounds 1, 7, 13)

2.4. No guilt through mere association

FEG & TU T–5/00 (ground 355)
Technische Unie C–113/04 (grounds 115, 147)

2.5. Distinction between a decision of an association of undertakings and a public authority decision

Belgian Architects 535 (paras 46–49)
Mauri C–250/03 (grounds 28–37)
Cipolla v Fazari C–95/04 (grounds 44–54)

2.6. Advice/assistance in the context of a dispute

Belgian Architects 535 (para.87)

2.7. Implementation of decision as element of infringement

⋆French Beef T–217/03 (grounds 110–118)

D. THE PREVENTION, RESTRICTION, OR DISTORTION OF COMPETITION

1. Concept

1.1. Interbrand or intrabrand competition

Grundig/Consten 5
DRU/Blondel 7
Hummel/Isbecque 8
Delta Chemie 292 (para.27)

[For the tables of case citations see Tables 1 to 4, 11 and 12 at the back of the book.]

Eco System 344a (paras 26, 27)
BASF/Accinauto 405 (para.89)
★Consten & Grundig C–56/64

1.2. Competition between the parties and competition with third parties

Transocean Marine Paint Association I 10
SAFCO 48
★Delaval/Stork I 114 (para.6)
EATE Levy 231 (para.47)
Atlantic Container Line T–395/94 (grounds 300 & 330)

1.3. Actual and potential competition

See also Part VI, Chapter 5, 1.1 on Joint Ventures
Chaufourniers 20
Clima Chappée 25
SOPELEM/Langen 49
Wild/Leitz 55
★Vacuum Interrupters 112 (para.16)
SOPELEM/Vickers I 125 (para.III.1)
Distillers-Victuallers 157 (paras 12–17)
U.K. Tractors 347 (para.51)
HOV SVZ/MCN 381 (paras 75–83)
BNP/Dresdner Bank 410
Iridium 416
Air France/Alitalia 529 (paras 110–126)
★European Night Services T–374/94

1.4. Price or non-price competition

Dyestuffs 27
Henkel/Colgate 52
Fatty Acids 254 (paras 34–41)
UK Tractors 347 (para.52)
VISA 477 (paras 54–58)
GlaxoSmithKline T–168/01 (ground 109)
★Metro C–26/76 (grounds 20–22)
VBVB & VBBB C–43/82 (grounds 41–46)

1.5. State interference and competition

FEDETAB 133 (para.83)
Cane Sugar Supply Agreements 150 (110–133)
SSI 181 (paras 88–96)
HOV SVZ/MCN 381 (paras 75–78)
COAPI 402 (para.44–46)
Glaxo Wellcome 473
DSD 478
Belgian Architects 535 (paras 50–54)
Cockerill Sambre T–144/89 (ground 67)
Ferriere Nord T–143/89 (grounds 29, 63–65)
Thyssen Stahl T–141/94
Luxembourg Brewers T–49e.s./02 (ground 81)
DaimlerChrysler T–49e.s./02 (grounds 146, 156)
★GlaxoSmithKline T–168/01 (grounds 114–147, 190)
★Suiker Unie C–40/73 (grounds 65–73)
FEDETAB C–209/78
SSI C–240/82 (grounds 12–45)
NSO C–260/82 (grounds 18–27)
Commission v Ladbroke C–359/95P (grounds 33 and 34)
Albany C–67/96 (grounds 46–70)
Brentjens C–115/97 (ground 45)
Drijvende Bokken C–219/97 (grounds 35–52)
Mauri C–250/03 (grounds 28–37)

1.6. Interaction between upstream and downstream agreements

Roberts T–25/99 (grounds 106–109)

2. Object and effect

2.1. Object of restriction alone suffices

WEA/Filipacchi Music S.A. 68
IFTRA Aluminium 92
BMW Belgium 126 (para.22)
Flat Glass (Benelux) 216 (para.42)
Zinc Producer Group 217 (para.71)
John Deere 226 (para.26)
Polypropylene 247 (para.90)
Roofing Felt 248 (para.78)
PVC 305 (para.37)
LdPE 306 (para.44)
Eurocheques; Helsinki 352 (para.48)
French African Shipping 353 (para.42)
Glaxo Wellcome 473 (paras 124–126)
Luxembourg Brewing Industry 493 (para.61)
German Bank charges 494 (para.144)
Specialty Graphite 510 (para.354)
Copper Tubes 538 (paras 508–509)
Needles 542 (para.265)
Choline Chloride 543 (paras 158–159)
Peugeot 549 (para.130)
Methacrylates 554 (para.234)
Dutch Brewers 559 (para.377)
Rhône Poulenc T–1/89 (grounds 210–211)
Enichem T–6/89 (grounds 215–216)
Hercules T–7/89 (grounds 271–272)
DSM T–8/89 (ground 242)
Hüls T–9/89 (ground 305)
Hoechst T–10/89 (ground 301)
Solvay T–12/89 (ground 271)
ICI T–13/89 (grounds 290–293)
Montedipe T–14/89 (ground 247)
Linz T–15/89 (ground 315)

[For the tables of case citations see Tables 1 to 4, 11 and 12 at the back of the book.]

Europay T–39/92 (ground 87)
PVC II T–305e.s./94 (ground 741)
Luxembourg Brewers T–49e.s./02 (grounds 85, 97, 108, 140, 185)
Roquette Frères T–322/01 (ground 201)
Archer Daniels Midland T–329/01 (ground 265)
GlaxoSmithKline T–168/01 (grounds 115–122)
French Beef T–217/03 (ground 85)
LTM v MBU C–56/95
⋆Consten & Grundig C–56/64
Zinc Producers C–29/83 (ground 26)
BNIC v Clair C–123/83 (ground 22)
Sandoz C–277/87 (grounds 14–18)
General Motors C–551/03P (grounds 64–70, 77–78)
FEG C–105/04 (grounds 136–143)

2.2. Definition of the relevant market in Article 81

WEA/Filipacchi Music S.A. 68 KEWA 103
Miller 108 (para.12)
Vaessen/Moris 143 (para.16)
Natursteinplatten 159 (para.30)
Whisky and Gin 237 Olivetti/Canon 280
⋆Mars/Langnese 369 (paras 76–102)
Night Services 390 (paras 17–29)
BASF/Accinauto 405 (paras 87–88)
LH/SAS 408 (paras 30–38)
BNP/Dresdner Bank 410 (para.13)
Iridium 416
Whitbread 439 (paras 95–99)
VISA 477 (paras 32–52)
German Bank charges 494 (para.258)
AuA/LH 495 (paras 44–61)
Visa II 496 (paras 43–53)
IFPI 498 (paras 32–44)
Luxembourg Brewing Industry 493 (para.76)
Christie's/Sotheby's 506 (para.28)
Specialty Graphite 510 (para.550)
Network Sharing UK 514 (paras 40 ff)
German Network Sharing 518 (paras 44 ff)
Organic Peroxides 524 (para.36)
REIMS II Renewal 523 (paras 70–77)
Telenor/Canal+ 527 (paras 25 ff)
Air France/Alitalia 529 (paras 39 ff)
Topps 530 (paras 33–48)
Air France/Alitalia 529 (paras 39 ff)
Belgian Architects 535 (para.93)
French Brewers 539 (paras 53 ff)
Spanish Raw Tobacco 540 (para.368)
Needles 542 (para.23)
Peugeot 549
Dutch Brewers 559 (para 360)
Vichy T–19/91 (grounds 61–64)
Flat Glass T–68/89 (grounds 158–171)
Danish Fur Breeders T–66/89 (ground 99)
Fiat Agri T–34/92 (grounds 49–57)
⋆SPO T–29/92 (grounds 74–75)
Langnese Iglo T–7/93 (grounds 60–69)
Schöller T–9/93 (grounds 39–54)
Enso Espanola T–348/94 (ground 232)
European Night Services T–374/94 (ground 136)
PVC II 467, T–305e.s./94 (ground 741)
Far Eastern Freight Conference T–86/95 (grounds 116–136)
Atlantic Container Line T–395/94 (grounds 83, 264–273)
Volkswagen T–62/98 (grounds 230–231)
Roberts T–25/99 (grounds 26–49)
Adriatica T–61/99 (grounds 27 ff)
FEG & TU T–5/00 (ground 123)
⋆Mannesmannröhren-Werke T–44/00 (grounds 132 & 202–205)
Eurovision T–185/00 (grounds 206–226)
GlaxoSmithKline T–168/01 (grounds 151–161)
Danone T–38/02 (ground 99)
Brouwerij Haacht T–48/02 (grounds 57–59)
Luxembourg Brewers T–49e.s./02 (ground 144)
Heubach T–64/02 (grounds 122–125)
Austrian Banks T–259/02 (grounds 172–174)
Miller C–19/77 (ground 10)
Hoffmann-La Roche C–85/76 (grounds 122–123)
Hasselblad C–86/82 (grounds 19–22)
Windsurfing C–193/83 (grounds 12–19)
⋆Delimitis v Henninger Bräu C–234/89 (grounds 10–27)
⋆LTM v MBU C–56/95
Adriatica C–111/04P (grounds 30–32)

3. Restriction must be appreciable

3.1. Commission Notice of December 22, 2001 on agreements of minor importance which do not appreciably restrict competition under Article 81(1) of the Treaty establishing the European Community (de minimis) [2001] O.J. C368/13

3.2. Cases regarding appreciability

Socemas 13
Chaufourniers 20
Burroughs/Delplanque 50
Burroughs/Geha 51

[For the tables of case citations see Tables 1 to 4, 11 and 12 at the back of the book.]

WEA/Filipacchi Music S.A. 68
(See also 2nd Comp. Rep. para.40)
Intergroup 91
★Penney 127 (para.II.4)
Vaessen/Moris 143 (paras 8, 16–17)
★Floral 148 (para.II.4)
Distillers-Victuallers 157 (paras 12–17)
Natursteinplatten 159 (paras 30, 40–41)
Villeroy & Boch 244 (paras 29, 30)
Peugeot 250 (para.35)
★Fatty Acids 254 (paras 45, 47)
ServiceMaster 296 (para.10)
Charles Jourdan 298 (para.35)
ARD 312 (para.43)
APB 314 (paras 33–42)
Alcatel/ANT 319 (paras 12–18)
Moosehead 320 (para.15)
Odin 322 (paras 22–28)
★GEC-Siemens/Plessey 325 (paras 19, 26, 35, 36)
Vichy 334 (para.19)
Quantel 357 (paras 43–44)
UER 373 (paras 54–57)
Grundig 378 (para.34)
BASF/Accinauto 405 (para.93)
VW-Audi 429 (paras 147–150)
DSD II 484 (paras 125–150)
Luxembourg Brewing Industry 493 (paras 82–85)
Yamaha 517 (paras 148–156)
German Network Sharing 518 (paras 112)
Austrian Waste 522 (paras 224–229)
Telenor/Canal+ 527 (paras 144 ff)
PME 7th Comp. Rep. (paras 21–26)
13th Comp. Rep. (paras 23, 24)
Recais & Châteaux 27th Comp. Rep. (page 141)
Gustave Boël T–142/89 (grounds 88–89)
Langnese Iglo T–7/93 (grounds 97–98)
Schöller T–9/93 (grounds 74–75)
VGB T–77/94 (ground 139)
★European Night Services T–374/94
Far Eastern Freight Conference T–86/95 (grounds 137–143)
Adriatica T–61/99 (grounds 27–29)
Ventouris T–59/99 (grounds 167–169)
JFE Engineering T–67e.s./00 (ground 384)
★Mannesmannröhren-Werke T–44/00 (grounds 196–197)
Luxembourg Brewers T–49e.s./02 (grounds 140–141)
Völk v Vervaecke C–5/69 (grounds 5–7)
Cadillon v Höss C–1/71
Tepea C–28/77 (ground 50)
Hoffmann-La Roche C–85/76 (grounds 122–123)
Distillers C–30/78 (grounds 27–28)
NSO C–260/82 (grounds 46–49)

4. Rule of reason/ancillary restraints: assessing the restriction in the context of the relevant market

Nicholas Frègeres Vitapro 4
Alliance des Constructeurs Français 12
Socemas 13
Chaufourniers 20
Pirelli/Dunlop 28
SAFCO 48
Reuter/BASF 107
AEG/Telefunken 179 (para.54)
Amersham Buchler 184 (para.13)
Nutricia 206 (paras 26, 27)
Mecaniver/PPG 225 (para.15)
Villeroy & Boch 244 (paras 29, 31–33)
Tetra Pak I 289 (paras 54–57)
Moosehead 320 (para.15)
Odin 322 (paras 29–35)
Konsortium ECR 900 323
UK Tractors 347 (paras 37–48)
Grundig 378 (para.34)
★IPSP 397
BNP/Dresdner Bank 410 (paras 15 and 16)
Sicasov 436 (para.50)
Luxembourg Brewing Industry 493 (para.76)
Network Sharing UK 514 (paras 68–78)
German Network Sharing 518 (paras 73–77)
REIMS II Renewal 523 (paras 78–93)
Telenor/Canal+ 527 (paras 134–136)
Flat Glass T–68/89 (grounds 158–171)
Montedipe T–14/89 (grounds 264–265)
Société Métallurgique de Normandie T–147/89 (ground 90)
Tréfilunion T–148/89 (ground 109)
Société des Treillis et Panneaux Soudés T–151/89 (grounds 88–90)
Langnese Iglo T–7/93 (grounds 94–119)
Schöller T–9/93 (grounds 71–88)
Métropole Télévision T–112/99 (grounds 72–80, 103–149)
Eurovision T–185/00 (ground 64)
Vanden Bergh Foods T–65/98 (paras 80 ff)
★O2 (Germany) T–328/03
GlaxoSmithKline T–168/01 (grounds 114–147, 167 ff)
Vanden Bergh Foods 244 (paras 80 ff)
★LTM v MBU C–56/95
Consten & Grundig C–56/64(pp. 342–343)
De Haecht v Wilkin I C–23/67
Kali & Salz C–19/74 (grounds 1–7)
★Metro C–26/76 (ground 43)
★Nungesser C–258/78 (grounds 44–58)

[For the tables of case citations see Tables 1 to 4, 11 and 12 at the back of the book.]

Coditel v Cine-Vog C–262/81 (grounds 7, 15–19)
Remia C–42/84 (grounds 18–20)
Pronuptia v Schillgalis C–161/84
Metro C–75/84 (grounds 40–47)
⋆Delimitis v Henninger Bräu C–234/89 (grounds 10–27)
Gøttrup-Klim v DLG C–250/92
Oude Luttikhuis C–399/93 (grounds 9–20)
Montecatini C–235/92P (grounds 130–133)
Wouters C–309/99 (grounds 97–109)
General Motors C–551/03P (grounds 72–74)
Asnef-Equifax C–238/05 (ground 49)
Meca-Medina C–519/04 (grounds 42–54)

5. Facilitating market entry

⋆O2 (Germany) T–328/03

CHAPTER 2

ARTICLE 81(2)

1. Concept of nullity

Bosch v De Geus C–13/61
⋆LTM v MBU C–56/95
Béguelin v GL C–22/71 (grounds 25–29)
Ciments et Bétons v Kerpen C–319/82 (grounds 11–12)
VAG v Magne C–10/86 (grounds 14–15)
Ahmed Saeed v Zentrale 66/86 (grounds 20, 26–29)
Italian Insurers C–295/04 (grounds 56–59)

2. Retroactive effect

Bosch v De Geus C–13/61
Bilger v Jehle C–43/69 (grounds 10–11)
⋆De Haecht v Wilkin II C–48/72 (ground 27)
Dijkstra C–319/93 (ground 22)
Italian Insurers C–295/04 (ground 57)

3. Severability of offending clauses

⋆LTM v MBU C–56/95
Consten & Grundig C–56/64
Ciments et Bétons v Kerpen C–319/82 (ground 11)
VAG v Magne C–10/86 (grounds 14–15)
Brünsteiner & Hilgert C–376/05 (grounds 47–50)

4. Effect of a Commission decision

Velcro/Aplix 233
⋆VBA 288 (para.168)
Ciments et Bétons v Kerpen C–319/82 (grounds 11–12)

CHAPTER 3

ARTICLE 81(3)

Guidelines on the application of Article 81(3) of the Treaty [2004] O.J. C101/97

A. CONDITIONS FOR THE APPLICATION OF ARTICLE 81(3)

1. Contribution to the improvement, production or distribution of goods, or promoting technical progress

Bayer/Gist-Brocades 100 (p.14, para.1)
United Reprocessors 102
Cobelpa/VNP 115 (para.41)
FEDETAB 133 (para.93)
WANO 138
Carlsberg 214 (para.8)
Optical Fibres 249 (para.59)
ENI/Montedison 256 (paras 30–31)
BBC Brown Boveri 291 (para.23)
GEC-Siemens/Plessey 325 (paras 20–25)
⋆Screensport/EBU 337 (para.71)
Van den Bergh Foods 431 (paras. 224–225)
Revised TACA 507 (paras 90–91, 96)
Network Sharing UK 514 (paras 137–141)
German Network Sharing 518 (paras 122–128)
UEFA 519 (paras 139–168)
Austrian Waste 522 (paras 268–271)
REIMS II Renewal 523 (paras 105 ff)
Telenor/Canal+ 527 (paras 200 ff)
Air France/Alitalia 529 (para.132)
Matra T–17/93 (grounds 108–111)
⋆SPO T–29/92 (grounds 286–300)
Joynson T–231/99 (grounds 46–76, 96–98)
Shaw T–131/99 (grounds 47–53)
Van den Bergh Foods 244 (grounds 139–143)
⋆GlaxoSmithKline T–168/01 (grounds 247 ff)
Metro C–26/76 (grounds 43–44)
FEDETAB C–209/78 (grounds 174–186)
Remia C–42/84 (grounds 42)
NSO C–260/82 (grounds 61)
Publishers' Association C–360/92P (grounds 24–29)
⋆Asnef-Equifax C–238/05 (ground 70)

[For the tables of case citations see Tables 1 to 4, 11 and 12 at the back of the book.]

2. Allowing consumers a fair share of the resulting benefit

★Synthetic Fibres 213 (paras 39–42)
P&I Clubs 243 (para.41)
Scottish Nuclear 339 (para.37)
Stichting Baksteen 383 (para.31)
REIMS II Renewal 523 (paras 118 ff)
Telenor/Canal+ 527 (paras 229–234)
Air France/Alitalia 529 (paras 133–137)
Matra T–17/93 (ground 122)
★SPO T–29/92 (grounds 286–300)
Metro C–26/76 (grounds 44–45)

3. No imposition on the undertakings concerned of restrictions which are not indispensable to the attainment of these objectives

Convention Faience 2
Bayer/Gist-Brocades 100
SOPELEM/Vickers I 125
Grundig 232
★Optical Fibres 249 (paras 62–63)
Net Book Agreements 301 (paras 73–75)
Astra 368 (paras 19–31)
Grundig 378
Eurotunnel 396 (para.102)
DSD II 484 (paras 150–157)
Visa II 496 (para.98)
IFPI 498 (paras 96–115)
UEFA 519 (paras 174–192)
REIMS II Renewal 523 (paras 131–144)
Telenor/Canal+ 527 (paras 235 ff)
Air France/Alitalia 529 (paras 138–140)
Publishers' Association T–66/89 (in particular grounds 71–76, 98)
Europay T–39/92 (grounds 111–119)
Matra T–17/93 (ground 135)
★Métropole T–528/93 (grounds 95–102)
GlaxoSmithKline T–168/01 (grounds 244, 247, 304–307)
Metro C–26/76 (grounds 40–48)
Publishers' Association C–360/92P

4. Not affording such undertakings the possibility of eliminating competition in respect of a substantial part of the products in question

Bayer/Gist-Brocades 100
United Reprocessors 102
IVECO/Ford 287 (paras 37–40)
Trans Atlantic 393A (paras 428–461)
Revised TACA 507 (paras 92 & 96)
Austrian Waste 522 (paras 280–293)
REIMS II Renewal 523 (paras 145–157)
Telenor/Canal+ 527 (paras 252–256)
Air France/Alitalia 529 (paras 142 ff)
PRB/Shell 17th Comp. Rep. (para.74)
Langnese Iglo T–7/93 (ground 152)
Atlantic Container Line T–395/94 (ground 300)
Eurovision T–185/00
Duales II T–289/01
Metro C–26/76 (grounds 49–59)
FEDETAB C–209/78 (grounds 187–189)
ANCIDES C–43/85 (ground 13)

B. ELEMENTS RELEVANT TO THE ASSESSMENT OF ARTICLE 81(3)

1. Balancing the pros and cons

NCH 53 (para.9)
MAN/SAVIEM 54 (para.28)
FEDETAB 133 (para.129)
Natursteinplatten 159 (paras 31–32)
VBBB/VBVB 169 (para.53)
Ford Werke AG 199 (paras 35, 43)
SABA II 208
Ivoclar 234 (para.21)
X/Open Group 263 (para.42)
GEC-Siemens/Plessey 325 (para.43)
Stichting Kraanverhuur 382 (para.29)
Dutch Cranes 407a (para.37)
Bass 447
Scottish and Newcastle 448
JCB 479 (paras 209–210)
German Network Sharing 518 (para.142)
UEFA 519 (para.137)
Far Eastern Freight Conference T–86/95 (grounds 342–348)
★FEDETAB C–209/78 (ground 185)

2. Social considerations

★Synthetic Fibres 213 (para.37)
Ford/Volkswagen 367 (para.36)
Stichting Baksteen 383 (para.27)
★Metro C–26/76 (ground 29)
FEDETAB C–209/78 (ground 182)
Remia C–42/84 (ground 42)
Metro C–75/84 (ground 65)

3. Environmental considerations

Carbon Gas Technologie 205
KSB 328
Assurpol 346 (para.38)
CECED 461
DSD II 484 (paras 143–144)
Austrian Waste 522 (paras 268–269)
EACEM 29th Comp. Rep. p.152

[For the tables of case citations see Tables 1 to 4, 11 and 12 at the back of the book.]

22nd Comp. Rep. (para.77)

4. Burden of proof

FEDETAB 133 (para.93)
Glaxo Wellcome 473 (para.153)
Publishers' Association T–66/89 (grounds 69–79)
John Deere T–35/92 (ground 105)
Fiat Agri T–34/92 (ground 99)
SPO T–29/92 (ground 262)
Langnese Iglo T–7/93 (ground 179–193)
Schöller T–9/93 (ground 141)
Far Eastern Freight Conference T–86/95 (ground 284)
JCB Service T–67/01 (ground 162)
Consten & Grundig C–56/64
⋆VBVB & VBBB C–43/82 (ground 52)
Remia C–42/84 (ground 45)
Metro C–75/84
Fire Insurance C–45/85 (grounds 58–59)

5. Unilateral behaviour extraneous to contractual terms

Ford Werke-Interim Measures 182 (paras 21–25, 36)
Ford Werke AG 199 (para.36)
Peugeot 250 (para.40)
⋆Ford C–25/84

6. Advantage must be objective

Convention Faience 2
Fire Insurance 220 (para.41)
ANSAC 333a (para.29)
Quantel 357 (para.52)
Dutch Cranes 407a (para.33)
Van den Bergh Foods 431 (paras. 224–225)
Matra T–17/93 (ground 135)
⋆Consten & Grundig C–56/64

7. Conditions are cumulative

FRUBO 80
Europe Asia Trade Agreements 449
Europay T–39/92 (grounds 110–114)
Matra T–17/93 (grounds 104)
SPO T–29/92 (grounds 267, 286)
Langnese Iglo T–7/93 (ground 177)
Schöller T–9/93 (ground 139)
Métropole T–528/93 (ground 93)
Dutch Cranes T–213/95 (ground 191)
Far Eastern Freight Conference T–86/95 (ground 367)
GlaxoSmithKline T–168/01 (ground 247)
Consten & Grundig C–56/64
JCB Service C–167/04 (grounds 186–188)

8. Discretion of the Commission

Ford Werke AG 199 (para.35)
Europay T–39/92 (ground 110)
Atlantic Container Line T–395/94 (grounds 262–264 & 348)
GlaxoSmithKline T–168/01 (ground 244)
⋆Metro C–26/76 (ground 45)

9. Can an Article 82 abuse be exempted?

Decca 304 (para.122)
TACA 441 (para.550)
⋆Tetra Pak T–51/89
Matra T–17/93 (grounds 153, 159)
CMB a.o./Commission T–24/93 (grounds 152, 188–190)
Ahmed Saeed v Zentrale C–66/86 (ground 32)

10. Contribution to other EC policies

IATA Passengers 342 (paras 68–71)
IATA Cargo 343 (paras 58–61)
⋆Ford/Volkswagen 367 (para.36)
Austrian Waste 522 (para.268)
21st Comp. Rep. (para.42)

11. An exemption is never extended per se

Matra T–17/93 (ground 85)

12. Relation with Article 82(2)

Métropole T–528/93 (grounds 114–126)

13. Ruinous competition

Europe Asia Trade Agreements 449

14. Restrictions by object under Article 81(3)

⋆GlaxoSmithKline T–168/01 (ground 233)

C. EXEMPTION BY CATEGORY

1. Delegation of the authority to adopt Regulations to the Commission

[For the tables of case citations see Tables 1 to 4, 11 and 12 at the back of the book.]

1.1. Council Regulation 19/65 of March 2, 1965 on application of Article 85(3) of the Treaty to certain categories of agreements and concerted practices J.O. 533/65; [1965] O.J. Spec. Ed. 35 as amended by Regulation 1/2003 O.J. L1/1

1.2. Council Regulation 2821/71 of December 20, 1971 on application of Article 85(3) of the Treaty to categories of agreements, decisions and concerted practices J.O. 46/71; [1971] O.J. Spec Ed. 1032 as amended by Regualtion 1/2003 [2003] O.J. L1/1

2. Effect of a group exemption regulation

JCB Service T–67/01 (ground 164)
Fonderies Roubaix v Fonderies Roux C–63/75 (grounds 10–11)
VAG v Magne C–10/86 (grounds 10–11)
Delimitis v Henninger Bräu C–234/89 (ground 46)
Grand Garage Albigeois C–226/94
Nissan France C–309/94
Fontaine 280
VAG/SYD-Consult C–41/96

3. Withdrawal of the benefit of a group exemption regulation

Tetra Pak I 289 (paras 53, 58–59)
Mars/Langnese 369 13th Comp. Rep. (para.73)
Tetra Pak T–51/89
Langnese Iglo T–7/93 (grounds 144–149, 173–176)

4. Letter of Commission

De Bloos v Bouyer C–59/77 (grounds 17–18)
Hydrotherm v Andreoli C–170/83 (ground 6)

[For the tables of case citations see Tables 1 to 4, 11 and 12 at the back of the book.]

PART III

HORIZONTAL AGREEMENTS

CHAPTER 1

CARTELS

A. LIST OF CARTEL CASES

Convention Faience 2
Cobelaz 15
Cobelaz Cokes 16
CFA 18
Chaufourniers 20
VVVF 22
SEIFA 23
Quinine Cartel 24
Dyestuffs 27
ASPA 30
Supexie 34
Ceramic Tiles 35
VCH 47
SAFCO 48
NCH 53
Central Heating 60
Dutch Cement 65
Cimbel 66
GISA 67
European Sugar Industry 69
SCPA/Kali & Salz 70
Heaters and Boilers 72
Kali & Salz/Kalichemie 76
IFTRA Glass 77
Belgian Wallpaper 78
FRUBO 80
Franco-Japanese Ball-Bearings 81
Tinned Mushrooms 88
Fireplaces 90
IFTRA Aluminium 92
Bomée-Stichting 97
Pabst & Richerz/BNIA 106
Cobelpa/VNP 115
Centraal Bureau voor de Rijwielhandel 118
Cauliflowers 119
Vegetable Parchment 129
SNPE/LEL 132 (paras 4–7, 13–15)
FEDETAB 133
CSV 134
White Lead 142
BP Kemi/DDSF 147
Floral 148
Rennet 149
IMA Rules 158
Natursteinplatten 159
Italian Cast Glass 163
Italian Flat Glass 164
VBBB/VBVB 169
SSI 181
Zinc 189
AROW/BNIC 190
Vimpoltu 195
Cast Iron & Steel Rolls 198
International Energy Agency 207
Synthetic Fibres 213
Flat Glass (Benelux) 216
Zinc Producer Group 217
Peroxide Products 218
Fire Insurance 220
Milchfoerderungsfonds 221
Woodpulp 227
Aluminium 228
Siemens/Fanuc 246
Polypropylene 247
Roofing Felt 248
Meldoc 253
Fatty Acids 254
VBA 288
Hudson Bay 294
Net Book Agreements 301
Flat Glass II 300
PVC 305
LdPE 306
Welded Steel Mesh 311
Sugar Beet 315
Solvay/ICI 330
Solvay/CFK 331
ANSAC 333a
UK Tractors 347
Dutch Building Cartel 349
French African Shipping 353
Eurocheques; Helsinki 352
Scottish Salmon 358

[For the tables of case citations see Tables 1 to 4, 11 and 12 at the back of the book.]

Railway Tickets 362
CEWAL 371
CNSD 375
HOV SVZ/MCN 381
Stichting Kraanverhuur 382
Stichting Baksteen 383
Carton Board 385
Cement 394
Far Eastern Freight 399
Trans Atlantic 393A
COAPI 402
Dutch Cranes 407a
Ferry Services 413
Alloy Surcharge 430
British Sugar II 434
Pre-Insulated Pipe Cartel 435
TACA 441
SAS/Maersk 475
Seamless Steel Tubes 499
Interbrew & Alken-Maes 500
Zinc Phosphate 501
Carbonless Paper 502
Austrian Banks 503
Methionine 504
Christie's/Sotheby's 506
Methylglucamine 508
Food Flavour Enhancers 509
Specialty Graphite 510
Italian Raw Tobacco 550
French Beef 513
Organic Peroxide 524
Belgian Architects 535
Copper Tubes 538
French Brewers 539
Spanish Raw Tobacco 540
Needles 542
Choline Chloride 543
Methacrylates 554
Dutch Bitumen 556
Alloy Surcharge Readoption 557
Gas Insulated Switchgear 558
Dutch Brewers 559
Lino Cartel 5th Comp. Rep. (para.35)
Rhône Poulenc T–1/89
Petrofina T–2/89
BASF T–4/89
Enichem T–6/89
Hercules T–7/89
DSM T–8/89
PVC T–79/89
Flat Glass T–68/89
Hüls T–9/89
Hoechst T–10/89
Shell T–11/89
Solvay T–12/89
ICI T–13/89
Montedipe T–14/89
Linz T–15/89
Publishers' Association T–66/89
Europay T–39/92
John Deere T–35/92
Fiat Agri T–34/92
SPO T–29/92
Ilro T–152/89
Baustahlgewebe T–145/89
Tréfileurope T–141/89
Gustave Boël T–142/89
Société Métallurgique de Normandie T–147/89
Tréfilunion T–148/89
Société des Treillis et Panneaux Soudés T–151/89
Cockerill Sambre T–144/89
Ferriere Nord T–143/89
Martinelli T–150/89
Sotralentz T–149/89
CMB a.o./Commission T–24/93
Buchmann T–295/94
Europa Carton T–304/94
Cascades T–308/94
Koninklijke KNP T–309/94
Gruber & Weber T–310/94
BPB de Eendracht T–311/94
Moritz J. Weig T–317/94
Fiskeby Board T–319/94
SCA Holding T–327/94
Sarrió T–334/94
Enso-Gutzeit T–337/94
Finnish Board Mills T–338/94
Metsä-Serla T–339/94
Mayr-Melnhof Kartongesellschaft T–347/94
Enso Espanola T–348/94
Mo och Domsjö T–352/94
Stora Kopparbergs Bergslags T–354/94
Thyssen Stahl T–141/94
PVC II T–305e.s./94
Daesang & Sewon Europe T–230/00
ADM & ADM Ingredients T–224/00
Kyowa Hakko Kogyo T–223/00
Cheil Yedang T–220/00
Minoan Lines T–66/99
Strintzis Lines T–65/99
Adriatica T–61/99
Ventouris T–59/99
Marlines T–56/99
Tokai Carbon et al. T–236e.s./01
JFE Engineering T–67e.s./00
Dalmine T–50/00
Corus UK T–48/00
Mannesmannröhren-Werke T–44/00

[For the tables of case citations see Tables 1 to 4, 11 and 12 at the back of the book.]

Dresdner Bank T–44/02
Vereins-und Westbank T–54/02
Bayerische Hypo-und Vereinsbank T–56/02
Deutsche Verkehrsbank T–60/02
Commerzbank T–61/02
Holcim (Germany) T–28/03
Holcim (France) T–86/03
Specialty Graphite T–71e.s./03
SAS T–241/01
Luxembourg Brewers T–49e.s./02
Sumitomo T–22/02
Danone T–38/02
Heubach T–64/02
Union Pigments T–62/02
SNCZ T–52/02
Britannia Alloys T–33/02
Brouwerij Haacht T–48/02
Daiichi T–26/02
BASF T–15/02
Degussa T–279/02
Archer Daniels Midland T–59/02
Jungbunzlauer T–43/02
Peróxidos Orgánicos T–120/04
Westfalen Gassen T–303/02
Austrian Banks T–259/02
French Beef T–217
Carbonless Paper T–109/02
ACF Chemiefarma C–41/69
Boehringer C–45/69
ICI C–48/69
BASF C–48/69
Bayer C–51/69
Ciba-Geigy C–52/69
Sandoz C–53/69
Francolor C–54/69
Cassella C–55/69
Hoechst C–56/69
ACNA C–57/69
Cement Dealers C–8/72
Boehringer C–7/72
Kali & Salz C–19/74
Frubo C–71/74
Papiers Peints C–73/74
Suiker Unie C–40/73
FEDETAB C–209/78
Stremsel C–61/80
Zuechner v Bayerische Vereinsbank C–172/80
VBVB & VBBB C–43/82
Zinc Producers C–29/83
BNIC v Clair C–123/83
SSI C–240/82
NSO C–260/82
Fire Insurance C–45/85
BNIC/Aubert C–136/86
Ahmed Saeed v Zentrale C–66/86
Belasco C–246/86
Woodpulp C–89/85
Ferriere Nord C–219/95P
John Deere C–7/95P
New Holland Ford C–8/95P
Aalborg 384
British Sugar C–359/01P
Greencore C–123/03P
CMA CGM C–236/03P
Dansk Rørindustri C–189e.a./02P
Acerinox C–57/02P
ThyssenKrupp Stainless C–65/02P
Marlines C–112/04P
Minoan Lines C–121/04P
Adriatica C–111/04P
Strintzis Lines C–110/04P
Archer Daniels Midland C–397/03
Graphite Electrodes C–301/04
SGL Carbon C–308/04
Showa Denko C–289/04
Salzgitter Mannesmann C–411/04
Sumitomo & Nippon Steel C–403/04
Dalmine C–407/04
Danone C–3/06
Britannia Alloys C–76/06

B. SPECIFIC CLAUSES OR AGREEMENTS TYPICAL OF CARTEL SCHEMES

1. Production related schemes or clauses

1.1. Production quotas for existing capacity

Chaufourniers 20
★Quinine Cartel 24 (para.30)
Vegetable Parchment 129 (paras 17–23)
Italian Cast Glass 163
Synthetic Fibres 213
Zinc Producer Group 217 (para.67)
Stichting Baksteen 383
Trans Atlantic 393A
Fruit Agreements. 5th Comp. Rep. (para.38)
Air-Forge 12th Comp. Rep. (para.85)

1.2. Provisions regulating capacity

1.2.1. Prohibition of new capacity

Chaufourniers 20

1.2.2. Prohibition on sale of capacity outside cartel

Cimbel 66 (paras 13–14)
★Roofing Felt 248 (para.73)

1.2.3. Matching supply and demand

Carton Board 385 (paras 51–60, 133–135)

1.3. Clauses relating to the nature of the product

1.3.1. Common product range

Roofing Felt 248
Belasco C–246/86 (ground 30)

1.3.2. Sharing of product ranges between competitors

Italian Cast Glass 163
Needles 542
BP/Montedison 23rd Comp. Rep. page 455

1.4. Supply agreements

1.4.1. Emergency supply agreements

Zinc 189
CECED 461
Zinc Producers C–29/83 (grounds 132–137)

1.4.2. Reciprocal supply arrangements

Flat Glass 300 (para.70)
Solvay/ICI 330 (paras 36–39)
Sand Producers 6th Comp. Rep. (paras 123–125)
Nitrogenous Fertilisers 6th Comp. Rep. (paras 126–127)
Flat Glass T–68/89 (grounds 338–339)

1.5. Production information exchange schemes

Cimbel 66
Tinned Mushrooms 88
Cobelpa/VNP 115 (paras 5, 9, 24–28)
⋆Italian Cast Glass 163
Zinc Producer Group 217 (para.68)
Carton Board 385 (paras 61–69, 105–106, 134)
Cement 394 (para.62)
2nd Comp. Rep. (para.18)
CEPI 26th Comp. Rep. p.145

1.6. Compensation schemes

Chaufourniers 20
Needles 542

2. Market sharing schemes, agreements or clauses

2.1. Dividing territories between competitors

2.1.1. Between Member States

Quinine Cartel 24 (para.28)
Cimbel 66 (para.13)
⋆European Sugar Industry 69
SCPA/Kali & Salz 70
Tinned Mushrooms 88
Vegetable Parchment 129 (paras 17–33, 55–62)
SNPE/LEL 132
⋆White Lead 142 (paras 12–17, 27–29)
Italian Flat Glass 164
Cast Iron & Steel Rolls 198 (paras 3, 5, 53–54)
Flat Glass (Benelux) 216
Zinc Producer Group 217 (para.77)
Peroxide Products 218
Woodpulp 227
Aluminium 228
Meldoc 253 (para.21)
Welded Steel Mesh 311
Solvay/ICI 330
CEWAL 371 (paras 37, 38)
Carton Board 385 (paras 51–60)
Cement 394 (para.45)
SAS/Maersk 475
Seamless Steel Tubes 499
Food Flavour Enhancers 509
Needles 542
Choline Chloride 543
Gas Insulated Switchgear 558
Sheet Glass 1st Comp. Rep. (paras 4, 6)
International Cable Development Corp. 1st Comp. Rep. (para.4)
Cleaning Products 1st Comp. Rep. (para.4)
Sand Producers 6th Comp. Rep. (para.122)
Nitrogenous Fertilisers 6th Comp. Rep. (paras 126–128)

2.1.2. Third country markets

DECA 6
Cobelaz 15
Cobelaz Cokes 16
CFA 18
VVVF 22
SEIFA 23
Quinine Cartel 24 (para.28)
Supexie 34
⋆CSV 134 (paras 18, 20–62, 77)
Cement 394 (paras 54, 58, 59, 61)
Seamless Steel Tubes 499
Gas Insulated Switchgear 558

2.2. Quotas

⋆Quinine Cartel 24 (para.28)
NCH 53
Thin Paper 59

[For the tables of case citations see Tables 1 to 4, 11 and 12 at the back of the book.]

Dutch Cement 65
Cimbel 66 (para.13)
European Sugar Industry 69
Tinned Mushrooms 88
CSV 134 (paras 18, 20, 62, 72)
White Lead 142 (paras 12, 15–17, 27–29)
BP Kemi/DDSF 147 (paras 28a, 38, 82)
Italian Cast Glass 163
Italian Flat Glass 164
Cast Iron & Steel Rolls 198 (paras 3, 5, 53c-d, 54)
Flat Glass (Benelux) 216 (para.44)
★Peroxide Products 218
★Aluminium 228 (para.11)
Polypropylene 247 (paras 52–53, 80, 89)
Roofing Felt 248 (paras 73–74)
Meldoc 253 (paras 21, 60)
Flat Glass 300 (para.67)
PVC 305 (para.10)
Welded Steel Mesh 311
Solvay/CFK 331
Pre-Insulated Pipe Cartel 435
Vitamins 491
Citric Acid 492
Seamless Steel Tubes 499 (para.111)
Interbrew & Alken-Maes 500
Zinc Phosphate 501
Carbonless Paper 502
Methylglucamine 508
Organic Peroxides 524
Copper Tubes 538
French Brewers 539
Spanish Raw Tobacco 540
Choline Chloride 543
Gas Insulated Switchgear 558
Sheet Glass 1st Comp. Rep. (paras 4, 6)
2nd Comp. Rep. (para.19)
Air-Forge 12th Comp. Rep. (para.85)
Cockerill Sambre T–144/89 (ground 28)
PVC II T–305e.s./94
BNIC/Aubert C–136/86 (grounds 1, 7)
ACF Chemiefarma C–41/69 (grounds 126–129)
Boehringer C–45/69 (grounds 41–44)

2.3. Dividing customers between competitors

FEDETAB 133
BP Kemi/DDSF 147 (paras 28e, 38, 80)
Peroxide Products 218
★Woodpulp 227 (paras 71–76, 133–134)
Roofing Felt 248 (para.74)
French African Shipping 353 (para.40)
CEWAL 371 (paras 37, 38)
Vitamins 491
Citric Acid 492
Luxembourg Brewing Industry 493
Interbrew & Alken-Maes 500
Zinc Phosphate 501
Methylglucamine 508
Food Flavour Enhancers 509
Specialty Graphite 510
Organic Peroxides 524
Copper Tubes 538
Choline Chloride 543
Gas Insulated Switchgear 558

2.4. Market and/or sales information exchange

Tinned Mushrooms 88
Cobelpa/VNP 115 (paras 5, 9, 24–28)
Vegetable Parchment 129 (paras 34–39, 63–70)
SNPE/LEL 132 (paras 7, 13)
CSV 134 (para.25)
White Lead 142 (paras 12–16, 25–27)
BP Kemi/DDSF 147 (paras.28c, 38, 51, 78–79)
Italian Cast Glass 163
Italian Flat Glass 164
Flat Glass (Benelux) 216 (para.45)
Peroxide Products 218
Polypropylene 247 (paras 66, 80)
★Fatty Acids 254
Solvay/ICI 330 (paras 30–33)
★UK Tractors 347
Carton Board 385 (paras 61–69, 105–106, 134)
★German Steel 427
Citric Acid 492
Seamless Steel Tubes 499 (para.153)
Interbrew & Alken-Maes 500
Zinc Phosphate 501
Methionine 50
Methylglucamine 508
Food Flavour Enhancers 509
Specialty Graphite 510
Organic Peroxides 524
Copper Tubes 538
Spanish Raw Tobacco 540
Choline Chloride 543
Gas Insulated Switchgear 558
Paper Machine Wire Manu 6th Comp. Rep. (para.134)
7th Comp. Rep. (paras 5–8)
EWIS 18th Comp. Rep. (paras 63)

[For the tables of case citations see Tables 1 to 4, 11 and 12 at the back of the book.]

John Deere T–35/92 (grounds 47–53, 78–98)
Fiat Agri T–34/92 (grounds 86–94)
Dalmine T–50/00 (grounds 188–191)
Corus UK T–48/00 (grounds 82–86)
Mannesmannröhren-Werke T–44/00 (grounds 166–170)
John Deere C–7/95P
New Holland Ford C–8/95P
Asnef-Equifax C–238/05 (grounds 51–63)

2.5. Compensation schemes

Transocean Marine Paint Assoc. I 10
Quinine Cartel 24 (para.28)
Cimbel 66 (para.13)
⋆CSV 134 (paras 18e, 62, 72)
White Lead 142 (para.12)
BP Kemi/DDSF 147 (paras 28b, 41, 82)
Roofing Felt 248 (para.73)
⋆Meldoc 253 (paras 21–60)
PVC 305 (para.11)
Solvay/CFK 331
Pre-Insulated Pipe Cartel 435
Vitamins 491
Citric Acid 492
Luxembourg Brewing Industry 493
Organic Peroxides 524
Spanish Raw Tobacco 540
BNIC/Aubert C–136/86 (grounds 1, 7)

3. Price agreements between competitors

3.1. Agreed minimum prices

VVVF 22
VCH 47 (para.16)
GISA 67
IFTRA Glass 77 (para.35)
⋆Centraal Bureau voor de Rijwielhandel 118 (paras 10, 25)
FEDETAB 133 (paras 19–21, 81, 96–97)
AROW/BNIC 190 (paras 11–47, 58–65, 67–71)
Cast Iron & Steel Rolls 198 (paras 3, 5–6, 10, 53a, 54)
Aluminium 228 (para.11)
Polypropylene 247 (paras 16, 22–23, 80, 89)
COAPI 402
Vitamins 491
Citric Acid 492
Industrial Gasses 497
Methionine 504
Food Flavour Enhancers 509
French Beef 513
Spanish Raw Tobacco 540 (para.302)
Herbage Seed 6th Comp. Rep. (para.119)
French Beef T–217/03
BNIC v Clair C–123/83

3.1a. Agreed maximum prices

Spanish Raw Tobacco 540 (para.301)

3.2. Agreed common prices

⋆Quinine Cartel 24 (paras 22–24)
VCH 47
NSH 53
Cimbel 66
Belgian Wallpaper 78
IFTRA Aluminium 92
Cobelpa/VNP 115 (paras 5, 21)
Vegetable Parchment 129 (paras 28, 40–52, 71–73)
CSV 134 (paras 18, 20, 62, 72)
BP Kemi/DDSF 147 (paras 28d, 40, 52–54, 81–82)
Natursteinplatten 159 (paras 7–12, 22, 27, 40–41)
Italian Flat Glass 164
SSI 181 (paras 107, 110d, 116d, 123, 127)
Flat Glass (Benelux) 216 (paras 40–43)
Zinc Producer Group 217 (para.66)
⋆Woodpulp 227 (paras 17–27)
Roofing Felt 248
Flat Glass 300 (para.61)
Welded Steel Mesh 311
Scottish Salmon 358 (para.20)
CNSD 375 (para.45)
Far Eastern Freight 399
Pre-Insulated Pipe Cartel 435
TACA 441
NVB-GSA 452
Reims II 453
German Bank Charges 494
Interbrew & Alken-Maes 500
Methionine 504
Christie's/Sotheby's 506
Methylglucamine 508
Specialty Graphite 510
Copper Tubes 538
Choline Chloride 543
Dutch Bitumen 556
Dutch Brewers 559
Sheet Glass 1st Comp. Rep. (para.6)
Lino Cartel 5th Comp. Rep. (para.35)
EBU 16th Comp. Rep. (para.62)
Verbändevereinbarung 28th Comp. Rep. p.165
Lif 29th Comp. Rep. p.170
⋆Europay T–39/92 (grounds 76–87)
Tate & Lyle T–202/98
Papiers Peints C–73/74 (grounds 6–12)
Zuechner v Bayerische Vereinsbank C–172/80 (ground 17)

[For the tables of case citations see Tables 1 to 4, 11 and 12 at the back of the book.]

Ahmed Saeed v Zentrale C–66/86 (ground 19)
Belasco C–246/86 (grounds 12–15)

3.3. Agreed recommended prices

VCH 47 (para.16)
IFTRA Aluminium 92
Vimpoltu 195 (paras 25–27, 39–40)
Fire Insurance 220 (para.23)
Lloyd's Underwriters 363 (paras 30–32)
Dutch Cranes 407a (para.20)
Fenex 409a
Belgian Architects 535 (paras 77–80)
Ship Chains 5th Comp. Rep. (para.40)
★Cement Dealers C–8/72 (grounds 21–25)
Woodpulp C–89/85 (ground 202)

3.4. Agreed price increase

★Dyestuffs 27
European Sugar Industry 69
Franco-Japanese Ball-Bearings 81
SSI 181 (para.110a)
Cast Iron & Steel Rolls 198 (paras 6, 8, 10, 20, 53a, 54)
Zinc Producer Group 217 (paras 75–76)
Fire Insurance 220
PVC 305 (paras 17–22, 35)
LdPE 306 (paras 26–27, 42)
Eurocheques; Helsinki 352 (paras 47–48)
Carton Board 385 (paras 72–102, 136)
Ferry Services 413
Alloy Surcharge 430
British Sugar II 434
Pre-Insulated Pipe Cartel 435
Vitamins 491
Industrial Gasses 497
Carbonless Paper 502
Austrian Banks 503
Methionine 504
Methylglucamine 508
Specialty Graphite 510
Organic Peroxides 524
Copper Tubes 538
Choline Chloride 543
Food Flavour Enhancers 509
Methacrylates 554
Dutch Brewers 559
Woollen Fabrics 12th Comp. Rep. (para.71)
VOTOB 22nd Comp. Rep. (paras 177–186)
PVC II 177
★ICI C–48/69 (grounds 83–103)

3.5. Collective R.P.M.

ASPA 30
Belgian Wallpaper 78
Fireplaces 90
Centraal Bureau voor de Rijwielhandel 118 (paras 10, 25)
FEDETAB 133 (paras 28–39, 82)
★VBBB/VBVB 169 (paras 9, 41–42, 48–63)
Net Book Agreements 301
Railway Tickets 362 (paras 70–84, 91–93)
Dutch Cartridges 3rd Comp. Rep. (paras 55–56)
SARABEX 8th Comp. Rep. (paras 35–37)
Dutch Pharmaceuticals 8th Comp. Rep. (paras 81–82)
VEB/Shell 16th Comp. Rep. (para.55)
Papiers Peints C–73/74 (grounds 6–12)
FEDETAB C–209/78 (grounds 96, 157–162)
VBBB & VBVB 43/82

3.6. Common rebate/discount policy

Quinine Cartel 24 (paras 22–24)
Ceramic Tiles 35
VCH 47 (para.16)
Cimbel 66 (para.15)
Heaters and Boilers 72
Belgian Wallpaper 78
Fireplaces 90
IFTRA Aluminium 92
Centraal Bureau voor de Rijwielhandel 118 (paras 11–12, 27)
★FEDETAB 133 (paras 35, 74–75, 86, 90, 98)
BP Kemi/DDSF 147 (paras 28, 81)
Natursteinplatten 159 (paras 8, 15, 27–28)
Italian Flat Glass 164
SSI 181 (paras 98–99, 114a-b, 133)
Vimpoltu 195 (paras 16–17, 35)
Roofing Felt 248 (paras 73–74)
Flat Glass 300 (para.61)
Net Book Agreements 301
Gosme/Martell 340 (paras 30–32)
FETTCSA 464
Citric Acid 492
Interbrew & Alken-Maes 500
Copper Tubes 538
Dutch Bitumen 556
Dutch Brewers 559
1st Comp. Rep. (para.24)
Dutch Liquorice 2nd Comp. Rep. (para.34)
Belgian & Dutch Electrodes 4th Comp. Rep. (para.78)
Glass Industry 4th Comp. Rep. (para.79)
Lino Cartel 5th Comp. Rep. (para.35)
FETTCSA T–213/00 (ground 175)
★FEDETAB C–209/78 (grounds 103, 142–146)
Vlaamse Reisbureaus C–311/85

3.7. Bidding agreements

DECA 6

[For the tables of case citations see Tables 1 to 4, 11 and 12 at the back of the book.]

European Sugar Industry 69
★Cast Iron & Steel Rolls 198 (paras 3, 5, 8, 10, 53a, 54)
Dutch Building Cartel 349
Pre-Insulated Pipe Cartel 435
Interbrew & Alken-Maes 500 (para.157)
Gas Insulated Switchgear 558
Irish Distillers 18th Comp. Rep. (para.80)
SPO T–29/92 (ground 119)

3.8. Aligning prices in another's territory

IFTRA Glass 77
★IFTRA Aluminium 92
Italian Flat Glass 164
Herbage Seed 6th Comp. Rep. (para.119)

3.9. Price information exchange agreements

IFTRA Glass 77 (paras 40–47)
Belgian Wallpaper 78
IFTRA Aluminium 92
★Cobelpa/VNP 115 (paras 5, 15, 29–30, 42)
Vegetable Parchment 129 (paras 34–39, 63–70)
Vimpoltu 195 (paras 23–27, 38)
Polypropylene 247 (para.80)
Dutch Building Cartel 349
British Midland 350 (paras 33–37)
Cement 394 (para.47)
Seamless Steel Tubes 499 (para.153)
Methylglucamine 508
Specialty Graphite 510
Copper Tubes 538
Spanish Raw Tobacco 540
Choline Chloride 543
Methacrylates 554
Dutch Brewers 559
Dutch Cartridges 3th Comp. Rep. (paras 55–56)
Paper Machine Wire Manu. 6th Comp. Rep. (para.134)
7th Comp. Rep. (paras 5–8)
EWIS 18th. Comp. Rep. (para.63)
Dalmine T–50/00 (grounds 188–191)
Corus UK T–48/00 (grounds 82–86)
Mannesmannröhren-Werke T–44/00 (grounds 166–170)
Ahmed Saeed v Zentrale 66/86 (ground 27)
Woodpulp C–89/85 (grounds 25, 148–163)

4. Sales agreements

4.1. Common or joint sales

Cobelaz 15
Cobelaz Cokes 16
CFA 18
SEIFA 23
Supexie 34
SAFCO 48
NCH 53
SCPA/Kali & Salz 70
Kali & Salz/KaliChemie 76
★CSV 134 (paras 18–19, 62, 72)
Floral 148
Siemens/Fanuc 246
Meldoc 253 (paras 38–44, 65–67)
Hudson Bay 294 (paras 9–10)
ANSAC 333a (para.19)
HOV SVZ/MCN 381 (paras 81–88)
1st Comp. Rep. (para.11)
CIM 1st Comp. Rep. (para.14)
3rd Comp. Rep. (paras 50–52)
Safety Glass 5th Comp. Rep. (para.34)

4.2. Common exports

Alliance de Constructeurs Français 12
Cobelaz 15 (para.6)
Cobelaz Cokes 16
CFA 18
SEIFA 23
Supexie 34
SAFCO 48
★Milchfoerderungsfonds 221

4.3. Common sales policy

Tinned Mushrooms 88
Meldoc 253 (paras 21, 60)
Cement 394 (paras 54, 58–61)
Feldmühle/Stora 12th Comp. Rep. (para.73)
Finnish Wood 26th Comp. Rep. p.144

4.4. Common purchasing policy, purchasing cartels

Quinine Cartel 24 (para.30)
★Italian Flat Glass 164
Aluminium 228 (para.11)
Cement 394 (paras 54, 56)
★Italian Raw Tobacco 550
Dutch Bitumen 556
Belgian Wood Cartel 5th Comp. Rep. (para.37)

4.5. Common sales conditions

Cobelaz 15 (para.7)
Cobelaz Cokes 16
CFA 18
SEIFA 23

[For the tables of case citations see Tables 1 to 4, 11 and 12 at the back of the book.]

Supexie 34
VCH 47 (para.16)
NCH 53
Cimbel 66 (para.13)
GISA 67
Heaters and Boilers 72
IFTRA Glass 77 (paras 36–37, 48–50)
Belgian Wallpaper 78
Pabst & Richerz/BNIA 106
Cobelpa/VNP 115 (paras 5, 21)
Centraal Bureau voor de Rijwielhandel 118 (paras 11–12, 25–26)
★FEDETAB 133 (paras 51–52, 63–73, 76, 86, 99–104)
BP Kemi/DDSF 147 (paras 28, 81)
Natursteinplatten 159 (paras 8–12, 27–28)
Vimpoltu 195 (paras 18–20, 28–30, 35–36, 39)
Zinc Producer Group 217 (para.67)
Roofing Felt 248 (paras 73–74)
★Net Book Agreements 301
Railway Tickets 362 TACA 441
Industrial Gasses 497
Specialty Graphite 510
Spanish Raw Tobacco 540
Lino Cartel 5th Comp. Rep. (para.35)
Finpap 19th Comp. Rep. (para.44)
★FEDETAB C–209/78 (grounds 99, 103, 147–156)

4.6. Information exchange on sales conditions

Cobelpa/VNP 115 (paras 5, 29–30, 42)
★Vegetable Parchment 129 (paras 34–39, 63–70)
CSV 134 (para.25)
PVC 305 (paras 12, 15, 35)
LdPE 306 (paras 10, 18–19, 42)
EWIS 18th Comp. Rep. (para.63)
Tractors 29th Comp. Rep. p.156

4.7. Mutual respect for distribution channels

Cobelpa/VNP 115 (paras 7–8, 16, 31–32, 43)
★Centraal Bureau voor de Rijwielhandel 118 (paras 2–7, 21–22)
IATA Passenger 342 (paras 48–99)
IATA Cargo 343 (paras 43–44)
Railway Tickets 362 (paras 70–72)
Europe Asia Trade Agreements 449
Luxembourg Brewing Industry 493
Interbrew & Alken-Maes 500 (para.242)
French Brewers 539
Tate & Lyle T–202/98 (grounds 58–61)
Luxembourg Brewers T–49e.s./02
FEDETAB C–209/78 (grounds 95–141)

4.8. Restrictions on advertising

Interbrew & Alken-Maes 500 paras 143–147
Austrian Banks 503
Christie's/Sotheby's 506 (paras 168–172)
Patent Agents T–144/99

5. Exclusionary practices

5.1. Collective exclusive dealing

Convention Faience 2
ASPA 30
VCH 47
Central Heating 60
GISA 67
Heaters and Boilers 72
FRUBO 80
Fireplaces 90
Bomée-Stichting 97
★Centraal Bureau voor de Rijwielhandel 118 (paras 5–9, 21–22)
Cauliflowers 119
FEDETAB 133
★Rennet 149 (paras 5–7, 22–23, 31)
IMA Rules 158 (paras 19–20, 43–47, 57–66, 68–73)
Natursteinplatten 159 (para.14)
VBBB/VBVB 169 (paras 9, 39–40, 48)
Sugar Beet 315 (paras 21–41, 73–87)
Ijsselcentrale 335
Railway Tickets 362
Stichting Kraanverhuur 382
Dutch Cranes 407a (para.23)
1st Comp. Rep. (paras 19–23)
Hibin 2nd Comp. Rep. (para.32)
Dutch Cartridges 3rd Comp. Rep. (para.55)
Dutch Record Agreement 4th Comp. Rep. (para.76)
Dutch Transport Insurers 6th Comp. Rep. (para.120)
SARABEX 8th Comp. Rep. (paras 35–37)
Dutch Pharmaceuticals 8th Comp. Rep. (paras 81–82)
Irish Timber Importers 20th Comp. Rep. (para.98)
FEG & TU T–5/00
Frubo C–71/74 (grounds 33–39)
FEDETAB C–209/78 (grounds 95–141)
Stremsel C–61/80

5.2. Agreements intended to control the supply of a product

FRUBO 80

[For the tables of case citations see Tables 1 to 4, 11 and 12 at the back of the book.]

Pabst & Richerz/BNIA 106 (prohibition of bulk sales)
Zinc Producer Group 217 (para.67)
★Aluminium 228 (para.11)
VBA 288
Hudson Bay 294 (paras 8–10)
Ijsselcentrale 335
Dutch Building Cartel 349 (paras 98–99)
French African Shipping 353 (para.41)
Spa Monopole 23rd Comp. Rep. (para.240)
Danish Fur Breeders T–66/89 (grounds 72–83)

5.3. Predatory price-cutting agreements

Meldoc 253 (paras 27–49, 65–69)
CEWAL 371
CMB T–24/93

5.4. Joint production with exclusive purchasing

Rennet 149 (paras 5–7, 22–23, 31)
Ijsselcentrale 335

5.5. Collective refusal to supply

Belgian Wallpaper 78
Bronbemaling 95
FEDETAB 133 (para.87)
Ministère Public v Tournier C–395/87 (grounds 23–26)
Lucazeau v SACEM C–110/88 (grounds 15–19)

5.6. Aggregate rebates

★Ceramic Tiles 35
Belgian Wallpaper 78
★FEDETAB 133 (paras 35, 74–75, 86, 90, 98)
Natursteinplatten 159 (paras 15, 28)
Citric Acid 492
Dutch Liquorice 2nd Comp. Rep. (para.34)
CMB a.o./Commission T–24/93 (ground 183)
★FEDETAB C–209/78 (grounds 103, 142–146)

5.7. Patent pooling

Bronbemaling 95
Concast/Mannesmann 11th Comp. Rep. (paras 92–93)
IGR Stereo TV 11th Comp. Rep. (para.94)
IGR 14th Comp. Rep. (para.92)
Philips/Matsushita 23rd Comp. Rep. (p.460)
Minidiscs 25th Comp. Rep. (p.123)
ETSI 25th Comp. Rep. (p.131)

5.8. Poaching of employees

Pre-Insulated Pipe Cartel 435

5.9. Agreements preventing imports

French Beef 513

5.10. Discriminating against non-members

Dutch Bitumen 556 (paras 156–158)

6. Practices used by cartels to enforce agreements

6.1. Boycotting non-members

Belgian Wallpaper 78
FEDETAB 133 (para.87)
Pre-Insulated Pipe Cartel 435
Luxembourg Brewing Industry 493
Gas Insulated Switchgear 558

6.2. Fines on cartel members for breach of rules

IFTRA Glass 77 (para.39)
Fire Places 90
Centraal Bureau voor de Rijwielhandel 118 (para.13)
Rennet 149 (paras 9, 22, 24, 31)
IMA Rules 158 (paras 20, 32–33)
★Vimpoltu 195 (paras 21–22, 37)
Synthetic Fibres 213
Stichting Baksteen 383
Luxembourg Brewing Industry 493
Dutch Bitumen 556 (para 157)
Gas Insulated Switchgear 558

6.3. Moratoria

Industrial Gasses 497

7. Crisis cartels

Chaufourniers 20
Zinc 189
International Energy Agency 207
★Synthetic Fibres 213
Stichting Baksteen 383
French Beef 513
Polyester Fibres 2nd Comp. Rep. (para.31)
Man-made Fibres 8th Comp. Rep. (para.42)
Man-made Fibres 11th Comp. Rep. (paras 46–48)
12th Comp. Rep. (paras 38–41)
Zinc Producers 13th Comp. Rep. (paras 56–61)
Société Métallurgique de Normandie T–147/89 (grounds 97–98)
Tréfilunion T–148/89 (grounds 116–117)
Société des Treillis et Panneaux Soudés T–151/89 (ground 98)

[For the tables of case citations see Tables 1 to 4, 11 and 12 at the back of the book.]

ACF Chemiefarma C–41/69 (grounds 126–131)
Boehringer C–45/69 (grounds 41–44)

8. Minority acquisitions

BT/MCI 387
Phoenix 412
Dresser/Ingersoll 25th Comp. Rep. (p. 116)
BAT v Philip Morris C–142/84

9. Agreement to purchase or not to purchase third parties

Organic Peroxides 524
French Brewers 539

10. Facilitating others' cartels

★Organic Peroxide 524 (para.331)

CHAPTER 2

CO-OPERATION AGREEMENTS

A. LIST OF CASES ON CO-OPERATION AGREEMENTS

Transocean Marine Paint Assoc. I 10
Eurogypsum 11
Alliance de Constructeurs Française 12
VVVF 22
Pirelli/Dunlop 28
ASBL 31
SAFCO 48
Video Cassette Recorders 122
SOPELEM/Vickers I 125
SNPE/LEL 132
SOPELEM/Vickers II 171
NAVEWA-ANSEAU 178
VW/MAN 203
International Energy Agency 207
Nuovo-CEGAM 209
Uniform Eurochèques 224
Irish Banks Standing Committee 252
Belgian Banking Association 261
ABI 262
X/Open Group 263
Eurotunnel 293
Uniform Eurochèques Manufacturing 302
Dutch Banking Association 310
APB 314
Concordato 316
TEKO 317
IATA Passengers 342
IATA Cargo 343
UER 373
International Energy Agency II 380
Eurotunnel 396
Network Sharing UK 514
German Network Sharing 518
Air France/Alitalia 529
BP-Ruhrgas 9th Comp. Rep. (para.94)
ICL/Fujitsu 16th Comp. Rep. (para.72)
FIEC-CFETB 18th Comp. Rep. (para.62)
EWIS 18th Comp. Rep. (para.63)
BDO Binder 21st Comp. Rep. (p.35)
Acriss 23rd Comp. Rep. (p.454)
Abim Card 23rd Comp. Rep. (para.458)
Gøttrup-Klim v DLG C–250/92
★O2 (Germany) T–328/03
Asnef-Equifax C–238/05

B. TEXT OF RELEVANT NOTICES

1. Co-operation agreements

1.1. Commission Notice Guidelines on the applicability of Article 81 of the EC Treaty to horizontal co-operation agreements [2001] O.J. C3/2

1.2. Cases on the interpretation of the Notice of July 29, 1968 on co-operation between enterprises [1968] O.J. C75/3, amended by corrigendum [1968] O.J. C84/14

IFTRA Glass 77
IFTRA Aluminium 92 Cobelpa/VNP 115 (para.27)
Vegetable Parchment 129 (para.65)
Beecham/Parke Davis 144 (para.33)
Roofing Felt 248 (para.73)
Siemens/Fanuc 246 (para.30)
★Eurotunnel 293
ANSAC 333a (para.30)

2. Commission Notice of December 18, 1978 concerning its assessment of certain sub-contracting agreements in relation to Article 85(1) of the EEC Treaty [1979] O.J. C1/2

C. TYPES/CATEGORIES OF CO-OPERATION AGREEMENTS

1. Sharing of research and development (R&D) costs

See R&D agreements, Chapter 4.

2. Patent pools

Video Cassette Recorders 122 (paras 12, 15, 24)
★Continental/Michelin 290
Concast/Mannesmann 11th Comp. Rep. (paras 92–93)
IGR Stereo TV 11th Comp. Rep. (para.94)
Minidiscs 25th Comp. Rep. (p.123)
ETSI 25th Comp. Rep. (p.131)

3. Sharing of capacity

Pirelli/Dunlop 28
Air France/Alitalia 529

4. Building consortia

Eurotunnel 293
Global Satellite 25th Comp. Rep. (p.132)

5. Uniform standards

VVVF 22
Video Cassette Recorders 122
SOPELEM/Vickers I 125
★X/Open Group 263
Uniform Eurochèques Manufacturing 302
European Cement Producers 548

6. Uniform sales conditions

★Nuovo-CEGAM 209
Uniform Eurochèque 224
Irish Banks Standing Committee 252
Belgian Banking Association 261
ABI 262 (para.41)
Olivetti/Digital 393

7. Joint or common advertising

ASBL 31

8. Adoption of common trademarks or quality marks

★Transocean Marine Paint Assoc. I 10
ASBL 31
Belgian Wallpaper 78
Intergroup 91
★NAVEWA-ANSEAU 178
APB 314
1st Comp. Rep. (para.39)
Poroton 10th Comp. Rep. (paras 130–132)

9. Joint sales

Alliance de Constructeurs Français 12
★SAFCO 48
SOPELEM/Vickers I 125
UEFA 519
Bundesliga Broadcasting Rights 544
FA Premier League 551

10. Inter-bank agreements

See Part IX, Chapter 3
Visa II 496
Asnef-Equifax C–238/05

11. Buying groups

Socemas 13
★Intergroup 91
Rennet 149
National Sulphuric Acid Assoc. I 156
IMA Rules 158
Fisher-Price 275 (para.18)
National Sulphuric Acid Assoc. II 308
★Dutch Bitumen 556 (paras 146–147, 162–167)
UER 373
1st Comp. Rep. (paras 40–41)
Orptie 20th Comp. Rep. (para.120)
Métropole T–528/93
Stremsel C–61/80
★Gøttrup-Klim v DLG C–250/92

12. Exploitation/sharing of infrastructure

Eurotunnel 396
Network Sharing UK 514
German Network Sharing 518
O2 (Germany) T–328/03

13. Collective lobbying

Cement 394 (para.53)

14. Shareholders' agreements

TPS 440
Identrus 476

CHAPTER 3

SPECIALISATION AGREEMENTS

A. LIST OF CASES ON SPECIALISATION AGREEMENTS

ACEC/Berliet 14
Clima Chappée 25
Jaz/Peter I 26

[For the tables of case citations see Tables 1 to 4, 11 and 12 at the back of the book.]

FN-CF 37
SOPELEM/Langen 49
MAN/SAVIEM 54
Wild/Leitz 55
Thin Paper 59
Prym/Beka 74
Kali & Salz/Kalichemie 76
Rank/SOPELEM 86
Bayer/Gist-Brocades 100
SOPELEM/Vickers I 125
Jaz/Peter II 128
Italian Cast Glass 163
SOPELEM/Vickers II 171
Zinc 189
VW/MAN 203
BPCL/ICI 215
ENI-Montedison 256
Alcatel/ANT 319
1st Comp. Rep. (paras 26–29)
2nd Comp. Rep. (paras 8–11, 35)
7th Comp. Rep. (paras 35, 36)
VFA/SAVER 15th Comp. Rep. (para.78)
Enimont/Orkem 23rd Comp. Rep. (p.457)

B. COMMISSION REGULATION 2658/2000 OF NOVEMBER 29, 2000 ON THE APPLICATION OF ARTICLE 81(3) OF THE TREATY TO CATEGORIES OF SPECIALISATION AGREEMENTS [2000] O.J. L304/3

C. CASES ON THE INTERPRETATION OF THE REGULATION

Italian Cast Glass 163
Needles 542

D. CATEGORIES OF SPECIALISATION AGREEMENTS

1. Agreements to expand the range of goods produced/sold by the parties

Clima-Chappée 25
★Jaz/Peter I 26
FN/CF 37
SOPELEM/Langen 49
MAN/SAVIEM 54
Wild/Leitz 55
Rank/SOPELEM 86
SOPELEM/Vickers I 125
SOPELEM/Vickers II 171
VW/MAN 203

2. Agreements to share R&D costs

★ACEC/Berliet 14
Rank/SOPELEM 86
Bayer/Gist-Brocades 100
Alcatel/ANT 319 (para.6c)

3. Joint distribution agreements

SOPELEM/Vickers I 125
★VW/MAN 203 (paras 8–9, 20, 28)

4. Restructuring agreements

Thin Paper 59
Prym/Beca 74
Cast Iron & Steel Rolls 198
BPCL/ICI 215
★ENI/Montedison 256

E. CLAUSES TYPICAL OF SPECIALISATION AGREEMENTS

1. Exchange of information/licences

ACEC/Berliet 14
★MAN/SAVIEM 54 (para.27)
Bayer/Gist-Brocades 100
SOPELEM/Vickers I 125
Alcatel/ANT 319 (paras 6d and 6f)

2. Reciprocal distribution rights

Clima Chappée 25
Jaz/Peter I 26 (paras 5–6)
FN/CF 37
SOPELEM/Langen 49
MAN/SAVIEM 54
Wild/Leitz 55
Rank/SOPELEM 86
SOPELEM/Vickers I 125
Jaz/Peter II 128

3. Obligation to supply or purchase from the other party

3.1. Exclusive purchasing obligation

★ACEC/Berliet 14
Clima Chappée 25
SOPELEM/Langen 49
Prym/Beca 74
Zinc 189
VW/MAN 203
Alcatel/ANT 319 (para.6c)
Perlite 19th Comp. Rep. (para.39)

[For the tables of case citations see Tables 1 to 4, 11 and 12 at the back of the book.]

3.2. Obligation to supply the other party

★ACEC/Berliet 14
Bayer/Gist-Brocades 100
Zinc 189
Alcatel/ANT 319 (paras 6c and 6h)
VFA/SAVER 15th Comp. Rep. (para.78)

3.3. Right of first refusal to sell new products

Jaz/Peter I 26 (paras 5–6, 126)

3.4. Most favoured customer clause

ACEC/Berliet 14

4. Non-competitive clause

Jaz/Peter I 26 (paras 5–6, 126)
FN/CF 37
SOPELEM/Langen 49
★MAN/SAVIEM 54 (paras 15–22)
Prym/Beca 74
Bayer/Gist-Brocades 100 (para.II.3)
SOPELEM/Vickers I 125
Zinc 189
VW/MAN 203 (paras 10, 17, 19, 26, 31)

5. Territorial restriction

MAN/SAVIEM 54
★Rank/SOPELEM 86

6. Trade mark related clauses

Jaz/Peter I 26 (paras 5–6)
Rank/SOPELEM 86

CHAPTER 4

RESEARCH AND DEVELOPMENT AGREEMENTS

A. LIST OF CASES ON R&D AGREEMENTS

Eurogypsum 11
ACEC/Berliet 14
Henkel/Colgate 52
MAN/SAVIEM 54
Rank/SOPELEM 86
Vacuum Interrupters I 112
Delaval/Stork I 114
GEC/Weir Sodium Circulators 117
Beecham/Parke Davis 144
Vacuum Interrupters II 161
VW/MAN 203
Carbon Gas Technologie 205
BP/Kellogg 235
Olivetti/Canon 280
Delaval/Stork II 281
Continental/Michelin 290
BBC Brown Boveri 291
Alcatel/ANT 319
Odin 322
Konsortium ECR 900 323
KSB 328
Asahi/St Gobain 398
1st Comp. Rep. (paras 31–35)
NCB 15th Comp. Rep. (para.71)
Bayer/Hoechst 20th Comp. Rep. (para.99)
UTC/MTU 22nd Comp. Rep. (p.415)
Exxon/Hoechst 25th Comp. Rep. (p.125)
Eurocar 27th Comp. Rep. (p.138)

B. COMMISSION REGULATION 2659/2000 OF NOVEMBER 29, 2000 ON THE APPLICATION OF ARTICLE 81(3) OF THE TREATY TO CATEGORIES OF RESEARCH AND DEVELOPMENT AGREEMENTS [2000] O.J. L304/7

C. CASES ON THE INTERPRETATION OF THE REGULATION

BP/Kellogg 235
Continental/Michelin 290 (para.21)
BBC Brown Boveri 291 (paras 16, 21)
Welded Steel Mesh 311 (paras 190–191)
Alcatel/ANT 319 (para.17)
★KSB 328
Quantel 357 (paras 45–49)
17th Comp. Rep. (para.31)
Sevel 23rd Comp. Rep. (para.227)

D. CATEGORIES OF R&D AGREEMENTS

1. Joint R&D without production

ACEC/Berliet 14
★Henkel/Colgate 52
MAN/SAVIEM 54
Rank/SOPELEM 86
Beecham/Parke Davis 144
Continental/Michelin 290
BBC/Brown Boveri 291
Alcatel/ANT 319
Asahi/St Gobain 398

2. Joint R&D with subsequent joint production

Vacuum Interrupters I 112

[For the tables of case citations see Tables 1 to 4, 11 and 12 at the back of the book.]

Delaval/Stork I 114
GEC/Weir Sodium Circulators 117
Vacuum Interrupters 161
Carbon Gas Technologie 205
BP/Kellogg 235
⋆Olivetti/Canon 280
Delaval/Stork II 281
Odin 322
Konsortium ECR 900 323
⋆KSB 328
Fujitsu AMD 395

E. CLAUSES COMMONLY FIGURING IN R&D AGREEMENTS

1. Territorial provisions

1.1. Division of the EC into exclusive territories between the contracting parties for exploitation of results

⋆ACEC/Berliet 14
MAN/SAVIEM 54 (para.17)
Rank/SOPELEM 86
Beecham/Parke Davis 144 (paras 20, 43)

1.2. Prohibition of active sales outside exclusive territory

Rank/SOPELEM 86

1.3. Prohibition of passive sales outside exclusive territory

MAN/SAVIEM 54 (para.17)

1.4. Export prohibition to the Common Market

BBC Brown Boveri 291 (paras 18, 22)

2. Supply and purchase obligations

2.1. Exclusive purchasing obligations

ACEC/Berliet 14
Vacuum Interrupters I 112
Vacuum Interrupters II 161
Alcatel/ANT 319 (para.6c)
⋆KSB 328 (para.22)

2.2. Mutual supply obligations

ACEC/Berliet 14
MAN/SAVIEM 54
Alcatel/ANT 319 (para.6h)

2.3. Most favoured customer clause

ACEC/Berliet 14

3. Non-competition clauses

3.1. Prohibition from engaging in competing R&D

MAN/SAVIEM 54 (paras 15, 22)
⋆GEC/Weir Sodium Circulators 117
Beecham/Parke Davis 144 (paras 14, 29)
Carbon Gas Technologie 205
⋆BP/Kellogg 235 (para.9)
Continental/Michelin 290 (para.13)
BBC Brown Boveri 291 (para.16)
Alcatel/ANT 319 (para.6c)
Konsortium ECR 900 323
Asahi/St Gobain 398 (paras 11, 21, 29)

3.2. Prohibition from engaging in R&D in unconnected fields

MAN/SAVIEM 54 (paras 15–16)
GEC/Weir Sodium Circulators 117
Vacuum Interrupters II 161
Carbon Gas Technologie 205
⋆BP/Kellogg 235 (paras 8–9)

4. Customer limitation clause

MAN/SAVIEM 54 (paras 20–21)

5. Clauses relating to intellectual property and related rights

5.1. Exchange of technical information

ACEC/Berliet 14
Henkel/Colgate 52
Vacuum Interrupters I 112
GEC/Weir Sodium Circulators 117
⋆Beecham/Parke Davis 144 (paras 9–11, 16–21, 33, 39–41)
Vacuum Interrupters II 161
Carbon Gas Technologie 205
BP/Kellogg 235
Continental/Michelin 290 (paras 7, 17)
BBC Brown Boveri 291 (para.19)
Alcatel/ANT 319 (paras 6d & 6f)
Odin 322 (paras 6–9)
Konsortium ECR 900 323
Asahi/St Gobain 398

5.2. Field of use restrictions

Article 5(1)(b)
ACEC/Berliet 14
Alcatel/ANT 319 (para.6d)
Odin 322 (paras 6–9)

5.3. Obligation to maintain confidentiality of know-how

MAN/SAVIEM 54 (para.27)

[For the tables of case citations see Tables 1 to 4, 11 and 12 at the back of the book.]

Carbon Gas Technologie 205
Alcatel/ANT 319 (para.6e)
Odin 322 (para.19)
KSB 328 (para.18)

5.4. Grant of licences to third parties/sub-licensing

Henkel/Colgate 52
Beecham/Parke Davis 144 (paras 9–11, 16–21, 33, 39–41)
BP/Kellogg 235
★KSB 328 (para.18)
Asahi/St Gobain 398

5.5. Patent pooling

Video Cassette Recorders 122 (paras 12, 15, 24)
Continental/Michelin 290 (para.15)
Alcatel/ANT 319 (para.6d)
See also Part IV, Chapter 1.

5.6. Post-term use ban of jointly developed technology

Carbon Gas Technologie 205

5.7. Patent no-challenge clause

5.8. Obligation to inform the other party of patent infringement

6. Duration of the agreement

6.1. Between competitors

Article 3(2)-(5)
Henkel/Colgate 52
★KSB 328

6.2. Between non-competitors

7. Royalty provisions

7.1. Obligation to pay royalties to the other party if contribution to R&D is unequal

Beecham/Parke Davis 144 (paras 18, 43c)

7.2. Obligation to share royalties received from third parties

Continental/Michelin 290 (para.15)

7.3. Profit-sharing through royalty payments

Beecham/Parke Davis 144 (paras 18, 43c)

CHAPTER 5

TRADE ASSOCIATIONS

A. CASES ON TRADE ASSOCIATIONS

1. General list

Eurogypsum 11
ASBL 31
London Sugar Market 238
London Cocoa Market 239
London Coffee Market 240
London Rubber Market 241
P&I Clubs 243
IPEL 255
London Grain Market 257
London Potato Market 258
London Meat Exchange 259
GAFTA 260
BIFFEX 271
Sarabex 8th Comp. Rep. (paras 35–37)
Department Stores 9th Comp. Rep. (para.89)
FEG C–105/04
Technische Unie C–113/04

2. List of cases where a trade association was acting as a cartel

VVVF 22
ASPA 30
Ceramic Tiles 35
Cimbel 66
GISA 67
Heaters and Boilers 72
Belgian Wallpaper 78
FRUBO 80
Bomée Stichting 97
Pabst & Richerz/BNIA 106
Centraal Bureau voor de Rijwielhandel 118
Cauliflowers 119
FEDETAB 133
Rennet 149
National Sulphuric Acid Assoc. I 156
IMA Rules 158
Natursteinplatten 159
Italian Flat Glass 164
VBBB/VBVB 170
SSI 181
Vimpoltu 195
Fire Insurance 220
Roofing Felt 248
VBA 288

[For the tables of case citations see Tables 1 to 4, 11 and 12 at the back of the book.]

Hudson Bay 294
National Sulphuric Acid Assoc. II 308
Sugar Beet 315
U.K. Tractors 347
Auditel 376
Dutch Cranes 407a
French Beef 513
Herbage Seed 6th Comp. Rep. (para.119)
Dutch Transport Insurers 6th Comp. Rep. (para.120)
Dutch Pharmaceuticals 8th Comp. Rep. (paras 81–82)
French Beef T–217/03
Frubo C–71/74 (grounds 33–39)
FEDETAB C–209/78
Stremsel C–61/80 (grounds 12–13)
FEG C–105/04
Technische Unie C–113/04

B. STIPULATIONS COMMON TO TRADE ASSOCIATION AGREEMENTS

1. Rules regarding membership of associations

1.1. Objective criteria for membership

Centraal Bureau voor de Rijwielhandel 118 (paras 3, 19–20)
Cauliflowers 119
★FEDETAB 133 (paras 6, 40–43, 84)
IMA Rules 158 (paras 12–18, 42–45)
Natursteinplatten 159 (paras 36–38)
Nuovo-CEGAM 209 (para.16)
London Sugar Market 238
London Cocoa Market 239
London Coffee Market 240
London Rubber Market 241
IPEL 255
GAFTA 260
London Grain Market 257
★X/Open Group 263
British Sheep Breeders 22nd Comp. Rep. (p.416)
Métropole T–528/93 (grounds 95–102)

1.2. Limit on numbers of members

FEDETAB 133 (paras 40–43, 84)
IMA Rules 158 (para.45)
SSI 181 (paras 99d, 116a, 134–137)
Dept. Stores 9th Comp. Rep. (para.89)
★FEDETAB C–209/78 (ground 97)

1.3. Provisions limiting withdrawal from association

Rennet 149 (paras 9, 22–24, 31)
★P&I Clubs 243

2. Pricing obligations

FEDETAB 133
Natursteinplatten 159
London Sugar Market 238
London Cocoa Market 239
London Coffee Market 240
London Rubber Market 241
P&I Clubs 243 IPEL 255
GAFTA 260
London Grain Market 257
London Potato Market 258
London Meat Exchange 259
BIFFEX 271
Sarabex 8th Comp. Rep. (paras 35–37)
Dutch Pharmaceuticals 8th Comp. Rep. (paras 81–82)
FEDETAB C–209/78 (grounds 96, 157–162)

3. Agreement to purchase minimum percentages from domestic producers

★GISA 67
Rennet 149 (paras 5–7, 22–23, 31)

4. Discriminatory conditions against non-members

Ceramic Tiles 35 (para.2c)
Belgian Wallpaper 78
SSI 181 (paras 99b, 111, 116c)
★EATE Levy 231 (para.47)
Sugar Beet 315

5. Industry organised distribution schemes

FEDETAB 133 (paras 19–27, 81, 96–97)
Rennet 149
National Sulphuric Acid Assoc. 156
IMA Rules 158

6. Collective exclusive dealing

See Cartels

7. Collective lobbying

French African Shipping 353 (para.68)
Scottish Salmon 358 (paras 12, 19)
French Beef T–217/03 (ground 102)

[For the tables of case citations see Tables 1 to 4, 11 and 12 at the back of the book.]

CHAPTER 6

TRADE FAIR AND EXHIBITION AGREEMENTS

A. CASES ON TRADE FAIR AND EXHIBITION AGREEMENTS

EMO I 19
Cematex I 43
UNIDI I 93
BPICA I 116
EMO II 140
BPICA II 180
Cematex II 193
UNIDI II 219
EMO III 303
SMM&T 201
VIFKA 251
International Dental Exhibition 274
British Dental Trade Association 285
Sippa 336
1st Comp. Rep. (paras 42–43)
British Dental Trade Association 27th Comp. Rep. (p.134)
Ancides C–43/85
JCB Service C–167/04

B. STIPULATIONS COMMON TO EXHIBITION AGREEMENTS

1. Agreement not to exhibit at other exhibitions

EMO I 19
Cematex I 43
UNIDI I 93
BPICA I 116
EMO II 140
BPICA II 180
Cematex II 193
UNIDI II 219
EMO III 303
SMM&T 201
★VIFKA 251
International Dental Exhibition 274
British Dental Trade Association 285

2. Objective criteria for admittance

BPICA I 116 (para.9)
★International Dental Exhibition 274
Sippa 336

3. Discrimination against foreign exhibitors

★British Dental Trade Association 285
EUMAPRINT Exhibition 3rd Comp. Rep. (para.57)

[For the tables of case citations see Tables 1 to 4, 11 and 12 at the back of the book.]

PART IV

VERTICAL AGREEMENTS

CHAPTER 1

LEGISLATION

A. COMMISSION REGULATION 2790/1999 OF DECEMBER 22, 1999 ON THE APPLICATION OF ARTICLE 81(3) OF THE TREATY TO CATEGORIES OF VERTICAL AGREEMENTS AND CONCERTED PRACTICES [1999] O.J. L336/21

B. COMMISSION NOTICE GUIDELINES ON VERTICAL RESTRAINTS [2000] O.J. C291/1

CHAPTER 2

DISTRIBUTION AGREEMENTS

A. LIST OF CASES ON EXCLUSIVE DISTRIBUTION

Grosfillex/Fillestorf 1
★Grundig/Consten 5
DRU/Blondel 7
Hummel/Isbecque 8
Maison Jallatte 9
Rieckerman 17
Omega 33
Pittsburgh Corning 63
DuroDyne 83
Goodyear Italiana/Euram 85
SABA I 99
Miller 108
Junghans 109
Theal/Watts 110
Pioneer 152
Hennessy/Henkel I 162
Moët et Chandon (London) Ltd 172
Hasselblad 173
National Panasonic 186
SABA II 208
Polistil/Arbois 211
Carlsberg 214
John Deere 226
Whisky and Gin 237
Sperry New Holland 245
Siemens/Fanuc 246
Tipp-Ex 269
ARG/Unipart 278
Gosme/Martell 340
Viho/Toshiba 341
Eco System 344a
Newitt/Dunlop 351
World Cup Football 360
Tretorn 401
BASF/Accinauto 405
Novalliance 415
Nintendo 505
Telenor/Canal+ 527 (paras 170–177 & 146–156)
Needles 542 (paras 305–307)
1st Comp. Rep. (paras 45–57)
2nd Comp. Rep. (para.40)
Beecham Pharma 6th Comp. Rep. (para.129)
Seita 10th Comp. Rep. (para.124)
18th Comp. Rep. (paras 21 and 50–56)
26th Comp. Rep. (paras 46–58)
Atlanta Olympic Games 26th Comp. Rep. p.165
1998 Football World Cup 27th Comp. Rep. p.146
Van Megen Sport T–49/95
JCB Service T–67/01
Consten & Grundig C–56/64
Italy v Council and Commission C–32/65
Völk v Vervaecke C–5/69
Cadillon v Höss C–1/71
Béguelin v GL C–22/71
Dassonville C–8/74 (grounds 12–15)
Ciments et Bétons v Kerpen C–319/82
ETA v DKI C–31/85
Volkswagen C–338/00P

[For the tables of case citations see Tables 1 to 4, 11 and 12 at the back of the book.]

B. LIST OF CASES ON NON-EXCLUSIVE DISTRIBUTION

Bendix/Mertens and Straet 3
Dupont de Nemours Germany 71
Deutsche Philips 73
Kali & Salz/Kalichemie 76
Gerofabriek 111
The Distillers Company 123
Spices 124
Arthur Bell & Sons Ltd 135
Teacher & Sons 136
Zanussi 139
Distillers-Victuallers 157
Johnson & Johnson 160
Moët et Chandon (London) Ltd 172
Cafeteros de Colombia 187
VIHO/Parker Pen 355
Topps 530 (para.138)
Joynson T–231/99
Shaw T–231/99
Van den Bergh Foods T–65/98

C. CLAUSES COMMONLY STIPULATED IN DISTRIBUTION AGREEMENTS

1. Territorial restrictions

1.1. Grant of an exclusive territory to the distributor

Grundig/Consten 5
DRU/Blondel 7
Hummel/Isbecque 8
Maison Jallatte 9
Omega 33 (paras 2, 5, 7)
DuroDyne 83
Goodyear Italiana/Euram 85
SABA I 99 (paras 13, 32, 46)
Junghans 109 (paras 28, 31)
Theal/Watts 110
Hennessy/Henkell 162
Hasselblad 173
Polistil/Arbois 211 (para.22)
Whisky and Gin 237
Sperry New Holland 245
Tipp-Ex 269
Nathan Bricolux 466 (paras 73–84)
1st Comp. Rep. (paras 45–52)
2nd Comp. Rep. (para.42)
7th Comp. Rep. (paras 9–16)
SEITA 10th Comp. Rep. (para.124)
⋆Consten & Grundig C–56/64
Italy v Council and Commission C–32/65

1.2. No active sales policy outside agreed territory

Goodyear Italiana/Euram 85
⋆SABA I 99 (paras 13, 32, 46)
Junghans 109 (paras 9, 29, 31)
Whisky and Gin 237
⋆Sperry New Holland 245 (paras 54–55)
Tipp-Ex 269 (para.13)
Maison des Bibliothèques 14th Comp. Rep. (para.68)

1.3. Profit pass-over clause

Polistil/Arbois 211 (para.22)
Ivoclar 234
JCB 479 (paras 155–167)

1.4. Export ban on direct sales by distributor

1.4.1. Between Member States

Grundig/Consten 5
Omega 33 (para.9)
Miller 108 (paras 5–6, 11–15)
Gerofabriek 111
The Distillers Company 123
Arthur Bell & Sons Ltd 135
Teacher & Sons 136
Moët et Chandon (London) Ltd 172
John Deere 226 (paras 16, 24)
Sperry New Holland 245 (paras 24, 26, 53)
Viho/Toshiba 341
Newitt/Dunlop 351 (paras 48–50)
VIHO/Parker Pen 355
BASF/Accinauto 405 (para.89)
Novalliance 415
JCB 479 (paras 141–149)
Mercedes Benz 490 (para.173)
Nintendo 505
Topps 530
1st Comp. Rep. (para.54)
Beecham Pharma 6th Comp. Rep. (para.129)
Dunlop T–43/92
Parker Pen T–77/92
Herlitz T–66/92
BASF T–175/95
Volkswagen T–62/98 (grounds 48–49)
JCB Service T–67/01
⋆Consten & Grundig C–56/64
Völk v Vervaecke C–5/69
Parfums Rochas v Bitsch C–1/70 (grounds 2, 5, 7)
Cadillon v Höss C–1/71 (grounds 9–10)
ETA v DKI C–31/85 (ground 10)

1.4.2. Into the EC

Grosfillex/Fillertorf 1

[For the tables of case citations see Tables 1 to 4, 11 and 12 at the back of the book.]

★Rieckermann 17
Haladjian Frères T–204/03 (ground 183)

1.4.3. Outside the EC

★Omega 33 (para.5)
Deutsche Philips 73
Goodyear Italian/Euram 85 (para.8)
Junghans 109 (paras 10, 24)
The Distillers Company 123
Arthur Bell & Sons Ltd 135
Teacher & Sons 136
JCB Service T–67/01 (ground 102)

1.5. Export ban on indirect sales, i.e. export ban reimposed upon customers

Grundig/Consten 5
Du Pont de Nemours Germany 71
Deutsche Philips 73
Miller 108 (paras 5–6, 11–15)
Theal/Watts 110
The Distillers Company 123
Johnson & Johnson 160 (paras 13–23, 29–34)
Hasselblad 173 (paras 10–29, 52–55)
Polistil/Arbois 211 (paras 26, 40–43)
Tipp-Ex 269 (paras 13, 51–52, 60–62)
Gosme/Martell 340 (para.35)
Tretorn 401
★Consten & Grundig C–56/64
Miller C–19/77 (ground 7)
Tepea C–28/77 (grounds 33–45, 53–57)

2. Clauses relating to the product that the distributor may sell

2.1. Non-competition clause

★Maison Jallatte 9
Goodyear Italian/Euram 85 (para.2)
SABA I 99 (paras 13, 32, 46)
Junghans 109 (paras 14, 28, 31)
Gerofabriek 111
Spices 124 (paras 12, 17, 19–20)
Hennessy/Henkell 162 (paras 5, 18–19)
Whisky and Gin 237
Telenor/Canal+ 527 (paras 157–168 & 179–183)
Microsoft Internet Explorer 29th Comp. Rep. (p.162)
Vanden Bergh Foods T–65/98

2.2. Minimum purchasing obligations

Goodyear Italian/Euram 85 (para.1)
Carlsberg 214 (para.3.1)
Microsoft Internet Explorer 29th Comp. Rep. (p.162)

2.3. Exclusive purchasing requirements

Rieckerman 17
Hennessy/Henkell 162 (paras 5, 19)
Neste C–214/99
JCB Service T–67/01 (grounds 111–118)

2.4. Guaranteed after-sales service

See also Part IV, Chapter 3.
Grundig/Consten 5
Omega 33 (paras 2, 5)
★Zanussi 139 (paras 10–13)
★Hasselblad 173 (paras 30–32, 52–55)
Ideal Standard Sales System 223 (para.16)
Constructa 4th Comp. Rep. (para.109)
7th Comp. Rep. (paras 17–20)
Moulinex 10th Comp. Rep. (para.122)
Matsushita 12th Comp. Rep. (para.77)
Ford Germany 13th Comp. Rep. (paras 104–106)
Fiat 14th Comp. Rep. (paras 70–71)
16th Comp. Rep. (para.56)
Sony 17th Comp. Rep. (para.67)
AKZO 19th Comp. Rep. (para.45)
★ETA v DKI C–31/85 (grounds 12–14)
★Hasselblad C–86/82 (grounds 33–34)

2.5. Assembly and manufacture by distributor

Omega 33 (paras 2, 5)

2.6. Stocking requirement

Omega 33 (paras 2, 5)
★Spices 124 (para.12)

3. Clauses related to the price of the product

3.1. Resale price maintenance

See Council Decision of September 22, 1997 on cross-border fixed book prices in European linguistic areas ([1997] O.J. C305/2) and Council Resolution of February 8, 1999 on fixed book prices in homogeneous cross-border linguistic areas ([1999] O.J. C42/3).
Omega 33 (para.3)
Dupont de Nemours Germany 71
★Deutsche Philips 73
Junghans 109 (paras 17–18)

[For the tables of case citations see Tables 1 to 4, 11 and 12 at the back of the book.]

★Gerofabriek 111
Spices 124 (paras 12, 17)
Hennessy/Henkell 162 (paras 5, 11–15, 20, 28–29, 32–33)
Novalliance 415 (para.61)
Nathan Bricolux 466
Volkswagen 474
JCB 479 (paras 168–173)
Mercedes Benz 490 (para.177)
1st Comp. Rep. (para.55)
VEB/Shell 16th Comp. Rep. (para.54)
Rover 23rd Comp. Rep. (para.228)
Belgian newspapers 29th Comp. Rep. p.161
FEG & TU T–5/00
JCB Service T–67/01 (grounds 131–133)
★AMP v Binon C–243/83 (grounds 44–46)
Louis Erauw v La Hesbignonne C–27/87 (ground 15)

3.2. Discriminatory pricing between different territories

★Pittsburgh Corning 63
The Distillers Company 123
Polistil/Arbois 211 (para.43–51)
Sperry New Holland 245 (paras 28, 54)
Gosme/Martell 340 (para.31)
★Newitt/Dunlop 351 (paras 54–57)
Glaxo Wellcome 473
1st Comp. Rep. (para.48)
Maison des Bibliothèques 14th Comp. Rep. (para.69)
Distillers 17th Comp. Rep. (para.65)

3.3. Obligation to transmit recommended prices

ARG/Unipart 278 (para.32)

4. Clauses relating to the customers to which the distributor may sell

Omega 33 (para.9)
Dupont de Nemours Germany 71
★Deutsche Philips 73
Junghans 109 (para.21)
Gerofabriek 111
Distillers-Victuallers 157 (paras 12–17)
Cafeteros de Colombia 187
World Cup Football 360 (paras 84–86)
Opel 467
Volkswagen 474
Mercedes Benz 490 (para.176)
Nintendo 505
Brazilian Coffee 5th Comp. Rep. (para.33)
Beecham Pharma 6th Comp. Rep. (para.129)
Brazilian Coffee 6th Comp. Rep. (para.54)
IBC 16th Comp. Rep. (para.54)
Volkswagen T–62/98
JCB Service T–67/01 (grounds 148–153)
★Ciments et Bétons v Kerpen C–319/82 (ground 6)

5. Distribution agreements between competing manufacturers

5.1. Reciprocal

SNPE/LEL 132 (paras 4, 13)
★Siemens/Fanuc 246
Fluke/Philips 19th Comp. Rep. (para.47)
ESK/Gist Brocades 26th Comp. Rep. p.164
Baustahlgewebe T–145/89 (grounds 101–106)
Tréfileurope T–141/89 (grounds 116–121)

5.2. Non-reciprocal

European Sugar Industry 69
Kali & Salz/Kalichemie 76
Carlsberg 214 (paras 3, 11)
★Whisky and Gin 237
Carlsberg/Courage 22nd Comp. Rep. (para.130)
Interbrew 24th Comp. Rep. (p.351)

CHAPTER 3

EXCLUSIVE PURCHASING AGREEMENTS

A. CASES ON EXCLUSIVE PURCHASING AGREEMENTS

Spices 124
BP Kemi/DDSF 147 (paras 26, 33–37, 57–71, 93–97)
Rennet 149
Cane Sugar Supply Agreements 150 (paras 11, 12, 19–24)
National Sulphuric Acid Assoc. I 156
IMA Rules 158
Schlegel/CPIO 204 (paras 4–5, 14–21)
National Sulphuric Acid Assoc. II 308
Ijsselcentrale 335 (para.28)
Scottish Nuclear 339
Mars/Langnese 369
Jahrhundertvertrag 370
Auditel 376
Olivetti/Digital 393
Van den Bergh Foods 431
Whitbread 439
Repsol 552

[For the tables of case citations see Tables 1 to 4, 11 and 12 at the back of the book.]

Sand Producers 6th Comp. Rep. (paras 123–125)
7th Comp. Rep. (paras 9–16)
Soda Ash 11th Comp. Rep. (paras 73–76)
Nutrasweet 18th Comp. Rep. (para.53)
Elders/Grand Metropolitan 21st Comp. Rep. (para.86)
Unilever/Mars 25th Comp. Rep. (p.137, para.41)
MD Foods 25th Comp. Rep. (p.136)
ISAB Energy 26th Comp. Rep. p.152
Ren Turbogas 26th Comp. Rep. p.153
Transgas 26th Comp. Rep. p.154
Langnese Iglo T–7/93
Schöller T–9/93
Duales II T–289/01
De Haecht v Wilkin I C–23/67
De Norre v Concordia C–47/76
Stremsel C–61/80
⋆Delimitis v Henninger Bräu C–234/89
Almelo v Ysselmij C–393/92 (grounds 34–39)
Langnese-Iglo C–279/95P
Neste C–214/99
CEEES v CEPSA C–217/05

B. CLAUSES COMMONLY FIGURING IN EXCLUSIVE PURCHASING AGREEMENTS

1. Exclusivity

BP Kemi/DDSF 147 (paras 26, 57–61, 67–71)
Mars/Langnese 369 (paras 71–72)
Natrium Carbonate 11th Comp. Rep. (paras 73–76)
Nutrasweet 18th Comp. Rep. (para.53)
Industrial Gases 19th Comp. Rep. (para.62)
Duales II T–289/01
⋆Delimitis v Henninger Bräu C–234/89

2. Non-competition clause

⋆Spices 124 (paras 12, 17, 19–20)
Rennet 149
Mars/Langnese 369 (paras 73–74)
Repsol 552
Langnese Iglo T–7/93 (ground 94)
Schöller T–9/93 (ground 71)
Roberts T–25/99 (grounds 65–69, 106–109)
Stremsel C–61/80 (grounds 12–13)

3. English clause

BP Kemi-DDSF 147 (paras 63–66)
Industrial Gases 19th Comp. Rep. (para.62)

4. Purchasing or supply obligations

BP Kemi/DDSF 147 (para.26)
Scottish Nuclear 339 (para.29)
Shotton Paper 20th Comp. Rep. (para.93)

5. Resale price maintenance

Spices 124 (paras 12, 17)
Repsol 552 (para.36)
CEEES v CEPSA C–217/05 (ground 64)

CHAPTER 4

SELECTIVE DISTRIBUTION AGREEMENTS

A. CASES ON SELECTIVE DISTRIBUTION AGREEMENTS

Omega 33
BMW 82
SABA I 99
Junghans 109
BMW Belgium 126
Kawasaki 141
Krups 155
Hasselblad 173
AEG/Telefunken 179
Ford Werke-Interim Measures 182
National Panasonic 186
Ford Werke AG 199
Murat 200
SABA II 208
IBM PC 210
Grohe Sales System 222
Ideal Standard Sales System 223
Grundig 232
Ivoclar 234
Villeroy & Boch 244
Peugeot 250
Charles Jourdan 298
D'Ieteren 329
Vichy 334
Eco System 344a
Yves Saint Laurent 345
Parfums Givenchy 356
Grundig 378
Volkswagen 474
Yamaha 517
Peugeot 549
1st Comp. Rep. (paras 56–57)
3rd Comp. Rep. (paras 7–12)
4th Comp. Rep. (paras 33–36)

[For the tables of case citations see Tables 1 to 4, 11 and 12 at the back of the book.]

Dior & Lancôme Sales 4th Comp. Rep. (paras 93–95)
5th Comp. Rep. (paras 12–13, 54, 57–61)
9th Comp. Rep. (paras 5, 6)
13th Comp. Rep. (paras 33–39)
Interlübcke 15th Comp. Rep. (para.15)
Memrad 15th Comp. Rep. (para.64)
Rodenstock 15th Comp. Rep. (para.65)
16th Comp. Rep. (paras 97–106)
Sony Peda 25th Comp. Rep. (p.135)
Chanel 25th Comp. Rep. (p.136)
Vichy T–19/91
Peugeot T–9/95
Kruidvat T–87/92
Leclerc T–19/92
Leclerc T–88/92
GM & Opel Netherlands T–368/00
Haladjian Frères T–204/03
Metro C–26/76
BMW Belgium C–32/78 (grounds 20–34)
FEDETAB C–209/78 (grounds 135–141)
L'Oréal v De Nieuwe AMCK C–31/80 (grounds 14–17)
Salonia v Poidomani & Baglieri C–126/80
Demo Schmidt C–210/81 (grounds 17–22)
AEG C–107/82
AMP v Binon C–243/83
Ford C–25/84
Metro C–75/84
Metro v Cartier C–376/92
Peugeot C–322/93P
Fontaine 280
VAG v SYD-Consult C–41/96
Cabour v Arnor C–230/96
Kruidvat C–70/97P
Volkswagen C–338/00P
General Motors C–551/03P

B. COMMISSION REGULATION 1400/2002 OF JULY 31, 2002 ON THE APPLICATION OF ARTICLE 81(3) OF THE TREATY TO CATEGORIES OF VERTICAL AGREEMENTS AND CONCERTED PRACTICES IN THE MOTOR VEHICLE SECTOR [2002] O.J. L203/30

C. CASES ON THE INTERPRETATION OF REGULATIONS 123/85, 1475/95 AND 1400/2002

Peugeot 250 (para.38)
ARG/Unipart 278 (para.35)
D'Ieteren 329
Eco System 344a
VW-Audi 429 (paras 154–187)
Opel Nederland 467
Mercedes Benz 490
Peugeot 549
Citroën 18th Comp. Rep. (para.56)
20th Comp. Rep. (para.42)
21st Comp. Rep. (paras 121–124)
Fiat 23rd Comp. Rep. (para.229)
23rd Comp. Rep. (paras 335–336)
Cicra 24th Comp. Rep. (page 361)
24th Comp. Rep. (page 363)
Smart 27th Comp. Rep. (page 147)
Food Services Outfit 27th Comp. Rep. (page 147)
Audi 33rd Comp. Rep. (paras 155–157)
Peugeot T–23/90R (grounds 19–22)
Peugeot T–23/90
★Peugeot T–9/92
SEP T–115/99 (ground 47)
DaimlerChrysler T–49e.s./02 (grounds 149–155)
VAG v Magne C–10/86
★Peugeot C–322/93P
Volkswagen C–266/93
BMW C–70/93
Grand Garage Albigeois C–226/94
Nissan France C–309/94
Fontaine C–128/95
VAG v SYD-Consult C–41/96
Cabour v Arnor C–230/96
VW-Audi Dealers C–125/05
Brünsteiner & Hilgert C–376/05
City Motors Groep C–421/05
Petschenig v Toyota C–273/06

D. THE ASSESSMENT OF SELECTIVE DISTRIBUTION AGREEMENTS

1. Nature of the product which justifies selective distribution

IBM PC 210 (para.14)
Grohe Sales System 222 (para.15)
Ideal Standard Sales System 223
★Villeroy & Boch 244 (paras 21–24)
Vichy 334 (para.6–7)
Yves Saint Laurent 345 (para.5)
Parfums Givenchy 356 (paras 4–5)
Vichy T–19/91 (grounds 69–70)
★Leclerc T–19/92 (grounds 113–123)
Leclerc T–88/92 (grounds 105–117)
FEDETAB C–209/78 (ground 138)
L'Oréal v De Nieuwe AMCK C–31/80 (ground 16)

[For the tables of case citations see Tables 1 to 4, 11 and 12 at the back of the book.]

★AMP v Binon C–243/83 (ground 32)
ETA v DKI C–31/85 (ground 16)
★Metro C–75/84 (grounds 53–56)

2. Selection of the dealer

2.1. Qualitative criteria (experience, professional qualifications, specialisation, after-sales service, shop opening hours)

Omega 33 (paras 2, 5)
BMW 82 (paras 13, 20–22)
SABA I 99 (paras 27–28)
Junghans 109 (paras 22–23)
Krups 155
Murat 200 (paras 6–7, 13–15)
SABA II 208
IBM PC 210 (para.16)
Grundig 232 (para.2)
D'Ieteren 329
Villeroy & Boch 244 (paras 24–28)
Vichy 334 (para.18)
Yves Saint Laurent 345 (page 25, para.5)
Parfums Givenchy 356 (pages 12 and 13, para.5)
Grundig 378 (paras 24 and 33)
Leclerc T–19/92 (grounds 131–155)
Leclerc T–88/92 (grounds 125–148)
★Metro C–26/76 (grounds 20, 34–37)
L'Oréal v De Nieuwe AMCK C–31/80 (grounds 15–16)
Salonia v Poidomani & Baglieri C–126/80 (grounds 21–27)
AMP v Binon C–243/83 (grounds 31–34)
Metro C–75/84 (grounds 40–47)

2.2. Quantitative criteria

2.2.1. Related to population in allotted territory

★Omega 33 (paras 2, 5)
BMW 82 (paras 13–15, 24, 30)
★Hasselblad 173 (paras 35, 63–66)
AEG/Telefunken 179 (paras 61, 64)
Ivoclar 234 (paras 29–30)
Vichy 334 (para.18)
Vichy T–19/91 (grounds 67–68)
L'Oréal v De Nieuwe AMCK C–31/80 (ground 17)

2.2.2. Related to the turnover of the distributor

SABA I 99 (paras 29, 40)
SABA II 208
Ivoclar 234
Yves Saint Laurent 345 (para.6B)
★Metro C–26/76 (grounds 37, 39–50)
L'Oréal v De Nieuwe AMCK C–31/80 (ground 16)

2.2.3. Stocking requirements

BMW 82 (para.13)
SABA I 99 (paras 29, 40)
Krups 155
Murat 200 (para.7)
SABA II 208
★Grundig 232 (para.3)
★Villeroy & Boch 244 (paras 29, 31–33)
Yves Saint Laurent 345 (para.6C)
Parfums Givenchy 356 (para.6D)
★Grundig 378 (para.35)
L'Oréal v De Nieuwe AMCK C–31/80 (ground 16)

2.2.4. Minimum purchase obligation

Parfums Givenchy 356 (para.63)

3. Procedure for the authorisation of the dealer

3.1. Objective

AEG/Telefunken 179 (paras 56, 61–64)
★SABA II 208
Grundig 232 (para.29)
Yves Saint Laurent 345 (para.6A)
Parfums Givenchy 356 (para.6A)
Grundig 378 (para.33)

3.2. Not related to prices

AEG/Telefunken 179 (paras 57–58)

3.2.1. Non-discriminatory application of the criteria

AEG/Telefunken 179 (para.54)
Leclerc T–19/92 (grounds 124–130)
Leclerc T–88/92 (grounds 118–123)
AEG C–107/82 (grounds 36–39)
★AMP v Binon C–243/83 (ground 37)
Metro C–75/84 (grounds 72–74)

3.2.2. Refusal to supply

Ford Werke-Interim Measures 182 (paras 11–15, 35–37)
★Ford Werke AG 199 (paras 21–25, 36–46)
Peugeot 250 (paras 38–41)
Opel Nederland 467

★Ford C–25/84

3.2.3. Impeding parallel trade in the framework of a selective distribution

★Kawasaki 141 (paras 4–25, 43–46)
Ford Werke-Interim Measures 182 (paras 11–15, 35–37)
National Panasonic 186 (paras 23–39, 48–54)
Ford Werke AG 199 (paras 21–25, 36–46)
★Peugeot 250 (para.38)
Eco System 344a
Opel Nederland 467
JCB 479 (paras 179–184)
Yamaha 517 (para.102)
Peugeot 549
Dior & Lancôme 4th Comp. Rep. (para.74)
Fiat 14th Comp. Rep. (paras 70–71)
VW 19th Comp. Rep. (para.48)
Peugeot T–9/92
Peugeot C–322/93P

3.3. No a priori exclusion of certain categories of shops

Leclerc T–19/92 (grounds 164–177)
Leclerc T–88/92 (grounds 156–169)

4. No rigidity in market

Leclerc T–19/92 (grounds 178–192)
Leclerc T–88/92 (grounds 170–184)
JCB Service T–67/01 (ground 131)
Metro C–75/84

5. Requirement that system is tight ("Lückenlosigkeit")

Metro v Cartier C–376/92
VAG v SYD-Consult C–41/96

E. FEATURES AND CLAUSES COMMON IN SELECTIVE DISTRIBUTION AGREEMENTS

1. Territorial restrictions

1.1. Exclusivity

BMW 82 (paras 15–16, 26–27, 30)
Ford Werke AG 199 (paras 14, 30–34)
Ivoclar 234
★Peugeot 250 (paras 12, 34)
Charles Jourdan 298 (paras 34–35)

1.2. No active sales policy outside agreed territory

BMW 82 (paras 17, 27, 30)
Junghans 109 (paras 29, 33)
Kawasaki 141 (paras 4–25, 43–46)
Ivoclar 234
★Peugeot 250 (paras 12, 34)
Yves Saint Laurent 345 (para.6D)
Parfums Givenchy 356 (para.6E)

1.3. Export bans

1.3.1. Between Member States

Dupont de Nemours Germany 71 (para.III)
Deutsche Philips 73
Junghans 109
BMW Belgium 126 (paras 3–5, 19–21)
★Kawasaki 141 (paras 4–25, 43–46)
Hasselblad 173 (paras 35, 59, 61, 69)
★Ford Werke-Interim Measures 182 (paras 11–15, 35–37)
National Panasonic 186 (paras 23–29, 48–54)
Ford Werke AG 199 (paras 21, 23–25, 36–46)
Opel Nederland 467
JCB 479 (paras 141–149)
Yamaha 517 (paras 102–115)
ADOX 2nd Comp. Rep. (para.43)
GM & Opel Netherlands T–368/00 (grounds 130 ff)
BMW Belgium C–32/78 (grounds 20–34)
Ford C–25/84

1.3.2. Outside the EC

SABA I 99 (para.35)
Junghans 109 (para.24)
Yamaha 517 (paras 119–122)

1.4. Control of sales by principal

★Yves Saint Laurent 345 (para.7)
Parfums Givenchy 356 (para.7)

2. Clauses relating to the customer to whom the dealer may sell

2.1. Inherent restriction (horizontal sales only to other authorised dealers)

★Omega 33 (para.9)
BMW 82 (para.14)
SABA I 99 (paras 23, 31, 34, 49)
Junghans 109 (paras 7, 21)
BMW Belgium 126 (paras 7–11)
Hasselblad 173 (paras 33, 59)
Ford Werke AG 199 (paras 31–33)
Murat 200 (para.10)
SABA II 208
Grundig 232 (para.3)

[For the tables of case citations see Tables 1 to 4, 11 and 12 at the back of the book.]

Villeroy & Boch 244 (para.34)
Bayonox 313 (para.93)
Vichy 334 (para.10)
Grundig 378 (paras 28 and 29)
Metro C–26/76 (grounds 26–27)
Hasselblad C–86/82 (ground 46)

2.2. Separation of wholesale and retail level

Dupont de Nemours Germany 71 (para.III)
Deutsche Philips 73
SABA I 99 (para.34)
Grundig 232 (para.2.f)
Villeroy & Boch 244 (para.36)
Yves Saint Laurent 345 (para.5)
Yamaha 517 (paras 90 & 93)
JCB Service T–67/01 (grounds 148–153)
★Metro C–26/76 (grounds 26–30)

2.3. Sales to specific types of customers

Omega 33 (para.9)
SABA I 99 (paras 15, 34)
Distillers-Victuallers 156 (paras 12–17)
Grohe Sales System 222 (paras 16, 20–22)
★Ideal Standard Sales System 223
Villeroy & Boch 244 (paras 37–38)
Peugeot 250 (paras 13, 35)
Yves Saint Laurent 345 (para.5)
★Metro C–26/76 (grounds 31–33)

2.4. Preventing sales between authorised dealers

Yamaha 517 (paras 89–99)

3. Clauses relating to the product which the dealer is authorised to sell

3.1. Exclusive purchase obligations imposed on the dealer

Omega 33 (para.9)
JCB 479 (paras 174–178)
Olio-Fiat 17th Comp. Rep. (para.84)

3.2. Non-competition clause

BMW 82 (paras 18, 28, 30)
Ford Werke AG 199 (paras 13, 31–34)
★Peugeot 250 (paras 12, 35)
Charles Jourdan 298 (paras 15, 31)

3.3. Guarantee and after-sales service

Omega 33 (paras 2, 5)
★Zanussi 139 (paras 10–13)
★Hasselblad 173 (paras 30–32, 52–55)
Ideal Standard Sales System 223 (para.16)
D'Ieteren 329 (para.11)
Constructa 4th Comp. Rep. (para.109)
7th Comp. Rep. (paras 17–20)
Moulinex 10th Comp. Rep. (para.122)
Matsushita 12th Comp. Rep. (para.77)
Ford Germany 13th Comp. Rep. (paras 104–106)
16th Comp. Rep. (para.56)
Hasselblad C–86/82 (grounds 33–34)
★ETA v DKI C–31/85 (grounds 12–14)
Metro v Cartier C–376/92 (grounds 31–33)

3.4. Obligation to sell product in specified packaging

Du Pont de Nemours Germany 71

3.5. Obligation not to sell incompatible products

Yves Saint Laurent 345 (pages 25, 26, para.5)
Parfums Givenchy 356 (page 13, paras 5, 6C)

4. Clauses relating to the prices of the contract products

4.1. Effect on prices resulting from selective distribution

Grohe Sales System 222 (paras 26, 27)
Ideal Standard Sales System 223
★AEG C–107/82 (grounds 42–43)

4.2. Resale price maintenance

Omega 33 (para.8)
Junghans 109 (para.17)
★Hasselblad 173 (paras 36–41, 65–66, 69–70)
Volkswagen 474
JCB 479 (paras 168–173)
Yamaha 517 (paras 124–146)
Interlübcke 15th Comp. Rep. (para.61)
Italian Specs 15th Comp. Rep. (paras 66–67)
★Vlaamse Reisbureaus C–311/85 (ground 17)
Louis Erauw v La Hesbignonne C–27/87 (ground 15)

CHAPTER 5

AGENCY AGREEMENTS

1. Cases on agency agreements

Pittsburgh Corning 63

[For the tables of case citations see Tables 1 to 4, 11 and 12 at the back of the book.]

European Sugar Industry 69
IMA Rules 158 (paras 61–63, 71–72)
Fisher-Price 275 (para.18)
ARG/Unipart 278
Eco System 344a (paras 26–32)
World Cup Football 360 (paras 76–78)
Railway Tickets 362 (paras 42–46)
Topps 530 (paras 97–104)
Repsol 552 (para.36)
Center Parcs 22nd Comp. Rep. (p.420)
Halifax 22nd Comp. Rep. (p.421)
Peugeot T–9/92
Minoan Lines T–66/99 (grounds 126–129)
★DaimlerChrysler T–49e.s./02 (grounds 81–118)
★Suiker Unie C–40/73 (grounds 473–498)
★Vlaamse Reisbureaus C–311/85 (grounds 19–20)
Volkswagen C–266/93 (ground 19)
CEEES v CEPSA C–217/05 (grounds 38–63)

CHAPTER 6

FRANCHISING AGREEMENTS

A. CASES ON FRANCHISING AGREEMENTS

Yves Rocher 265
Pronuptia 266
Computerland 270
ServiceMaster 296
Charles Jourdan 298
16th Comp. Rep. (paras 107–111)
19th Comp. Rep. (para.20)
BWI 27th Comp. Rep. (p.148)
Pronuptia v Schillgalis 161/84

B. CLAUSES COMMONLY STIPULATED IN FRANCHISING AGREEMENTS

1. Clauses relating to the franchisee

1.1. Selection of the franchisee

Yves Rocher 265 (paras 16, 41)
Pronuptia 266 (paras 11, 25)
Computerland 270 (paras 4, 9, 23)
ServiceMaster 296 (para.21)
Charles Jourdan 298 (paras 8, 27, 30)
★Pronuptia v Schillgalis C–161/84 (ground 16)

1.2. Non-competition restraint of trade clauses

1.2.1. Obligation not to engage in competing activities during agreement

Yves Rocher 265 (para.47)
Pronuptia 266 (para.27)
Computerland 270 (paras 12, 22)
ServiceMaster 296 (para.10)
Charles Jourdan 298 (paras 15, 27)
★Pronuptia v Schillgalis C–161/84 (ground 16)

1.2.2. Post-term non-competition clause

Yves Rocher 265 (paras 27, 48)
Pronuptia 266 (para.25)
★Computerland 270 (paras 12, 22)
ServiceMaster 296 (para.11)

1.3. Best endeavours clause

ServiceMaster 296 (para.16)

2. Licensing of know-how or trade marks

2.1. Grant of licence

Yves Rocher 265 (paras 22, 39–40)
Pronuptia 266 (paras 11, 25)
Computerland 270 (paras 5, 23)
ServiceMaster 296 (paras 13, 22)
Charles Jourdan 298 (paras 11–12, 23, 27)
★Pronuptia v Schillgalis C–161/84 (ground 16)

2.2. Royalties

Yves Rocher 265 (para.24)
★Pronuptia 266 (paras 11, 26)
Computerland 270 (paras 11, 24)
Charles Jourdan 298 (para.14)

2.3. Field of use restrictions

Yves Rocher 265 (paras 21, 40)
★Pronuptia 266 (para.26)
ServiceMaster 296 (para.8)

2.4. Grant back of improvements

Computerland 270 (paras 5, 23)
★ServiceMaster 296 (para.14)

2.5. Post-term use ban

Computerland 270 (paras 5, 23)
★ServiceMaster 296 (para.9)
Charles Jourdan 298 (paras 21, 27)

3. Clauses promoting the uniformity of the franchise network

3.1. Regarding the decoration of the shop

Yves Rocher 265 (paras 43, 44, 49)
★Pronuptia 266 (paras 11, 25–26)

[For the tables of case citations see Tables 1 to 4, 11 and 12 at the back of the book.]

Computerland 270 (paras 8, 23)
ServiceMaster 296 (para.18)
Charles Jourdan 298 (para.28)

3.2. Collective advertising provisions

Yves Rocher 265 (paras 43, 44, 49)
⋆Pronuptia 266 (paras 25, 26)
Computerland 270 (paras 8, 23)
ServiceMaster 296 (para.18)
⋆Pronuptia v Schillgalis C–161/84 (ground 22)

3.3. Business methods

Yves Rocher 265 (paras 43, 49)
Pronuptia 266 (paras 11, 25)
Computerland 270 (para.23)
⋆Pronuptia v Schillgalis C–161/84 (ground 16)

4. Territorial restrictions

4.1. Fixed location of retail outlet

Yves Rocher 265 (paras 18, 42)
Pronuptia 266 (para.25)
ServiceMaster 296 (paras 15, 22)
Charles Jourdan 298 (paras 10, 32)
⋆Pronuptia v Schillgalis C–161/84 (grounds 17, 24)

4.2. Exclusivity in the contract territory

Yves Rocher 265 (paras 19, 54, 63)
Pronuptia 266 (paras 28, 36)
Computerland 270 (paras 7, 25)
ServiceMaster 296 (para.22)
Charles Jourdan 298 (paras 10, 32)
⋆Pronuptia v Schillgalis C–161/84 (ground 24)

4.3. Obligation not to open a new outlet outside agreed territory

Yves Rocher 265 (para.54)
Pronuptia 266 (para.28)
Computerland 270 (para.25)
ServiceMaster 296 (para.22)
⋆Pronuptia v Schillgalis C–161/84 (ground 24)

5. Clauses related to the product the franchisee is authorised to sell

5.1. Obligation not to sell competing products in authorised outlet

Yves Rocher 265 (para.47)
⋆Computerland 270 (para.23)

5.2. Purchase obligations on the franchisee

5.2.1. General

Pronuptia 266 (para.25)
Charles Jourdan 298 (paras 16, 28)

5.2.2. Obligation to purchase goods of defined quality

⋆Computerland 270 (para.23)
ServiceMaster 296 (para.17)

5.2.3. Exclusive purchasing

Pronuptia 266 (paras 11, 25)
Pronuptia v Schillgallis 161/84 (ground 21)

6. Clauses relating to the customers the franchisee may serve

6.1. Obligation not to sell outside the network

Yves Rocher 265 (para.46)
⋆Pronuptia 266 (para.25)
Computerland 270 (paras 26, 34)
Charles Jourdan 298 (paras 6, 28)

6.2. Restrictions on the franchisee regarding the customers to which it may sell

Yves Rocher 265 (para.46)
Pronuptia 266 (paras 11, 25)
⋆Computerland 270 (paras 26, 34)

7. Recommended prices

Yves Rocher 265 (paras 30, 51)
⋆Pronuptia 266 (paras 11, 26)
Charles Jourdan 298 (paras 18, 29)

CHAPTER 7

AGREEMENTS PREVENTING PARALLEL TRADE

A. CASES ON AGREEMENTS PREVENTING PARALLEL TRADE

Kodak 29
Pittsburgh Corning 63
GISA 67
WEA/Filipacchi Music S.A. 68
Dupont de Nemours Germany 71
Deutsche Philips 73
Pabst & Richerz/BNIA 106

[For the tables of case citations see Tables 1 to 4, 11 and 12 at the back of the book.]

Gerofabrik 111
The Distillers Company 123
BMW Belgium 126
Arthur Bell & Sons 135
Teacher & Sons 136
Zanussi 139
Kawasaki 141
Pioneer 152
Johnson & Johnson 160
Moët et Chandon (London) Ltd 172
Hasselblad 173
NAVEWA-ANSEAU 178
Ford Werke-Interim Measures 182
National Panasonic 186
Cafeteros de Colombia 187
Cast Iron & Steel Rolls 198
Ford Werke AG 199
John Deere 226
Sperry New Holland 245
Tipp-Ex 269
Sandoz 272
Fisher-Price 275
Konica 277
Bayonox 313
Gosme & Martell 340
Eco System 344a
Newitt/Dunlop 351
Ford Agricultural 364
ZERA 374
Tretorn 401
Adalat 408
VW-Audi 429
Opel 467
Glaxo Wellcome 473
JCB 479
Nintendo 505
Topps 530
Peugeot 549
2nd Comp. Rep. (para.43)
Ford Germany 13th Comp. Rep. (paras 104–106)
Euglucon 13th Comp. Rep. (paras 107–109)
BIEM-IFPI 13th Comp. Rep. (paras 147–150)
Citroën 18th Comp. Rep. (para.56)
AKZO Coatings 19th Comp. Rep. (para.45)
Peugeot T–23/90R
Dunlop T–43/92 (grounds 52–56)
Parker Pen T–77/92
Herlitz T–66/92
Van Megen Sport T–49/95
GM & Opel Netherlands T–368/00
JCB Service T–67/01
Haladjian Frères T–204/03
GlaxoSmithKline T–168/01
Dassonville C–8/74
BMW Belgium C–32/78
Sandoz C–277/87
Tipp-Ex C–279/87
Volkswagen C–338/00P

B. CLAUSES OR PRACTICES WHICH MAY HAVE THE OBJECT/EFFECT OF PREVENTING PARALLEL TRADE

1. General sales conditions

⋆Kodak 29
Dupont de Nemours Germany 71
Deutsche Philips 73
The Distillers Company 123
⋆Kawasaki 141 (paras 2–6, 43–46)
Johnson & Johnson 160 (paras 13–23, 29–34)
Moët et Chandon (London) Ltd 172
Cafeteros de Colombia 187
Zinc 189
Sandoz 272
Bayer/Dental 327
Nintendo 505
Citroën 18th Comp. Rep. (para.56)
Sandoz C–277/87 (grounds 6–12)

2. Circular sent by principal to distributors

WEA/Filipacchi Music S.A. 68
BMW Belgium 126
Kawasaki 141 (paras 7–13, 43–46)
⋆Konica 277
Bayonox 313 (paras 17–22, 36–38)
Eco System 344a
⋆BMW Belgium C–32/78 (grounds 20–34)

3. Pressure exercised by principal on distributor

Pittsburg Corning 63
BMW Belgium 126
Kawasaki 141 (paras 7–13, 43–46)
Pioneer 152 (paras 48–49)
Johnson & Johnson 160 (paras 15–23)
Hasselblad 173
National Panasonic 186
⋆John Deere 226
⋆Tipp-Ex 269
Fisher-Price 275
Adalat 408
VW-Audi 429
Nintendo 505 (paras 271, 275 & 330)
Topps 530
Philips Lightbulbs 1st Comp. Rep. (para.54)

[For the tables of case citations see Tables 1 to 4, 11 and 12 at the back of the book.]

Euglucon 13th Comp. Rep. (para.109)
Tipp-Ex C–279/87 (grounds 18–24)

4. Discriminatory trading conditions

4.1. Quality marks

NAVEWA-ANSEAU 178
Newitt/Dunlop 351 (para.60)

4.2. On grounds of nationality

GISA 67
Luxembourg Car Insurance 15th Comp. Rep. (para.71)

4.3. State of the product

★Pabst & Richerz/BNIA 106
The Distillers Company 123
Arthur Bell & Sons 135
Teacher & Sons 136
Cafeteros de Colombia 187
Bayer/Dental 327 (paras 10–12)
IBC 5th Comp. Rep. (para.33)
12th Comp. Rep. (para.76)
16th Comp. Rep. (para.54)

4.4. Prices and rebates

Sperry New Holland 245
Ford Agricultural 364 (paras 13–14)
VW-Audi 429
Glaxo Wellcome 473
Organon 25th Comp. Rep. (paras 37–38)
GM & Opel Netherlands T–368/00 (grounds 97–105)
JCB Service T–67/01 (grounds 131–133)
GlaxoSmithKline T–168/01 (grounds 176–179)

[For the tables of case citations see Tables 1 to 4, 11 and 12 at the back of the book.]

PART V

INDUSTRIAL AND INTELLECTUAL PROPERTY AGREEMENTS

CHAPTER 1

TECHNOLOGY TRANSFER AGREEMENTS

A. CASES ON LICENSING AGREEMENTS

Julien/Van Katwijk 32
Burroughs/Delplanque 50
Burroughs/Geha 51
Davidson Rubber 56
Raymond/Nagoya 57
Kabelmetal/Luchaire 94
Bronbemaling 95
AOIP/Beyrard 98
Video Cassette Recorders 122
Campari 130
Vaessen/Moris 143
Windsurfing International 194
Schlegel/CPIO 204
Velcro/Aplix 233
Boussois/Interpane 264
Mitchell Cotts/Solfiltra 267 (Joint venture)
Rich Products 283
Tetra Pak I 289
Delta Chemie 292
Moosehead 320
Sicasov 436 (paras 72–77)
Copper Tubes 538 (para.456)
1st Comp. Rep. (paras 66, 69–80)
4th Comp. Rep. (paras 19–32)
5th Comp. Rep. (paras 10–11, 63)
Peugeot/Zimmern 6th Comp. Rep. (para.159)
Pentacon 8th Comp Rep. (paras 118–120)
Clutch-type disc brakes 8th Comp. Rep. (para.121)
Spitzer/Van Hool 12th Comp. Rep. (para.86)
ICL/Fujitsu 16th Comp Rep. (para.72)
16th Comp. Rep. (paras 112–116)
Pilkington/Covina 19th Comp. Rep. (para.60)
Cyclopore 23rd Comp. Rep. (para.241)
Minidiscs 25th Comp. Rep. (p.123)
ETSI 25th Comp. Rep. (p.131)
Video Games 27th Comp. Rep. (p.148)
Philips/Sony 33rd Comp. Rep. (paras 65–67)
Ladbroke T–504/93
Parke, Davis v Centrafarm C–24/67
Pharmon v Hoechst C–19/84
Windsurfing C–193/83
Bayer v Süllhöfer 65/86
Ottung v Klee C–320/87

B. LEGISLATION

1. **Text of Commission Regulation 772/2004 on the application of Article 81(3) of the Treaty to categories of technology transfer agreements [2004] O.J. L123/11**
2. **Guidelines on the application of Article 81 of the EC Treaty to technology transfer agreements [2004] C101/2**

C. CLAUSES COMMONLY STIPULATED IN TECHNOLOGY TRANSFER AGREEMENTS

1. Territorial provisions

1.1. Right to use the technology exclusively within an agreed territory

1.1.1. To manufacture the product

★Burroughs/Delplanque 50
Burroughs/Geha 51
Kabelmetal/Luchaire 94
Campari 130
Boussois/Interpane 264
★Rich Products 283 (paras 28–30)
Tetra Pak I 289 (paras 8, 53–59)
Delta Chemie 292

1.1.2. To exploit the product

Burroughs/Geha 51
★Davidson Rubber 56
Raymond/Nagoya 57 (para.1)

[For the tables of case citations see Tables 1 to 4, 11 and 12 at the back of the book.]

AOIP/Beyrard 98
Campari 130
Velcro/Aplix 233
Boussois/Interpane 264 (paras 4, 5, 16)
Mitchell Cotts/Solfiltra 267 (para.23)
Tetra Pak I 289 (paras 53, 58–59)
★Delta Chemie 292 (paras 25–26)
Clutch-type disc brakes 8th Comp. Rep. (para.121)

1.2. Obligation not to pursue an active sales policy outside agreed territory

Campari 130
★Boussois/Interpane 264 (para.16)
Mitchell Cotts/Solfiltra 267 (para.23)

1.3. Obligation not to export outside agreed territory (passive sales)

1.3.1. Between Member States

Julien/Van Katwijk 32
★Davidson Rubber 56
AOIP/Beyrard 98
Velcro/Aplix 233
★Boussois/Interpane 264 (paras 16, 20)
Fondasol 9th Comp. Rep. (paras 112–113)
Pilkington-Covina 19th Comp. Rep. (para.60)

1.3.2. To third countries

Kabelmetal/Luchaire 94
★Campari 130

1.3.3. Into the Common Market

Raymond/Nagoya 57 (para.2)

1.4. Limitation on site of manufacture

Windsurfing International 194
★Windsurfing C–193/83 (grounds 85–88)

1.5. Grant of a non-exclusive licence authority for exclusive territory

★Boussois/Interpane 264 (para.5)
Rich Products 283 (para.31)

1.6. Obligation to respect confidentiality

Davidson Rubber 56 (para.9)
Kabelmetal/Luchaire 94
Campari 130
Boussois/Interpane 264 (para.22)
Mitchell Cotts/Solfiltra 267 (para.21)
★Rich Products 283 (para.32)
Delta Chemie 292 (para.32)

2. Clauses relating to the product that the licensee may sell

2.1. Non-competition clause

★AOIP/Beyrard 98
Campari 130
Velcro/Aplix 233
Mitchell Cotts/Solfiltra 267 (para.22)
Spitzer/Van Hool 12th Comp. Rep. (para.86)
Video Games 27th Comp. Rep. (p.148)

2.2. Obligation on licensee to restrict output

See Article 4(1)(b); Article 4(1)(c) i-ii, vi-vii; Article 4(2)(b) (iii-v) Regulation 772/2004

2.3. Quality norms

Burroughs/Geha 50
Burroughs/Delplanque 51
Raymond/Nagoya 57
Video Cassette Recorders 122
Campari 130
★Rich Products 283 (para.37)
Delta Chemie 292 (para.30)
★Windsurfing C–193/83 (grounds 45–53)

2.4. Purchase or supply obligations

2.4.1. Purchasing

★Vaessen/Moris 143 (paras 1–2, 5–6, 15, 23)
Schlegal/CPIO 204 (paras 4–5, 14–21)
Velcro/Aplix 233
★Rich Products 283
Moosehead 320 (paras 9.2, 15.3)
Bramley/Gilbert 10th Comp. Rep. (para.128)

2.4.2. Tying

Video Cassette Recorders 122
Vaessen/Moris 143
Windsurfing International 194
★Windsurfing C–193/83

2.5. Trade mark clauses

Burroughs/Geha 50
Burroughs/Delplanque 51
Campari 130
Windsurfing International 196
★Velcro/Aplix 233
Delta Chemie 292 (paras 6, 16)
Moosehead 320
Windsurfing C–193/83 (grounds 81)

[For the tables of case citations see Tables 1 to 4, 11 and 12 at the back of the book.]

2.6. Best endeavours clause

Delta Chemie 292 (para.3)

3. Pricing restrictions on the licensee

Plastic Omnium (Bulletin 6–1988 pt 2.1.107)

4. Restrictions upon the customers which the licensee may serve

Campari 130
Bramley/Gilbert 10th Comp. Rep. (para.128)

5. Clauses relating to the protection of the technology

5.1. Field of use restrictions

Windsurfing International 194
⋆Rich Products 283 (para.35)
Delta Chemie 292 (para.31)
France/Suralmo 9th Comp. Rep. (paras 114–115)
⋆Windsurfing C–193/83

5.2. No-challenge clause

Burroughs/Geha 51
Davidson Rubber 56 (para.16)
Raymond/Nagoya 57 (para.3)
Bronbemaling 95
⋆AOIP/Beyrard 98
Bayer/Gist-Brocades 100
Vaessen/Moris 143 (paras 4–6, 14, 17, 23)
Windsurfing International 194
Delta Chemie 292 (para.33)
Pentacon-Dresden 8th Comp. Rep. (paras 118–120)
ACC/Fabry 9th Comp. Rep. (paras 107–108)
Spitzer/Van Hool 12th Comp. Rep. (para.86)
⋆Windsurfing C–193/83 (grounds 92–93)
⋆Bayer v Süllhöfer 65/86

5.3. Guaranteed rights to any subsequent improvements

Burroughs/Delplanque 50
Burroughs/Geha 51
⋆Davidson Rubber 56 (para.9)
Raymond/Nagoya 57 (paras 5–6)
Kabelmetal/Luchaire 94
⋆Velcro/Aplix 233
⋆Boussois/Interpane 264 (para.22)
Mitchell Cotts/Solfiltra 267 (paras 10, 21)
Rich Products 283 (para.36)
⋆Delta Chemie 292 (para.36)
Nodet/Gougis 10th Comp. Rep. (para.127)
Spitzer/Van Hool 12th Comp. Rep. (para.86)

5.4. Restrictions on sub-licensing

Burroughs/Geha 50
Burroughs/Delplanque 51
⋆Davidson Rubber 56 (para.9)
AOIP/Beyrard 98
Mitchell Cotts/Solfiltra 267 (para.21)
Rich Products 283 (para.33)
⋆Delta Chemie 292 (para.36)
France/Suralmo 9th Comp. Rep. (paras 114, 115)

5.5. Requirement that the know-how is unintentional and identified

Boussois/Interpane 264 (para.2)
⋆Delta Chemie 292 (para.23)

6. Royalties

6.1. Obligation to pay minimum royalties/produce minimum quantities

AOIP/Beyrard 98
Windsurfing C–193/83 (grounds 65–66)

6.2. Obligation to pay royalties after expiration or invalidity of the patent

Kabelmetal/Luchaire 94
AOIP/Beyrard 98
⋆Windsurfing International 194
Preflex/Lipski 10th Comp. Rep. (para.126)
UNARCO 14th Comp. Rep. (para.93)
⋆Ottung v Klee C–320/87

6.3. Most favoured licensee clause

Kabelmetal/Luchaire 94

6.4. Obligation to pay royalty even if patent not used

AOIP/Beyrard 98
Spitzer/Van Hool 12th Comp. Rep. (para.86)
Microsoft/Santa Cruz 27th Comp. Rep. (p.140)

6.5. Obligation to pay royalties on a know-how if in the public domain

Boussois/Interpane 264 (paras 7, 22)
Spitzer/Van Hool 12th Comp. Rep. (para.86)

7. Clauses relating to the duration of the agreement, post-term provisions

7.1. Automatic extension of agreement

AOIP/Beyrard 98

[For the tables of case citations see Tables 1 to 4, 11 and 12 at the back of the book.]

★Velcro/Aplix 233
Boussois/Interpane 264 (paras 6, 21)
★Delta Chemie 292 (paras 19, 47, 49)

7.2. Post-term use restrictions

Burroughs/Geha 50
★Burroughs/Delplanque 51
Rich Products 283 (para.34)
★Delta Chemie 292 (para.35)
Cartoux/Terrapin 10th Comp. Rep. (para.129)
Ottung v Klee C–320/87

8. Patent dispute settlements

Bronbemaling 95
Vaessen/Moris 143 (paras 4–6)
Zoller & Frölich 9th Comp. Rep. (paras 109–111)
★Bayer v Sülhöffer 65/86

9. Patent pooling

See paras 210–235 of Commission Notice — Guidelines on the application of Artricle 81 of the EC Treaty to technology transfer agreements [2004] O.J. C101/2.

CHAPTER 2

TRADE MARK AGREEMENTS

A. CASES ON TRADE MARK LICENSING AGREEMENTS

Jaz/Peter I 26
Burroughs/Delplanque 50
Burroughs/Geha 51
Theal/Watts 110
Campari 130
Moosehead 320
Copper Tubes 538 (para.456)
1st Comp. Rep. (paras 61–65)
Tyler/Linde 11th Comp. Rep. (para.96)
Campari 18th Comp. Rep. (para.69)
Duales T–151/01
Tepea C–28/77

B. CASES ON TRADE MARK ASSIGNMENTS

Grundig/Consten 5
Advocaat Zwarte Kip 79
Moosehead 320 (para.16)
1st Comp. Rep. (paras 61–65)
Remington Rand 1st Comp. Rep. (para.64)
Consten & Grundig C–56/64
Sirena v Eda C–40/70
EMI-CBS 51/75; 86/75; 96/75

C. CASES ON THE CREATION OF A JOINT TRADE MARK

Transocean Marine Paint Assoc. I 10
Transocean Marine Paint Assoc. II 75
Transocean Marine Paint Assoc. III 96
Transocean Marine Paint Assoc. IV 151
Transocean Marine Paint Assoc. V 297
Poroton 10th Comp. Rep. (paras 130–132)

D. TRADE MARK DELIMITATION AGREEMENTS

Nicholas Frègeres Vitapro 4
Sirdar/Phildar 89
Penney 127
Toltecs/Dorcet 191
Leopold/AFS 5th Comp. Rep. (para.70)
Bayer/Tanabe 8th Comp. Rep. (paras 125–127)
Winninger Domgarten 10th Comp. Rep. (paras 133–134)
Osram/Airam 11th Comp. Rep. (para.97)
Syntex/Synthelabo 19th Comp. Rep. (para.59)
Hershey/Herschi 20th Comp. Rep. (para.111)
Terrapin v Terranova C–119/75
BAT C–35/83

E. CLAUSES COMMONLY FIGURING IN TRADE MARK LICENSING OR ASSIGNMENT AGREEMENTS

1. Territorial restrictions

1.1. Right to use the trade mark exclusively within an agreed territory

Theal/Watts 110
Moosehead 320 (paras 7, 15, 16)
Consten & Grundig C–56/64
★Tepea C–28/77 (grounds 33–45, 53–57)

1.2. Export ban

Advocaat Zwarte Kip 79

1.3. Grant of exclusivity gives licensee ability to prevent parallel imports

Theal/Watts 110

[For the tables of case citations see Tables 1 to 4, 11 and 12 at the back of the book.]

Consten & Grundig C–56/64
Sirena v Eda C–40/70 (ground 11)
EMI-CBS C–51/75 (grounds 26–29)
★Terrapin v Terranova C–119/75 (grounds 5, 8)
★Tepea C–28/77 (grounds 33–45, 53–57)

2. Trade mark no-challenge clause

★Goodyear Italiana/Euram 85 (para.2)
Penney 127 (paras I.5, I.7, II.4.c)
Windsurfing International 194
Moosehead 320

3. Duration of the validity of the trade mark

Velcro/Aplix 233
Tyler/Linde 11th Comp. Rep. (para.96)

4. Non-use clause

Chiquita/Fyffes 22nd Comp. Rep. (paras 168–176)

5. Between competitors

Swedish Match 27th Comp. Rep. (p.132)

CHAPTER 3

COPYRIGHT AND DESIGN RIGHT AGREEMENTS

A. CASES ON COPYRIGHT AGREEMENTS

Decca 304 (paras 104–107, 117–119)
ARD 312
PMI-DSV 404
IFPI 498
Telenor/Canal+ 527 (para.196)
1st Comp. Rep. (para.67)
BBC 6th Comp. Rep. (para.163)
The Old Man and the Sea 6th Comp. Rep. (para.164)
English Football Assoc. 9th Comp. Rep. (paras 116, 117)
Ernest Benn 9th Comp. Rep. (para.118)
STEMRA 11th Comp. Rep. (para.98)
Nielson-Hordell 12th Comp. Rep. (paras 88–89)
Knoll/Hille-Form 13th Comp. Rep. (paras 142–146)
BIEM-IFPI 13th Comp. Rep. (paras 147–150)
GEMA 15th Comp. Rep. (para.81)
18th Comp. Rep. (para.42)
BBC 23rd Comp. Rep. (para.459)
Sport 7/KNVB 27th Comp. Rep. (p.145)
Ladbroke T–504/93
Coditel v Cine-Vog C–262/81
EMI v Patricia C–341/87
Ministère Public v Tournier C–395/87
Lucazeau v SACEM C–110/88

B. CASES ON DESIGN RIGHT AGREEMENTS

Dutch Design Institute 5th Comp. Rep. (para.69)
ICL/Fujitsu 16th Comp. Rep. (para.72)
Ford 20th Comp. Rep. (para.112)

C. CLAUSES TYPICALLY STIPULATED IN COPYRIGHT/DESIGN RIGHT AGREEMENTS

1. Territorial restrictions

1.1. Exclusivity

PMI-DSV 404
Telenor/Canal+ 527 (paras 46–156 & 170–177)
BSB 23rd Comp. Rep. (para.459)
Ladbroke T–504/93
Coditel v Cine-Vog C–262/81 (grounds 14–19)
Ministère Public v Tournier C–395/87
Lucazeau v SACEM C–110/88

1.2. Export bans

BBC 6th Comp. Rep. (para.163)
The Old Man and the Sea 6th Comp. Rep. (para.164)
Ernest Benn 9th Comp. Rep. (para.118)
STREMSA 11th Comp. Rep. (para.98)
Nielson-Hordell 12th Comp. Rep. (paras 88–89)
★Coditel v Cine-Vog C–262/81 (grounds 14–19)

2. No-challenge clause

Vaessen/Moris 143
Nielson-Hordell 12th Comp. Rep. (paras 88–89)

3. Royalties

IFPI 498
Nielson-Hordell 12th Comp. Rep. (paras 88–89)

[For the tables of case citations see Tables 1 to 4, 11 and 12 at the back of the book.]

GEMA 15th Comp. Rep. (para.18)

4. Non-competition restraint of trade clause

Telenor/Canal+ 527 (paras 157 et seq., 179 et seq., 187 et seq.)
Nielson-Hordell 12th Comp. Rep. (paras 88–89)

5. Improvements

Nielson-Hordell 12th Comp. Rep. (paras 88–89)

6. Tying

Ministère Public v Tournier C–395/87 (grounds 31–32)

7. Sub-licensing

PMI-DSV 404
Ladbroke T–504/93

CHAPTER 4

BREEDERS' RIGHTS LICENSING AGREEMENTS

A. CASES ON BREEDERS' RIGHTS

Maize Seeds 137
Breeders' rights; roses 236
⋆Sicasov 436
Plant Royalty Bureau 9th Comp. Rep. (para.120)
Nungesser C–258/78 (ground 43)
Louis Erauw v La Hesbignonne C–27/87

B. CLAUSES COMMONLY FIGURING IN BREEDERS' RIGHTS AGREEMENTS

1. Territorial restrictions

1.1. Exclusivity

Maize Seeds 137
⋆Nungesser C–258/78 (grounds 49, 53–58)

1.2. Export ban

Maize Seeds 137
Sicasov 436
⋆Nungesser C–258/78 (grounds 53, 61, 77–78)
⋆Louis Erauw v La Hesbignonne C–27/87

2. Non-competition restraint of trade clause

Maize Seeds 137

3. Control of prices by licensor

Maize Seeds 137
⋆Louis Erauw v La Hesbignonne C–27/87 (ground 15)

4. No-challenge clause

Breeders' rights; roses 236

5. Grant back of improvements

Breeders' rights; roses 236

6. Purchasing obligations on licensee

Maize Seeds 137

7. Customer limitation clause

Maize Seeds 137

[For the tables of case citations see Tables 1 to 4, 11 and 12 at the back of the book.]

PART VI

JOINT VENTURES

CHAPTER 1

LIST OF CASES ON JOINT VENTURE AGREEMENTS

[For the tables of case citations see Tables 1 to 4, 11 and 12 at the back of the book.]

Continental Michelin 27th Comp. Rep. (p.129)
Scandairy 27th Comp. Rep. (p.131)
Sanofi 27th Comp. Rep. (p.130)
Hydro Texaco 27th Comp. Rep. (p.131)
HFC Bank 27th Comp. Rep. (p.132)
Matra T–17/93
European Night Services T–374/94
Métropole Télévision T–112/99
Stremsel C–61/80

CHAPTER 2

TYPES OF JOINT VENTURES

A. JOINT VENTURES UNDER THE MERGER REGULATION

1. **Article 2(4) of Council Regulation 139/2004 on the control of concentrations between undertakings (the EC Merger Regulation) [2004] O.J. L24/1**

2. **Commission Notice on the concept of full-function joint ventures under Council Regulation 4064/89 on the control of concentrations between undertakings**

B. JOINT VENTURES UNDER ARTICLE 81(1)

1. Joint R&D

Eurogypsum 11
⋆Henkel/Colgate 52
Vacuum Interrupters I 112
Delaval/Stork I 114
GEC/Weir Sodium Circulators 117
Vacuum Interrupters II 161
Carbon Gas Technologie 205
BP/Kellogg 235
Olivetti/Canon 280
Delaval/Stork II 281
BP/Bayer 284 (para.22), 386
BBC Brown Boveri 291
Odin 322
Asahi/St Gobain 398

2. Joint buying

See also Buying Groups, Part III, page 176
⋆Rennet 149
National Sulphuric Acid Assoc. I 156 (paras 20, 26–27, 32, 36, 39–54)
Enichem/ICI 279
GEC/Siemens/Plessey 325
Irish Distillers 18th Comp. Rep. (para.80)

3. Joint production

Bayer/Gist-Brocades 100
KEWA 103
Vacuum Interrupters I 112
Delaval/Stork I 114
GEC/Weir Sodium Circulators 117
SNPE-LEL 132
WANO 138
Rennet 149
Vacuum Interrupters II 161
Langenscheidt/Hachette 168
Amersham/Buchler 184
Rockwell/IVECO 196
IVECO/Ford 207
Optical Fibres 249
Mitchell Cotts/Sofiltra 267
⋆Olivetti/Canon 280
Delaval/Stork II 281
BP/Bayer 284 (para.21)
Odin 322
Cekacan 326
Ford/Volkswagen 367
Exxon/Shell 384
Fujitsu AMD 395
Feldmühle/Stora 12th Comp. Rep. (paras 73–74)
Shell/AKZO 14th Comp. Rep. (para.85)
EMC/DSM 18th Comp. Rep. (para.50)
Stremsel C–61/80

4. Joint sales

SHV/Chevron 87
United Reprocessors 102
KEWA 103
Vacuum Interrupters I 112
⋆Delaval/Stork I 114
Sopelem/Vickers I 125
CSV 134
WANO 138
Floral 148
Langenscheidt/Hachette 168
Amersham/Buchler 184
Optical Fibres 249
Mitchell Cotts/Sofiltra 267
BP/Bayer 284, 386 (paras 11, 20)
IVECO/Ford 287
UIP 309 (para.41)
Odin 322
Cekacan 326
Screensport/EBU 337

Gosme/Martell 340 (para.30)
Eirpage 344 (para.21)
Fiat/Hitachi 366
Astra 368
BT/MCI 387
ACI 388
Night Services 390
Pasteur Merck 392
IPSP 397
Philips/Osram 400
LH/SAS 409
Feldmuhle/Stora 12th Comp. Rep. (paras 73–74)
AIR-Forge 12th Comp. Rep. (para.85)
Finnpap 19th Comp. Rep. (para.44)

5. Co-ordination centres

Enichem/ICI 279
BF-Goodrich/Messier-Bugatti 26th Comp. Rep. p.143

6. Shareholders agreements

TPS 440

CHAPTER 3

PURPOSE OF THE CO-OPERATION

1. Market extension

KEWA 103
Delaval/Stork I 114
★Langenscheidt/Hachette 168
Amersham/Buchler 184 (para.11)
Mitchell Cotts/Sofiltra 267
Delaval/Stork II 281
IVECO/Ford 287
Odin 322
Cekacan 326
Screensport/EBU 337
Eirpage 344
Ford/Volkswagen 367
Atlas 411
Phoenix 412
Unisource 425
Uniworld 426

2. Technological progress/transfer of technology

Henkel/Colgate 52
GEC/Weir Sodium Circulators 117
Vacuum Interrupters II 161
Rockwell/IVECO 196
Carbon Gas Technologie 205
★Optical Fibres 249
Olivetti/Canon 280 (para.54)
BBC Brown Boveri 291

3. Restructuring operations

Enichem/ICI 279
BP/Bayer 284
IVECO/Ford 287
UIP 309
FIAT/Hitachi 366
12th Comp. Rep. (paras 38–41)
Shell/AKZO 14th Comp. Rep. (para.85)

4. Market sharing

United Reprocessors 102
CSV 134
★WANO 138
Floral 148
Feldmühle/Stora 12th Comp. Rep. (paras 73–74)
Papeteries de Golbey 23rd Comp. Rep. (para.244)

5. Rationalisation of production capacity

United Reprocessors 102

CHAPTER 4

LEGISLATION

1. Commission Regulation 2658/2000 on the application of Article 81(3) of the Treaty to categories of specialisation agreements [2000] O.J. L304/3

2. Commission Regulation 2659/2000 on the application of Article 81(3) of the Treaty to categories of research and development agreements [2000] O.J. L304/7

3. Commission Regulation 773/2004 on the application of Article 85(3) of the Treaty to certain categories of technology transfer agreements [2004] O.J. L123/11

4. Other information

23rd Comp. Rep. (paras 193–197)

[For the tables of case citations see Tables 1 to 4, 11 and 12 at the back of the book.]

CHAPTER 5

OPERATIONS/CLAUSES TYPICAL OF JOINT VENTURE AGREEMENTS

1. Restriction of competition which may result from the creation of the joint venture

1.1. Competition between the parent companies

1.1.1. Actual competition

United Reprocessors 102
GEC/Weir Sodium Circulators 117
WANO 138
Amersham/Buchler 184 (para.7)
Enichem/ICI 279 (paras 27, 29)
⋆Olivetti/Canon 280 (paras 37, 40)
FIAT/Hitachi 366 (para.20)
⋆Astra 368 (paras 12–17)
Fujitsu AMD 395 (para.29)
LH/SAS 409 (paras 44–62)
AuA/LH 495

1.1.2. Potential competition

KEWA 103
Delaval/Stork I 114
GEC/Weir Sodium Circulators 117
WANO 138
⋆Vacuum Interrupters II 161
Amersham/Buchler 184 (para.8)
Rockwell/IVECO 196
Optical Fibres 249
Enichem/ICI 279 (para.28)
Olivetti/Canon 280 (para.39)
⋆Delaval Stork II 281
BP/Bayer 284 (para.23)
IVECO/Ford 287 (para.24)
UIP 309 (para.3a)
Odin 322
Konsortium ECR 900 323
Cekacan 326 (para.30)
Screensport/EBU 337 (paras 54–56)
Eirpage 344 (paras 11, 12, 18)
Ford/Volkswagen 367 (para.19)
BT/MCI 387 (paras 36–43)
Pasteur/Merck 392 (para.59)
IPSP 397 (para.55–58)
13th Comp. Rep. (para.55)
European Night Services T–374/94

1.1.3. Spill-over effect

Bayer/Gist-Brocades 100
⋆GEC/Weir Sodium Circulators 117
CSV 134 (para.76)
WANO 138
Odin 322 (para.36)
Ford/Volkswagen 367 (para.20)
Exxon/Shell 384 (paras 60–63)
P&O Stena Line 445

1.2. Effect of the joint venture on the competitive position of third parties

Optical Fibres 249 (para.46)
Mitchell-Cotts/Sofiltra 267 (para.19)
⋆Screensport/EBU 337 (paras 57–66)
Eirpage 344 (paras 7, 20, 22, 23)
Astra 368 (para.17)
Night Services 390 (para.46–48)
Pasteur/Merck 392 (paras 70–71)
LH/SAS 409 (paras 51–56)
P&O Stena Line 445
DHL International 21st Comp. Rep. (para.88)
Carlsberg/Tetley 22nd Comp. Rep. (paras 131–137)
INTRAX 23rd Comp. Rep. (para.218)
European Night Services T–374/94

1.3. Restriction of future competition resulting from the joint venture agreements

1.3.1. Between parents and the joint venture

Delaval/Stork 114 (para.4)
Mitchell-Cotts/Sofiltra 267 (para.20)
FIAT/Hitachi 366 (para.21)
Fujitsu AMD 395 (para.30)
Du Pont/Merck 21st Comp. Rep. (para.85)
Apollinaris/Schweppes 21st Comp. Rep. (para.87)

1.3.2. Between several joint ventures having a common parent company

⋆Optical Fibres 249 (para.48)
Mitchell-Cotts/Sofiltra 267 (para.19)
ACI 388 (paras 33–36)
European Night Services 390 (grounds 49–52)

1.4. Need to have joint control

TPS 440

1.5. Creation of an oligopolistic market structure

P&O Stena Line 445

[For the tables of case citations see Tables 1 to 4, 11 and 12 at the back of the book.]

2. Ancillary clauses which may restrict competition

2.1. Non-competition clauses

United Reprocessors 102
KEWA 103
Vacuum Interrupters I 112
GEC/Weir Sodium Circulators 117
WANO 138
Floral 148 (para.II.1)
Rennet 149
Vacuum Interrupters II 161
Langenscheidt/Hachette 168 (para.II.8)
Amersham/Buchler 184 (paras 2, 13)
Rockwell/IVECO 196
★BP Kellogg 235
Mitchel-Cotts/Sofiltra 267 (para.22)
IVECO/Ford 287 (paras 14, 15, 24–25)
BBC Brown Boveri 291 (para.16)
Odin 322 (paras 7 & 9)
Cekacan 326 (paras 16, 34–35)
Eirpage 344 (para.12)
BT/MCI 387 (paras 46, 48)
Fujitsu AMD 396 (paras 6, 10, 33, 39)
IPSP 397 (para.61)
Philips/Osram 400 (paras 19 and 20)
Atlas 411
Phoenix 412 (paras 52, 53)
Unisource 425 (paras 81–83)
Uniworld 426 (paras 64–65)
TPS 440 (para.77)
6th Comp. Rep. (paras 60–63)
Stremsel C–61/80

2.2. Co-ordination of investment policy

United Reprocessors 102
★Enichem/ICI 282
BP/Bayer 284 (paras 11, 21)
Alenia/Honeywell 23rd Comp. Rep. (para.216)

2.3. Post-termination provisions

★Delaval/Stork I 114 (paras 7, 14)
Odin 322 (paras 10–13)
Eirpage 344 (para.19)
Fujitsu AMD 395 (para.10, 33, 35)
Roquette/National Starch 14th Comp. Rep. (paras 87–89)

2.4. Licensing and exchange of technical information

Henkel/Colgate 52
United Reprocessors 102
Delaval/Stork I 114 (paras 7, 14)
GEC/Weir Sodium Circulators 117
WANO 138
Langenscheidt/Hachette 168 (para.II.12)
Rockwell/IVECO 196
BP/Kellogg 235
★Optical Fibres 249 (paras 38, 49, 59)
Mitchell-Cotts/Sofiltra 267 (paras 9–10)
Olivetti/Canon 280 (paras 48–50)
BP/Bayer 284 (para.21)
BBC Brown Boveri 291 (para.19)
Odin 322 (paras 6–9)
Fujitsu AMD 395 (paras 12, 36, 38, 39)
Asahi/St Gobain 398 (paras 9, 19)

2.5. Joint price-fixing

United Reprocessors 102
Feldmuhle-Stora 12th Comp. Rep. (paras 73–74)

2.6. Purchasing and supply obligations

WANO 138
Vacuum Interrupters II 161
★Rockwell/IVECO 196
Olivetti/Canon 280 (para.43)
Enichem/ICI 282 (para.26)
BP/Bayer 284 (paras 11, 20)
IVECO/Ford 287 (paras 8, 9, 27, 28)
Cekacan 326 (paras 17, 18, 21–22, 36, 39)
BT/MCI 387 (para.46)
IPSP 397 (para.61)
Philips/Osram 400 (paras 19, 20)
Atlas 411
Phoenix 412
Feldmuhle/Stora 12th Comp. Rep. (paras 73–74)

2.7. Grant of exclusive distribution rights

Delaval/Stork I 114 (para.7)
WANO 138
Langenscheidt/Hachette 168 (para.9)
Amersham/Buchler 184 (paras 3–4)
Rockwell/IVECO 196
Optical Fibres 249 (paras 37–38)
★Mitchell-Cotts/Sofiltra 267 (para.10)
IVECO/Ford 287 (paras 13, 27, 28)
UIP 309 (paras 17, 25, 26, 42, 55)
FIAT/Hitachi 366 (para.22)
BT/MCI 387 (paras 47–59)
★Pasteur/Merck 392 (paras 72–80, 103, 111–112)
IPSP 397 (para.59)
Atlas 411
Phoenix 412

[For the tables of case citations see Tables 1 to 4, 11 and 12 at the back of the book.]

Iridium 416 (para.44)
Unisource 425 (para.83)
Uniworld 426 (para.66)
TPS 440 (paras 78–79)
Finnpap 19th Comp. Rep. (para.44)

2.8. Territorial restrictions

Optical Fibres 249 (paras 37–39, 54, 67)
★Mitchell-Cotts/Sofiltra 267 (paras 11, 23)
IVECO/Ford 287 (paras 10, 13–15, 27–28)
BBC Brown Boveri 291 (paras 18, 30)
Cekacan 326 (paras 40–42)
Fujitsu AMD 395 (paras 8, 12, 32, 43)
Feldmühle/Stora 12th Comp. Rep. (paras 73–74)

2.9. Trade mark related clauses

Olivetti/Canon 280 (para.45)
IVECO/Ford 287 (paras 11, 26)

[For the tables of case citations see Tables 1 to 4, 11 and 12 at the back of the book.]

PART VII

ARTICLE 82

CHAPTER 1

THE ESTABLISHMENT OF A DOMINANT POSITION

A. THE RELEVANT MARKET

1. The relevant product market

1.1. Definition of the term "relevant product market"

See Notice on relevant market
European Sugar Industry 69 (para.E.I)
Chiquita 101 (para.II.A.2)
ECS/AKZO 242 (paras 62, 64)
★Hilti 282 (para.60)
Solvay 332 (paras 42, 44)
Hilti T–30/89 (ground 64)
Tetra Pak II T–83/91 (ground 63)
British Airways T–219/99 (ground 91)
Continental Can C–6/72 (ground 32)
Michelin C–322/81 (grounds 37, 48, 51)
AKZO C–62/86 (grounds 37–45)
Tetra Pak C–333/94P

1.2. Relevant factors

1.2.1. Physical characteristics/end use

Continental Can 46 (paras I.H, I.I)
Chiquita 101 (para.II.A.2)
Vitamins 104 (para.20)
GVL 166 (para.43)
Michelin 165 (paras 31–33)
ECS/AKZO 242 (paras 64–65)
Hilti 282 (paras 55, 61–63)
British Sugar 286 (para.42)
Tetra Pak I 289 (paras 29–32)
SABENA 295 (para.14)
Flat Glass 300 (para.76)
Decca 304 (paras 83–87)
Magill 307 (para.20)
Tetra Pak II 348 (para.93)
British Midland 350 (para.14)
French African Shipping 353 (paras 4–7, 60–61)
Gillette 361 (para.6)
HOV SVZ/MCN 381 (paras 59, 126–130)
Italian GSM 406 (para.11)
Michelin 481 (paras 116–117)
AstraZeneca 545 (paras 368–370, 373, 380)
Hilti T–30/89 (grounds 69–72)
Tetra Pak II T–83/91 (ground 64)
United Brands C–27/76 (grounds 22–34)
Hoffmann-La Roche C–85/76 (grounds 28–30)
Michelin C–322/81 (grounds 39, 51–52)

1.2.2. Price

Michelin 165 (para.32)
Hilti 282 (paras 62–65)
British Midland 350 (para.14)
Gillette 361 (para.6)
HOV SVZ/MCN 381 (para.59)
Microsoft 528 (paras 369–382)
Clearstream 531 (paras 142, 150–153)
AstraZeneca 545 (paras 364–366, 385, 459–460)
Tetra Pak II T–83/91 (ground 64)

1.2.3. Consumer preference

Clearstream 531 (paras 138–148, 173–175)
Tetra Pak I 289 (paras 32–33)
RTE T–69/89 (ground 62)
BBC T–70/89 (ground 50)
ITV T–76/89 (ground 48)

1.2.4. Exclusion of in-house production

Continental Can 46 (para.I.K)

1.2.5. Existence of specialised producers

UEFA Broadcasting 471
HOV SVZ/MCN 381 (para.137)
Hilti T–30/89 (ground 67)

1.2.6. Specific distribution channels

Tetra Pak I 289 (para.39)

[For the tables of case citations see Tables 1 to 4, 11 and 12 at the back of the book.]

Coca-Cola 546 (para.21)
British Airways T–219/99 (grounds 92–100)
Michelin C–322/81 (ground 40)

1.2.7. Product represents small part of overall final product cost

Hilti 282 (paras 63, 65)
★Tetra Pak I 289 (paras 30–31, 34–35)
Tetra Pak II 348 (para.93)
Tetra Pak II T–83/91 (grounds 67, 68, 72)

1.2.8. Supply-side substitutability/potential competition

Hilti 282 (paras 55–56, 59)
Tetra Pak I 289 (paras 30, 36–37)
Duales 472 (paras 75–79)
Deutsche Telekom 515 (para.82)
Microsoft 528 (paras 322, 334–341)
AstraZeneca 545 (para.403)
Continental Can C–6/72 (grounds 33–35)
Michelin C–322/81 (ground 41)

1.2.9. Relevant product market defined in light of product range of alleged dominant firm

Solvay 332 (paras 42–43)
ICI 333 (paras 43–44)
Microsoft 528 (paras 360–368)

1.2.10. Cellophane fallacy

★AstraZeneca 545 (para. 466)

1.3. Relevant evidence

1.3.1. Consumer surveys

1.3.2. Conditions of competition

1.3.3. Historical evidence on cross-elascticity

Chiquita 101 (para.II.A.2)
AstraZeneca 545 (paras 366, 391, 397, 401, 494, 500)
RTE T–69/89 (ground 62)
BBC T–70/89 (ground 50)
ITV T–76/89 (ground 48)
Hilti T–30/89 (grounds 73–76)
United Brands C–27/76 (ground 32)

1.3.4. Definition given by defendant

Boosey & Hawkes 273 (para.17)
HOV SVZ/MCN 381 (paras 130–136)
Hilti T–30/89 (ground 78)
Michelin C–322/81 (ground 42)

1.3.5. Industry product classifications

ABG/Oil Companies 113 (para.I.D)
AstraZeneca 545 (paras 371–372, 504)

1.3.6. One-way sustitutability

Deutsche Telekom 515 (para.77)
Microsoft 528 (para.415)
AstraZeneca 545 (paras 489–491)

1.3.7. Dependence on competitors for input

Microsoft 528 (paras 411–413)

1.4. Narrow definition of relevant product market

General Motors 84
Hugin/Liptons 121 (para.II.A)
British Leyland 212 (para.25)
Boosey & Hawkes 273 (para.17)
AstraZeneca 545 (paras 380–381)
★25th Comp. Rep. (para.86)
Pelikan/Kyocera 25th Comp. Rep. (para.87)
RTE T–69/89
Deutsche Bahn T–229/94 (grounds 56 and 57)
General Motors C–26/75 (grounds 7–9)
Hugin C–22/78 (grounds 6–8)
British Leyland C–226/84 (grounds 4–6)

2. Relevant geographic market

2.1. Definition of the term "relevant geographic market"

Tetra Pak II T–83/91 (ground 91)
Italian Tobacco T–139/98 (ground 39)
United Brands C–27/76 (ground 44)

2.2. Relevant factors

2.2.1. Regulatory trade barriers

British Sugar 286 (paras 43–44)
Solvay 332 (para.45)
ICI 333 (para.48)
United Brands C–27/76 (grounds 46–51)

2.2.2. Local specification requirements/differing national standards

Georg/Ferrovie 521 (para.57)

2.2.3. National procurement policies

2.2.4 Adequate distribution facilities/different distribution systems

Chiquita 101 (para.II.A.2)
British Midland 350 (para.15)

[For the tables of case citations see Tables 1 to 4, 11 and 12 at the back of the book.]

Michelin 481

2.2.5. Transport costs

Chiquita 101 (para.II.A.2)
ECS/AKZO 242 (para.66)
British Sugar 286 (para.44)
Tetra Pak I 289 (para.41)
British Plasterboard 299 (para.111)
Flat Glass 300 (para.77)
Hilti T–30/89 (ground 81)
Tetra Pak II T–83/91 (ground 94)
Continental Can C–6/72 (ground 35)
United Brands C–27/76 (ground 55)

2.2.6. Language

2.2.7. Consumer preferences

British Sugar 286 (para.44)

2.2.8. Need for secure/regular supplies or rapid after-sales service and thus locally based suppliers

British Sugar 286 (para.44)
Tetra Pak I 289 (para.41)
Flat Glass 300 (para.77)
Michelin 481 (para.128)
Georg/Ferrovie 521 (para.58)

2.2.9. Supply side substitutability; potential competition

Solvay 332 (para.43)
Duales 472 (para.96)

2.2.10. Market defined on basis of geographic scope of alleged dominant firms' scope of activities

ABG/Oil Companies 113 (para.I.D)
Michelin 165 (para.34)
Decca 304 (paras 88–89)
Magill 307 (para.21)
Solvay 332 (para.49)
Soda Ash (ICI) 489 (para.124)

2.3. Relevant evidence

2.3.1. Price difference between neighbouring areas

Solvay 332 (para.43)
British Midland 350 (para.15)
HOV SVZ/MCN 381 (para.65)
Michelin 481 (paras 134, 158–167)
Hilti T–30/89 (ground 81)
Tetra Pak II T–83/91 (ground 95)

2.3.2. Market share differences between neighbouring areas

Michelin 481 (paras 132–133)

2.3.3. Significant trade flows between neighbouring areas

Chiquita 101 (para.II.A.2)
ECS/AKZO 242 (para.66)
Tetra Pak I 289 (para.41)
Solvay 332 (para.43)
Michelin 481 (paras 127–151)

3. A substantial part of the Common Market

3.1. Local/regional markets

Suiker Unie C–40/73 (grounds 370–375, 441–449)
Alsatel v Novasam C–247/86
Almelo v Ysselmij C–393/92 (ground 41)

3.2. National markets

RTE T–69/89 (ground 64)
Tetra Pak II T–83/91 (ground 92–93)
Deutsche Bahn T–83/97 (ground 58)
BRT v SABAM II C–127/73 (ground 5)
Michelin C–322/81 (grounds 25–28)

3.3. Transport infrastructure/essential facilities

SABENA 295 (para.16)
British Midland 350
Rodby 379 (para.8)
Brussels Airport 403
Frankfurt Airport 428
Alpha Flight Services 432
Portuguese Airports 437
Finnish Airports 438
Georg/Ferrovie 521
Microsoft 528 (paras 585–589, 621–622, 631)
B&I/Sealink, Holyhead 22nd Comp. Rep. (para.219)
Morlaix 25th Comp. Rep. (para.43)
Vanden Bergh Foods T–65/98 (ground 161)
Merci v Siderurgica C–179/90 (ground 15)
Corsica Ferries C–18/93 (ground 41)
RTE C–241/91P
GT-Link v DSB C–242/95 (paras 35–37)
⋆Oscar Bronner C–7/97
IMS Health C–418/01

[For the tables of case citations see Tables 1 to 4, 11 and 12 at the back of the book.]

B. DOMINANCE

1. Definition of the term "dominant position"

Continental Can 46 (para.II.B.3)
European Sugar Industry 69 (para.E.I)
Chiquita 101 (para.II.A.2)
ABG/Oil Companies 113 (para.II.A)
Michelin 165 (para.35)
ECS/AKZO 242 (para.67)
Solvay 332 (paras 40–41)
ICI 333 (paras 41–43)
Soda Ash (ICI) 489 (paras 117–119)
10th Comp. Rep. (para.150)
Hilti T–30/89 (ground 90)
Tetra Pak II T–83/91 (grounds 113–116)
Vanden Bergh Foods T–65/98 (ground 154)
★United Brands C–27/76 (grounds 63–66)
★Hoffmann-La Roche C–85/76 (grounds 38–39)
Michelin C–322/81 (ground 57)
Bodson v Pompes Funébres C–30/87 (grounds 26–27)
Télémarketing v CLT C–311/84 (ground 16)

2. Relevant factors

2.1. Market share

Continental Can 46 (para.II.B.4–7)
Chiquita 101 (para.II.A.2)
Vitamins 104 (para.21)
Michelin 165 (para.35)
ECS/AKZO 242 (para.68)
Boosey & Hawkes 273 (para.18)
Hilti 282 (paras 66–68)
Tetra Pak I 289 (para.44)
SABENA 295 (para.24)
British Plasterboard 299 (para.116)
Decca 304 (paras 93, 95–96)
Solvay 332 (paras 44–45)
ICI 333 (para.47)
Tetra Pak II 348 (paras 100–102)
British Midland 350 (para.18)
French African Shipping 353 (paras 62, 64)
Gillette 361 (para.22)
CEWAL 371 (para.57)
Irish Sugar 418 (paras 102–108)
Van den Bergh Foods 431 (paras 258–259)
DSD 478 (para.95)
Michelin 481 (paras 174–180)
Deutsche Telekom 515 (paras 97–100)
Microsoft 528 (para.435)
AstraZeneca 545 (para.515)
★10th Comp. Rep. (para.150)
Hilti T–30/89 (grounds 91–92)
Tetra Pak II T–83/91 (ground 109)
CMB a.o./Commission T–24/93 (grounds 76–77)
Italian Tobacco T–139/98 (grounds 51–52)
Vanden Bergh Foods T–65/98 (ground 154)
British Airways T–219/99 (grounds 210–211)
United Brands C–27/76 (grounds 105–109) (ground 46)
★Hoffmann-La Roche C–85/76(grounds 40–41)
Michelin C–322/81 (grounds 52, 59–60)
★AKZO C–62/86
Gøttrup-Klim v DLG C–250/92 (grounds 46–48)

2.2. Size and resources of the group

Continental Can 46 (para.II.B.12–13)
Vitamins 104 (para.20)
Michelin 165 (para.35)
Hilti 282 (para.67)
Tetra Pak I 289 (para.44)
British Plasterboard 299 (para.116)
Tetra Pak II 348 (para.101)
AstraZeneca 545 (paras 565–566)
Hoffmann-La Roche C–85/76 (ground 47)
Michelin C–322/81 (ground 55)
Bodson v Pompes FunébresC-30/87 (ground 29)

2.3. Size and importance of competitors

Continental Can 46 (para.I.J, I.K)
Chiquita 101 (para.II.A.2)
Michelin 165 (para.35)
Hilti 282 (para.67)
SABENA 295 (para.25)
British Plasterboard 299 (para.117)
ICI 333 (para.48)
Gillette 361 (para.22)
CEWAL 371 (para.59)
ICI & CSC C–6/73 (grounds 15–16)
United Brands C–27/76 (grounds 110–111)
Hoffman-La Roche C–85/76 (ground 48)

2.4. Commercial advantage over competitors

2.4.1. Product range

Continental Can 46 (para.II.B.11)
Vitamins 104 (para.21)
Michelin 165 (para.36)
ECS/AKZO 242 (para.69)
British Plasterboard 299 (para.117)
Solvay 332 (para.45)

[For the tables of case citations see Tables 1 to 4, 11 and 12 at the back of the book.]

CEWAL 371 (para.45)
Hoffmann-La Roche C–85/76 (ground 46)
Michelin C–322/81 (ground 58)

2.4.2. Established trade marks; customer loyalty

Chiquita 101 (para.II.A.2)
Boosey & Hawkes 273 (para.18)
Microsoft 528 (para.523)
AstraZeneca 545 (paras 542, 551–552)
United Brands C–27/76 (grounds 86–96)

2.4.3. Vertical integration of firm

Continental Can 46 (para.II.B.9)
Chiquita 101 (para.II.A.2)
British Plasterboard 299 (para.116)
Solvay 332 (para.45)
Michelin 481 (paras 193–195)
United Brands C–27/76 (grounds 69–81)

2.4.4. Extensive sales/service network

Michelin 165 (para.36)
Hilti 282 (para.69)
Tetra Pak I 289 (para.44)
Solvay 332 (para.45)
Michelin 481 (paras 191–192)
Italian Tobacco T–139/98 (ground 52)

2.5. Technical advantages

2.5.1. General

Boosey & Hawkes 273 (para.18)
Michelin 481 (paras 182–184)
Microsoft 528 (para.453)
Hoffmann-La Roche C–85/76 (ground 48)
Michelin C–322/81 (ground 61)

2.5.2. Patents

Continental Can 46 (para.II.B.10)
Hilti 282 (paras 56, 67, 69)
Tetra Pak I 289 (paras 36, 44)
Tetra Pak II 348 (para.101)
AstraZeneca 545 (paras 517–540)
Hilti T–30/89 (ground 93)

2.5.3. Know-how

Continental Can 46 (para.II.B.10)
Chiquita 101 (para.II.A.2)
Tetra Pak I 289 (paras 36, 44)
Tetra Pak II 348 (para.101)
United Brands C–27/76 (grounds 82–92)

2.5.4. Copyright

Magill 307 (para.22)
RTE C–241/91P (ground 47)

2.5a. Advantages of a regulatory nature

AstraZeneca 545 (paras 517–518, 527)

2.6. Dependence of consumers

ABG/Oil Companies 113 (para.II.A)
Boosey & Hawkes 273 (para.18)
British Plasterboard 299 (para.117)
ICI 333 (para.48)
Michelin 481 (paras 200–207)
British Airways T–219/99 (grounds 216)

2.7. Statutory dominance or monopoly

Gema I 38
General Motors 84 (para.7)
GVL 166 (para.45)
British Telecommunications 188 (paras 25–27)
British Leyland 212 (para.25)
Magill 307 (para.22)
Rodby 379 (para.10)
HOV SVZ/MCN 381 (paras 141 and 149)
Irish Sugar 418 (para.104)
Alpha Flight Services 432 (paras 72–76)
DPAG Cross-border mail 483 (paras 88–96)
Georg/Ferrovie 521 (paras 82–85)
German Postal Law 541 (para.53)
RTE T–69/89 (ground 63)
BBC T–70/89 (ground 51)
ITV T–76/89 (ground 49)
Aéroports de Paris T–128/98 (grounds 8, 148–14)
GVL C–7/82 (ground 44)
British Leyland C–226/84 (grounds 8–9)
Bodson v Pompes FunébresC-30/87 (grounds 28–29)
GT-Link v DSB C–242/95 (ground 35)

2.8. Supply side substitutability; entry barriers

2.8.1. Basic concept

Vitamins 104 (para.21)
Solvay 332 (para.45)
ICI 333 (para.48)
Gillette 361 (para.9)
Microsoft 528 (paras 450–451)

2.8.2. Regulatory barriers

Decca 304 (para.8)
British Midland 350 (para.19)
French African Shipping 353 (para.63)

[For the tables of case citations see Tables 1 to 4, 11 and 12 at the back of the book.]

Irish Sugar 418 (para.104)
Georg Ferrovie 521 (paras 100–101, 114)
Clearstream 531 (para.211)

2.8.3. Financial risk (likely return on investment if market already mature or saturated)

Hilti 282 (para.69)
Tetra Pak I 289 (para.44)
British Plasterboard 299 (para.120)
Gillette 361 (para.9)

2.8.4. High capital cost of entry

British Plasterboard 299 (para.120)
Decca 304 (para.8)
Gillette 361 (para.9)
Deutsche Telekom 515 (para.101)
Georg Ferrovie 521 (paras 104–105)
Clearstream 531 (para.214)
United Brands C–27/76 (ground 122)
Hoffmann-La Roche C–85/76 (ground 48)

2.8.5. Marketing entry barriers

See point 2.4 above

2.8.6. Technical entry barriers

See point 2.5 above

2.8.7. Economies of scale

Gillette 361 (para.9)
Clearstream 531 (para.210)
Hoffmann-La Roche C–85/76 (ground 48)

2.8.8. Historical evidence of past entry indicates entry barriers surmountable

ECS/AKZO 242 (para.70)
Boosey & Hawkes 273 (para.18)
Hilti 282 (para.67)
British Midland 350 (para.22)
British Gypsum 22nd Comp. Rep. (page 422)

2.8.9. Entry must be likely in the short term

Tetra Pak II 348 (paras 94–96)
Microsoft 528 (para.453)

2.8.10. Opinions of customers and competitors regarding possibility for new entry

Gillette 361 (para.9)
Microsoft 528 (para.523)

2.8.11. High switching costs for customers

Tetra Pak I 289 (para.37)
Microsoft 528 (para.463)

2.8.12. Network effects

Microsoft 528 (paras 448–463, 520–522, 878–882)
Clearstream 531 (para.213)

2.9. Imperfect substitutes

Continental Can 46 (para.II.B.8, 16)
Hilti 282 (para.72)
British Plasterboard 299 (paras 106–109, 118–119)
Solvay 332 (paras 46–48)
ICI 333 (paras 49–51)
Tetra Pak II 348 (para.103)
French African Shipping 353 (paras 60–61)

2.10. Countervailing buying power

AstraZeneca 545 (paras 553–561)
Irish Sugar T–228/97 (grounds 98–104)

2.11. Dominance in rapidly evolving markets

Microsoft 528 (paras 465–470)

2.12. Superdominance

Microsoft 528 (paras 435 & 472)

3. Relevant evidence for determining dominance

3.1. Historical evidence of ability to maintain prices unilaterally

ECS/AKZO 242 (para.69)
Boosey & Hawkes 273 (para.18)
Solvay 332 (para.45)
ICI 333 (para.48)
British Midland 350 (para.21)
AstraZeneca 545 (paras 544–552)
United Brands C–27/76 (grounds 125–128)

3.2. Ability to engage in abusive conduct (circular argument)

Michelin 165 (para.36)
Boosey & Hawkes 273 (para.18)
Hilti 282 (paras 71–72)
TACA 441 (paras 534–537)
Michelin 481 (para.198)
Microsoft 528 (para.524)
AstraZeneca 545 (paras 528, 561)
Tetra Pak II T–83/91 (ground 110)

3.3. Ability to maintain market share over time

ECS/AKZO 242 (para.69)

[For the tables of case citations see Tables 1 to 4, 11 and 12 at the back of the book.]

ICI 333 (paras 47–48)
AstraZeneca 545 (paras 569 ff)
Hoffmann-La Roche C–85/76 (ground 44)

3.4. Econometric studies provided by parties

Hilti 282 (para.73)
★Microsoft 528

4. Joint and collective dominance

Flat Glass 300 (paras 78–79)
French African Shipping 353 (paras 55–58)
CEWAL 371 (para.49)
Rodby 379 (para.11)
Irish Sugar 418 (paras 111–113)
TACA 441 (paras 520–531)
P&I Clubs 446
Coca-Cola 546 (para.23)
TACA 28th Comp. Rep. p.145
Flat Glass T–68/89
★CMB a.o./Commission T–24/93 (grounds 59–68)
★Gencor T–102/96 (grounds 273–297)
Irish Sugar T–228/97 (grounds 46, 60–63)
Piau T–193/02 (grounds 110–116, 118)
Almelo v Ysselmij C–393/92 (grounds 42–43)
CMB C–395/96P (grounds 32–58)

5. Monopsonistic dominant position

Railway Rolling Stock 3rd Comp. Rep. (para.67)
Filtrona/Tabacalera 19th Comp. Rep. (para.61)
UK Small Mines 21st Comp. Rep. (para.107)
British Airways T–219/99 (grounds 101–109)

CHAPTER 2

ABUSE OF A DOMINANT POSITION

A. CONCEPT OF AN ABUSE OF A DOMINANT POSITION

Continental Can 46
Zoja CSC-ICI 64
ECS/AKZO 242 (para.73)
Decca 304 (para.96)
Irish Sugar 418 (para.115)
★AstraZeneca 545 (paras 325–328, 758, 848)
Tetra Pak II T–83/91 (paras 113–116)
Irish Sugar T–228/97
Vanden Bergh Foods T–65/98 (grounds 157–159)
Continental Can C–6/72
ICI & CSC C–6/73 (ground 22)
★Hoffmann-La Roche C–85/76 (ground 91)
Ahmed Saeed v Zentrale C–66/86 (grounds 37–38)
Tetra Pak C–333/94P

B. EXAMPLES OF ABUSE

1. Unfair terms imposed on clients

Gema I 38
Chiquita 101 (para.II.A.3.a)
Gema Statutes 174
British Telecommunications 188 (paras 28–36)
Tetra Pak II 348 (paras 108, 110, 115, 123–127)
TACA 441 (paras 551–558)
Duales 472 (para.112)
Michelin 481
DPAG Cross-border mail 483 (paras 155–156)
Railway Rolling Stock 3rd Comp. Rep. (paras 68–69)
SACEM & SABAM 4th Comp. Rep. (para.112)
Instituto/IMC & Angus 16th Comp. Rep. (para.76)
Deutsche Bahn T–229/94 (ground 79)
BRT v SABAM II C–127/73 (grounds 8–15)
Sacchi C–155/73 (grounds 6–1)
Suiker Unie C–40/73 (grounds 383–402)
★United Brands C–27/76 (grounds 130–162)
Ahmed Saeed v Zentrale C–66/86 (grounds 42–44)

2. Unfair or excessive prices

General Motors 84
Chiquita 101 (para.II.A.3.b,c)
British Leyland 212
SABENA 295 (para.29)
Duales 472 (para.111)
Deutsche Telekom 515
IMAX 534
★Scandlines 236
★Sundbusserne 537
Sterling Airways 10th Comp. Rep. (paras 136–138)
ITT/Belgacom 27th Comp. Rep. (p.152)
Dutch electricity grid 29th Comp. Rep. (p.165)
ITT Promedia T–111/96
Poudres Sphériques T–5/97 (ground 178)
Duales T–151/01
Parke, Davis v Centrafarm C–24/67
★General Motors C–26/75 (grounds 11–24)
★United Brands C–27/76 (grounds 235–268)

[For the tables of case citations see Tables 1 to 4, 11 and 12 at the back of the book.]

Bodson v Pompes Funébres C–30/87 (grounds 31–34)
Ministère Public v Tournier C–395/87 (ground 38–43)
Lucazeau v SACEM C–110/88 (ground 25–30)
La Crespelle C–323/93 (grounds 23–27)
Deutsche Post C–147/97 (grounds 57–58)

3. Exclusive purchasing

Vitamins 104 (paras 11–18, 22–27)
Solvay 332 (paras 56–59)
ICI 333 (paras 57–60)
Tetra Pak II 348 (paras 116–117, 143)
CEWAL 371 (paras 63–66)
Van den Bergh Foods 431
Duales 472 (paras 114–115)
Michelin 481 (paras 329–330)
Soda Ash (Solvay) 488 (paras 166–178)
Soda Ash (ICI) 489 (paras 142–150)
CIK-FIA 533 (paras 78–79)
Coca-Cola 546 (paras 27–31, 46)
Instituto/IMC & Angus 16th Comp. Rep. (para.76)
Industrial cases 19th Comp. Rep. (para.62)
UCB 24th Comp. Rep. (p.362)
AMEX/VISA 26th Comp. Rep. p.160
Pelika Ray 26th Comp. Rep. p.161
British Gypsum T–65/89 (grounds 65–77)
Tetra Pak II T–83/91 (grounds 134–135, 737)
Michelin T–203/01 (grounds 178 ff, 223 ff)
⋆Hoffmann-La Roche C–85/76 (grounds 89–120)
AKZO C–62/86 (ground 149)
Almelo v Ysselmij C–393/92 (ground 44)

3a. Purchasing from a competitor

De Beers 553 (paras 28–32, 46–48)

4. Exclusive distribution systems

Decca 304 (paras 97, 100–103)
De Beers 553 (paras 28–32, 46–48)
Hachette 8th Comp. Rep. (paras 114–115)
SEITA 10th Comp. Rep. (para.124)
CSK/Gist-Brocades 26th Comp. Rep. p.163

5. Discriminatory pricing

Chiquita 101 (para.II.A.3.b)
British Leyland 212
⋆ECS/AKZO 242
Hilti 282 (paras 75, 80–81)
Tetra Pak II 348 (paras 154–155, 160)
⋆HOV SVZ/MCN 381 (paras 157–159)
Irish Sugar 418
Alpha Flight Services 432
Portuguese Airports 437
Finnish Airports 438
DPAG Cross-border mail 483 (paras 121–134)
Clearstream 531 (paras 302, 310)
⋆Scandlines 536 (paras 249–287)
Magnetti Marelli 22nd Comp. Rep. (page 421)
AFS/ADP 28th Comp. Rep. p.144
Tetra Pak II T–83/91 (grounds 160–173, 207–209)
Deutsche Bahn T–229/94
Irish Sugar T–228/97 (grounds 164, 183)
Aéroportsde Paris T–128/98 (grounds 201–202, 206–220)
British Airways T–219/99 (grounds 23–240)
⋆United Brands C–27/76 (grounds 204–234)
British Leyland C–226/84
GT-Link v DSB C–242/95
Portugal C–163/99

6. Discriminatory conditions between different customers

Michelin 165 (paras 25, 41)
GVL 166 (paras 49–60)
⋆British Telecommunications 188 (para.30)
British Sugar 286 (paras 33–35, 73)
⋆British Plasterboard 299 (paras 81–85, 142–147)
Solvay 332 (paras 62–64)
Tetra Pak II 348 (paras 138, 161)
Football tickets 455
Virgin/BA 456
DPAG Cross-border mail 483 (paras 121–134)
Soda Ash (Solway) 488 (paras 181–185)
German Postal Law 541 (paras 64–66, 86–87, 92–95)
Clearstream 531 (paras 293–299)
UK Small Mines 21st Comp. Rep. (para.107)
British Gypsum T–65/89 (grounds 94–97)

7. Discrimination on grounds of nationality

Gema I 38
GVL 166 (paras 46–47)
SACEM & SABAM 4th Comp. Rep. (para.112)
Boat Equipment 10th Comp. Rep. (paras 119–120)
Italian Tobacco T–139/98
⋆GVL C–7/82 (ground 56)

8. Discriminatory allocation of products during supply shortages

ABG/Oil Companies 113
British Sugar 286 (paras 20–23, 61–64)

9. Predatory pricing

⋆ECS/AKZO 242

[For the tables of case citations see Tables 1 to 4, 11 and 12 at the back of the book.]

Hilti 282 (paras 80–81)
⋆British Sugar 286 (paras 24–31, 65–68)
Tetra Pak II 348 (paras 147–152, 156–159)
CEWAL 371 (paras 73–83)
Deutsche Post 470 (para.35)
Macron/Angus 17th Comp. Rep (para.81)
Tetra Pak II T–83/91 (grounds 147–152, 185–193, 199–203)
CMB a.o./Commission T–24/93 (ground 138)
⋆AKZO C–62/86 (grounds 69–72)
CMB C–395/96P (grounds 115–120)

10. Refusal to supply

Zoja CSC-ICI 64
European Sugar Industry 69
Chiquita 101 (para.II.A.3.d)
ABG/Oil Companies 113
Hugin/Liptons 121
British Telecommunications 188 (paras 28–36)
British Leyland 212
⋆Boosey & Hawkes 273 (para.19)
Hilti 282 (paras 76–84)
British Sugar 286 (paras 20–23, 61–64)
SABENA 295 (paras 29–32)
Seacontainers 377 (paras 66–76)
DPAG Cross-border mail 483 (paras 135–143)
Georg/Ferrovie 521 (paras 119 ff, 144 ff)
⋆Microsoft 528 (paras 564–559, 704–705)
Clearstream 531 (paras 217 ff)
Sundbusserne 537 (paras 238–249)
7th Comp. Rep. (paras 27, 28)
Boat equipment 10th Comp. Rep. (paras 119–120)
Polaroid 13th Comp. Rep. (paras 155–157)
Instituto/IMC & Angus 16th Comp. Rep. (para.76)
Volvo 17th Comp. Rep. (para.82)
London European/SABENA 17th Comp. Rep. (para.86)
Info-Lab/Ricoh 29th Comp. Rep. p.169
ITT Promedia T–111/96
Microsoft T–201/04 (grounds 203–204)
ICI & CSC C–6/73 (ground 25)
⋆United Brands C–27/76 (grounds 163–196)
Benzine & Petroleum BV C–77/77 (grounds 19–34)
British Leyland C–226/84
Volvo v Veng C–238/87
Maxicar v Renault C–53/87
Höfner v Macrotron C–41/90
⋆Oscar Bronner C–7/97
⋆IMS Health C–418/01

11. Refusal to do business with competition

British Midland 350
French African Shipping 353 (paras 68–69)
Frankfurt Airport 428
Georg/Ferrovie 521 (paras 119–125)
Clearstream 531 (paras 234, 236)
Italian Tobacco T–139/98

12. Tying

Article 86(d) EEC
Gema I 38
European Sugar Industry 69
Michelin 165 (paras 20–24, 28, 37–50)
British Sugar 286 (paras 32, 69–72)
Hilti 292
SABENA 295 (para.31)
Tetra Pak II 348 (paras 116, 117, 140)
Frankfurt Airport 428
Michelin 481 (paras 256–258)
De Post/La Poste 486 (paras 53–62)
⋆Microsoft 528 (paras 794, 800–803, 830–832, 835–838, 841, 960–961)
IMAX 534
Coca-Cola 546 (paras 33–37)
SACEM & SABAM 4th Comp. Rep. (para.112)
IBM 14th Comp. Rep. (paras 94–95)
IBM 16th Comp. Rep. (para.75)
Olio Fiat 17th Comp. Rep. (para.84)
IRI/Nielsen 26th Comp. Rep. p.164
Novo/Nordisk 26th Comp. Rep. p.162
Digital 27th Comp. Rep. (p.153)
Tetra Pak II T–83/91 (grounds 134–135)
Microsoft T–201/04 (grounds 390–404)
Michelin C–322/81 (grounds 93–99)
Télémarketingv CLT C–311/84 (grounds 18–26)
Tetra Pak C–333/94P

13. Rebates and discounts

European Sugar Industry 69
Vitamins 104 (paras 11–18, 22–27)
⋆Michelin 165 (paras 20–24, 28, 37–50)
Hilti 282 (para.74)
British Sugar 286 (paras 36–39, 74–76)
British Plasterboard 299 (paras 58–59, 123-129, 86–92, 148–152)
Solvay 332 (paras 50–64)
ICI 333 (paras 53–62)
Tetra Pak II 348 (paras 111–114)
CEWAL 371 (paras 84–91)
⋆Brussels Airport 403 Irish Sugar 418
Virgin/BA 456
Michelin 481
Soda Ash (Solvay) 488 (paras 152–154, 162–163)
Soda Ash (ICI) 489 (paras 139–141)

[For the tables of case citations see Tables 1 to 4, 11 and 12 at the back of the book.]

Coca-Cola 546 (paras 32 & 36)
Coca-Cola 19th Comp. Rep. (para.50)
British Gypsum 22nd Comp. Rep. (page 422)
Cicra 24th Comp. Rep. (para.361)
British Gypsum T–65/89 (ground 120)
Irish Sugar T–228/97 (grounds 114, 194–197, 203–210)
⋆Michelin T–203/01 (grounds 56–60, 95–100)
British Airways T–219/99 (grounds 244–249)
Suiker Unie C–40/73 (grounds 421, 499–528)
⋆Hoffmann-La Roche C–85/76 (grounds 89–108)
Michelin C–322/81 (grounds 63–99)
Portugal C–163/99 (grounds 50–57)
Deutsche Post 470 (grounds 33–34, 38–39)

14. Using dominance to move into or protect ancillary markets

⋆Zoja CSC-ICI 64
Michelin 165 (para.50)
Hilti 282 (para.74)
Tetra Pak II 348 (para.104)
Seacontainers 377 (paras 66–76)
Rodby 379 (para.12)
Atlas 411
Phoenix 412
Italian Tobacco 433
Italian Post 468
Michelin 481 (paras 256–258, 297–304)
Deutsche Telekom 515
Georg/Ferrovie 521 (paras 124, 140–141)
Microsoft 528 (paras 526–534, 772–778)
Scandlines 536 (paras 271–272)
Sundbusserne 537 (paras 223–237)
German Postal law 541 (paras 59–63, 82–85)
Filtrona/Tabacalera, 19th Comp. Rep. (para.61)
Frankfurt/Main 28th Comp. Rep. P. 145
Irish Sugar T–228/97 (grounds 166–167)
Aéroportsde Paris T–128/98 (grounds 163–166)
Microsoft T–201/04
ICI & CSC C–6/73
⋆Télémarketingv CLT C–311/84 (grounds 18–26)
Glöckner C–475/99 (paras 40–43)

15. Actions preventing parallel trade

Gema I 38
European Sugar Industry 69
General Motors 84
Chiquita 101 (para.II.A.3.a)
Hilti 282 (paras 76–77)
Michelin 481 (paras 240–247)
Interbrew 26th Comp. Rep. p.159
⋆General Motors C–26/75 (grounds 11–24)
Hoffmann-La Roche v Centrafarm C–102/77 (grounds 15–16)

16. Refusal to disclose technical information, e.g. details of products

Hilti 282 (para.79)
Decca 304 (paras 97, 108–110)
Tetra Pak II 348 (para.162)
Georg/Ferrovie 521 (paras 124–131)
⋆Microsoft 528 (paras 546–559)
Sundbusserne 537 (paras 238–244)
⋆IBM 14th Comp. Rep. (paras 94–95)
Microsoft T–201/04 (grounds 203–224)

17. Abusive registration of a trade mark

Osram/Airam 11th Comp. Rep. (para.97)

18. Restricting intra-band competition

Tetra Pak II 348 (paras 162–164)

19. Abuse of intellectual/industrial property rights

Hilti 282 (para.78)
Decca 304 (paras 104–107)
Magill 307 (para.23)
DSD 478
⋆Microsoft 528 (paras 546–558, 709–712, 740–741, 785)
GEMA 15th Comp. Rep. (para.81)
Chiquita/Fyffes 22nd Comp. Rep. (paras 168–176)
Microsoft 24th Comp. Rep. (p.365)
Lederle 24th Comp. Rep. (p.353)
⋆RTE T–69/89 (grounds 65–75)
BBC T–70/89 (grounds 52–63)
ITV T–76/89 (grounds 50–61)
Hilti T–30/89 (grounds 99–100)
⋆Ladbroke T–504/93 (grounds 123–134)
Microsoft T–201/04 (grounds 203–224)
Duales T–151/01
Parke, Davis v Centrafarm C–24/67
Sirena v Eda C–40/70 (ground 17)
Deutsche Grammophon v Metro C–78/70 (ground 19)
GVL C–7/82 (grounds 53–56)
Basset v SACEM C–402/85
Volvo v Veng C–238/87
Maxicar v Renault C–53/87
⋆Ministère Public v Tournier C–395/87 (grounds 38–43)

[For the tables of case citations see Tables 1 to 4, 11 and 12 at the back of the book.]

★Lucazeau v SACEM C–110/88 (grounds 25–30)
RTE C–241/91P (grounds 52–58)
★IMS Health C–418/01

19a. Abuse of intellectual/industrial property procedures

★AstraZeneca 545 (paras 626–749)

19b. Misleading representations to regulatory authorities

★AstraZeneca 545 (paras 626–749)

19c. Misleading representations in legal proceedings

★AstraZeneca 545 (paras 736–740)

20. Acquisition

(See also Book Two, Chapter 2, D, 3)
Gillette 361
UPS Europe T–175/99 (grounds 51–64)
Continental Can C–6/72

21. Pressure on dependent market players

Irish Sugar 418 (paras 120–122)
TACA 441 (paras 559–567)
Michelin 481 (paras 321–327)
Michelin T–203/01 (grounds 215–219)

22. Product swaps

Irish Sugar 418 (paras 125–126)

23. Litigation and complaints

Astra Zeneca 545 (paras 736–740)
IPS/Péchiney 26th Comp. Rep. p.157
ITT/Promedia T–111/96 (grounds 30 & 60)
Poudres Sphériques T–5/97 (grounds 211–218)

24. Abuse of collective or joint dominant position

Irish Sugar T–228/97 (ground 66)

25. Limiting production, markets or technical development

DPAG Cross-border mail 483 (paras 168–178)
Microsoft 528 (paras 693 ff)

26. Long-term/indefinite duration contracts/excessive notice periods

Coca-Cola 546 (paras 29, 31 & 44)
Soda Ash (Solvay) 488 (grounds 154–176)

27. Margin squeeze/raising rivals' costs

Deutsche Telekom 515 (paras 100 ff, 176 ff)

28. Abusive tender procedures

CIK-FIA 533

29. Abuse of regulatory procedures

★AstraZeneca 545 (paras 788–862)

30. Exploiting legal uncertainty or legal loopholes

★AstraZeneca 545 (paras 836–843, 847)

C. OBJECTIVE JUSTIFICATION

Hilti 282 (paras 89–96)
Tetra Pak 289 (para.49)
British Plasterboard 299 (paras 70, 131–134)
Decca 304 (paras 111–113)
Tetra Pak II 348 (paras. 118, 119, 120, 124–127)
Rodby 379 (paras. 15–16)
★HOV SVZ/MCN 381 (paras 157–159)
★Frankfurt Airport 428
Duales 472 (paras 136–154)
DSD 478 (paras 136–153)
Microsoft 528 (paras 955–969)
Clearstream 531 (paras 253–269, 278–288, 313–332)
Hilti T–30/89 (grounds 117–119)
British Gypsum T–65/89 (grounds 117–118)
Tetra Pak II T–83/91 (grounds 83–89, 138)
Aéroportsde Paris T–128/98 (grounds 201–202)
Microsoft T–201/04
Duales T–151/01
★General Motors C–26/75 (grounds 11–24)
United Brands C–27/76 (grounds 189–190)
★Ministère Public v Tournier C–395/87
★Lucazeau v SACEM C–110/88 (grounds 131–134)
Gøttrup-Klim v DLG C–250/92 (grounds 49–51)

[For the tables of case citations see Tables 1 to 4, 11 and 12 at the back of the book.]

PART VIII

STATE INTERVENTION

CHAPTER 1

ARTICLE 86

1. Cases on the interpretation of Article 86(1)

Gema I 38
Rodby 379
Brussels Airport 403
Italian GSM 406
SNELPD 485 (paras 62–93)
German Postal Law 541
Postal Cases 25th Comp. Rep. (page 141)
SPEGNN 28th Comp. Rep. (p.170)
VTM T–266/97
Van Ameyde v UCI C–90/76 (ground 22)
GB-INNO v ATAB C–13/77 (grounds 39–51)
Commission v Italy C–118/85
★Bodson v Pompes Funébres C–30/87 (grounds 33–34)
Ahmed Saeed v Zentrale C–66/86 (grounds 50–52)
★France C–202/88 (grounds 22, 55–57)
Höffner v Macrotron C–41/90
ERT v DEP C–260/89 (grounds 34–38)
Merci v Siderurgica C–179/90
RTT v GB-Inno C–18/88
Spain C–271/90
Corbeau C–320/91
Corsica Ferries C–18/93
La Crespelle 239
Banchero C–387/93 (grounds 45–56)
GT-Link v DSB C–242/95
Job Centre C–55/96
Corsica Ferries France C–266/96
Chemische Afvalstoffen Dusseldorp C–203/96
Deutsche Post C–147/97 (grounds 36–48)
Glöckner C–475/99 (grounds 18–25)
T-Mobile Austria C–141/02P (grounds 66–74)

2. Article 86(2)

2.1. Direct effect

Muller C–10/71
Inter-Huiles C–172/82
Ahmed Zaeed v Zentrale 66/86 (paras 54–57)
★ERT v DEP C–260/89 (grounds 33–34)
Corbeau C–320/91
Almelo v Ysselmij C–393/92 (grounds 46–50)

2.2. Cases on the interpretation of Article 86(2).

See also Communication from the Commission — Services of general interest in Europe
Gema I 38
Pabst & Richerz/BNIA 106 (para.IV)
Maize Seeds 137
GVL 166 (paras 65–68)
NAVEWA-ANSEAU 178 (paras 64–67)
British Telecommunications 188 (paras 41–43)
Uniform Eurochèques 224 (paras 29–30)
Decca 304
Magill 307 (para.25)
Ijsselcentrale 335 (paras 39–52)
Screensport/EBU 337 (paras 68–69)
Jahrhundertvertrag 370 (paras 28–30)
UER 373 (paras 78–79)
Rodby 379 (para.18)
Irish Telecommunications 414
Italian Post 468
Deutsche Post 470
Frankfurt Airport 482 (paras 99–102)
Deutsche Telekom 515 (paras 186–198)
German Postal Law 541 (paras 104 ff)
RTE T–69/89 (grounds 82–84)
Rendo T–16/91 (grounds 96–112)
Métropole T–528/93 (grounds 116–117)
★FFSA T–106/95
Air Inter T–260/94
Aéroports de Paris T–128/98 (grounds 227–229)
Duales T–151/01 (grounds 207–211)
Duales II T–289/01 (grounds 206 ff)

⋆BRT v SABAM II C–127/73 (grounds 17–23)
⋆Sacchi C–155/73 (grounds 16–18)
Zuechner v Bayerische Vereinsbank C–172/80 (grounds 6–9)
Nungesser C–258/87 (ground 9)
GVL C–7/82 (grounds 31–32)
⋆Italy C–41/83 (grounds 33, 34)
Télémarketingv CLT C–311/84 (ground 17)
Ahmed Saeed v Zentrale C–66/86 (grounds 54–57)
⋆France C–202/88 (grounds 11–12)
Höfner v Macrotron C–41/90 (grounds 24–25)
ERT v DEP C–260/89 (grounds 33–34)
Commission v Netherlands C–353/89 (grounds 33–36)
Merci v Siderurgica C–179/90
RTT v GB-Inno C–18/88
⋆Corbeau C–320/91
Banco de Credito v Valencia C–387/92
Almelo v Ysselmij C–393/92
GT-Link v DSB C–242/95 (grounds 47–55)
Commission v Netherlands C–157/95
Commission v Italy C–158/95
Commission v France C–159/95
Commission v Spain C–160/94
Job Centre C–55/96
Albany C–67/96 (grounds 88–123)
Brentjens C–115/97 (grounds 88–123)
Drijvende blokken C–219/97 (grounds 78–113)
Deutsche Post C–147/97 (grounds 49–61)
Pavlov C–180/98 (grounds 120–130)
Glöckner C–475/99 (grounds 51–65)
European Broadcasting Union C–470/02P (grounds 47–48)

3. Article 86(3)

Greek Insurance 230
⋆Canary Islands 268
Dutch Express Delivery 318
Spanish Courier Services 324
Rodby 379
Brussels Airport 403
Italian GSM 406
Spanish GSM 417
VTM/VT4 422
Italian Ports 423
Italian Pilots 424
Portuguese Airports 437
Danish PTT 20th Comp. Rep. (para.358)
Flying German Officials 20th Comp. Rep. (para.357)
Flying Belgian Officials 21st Comp. Rep. (para.33)
Transmediterranean 21st Comp. Rep. (paras 334–336)
⋆Ladbroke T–32/93
German Accountants T–84/94
Ladbroke T–548/93 (ground 45)
Koelman T–575/93 (grounds 71–72)
ITT Promedia T–111/96 (ground 97)
VTM T–266/97
Coe Clerici T–52/00
France C–188/80
Commission v Greece C–226/87
⋆France C–202/88 (grounds 16–18, 21)
⋆Netherlands C–48/90
Spain C–271/90
France C–325/91
German Accountants C–107/95P
Portugal C–163/99 (grounds 19–34)

CHAPTER 2

APPLICATION OF ARTICLE 86

A. GENERAL

1. Communication from the Commission on services of general interest in Europe [2001] O.J. C17/4

2. References

Report to the Laeken European Council—Services of General Interest (COM (2001) 598—final, 17.10.2001)
Green Paper on Services of General Interest (COM (2003) 270 final, 21.5.2003)

B. TELECOMMUNICATIONS

1. Commission Directive 2002/77 of September 16, 2002 on competition in the markets for electronic communication networks and services [2002] O.J. L249/21

2. Commission guidelines on market analysis and the assessment of significant market power under the Community regulatory framework for electronic communications networks and services [2002] O.J. C165/6

3. Notice on the application of the competition rules to access agreements in the telecommunications sector [1998] O.J. C265/2

[For the tables of case citations see Tables 1 to 4, 11 and 12 at the back of the book.]

4. Reference to old notice

Commission Guidelines on the application of the EEC competition rules in the telecommunications sector ([1991] O.J. C233/2)

5. Cases on previous Directives

France C–202/88
Decoster C–69/91
Lagauche C–46/90
Taillandier C–92/91
Rouffeteau C–314/93
Tranchant C–91/94

C. POSTAL SERVICES

1. Notice on the application of the competition rules to the postal service and on the assessment of certain State measures relating to postal services [1998] O.J. C39/2

2. Cases on postal services

DPAG Cross-border mail 483 (paras 180–186)
SNELPD 485
De Post/La Poste 486 (paras 80–81)
German Postal Law 541
UPS Europe T–175/99

CHAPTER 3

STATE RESPONSIBILITY

A. STATE RESPONSIBILITY UNDER ARTICLES 3F AND 5 OF THE TREATY FOR FACILITATING OR ENCOURAGING BEHAVIOUR CONTRARY TO ARTICLES 81 AND 82

GB-INNO v ATAB C–13/77 (paras 24–38)
⋆Leclerc C–229/83
Cullet v Leclerc C–231/83
St. Herblain v Syndicat des Libraires C–299/83
⋆Nouvelles Frontières C–209/84 (grounds 75–77)
Procureur v Cognet C–355/85
⋆Vlaamse Reisbureaus C–311/85
BNIC/Aubert C–136/86 (grounds 5, 7–8, 23–24)
Syndicat v Leclerc Aigle C–254/87
⋆Van Eycke v Aspa C–267/86
Ahmed Saeed v Zentrale C–66/86 (grounds 48–49, 52)
Batista Morais C–60/91
Marchandise C–332/89
⋆Meng C–2/91
⋆Reiff C–185/91
⋆Ohra C–245/91
Tankstation t'Heukske C–401/92
Delta Schiffahrt C–153/93
Mateo Peralta C–379/92
Leclerc-Siplec C–412/93
Spediporto C–96/94
DIPA C–140/94
Esso Espanola C–134/94
Sodemare C–70/95
Commission v Ladbroke C–359/95P
⋆Commission v Italy C–35/96
Corsica Ferries C–266/96
Autotransporti Librandi C–38/97
Brentjens C–115/97 (grounds 63–70)
Drijvende Bokken C–219/97 (grounds 53–60)

B. GOVERNMENTAL SILENCE, ENCOURAGEMENT OR APPROVAL IS NO EXCUSE FOR INFRINGING

ARTICLES 81 AND 82
Franco-Japanese Ball-Bearings 81 FEDETAB 133 (paras 83, 88, 107)
SSI 181 (paras 88–96)
AROW/BNIC 190
Zinc Producer Group 217 (paras 73–74)
Fire Insurance 220 (para.28)
Aluminium 228 (paras 10–12)
ENI/Montedison 256 (para.5)
Welded Steel Mesh 311 (paras 201, 202, 206)
Ijsselcentrale 335 (paras 21, 33–38)
Dutch Building Cartel 349 (paras 66–69)
French African Shipping 353 (paras 9–15, 25, 26, 34–38, 68)
CEWAL 371 (paras 70–72)
CNSD 375 (paras 42–44)
COAPI 402 (paras 47–48)
DPAG Cross-border mail 483 (paras 81–82, 98–102)
Interbrew & Alken Maes 500 (paras 247–248)
Spanish Raw Tobacco 540 (paras 349–355)
Italian Raw Tobacco 550 (paras 315–324)
Dutch Pharmaceuticals 8th Comp. Rep. (paras 81–82)
Beuc T–37/92 (ground 69)
John Deere T–35/92 (grounds 50)

[For the tables of case citations see Tables 1 to 4, 11 and 12 at the back of the book.]

Asia Motor France T–7/92 (grounds 37–56 and 71)
Asia Motor France T–387/94
CMB a.o./Commission T–24/93 (grounds 80–81, 102–109)
French Beef T–217/03 (ground 92)
Van Ameyde v UCI C–90/76
BP 77/77 (ground 15)
★VBVB & VBBB C–43/82 (grounds 38–40)
BNIC v Clair C–123/83 (grounds 17, 20–21)
★SSI C–240/82 (grounds 38–40)
NSO C–260/82 (grounds 28–30)

[For the tables of case citations see Tables 1 to 4, 11 and 12 at the back of the book.]

PART IX

SECTORAL APPLICATION OF EC COMPETITION RULES

CHAPTER 1

AGRICULTURE

A. COUNCIL REGULATION 26/62 APPLYING CERTAIN RULES OF COMPETITION TO PRODUCTION OF AND TRADE IN AGRICULTURAL PRODUCTS [1962] O.J. SPEC. ED. 129

B. CASES REGARDING AGRICULTURE AND COMPETITION

1. General cases

Milk Marque 379
French Beef 513
Spanish Raw Tobacco 540
Italian Raw Tobacco 550 (para.60)
2nd Comp. Rep. (para.74)
Milk Marketing Board 22nd Comp. Rep. (paras 161–167)
Danish Fur Breeders T–61/89 (grounds 49–56)
Florimex T–70/92
Cerafel v Le Campion C–218/85
★UNILEC v Larroche C–212/87
★Dijkstra C–319/93
Oude Luttikhuis C–399/93

2. Cases in which Regulation 26/62 was applicable

New Potatoes 276

3. Cases in which Regulation 26/62 was not applicable

European Sugar Industry 69
FRUBO 80
Tinned Mushrooms 88
Pabst & Richerz/BNIA 106 (para.II.5)
Cauliflowers 119
Maize Seeds 137
Rennet 149 (paras 26–27)
★Milchförderungsfonds 221 (paras 18–25)
Meldoc 253 (paras 53–55)
VBA 288
Sugar Beet 315 (paras 87–88)
Scottish Salmon 358 (para.22)
British Sugar II 434 (paras 185–188)
French Beef 513 (paras 135–149)
Spanish Raw Tobacco 540 (paras 337–348)
Italian Raw Tobacco 550 (paras 303–314)
Campina 21st Comp. Rep. (paras 83–84)
Danish Fur Breeders T–61/89 (grounds 36–39)
French Beef T–217/03 (grounds 197–206)
Frubo C–71/74 (grounds 11, 22–29)
Suiker Unie C–40/73
Stremsel C–61/80 (grounds 19–21)
★Nungesser C–258/87 (grounds 18–22)
BNIC v Clair C–123/83 (ground 15)
BNIC/Aubert C–136/86 (grounds 14–15)
Gøttrup-Klim v DLG C–250/92 (grounds 21–27)

CHAPTER 2

TRANSPORT

A. INLAND WATERWAYS, RAIL AND ROAD TRANSPORT

1. Legislation

Council Regulation 1017/68 of July 19, 1968 applying rules of competition to transport by rail, road and inland waterway [1968] O.J. Spec. Ed. 302, as amended by Regulation 1/2003 [2003] O.J. L1/1.

2. Cases on the interpretation and application of the Regulations

EATE Levy 231
RailwayTickets 362 (paras 47–59)
Combined Transport 372
HOV SVZ/MCN 381

[For the tables of case citations see Tables 1 to 4, 11 and 12 at the back of the book.]

ACI 388
Night Services 390
Eurotunnel 396
Trans Atlantic 393A (paras 304–306, 375–381, 462–491)
Far Eastern Freight 399
FETTCSA 464
Revised TACA 507
Georg/Ferrovie 521
Eurotunnel II 19th Comp. Rep. (para.57)
Railway Companies 20th Comp. Rep. (para.115)
ACE 25th Comp. Rep. (page 127)
CIA 29th Comp. Rep. p.153
SNCF T–79/95
Deutsche Bahn T–229/94 (grounds 34–44)
European Night Services T–374/94
Far Eastern Freight Conference T–86/95 (grounds 231–276)
Atlantic Container Line T–395/94 (ground 391)
Atlantic Container Line II T–18/97 (grounds 48–63)
FETTCSA T–213/00
★UICF T–14/93
ANTIB C–272/85
Commission v UIC C–264/95P

B. MARITIME TRANSPORT

1. **Council Regulation 4056/86 of December 22, 1986 laying down detailed rules for the application of Articles 85 and 86 of the Treaty to maritime transport [1986] O.J. L378/4, as amended by Regulation 1/2003 [2003] O.J. L1/1**
2. **Council Regulation 479/92 of February 25, 1992 on the application of Article 85(3) of the Treaty to certain categories of agreements, decisions and concerted practices between liner shipping companies (consortia) [1992] O.J. L55/3, as amended by Regulation 1/2003 [2003] O.J. 11/1**
3. **Commission Regulation 823/2000 of April 19, 2000 on the applicability of Article 81(3) of the Treaty to certain categories of agreements, decisions and concerted practices between liner shipping companies (consortia) [2000] O.J. L100/24 as amended by Regulation 463/2004 [2004] O.J. L77/23**

4. Cases

Secrétama 329a
French African Shipping 353
UKWAL 354
MEWAC 365
CEWAL 371
★Trans Atlantic 393A
★Far Eastern Freight 399
Ferry Services 413
TACA 441
Europe Asia Trade Agreements 449
FETTCSA 464
Revised TACA 507
Holyhead 22nd Comp. Rep. (para.219)
DSB 22nd Comp. Rep. (page 418)
EAL 23rd Comp. Rep. (para.230)
Irish Club 23rd Comp. Rep. (para.233)
25th Comp. Rep. (paras 66–72)
26th Comp. Rep. (paras 84–91)
27th Comp. Rep. (paras 134–137)
Revised TACA 29th Comp. Rep. p.150
VSA2/CSVA 29th Comp. Rep. p.151
CMB a.o./Commission T–24/93 (grounds 46–52, 174–178)
Far Eastern Freight Conference T–86/95 (grounds 231–276)
Atlantic Container Line T–395/94 (grounds 134–178 & 391)
Atlantic Container Line II T–18/97 (ground 44)
Minoan Lines T–66/99
Strintzis Lines T–65/99
Adriatica T–61/99
Ventouris T–59/99
Marlines T–56/99
CMA CGM C–236/03P
CMB C–395/96P (grounds 46–52, 445–118, 129–136)

C. AIR TRANSPORT

1. **Council Regulation 3976/87 of December 14, 1987 on the application of Article 85(3) of the Treaty to certain categories of agreements and concerted practices in the air transport sector [1987] O.J. L374/9 as amended by Regulation 2344/90 [1990] O.J. L217/15, Regulation 2411/92 [1992] O.J. L240/19 and Regulation 411/2004 [2004] O.J. L68/1**

[For the tables of case citations see Tables 1 to 4, 11 and 12 at the back of the book.]

2. **Commission Regulation 1617/93 of June 25, 1993 on the application of Article 85(3) of the Treaty to certain categories of agreements, and concerted practices concerning joint planning and co-ordination of schedules, joint operations, consultations on passenger and cargo tariffs on scheduled air services and slot allocation at airports [1993] O.J. L155/18, as amended by Regulation 1523/96 [1996] O.J. L190/11, Regulation 1083/1999 [1999] O.J. L131/27, Regulation 1324/2001 [2001] O.J. L177/56 and the Act of Accession of Austria, Sweden and Finland [1994] O.J. C241/21 (adapted by Council Decision 95/1/EC, Euraton, ECSC [1995] O.J. L1/1), corrigendum in [1994] O.J. L15/20**
3. **Commission Regulation 1324/2001 of June 29, 2001 amending Regulation 1617/93 as regards consultations on passenger tariffs and slot allocation at airports [2001] O.J. L177/56**
4. **Notice concerning procedures for communications to the Commission pursuant to Articles 4 and 5 of Commission Regulation 1617/93 of June 25, 1993 on the application of Article 85(3) of the Treaty to certain categories of agreements and concerted practices concerning joint planning and co-ordination of schedules, joint operations, consultations on passenger and cargo tariffs on scheduled air services and slot allocation at airports [1993] O.J. C177/6**

5. Cases

Olympic Airways 229
SABENA 295
IATA Passengers 342
IATA Cargo 343
⋆British Midland 350
LH/SAS 409 SAS/Maersk Air 475
Air France/Alitalia 529
5th Comp. Rep. (para.14)
9th Comp. Rep. (paras 12–15)
Sterling Airways 10th Comp. Rep. (paras 136–138)
11th Comp. Rep. (para.5)
15th Comp. Rep. (paras 27–33)
17th Comp. Rep. (paras 43–46)
IATA 19th Comp. Rep. (para.58)
19th Comp. Rep. (para.44)
20th Comp. Rep. (paras 73–76, 106–109)
Amadeus/Sabre 21st Comp. Rep. (paras 93–95)
IATA 23rd Comp. Rep. (para.238)
Sabre 23rd Comp. Rep. (para.239)
⋆Premiair 25th Comp. Rep. (page 134)
26th Comp. Rep. (paras 99–102)
Aéroportsde Paris 26th Comp. Rep. p.162
Aéroportsde Paris T–128/98 (grounds 34–47)
British Airways T–219/99 (grounds 155–173)
SAS T–241/01
AFS/ADP 28th Comp Rep p.144
Lord Bethell C–246/81
Nouvelles Frontières C–209/84
Ahmed Saeed v Zentrale C–66/86
Portugal C–163/99

CHAPTER 3

FINANCIAL SERVICES

A. LEGISLATION

1. **Council Regulation 1534/91 of May 31, 1991 on the application of Article 85(3) of the Treaty to certain categories of agreements, decisions and concerted practices in the insurance sector [1991] O.J. L143/1, as amended by Regulation 1/2003 [2003] O.J. L1/1**
2. **Commission Regulation 358/2003 of February 27, 2003 on the application of Article 85(3) of the Treaty to certain categories of agreements, decision and concerted practices in the insurance sector [2003] O.J. L53/8**
3. **Notice on the application of the EC competition rules to cross-border credit transfers [1995] O.J. C25/3**

B. CASES

1. Banking

Uniform Eurochèques 224
Irish Banks Standing Committee 252
Belgian Banking Association 261
ABI 262
Dutch Banking Association 310
Eurocheques; Helsinki 352

[For the tables of case citations see Tables 1 to 4, 11 and 12 at the back of the book.]

★BNP/Dresdner Bank 410
Identrus 476
VISA 477
Austrian Banks 503 (paras 392–400)
Clearstream 531
2nd Comp. Rep. (paras 52–53)
8th Comp. Rep. (paras 32–37)
13th Comp. Rep. (paras 67–69)
21st Comp. Rep. (paras 33–34)
Halifax Building Society 21st Comp. Rep. (page 335)
TEPAR 21st Comp. Rep. (para.336)
Interest Rates 22nd Comp. Rep. (para.417)
ISMA 23rd Comp. Rep. (para.453)
25th Comp. Rep. (paras 45–48)
IBOS 26th Comp. Rep. p.146
Eurogiro 26th Comp. Rep. p.148
Finanzrädet 26th Comp. Rep. p.148
Europay 26th Comp. Rep. p.154
Amex/Visa 26th Comp. Rep. p.161
Europay T–39/92
Dresdner Bank T–44/02
Vereins-und Westbank T–54/02
Bayerische Hypo-und Vereinsbank T–56/02
Deutsche Verkehrsbank T–60/02
Commerzbank T–61/02
Zuechner v Bayerische Vereinsbank C–172/80
Van Eycke v Aspa C–267/86
Carlo Bagnasco C–215/96
NVB-GSA 452

2. Insurance

Nuovo/CEGAM 209
Fire Insurance 220
Greek Insurance 230
P&I Clubs 243
Concordato 316
TEKO 317
Assurpol 346
Lloyd's Underwriters 363
P&I Clubs 446
2nd Comp. Rep. (paras 52–53)
8th Comp. Rep. (paras 32–37)
Luxemburg Car Insurance 15th Comp. Rep. (para.71)
26th Comp. Rep. p.149
Van Ameyde v UCI C–90/76
Fire Insurance C–45/85
Poucet C–159/91
French Insurance C–244/94

CHAPTER 4

SPORTS

A. CASES

Meca-Medina T–313/02
★Meca-Medina C–519/04

[For the tables of case citations see Tables 1 to 4, 11 and 12 at the back of the book.]

PART X

PROCEDURE AND REMEDIES

CHAPTER 1

PROCEDURAL LEGISLATION

A. RELEVANT PROVISIONS OF THE TREATY

1. Article 83 (ex 87)

2. Cases on the interpretation of Article 83 (ex 87)

★Bosch v De Geus C–13/61
Italy v Council and Commission C–32/65
Walt Wilhelm C–14/68 (grounds 4–5)
ACF Chemiefarma C–41/69
Ahmed Saeed v Zentrale C–66/86

3. Articles 84–85 (ex 88–89)

4. Cases on the interpretation of Articles 84–85 (ex 88–89)

Parker Pen v Commission T–77/92 (ground 63)
★Nouvelles Frontieres C–209/84
Ahmed Saeed v Zentrale C–66/86

B. RELEVANT LEGISLATIVE PROVISIONS

1. Council Regulation 1/2003 of December 16, 2002 on the interpretation of the rules on competition laid down in Articles 81 and 82 of the Treaty [2003] O.J. L1/1 as amended by Regulation 411/2004 [2004] O.J. L68/1

2. Commission Regulation 773/2004 on the conduct of proceedings by the Commission pursuant to Articles 81 and 82 of the EC Treaty [2004] O.J. L123/18

3. Notice on informal guidance relating to novel questions concerning Articles 81 and 82 of the EC Treaty that arise in individual cases (guidance letters) [2004] O.J. C101/78

4. Notice on the handling of complaints by the Commission under Articles 81 and 82 of the EC Treaty [2004] O.J. C101/65

CHAPTER 2

THE HANDLING OF A CASE

A. THE OPENING OF A FILE

1. Method of notification; what constitutes a valid notification (Former Regulation 17)

Regulation 3385/94
Grundig/Consten 5
Cobelpa/VNP 115 (paras 5, 9, 40)
★The Distillers Company 123
BMW Belgium 126 (para.25)
Hasselblad 173 (para.72)
AEG/Telefunken 179 (para.75)
Zinc Producers Group 217
Aluminium 228 (para.16)
Sperry New Holland 245 (para.65)
Eco System 344a (para.29)
U.K. Tractors 347 (para.59)
★Eurocheques; Helsinki 352 (para.84)
15th Comp. Rep. (para.48)
GEC Alstom/Fiat 22nd Comp. Rep. (page 415)
Parfums Rochas v Bitsch C–1/70 (grounds 4–6, 7, 11)
De Haecht v Wilkin II C–48/72 (grounds 14–23)
Boekhandels v Eldi Records C–106/79 (grounds 8–11)
★Distillers C–30/78 (grounds 19–24)
FEDETAB C–209–215, C–218/78 (grounds 48–56)

[For the tables of case citations see Tables 1 to 4, 11 and 12 at the back of the book.]

1.1. When is notification necessary (Former Regulation 17)

Articles 4(2), 5(2) Regulation 17/62
Article 7 Regulation 19/65
Kabelmetal/Luchaire 94
Vaessen/Moris 143 (paras 21–22)
BP Kemi/DDSF 147 (paras 98–102)
NAVEWA–ANSEAU 178 (para.62)
⋆SSI 181 (para.143)
Windsurfing International 194
Fire Insurance 220 (para.38)
Roofing Felt 248 (paras 96–98)
Meldoc 253 (para.74)
COAPI 402 (para.41)
Whitbread 439 (paras 182–185) 1st Comp. Rep. (para.39)
JCB Service T–217/03 (grounds 77–82)
Bilger v Jehle C–43/69 (grounds 4–6)
De Haecht v Wilkin II C–48/72 (grounds 19–23)

1.2. Conversion of notification (Former Regulation 17)

Article 5 Regulation 2367/90 BT/MCI 387 (para.7)
Pasteur/Merck 392

1.3. Effect of notification

1.3.1. Possibility of the grant of an exemption

Article 4 Regulation 17/62
L'Oréal v De Nieuwe AMCK C–31/80 (ground 13)

1.3.2. Immunity from fines (Former Regulation 17)

Article 15(5) Regulation 17/62
Theal/Watts 110
AEG/Telefunken 179 (para.75)
John Deere 226 (para.38)
Sperry New Holland 245 (para.65)
Dutch Building Cartel 349 (paras 138–139)
Eurocheques; Helsinki 352 (paras 57 and 84)
Quantel 357 (para.50)
SPO T–29/92 (ground 342)
Volkswagen T–62/98 (ground 342)
Atlantic Container Line II T–18/97 (grounds 48–63)
Tepea C–28/77 (grounds 67–72)
Hasselblad C–86/82 (grounds 54–55)
⋆SSI C–240/82 (ground 75)

1.3.3. Provisional validity for old agreements (Former Regulation 17)

Article 25 Regulation 17/62
Julien/Van Katwijk 32
De Haecht v Wilkin I C–23/67
Portelange v Smith Corona C–10/69
Bilger v Jehle C–43/69 (grounds 4–6)
Parfums Rochas v Bitsch C–1/70 (grounds 6–7)
De Haecht v Wilkin II C–48/72
De Bloos v Bouyer C–59/77 (grounds 8–15)
Boekhandels v Eldi Records C–106/79 (grounds 8–11)
⋆Nouvelles Frontieres C–209/84 (grounds 61–69)
Ahmed Saeed v Zentrale C–66/86 (grounds 5, 21, 32–33)
KVBB v Free Record Shop C–39/96

2. Complaints

2.1. Method of lodging a complaint/*locus standi*

Article 7 Regulation 1/2003
Herbage Seed 6th Comp. Rep. (para.119)
BBC 6th Comp. Rep. (para.163)
PSA Peugeot-Citroën 8th Comp. Rep. (para.149)
BB/TGWU 16th Comp. Rep. (para.43)
BEMIM T–114/92 (grounds 26–30, 63)

2.2. Rights and obligations of complainant

Pabst & Richerz/BNIA
Tremblay T–5/93 (grounds 78, 91)
Langnese Iglo T–7/93 (ground 41)
Kruidvat T–87/92
VGB T–77/94 (grounds 76–88)
TF1 T–17/96 (grounds 88–95)
SGA T–189/95 (grounds 39–41)
Europeenne automobile T–9/96
Kish Glass T–95/96 (grounds 32–34)
Ufex T–77/95 (grounds 36–45)
Sodima T–62/99 (grounds 35–58)
Metropole Television T–206/99 (grounds 57–59, 64–66)
⋆Osterreichische Postsparkasse T–213/01
GEMA C–125/78 (grounds 10–23)
⋆CICCE C–298/83
BAT v Commission & Philip Morris C–142 (grounds 19–20, 23–24)
Koelman C–59/96P (ground 42)
Florimex C–265/97P (grounds 93–107)
Fonderies Roubaix v Fonderies Roux C–63/75 (grounds 5–8)
De Bloos v Bouyer C–59/77 (grounds 11–13)
⋆NA VE WA C–96–102 (grounds 30–35)
⋆SSI v Commission 127 (ground 75)
Windsurfing C–193/83 (ground 100)

[For the tables of case citations see Tables 1 to 4, 11 and 12 at the back of the book.]

3. *Ex-officio* investigation

Article 7 Regulation 1/2003
Bayer/Dental 327 (para.20)
GAARM C–289/83 (grounds 21–24)
Otto C–60/92 (grounds 18–20)

B. THE INVESTIGATION OF A CASE

1. By letter

1.1. Potential addresses of a letter pursuant to Article 8 Regualtion 1/2003

Article 18(1)(4) Regualtion 1/2003

1.2. Simple request for information

Article 18(2), (3) Regulation 1/2003

1.2.1. Text of a typical request for information letter sent pursuant to Article 18 of Regulation 1/2003

1.2.2. Cases

Comptoir d'Importation 167
Telos 170
National Panasonic (Belgium) 176
National Panasonic (France) 177
Spanish Banks 196
★Peugeot 250 (paras 27–31, 48–53)
Austrian Banks 503 (paras 486–490)
Specialty Graphite 510 (paras 539–540)
PVC II T–305e.s./94
Mannesmann T–112/98
★Brouwerij Haacht T–48/02 (grounds 107 & 113)
Boekhandels v Eldi Records T–46/92 (grounds 12–13)
CICCE C–298/83 (grounds 5–6)
Aalborg C–204e.s./00p (grounds 62–65 & 207–208)

1.3. Request for information by decision

Article 18(1)(3) Regulation 1/2003
CICG 36
Alba 39
Union des Brasseries 40
Maes 41
SIAE 44 Rodenstock 61
Misal 62
CSV 105
RAI/UNITEL 131
Fire Insurance 175
Castrol 192
★Olympic Airways 229
Specialty Graphite 510 (paras 539–540)
SEP T–39/90R
SEP T–39/90 (grounds 25, 30, 51, 52)
Scottish Football Association T–46/92
Dalmine T–596/97
PVC II T–305e.s./94 (grounds 444–449)
★Brouwerij Haacht T–48/02 (grounds 107 & 113)
★Orkem C–374/87
Acerinox C–57/02P (grounds 86–89)
ThyssenKrupp Stainless C–65 (grounds 49–52)

1.4. Oral questions

Kish Glass T–65/96 (grounds 37–38)

2. By inspection

2.1. Inspectors

2.1.1. National inspectors

Article 22 Regulation 1/2003

2.1.2. Commission inspectors

Articles 20, 21, 22 Regulation 1/2003

2.2. Powers of inspectors

Article 20 Regulation 1/2003
★Hoechst v Commission III C–46/87 (grounds 10–38)
Dow Benelux C–85/87
Dow Iberica C–97/99/87

2.3. Inspection without decision

Article 20 Regulation 1/2003

2.3.1. Text of typical authorisation to investigate under Article 20 of Regulation 1/2003

2.3.2. Cases on inspections without decisions

AM & S Europe 146
Fabbrica Pisana 153 (paras 10, 12)
Fabbrica Lastre 154
F'ed'eration Chaussure de France 183 (para.8)
11th Comp. Rep. (paras 17–21)
12th Comp. Rep. (para.32)
13th Comp. Rep. (para.74)
Elf Atochem T–9/976
★AM & S C–155/79

2.4. Inspection with decision

Article 20(4) Regulation 1/2003

2.4.1. Cases on inspections with decisions

German Blacksmiths 120
Fides 145
AM & S Europe 146
UKWAL 354
11th Comp. Rep. (paras 17–20)
12th Comp. Rep. (para.32)
17th Comp. Rep. (para.57)
★Minoan Lines T–66/99 (grounds 41–97)
★Strintzis Lines T–65/99 (grounds 27–83)
Ventouris T–59/99 (grounds 111–162)
National Panasonic C–136/79
★AM & S C–55/79
★AKZO v Commission II C–5/85
Hoechst v Commission II C–46/87R
Dow C–85/87R
★Hoechst v Commission III C–46/87 (grounds 10–38)
Dow Benelux C–85/87
Dow Iberica C–97/87
★Minoan Lines C–121/04P (grounds 27–47)
Strintzis Lines C–110/04P (grounds 30–49)

3. Sectoral investigation

Alba 39
Union des Brasseries 40
Maes 41

4. Co-operation with national authorities

FA Premier League 551 (para.35)
★SEP T–39/90 (ground 53)
SEP C–36/92P
Roquette Freres/DGCCRF C–94/00

5. Power to take statements

Article 19 Regulation 1/2003

C. PROCEDURAL STEPS AND SAFEGUARDS

1. In relation to an infringement decision

1.1. Initiation of proceedings

ACF Chemiefarma C–41/69
★De Haecht v Wilkin II C–48/72 (ground 16)
BRT v SABAM II C–127/73
Anne Marty v Estee Lauder C–37/79 (grounds 12–16)
IBM C–60/81
Nouvelles Frontieres C–209/84 (grounds 55–56)

1.2. Statement of objections

Vichy T–19/91 (ground 121)
Cement Industries T–10/92 (grounds 28–36)
★Europay T–39/92 (grounds 46–48, 58)
Postbank T–353/94
PVC II T–305e.s./94 (grounds 85–88)
Irish Sugar T–228/97 (grounds 32–37)
CMB C–395/96P (grounds 142–147)
Cement T–25/95 (grounds 476, 480–481, 483–485)
LR AF 1998 T–23/99 (grounds 206–209)
JCB Service T–67/01
Specialty Graphite T–71e.s./03 (grounds 138–141)
DaimlerChrysler T–325/01 (grounds 188–194)
Danone T–38/02 (grounds 50–57)
ACF Chemiefarma C–41/69 (ground 27)
Boehringer C–45/69
ICI C–48/69 (grounds 17, 24)
BASF C–49/69
Bayer C–51/69
Ciba-Geigy C–52/69
Sandoz C–53/69
Francolor C–54/69
Cassella C–55/69
Hoechst I C–56/69
ACNA C–57/69
Continental Can C–6/72 (ground 5)
★FEDETAB C–209/78 (grounds 29–35, 67–78)
IBM C–60/81
Pioneer C–100/80 (ground 14)
Woodpulp C–89/85 (ground 153)
Aalborg C–204e.s./00P (grounds 60 & 192)
ThyssenKrupp Stainless C–65/02P (grounds 92–96)

[For the tables of case citations see Tables 1 to 4, 11 and 12 at the back of the book.]

1.3. Access to file

1.3.1. Grant of access to all documents upon which the Commission relies

British Sugar 286 (paras 67–68)
PVC 305 (para.27)
LdPE 306 (para.34)
BASF/Accinauto 405 (para.62)
Seamless Steel Tubes 499 (paras 124–126)
★11th Comp. Rep. (paras 22–25)
★12th Comp. Rep. (paras 34–35)
★13th Comp. Rep. (para.74)
20th Comp. Rep. (para.89)
★23rd Comp. Rep. (paras 189–206)
BASF T–4/89 (ground 36)
Hercules T–7/89 (grounds 45–56)
DSM T–52/69 (ground 37)
Huls T–57/69 (grounds 46–49)
Hoechst T–8/72 (grounds 51–54)
Cement Industries T–51/75 (grounds 37–49)
British Gypsum T–86/75 (grounds 29–35)
★Matra T–17/93 (ground 34)
★ICI T–36/91
Sodima T–62/99 (grounds 65–66)
HFB et al. T–9/99 (grounds 327–331)
LR AF T–23/99 (grounds 170–179)
JCB Service T–67/01 (grounds 64–71)
Danone T–38/02 (grounds 33–44, 64–80)
Consten & Grundig C–56 & C–58/64
ACF Chemiefarma C–41/69 (grounds 37–43)
Buchler & Co. C–44/69 (grounds 12–15)
Boehringer C–45/69 (grounds 12–15)
★FEDETAB C–209–215 & 218/78 (grounds 36–40)
AEG C–107/82
Michelin C–322/81 (grounds 5, 8–10)
★VBVB & VBBB C–43 & C–63/82 (grounds 24–25)
AKZO v Commission III C–62/86 (grounds 1524)
BPB C–310/93
Aalborg C–204e.s./00P (grounds 70–77 & 156–163)

1.3.2. Text of Commission Notice on the internal rules of procedure for processing requests for access to the file in cases pursuant to Articles 85 and 86 of the EC Treaty, Articles 65 and 66 of the ECSC Treaty and Council Regulation 4064/89 [1997] O.J. C23/3

1.3.3. Text of Commission Notice on the rules for access to the Commission file in cases pursuant to Articles 81 and 82 of the EC Treaty, Articles 53, 54 and 57 of the EEA Agreement and Council Regulation 139/2004 [2005] O.J. C325/7

1.4. Reply to the statement of objections by the parties

1.4.1. In writing

Copper Tubes 538 (para.762)
18th Comp. Rep. (para.44)
Volkswagen T–62/98 (grounds 311–317)
HFB et al. T–9/99 (grounds 342–354)
LR AF 1998 T–23/99 (ground 190)
FEDETAB C–209/78

1.4.2. Oral hearing

11th Comp. Rep. (paras 26–28)
12th Comp. Rep. (paras 36–37)
13th Comp. Rep. (para.75)
18th Comp. Rep. (para.44)
23rd Comp. Rep. (paras 189–206)
★Tetra Pak II T–83/91 (grounds 36–39)
PVC II T–305e.s./94
Far Eastern Freight Conference T–86/95 (grounds 465–469)
ACF Chemiefarma C–41/69 (grounds 44–53)
Buchler & Co. C–44/69 (grounds 16–17, 19–22)
Boehringer C–45/69 (grounds 16–18)
ICI C–48/69 (grounds 28–32, 63)
BASF C–49/69 (grounds 10–12)
Bayer C–51/69 (grounds 13–15)
Ciba-Geigy C–52/69
Sandoz C–53/69
Cassella C–55/69
Hoechst I C–56/69
ACNA C–57/69
★FEDETAB C–209/78 (grounds 16–18, 22–24, 64–66)
★VBVB & VBBB C–43/82 (grounds 15–18)
ANCIDES C–43/85 (grounds 7–8)

1.4.3. Notice on the internal rules of procedure for processing requests for access to the file in cases pursuant to Articles 85 and 86 of the EC Treaty, Articles 65 and 66 of the ECSC Treaty and Council Regulation 4064/89 [1997] O.J. C23/3

1.4.4. Role of the Hearing Officer

10th Comp. Rep. (para.44)

[For the tables of case citations see Tables 1 to 4, 11 and 12 at the back of the book.]

13th Comp. Rep. (paras 273–274)
23rd Comp. Rep. (paras 203–206)
BASF T–4/89 (ground 51)
Enichem T–6/89 (grounds 53–55)
Hercules T–7/89 (grounds 30–34)
Peugeot T–90/96
PVC II T–305e.s./94 (grounds 60, 125–126, 365–370, 375–377)
HFB et al. T–9/99 (grounds 403–413)
Tokai Carbon et al. T–236e.s./01 (grounds 52–53)

1.4.5. General considerations on the right to be heard

Copper Tubes 538 (para.762)
★Hilti T–30/89 (grounds 36–38)
PublishersAssociation T–66/89 (grounds 64–65)
Solvay T–30/91
ICI T–36/91 (grounds 91–94, 111)
PVC II T–305e.s./94 (grounds 246–252)
HFB et al. T–305e.s./94 (grounds 381–392)
VEG & TU T–5/00 (grounds 32–35, 44–45)
Boehringer C–45/69 (grounds 8–11)
Komponistenverband C–8/71
FEDETAB C–209/78 (grounds 29–35, 64–74, 79–81)
★AM&S C–155/79 (ground 23)

1.4.6 Minutes of the hearing

Accinauto T–176/95 (paras 39–43)

1.5. Advisory committee

13th Comp. Rep. (para.79)
RTE T–69/89 (grounds 21–28)
Petrona T–2/89 (grounds 43–51)
★BASF T–4/89 (grounds 43–45)
Enichem T–6/89 (grounds 45)
Vichy T–19/91 (grounds 31–41)
Tetra-Pak II T–83/91 (grounds 36–39)
Fiat Agri T–34/92 (ground 30)
Cement T–191 (grounds 742, 744, 748)
★Buchler & Co. C–44/69 (ground 17)
Frubo C–71/74 (ground 11)
Pioneer C–100/80 (ground 36)

2. Relating to a positive decision

2.1. Publication of Notice (Former Regulation 17)

Regulation 17/62
Ladbroke T–74/92 (grounds 65 and 72)
Kruidvat T–87/92
Leclerc T–19/92 (grounds 58 and 62)
Leclerc T–88/92 (grounds 49 and 53)
ANCIDES C–43/85

2.2. Advisory committee

13th Comp. Rep. (para.79)
PVC II T–305e.s./94 (grounds 114–118)

3. Relating to a rejection of a complaint

Article 6 Regulation 2842/98
GEC-Siemens/Plessey 325 11th Comp. Rep. (para.118)
British Sugar-Berisford 12th Comp. Rep. (paras 104–106)
★Standardised bottles in Germany 17th Comp. Rep. (para.75)
★Automec T–64/89
Matra T–17/93 (ground 34)
Ladbroke T–74/92 (ground 40)
UPS T–127/98
Ufex C–119/97P

4. General procedural safeguards

4.1. Legal professional privilege

★AM & S Europe 146
11th Comp. Rep. (para.21)
12th Comp. Rep. (para.33)
13th Comp. Rep. (para.78)
★Nobel T–125 & T–253/03R
★AM&S T–155/79

4.2. Obligation of the Commission as to confidentiality

4.2.1. General obligation

SEP T–39/90R
SEP T–39/90 (grounds 52–60)
Cement Industries T–10/92R
Postbank T–353/94R
Solvay T–30/91 (grounds 90–95)
ICI T–36/91 (grounds 97–105)
Postbank T–353/94
PVC II T–305e.s./94 (grounds 460–478)
Volkswagen T–62/98 (grounds 279–283)
Bank Austria T–198/03R
★Bank Austria II T–198/03 (grounds 29, 71, 95–96)
BASF T–15/02 (grounds 604–606)
Degussa T–279/02 (ground 411)
Osterreichische Postsparkasse T–213/01
Michelin C–322/81 (ground 8)
★Stanley Adams C–145/83
★Dow Benelux C–85/87 (grounds 13–21)

[For the tables of case citations see Tables 1 to 4, 11 and 12 at the back of the book.]

Spanish Banks C–67/91
Otto C–60/92 (grounds 18–20)
SEP C–36/92P (grounds 27–32)
Volkswagen C–338/00P (grounds 163–165)

4.2.2. Business secrets

CSV 105
Solvay T–30/91 (grounds 92–93)
ICI T–36/91 (grounds 102–103)
Postbank T–353/94
Peugeot T–90/96
HFB et al. T–9/99 (grounds 363–365)
Michelin T–203/1 (grounds 123–126)
Bank Austria T–198/03R
Dalmine T–50/00 (grounds 88–89)
★Bank Austria II T–198/03
ACF Chemiefarma C–41/69 (grounds 37–43)
Boehringer C–45/69 (grounds 12–15)
Hoffmann-La Roche C–85/76 (grounds 14–15)
FEDETAB C–209/78 (grounds 41–47)
★AKZO v Commission C–53/85
BAT v Commission & Philip Morris C–142/84 (ground 21)

4.2.3. Result of disclosure of business secrets or confidential information

★FEDETAB C–209/78 (para.47)
Stanley Adams v Commission C–145/83
★AKZO C–53/85

4.3. Statement of position prior to a decision

4.4. Objective and impartial investigation

ABB T–31/99 (grounds 99–106)
BASF T–15/02 (grounds 609–610)
Degussa T–292/02 (grounds 414–415)

4.5. Duty to make a record of meetings

BASF T–15/02 (grounds 501–502 & 509)

D. INFORMAL STEPS OFTEN TAKEN BY THE COMMISSION

1. Negotiations and modifications of agreements

ACEC/Berliet 14
Cobelaz 15
Cobelaz Cokes 16 (para.8)
CFA 18
VVVF 22
SEIFA 23
Supexie 34
Du Pont de Nemours Germany 71
Transocean Marine Paint Assoc. II 75
SABA I 99
CSV 134 (paras 81–87)
Zanussi 139
White Lead 142 (para.19)
Natursteinplatten 159 (paras 17–24, 46–47)
VBBB/VBVB 169 (paras 24–31)
National Panasonic 186 (para.5)
Grundig 232
Velcro/Aplix 233
British Sugar 286 (paras 9–10, 82)
Tetra Pak I 289 (para.69)
UIP 309 (paras 25–33)
APB 314 (paras 28–33)
Man-made fibres 8th Comp. Rep. (para.42)
Hachette 8th Comp. Rep. (paras 114–115)
Feldmühle-Stora 12th Comp Rep. (paras 73–74)
13th Comp Rep. (para.81)
Philip Morris 14th Comp. Rep. (paras 98–100)
★IBM 14th Comp. Rep. (paras 94–95); 16th Comp. Rep. (para.75); 17th Comp. Rep. (para.85); (Bulletin 12/88. Pt. 2.1.116)
Instituto/IMC & Angus 16th Comp. Rep. (para.76)
Macron/Angus 17th Comp. Rep. (para.81)
Irish Distillers 18th Comp. Rep. (para.80)
De Haecht v Wilkin II T–12/89 (ground 6)
BAT & Philip Morris 145

2. Informal settlement

2.1. Undertakings

★British Sugar 286 (paras 9–10, 82)
GEC-Siemens/Plessey 325
Pilkington/BSN 10th Comp. Rep. (paras 152–155)
IBM 17th Comp. Rep. (para.85)
Carnaud/Sofreb 17th Comp. Rep. (para.70)
IBM 18th Comp. Rep. (para.78)
Irish Distillers 18th Comp. Rep. (para.80)
AKZO Coatings 19th Comp. Rep. (para.45)
Coca-Cola 19th Comp. Rep. (para.50)
Consolidated Goldfields 19th Comp. Rep. (para.68)
IBM 21st Comp. Rep. (para.106)
Unilever/Mars 25th Comp. Rep. (page 137)
IRI/Nielsen 26th Comp. Rep. p.164 hrt SWIFT, [1997] O.J. C335/3
Woodpulp C–89/85 (grounds 178–185)

3.1. Text of a typical comfort letter issued under Former Regulation 17

Registered with advice of delivery

[For the tables of case citations see Tables 1 to 4, 11 and 12 at the back of the book.]

Re Case No. COMP/
Notification of
(date), by
Agreement between

Dear Sirs,

I refer to the notification of the above agreement.
On the basis of the information provided on notification of the agreement (as well as contained in documents subsequently received), the Commission's Directorate General for Competition has now completed a preliminary examination of this case.
This examination has not revealed the existence of any grounds under Article (85(1)) (86) for further action on the part of the Commission in respect of the notified agreement.
(A notice containing a summary of the agreement was published in the Official Journal of the European Communities No. C . . . of . . . The Directorate General for Competition has received no observations from interested third parties following publication of that Notice.
As it was indicated in the Notice–and as it has been agreed with you–the notification under consideration might be dealt with by means of an administrative letter closing the file.)
(You have indicated that you can agree to the notification under consideration being dealt with by means of an administrative letter closing the file.)
However, the case could be reconsidered if the factual or legal situation changes as concerns as essential aspect of the agreement which affects its evaluation.
Naturally, any reopening of the file would be without prejudice to the legal consequences of the notification, particularly as regards the immunity from fines provided by Article 15(5) of Council Regulation No. 17/62.
Yours faithfully,
Director cc: All Member States

3.2. Cases on comfort letters

GEC-Siemens/Plessey 325 11th Comp. Rep. (para.15)
12th Comp. Rep. (para.30)
13th Comp. Rep. (para.72)
Air France T–3/93 (ground 50)
Langnese Iglo T–7/93 (grounds 2, 35–41)
Scholler T–9/93 (grounds 1, 110–114)
Koelman T–575/93 (grounds 41–43)
Frubo C–71/74 (grounds 18–21)
De Bloos v Bouyer C–59/77 (grounds 17–18)
Procureur v Guerlain C–253/78, 1–3/79 (grounds 9–13)
★Anne Marty v Estee Lauder C–37/79 (grounds 5–10)
Lancome v Etos C–99/79 (grounds 6–18)
L'Oréal v De Nieuwe AMCK C–31/80 (grounds 7–12)
Koelman C–59/96P (ground 44)

E. LENGTH OF PROCEDURE

See also Part VI, 4.1
Far Eastern Freight 399 (para.158)
23rd Comp. Rep. (para.207)
Dunlop T–43/92 (ground 167)
Tetra Pak II T–83/91 (grounds 30–31)
Tremblay T–5/93 (grounds 87–90)
Societe Metallurgique de Normandie T–147/89 (ground 108)
Trelunion T–148/89 (grounds 125–128)
Societe des Treillis et Panneaux Soudes T–151/89 (grounds 106–109)
★Dutch Cranes T143
Siderurgica T–175h, CS40 (ground 169–172)
PVC II T–305e.s./94 (grounds 169, 180–184, 187–189, 169–234, 272–279)
Sodima T–62/99 (grounds 93–95)
Trabisco T–26/99 (grounds 51–53)
VEG & TU T–5 & T–6/00 (grounds 73–74, 79–80 & 87)
ICI & CSC C–6 & C–7/73
Baustahlgewebe C–185/95P

F. COMMISSION DECISIONS

1. Administrative decisions

Articles 10, 20 Regulation 1/2003 (see above)

1a. Decisions of the Hearing Officer

Bank Austria II T–198/03

2. Provisional decisions

2.1. Removal of immunity from fines (Former Regulation 17)

Article 15(6) Regulation 17
★Sirdar-Phildar 89

[For the tables of case citations see Tables 1 to 4, 11 and 12 at the back of the book.]

Bronbemaling 95
SNPE/LEL 132
P&I Clubs 243 (para.2)
Decca 304 (paras 77–78)
Vichy 334 (para.32)
Stichting Kraanverhuur 382
Dutch Cranes 407a (para.46)
Beecham Pharma 6th Comp. Rep. (para.133)
Prodifarma v Commission II T–3/90 (grounds 39–49)
★Cimenteries C–8/66
IBM C–60/81 (ground 19)
Ford C–228/82 (ground 23)

2.2. Interim measures

Ford Werke-Interim Measures 182
ECS/AKZO-Interim Measures 197
Boosey & Hawkes 273
Hilti 282 (paras 27–29)
British Sugar 286 (para.9)
Holyhead 22nd Comp. Rep. (para.219)
Cosimex T–131/89R
Peugeot T–23/90
★La Cinq T–44/90
IMS T–184/01R
★Camera Care C–792/79 R
Hasselblad C–86/82 (ground 19)
Ford C–228/82 (ground 19)

2.3. Rejecting request for interim measures

Sea Containers 377
EBU-Eurovision 22nd Comp. Rep. (page 425)
Phoenix/IBM 22nd Comp. Rep. (page 426)
TESN 22nd Comp. Rep. (page 426)
La Cinq T–44/90
Goldstein T–235/94 R

3. Recommendation

Convention Faience 2

4. Final decisions

4.1. Negative clearance (Former Article 2 Regulation 17)

Gema Statutes 174
Dutch Banks T–138/89

4.2. Exemption (Former Article 8 Regulation 17)

4.2.1. Duration of exemption (Former Article 8 Regulation 17)

4.2.2. Conditions or obligations for exemption (Former Article 8 Regulation 17)

★Transocean Marine Paint Assoc. I 10
United Reprocessors 102
Ford/Volkswagen 367 (para.41)
Eurotunnel 396 (paras 102, 109–124)
★LH/SAS 408 Atlas 411
★Phoenix 412
Unisource 425
Uniworld 426
Reims II 453
BIB/Open 454
GEAE 459
Eurovision 460
Air France/Alitalia 529 (paras 160ff)
SNCF T122

4.2.3. Renewal of exemption (Former Article 8 Regulation 17)

Transocean Marine Paint Association 40b
★Transocean Marine Paint Assoc. II 75
Cematex II 193
★Bayer/BP 386
DIR T–369/94 (ground 105)
Metro v Commission II C–75/84 (grounds 30–32)

4.2.4. Revocation of exemption (Former Article 8 Regulation 17)

Tetra Pak I 289
Eco System 344a (paras 25, 33)
Automec v Commission II T–24/90 (ground 75)
CMB T–24/93 (grounds 188–190)

4.2.5 Effect of an exemption (Former Article 8 Regulation 17)

DIR T–369/94 (ground 105)
L'Oreal v De Nieuwe AMCK 31/80 (grounds 22–23)

4.3. Prohibition

Article 7 Regulation 1/2003

4.3.1. Order to cease

Gema I 38
Aluminium 228 (para.18)
Decca 304 (para.131)
Ijsselcentrale 335 (para.55)
Dutch Building Cartel 349 (para.133)
British Midland 350 (paras 43–44)
Quantel 357 (para.55)
Gillette 361 (para.43)
Astra 368 (paras 32–33)
Auditel 376 (para.38)

[For the tables of case citations see Tables 1 to 4, 11 and 12 at the back of the book.]

Microsoft 528 (paras 995–997)
⋆Automec v Commission II T–24/90 (grounds 47–54)
IECC T–133/95
Aeroports de Paris T–128/98 (grounds 82–83)
Atlantic Container Line T–395/94 (grounds 410–420)
⋆GVL C–7/82 (grounds 23–28)
Ufex C–119/97P

4.3.2. Order to act

Zoja CSC-ICI 64
ECS/AKZO–Interim Measures 197 (paras 36–38)
ECS/AKZO 242 (para.99)
Net Book Agreements 301 (para.89)
Magill 307 (para.27)
Microsoft 528 (paras 995–997)
RTE T–69/89 (grounds 97–99)
BBC T–70/89 (grounds 71–73)
ITV T–76/89 (grounds 70–72)
⋆Automec v Commission II T–24/90 (grounds 47–54)
Gruber & Weber T–310/94
BPB de Eendracht T–311/94
Moritz J. Weig T–317/94
Sarrio T–334/94
Finnish Board Mills T–338/94
Mayr-Melnhof Kartongesellschaft T–347/94
Mo och Domsjo T–352/94
Stora Kopparbergs Bergslags T–354/94
Aeroports de Paris T–128/98 (grounds 82–83)
⋆ICI & CSC C–6/73

4.3.3. Neutral; obligation of parties to suggest remedy

VBBB/VBVB 169 (paras 64–65)
Microsoft 528 (paras 995–997)

4.3.3a. Monitoring mechanism

Microsoft 528 (paras 1043–1048)
Microsoft Monitoring trustee 547

4.3.4. Date of commencement of prohibition

Velcro/Aplix 233
⋆VBA 288 (paras 164–168)

4.3.5. Effects in time

4.3.6. Findings of past infringements: Legitimate interest

Dupont de Nemours Germany 71
Bosch v De Geus C–13/61
Sumitomo T297 (grounds 129–39)
GVL C–7/82 (ground 24)

4.4. Rejection of complaint

GEC-Siemens/Plessey 325
IMAX 534 (p.10, para.3; p.13, paras 4–7)
European Cement Producers 548
11th Comp. Rep. (para.118)
VEB/Shell 16th Comp. Rep. (para.55)
Standardised bottles in Germany 17th Comp. Rep. (para.75)
New Focus Health Care 21st Comp. Rep.
Iqbal 21st Comp. Rep.
SACEM 22nd Comp Rep.
Howden 22nd Comp. Rep.
23rd Comp. Rep. (pp.460–464)
Automec T–64/89 (grounds 46–58)
⋆Automec v Commission II T–24/90 (grounds 71–98)
Rendo v Commission I T–16/91
SFEI T–36/92
Rendo v Commission II T–2/92
Asia Motor France T–7/92
BEUC T–37/92
Ladbroke T–74/92 (grounds 40, 58, 63, 67)
⋆BEMIM T–114/92 (grounds 9–75, 78, 91)
Guerin Automobiles T–186/94
Ladbroke T–548/93
Koelman T113
Asia Motor France T–387/94
SFEI T–77/95
Intertronic T–117/96
Florimex T–70/92
VGB T–77/94
Ladbroke T–504/93
Tremblay T–224/95
ITT Promedia T–111/96
IECC T–110/95
IECC T–133/95
Riviera T–185/96
Max Mobil T–54/99 (grounds 48–55)
Piau T–193/02
Centro Europa 7 T–338/04 (grounds 36–40)
Gema T–125/78 (grounds 10–23)
Lord Bethell C–246/81
Demo Schmidt C–210/81
CICCE C–298/83
BAT v Commission & Philip Morris C–142/84 (grounds 26–27, 70)
SFEI C–322/93P
Rendo C–19/93 (ground 28)
Tremblay C–91/95P
Guerin C–282/95P
Koelman C–59/96P
Commission v Ladbroke C–359/95P

[For the tables of case citations see Tables 1 to 4, 11 and 12 at the back of the book.]

Ufex C–119/97P

4.5. Commitment decisions

Bundesliga Broadcasting Rights 544
FA Premier League 551
Repsol 552

5. Formal requirements regarding the form/content of decisions

5.1. Decisions must be reasoned

PVC 305 (paras 45–46)
LdPE 306 (paras 28–29)
DSM T–8/89 (ground 257)
Danish Fur Breeders T–61/89 (grounds 129–137)
★British Gypsum T–65/89 (ground 98)
BEUC T–37/92 (grounds 47–67)
Societe Metallurgique de Normandie T–147/89 (ground 108)
Trelunion T–148/89 (grounds 141–142)
★Societe des Treillis et Panneaux T–151/89 (grounds 121–123)
Asia Motor France T–387/94
Rendo T–16/91RV) (grounds 43–60)
★Buchmann T–295/94 (ground 45)
★BPB de Eendracht T–311/94 (ground 66)
Fiskeby Board T–319/94 (grounds 118–131)
PVC II T–305e.s./94 (grounds 449, 463–464)
Stork T–241/97 (grounds 70–81)
Cement T25/95 (grounds 4725–4726, 4734–4737)
Poudres Spheriques T–5/97 (grounds 198–199)
Atlantic Container Line T–395/94 (grounds 253–254)
FETTCSA T–213/00 (grounds 217, 439)
Vanden Bergh Foods T–65/98 (grounds 176–179)
Adriatica T–61/99 (grounds 47–50)
Ventouris T–59/99 (ground 31)
Tokai Carbon et al. T–236e.s./01 (grounds 231–233, 248, 285)
JFE Engineering T–67e.s./00 (grounds 413–414)
Dalmine T–50/00 (ground 146)
Piau T–193/02 (grounds 48–52)
Specialty Graphite T–71e.s./03 (grounds 126–127)
Danone T–38/02 (grounds 95–102)
Heubach T–64/02 (grounds 217–222)
Brouwerij Haacht T–48/02 (grounds 45–46)
Greencore T–135/02 (grounds 55–58)
Daiichi T–26/02 (grounds 178–179)
BASF T–15/02 (grounds 205–215, 303, 417–419, 452–453)
Degussa T–279/02 (grounds 192–194, 197)
Osterreichische Postsparkasse T–328/03 (grounds 131, 134–135)
Consten & Grundig C–56 & 58/64
BASF C–49/69 (grounds 13–15)
Cassella C–55/69
Hoechst C–56/69
Kali & Salz C–19/74 (grounds 8–15)
Papiers Peints C–73/74 (grounds 28–33)
★FEDETAB C–209/78 (grounds 75–78)
GVL C–7/82 (ground 12)
Michelin C–322/81 (grounds 14, 17–21)
★VBVB & VBBB C–43/82 (ground 22)
Hasselblad C–86/82 (ground 17)
KNP BT C–248/98P (grounds 37–50)
Cascades C–279/98P (grounds 30–50)
Moritz Weig C–280/98P (grounds 30–50)
Enso Espanola C–282/98P (grounds 29–48)
Mo och Domsjo C–283/98P (grounds 32–51)
Stora Kopparbergs Bergslags C–286/98 (grounds 47–66)
Sarrio C–219/98 (grounds 61–80)
Metsa Serla (Finnboard) C–298/98P (grounds 32–51)
SCA Holding C–297/98 (grounds 45–64)
Dansk Rørindustri C–189e.a./02P (grounds 453–468)
Marlines C–112/04P (grounds 15–18)

5.2. Burden and standard of proof

John Deere 226 (para.26)
★Woodpulp 227 (paras 101, 107)
Seamless Steel Tubes 499 (paras 121–122)
Interbrew & Alken Maes 500 (paras 253 & 255)
Specialty Graphite 510 (para. 327)
Topps 530 (paras 138, 164–165)
Copper Tubes 538 (paras 440, 464, 470, 483–490, 542)
Spanish Raw Tobacco 540 (para.282)
Needles 542 (para.239)
Choline Chloride 543 (paras 129, 134)
AstraZeneca 545 (paras 750–757)
Peugeot 549 (para. 149)
Fiat Agri T–34/92 (ground 35)
Volkswagen T–62/98 (grounds 270–272)
HFB et al. T–9/99 (ground 231)
ADM & ADM Ingredients T–224/00 (grounds 227 & 237)
Michelin T–203/1 (grounds 123–126)
Adriatica T–61/99 (grounds 125 & 135)
VEG & TU T–5/00 (ground 359)
JCB Service T–67/01 (grounds 53–60)
Marlines T–56/99 (ground 56)
Tokai Carbon et al. T–257 (grounds 106–109)

JFE Engineering T–67e.s./00 (grounds 176–180, 192, 203, 219–220, 273, 293, 329, 343–344)
★Dalmine T–50/00 (grounds 72–73, 308–309)
Corus UK T–48/00 (grounds 125–126)
Mannesmannrohren-Werke T–44/00 (grounds 84–85 & 262–263)
Dresdner Bank T–44/02
Vereins-und Westbank T–54/02
Bayerische Hypo-und Vereinsbank T–56/02
Deutsche Verkehrsbank T–60/02
Commerzbank T–61/02
Specialty Graphite T–71e.s./03 (grounds 65–66)
SAS T–241/01 (ground 192)
DaimlerChrysler T–325/01 (grounds 201–206, 220)
Danone T–38/02 (grounds 215–218, 245, 285)
Union Pigments T–62/02 (grounds 36–42)
02 (Germany) T–328/03 (ground 94)
BASF T–15/02 (ground 298)
★Papiers Peints T–73/74 (grounds 15–21)
Commission v Anic C–49/92P (grounds 85–88, 93–100)
Huls C–199/92 (grounds 149–155, 162, 174)
Montecatini C–235/92P (grounds 175–182)
Aalborg C–204e.s./00P (grounds 55–57, 78–86, 236ff)
Acerinox C–251/95 (grounds 33–38)
Dansk Rørindustri C–189e.a./02P (grounds 142–150)

5.3. Must contain only that which figured in the statement of objections

Amino Acids 465 (paras 296, 380, 391)
★Europay T–39/92)
PVC II T–305e.s./94 (ground 497)
Cement T191 (grounds 323, 364, 480–481, 483–485, 643, 1838, 4270, 4281, 4283)
Far Eastern Freight Conference T–86/95 (grounds 442–452)
Atlantic Container Line T–395/94 (grounds 412–420)
FETTCSA T–213/00 (ground 116)
Tokai Carbon et al. T–236e.s./01 (ground 47)
JFE Engineering T–67e.s./00 (grounds 429–430, 453)
Dalmine T–50/00 (grounds 59–64)
Mannesmannrohren-Werke T–44/00 (grounds 98–100)
Specialty Graphite T–71e.s./03 (grounds 148–153)
DaimlerChrysler T–325/01 (grounds 188–195)
BASF T–15/02 (grounds 48, 59, 62, 90–96)
ACF Chemiefarma C–41/69)
★FEDETAB C–209/78 (grounds 67–74)
Pioneer C–100–103/80
AEG C–107/82 (grounds 27)
Michelin C–322/81 (ground 19)
★Woodpulp C–89/85 (grounds 40–54)
Aalborg C–204e.s./00P (grounds 65 & 192)

5.4. Obligation to take account of the defendant's views in the decision

★La Cinq T–44/90)
★Asia Motor France T–7/92 (grounds 30–32)
All Weather Sports T–7/92
BEMIM T–114/92 (grounds 41–57)
Tremblay T–5/93 (grounds 29–49)
Aeroports de Paris T–128/98 (grounds 59–70)
★BAT v Commission & Philip Morris C–142/84 (ground 72)
Publishers Association C–360/92P (grounds 39–49)

5.5. Obligation to respect internal procedural and linguistic rules

PVC T–79/91
Dunlop T–43/92 (ground 24)
John Deere T–35/92 (ground 31)
Fiat Agri T–34/92 (ground 27)
ICI T–37/91)
PVC II T–305e.s./94 (grounds 299–309, 337–339)
Cimenteries C–8–11/66 (grounds 10–14)
ICI C–48/69 (grounds 11–15)
VBVB & VBBB C–43/82 (ground 19)
★AKZO v Commission II (C–5/85)
ICI C–286/95P (grounds 38–52, 59–63)

5.6. Notification of decision

Carton Board 385 (paras 173–174)
Bayer T–12/90
Dunlop T–43/92 (grounds 25)
John Deere T–35/92 (ground 31)
Fiat Agri T–34/92 (ground 27)
Continental Can T–13/89 (ground 10)
ICI T–4/89 (grounds 39–40)
Bayer C–195/91P

5.7. Withdrawal of decision

NDC/IMS 520

5.8. Publication of decision

Bank Austria II T–198/03 (grounds 58, 69–79, 102)

[For the tables of case citations see Tables 1 to 4, 11 and 12 at the back of the book.]

G. FINES AND PERIODIC PENALTY PAYMENTS

1. Fines for substantive infringements

1st Comp. Rep. (para.98)
13th Comp. Rep. (paras 62–66)
Europay T–39/92 (ground 136)
Cartes Bancaires T–275/94)
Cement T–25/95 (grounds 5009, 5022–5023, 5040, 5049, 5054–5056)

1.1. Requirements

1.1.1. Intentional infringement

⋆Quinine Cartel 24 (para.27)
Vegetable Parchment 129 (para.83)
Kawasaki 141 (paras 51–55, 57)
Fatty Acids 254 (para.55)
⋆Carton Board 386 (para.167)
BASF/Accinauto 405 (para.103)
VW-Audi 429 (paras 219–220)
FEG & TU 457
Luxembourg Brewing Industry 493 (para.89)
Austrian Banks 503 (paras 494–501)
Nintendo 505 (para.377)
Microsoft 528 (para.1057)
Belgian Architects 535 (paras 123–125)
AstraZeneca 545 (para. 905)
SPO T83 (grounds 362))
Treleurope T–141/89 (ground 176)
Gustave Boel T–142/89 (ground 116)
Ferriere Nord T–143/89 (ground 41)
Martinelli T–150/89 (ground 36)
Sarrio T–334/94 (ground 169)
Mayr-Melnhof Kartongesellschaft T–347/94 (ground 175)
VEG & TU T–5/00 (ground 396)
Dalmine T–50/00 (ground 333)
Luxembourg Brewers T–49e.s./02 (ground 156)
Miller C–19/77)
Belasco C–246/86 (ground 41)
Tipp-Ex C–279/87 (grounds 29–30)
Metsa Serla Oyj C–294/98P (grounds 25–30)
Volkswagen C–338/00P (grounds 95–98)

1.1.2. Negligence

⋆Deutsche Philips 73
BMW Belgium 126 (para.27)
FEG & TU 457
Microsoft 528 (para.1057)
Belgian Architects 535 (paras 123–125)
⋆United Brands C–27/76 (grounds 289–304)
SSI 127 (ground 65)
Sandoz C–277/87 (grounds 6–8)

1.2. Relevant Legislation

1.2.1. Articles 23–26 of Regulation 1/2003

1.2.2. Guidelines on the method of setting fines imposed pursuant to Article 15(2) of Regulation 17 and Article 65(5) of the ECSC Treaty [1998] O.J. C9/3

1.2.3. Commission Notice on immunity from fines and reduction of fines in cartel cases [2002] O.J. C45/3

1.3 List of cases on the fining guidelines

Amino Acids 46 (paras 255–396)
Michelin 481 (para.361)
Seamless Steel Tubes 499
Zinc Phosphates 501
Carbonless Paper 502
Austrian Banks 503
Methionine 504 (paras 269–331)
Nintendo 505 (paras 372–451)
Methylglucamine 508 (paras 224–261)
Food Flavour Enhancers 509 (paras 220–280)
Specialty Graphite 510
French Beef 513 (paras 164–186)
Deutsche Telekom 515 (paras 201–212)
Yamaha 517 (paras 188–199)
Italian Raw Tobacco 550
LR AF 1998 T–23/99 (grounds 233–246, 272–290)
FETTCSA T–213/00
Daesang & Sewon Europe T–230/00
ADM & ADM Ingredients T–224/00
Kyowa Hakko Kogyo T–223/00
Cheil Yedang T–220/00
GM & Opel Netherlands T–368/00 (grounds 182–204)
Minoan Lines T–66/99 (grounds 270–354)
Strintzis Lines T–65/99 (grounds 158–170 & 192–194)
Ventouris T–59/99 (grounds 204–213)
JCB Service T–67/01 (grounds 180ff)
Tokai Carbon et al. T–236e.s./01 (grounds 352–354)
JFE Engineering T–67e.s./00 (grounds 537ff)
Mannesmannrohren-Werke T–44/00 (grounds 212–213, 274)
SAS T–241/01 (grounds 64–75, 160–166)
Luxembourg Brewers T–49e.s./02 (grounds 168–169, 191–195)
Danone T–38/02 (grounds 138, 339–344, 520–524)

[For the tables of case citations see Tables 1 to 4, 11 and 12 at the back of the book.]

Heubach T–64/02 (grounds 35–45, 205–210)
Union Pigments T–62/02
Brouwerij Haacht T–48/02
Daiichi T–26/02
BASF T–15/02
Degussa T–279/02 (grounds 388–395)
Volkswagen C–338/00P (grounds 145–146)
Dansk Rørindustri C–189e.a./02P (grounds 160ff)
Acerinox C–57/02P (grounds 75–80)
Archer Daniels Midland C–397/03 (grounds 15–25, 91–95)

1.4. List of cases on the leniency notices

Greek Ferries 443
Amino Acids 465 (paras 397–435)
SAS/Maersk Air 475 (paras 120–124)
Graphite Electrodes 482
Seamless Steel Tubes 499 (paras 170–175)
Interbrew & Alken Maes 500 (paras 322ff)
Zinc Phosphate 501 (paras 346–366)
Carbonless Paper 502 (paras 435–458)
Austrian Banks 503 (paras 543–559)
Methionine 504 (paras 333–355)
Nintendo 505 (paras 453)
Methylglucamine 508 (paras 262–282)
Food Flavour Enhancers 509 (paras 281–295)
Christie's/Sotheby's 506 (paras 227–231)
Specialty Graphites 510 (paras 519ff)
Organic Peroxides 524 (paras 501–518)
Copper Tubes 538 (paras 768ff)
Needles 542 (paras 336–339)
Choline Chloride 543 (paras 220–236)
Italian Raw Tobacco 550 (paras 405–460)
ABB T–31/99 (grounds 234–239)
Danone T–38/02 (grounds 445–517)
Union Pigments T–62/02 (grounds 137–140)
⋆Brouwerij Haacht T–48/02 (ground 107)
Daiichi T–26/02 (grounds 146–163, 175–183)
⋆BASF T–15/02 (grounds 492–506, 517, 522–526, 543–546, 571–574)
Degussa T–279/02 (grounds 367–385)
Metsa Serla (Finnboard) C–298/98P (grounds 53–60)
LR AF 1998 (T–23/99)
Daesang & Sewon Europe T–230/00 (grounds 121–145)
ADM & ADM Ingredients T–224/00 (grounds 289–312)
⋆Adriatica T–61/99 (grounds 208–209)
Tokai Carbon et al. T–236e.s./01 (grounds 352–354, 402–416, 431 & 435–436)
JFE Engineering T–67e.s./00 (grounds 499ff)
Corus UK T–48/00 (grounds 192–199)
Mannesmannrohren-Werke T–44/00 (grounds 295ff)
Specialty Graphite T–71e.s./03 (grounds 358–374)
SAS T–241/01 (grounds 211–213, 218)
Dansk Rørindustri C–189e.a./02P (grounds 183–196, 375–382, 392–399)
Acerinox C–57/02P (grounds 85–95)
ThyssenKrupp Stainless C–231/03 (grounds 54–60)

1.5. Factors taken into account

1.5.1. Gravity

Quinine Cartel 24 (para.38)
BMW Belgium 126 (para.26)
PVC 305 (para.52)
LdPE 306 (para.64)
HOV SVZ/MCN 381 (paras 261–262)
Ferry Services 413 (para.65)
Greek Ferries 443
JCB 479 (paras 248–251)
Graphite Electrodes 482 (paras 131–134)
Zinc Phosphates 501 (paras 273 & 276)
Carbonless Paper 502 (paras 379–381)
Christie's/Sotheby's 506 (paras 198–213)
Deutsche Telekom 515 (paras 201–207)
Organic Peroxides 524 (paras 433ff)
Topps 530 (paras 174ff)
Belgian Architects 535 (paras 126ff)
Copper Tubes 538 (paras 605ff)
French Brewers 539 (paras 83, 98)
Choline Chloride 543 (paras 189ff)
AstraZeneca 545 (paras 900–915)
Peugeot 549 (paras 163–172)
Italian Raw Tobacco 550 (paras 365–376)
Europay T–39/92 (grounds 143–145)
Tate & Lyle T–202/98 (grounds 107–110)
Sigma Tecnologie T–28/99 (grounds 81–90)
FETTCSA T–213/00 (grounds 261–266)
ADM & ADM Ingredients T–224/00 (grounds 117–132)
SAS T–241/01 (grounds 82ff)
Luxembourg Brewers T–49e.s./02 (ground 170)
Danone T–38/02 (grounds 139ff)
Heubach T–64/02 (grounds 65–91, 144–148)
Sumitomo T–62/02 (grounds 103–106)
Degussa T–279/02 (grounds 192–197)
ACF Chemiefarma C–41/69 (ground 176)
⋆Pioneer C–100/80 (grounds 106, 120)
Michelin C–322/81 (ground 11)
Windsurfing C–193/83 (grounds 112–114)
Cascades C–279/98P (grounds 52–62)
Mo och Domsjo C–283/98P (grounds 53–62)
Metsa Serla (Finnboard) C–298/98P (grounds 70–73)

[For the tables of case citations see Tables 1 to 4, 11 and 12 at the back of the book.]

1.5.2. Size and profitability of the undertaking

Deutsche Philips 73
BMW Belgium 126 (para.26)
Cast Iron & Steel Rolls 198 (paras 72–73)
Fatty Acids 254 (para.56)
Tipp-Ex 269 (para.75)
Sandoz 272 (para.39)
Hudson Bay 294 (para.14)
PVC 305 (para.52)
BASF/Accinauto 405 (para.103)
Greek Ferries 443
Graphite Electrodes 482
Zinc Phosphates 501 (para.343)
Carbonless Paper 502 (paras 406–410)
Nintendo 505 (para.386)
Methylglucamine 508 (para.237)
Food Flavour Enhancers 509 (para.247)
Specialty Graphite 510 (paras 471–478, 555)
Organic Peroxides 524 (paras 450–458, 488)
Copper Tubes 538 (paras 680, 697, 821–841)
Spanish Raw Tobacco 540 (paras 415–423)
Needles 542 (paras 323–325)
Choline Chloride 543 (paras 200–202)
Italian Raw Tobacco 550 (paras 370–373)
Europay T–39 & T–40/92 (ground 137)
★Gustave Boel T–142/89 (ground 131)
LR AF 1998 T–23/99 (grounds 308 & 338)
FETTCSA T–213/00 (grounds 351–352, 395–400)
Daesang & Sewon Europe T–230/00 (grounds 37–64)
ADM & ADM Ingredients T–224/00 (grounds 187–206)
Kyowa Hakko Kogyo T–223/00 (grounds 61–89)
Cheil Yedang T–220/00 (grounds 82–103)
★Tokai Carbon et al. T–236e.s./01 (grounds 195, 200–201 & 219–233)
JFE Engineering T–67e.s./00 (grounds 551–554)
Dalmine T–50/00 (grounds 283–287)
Corus UK T–48/00 (grounds 179–182)
Mannesmannrohren-Werke T–44/00 (grounds 245–247)
Specialty Graphite T–71e.s./03 (grounds 180–181, 193–196, 225ff, 333, 405)
SAS T–241/01 (grounds 160–166)
Danone T–38/02 (grounds 156–165, 175, 413)
Heubach T–64/02 (grounds 161–164)
Union Pigments T–62/02 (grounds 149–164, 175–179)
SNCZ T–52/02 (grounds 61–85, 99–101)
Brouwerij Haacht T–48/02 (grounds 64–67)
Daiichi T–26/02 (grounds 61–65, 74)
BASF T–15/02 (grounds 144ff)
Degussa T–279/02 (ground 95)
ACF Chemiefarma C–41/69 (ground 186)
Boehringer C–45/69 (grounds 52–61)
★United Brands C–27/76 (grounds 125–128)
Hoffmann-La Roche C–85/76
Belasco C–246/86 (ground 60)
Tipp-Ex C–279/87 (grounds 37–39)
Huls C–199/92 (ground 195)
Sarrio C–219/98 (grounds 82–89)
Dansk Rørindustri C–189e.s./02P (ground 327)
Acerinox C–57/02P (grounds 75–80)
ThyssenKrupp Stainless C–65 & 73/02P
Archer Daniels Midland C–397/03 (grounds 33–35, 100–102)

1.5.3. Multi-product undertaking

Interbrew & Alken Maes 500 (para.305)

1.5.4. Mark-up for deterrent effect[1]

Pre-insulated pipe cartel 435 (paras 168–169) (x2.5)
Graphite Electrodes 482 (paras 152–154) (x1.25; x2.5)
Citric Acid 492 (paras 240–246) (x2; x2.5)
Luxembourg Brewers 493 (para.96) (x3)
German Bank Charges 494 (paras 192–194) (x2)
Carbonless Paper 502 (paras 410–412) (x2)
Methionine 504 (paras 303–305) (x2)
Nintendo 505 (paras 392–396) (x3; x1.25)
Methylglucamine 508 (paras 239–247) (x2)
Food Flavour Enhancers 509 (paras 252–254) (x2)
Microsoft 528 (para.1076) (x2)
Organic Peroxides 524 (paras 460–463) (x2)
Copper Tubes 538 (paras 701–705) (x1.5)
Choline Chloride 542 (paras 203–204) (x1.5; x2)
Italian Raw Tobacco 550 (paras 374–375 (x1.25; x1.5)
Specialty Graphite T–71e.s./03 (grounds 334–337)
Danone T–38/02 (grounds 169–182)
★BASF T–15/02 (grounds 218–262)
Degussa T–279/02 (grounds 278–290, 302, 316–317, 329–342)

1.5.5. Size of the relevant geographic market

Zinc Phosphates 501 (paras 302–303)

[1] The Commission may express the mark-up for deterrence as a percentage (e.g. + 100%) or as a factor (e.g. x2). For ease of comparison, all mark.

[For the tables of case citations see Tables 1 to 4, 11 and 12 at the back of the book.]

Carbonless Paper 502 (para.403)
Austrian Banks 503 (para.511)
Christie's/Sotheby's 506 (para.212)
Specialty Graphite 510 (para.456)
Organic Peroxides 524 (para.447)
Topps 530 (para.177)
Copper Tubes 538 (paras 674–677)
French Brewers 539 (para.86)
Spanish Raw Tobacco 540 (para.408)
Needles 542 (para.321)
Choline Chloride 543 (para.197)
Corus UK T–48/00 (grounds 169–170)
SAS T–241/01 (grounds 86–89, 99)
Danone T–38/02 (grounds 150–152)

1.5.6. Size of the relevant product market

Food Flavour Enhancers 509 (paras 242–243)
Copper Tubes 538 (paras 678–679)
French Brewers 539 (para.86)
Spanish Raw Tobaco 540 (para.414)
Choline Chloride 543 (para.199)
Dalmine T–50/00 (grounds 264–265)
Mannesmannrohren-Werke T–44/00 (grounds 234–235)
Luxembourg Brewers T–49e.s./02 (grounds 176–177)
BASF T–15/02 (grounds 130–136)

1.5.7. Duration

PVC 305 (paras 48–49)
LdPE 306 (paras 60–61)
Dutch Cranes 407a (para.46)
Graphite Electrodes 482 (paras 155–159)
Zinc Phosphates 501 (paras 310–312)
Carbonless Paper 502 (paras 413–416)
Methionine 504 (paras 308–311)
Nintendo 505 (paras 397–404)
Food Flavour Enhancers 509 (para.259–261)
Specialty Graphite 510 (paras 364, 479–483)
Christie's/Sotheby's 506 (paras 214–217)
Organic Peroxides 524 (paras 464–468)
Belgian Architects 535 (paras 132–133)
Copper Tubes 538 (para.464, 483, 490, 706–714)
French Brewers 539 (paras 73, 89)
Spanish Raw Tobacco 540 (paras 297–298, 327–328, 432–433)
Needles 542 (paras 327–328)
Choline Chloride 543 (para.206)
AstraZeneca 545 (paras 916–920)
Peugeot 549 (para. 149, 174)
Italian Raw Tobacco 550 (paras 377–378)
Italian Tobacco T–184/01R (ground 105)
Dansk Rørindustri T–21/99 (grounds 56–62, 213–216)
Cheil Yedang T–220/00 (grounds 133–139)
Michelin T–203/1 (ground 278)
Adriatica T–61/99 (grounds 125–130 & 204–207)
Ventouris T–59/99 (grounds 181–193)
Tokai Carbon et al. T–236e.s./01 (grounds 257–259, 277)
Specialty Graphite T–71e.s./03 (ground 275)
SAS T–241/01 (grounds 186, 192–194)
⋆Luxembourg Brewers T–49e.s./02 (ground 185)
Danone T–38/02 (grounds 206–247)
Union Pigments T–62/02 (grounds 36–42)
Degussa T–279/02 (grounds 114, 128–129, 178–181)
⋆SSI 127 (ground 95)
Volkswagen C–338/00P (grounds 175–179)
Acerinox C–57/02P (grounds 46–52, 103–108)
ThyssenKrupp Stainless C–65 & C–73/02 (grounds 31–39)

1.5.8. Effect/impact of infringement

Quinine Cartel 24 (para.38)
Tinned Mushrooms 88
Theal/Watts 110
Vegetable Parchment 129 (para.82)
⋆White Lead 142 (paras 41–42)
Floral 148
Zinc Producer Group 217
Woodpulp 227 (para.148)
Polypropylene 247 (para.108)
Meldoc 253 (para.76)
Fatty Acids 254 (para.56)
Hudson Bay 294 (para.13)
⋆British Plasterboard 299 (para.169)
SAS/Maersk Air 475 (paras 92–95)
JCB 479 (paras 252–254)
Graphite Electrodes 482 (paras 135–142)
Zinc Phosphates 501 (para.281)
Carbonless Paper 502 (paras 388–392 & 401)
Christie's/Sotheby's 506 (paras 203–211)
Methylglucamine 508 (paras 232–233)
Specialty Graphite 510 (paras 443–455)
Organic Peroxide 524 (paras 437–446)
Topps 530 (para.176)
Belgian Architects 535 (paras 128–129)
Copper Tubes 538 (paras 609ff)
Spanish Raw Tobacco 540 (paras 412–413)
Needles 542 (paras 318–320)
Choline Chloride 543 (paras 191–199)
Volkswagen T–62/98 (grounds 188–192)
Strintzis Lines T–65/99 (ground 172)
Dalmine T–50/00 (ground 265)
SAS T–241/01 (grounds 122, 130)

[For the tables of case citations see Tables 1 to 4, 11 and 12 at the back of the book.]

Luxembourg Brewers T–49e.s./02 (ground 178)
Danone T–38/02 (grounds 188–192)
Heubach T–64/02 (grounds 104–134)
SNCZ T–52/02 (grounds 86–88)
⋆Degussa T–279/02 (grounds 215–216, 224, 231, 250)

1.5.9. Extent of culpability

Quinine Cartel 24 (para.40)
BMW Belgium 126 (para.26)
AEG/Telefunken 179 (para.74)
AROW/BNIC 190 (para.77)
Windsurfing International 194
Polypropylene 247 (para.109)
Roofing Felt 248 (paras 75, 114–115)
Meldoc 253 (paras 80, 81)
Tipp-Ex 269 (paras 76–79)
Sandoz 272 (para.33)
⋆Fisher-Price 275 (para.26)
Konica 277
PVC 305 (paras 53–54)
LDPE 306 (paras 65–67)
Eurocheques; Helsinki 352 (para.79)
HOV SVZ/MCN 381 (paras 111–112)
Amino Acids 465 (paras 352–356)
Opel Nederland 467
Graphite Electrodes 482
Zinc Phoshates 501 (paras 314–323)
Carbonless Paper 502 (paras 418–427)
Nintendo 505 (paras 421–433 & 443)
Specialty Graphite 510 (paras 485–501)
Organic Peroxides 524 (paras 458, 478–480)
Copper Tubes 538 (para.756)
Spanish Raw Tobacco 540 (paras 435–438)
Italian Raw Tobacco 550 (para. 380)
Tate & Lyle T–202/98 (grounds 118–120)
Cheil Yedang T–220/00 (ground 168)
Adriatica T–61/99 (ground 187)
Ventouris T–59/99 (grounds 214–222)
Tokai Carbon et al. T–236/e.s.01 (ground 307)
Dalmine T–50/00 (grounds 294–295)
Specialty Graphite T–71e.s./03 (grounds 295–296, 316–331)
Union Pigments T–62/02 (grounds 63, 73, 82–88, 125–126)
Brouwerij Haacht T–48/02 (grounds 74–80)
⋆BASF T–15/02 (grounds 280–463)
BAT v Commission & Philip Morris C–142/84 (ground 43)
Tipp-Ex C–279/87 (grounds 40–41)
Commission v Anic C–49/92P (grounds 190–204)
Aalborg C–204e.s./00P (ground 373)
Dansk Rørindustri C–189e.a./02P (grounds 366–370)

1.5.10. Non-enforcement/non-implementation of agreement

British Telecommunications 188 (para.45)
Zinc Phosphates 501 (para.327)
Specialty Graphite 510 (paras 509–510)
Organic Peroxides 524 (para.486)
Belgian Architects 535 (para.129)
Copper Tubes 538 (paras 728–736)
FETTCSA T–213/00 (grounds 289–293)
ADM & ADM Ingredients T–224/00 (grounds 264–265)
Cheil Yedang T–220/00 (grounds 288–289)
JFE Engineering T–67e.s./00 (grounds 549–550)
⋆Dalmine T–50/00 (grounds 291–293)
Mannesmannrohren-Werke T–44/00
Danone T–38/02 (grounds 384–392)
Heubach T–64/02 (grounds 104–134)
Union Pigments T–62/02 (ground 130)
Daiichi T–26/02 (grounds 105–130)

1.5.11. Use of violence/physical force

French Beef 513 (paras 173 & 177)

1.5.12. Difficult market conditions

Quinine Cartel 24 (para.38)
ABG/Oil Companies 113
Cast Iron & Steel Rolls 198 (paras 72–73)
Flat Glass (Benelux) 216
⋆Zinc Producer Group 217 (para.104)
Polypropylene 247 (para.108)
Roofing felt 248
Meldoc 253 (para.79)
Flat Glass 300 (para.84)
LdPE 306 (para.64)
Welded Steel Mesh 311 (para.200)
Graphite Electrodes 482 (paras 195–197)
Citric Acid 492 (paras 287 & 290)
Interbrew & Alken Maes 500 (para.321)
Zinc Phosphate 501 (paras 339–340)
Carbonless Paper 502 (paras 430–431)
Methylglucamine 508 (paras 253)
French Beef 513 (paras 182–185)
Copper Tubes 538 (paras 741–746)
Choline Chloride 543 (para.216)
Italian Raw Tobacco 550 (para. 384)
Rhone Poulenc v Commission T–1/89 (grounds 159–167)
Hercules T–7/89 (grounds 331–335)
Societe Metallurgique de Normandie T–147/89 (grounds 97–98)
Trelunion T–148/89 (grounds 116–117)
Societe des Treillis et Panneaux Soudes T–151/89 (ground 98)

[For the tables of case citations see Tables 1 to 4, 11 and 12 at the back of the book.]

Danone T–38/02 (ground 414)
Heubach T–64/02 (grounds 139–140)

1.5.13. Co-operative or unco-operative attitude of the undertaking

1.5.13.1. Undertakings and modification of the agreements at the Commission's request

General Motors 84
Chiquita 101 (para.II.B)
Miller 108 (para.7)
Kawasaki 141 (para.61)
Floral 148
John Deere 226 (para.41)
Hilti 282 (para.103)
★Hudson Bay 294 (para.14)
Fenex 409a (para.89)
Amino Acids 465 (paras 319–328)
★Sandoz v Commission C–277/87 (paras 21–22)
Woodpulp C–89/85 (ground 194)

1.5.13.2. Introduction of a compliance programme

National Panasonic 186 (paras 5, 43–47)
Sperry New Holland 245 (para.68)
Tipp-Ex 269 (para.75)
Fisher-Price 275 (para.27)
★British Sugar 286 (paras 10, 82, 85)
★Viho/Toshiba 341 (paras 28–30)
Ford Agricultural 364 (para.23)
British Sugar II 434 (paras 149–151)
Graphite Electrodes 482 (paras 193–194)
Zinc Phosphates 501 (paras 331–332)
Methionine 504 (paras 331–332)
Nintendo 505 (paras 450–451)
Methylglucamine 508 (paras 259–260)
Food Flavour Enhancers 509 (para.279)
Organic Peroxides 524 (para.490)
Topps 530 (para.181)
Copper Tubes 538 (para.754)
Choline Chloride 543 (para.217)
ICI T–13/89 (ground 395)
Parker Pen T–196/89Rev (ground 94)
LR AF 1998 T–23/99 (ground 345)
ADM & ADM Ingredients T–224/00 (grounds 280–281)
Strintzis Lines T–65/99 (ground 201)
Tokai Carbon et al. T–236e.s./01 (ground 343)
BASF T–15/02 (ground 266)
Degussa T–279/02 (grounds 350, 361)
British Leyland C–226/84 (ground 44)
Dansk Rørindustri C–189e.a./02P (grounds 371–373)

1.5.13.3. Active participation of company

Carton Board 385 (ground 71)
Novalliance 415 (para.82)
Greek Ferries 443
Graphite Electrodes 482
Nintendo 505 (paras 455–462)
Organic Peroxides 524 (paras 493–496)
Copper Tubes 538 (paras 757–761)
French Brewers 539 (paras 100–103)
Choline Chloride 543 (para.218)
Italian Raw Tobacco 550 (paras 387–398)
ICI T–13/89 (grounds 391–394)
BPB de Eendracht T–311/94 (ground 325)
Moritz J. Weig T–317/94 (ground 283)
Mayr-Melnhof Kartongesellschaft T–347/94 (grounds 331–339)
ABB T–31/99 (grounds 234–239)
FETTCSA T–213/00 (grounds 289–308)
Michelin T–203/1 (grounds 296–299)
Tokai Carbon et al. T–236e.s./01 (grounds 431 & 435–436)
BASF T–15/02 (grounds 585–589)
Metsa Serla (Finnboard) C–398/98P (grounds 53–60)
SCA Holding C–297/98 (grounds 34–37)
Acerinox C–57/02P (grounds 85–90)
ThyssenKrupp Stainless C–65/02P (grounds 48–60)

1.5.13.4. Offering victims compensation

Nintendo 505 (paras 440–441)
Tokai Carbon et al. T–236e.s./01 (ground 348)

1.5.13.5. Unco-operative attitude

Bayonox 313 (para.69)
Eurocheques; Helsinki 352 (para.89)
Graphite Electrodes 482 (para.160)
Nintendo 505 (paras 413–419)
HFB et al. T–9/99 (grounds 555–564)
FETTCSA T–213/00 (grounds 289–308)
Minoan Lines T–248 (grounds 335–338)
Tokai Carbon et al. T–66/99 (grounds 312–315)
SCA Holding C–297/98 (grounds 34–37)

1.5.13.6. Disputing the facts for the first time on appeal

★Tokai Carbon et al. T–66/99 (grounds 112–113, 288 & 417–418)
SAS T–241/01 (grounds 231–242)
Dansk Rørindustri C–189e.a./02P (grounds 351–353)
Minoan Lines C–121/04P (grounds 65–66)
Adriatica C–111/04P (grounds 90–91)
Strintzis C–110/04P (ground 63)

1.5.13.7. Dismissal of persons involved in infringement

BASF T–15/02 (ground 266)

[For the tables of case citations see Tables 1 to 4, 11 and 12 at the back of the book.]

1.5.14. State of the law

1.5.14.1. State of legal development

Chiquita 101 (para.II.B)
Vitamins 104
Vegetable Parchment 129 (para.83)
Italian Cast Glass 163
Windsurfing International 194
Woodpulp 227 (para.146)
Roofing Felt 248
Fatty Acids 254 (para.58)
⋆British Sugar 286 (paras 87–88)
SABENA 295 (para.40)
Flat Glass 300 (para.84)
Decca 304 (para.133)
Eco System 344a (para.34)
British Midland 350 (para.42)
World Cup Football 360 (para.125)
Ford Agricultural 364 (para.21)
Far Eastern Freight 399 (para.188)
DPAG Cross-border mail 483 (para.193)
Montedipe T–14/89 (ground 346)
Dunlop T–89/91 (ground 143)
Irish Sugar T–228/97 (grounds 290–293)
Far Eastern Freight Conference T–86/95 (grounds 484–487)
Degussa T–279/02 (grounds 72, 82–83, 395)
Hoffmann-La Roche C–85/76 (grounds 128–137)
⋆Michelin C–322/81 (ground 107)
AKZO C–62/86
⋆Johnson & Johnson 160 (para.41)
⋆Roofing Felt 248 (para.109)
Spanish Raw Tobacco 540 (paras 427–429)
AstraZeneca 545 (para. 921)
Italian Raw Tobacco (paras 358–362)
Far Eastern Freight Conference T–86/95 (grounds 484–487)
Minoan Lines T–66/99 (grounds 294 & 347)
Danone T–35/02 (grounds 405–408)
⋆Miller C–19/77 (ground 18)

1.5.14.2. Well-documented infringement

WEA/Filipacchi Music S.A. 68
Miller 108 (para.21)
BMW Belgium 126 (para.26)
Kawasaki 141 (para.56)
⋆Pioneer 152 (para.93)
Michelin 165 (para.55)
Möet et Chandon (London) Ltd 172 (para.21)
AEG-Telefunken 179 (para.78)
AROW/BNIC 190
Windsurfing International 194
Polistil/Arbois 211
British Leyland 212
Flat Glass (Benelux) 216
Peroxide Products 218
John Deere 226 (para.42)
Sandoz 272 (para.39)
Tate & Lyle T–202/98 (grounds 43–145)
Danone T–38/02 (grounds 405–408)
BMW Belgium C–32 & 36–82/78 (grounds 52–55)

1.5.14.3. Ignorance of the law, obtaining wrong legal opinion

Kawasaki 141 (paras 30, 36–37)

1.5.15. Repeated infringement

Möet et Chandon (London) Ltd 172 (para.20)
Hasselblad 173 (para.72)
Flat Glass (Benelux) 216
Polypropylene 247 (para.107)
⋆Flat Glass 300 (para.84)
PVC 305 (para.52)
⋆Solvay/ICI 330 (para.64)
Michelin 481 (paras 361–363)
Interbrew & Alken Maes 500 (paras 314–316)
Specialty Graphite 510 (paras 513, 557–558)
Organic Peroxides 524 (paras 470–477)
Copper Tubes 538 (paras 720–726)
French Brewers 539 (paras 91–94)
Choline Chloride 543 (para.208)
Enichem T–6/89 (ground 295)
Hercules T–7/89 (ground 348)
Michelin T–203/1 (grounds 284–288)
⋆Danone T–38/02 (grounds 345–369)

1.5.16. Continuation of infringement following clarification of the law

ECS/AKZO 242 (para.97)Far Eastern Freight 399 (para.149)
Irish Sugar 418 (para.167)
Dunlop T–83/91 (grounds 146–150)

1.5.17. Continuation or cessation of the infringement following Commission action

Nintendo 505 (paras 407–410)
French Beef 513 (para.174)
Yamaha 517 (para.198)
Topps 530 (para.183)
Copper Tubes 538 (para.750)
Tokai Carbon et al. T–236e.s./01 (grounds 292–296)
Union Pigments T–62/02 (grounds 92–93)
General Motors C–551/03P (grounds 86–88)

1.5.17a. Cessation of the infringement prior to Commission action

Organic Peroxides 524 (paras 483–485)

[For the tables of case citations see Tables 1 to 4, 11 and 12 at the back of the book.]

Choline Chloride 543 (para.210)

1.5.18. Governmental pressure, encouragement or approval

AROW/BNIC 190 (para.77)
British Sugar II 434 (paras 203–205)
Huls T–9/89 (grounds 365–366)
Hoechst T–10/89 (grounds 358–359)
Minoan Lines T–66/99 (ground 281)
Ventouris T–59/99 (ground 211)
★SSI 127 (ground 94)

1.5.18a. Acting under other participant's instructions

★Specialty Graphite 510 (paras 515–516)

1.5.19. Additional profit from infringement

Kawasaki 141 (paras 58–59)
Eurocheques; Helsinki 352 (paras 80–82)
Copper Tubes 538 (paras 737–740)
SNCZ T–52/02 (grounds 89–92)

1.5.20. Non bis in idem (double jeopardy)

Cast-iron & Steel Rolls 198 (para.71)
Flat Glass 300 (para.84)
Welded Steel Mesh 311 (para.205)
Graphite Electrodes 482 (paras 177–183)
Specialty Graphite 510 (paras 545ff)
Belgian Architects 535 (paras 115–119)
Copper Tubes 538 (paras 715–718)
1st Comp. Rep. (para.130)
2nd Comp. Rep. (para.26)
Treleurope T–141/89 (ground 191)
Société Metallurgique de Nomandie T–147/89 (grounds 132)
Trelunion T–148/89 (ground 151)
Societe des Treillis et Panneaux Soudes T–151/89 (ground 132)
Sotralentz T–149/89 (ground 29)
PVC II T97 (ground 29)
Specialty Graphite T–71e.s./03 (grounds 112–124, 334–337)
Danone T–38/02 (grounds 184–187)
Walt Wilhelm C–14/68 (grounds 10–11)
★Boehringer C–45/69
Boehringer C–7/72
Aalborg C–204e.s./00P (grounds 338–340)
Dansk Rørindustri C–189e.a./02P (grounds 402–403)
Archer Daniels Midland C–397/03 (grounds 46–74)

1.5.21. Sanctions imposed by other authorities

Graphite Electrodes 482 (paras 177–183)
Food Flavour Enhancers 509 (paras 274–275)
ADM & ADM Ingredients T–224/00 (grounds 85–104)
Kyowa Hakko Kogyo T–223/00 (grounds 96–114)
★Tokai Carbon et al. T–236e.s./01 (grounds 130–148)
★Archer Daniels Midland C–397/03 (grounds 46–74)

1.5.22. Duration of proceedings

FEG & TU 457
FETTCSA 464
Christie's/Sotheby's 506 (paras 223, 232)
Choline Chloride 543 (paras 212–214)
Irish Sugar T–228/97 (grounds 277–286)
Volkswagen T–62/98 (grounds 337–338)
FETTCSA T–213/00 (grounds 321–325)
JCB Service T–67/01 (grounds 36–45)

1.5.23. The existence of sector-specific regulation

Deutsche Telekom 515 (para.212)
Italian Raw Tobacco 550 (paras 358–362)

1.5.24. Non-discrimination; undertakings involved in the same infringement should be fined equally

Austrian Banks 503 (paras 470–472)
Specialty Graphite 510 (paras 409–410)
Hercules T–7/89 (ground 295)
Treleurope T–141/89 (ground 185)
Gustave Boel T–142/89 (grounds 128–135)
★Ferriere Nord T–143/89 (grounds 54–56)
Martinelli T–150/89 (grounds 57–61)
Van Megen Sport v Commission T–49/95 (ground 56)
Finnish Board Mills T–338/94)
Mayr-Melnhof Kartongesellschaft T–347/94 (grounds 334–336, 352–354)
Tate & Lyle T–202/98 (grounds 111, 118–120)
Cascades II T–308/94 (ground 65)
ABB T–31/99 (grounds 240–245)
LR AF 1998 T–23/99 (grounds 290–300)
Ke Kelit T–17/99 (ground 101)
FETTCSA T–213/00 (grounds 406–426)
Daesang & Sewon Europe T–230/00 (grounds 65–76)
ADM & ADM Ingredients T–224/00 (grounds 69–74 & 208–212)
Cheil Yedang T–220/00 (grounds 104–115)
Michelin T–203/01 (grounds 251–254 & 277)
Minoan Lines T–66/99 (grounds 330–334)

[For the tables of case citations see Tables 1 to 4, 11 and 12 at the back of the book.]

Adriatica T–61/99 (grounds 157–159 & 191)
VEG & TU T–5/00 (grounds 428–432)
JCB Service T–67/01 (grounds 187–189)
★Tokai Carbon et al. T–236e.s./01 (grounds 219–233)
Dalmine T–50/00 (grounds 340–345)
Danone T–38/01 (grounds 153–154, 459–476)
Heubach T–64/02 (grounds 195–200)
Union Pigments T–62/02 (grounds 155–159)
SNCZ T–52/02 (grounds 109–116)
Britannia Alloys T–33/02 (grounds 60–63)
Brouwerij Haacht T–48/02 (ground 109)
Daiichi T–26/02 (grounds 81–93)
BASF T–15/02 (grounds 133–134, 149–150, 156–168, 179–182)
Degussa T–279/02 (grounds 327–335)
Moritz Weig C–280/98P (grounds 54–68)
Enso Espanola C–282/98P (grounds 50–59)
Sarrio C–219/98 (grounds 92–99)
Volkswagen C–338/00P (ground 146)
Archer Daniels Midland C–397/03 (grounds 28–35)

1.5.25. Single fine for multiple infringements

AstraZeneca 545 (para. 915)
Michelin T–203/01 (ground 265)
Adriatica T–61/99 (ground 191)
Ventouris T–59/99 (grounds 214–222)
Dansk Rørindustri C–189e.a./02P (grounds 304–313, 328–340)

1.6. No more than 10% of turnover

Carbonless Paper 502 (para.434)
Organic Peroxides 524 (paras 498–499)
Copper Tubes 538 (paras 766–767)
Spanish Raw Tobacco 540 (paras 440–446)
HFB et al. T–9/99 (grounds 528–543)
Specialty Graphite T–71e.s./03 (grounds 377, 387–393)
Union Pigments T–62/02 (ground 161)
SNCZ T–52/02 (grounds 36–41, 96)
★Britannia Alloys T–33/02 (grounds 33–51, 69–74)
BASF T–15/02 (ground 70)
Degussa T–279/02 (ground 96)
Dansk Rørindustri C–189e.a./02P (grounds 277–283, 321–323)

1.7. Limitation periods

Quinine Cartel 24 (para.36)
Vegetable parchment 129 (para.54)
Toltecs/Dorcet 191
Cast Iron & Steel Rolls 198 (paras 67–68)
★Aluminium 228
Polypropylene 247 (para.103)
PVC 305 (para.47)
LDPE 306 (paras 58–59)
Welded Steel Mesh 311 (para.196)
★PVC II 389 (paras 55–58)
Organic Peroxides 524 (paras 262, 326–330, 419)
Belgian Architects 535 (para.121)
Copper Tubes 538 (paras 591–592)
Choline Chloride 543 (paras 183–184)
2nd Comp. Rep. (paras 13–14)
4th Comp. Rep. (paras 48–50)
Hercules T–7/89 (grounds 309–310)
PVC II T–305e.s./94 (grounds 1089–1106)
FETTCSA T–213/00 (grounds 484–488, 506)
★Sumitomo T–22/02 (grounds 34–63)
★Greencore T–135/02 (grounds 59–68)
ACF Chemiefarma C–41/69 (grounds 17–20)
Boehringer C–45/69 (grounds 5–7)
ICI C–48/69 (grounds 45–50)
BASF C–49/69
Bayer C–51/69
Ciba-Geigy C–52/69
Sandoz C–53/69
Francolor C–54/69
Cassella C–55/69
Hoechst v Commission I C–56/69
ACNA C–57/69
★CMA CGM C–236/03P

1.8. Recovery of fine/interest upon annulment/reduction

Tokai Carbon et al. T–236e.s./01 (grounds 475–479)
Holcim (France) T–86/03
Greencore T–135/02
Greencore 389

2. Fines for infringement of procedural rules

Fides 145
Fabbrica Pisana 153
Fabbrica Lastre 154
Comptoir d'Importation 167
Telos 170
National Panasonic (Belgium) 176
National Panasonic (France) 177
Fédération Chaussure de France 183
★Peugeot 250 (para.52)
Secrétama 329a
UKWAL 354
CSM 359
MEWAC 365
AKZO 391

1st Comp. Rep. (para.99)
Tepea C–28/77 (grounds 67–72)
Scottish & Newcastle II 458

3. Periodic penalty payments

Article 16 Regulation 17/62
⋆Hugin/Liptons 121
Baccarat 338
Dalmine T–596/97
Mannesmann T–128/98
Hoechst v Commission II C–46/87R
⋆Hoechst v Commission III C–46/87 & 227/88 (grounds 49–66)

CHAPTER 3

JUDICIAL REVIEW

A. JURISDICTION

1. Text of Article 220 (ex 164)

2. Article 229 (ex 172)

2.1. Text of Article 229 (ex 172)

2.2. Cases on the interpretation of Article 229 (ex 172)

CMB T–24/93 (ground 242)
⋆Europa Carton T–304/94 (ground 100)
Hilti C–53/92P (grounds 48–50)

3. Article 31 Regulation 1/2003

Reproduced in the Legislation section below.

4. Competence of the Court of First Instance

PTT T–42/91
Sofacar T–27/91
PTT C–66/90

B. TYPES OF PROCEDURE

1. Article 226 (ex 169)

1.1. Text of Article 226 (ex 169)

1.2. Cases on the interpretation of Article 226 (ex 169)

Rendo v Commission I T–16/91 (grounds 39–57, 96–112)
Intertronic T–117/96
Sateba T–83/97 (ground 32)
Commission v Greece C–226/87
Commission v Italy C–35/96
Commission v Luxembourg C–59/98

2. Article 230 (ex 173)

2.1. Text of Article 230 (ex 173)

2.2. Direct and individual concern

Zunis T–83/92
⋆Métropole T–528/93 (grounds 59–65)
⋆Kruidvat T–87/92
Leclerc T–19/92 (grounds 53–69)
Leclerc T–88/92 (grounds 41–55)
Conseil National T–62/98
Joynson T–231/99 (grounds 28–34)
Shaw T–131/99 (grounds 25–29)
Piau T–193/02 (ground 38)
⋆Metro v Commission I C–26/76 (grounds 5–13)
Metro v Commission II C–75/84
ANCIDES C–43/85
Kruidvat C–70/97P

2.3. Challengeable acts

SGA T–189/95 (grounds 25–29)
Stork T–241/97 (grounds 49–63)
Patent Agents T–144/99 (grounds 29–35)
Max Mobil T–54/99 (paras 48–71)
Atlantic Container Line II T–18/97 (grounds 41–42)

2.3.1. Challengeable steps

Automec T–64/89
Nefarma T–113/89
VNZ T–114/89
Prodifarma T–116/89
Cement Industries T–10/92 R
Rendo v Commission II T–2/92
Ladbroke T–74/92 (ground 72)
Ladbroke T–104/95R
Peugeot T–136/96, T–90/96
Elf Atochem T–9/97
Dalmine T–596/97
TF1 T–17/96 (paras 29–33)
Atlantic Container Line II T–18/97 (grounds 41–42)
Satellimages TV5 T–95/99 (grounds 32–41)
Greencore T–135/02 (grounds 18–37)
Österreichische Postsparkasse T–328/03 (grounds 64–72)
⋆IBM C–60/81

[For the tables of case citations see Tables 1 to 4, 11 and 12 at the back of the book.]

Greencore C–123/03P (grounds 44–47)

2.3.2. Interim decisions

Cimenteries C–8/66
⋆Ford C–228/82

2.3.3. Disclosure of confidential information

Postbank T–353/94
AKZO v Commission I C–53/85 (grounds 17–22)

2.3.4. Rejection of a complaint

Automec T–64/89
Asia Motor France T–28/90 (ground 42)
Rendo v Commission I T–16/91
SFEI T–36/92
BEUC T–37/92 (grounds 27–39)
BEMIM T–114/92 (grounds 26–37)
Tremblay T–5/93
Guérin Automobiles T–186/94
Ladbroke T–104/95R
Intertronic T–117/96
VGB T–77/94 (grounds 69–80)
Guérin T–38/96
Piau T–193/02 (ground 38)
Centro Europa 7 T–338/04 (grounds 36–40)
Lord Bethell C–246/81
⋆Demo Schmidt C–210/81
CICCE C–298/83
BAT v Commission & Philip Morris C–142/84 (ground 12)
⋆SFEI C–39/93P
Rendo C–19/93 (ground 28)
German Accountants C–107/95P
T-Mobile Austria C–141/02P (grounds 66–74)

2.3.5. Absence of legal effect

Métropole Télévision T–112/99 (grounds 35–43)
IMS T–184/01
Centro Europa 7 T–338/04 (grounds 36–40)
Österreichische Postsparkasse T–328/03 (grounds 64–72)
Bosman C–117/91
Hüls C–199/92 (grounds 53–55, 90–92, 130–131)
ICI C–200/92P (grounds 69–73)
Hoechst C–227/92P (grounds 69–78)
Shell C–234/92P (grounds 55–59)
Montecatini C–235/92P (grounds 96–100)
Chemie Linz C–245/92P (grounds 92–97)
DSM C–5/93 (grounds 30–33)
T-Mobile Austria C–141/02P (grounds 70–72)

2.3.6. Undertakings

Woodpulp C–89/85 (grounds 178–181)

2.3.7. Negative clearance

Dutch Banks T–138/89
First Data T–28/02

2.3.8. Comfort letters

Air France T–3/93 (ground 50)

2.3.9. Exemption

O2 (Germany) T–328/03 (grounds 46–49)

2.3.10. Decisions of the Hearing Officer

Bank Austria II T–198/03

2.4. Limitation periods

Guérin C–154/98P (paras 12–13)
Guérin C–153/98P (paras 12–16)
Sodima C–44/00
Norsk Hydro T–106/89
Filtrona T–125/89
⋆Bayer T–12/90
Florimex T–70/92 (grounds 71–77)
FNICGV T–252/03
AssiDomän C–310/97 (grounds 57–63)

2.5. Estoppel

Hilti T–30/89 (grounds 25, 34–39)
Specialty Graphite T–71e.s./03 (ground 324)

2.6. Scope of judicial review

La Cinq T–44/90
Flat Glass T–68/89 (grounds 315–320)
Asia Motor France T–7/92 (grounds 33–35)
Europay T–39/92 (grounds 85, 110)
BEUC T–37/92 (ground 45)
Matra T–17/93 (ground 104)
Viho Europe T–102/92 (grounds 28–29)
Ladbroke T–74/92 (ground 75)
BEMIM T–114/92 (grounds 33, 72)
SPO T–29/92 (grounds 288, 330–331)
Langnese Iglo T–7/93 (ground 178)
Schöller T–9/93 (ground 140)
Solvay T–30/91 (grounds 98–103)
ICI T–36/91 (ground 108)
Ladbroke T–104/95R (ground 54)
Koelman T–575/93 (grounds 29–33, 56)
⋆Métropole T–528/93 (ground 93)
SNCF T–79/95 (ground 64)
PVC II T–305e.s./94 (grounds 167–174)

[For the tables of case citations see Tables 1 to 4, 11 and 12 at the back of the book.]

Kish Glass T–65/96 (ground 64)
Asia Motor France T–154/98 (ground 53)
Italian Tobacco T–139/98 (grounds 77–79)
Max Mobil T–54/99 (grounds 58–59)
Far Eastern Freight Conference T–86/95 (ground 339)
Atlantic Container Line T–395/94 (ground 257)
Joynson T–231/99 (ground 36)
Shaw T–131/99
ADM & ADM Ingredients T–224/00 (grounds 360–370)
Michelin T–203/01 (grounds 129 ff)
Vanden Bergh Foods T–65/98 (ground 135)
Minoan Lines T–66/99 (grounds 356–358)
Adriatica T–61/99 (grounds 208–209)
Hoechst T–410/03 (grounds 16–19)
Piau T–193/02 (grounds 76–79)
Holcim (Germany) T–64/02 (grounds 95–99)
Brouwerij Haacht T–48/02 (44)
BASF T–15/02 (grounds 293, 303, 338, 420, 455, 534, 542, 546, 571, 582)
Remia C–42/84
Woodpulp C–89/85 (grounds 31–32)
Hilti C–53/92P
Aalborg Portland C–204e.s./00P (grounds 70–77)
European Broadcasting Union C–470/02P (grounds 61–74)
Dansk Rørindustri C–189e.a./02P (ground 445)
Strintzis Lines C–110/04P (54–56)
General Motors C–551/03P (grounds 50–57)

2.6a. Impact of admission of facts on standing

Strintzis Lines C–110/04P (ground 28)

2.7. Article 233 (ex 176)

AnniDomän T–227/95
Tremblay T–224/95
PVC II T–305e.s./94 (grounds 77–84, 95–99, 148–154)
Assi/Domän C–310/97 (grounds 49–56)

2.8. Relationship with Article 229

FNICGV T–252/03

3. Article 232 (ex 175)

3.1. Text of Article 232 (ex 175)

3.2. Cases on the interpretation of Article 232 (ex 175)

Solomon v Commission T–55/89
Prodifarma v Commission II T–3/90 (grounds 35–37)
Asia Motor France T–28/90
Ladbroke T–74/92
Koelman T–56/92
Ladbroke T–74/92
Guérin Automobiles T–186/94
Koelman T–575/93 (grounds 71–72)
Guérin T–195/95
ITT Promedia T–111/96 (ground 97)
IECC T–28/95
TF1 T–17/96 (grounds 26–36)
Holcim (France) T–86/03 (grounds 33–36)
⋆Komponistenverband C–8/71
⋆GEMA C–125/78
Lord Bethell C–246/81
Guérin C–282/95P
Sodima C–44/00 (grounds 42–54)

4. Article 234 (ex 177)

4.1. Text of Article 234 (ex 177)

4.2. Cases on the interpretation of Article 234 (ex 177)

German Postal Law 541 (paras 142–143)
Solvay T–30/91 (grounds 71–73)
ICI T–36/91 (grounds 81–82)
Bosch v De Geus C–13/61
De Haecht v Wilkin II C–48/72
BRT v SABAM I C–127/73
⋆Hoffmann-La Roche v Centrafarm C–107/76
Van Eycke v Aspa C–267/86
Ministère Public v Tournier C–395/87 (ground 25)
Lucazeau v SACEM C–110/88 (ground 1a)
Spanish Banks C–67/91
Telemarsicabruzzo C–320/90
Banchero C–157/92
Monin C–386/92
SAT v Eurocontrol C–364/92 (grounds 12–14)
Banks v British Coal C–128/92
Monin II C–428/93
Saddik C–458/93
Gomis C–167/94
⋆Oscar Bronner C–7/97
Viacom C–134/03
Mauri C–250/03 (grounds 18–22)
Syfait C–53/03 (grounds 21–37)

5. Articles 235 (ex 178), 288 (ex 215)

5.1. Text of Articles 235 (ex 178), 288 (ex 215)

5.2. Cases on the interpretation of Articles 235 (ex 178), 288 (ex 215)

Koelman T–575/93

[For the tables of case citations see Tables 1 to 4, 11 and 12 at the back of the book.]

Asia Motor France T–387/94 (grounds 106–111)
Guérin T–195/95, T–38/96
Dutch Cranes T–213/95
★Holcim (Germany) T–28/03
Holcim (France) T–86/03
GAARM C–289/83
★Stanley Adams C–145/83
Bosman C–117/91
Baustahlgewebe C–185/95P

6. Interim measures

6.1. Text of Articles 242 (ex 185) and 243 (ex 186)

6.2. Cases on the interpretation of Articles 242 (ex 185) and 243 (ex 186)

6.2.1. General

Cosimex T–131/89R
Peugeot T–23/90R
SEP T–39/90R
Vichy T–19/91R
Cement Industries T–10/92R
Langnese Iglo T–24/92R
Dutch Builders T–29/92R
Perrier's Employees T–96/92R
Langnese T–789/93R
CMBT T–24/93R
Vittel's Employees T–12/93R
SCPA T–88/94R
Postbank T–353/94R
Square d'Auvergne T–5/95R
Atlantic Container T–395/94R
SNCF & BR T–79/95R
Atlantic Container T–395/94RII
IMS T–184/01R
Goldstein T–235/94R
★Bayer T–41/96R
Van den Bergh Foods T–65/98R
Ventouris T–59/99R
DSR Senator T–191/98R
★Akzo Nobel T–215/03R
Bank Austria T–198/03R
Microsoft T–201/04
Camera Care C–792/79R
Hoechst v Commission II C–46/87R
Dow C–85/87R
RTE & BBC C–76/89R
Publisher's Association C–56/89R
Atlantic Container C–149/95P(R)

6.2.2. In respect of fines

Laackman Karton T–301/94R
Buchman T–295/94R
Cascades T–308/94R
Halkidos T–104/95R
Dutch Cranes T–18/86R
Cho Yang Shipping T–191/98R
Linea T–398/02R
FEG T–5/00R
Microsoft T–201/04
Dutch Cranes C–268/96P(R)
DSR Senator Lines C–364/99P(R)
Cho Yang Shipping C–361/00P(R)

7. Request of interpretation of court judgment

Générale Sucrière C–41/73

8. Articles 56–57 (ex49) Statute Court

SPO C–137/95P
Goldstein C–148/96P
John Deere C–7/95P
New Holland Ford C–8/95P
Deutsche Bahn C–436/97P
PVC II T–305e.s./94 (grounds 423, 528–534, 537, 614)
Aéroports de Paris T–128/98 (grounds 41, 56, 67, 94)
Commission v Anic C–49/92P (grounds 64–70)
Hüls C–199/92 (grounds 64–68, 84–88, 152)
ICI C–200/92P (grounds 57–59)
Hoechst C–227/92P (grounds 38–41, 79–81)
Shell C–234/92P (grounds 60–62)
Montecatini C–235/92P (grounds 109–111, 119–120)
Chemie Linz C–245/92P (grounds 98–100)
Aalborg Portland C–204e.s./00P (grounds 47–52 & 125)
British Sugar C–359/01P (ground 48)
European Broadcasting Union C–470/02P
Greencore C–123/03P
T-Mobile Austria C–141/02P (grounds 45–51)

[For the tables of case citations see Tables 1 to 4, 11 and 12 at the back of the book.]

Akzo Nobel C–7/04 (grounds 36–44)
Dansk Rørindustri C–189e.a./02P (grounds 122,129, 165, 245, 301–302)
ThyssenKrupp Stainless C–65/02P (ground 34)
Marlines C–112/04P (grounds 28–34)
Minoan Lines C–121/04P (grounds 17–20, 58–63)
Adriatica C–111/04P (grounds 49–52, 62–64, 75)
Archer Daniels Midland C–397/03 (ground 47)

9. Restrictive list of remedies available

Holcim (Germany) T–28/03 (grounds 31–36)

CHAPTER 4

NATIONAL JURISDICTIONS AND AUTHORITIES

A. NATIONAL AUTHORITIES

1. What is a national authority?

BRT v SABAM I C–127/73 (ground 19)
Nouvelles Frontières C–209/84 (grounds 55–56)

2. Competence

Article 84 EC
Article 6 Regulation 1/2003
Anne Marty v Estée Lauder C–37/79 (grounds 12–16)

3. Co-operation between the national authorities and the Commission

FA Premier League 551 (para.35)
6th Comp. Rep. (paras 114–116)
16th Comp. Rep. (paras 41–42)
23rd Comp. Rep. (para.189–191)
SEP T–39/90R
Mannesmann T–112/98 (paras 85–88)
⋆Spanish Banks C–67/91
Dalmine T–50/00 (grounds 84–85)
SEP C–36/92P

4. Notice on co-operation within the Network of Competition Authorities [2004] O.J. C101/43

B. NATIONAL JURISDICTIONS

1. Direct effect of Articles 81 and 82

Tetra Pak T–51/89 (grounds 40–42)
Automec v Commission II T–24/90
BEMIM T–114/92 (ground 62)
Tremblay T–5/93 (ground 59)
Bosch v De Geus C–13/61
BRT v SABAM I C–127/73 (ground 16)
Ahmed Saeed v Zentrale C–66/86
⋆Van Shijndel T–430/93
Application des Gaz SA v Falks Veritas Ltd. [1974] C.M.L.R. 75 at 84
Garden Cottage Foods Ltd. v Milk Marketing Board ([1982] A.C. 130; [1983] 2 All E.R. 770)

2. Conflict rules

2.1. General

Chaufourniers 20
Fireplaces 90
Bronbemaling 95
AOIP/Beyrard 98
VBBB/VBVB 169 (para.33)
VBA 288 (para.168)
Stichting Kraanverhuur 382 (paras 14–15)
13th Comp. Rep. (paras 217–218)
De Haecht v Wilkin II C–48/72 (grounds 10–13)
⋆BRT v SABAM I C–127/73 (grounds 20–23)
Procureur v Gueralin C–253/78 (ground 13)
Anne Marty v Estée Lauder C–37/79 (grounds 5–10, 14)
Lancôme v Etos C–99/79 (grounds 6–11)
L'Oréal v De Nieuwe AMCK C–31/80 (grounds 7–12)
VBVB & VBBB C–43/82 (ground 5)
⋆Delimitis v Henninger Bräu C–234/89 (grounds 43–55)
Otto C–60/92 (grounds 18–20)
Gøttrup-Klim v DLG C–250/92 (grounds 58–59)
Dijkstra C–319/93 (grounds 25–36)

2.2. Provisional validity for old agreements

Julien/Van Katwijk 32
Velcro/Aplix 233
Bosch v De Geus C–13/61
Portelange v Smith Corona C–10/69

Bilger v Jehle C–43/69 (grounds 4–6)
Parfums Rochas v Bitsch C–1/70 (grounds 6–7)
★De Haecht v Wilkin II C–48/72 (ground 9)
De Bloos v Boyer C–59/77 (grounds 8–15)
Boekhandels v Eldi Records C–106/79 (grounds 8–11)
Lancôme v Etos C–99/79 (grounds 12–18)
★Nouvelles Frontières C–209/84 (grounds 61–69)
Ahmed Saeed v Zentrale C–66/86 (grounds 5, 21, 32–33)
Delimitis v Henninger Bräu C–234/89 (grounds 48–49)

3. Commission desire to encourage national enforcement of Articles 81 and 82

3.1. Notice on the co-operation between the Commission and the courts of the EU Member States in the application of Articles 81 and 82 EC [2004] O.J. C101/54

3.2. Cases

ECS/AKZO-Interim Measures 197 (paras 6, 35)
Van den Bergh Foods 431 (paras 1–7)
German Postal Law 541 (paras 142–143)
★Clutch-type disc brakes 8th Comp. Rep. (para.121)
13th Comp. Rep. (paras 217–218)
15th Comp. Rep. (paras 38–43)
20th Comp. Rep. (para.4)
21st Comp. Rep. (paras 69–70)
New Focus Health Care 21st Comp. Rep. (page 333)
22nd Comp. Rep
SACEM 22nd Comp. Rep. (page 423)
Howden 22nd Comp. Rep. (page 423)
23rd Comp. Rep. (paras 189–191)
24th Comp. Rep. (paras 40–52)
25th Comp. Rep. (paras 92–95)
Postbank T–353/94R
BEMIM T–114/92 (grounds 62–94, see in particular 89)
Tremblay T–145/89 (grounds 59–75, see in particular 69)
Koelman T–575/93 (grounds 41–43)
Postbank T–353/94
Leclerc T–19/92 (grounds 124–130)
Leclerc T–88/92 (grounds 118–123)
Van der Wal T–83/96
★Delimitis v Henninger Bräu C–234/89 (ground 53)
Dijkstra C–319/93 (ground 34)
Van Shijndel C–430/93
Tremblay C–91/95P (ground 41)
Van der Wal C–174/98 (grounds 17–33)
Masterfoods C–344/98 (grounds 45–60)

4. Damages for breach of competition rules

Garden Cottage Foods Ltd v Milk Marketing Board [1982] A.C. 130; [1983] 2 All E.R. 770
Atlantic Container Line T–395/94 (ground 414)
Courage C–453/99

5. National procedural rules limiting application of competition law

Eco Swiss C–126/97

[For the tables of case citations see Tables 1 to 4, 11 and 12 at the back of the book.]

PART XI

RELATIONS WITH OTHER AREAS OF LAW

CHAPTER 1

RELATIONS WITH OTHER EC LAWS

1. Anti-dumping law

Scottish Salmon 358 (paras 12, 19)
Poudres Sphériques T–5/97 (grounds 211–218)
⋆Extramet v Council C–358/89

2. Free circulation law

World Cup Football 360 (paras 109–120)
ZERA 374 (para.126)
Whitbread 439
Asia Motor France II T–7/92 (grounds 62–73)
Meca-Medina T–313/02
Sirena v Eda C–40/70
Terrapin v Terranova C–119/75
⋆CMC Motorrad C–93/92
⋆Mars C–470/93

3. State aid

Ford/Volkswagen 367
Jahrhundvertrag 370 (paras 17–18, 44)
Cement 394 (paras 53)
Matra T–17/93 (grounds 44–48)
Weyl Beef T–197/97 (grounds 75–77)
⋆Matra C–255/91
Banco de Credito v Valencia C–387/92

4. Environmental law

VOTOB 22nd Comp. Rep. (paras 177–186)
Spa Monopole 23rd Comp. Rep. (para.240)
Oliebranches 24th Comp. Rep. (page 368)
25th Comp. Rep. (paras 83–85)

5. ECSC Treaty

Concrete Reinforcing Bars 32nd Comp. Rep. (paras 56–60)
Ferrière Nord T–143/89 (grounds 63–65)
Banks v British Coal C–128/92

6. Trade policy

Asia Motor France T–7/92
BEUC T–37/92

7. Charter of Fundamental Rights

French Beef 513 (paras 109–117)
JCB Service T–67/01 (grounds 36 ff)
Tokai Carbon et al. T–236e.s./01 (ground 137)
JFE Engineering T–67e.s./00 (ground 178)
Sumitomo T–22/02 (ground 103)
Danone T–38/02 (ground 216)
Degussa T–279/02 (ground 115)

CHAPTER 2

NATIONAL LAW

1. Supremacy of EC competition law over national law in general

Grundig/Consten 5
CNSD 375 (paras 42–44)
Grundig 378 (paras 12, 22, 25, 27)
Van den Bergh Foods 431 (paras 211–229)
1st Comp. Rep. (para.129)
4th Comp. Rep. (paras 43–47)
Sotralentz T–149/89 (grounds 26–30)
Costa v ENEL C–6/64
⋆Walt Wilhelm C–14/68
Fire Insurance C–45/85 (grounds 22–24)
Metro v Cartier C–376/92 (grounds 25–28)
⋆Fiammiferi C–198/01

2. Supremacy of EC law over national competition rules

Dyestuffs 27
Centraal Bureau voor de Rijwielhandel 118
SSI 181 (para.101)
Fire Insurance 220 (para.28)
Net Book Agreements 301 (para.43)
Welded Steel Mesh 311 (para.206)
2nd Comp. Rep. (para.27)

[For the tables of case citations see Tables 1 to 4, 11 and 12 at the back of the book.]

4th Comp. Rep. (paras 43–47)
Pilkington v BSN 10th Comp. Rep. (paras 152–154)
JCB Service T–67/01 (ground 93)
★Walt Wilhelm C–14/68
Procureur v Guerlain C–253/78 (grounds 14–19)
CICCE C–298/83 (grounds 26–27)
Spanish Banks C–67/91
Mörlins C–134/92
★Oscar Bronner C–7/97

3. National property law

Article 295 EC
VBA 288
AstraZeneca 454 (para. 741)
Vanden Bergh Foods T–65/98 (grounds 170–173)
★Consten & Grundig C–56/64
Italy C–32/65 (ground 22)
Portugal C–163/99 (grounds 58–59)

4. National defence interests

Articles 296(b), 297 EC
SNPE/LEL 132
WANO 138

5. National social security legislation

Albany C–67/96
Brentjens C–115/97
Drijvende bokken C–219/97
Pavlov C–180/98 (grounds 59–70, 98)
Van der Woude C–222/95 (grounds 22–32)

CHAPTER 3

INTERNATIONAL LAW

A. GENERAL

British Telecommunications 188 (para.43)
Woodpulp 227 (paras 78–80)
French African Shipping 353 (paras 33, 37)
Railway Tickets 362 (paras 85–90)
CEWAL 371 (paras 68–69)
Transatlantic 393A
Eurocontrol 532 (paras 21–24)
2nd Comp. Rep (paras 4–6)
RTE T–69/89 (grounds 102–104)
BBC T–40/89 (grounds 76–79)
ITV T–76/89 (grounds 75–77)
Gencor T–102/96
Specialty Graphite T–71e.s./03 (grounds 112–116)
Consten & Grundig C–56/64
National Panasonic C–136/79 (grounds 17–23)
FEDETAB C–209/78 (ground 81)
AM & S C–155/79
VBVB & VBBB C–43/82 (grounds 34–37)
Woodpulp C–89/85
Italy C–41/83 (ground 40)
Orkem C–374/87 (ground 30)
RTE C–241/91P (grounds 83–87)

B. EUROPEAN CONVENTION ON HUMAN RIGHTS

1. Selected Articles

Article 6: Right to a Fair and Public Hearing

1. In the determination of his civil rights and obligations or of any criminal charge against him, everyone is entitled to a fair and public hearing within a reasonable time by an independent and impartial tribunal established by law. Judgement shall be pronounced publicly but the press and public may be excluded from all or part of the trial in the interest of morals, public order or national security in a democratic society, where the interests of juveniles or the protection of the private life of the parties so require, or to the extent strictly necessary in the opinion of the court in special circumstances where publicity would prejudice the interests of justice.
2. Everyone charged with a criminal offence shall be presumed innocent until proved guilty according to law.
3. Everyone charged with a criminal offence has the following minimum rights:
   (a) to be informed promptly, in a language which he understands and in detail, of the nature and cause of the accusation against him;
   (b) to have adequate time and facilities for the preparation of his defence;

(c) to defend himself in person or through legal assistance of his own choosing or, if he has not sufficient means to pay for legal assistance, to be given it free when the interests of justice so require;
(d) to examine or have examined witnesses on his behalf under the same conditions as witnesses against him;
(e) to have the free assistance of an interpreter if he cannot understand or speak the language used in court.

Article 7: Freedom From Retrospective

Effect of Penal Legislation

1. No one shall be held guilty of any criminal offence on account of any act or omission which did not constitute a criminal offence under national or international law at the time when it was committed. Nor shall a heavier penalty be imposed than the one that was applicable at the time the criminal offence was committed.
2. This Article shall not prejudice the trial and punishment of any person for any act or omission which, at the time when it was committed, was criminal according to the general principles of law recognised by civilised nations.

Article 8: Right to Respect for Privacy

1. Everyone has the right to respect for his private and family life, his home and his correspondence.
2. There shall be no interference by a public authority with the exercise of this right except such as in accordance with the law and is necessary in a democratic society in the interests of national security, public safety or the economic well-being of the country, for the prevention of disorder or crime, for the protection of health or morals, or for the protection of the rights and freedoms of others.

Article 10: Freedom of Expression

1. Everyone has the right to freedom of expression. This right shall include freedom to hold opinions and to receive and impart information and ideas without interference by public authority and regardless of frontiers. This Article shall not prevent States from requiring the licensing of broadcasting, television or cinema enterprises.
2. The exercise of these freedoms, since it carries with it duties and responsibilities, may be subject to such formalities, conditions, restrictions or penalties as are prescribed by law and are necessary in a democratic society, in the interests of national security, territorial integrity or public safety, for the prevention of disorder or crime, for the protection of health or morals, for the protection of the reputation or rights of others, for preventing the disclosure of information received in confidence, or for maintaining the authority and impartiality of the judiciary.

Article 11: Freedom of Association and Assembly

1. Everyone has the right to freedom of peaceful assembly and to freedom of association with others, including the right to form and to join trade-unions for the protection of his interests.
2. No restrictions shall be placed on the exercise of these rights other than such as prescribed by law and are necessary in a democratic society in the interests of national security or public safety, for the prevention of disorder or crime, for the protection of health or morals or for the protection of the rights and freedoms of others. This Article shall not prevent the imposition of lawful restrictions on the exercise of the administration of the State.

2. Cases

2.1. Community cases

Montedipe v Commission T–14/89 (para.319)
Mayr-Melnhof Kartongesellschaft T–347/94 (grounds 309–316)
Enso Espanola T–348/94 (grounds 55–65)
Siderurgica T–175h, T–156/94 (grounds 95–105)
PVC II T–305e.s./94
Mannesmann T–112/98 (grounds 59–60)
ADM & ADM Ingredients T–224/00 (grounds 91 & 339–341)
Cheil Yedang T–220/00 (ground 43)
Tokai Carbon et al. T–236e.s./01 (grounds 134–135 & 402–412)
JFE Engineering T–67e.s./00 (ground 178)

[For the tables of case citations see Tables 1 to 4, 11 and 12 at the back of the book.]

Sumitomo T–22/02 (grounds 103–110)
Danone T–38/02 (ground 216)
Heubach T–64/02 (grounds 205–210)
Degussa T–279/02 (grounds 66–84, 115, 395, 411)
National Panasonic C–136/79 (ground 17)
Fedetab C–209/78 (grounds 79–81)
Pioneer C–100/80 (grounds 6–7)
VBVB & VBBB C–43/82 (grounds 21, 32, 33)
Cinéthèque C–60/84 (ground 25)
Stanley Adams C–145/83 (ground 19, 45)
AKZO v Commission II C–5/85 (ground 25, 27)
Bond van Adverteerders C–352/85 (grounds 2, 40)
Hoechst v Commission III C–46/87 (ground 13, 18)
Dow Benelux C–85/87 (grounds 24, 29)
Dow Iberica C–97/87 (grounds 10, 15)
Orkem C–374/87 (grounds 18, 30)
ERT v DEP C–260/89 (grounds 42–45)
Otto C–60/92 (grounds 11–12)
Baustahlgewebe C–185/95P
Van der Wal C–174/98 (grounds 17–33)
Roquette C–94/00
Aalborg Portland C–204e.s./00P (grounds 63–67 & 200)
Dansk Rørindustri C–189e.a./02P (grounds 65–71, 202, 215–219)
Archer Daniels Midland C–397/03 (grounds 15–26)

2.2. Strasbourg cases

SA Stenuit v France, Report of Commission No. 11598/85, 11.7.89, Series A, No. 232A.
CM & Co v Germany, Decision of Commission No. 1258/87, 9.2.90.
Niemitz v Germany, Judgment of Court, Series A, No. 251B, 16.12.93.
Funke v France, Judgment of Court, Series A, No. 256A, 25.2.93.
Lentia v Austria, Series A, No. 276, 24.11.93.
Bendenoun v France, Series A, No. 284, 24.2.94.
Société Colas Est and Others v France, No. 37971/97, ECHR 2002–111

C. AGREEMENTS CONCLUDED BY THE COMMUNITY

1. Co-operation Agreements EC-USA

1.1. Agreements

1.1.1. First Agreement

1.1.2. Second Agreement

1.1.3. Exchange of interpretative letters

1.2. Comments

22nd Comp. Rep. (paras 109–111, p.554)
France C–327/91

2.1. Decision of the Council and the Commission of April 1995 concerning the conclusion of the Agreement between the European Communities and the Government of the United States of America regarding the application of their competition laws 95/145/EC, ECSC, [1995] O.J. L95/45, [1995] O.J. L131/38)

2.2. Decision of the Council and the Commission of May 29, 1998 concerning the conclusion of the Agreement between the European Communities and the Government of the United States of America on the application of positive comity principles in the enforcement of their competition laws 98/386/EC, ECSC [1998] O.J. L173/26

2.3. Agreement between the European Communities and the Government of the United States of America on the application of positive comity principles in the enforcement of their competition laws [1998] O.J. L173/28

2.4. Agreement between the European Communities and the Government of Canada regarding the application of their competition laws [1999] O.J. L175/50

2.5. Agreement between the EC and the Government of Japan on co-operation regarding anti-competitive activities

3. European Economic Area

[For the tables of case citations see Tables 1 to 4, 11 and 12 at the back of the book.]

3.1. Comments

20th Comp. Rep. (para.15)
21st Comp. Rep. (paras 59–61)
22nd Comp. Rep. (paras 86–99)

3.2. Commission Regulation 3666/93 of December 15, 1993 amending Regulation 27 and Regulations 1629/69, 4260/88, 4261/88 and 2367/90 with a view to implementing the competition provisions laid down in the Agreement on the European Economic Area [1993] O.J. L336/1

3.3. Cases

TFB [1997] O.J. L284/91
NSF [1997] O.J. L284/69
Jaeger v Opel Norge E–3/97 1.4.1998
Mag Instrument/California Trading E–2/97 3.12.1997
Seamless Steel Tubes 499 (paras 118–120)
Austrian Banks 503 (paras 401–406)
Methionine 504 (paras 224–227)
Christie's/Sotheby's 506 (paras 138–143, 181–184)
Methylglucamine 508 (paras 194–197)
Food Flavour Enhancers 509 (paras 183–186)
Specialty Graphite 510 (paras 314–318, 360–363)
Organic Peroxides 524 (paras 287–293, 368–372)
Choline Chloride 543 (paras 122–125)
JFE Engineering T–67e.s./00 (grounds 482–492)
Dalmine T–50/00 (grounds 103–107)

[For the tables of case citations see Tables 1 to 4, 11 and 12 at the back of the book.]

BOOK TWO

MERGERS

BOOK TWO—CONTENTS

Chapters

USER GUIDE

Book Two is divided into five Chapters, each of which is further subdivided into headings. For example in Chapter 2, which covers questions of Jurisdiction, heading A deals with the concept of a concentration, heading B with the concept of Community dimension, and heading E with Article 9 referrals.

Each case or judgment bears its *official case number* next to it. Users should therefore be able to either move straight from the digest to an online search for the full text of the case/judgment or can consult the corresponding Tables to find its full reference.

The most important or interesting cases are marked with an asterisk.

CHAPTER 1

LEGISLATION

See table 12 at the back of the book.

CHAPTER 2

JURISDICTION: CASES AND REFERENCES

A. CONCENTRATION

1. Definition of the term "concentration" (control)

Article 3, Regulation 139/2004
Consolidated Jurisdictional Notice (paras 7–35)
Renault/Volvo M.4 (para.2)
★Arjomari/Wiggins Teape M.25 (para.4)
MBB/Aerospatiale M.17 (para.1)
CONAGRA/IDEA M.10 (paras 5–14)
Pechiney-Usinor/Saciller M.97 (paras 3–8)
ELF/Enterprise M.88 (paras 3–4)
★Eridania/ISI M.62 (paras 3–5)
Lucas/Eaton M.149 (paras 6–9)
★Ingersoll Rand/Dresser M.121 (para.8)
Mediobanca/Generali M.159 (paras 6–11)
Gambogi/Cogei M.167 (paras 5–8)
Sunrise M.176 (paras 15–17)
Costa Crociere/Chargeus Accor M.334 (paras 5–7)
★Société Générale de Belgique/Générale de Banque M.343 (paras 6–14)
British Telecom/MCI M.353 (paras 15–17)
Arvin/Sogefi M.360 (paras 7–9)
Knorr-Bremse/Allied Signal M.337 (para.8)
Abertis/Autostrade M.4249 (paras 8–12)

2. Mergers

2.1. De jure merger

Notice on concentration (para.6)
Consolidated Jurisdictional Notice (para.10)

2.2. De facto merger

2.2.1. Creation of a single economic unit

Notice on concentration (para.7)
Consolidated Jurisdictional Notice (para.10)
RTZ/CRA M.660 (paras 8–9)
Price Waterhouse/Coopers & Lybrand M.1016 (paras 7–17)
Ernst & Young France/Andersen France M.2816 (paras 23–25)
Sonae industria/Tarkett/JV M.4048 (para.8)
Atos Origing/Banksys/BCC M.4316 (paras 6–9)

2.2.2. Common single management

Notice on concentration (para.7)
Consolidated Jurisdictional Notice (para.10)

2.2.3. Other factors

Notice on concentration (para.7)

3. Acquisitions

3.1. Underlying concept: definition of the term "control" (de jure or de facto)

Notice on concentration (paras 8–12)
Consolidated Jurisdictional Notice (paras 11–13, 16–23)

3.2. Sole control

Notice on concentration (paras 13–17)
Consolidated Jurisdictional Notice (para.54–61)
SITA-RPC/Scori M.295 (paras 8–11)

3.2.1. Acquisition of majority of shares

Notice on concentration (para.13)
Consolidated Jurisdictional Notice (para.56)

3.2.2. Specific rights attached to minority shareholding

Notice on concentration (para.14)
Consolidated Jurisdictional Notice (para.57)
Ford/Hertz M.397

3.2.3. Majority of votes at shareholders' meetings

Notice on concentration (para.14)
Consolidated Jurisdictional Notice (para.59)
★Arjomari/Wiggins Teape M.25 (para.4)
Mediobanca/Generali M.159 (paras 6–11)
Solvay-Laporte/Interox M.197 (paras 9–13)
★Société Générale de Belgique/Générale de Banque M.343 (paras 6–14)
★Jefferson/Smurfitt/Munksjo M.613 (paras 4–7)
CGER/SNCI M.643 (para.5)
★Coca-Cola/Amalgamated Beverages GB M.794 (para.5–13)
Mannesmann/Vallourec M.906 (paras 11–20)

MERGERS: JURISDICTION

[For the tables of case citations see Tables 5 to 8 and 12 at the back of the book.]

★Ameritech/Tele Danmark M.1046 (para.4)
Alliance Unichem plc/Safa Galenica SA M.1243
Skanska/Scancem M.1157 (paras 14–16)
Elkem/Sapa M.2404 (paras 3–7)

3.2.4. Contractual right to manage the company

Notice on concentration (para.14)
Consolidated Jurisdictional Notice (para.61)
★CCIE/GTE M.258 (paras 6–12)
Fortis/CGER M.342 (paras 7, 11)
Renault/Nissan M.1519 (paras 8–14)
Siemens/Dematic/VDO/Sachs M.2059 (paras 13–38)
Bosch/Rexroth M.2060 (paras 10–12)
Celsa/Fundia M.4225 (para.6)

3.2.5. Sole shareholder with ability to veto strategic decisions

Notice on concentration (para.39)
Consolidated Jurisdictional Notice (para. 58)
Pepsico/General Mills M.232 (paras 7–8)
General Re/Kölnische Rück M.491 (paras 6–9)
★Albacom M.604 (paras 7–19)
Renault/Nissan M.1519 (para.7)
Nabisco/United Biscuit M.1920 (para.5)
Civen/Angel Street M.2777 (para.8)

3.2.6. Economic dependency

Notice on concentration (para.9)
Consolidated Jurisdictional Notice (para.20)
Blokker/Toys "R" Us M.890 (para.15)

3.3. Acquiring control via holding/management companies ("hidden control")

Notice on concentration (para.10)
Consolidated Jurisdictional Notice (para.13)
Nomura/Blueslate M.1037 (paras 6–7)
TPG/Technologistica M.1500 (para.5)
Rhodia/Donau Chemie/Albright & Wilson M.1517 (paras 7–11)
Industri Kapital (Nordkem)/Dyno M.1813 (paras 9–12)

3.4. Acquisition of part of an undertaking

Notice on concentration (para.11)
Consolidated Jurisdictional Notice (paras 24–27)

3.4.1. Outsourcing of in-house activities

Consolidated Jurisdictional Notice (paras 25–27)

3.5. Acquisition of assets

Notice on concentration (para.11)
Consolidated Jurisdictional Notice (paras 24–27)
E.ON/TXU Europe Group M.3007 (para.1)
Arvin Meritor/Volvo (Assets) M.3351 (para.3)
Flextronics/Nortel M.3583 (para.4)
Société Générale/Ford Lease Business Partner M.3969 (para.5)

3.6. Passive acquisition

Consolidated Jurisdictional Notice (para.21)
RTL/M6 M.3330 (paras 7–12)

3.7. Interrelated transactions

Recital 20 Regulation 139/2004
Consolidated Jurisdictional Notice (paras 36–50)
Gencor/Shell IV/M.470 (para.7)
Total/Gaz de France M.3410 (para.7)
Lóreal/Procasa/Cosmetique Iberica/Albesa M.957 (paras 4–5)
Textron/Kautex IV/M.861 (para.4)
Sonae industria/Tarkett/JV M.4048 (para.9)
Cinven/Warburg Pincus/Casema/Multikabel M.4338 (paras 5–11)
Smithfield/Oaktree/Sara Lee Foods Europe M.4257 (paras 7–13)
En+/Glencore/Sual/UC Rusal M.4441 (para.8)
★Cementbouw Handel T–282/02 (grounds 104–119)
★LGI/Telenet M.4521 (paras 6–20)

4. Joint ventures: joint control

4.1. Definition of joint control: joint strategic decision making

Notice on concentration (para.18–19)
Consolidated Jurisdictional Notice (paras 62–82)
Cementbouw Handel T–282/02 (grounds 54–59)

4.2. Equality in voting/decision making

Notice on concentration (para.20)
Consolidated Jurisdictional Notice (para.64)

[For the tables of case citations see Tables 5 to 8 and 12 at the back of the book.]

UAP/Transatlantic/Sunlife M.141 (paras 7–10)
Leisureplan M.662 (para.7)

4.3. De jure veto rights over strategic decisions (usually by agreement)

Notice on concentration (paras 21–29)
Consolidated Jurisdictional Notice (paras 65–73)
Renault/Volvo M.4 (paras 5–7)
★CONAGRA/IDEA M.10 (paras 5–14)
ELF/Enterprise M.88 (paras 3–8)
★Eridania/ISI M.62 (paras 3–5)
Lucas/Eaton M.149 (paras 6–9)
★Ingersoll Rand/Dresser M.121 (para.8)
Gambogi/Cogei M.167 (paras 5–8)
Ericsson/Ascom M.236 (paras 9–10)
Thomas Cook/LTU/West LB M.229 (paras 7–11)
Elf Atochem/Rohm & Haas M.160 (paras 6–8)
Linde AG/Fiat M.256 (para.5)
Air France/Sabena M.157 (paras 7–11)
★Philips/Thompson/SAGEM M.293 (paras 8–11)
SITA-RPE/Scori M.295 (paras 8–11)
★Fletcher Challenge/Methanex M.331 (paras 6–12)
Harrisons & Crosfield/AKZO M.310 (paras 5–8)
Dasa/Fokker M.237 (paras 4–6)
Kali-Salz/MDK/Treuhand M.308 (para.7)
CWB/Goldman Sachs/Tarkett M.395 (para.7)
Newspaper Publishing M.423 (paras 8–9)
GE/ENI/Nuovo Pignone M.440 (paras 6–9)
Sidmar/Köckner M.444 (paras 7–9)
Elf Atochem/Rütgers M.442 (paras 7–8)
Nordic Capital/Transpool M.625 (para.16)
★Albacom M.604 (paras 7–19)
Channel Five M.673 (paras 8–14)
Hermes Europe/Railtel M.683 (paras 7–12)
Saint Gobain/Wacker Chemie/NOM M.774 (para.11)
Birmingham International Airport M.786 (paras 8–10)
BT/Tele DK/SBB/Migros/UBS M.900 (para.11)
Mederic/Urrpimmec/CRI/Munich Re M.949 (para.7)
OBS! Danmark M.998 (para.9)
★Albacom/BT/ENI/Mediaset M.975 (paras 10–12)
Cummins/Wärtsilä M.1015 (para.5)
Mannesmann/Olivetti/Infostrada M.1025 (paras 12–13)
Alcatel/Thomson SA-Thomson CSF M.1121 (paras 13–14)
Westdeutsche Landesbank/Carlson/Thomas Cook M.1341 (para.5)
Carrier Corporation/Toshiba M.1433 (paras 8–9)
Pirelli/Edizione/Olivetti/Telecom Italia M.2574 (paras 12–26)
Fortis/BCP M.3556 (paras 7–14)
Gencor T–106/96 (grounds 176–194)
Cementbouw Handel T–282/02 (grounds 70–75)
Toshiba/Westinghouse M.4153 (paras 76–80)
Alfa Acciai/Cronimet/Remondis/TSR Group M.4495 (paras 8–10)

4.4. De facto veto rights over strategic decisions

Ford/Hertz M.397
Nordic Capital/Transpool M.625 (para.16)
★Albacom M.604 (paras 7–19)
RTL/Veronica/Endemol M.553 (paras 10–13)
Channel Five M.673 (paras 8–14)
Lockheed Martin/Loral M.697 (para.6)
KLM/Air UK M.967 (paras 8–17)
SAir Group/LTU M.1354 (paras 8–10)
Endemol T–221/95 (paras 148–164)

4.5. Joint exercise of voting rights by minority shareholders (through common interest, agreement or common mandated manager)

Notice on concentration (paras 30–35)
Consolidated Jurisdictional Notice (paras 74–80)
TNT/Canada Post M.102 (para.12)
★Fletcher Challenge/Methanex M.331 (paras 6–12)
Costa Crociere/Chargeus Accor M.334 (paras 5–7)
★Philips/Grundig M.382 (para.14)
Nordic Capital/Apax Industri M.1026 (paras 4–8)
Nordic Capital/Mölnlycke Clinical/Kolmi M.1075 (paras 2–5)
NEC/Bull/PBN M.1095 (para.5)
Nordic Capital/Hilding Anders M.1357

4.6. One parent company exercises day-to-day management of JV

Notice on concentration (para.36)
Consolidated Jurisdictional Notice (para.81)
★Ingersoll Rand/Dresser M.121 (para.8)
Shell/Montecatini M.269 (para.10)

[For the tables of case citations see Tables 5 to 8 and 12 at the back of the book.]

★Unisource/Telefonica M.544 (paras 5–14)
Arcelor/Oyak/Erdemir M.4085 (paras 10–14)
Gencor T–106/96 (grounds 171–175)

4.7. Both parents provide contribution to JV vital to its success

Consolidated Jurisdictional Notice (paras 95–102)
RTL/Veronica/Endemol M.553 (paras 10–13)
★Albacom/BT/ENI/Mediaset M.975 (para.12)

4.8. Joint control for an initial period only

Notice on concentration (para.38)
Consolidated Jurisdictional Notice (para.34)
Kali-Salz/MDK/Treuhand M.308 (para.7)
★Banco Santander/BT M.425 (paras 1–22)
★GE/ENI/Nuovo Pignone M.440 (paras 6–9)
★Albacom M.604 (paras 7–19)
Promodes/S21/Gruppo GS M.1086 (paras 7–8)
Smurfit Condat/CVC M.1319

4.9. Joint control following initial "running-in" period of sole control

Prudential/HSBC/Finnish Chemicals M.883 (para.11)
LGV/BTR M.1054 (paras 9–11)

4.10. Change in identity of parties sharing joint control in an existing JV

Notice on concentration (para.40)
Notice on 'undertakings concerned' (paras 33–45)
Consolidated Jurisdictional Notice (para. 87–88)
CAMPSA M.138 (paras 8–9)
★SolvayLaporte/Interox M.197 (paras 14–19)
★Avesta II M.452
Warner Bros./Lusomundo/Sogecable M.902 (paras 6–8, 13)
British Steel/Europipe M.1014 (para.61)
BellSouth/Vodafone (E-Plus) M.1817 (para.7)
CLT-UFA/Canal+Vox M.1889 (paras 9–10)
Vodafone/BT/Airtel JV M.1863 (paras 7–11)

4.11. Change in quality of control

Consolidated Jurisdictional Notice (paras 83–88)
Vodafone/BT/Airtel M.1863 (paras 7–11)
Umicore/Zinifex/Neptune M.4450 (paras 8–9)

4.12. Financing and commercial agreements do not give control

Consolidated Jurisdictional Notice (para. 20)
★CCIE/GTE M.258 (paras 6–12)
Nomura/Blueslate M.1037 (paras 4–7)

4.13. Member State has right to determine behaviour on public service grounds ("Golden Share")

Notice on concentration (para.37)
Consolidated Jurisdictional Notice (paras 52–53)
Tractebel/Synatom M.466
★Tractebel/Distrigaz M.493 (paras 9–19)

4.14. Other circumstances leading to joint control

Consolidated Jurisdictional Notice (paras 81–82)
Pirelli/Edizione/Olivetti/Telecom Italia M.2574 (paras 12–26)

5. Possibility of "changing alliances" between parents

Consolidated Jurisdictional Notice (para.80)
Eureko M.207 (paras 6–12)
★Koipe-Tabacalera/Elosua M.117 (paras 6–9)
★Philips/Thomson/SAGEM M.293 (paras 8–11)
★Fletcher Challenge/Methanex M.331 (paras 6–12)
★Philips/Grundig M.382 (para.14)
Channel Five M.673 (paras 8–14)

6. Asset swaps

Notice on "undertakings concerned" (paras 49–50)
Consolidated Jurisdictional Notice (paras 17, 41)
Stinnes/BTL M.1056 (paras 5–7)

7. Acquisitions by individuals and management buy-outs

Notice on "undertakings concerned" (paras 51–52)
Consolidated Jurisdictional Notice (para.12)
LGV/BTR M.1054 (paras 9–11)

[For the tables of case citations see Tables 5 to 8 and 12 at the back of the book.]

8. Passage from joint to sole control ("demergers")

Notice on concentration (para.16)
Notice on "undertakings concerned" (paras 46–48)
Notice on "simplified procedure" (para.9)
Consolidated Jurisdictional Notice (paras 41, 89–90, 148)
ICI/Tioxide M.23 (paras 2–47)
Metallgesellschaft/Safic Alcan II M.146 (paras 1–5)
VIAG/Brühl M.139
ABB/BREL M.221 (para.3)
Generali/Central Hispano-Generali M.404
GE/Power Controls M.577 (para.4)
UPM-Kymmene/Finnpap M.871 (para.6)
MAN Roland/Omnigraph (II) M.1448 (paras 4–6)
BP/JV Dissolution M.1820 (para.1)
Mobil/JV-Dissolution M.1822 (para.1)
Sampo/IF Skadeförsäkring M.3395 (paras 16–22)
Vodafone/Airtel M.2469 (paras 11–19)
Deutsche Post/DHL II M.2908 (paras 22–44)

9. Internal restructuring by private companies

Notice on concentration (para.8)
Consolidated Jurisdictional Notice (para.51)
Neste/Ivo M.931

10. State-owned companies (restructuring/concentration)

Notice on concentration (para.8)
Consolidated Jurisdictional Notice (para.52)
⋆Neste/Ivo M.931

11. Option to purchase shares

Notice on concentration (para.15)
Consolidated Jurisdictional Notice (para.60)
British Telecom/MCI M.353 (paras 15–17)
⋆Ford/Hertz M.397
⋆BS/BT M.425
⋆GE/ENI/Nuovo Pignone M.440 (paras 6–9)
Ingersoll Rand/MAN M.479 (para.10)
Tractebel/Distrigaz M.493 (paras 18–19)
Dow Buna M.591 (paras 7–10)
Nordic Capital/Transpool M.625 (para.16)
Albacom M.604 (para.19)
⋆KLM/Air UK M.967 (paras 8–17)
Nomura/Blueslate M.1037 (paras 5–7)
Rhodia/Donau Chemie/Albright & Wilson M.1517 (paras 7–8)
Scottish & Newcastle/Groupe Danone M.1925 (paras 6–7)
Air France T–2/93 (paras 67–72)
Ineos/BP Dormagen M.4094 (paras 7–9)

12. Exceptions

Article 3(5)(a), Regulation 139/2004 Notice on concentration (para.42)
Consolidated Jurisdictional Notice (paras 110–116)

12.1. Acquisition of shares by trading/financial companies

Consolidated Jurisdictional Notice (para.113)
Article 3(5)(a), Regulation 139/2004 Notice on concentration (para.42)

12.2. Liquidation, etc.

Article 3(5)(b), Regulation 139/2004
Notice on concentration (para.43)
Consolidated Jurisdictional Notice (para.112)

12.3. Rescue operations

Notice on concentration (para.45)
Consolidated Jurisdictional Notice (para. 116)

B. COMMUNITY DIMENSION (TURNOVER)

1. Companies taken into account in calculation: definition of control for the purposes of turnover calculation

1.1. Mergers

Notice on "undertakings concerned" (para.12)
Consolidated Jurisdictional Notice (para.132)

1.2. Acquisition by a subsidiary of a group of companies

Notice on "undertakings concerned" (paras 9, 18–20)
Consolidated Jurisdictional Notice (para.135)

1.3. Acquisition of sole control

Notice on "undertakings concerned" (paras 13–17)
Solvay-Laporte/Interox M.197 (paras 9–13)
Consolidated Jurisdictional Notice (paras 134–135)

[For the tables of case citations see Tables 5 to 8 and 12 at the back of the book.]

1.4. Acquisition of joint control

Notice on "undertakings concerned" (paras 21–25)
Consolidated Jurisdictional Notice (paras 139–141)
Article 5(4)–(5), Regulation 139/2004
TNT/Canada Post M.102 (paras 9–11)

1.5. Acquisition of control by a JV ("lifting the veil")

Notice on "understandings concerned" (paras 26–29)
Consolidated Jurisdictional Notice (paras 145–147)
TNT/Canada Post M.102 (paras 9–11)

1.6. Acquisition of part of an undertaking

Article 5(2), Regulation 139/2004
Consolidated Jurisdictional Notice (paras 136–137)
British Airways/Dan Air M.278 (para.6)
Bank of Scotland/Bank of Ireland M.681 (paras 9–15)

1.7. Change from joint to sole control

Notice on "undertakings concerned" (paras 30–32)
Consolidated Jurisdictional Notice (para.138)

1.8. Change in indentity of parties sharing joint control in an existing JV

Notice on "undertakings concerned" (paras 33–45)
Consolidated Jurisdictional Notice (paras 142–144)
PTT Post/TNT M.787 (para.10)

1.9. "Demergers" and the break-up of companies

Notice on "undertakings concerned" (paras 46–48)
Consolidated Jurisdictional Notice (paras 148–150)
⋆Solvay-Laporte/Interox M.197 (paras 14–19)
CAMPSA M.319 (paras 4–10)

1.10. Asset swaps

Notice on "undertakings concerned" (paras 49–50)
Consolidated Jurisdictional Notice (para 148–150)
Du Pont/ICI M.214 (paras 1–5)

1.11. Acquisitions by individuals and management buy-outs

Notice on "undertakings concerned" (paras 51–52)
Consolidated Jurisdictional Notice (paras 151–152)

1.12. Acquisitions by state-owned companies

Notice on "undertakings concerned" (paras 55–56)
Consolidated Jurisdictional Notice (para.153)

2. Turnover calculation

2.1. Underlying concept

Article 5, Regulation 139/2004
Calculation of turnover notice (paras 9–14)
Consolidated Jurisdictional Notice (paras 157–160)

2.2. Turnover thresholds

Article 1(2), Regulation 139/2004
Article 1(3), Regulation 139/2004
Article 1(3)(c), Regulation 139/2004
ICI/Williams M.1167
Agfa-Gevaert/Sterling M.1432 (para.7)
Sanitec/Sphinx M.1578 (para.8)

2.3. "Net" turnover

Consolidated Jurisdictional Notice (para. 164)

2.3.1. Rebates and taxes

Calculation of turnover notice (paras 19–21)
Consolidated Jurisdictional Notice (paras 165–166)

2.3.2. Intra-group turnover

Article 5(1), Regulation 139/2004
Calculation of turnover notice (paras 22–23)
Consolidated Jurisdictional Notice (paras 167–168)
⋆British Airways/TAT (II) M.806 (paras 9–14)

2.3.3. State aid

Calculation of turnover notice (para.16)
Consolidated Jurisdictional Notice (para.162)
Cereol/Continentale Italiana M.156

[For the tables of case citations see Tables 5 to 8 and 12 at the back of the book.]

2.3.4. Turnover generated under contracts to manage assets

Accor/Wagon-Lits M.126 (paras 5–10)

2.3.5. Franchisees

★UBS/Mister Minit M.940 (paras 10–18)

2.4. Which accounts to use?

Calculation of turnover notice (paras 24–29)
Consolidated Jurisdictional Notice (paras 169–174)
Endesa T–417/05 (paras 128–129, 132)

2.5. Services (including airlines)

Calculation of turnover notice (paras 12–13, 17, 45–48)
Consolidated Jurisdictional Notice (paras 199–202)
Delta Airlines/Pan Am M.130 (para.9)
★Air France/Sabena M.157 (paras 17–20)
British Airways/TAT M.259 (para.14)
British Airways/Dan Air M.278 (para.6)
Nomura/Blueslate M.1037 (para.15)

2.6. Staggered operations ("salami operations")

Article 5(2), Regulation 139/2004
Calculation of turnover notice (paras 32–35)
Consolidated Jurisdictional Notice (paras 136–137)
Volvo/Lex II M.261 (para.1)
Alcatel/STC M.366 (paras 1–3)
Norsk Hydro/Enichem Agricoltura Terni (II) M.832 (para.5)
Kingfisher/Grosslabor M.1482 (paras 10–13)
Alcoa/British Aluminium M.2111 (para.6)
Compass/Restorama/Rail Gourmet/Gourmet Nova M.2639 (para.11)
Siemens/Alstom M.3148 (para.6)
Société Générale/Ford Lease-Business Partner M.3969 (paras 5–7)
Cementbouw Handel T–282/02 (grounds 112–122)
Ineos/BP Dormagen M.4094 (para.11)

2.7. Timing of disposal of assets if excluded from turnover calculation

Rhône-Poulenc/Fisons M.632 (paras 9–11)

2.8. Group turnover

Article 5(4), Regulation 139/2004
Calculation of turnover notice (paras 36–42)
Consolidated Jurisdictional Notice (paras 175–184)
Arjomari/Wiggins Teape M.25 (paras 5–7)
Eridania/Isi M.62 (para.6)
Eurocom/RSCG M.147 (paras 5–6)
★Infint/Exor M.187 (paras 7–10)
Nomura/Blueslate M.1037 (paras 13–14)
Arla/Ingman Foods M.4323 (paras 9–10)

2.9. State-owned companies

Calculation of turnover notice (paras 43–44)
Consolidated Jurisdictional Notice (paras 192–194)

2.10. Geographical allocation of turnover

Article 5(1), Regulation 139/2004
Calculation of turnover notice (paras 45–48)
Consolidated Jurisdictional Notice (paras 195–202)
★Alcatel/STC M.366 (paras 7–16)
Ingersoll Rand/Clark Equipment M.560
Boeing/Hughes M.1879 (paras 9–15)
★Air France (DAN AIR) T–3/93 (paras 87–108)

2.11. Conversion into Euros

Calculation of turnover notice (paras 49–50)
Consolidated Jurisdictional Notice (paras 204–205)

2.12. Special cases

2.12.1. Banks and other financial institutions

Article 5(3)(a), Regulation 139/2004
Calculation of turnover notice (paras 51–54)
Consolidated Jurisdictional Notice (paras 210–220)
Torras/Sarrio M.166 (paras 4–7)
★Hong Kong & Shanghai Bank/Midland Bank M.213 (paras 7–12)
GECC/Avis M.234 (paras 6–10)

2.12.2. Leasing companies

Calculation of turnover notice (para.55)
Consolidated Jurisdictional Notice (paras 211–213)

[For the tables of case citations see Tables 5 to 8 and 12 at the back of the book.]

2.12.3. Insurance companies

Article 5(3)(b), Regulation 139/2004
Calculation of turnover notice (paras 56–58)
Consolidated Jurisdictional Notice (paras 214–216)
AG/AMEV M.18 (paras 3–6)
Allianz/DKV M.251 (paras 4–5)
★AGF/Camat M.777

2.12.4. Financial holding companies

Calculation of turnover notice (paras 59–61)
Consolidated Jurisdictional Notice (paras 217–220)

C. CONCENTRATIVE AND CO-OPERATIVE JOINT VENTURES

1. Autonomous Economic Entity

1.1. Full function JV (all assets necessary to carry out independent market role)

Article 3(2), Regulation 139/2004
Consolidated Jurisdictional Notice (paras 91–93)

1.1.1. Own management (commercial policy)

JV Notice (para.12)
Consolidated Jurisdictional Notice (para. 94)
Sanofi/Sterling Drugs M.72 (para.7)
Courtaulds/SNIA M.113 (paras 7–8)
Generali/BCHA M.189 (para.7)
Eucom/Digital M.218 (para.7)
Fortis/La Caixa M.254 (para.4.1)
Mannesmann/Hoesch M.222 (paras 8–9)
Rhône-Poulenc Chimie/Lyonnaise des Eaux M.266 (paras 12–15)
Harrisons & Crosfield/AKZO M.310 (paras 8–14)
Pasteur Merieux/Merck M.285 (paras 14–26, 31)
Rhône-Poulenc/Caffaro M.427 (para.9)
Daimler Benz/RWE M.441 (para.17)
Mederic/Urrpimmec/CRI/Munich Re M.949 (para.8)
Elf/Texaco/Antifreze JV M.1135 (paras 6–8)
Campina/Fonterra JV M.4207 (para.16)

1.1.2. Own resources

JV Notice (para.12)
Consolidated Jurisdictional Notice (para. 94)
Baxter/Nestlé/Salvia M.58 (paras 6–8)
Sanofi/Sterling Drugs M.72 (para.7)
★Draeger/IBM/HMP M.101 (para.5)
ABC/Générale des Eaux/Canal + W.H. Smith M.110 (para.8)
Thompson/Pilkington M.86 (para.8)
UAP/Transatlantic/Sunlife M.141 (para.11)
TNT/Canada Post M.102 (paras 13–15)
★Lucas/Eaton M.149 (paras 11–12)
★Courtaulds/SNIA M.113 (paras 7–9)
BSN/Nestlé/Cokoladovni M.90 (paras 9–10)
★Flachglas/VEGLA JVC M.168
Ericsson/Ascom M.236 (para.11)
Elf Atochem/Rohm & Haas M.160 (para.9)
Péchiney/VIAG M.198 (para.6)
Rhône-Poulenc/SNIA M.206 (para.502)
Avesta/British Steel/NCC M.239 (para.13)
Linde AG/Fiat M.256 (para.6)
Rhône-Poulenc Chimie/Lyonnaise des Eaux M.266 (paras 12–15)
Philips/Thomson/SAGEM M.293 (paras 12–14)
Ericsson/Hewlett Packard M.292 (para.7)
Harrisons & Crosfield/AKZO M.310 (paras 8–14)
Aegon/Scottish Equitable M.349 (paras 9–13)
Pasteur-Merieux/Merck M.285 (paras 14–21, 22–26, 31)
Rhône-Poulenc/SNIA M.355 (para.9)
British Telecom/MCI M.353 (paras 5–7)
Arvin/Sogefi M.360 (para.10)
SNECMA/TI M.368 (para.11)
Mannesmann/Vallourec/Ilva M.315 (paras 7–9)
Rhône-Poulenc/Caffaro M.427 (paras 9–10)
Daimler Benz/RWE M.441 (para.15)
Powergen/NRG/Morrison Knudsen/MIB M.402
Elf Atochem/Rütgers M.442 (paras 10–13)
British Steel/Svensk Stal/VSO M.503 (paras 10–13)
MSG Media Service M.469 (paras 10–13)
ATR/Bae M.551
Unisource/Telefonica M.544
Dow/Dupont M.663 (paras 11–13)
Teneo/Merill Lynch/Bankers Trust M.722 (paras 13–16)
RSB/Tenex/Fuel Logistic M.904 (para.8–13)
Mederic/Urrpimmec/CRI/Munich Re M.949 (para.7)
Merck/Rhône-Poulenc-Merial M.885 (paras 9–22, 83)
Cummins/Wärtsilä M.1015 (para.6)
ENW/Eastern M.1315
Assicurazioni Generali T–87/96
Campina/Fonterra JV M.4207 (para.16)

[For the tables of case citations see Tables 5 to 8 and 12 at the back of the book.]

1.1.3. Need for JV to have access to market

JV Notice (para.13)
Consolidated Jurisdictional Notice (paras 95–96)
Metronet/Infraco M.2694 (para.21)
ECT/PONL/Euromax M.3576 (paras 11–13)

1.1.4. Existence of purchase/supply agreements between parent and JV

1.1.4.1. During start-up period

JV Notice (para.14)
Consolidated Jurisdictional Notice (paras 97–102)
ESPN/Star M.826 (para.6)
BT/NS-Telefort M.855 (para.15)
Valinox/Timet M.917 (paras 17–18, 32–35)
Mederic/Urrpimmec/CRI/Munich Re M.949 (para.9)
Merck/Rhône-Poulenc-Merial M.885 (paras 9–22, 83)
Dupont/Hitachi M.994 (paras 9–12)
Areva/Urenco/ETC JV M.3099 (paras 15–17)

1.1.4.2. Longer-term dependence relationship (no full-function JV)

JV Notice (para.13)
Consolidated Jurisdictional Notice (paras 97–102)
RSB/Tenex/Fuel Logistic M.904 (paras 8–14)

1.1.4.3. Normal long-term commercial activities between parents and JV

JV Notice (paras 13–14)
Consolidated Jurisdictional Notice (paras 97–102)
Lucas/Eaton M.149 (paras 11–12)
Rhône-Poulenc/SNIA M.206 (para.5.2)
Northern Telecom/Matra Communication M.249
Mannesmann/Hoesch M.222 (paras 10–12)
Rhône-Poulenc Chimie/Lyonnaise des Eaux M.266 (paras 12–15)
Sextant/BTG-VDO M.290 (para.12)
⋆Philips/Thomson/SAGEM M.293 (paras 12–14)
SITA-RPC/Scori M.295 (para.12)
Alcan/Inespal/Palco M.322 (para.8)
Harrisons & Crosfield/AKZO M.310 (paras 8–14)
⋆British Telecom/MCI M.353 (paras 5–7)
SNECMA/TI M.368 (para.11)
Mannesmann/Vallourec/Ilva M.315 (para.8)
CGP/GEC/KPR/KONE M.420 (para.11)
Rhône-Poulenc/Caffaro M.427 (paras 10–14)
Schneider/AEG M.447 (para.8)
Vesuvius/Wülfrath M.472 (paras 9–13)
Elf Atochem/Shell Chimie M.475 (paras 12–14)
Cable and Wireless/Schlumberg ER M.532 (para.7)
Texaco/Norsk Hydro M.511 (paras 9–12)
AZKO Nobel/Monsanto M.523 (paras 10–11)
Havas/American Express M.564 (para.12)
EDS/Lufthansa M.584 (para.11)
Dow Buna M.591 (para.11)
Nordic Satellite M.490 (paras 34–38)
Rhône-Poulenc/Engelhard M.615 (paras 9–13)
Unisource/Telefonica M.544 (paras 15–16)
Nokia/Autoliv M.686 (para.7)
Siemens/Lagardere M.685 (para.11)
IP/Reuters M.730 (paras 7–11)
British Gas Trading/Group 4 M.791 (paras 9–11)
Recticel/Greiner M.835 (para.8)
Cereol/Ösat-Ölmühle M.866 (paras 11–12)
Merck/Rhône-Poulenc-Merial M.885 (paras 9–22, 83)
Cummins/Wärtsilä M.1015 (paras 7–8)
AKZO/PLV-EPL M.1049 (paras 8–10)
Fortis/BCP M.3556 (paras 15–18)
Sonae industria/Tarkett/JV M.4048 (para. 9)

1.1.4.4. Supply relationship of de minimis importance

Consolidated Jurisdictional Notice (para. 98)
P&O/Royal Nedlloyd M.831 (para.12)
Valinox/Timet M.917 (paras 17–18, 32–35)
Mezzo/Muzzik M.2550 (paras 15–16)
Adecco/Manpower/Vediorbis/JV M.3419 (paras 8–9)

1.1.4.5. JV as a trading company

JV Notice (para.14)
Consolidated Jurisdictional Notice (para.102)
⋆Agrevo/Marubeni M.788 (paras 8–11)

1.1.4.6. Value added to JV to purchases from parents

JV Notice (para.14)
Consolidated Jurisdictional Notice (para. 98)
Metronet/Infraco M.2694 (para.20)

MERGERS: JURISDICTION

1.1.5. JV exercises activities purely ancillary to those of parents

Consolidated Jurisdictional Notice (paras 95–96)

1.1.5.1. R&D JV

JV Notice (para.13)
Consolidated Jurisdictional Notice (para.95)

1.1.5.2. Production JV

JV Notice (para.13)
Consolidated Jurisdictional Notice (para.95)

1.1.5.3. Joint sales agency

JV Notice (para.13)
Consolidated Jurisdictional Notice (para.96)

1.1.5.4. Real-estate holding JVs

Consolidated Jurisdictional Notice (para.96)

1.2. Structural change must be permanent

1.2.1. Commitment of resources/sunk costs

JV Notice (para.15)
Consolidated Jurisdictional Notice (para.94)
★Baxter/Nestlé/Salvia M.58 (para.6)
Sanofi/Sterling Drugs M.72 (paras 7–8)
Draeger/IBM/HMP M.101 (paras 6–12)
★Lucas/Eaton M.149 (paras 11–12)
BSN/Nestlé/Cokoladovni M.90 (paras 9–10)
Rhône-Poulenc Chimie/Lyonnaise des Eaux M.266 (paras 12–15)
British Airways/TAT M.259 (para.10)
Waste Management/SAE M.283 (para.8)
Aegon/Scottish Equitable M.349 (paras 9–13)
Pasteur Merieux/Merck M.285 (paras 27–28)
Daimler Benz/RWE M.441 (paras 14–17)
Assicurazioni Generali T–87/96

1.2.2. Contingency clause on modification/dissolution of JV

JV Notice (para.15)
Consolidated Jurisdictional Notice (para.103)

1.2.3. JV agreement specifies term of JV

JV Notice (para.15)
Consolidated Jurisdictional Notice (para.104)

1.2.3.1. JV constituted for a lengthy period

JV Notice (para.15)
Mederic/Urrpimmec/CRI/Munich Re M.949 (para.8)

1.2.3.2. Possible prolongation after initial term

JV Notice (para.15)
Consolidated Jurisdictional Notice (para.103)

1.2.3.3. Short fixed period/single project JVs

JV Notice (para.15)
Consolidated Jurisdictional Notice (para.104)
Cereol/Sofiproteol-Saipol M.1125 (para.11)

1.3. Gradual transfer of business to JV

SNECMA/TI M.368 (para.12)
ATR/BAe M.551

2. Co-ordination of competitive behaviour

2.1. Actual competition between parents

Article 2(4), Regulation 139/2004
Baxter/Nestlé/Salvia M.58 (para.8)
Apollinaris/Schweppes M.93 (paras 5–8)
ELF/Enterprise M.88 (paras 6–7)
ABC/Générale des Eaux/Canal + W.H. Smith M.110 (para.9)
★Thomson/Pilkington M.86 (paras 9–10)
UAP/Transatlantic/Sunlife M.141 (para.12)
TNT/Canada Post M.102 (paras 14–17)
★Sunrise M.176 (paras 30–42)
Generali/BCHA M.189 (paras 9–14)
Eureko M.207 (paras 14–16)
Koipe-Tabacalera/Elosua M.117 (paras 10–14)
Rhône-Poulenc/SNIA M.206 (para.5.3)
Avesta/British Steel/NCC M.239 (paras 14–16)
Del Monte/Royal Foods/Anglo-American M.277 (paras 13–21)
Sextant/BTG-VDO M.290 (paras 13–18)
British Telecom/MCI M.353 (para.8)
Bertelsmann/News International/Vox M.489 (para.9)
MSG Media Service M.469 (para.14)
★VOX M.525 (para.12)
Inchcape/Gestetner M.583 (para.10)
★Unisource/Telefonica M.544 (paras 18–26)
BPB/Isover M.735 (paras 11–15)
Elf/Texaco/Antifreze JV M.1135

[For the tables of case citations see Tables 5 to 8 and 12 at the back of the book.]

2.2. Potential competition between parents

Article 2(4), Regulation 139/2004
Mitsubishi/UCAR M.24 (paras 7–8)
Baxter/Nestlé/Salvia M.58 (para.6)
Sanofi/Sterling Drugs M.72 (para.9)
Apollinaris/Schweppes M.93 (para.8)
Draeger/IBM/HMP M.101 (paras 6–12)
ABC/Générale des Eaux/Canal + W.H. Smith M.110 (para.9)
★Thomson/Pilkington M.86 (para.11)
UAP/Transatlantic/Sunlife M.141 (para.15)
★BSN/Nestlé/Cokoladovni M.90 (paras 11–16)
Eureko M.207 (para.16b)
Herba/IRR M.188 (para.10)
Mondi/Frantschach M.210 (para.7)
Eucom/Digital M.218 (para.7)
Ericsson/Ascom M.236 (para.8)
Thomas Cook/LTU/West LB M.229 (para.10)
Elf Atochem/Rohm & Haas M.160 (para.10)
Péchiney/VIAG M.198 (para.8)
Rhône-Poulenc/SNIA M.206 (para.5.3)
Avesta/British Steel/NCC M.239 (paras 14–16)
Linde AG/Fiat M.256 (para.7)
VTG/BPTL M.265
Sextant/BTG-VDO M.290 (paras 13–18)
Ericsson/Hewlett Packard M.292 (para.8)
Thomson/Shorts M.318 (paras 13–14)
Alcan/Inespal/Palco M.322 (para.8)
Harrisons & Crosfield/AKZO M.310 (para.15)
Arvin/Sogefi M.360 (para.12)
Knorr-Bremse/Allied Signal M.337 (para.11)
Synthomer/Yule Catto M.376 (para.9)
ABB/Renault Automation M.409 (para.8)
Philips/Hoechst M.406 (para.4)
Daimler Benz/RWE M.441 (paras 20–22)
British Steel/Svensk Stal/VSO M.503 (para.12)
MSG Media Service M.469 (para.15)
Inchcape/Gestetner M.583 (para.10)
Cable & Wireless/Vebacom M.618 (para.11)
Rhône-Poulenc/Engelhard M.615 (para.13)
BP/Sonatrach M.672 (paras 11–15)
ADSB/Belgacom M.689 (paras 21–27)

2.3. Non-competition clause excludes competition between parents

Baxter/Nestlé/Salvia M.58 (para.10)
★Apollinaris/Schweppes M.93 (para.8)
ABC/Générale des Eaux/Canal + W.H. Smith M.110 (para.9)
UAP/Transatlantic/SunlifeM.141 (para.14–15)
★Lucas/Eaton M.149 (paras 14–19)
Ingersoll Rand/Dresser, M.121 (paras 9–10)
Courtaulds/SNIA M.113 (para.6)
Rhône-Poulenc Chimie/SITA M.266 (para.17)
Matra/Cap Gemini Sogeti M.272 (para.9)
Aegon/Scottish Equitable M.349 (paras 14–15)
Arvin/Sogefi M.360 (para.12)
Rhône-Poulenc/Caffaro M.427 (para.17)
Marconi/Finmeccanica M.496 (para.11)
MSG Media Service M.469 (para.14)
Toepfer/Champagne Cereales M.557 (para.10)
Telenordic/BT/TeleDanmark/Telenor M.565 (para.25)
Burda/Blockbuster M.579 (para.10)
Babcock/Siemens/BS Railcare M.542 (paras 8–9)
Cable & Wireless/Vebacom M.618 (para.11)
★Unisource/Telefonica M.544 (paras 22–23, 27–29)
BT/Tele-DK/SBB/Migros/UBS M.900 (para.17)
Merck/Rhône-Poulenc-Merial M.885 (para.23, 82)
Albacom/BT/ENI/Mediaset M.975 (para.15)
Cummins/Wärtsilä M.1015 (para.4)

2.4. Neighbouring market spill-over

Article 2(4), Regulation 139/2004
Draege/IBM/HMP M.101 (para.11)
ABC/Générale des Eaux/Canal + W.H. Smith M.110 (para.9)
Courtaulds/SNIA M.113 (para.7)
James River/Rayne M.162 (para.4)
Ericsson/Ascom M.236 (paras 16–19)
Avesta/British Steel/NCC M.239 (paras 17–18)
Waste Management/SAE M.283 (paras 9–11)
Sextant/BTG-VDO M.290 (paras 13–18)
Philips/Thomson/SAGEM M.293 (paras 15–19)
Alcan/Inespal/Palco M.322 (paras 9–10)
Harrisons & Crosfield/AKZO M.310 (paras 15–21)
BHF/CCF/Charterhouse M.319 (paras 6–7)
Rhône-Poulenc/SNIA M.355 (para.11)
British Telecom/MCI M.353 (paras 9–12)
Arvin/Sogefi M.360 (para.13)
Knorr-Bremse/Allied Signal M.337 (paras 12–15)
Synthomer/Yule Catto M.376 (paras 9, 12)
SNECMA/TI M.368 (para.13)
Mannesmann/Vallourec/Ilva M.315 (para.10)
Newspaper Publishing M.423 (para.10)
Powergen/NRG/Morrison Knudsen/MIB M.402 (para.7)
Elf Atochem/Rütgers M.442 (para.15)
Vesuvius/Wülfrath M.472 (para.14)
MSG Media Service M.469 (para.16)
Elf Atochem/Shell Chimie M.475 (paras 15, 19–20)

[For the tables of case citations see Tables 5 to 8 and 12 at the back of the book.]

Texaco/Norsk Hydro M.511 (para.13)
Torrington/Ingersoll M.536 (para.9)
Havas Voyage/American Express M.564 (paras 14–16)
EDS/Lufthansa M.560 (para.13)
ADSB/Belgacom M.689 (paras 21–27)
Exxon/DSM M.708 (paras 26–31)
⋆BPB/Isover M.735 (paras 11–15)
IP/Reuters M.730 (paras 12–17)
BP Mobil M.727 (paras 21–22)
BT/Tele DK/SBB/Migros/UBS M.900 (paras 19–20)
Mederic/Urrpimmec/CRI/Munich Re M.949 (para.10)
Merck/Rhône-Poulenc-Merial M.885 (para.26)
Messer Griesheim/Hydrogas M.926 (para.11)
Albacom/BT/ENI/Mediaset M.975 (paras 15–22)
Cummins/Wärtsilä M.1015 (paras 11–12)
BASF/Shell (II) M.1041 (paras 24–30)

2.5. Upstream/downstream market spillover

Article 2(4), Regulation 139/2004
⋆Thomson/Pilkington M.86 (para.12)
UAP/Transatlantic/Sunlife M.141 (paras 16–17)
Sunrise M.176 (paras 30–42)
Elf Atochem/Rohm & Haas M.160 (para.11)
Mannesmann/Hoesch M.222 (paras 13–19)
Alcan/Inespal/Palco M.322 (paras 11–12)
SNECMA/TI M.368 (para.13)
ABB/Renault Automation M.409 (paras 9–10)
CGP/GEC/KPR/KONE M.420 (para.7)
Shell/Montecatini M.269 (paras 14–17
Daimler Benz/RWE M.441 (paras 20–22)
Texaco/Norsk Hydro M.511 (paras 14–17)
Burda/Blockbuster M.579 (para.10)
Nordic Satellite M.490 (paras 49–54)
Ericsson/Ascom II M.676 (para.9)
Emerson/Caterpillar M.700 (para.12)
BT/Tele-DK/SBB/Migros/UBS M.900 (para.19)
Merck/Rhône-Poulenc-Merial M.885 (para.25)
BASF/Shell (II) M.1041 (paras 24–30)

2.6. Actual/potential competition between parents and the JV

⋆BSN/Nestlé/Cokoladovni M.90 (paras 9–10)
Herba/IRR M.188 (para.10)
Mondi/Frantschach M.210 (para.8)
Ericsson/Ascom M.236 (para.15)
Linde AG/Fiat M.256 (para.8)
Ahold/Jeronimo Martins M.263 (paras 4–9)
Waste Management/SAE M.283 (paras 9–11)
British Telecom/MCI M.353 (paras 9–12)
Mannesmann/Vallourec/Ilva M.315 (paras 11–12)
Philips/Hoechst M.406 (para.4)
Newspaper Publishing M.423 (para.10)
Vesuvius/Wülfrath M.472 (para.14)
Bertelsmann/News International/Vox M.489 (para.11)
Swissair/Sabena M.616 (para.14)
Telecom Eireann M.802 (paras 14–15)

2.7. One parent company remains on the same market as the JV

Article 2(4), Regulation 139/2004
Thomson/Pilkington M.86
Ericsson/Ascom M.236 (para.15)
Northern Telecom/Matra Communication M.249
Linde AG/Fiat M.256 (para.8)
⋆Air France/Sabena M.157 (para.14)
⋆Fortis/La Caixa M.254 (para.5.6)
British Airways/TAT M.259 (paras 11–13)
⋆Arvin/Sogefi M.360 (para.12)
Shell/Montecatini M.269 (paras 12–13)
⋆Elf Atochem/Rütgers M.442 (para.17)
Vesuvius/Wülfrath M.472 (para.15)
Marconi/Finmeccanica M.496 (para.12)
Ericsson/Raychem M.519 (para.8)
Mannessmann Demag/Delaval Stork M.535 (para.12)
Cable and Wireless/Schlumberg ER M.532 (para.8)
Siemens/Italtel M.468 (para.13)
Telenordic/BT/TeleDanmark/Telenor M.565 (para.25)
Emerson/Caterpillar M.596 (para.12)
Orkla/Volvo M.582 (paras 17–18)
Exxon/DSM M.708 (para.32)
Cardo/Thyssen M.818 (para.9)
Saint Gobain/Wacker Chemie/NOM M.774 (para.14)
P&O/Royal Nedlloyd M.831 (para.17)
Cereol/Ösat-Ölmühle M.866 (para.9)
BT/Tele-DK/SBB/Migros/UBS M.900 (para.19)
Valinox/Timet M.917 (paras 19–20)
Mederic/Urrpimmec/CRI/Munich Re M.949 (para.10)
Cable & Wireless/Maerska data-Nautec M.951 (para.12)
⋆Norsk Alcoa/Elkem M.723 (paras 10–12)
⋆Albacom/BT/ENI/Mediaset M.975 (para.19)
British Steel/Europipe M.1014 (paras 12–14)

[For the tables of case citations see Tables 5 to 8 and 12 at the back of the book.]

2.8. Spill-over effects must be appreciable

Article 2(4), Regulation 139/2004
Aegon/Scottish Equitable M.349 (para.15)
Toyota/Walter Frey/Toyota M.326 (para.7)
Costa Crociere/Chargeus/Accor M.334 (para.10)
BHF/CCF/Charterhouse M.319 (para.8)
★Knorr-Bremse/Allied Signal M.337 (para.16)
Synthomer/Yule Catto M.376 (paras 9–12)
Mannesmann/Vallourec/Ilva M.315 (para.10)
ABB/Renault Automation M.409 (para.10)
Newspaper Publishing M.423 (para.10)
Siemens/Italtel M.468 (para.13)
Burda/Blockbuster M.579 (para.10)
Inchcape/Gestetner M.583 (para.10)
CGER/SNCI M.643 (para.7)
★ADSB/Belgacom M.689 (paras 21–27)
CEC/Thomson-CSF II M.724 (para.8)
Exxon/DSM M.708 (para.26)
Credit Agricole/Banque Indosuez M.719 (paras 7–11)
Cardo/Thyssen M.818 (para.9)
Telecom Eireann M.802 (para.16)
P&O/Royal Nedlloyd M.831 (paras 17–21)
BT/Tele-DK/SBB/Migros/UBS M.900 (paras 19–20)
CNN/Sogelfa-CIM M.1021 (paras 4–5)
Cereol/Sofiproteol-Saipol M.1125 (paras 14–16)

3. Full-function JVs resulting in the co-ordination of competitive conduct (Article 81 and Merger Regulation)

3.1. Concept

Article 2(4), Regulation 139/2004
Skandia/Storebrand/Pohjola JV21 (paras 32–34)
TXU Europe/EDF-London Investments JV36 (paras 41–42)
Asahi Glass/Mitsubishi/F2 Chemicals JV42 (paras 17–18, 21)
Wegener/PCM/JV M.3817 (para.62)
Boeing/Lockheed Martin/United Launch Alliance JV M.3856 (paras 13–36)
Intracom/Siemens/STI M.2851 (paras 41–44)

3.2. Likelihood of co-ordination

3.2.1. JV will do business with third parties

@ Home Benelux B.V. JV11 (para.38)
Ericsson/Nokia/Psion/Motorola JV12 (para.37)
Bertelsmann/Planeta/Bol Spain JV24 (para.26)
Stora Enso/AssiDomän/JV M.2243 (para.37)

3.2.2. Low competition of parents in the past

Enel/FT/DT JV2 (para.37)
Telefonica/Portugal Telecom/Medi Telecom JV23 (para.29)

3.2.3. Links between parents

Viag/Orange UK JV4 (para.32)
Telefonica/Portugal Telecom/Medi Telecom JV23 (paras 22–24)

3.2.4. Market shares

Telia/Telenor/Schibsted JV1 (para.43)
Ericsson/Nokia/Psion JV6 (paras 35–36)
@ Home Benelux B.V. JV11 (paras 36–40)
Fujitsu/Siemens JV22 (para.62)
Asahi Glass/Mitsubishi/F2 Chemicals JV42 (para.23)
Hitachi/Nec-Dram/JV JV44 (paras 38–39)
Telenor/ErgoGroup/DNB/Accenture JV M.2374 (paras 16–18)

3.2.5. Size and importance of competitors

Fujitsu/Siemens JV22 (para.74)
Asahi Glass/Mitsubishi/F2 Chemicals JV42 (para.22)
Hitachi/Nec-Dram/JV JV44 (para.39)
General Electric/Honeywell M.2220 (paras 174–223, 298–329)

3.2.6. Size of the JV market/size of the parents' market

Telia/Telenor/Schibsted JV1 (para.45)
Telia/Sonera/Lithuanian Telecommunications JV7 (para.30)
Bertelsmann/Planeta/Bol Spain JV24 (para.26)
Lafarge/Readymix JV28 (para.20)

3.2.7. Buying power

Fujitsu/Siemens JV22 (para.57)
Hitachi/Nec-Dram/JV JV44 (para.39)

3.2.8. Low barriers to entry

Telia/Telenor/Schibsted JV1 (para.42)
Sydkraft/Hew/Hansa Energy Trading JV22 (para.26)
Telenor/ErgoGroup/DNB/Accenture - JV M.2374 (para.20)

MERGERS: JURISDICTION

3.2.9. Non-transparent market

Fujitsu/Siemens JV22 (para.57)

3.2.10. Innovation

Fujitsu/Siemens JV22 (para.57)
Hitachi/Nec-Dram/JV JV44 (para.39)

3.2.11. Oligopolistic market

Fujitsu/Siemens JV22 (paras 63–64)

3.2.12. Examples of possible co-ordination

BT/AT&T JV15 (paras 174, 181–187)
Areva/Urenco/ETC JV M.3099 (paras 158–219)

3.3. Appreciable restriction of competition

Cegetel/Canal+/AOL/Bertelsmann JV5 (paras 35–36, 38)
@ Home Benelux B.V. JV11 (paras 36–37)
BT/AT&T JV15 (paras 175, 188–190)
Fujitsu/Siemens JV22 (para.64)

3.4. Effect on trade between Member States

BT/AT&T JV15 (paras 176, 191)
Fujitsu/Siemens JV22 (para.65)

3.5. Causality link

Enel/FT/DT JV2 (para.39)
Cegetel/Canal+/AOL/Bertelsmann JV5 (paras 35–36, 38)
Stora Enso/AssiDomän/JV M.2243 (para.41)

D. RESIDUAL APPLICABILITY OF ARTICLES 81 AND 82

1. Do Articles 81 and 82 still apply to concentrations?

Article 22(2), Regulation 139/2004

2. List of cases relevant to Article 81(1)

Nicholas Frères Vitapro 4
SHV/Chevron 87
Reuter/BASF 107
Nutricia 206
BPCL/ICI 215
Mecaniver/PPG 225
ENI/Montedison 256
GEC-Siemens/Plessey 325
Gillette 361
Ist Comp. Rep. (para.81)
2nd Comp. Rep. (paras 19–20)
3rd Comp. Rep. (paras 22–38)
4th Comp. Rep. (paras 17–18)
★Philip Morris, 14th Comp. Rep. (paras 98–100)
★Carnaud/Sofreb. 17th Comp. Rep. (para.70)
British Airways/British Caledonian 18th Comp. Rep. (para.81)
★Irish Distillers Group 18th Comp. Rep. (para.80)
Carnaud/Metal Box 19th Comp. Rep. (para.69)
Stena-Holder 19th Comp. Rep. (para.70)
KLM/Transavia 21st Comp. Rep. (paras 89–92)
Stora/Feldmhle 21st Comp. Rep.
Remia 42/84
★BAT & Philip Morris 142/84

3. List of cases relevant to Article 82

★Continental Can 46
★Tetra Pak I 289
Metaleurop 321
★Gillette 361
Michelin 165 8th Comp. Rep. (para.146)
Avebe/KSH 8th Comp. Rep. (paras 147–148)
PSA Peugeot-Citroën 8th Comp. Rep. (para.149)
BP-Ruhrgas 9th Comp. Rep. (paras 94–95)
ITA-Tubi 9th Comp. Rep. (paras 126, 127)
Vallourec 9th Comp. Rep. (paras 128, 129)
Kaiser/Estel 9th Comp. Rep. (para.131)
Coats Patons 9th Comp. Rep. (para.132)
Fichtel 9th Comp. Rep. (para.133)
10th Comp. Rep. (paras 150–151)
Pilkington/BSN 10th Comp. Rep. (paras 152–155)
Michelin/Kleber-Colombes 10th Comp. Rep. (para.156)
Baxter Tavenol Labs 10th Comp. Rep. (para.157)
Amicon/Fortia & Wright 11th Comp. Rep. (para.112)
Eagle Star 12th Comp. Rep. (para.103)
British Sugar-Berisford 12th Comp. Rep. (paras 104–106)
British Bright Bar 13th Comp. Rep. (para.160)
Dillingen 13th Comp. Rep. (para.162)
British Steel 13th Comp. Rep. (para.163)
Fagersta 13th Comp. Rep. (para.164)
Berisford-Napier Brown 13th Comp. Rep. (paras 165–166)
Ashland Oil Inc. 14th Comp. Rep. (para.109)
Stanton & Stavely 14th Comp. Rep. (para.110)

[For the tables of case citations see Tables 5 to 8 and 12 at the back of the book.]

Rhône-Poulenc/Monsanto 19th Comp. Rep. (para.67)
Consolidated Goldfields 19th Comp. Rep. (para.68)
★Continental Can 6/72
★BAT & Philip Morris 142/84

E. ARTICLE 4(4) AND 9: REFERRAL TO A MEMBER STATE

1. Concept

Article 4(4) and 9, Regulation 139/2004
Notice on Case Referral in respect of concentrations

2. List of article 4(4) decisions

Suhler Stevenson/Landesbank Berlin/Berlinonline Stadtportal M.4457
INCHCAPE/eUROPEAN MOTOR HOLDINGS M.4534
Cinven/Warburg Pincus/Essent Kabelcom M.4400
Metro/Wal-Mart M.4364
GENERALI/TORO M.4312
O2/THE LINK M.4302
Agis/Delta Lloyd/Menzis M.4287
Ahold/Konmar M.4276
RWE/Saar Ferngas M.4263
CELESIO/TJELLESEN/MAX JENNE M.4120
LONDON SOUTH EASTERN RAILWAY/THE INTEGRATED KENT RAIL FRANCHISE M.4070
Sulo/Cleanaway M.4012
BOOTS/ALLIANCE UNICHEM M.3990
SCHWARZ-GRUPPE/MEG M.3967
Southern Cross Healthcare/Cannon Capital (Ashbourne Healthcare) M.3955
Apollo/BC Partners/Iesy — Ish — Telecolumbus M.3953
FEM/ENTREMONT/UNICOPA M.3904 Article 4(4)
Dia/Penny Market M.3898
Industri Kapital/Tradeka/Wihuri M.3795
ALFAMAD/GRUPO FARMACÉN M.3758
Yara/DLG/Agro DK M.3737
BC Partners/Ish M.3684
Cargill-BCA/ABF-Allied Grain/JV M.3534
Metsäliitto Osuuskunta/Vapo M.3473
Aggregate Industries/Foster Yeoman UK M.10

3. Accepted requests

3.1. Total referral

Tarmac/Steetley M.180
McCormick/CPC M.330
REW-DEA/Hüls M.1174
Krauss-Maffei/Wegmann M.1206
ECS/Sibelga M.3318
Blackstone/NHP M.3669

3.2. Partial referral

Promodes/Casino M.991 (paras 2–3)
CNN/Sogelfa-CIM M.1021 (paras 2–3)
Lafarge/Redland M.1030 (paras 3–5)
Promodes/S21/Gruppo GS M.1086 (paras 2–3)
Vendex/Bijenkorf M.1060
Alliance Unichem/Unifarma M.1220
Carrefour/Promodes M.1684 (paras 27, 32–35, 107–109)
SEB/Moulinex M.2621 (paras 11–14)
Aker Maritime/Kvaerner (II) M.2683
Danish Crown/Steff Houlberg M.2662
Leroy Merlin/Brico M.2898
Arla Foods/Express Dairies M.3130
Alfa Acciai/Cronimet/Remondis/TSR Group M.4495
Aggregate Industries/Foster Yeoman M.4298
Tesco/Carrefour M.3905
Fimag/Züblin M.3864
Strabag/Dywidag M.3754

4. Rejected requests

Alcatel/AEG Kabel M.147
Holderchim/Cedest M.460 (para.2)
Exxon/Mobil M.1383 (paras 1–3)
Lagardère/Natexis/VUP M.2978

5. Cases in which request received and proceedings opened

Lafarge/Redland M.1030
Interbrew/Bass M.2044
Seb/Moulinex M.2621
Leroy Merlin/Brico M.2898
ECS/IEH M.2857

6. Referral challenged before the CFI

Royal Philips Electronics T–119/02 (paras 320–359)
Cableuropa T–346/02

F. ARTICLES 4(5) & 22: REFERRAL TO THE COMMISSION

Articles 4(5) & 22, Regulation 139/2004
Notice on Case Referral in respect of concentrations

MERGERS: JURISDICTION

[For the tables of case citations see Tables 5 to 8 and 12 at the back of the book.]

1. Article 22

British Airways/Dan Air M.278
CLT/Veronica/Endemol M.553 (para.1)
Blokker/Toys "R" Us M.890
Areva/Urenco/ETC JV M.3099 (paras 1–2)
Endemol T–221/95 (paras 37–47)
Kesko Oy T–22/97 (paras 67–93)

2. Pre-filing referral (Article 4(5))

Agfa-Gevaert/Lastra M.3439 (para.6)
Piaggio/Aprilia M.3570 (para.1)

G. LEGITIMATE INTERESTS (ARTICLE 21)

Article 21(4) Regulation 139/2004
Article 296 EEC
Newspaper Publishing M.423
Lyonnaise des Eaux/Northumbrian Water M.567 (paras 7–8)
Sun Alliance/Royal Insurance M.759 (paras 16–17)
EDF/South Western Electricity M.1471 (paras 6–7)
Antonio de Sommer Champalimaud/Banco Santander Central Hispanoamericano M.1616 (paras 39–45)
Sampo/Storebrand M.2491 (paras 38–39)
Portuguese Republic T–42/01
E.ON/Endesa M.4197
Unicredito/HVB M.4125

H. ARTICLE 296: MILITARY PRODUCTS

Marconi/Finmeccanica M.496
British Aerospace/VSEL M.528
GEC/VSEL M.529
Teneo/Merrill Lynch/Bankers Trust M.722 (paras 1, 12)
GEC/Thomson-CSF II M.724
British Aerospace/Lagadere SCA M.820 (paras 12–13)
GEC Marconi/Alenia M.1258
Matra/Aerospatiale M.1309 (paras 15–17, 18–23, 41–48)
British Aerospace/GEC Marconi M.1438 (paras 7–9)
Preussag/Babcock/Celsius M.1709 (paras 25–28)
Saab/Celsius M.1797 (paras 2, 11, 49)
MMS/Dasa/Astrium M.1636 (paras 24, 38–40, 85–92)
EADS M.1745
Snecma/Labinal M.2021 (paras 14, 34, 35–37)
SNPE/Saab/Patria JV (Eurenco) M.3205

I. RELATIONS WITH EEA

Orkla/Volvo M.582 (paras 7–9, 19)
Schneider/Lexel M.1434 (paras 8, 22)
Sanitec/Sphinx M.1578 (para.8, 201–207)
Volvo/Scania M.1672 (paras 11, 161–173)
Industri Kapital (Nordkem)/Dyno M.1813 (para.13)
Sampo/Storebrand M.2491 (paras 38–39)

J. EXTRATERRITORIAL JURISDICTION

Gencor T–106/96 (grounds 48–88)

CHAPTER 3

SUBSTANTIVE ISSUES: CASES AND REFERENCES

A. RELEVANT MARKET

1. Relevant product market

1.1. Definition of the term "relevant product market"

Notice on market definition (paras 2, 7, 10–13)
Aérospatiale-Alenia/de Havilland M.53 (paras 8–19)
Air France T–2/93 (paras 73–87)
(see also position under Article 82)

1.2. Relevant factors

1.2.1. Physical characteristics/end use

MBB/Aérospatiale M.17 (para.9)
VIAG/Continental Can M.81 (para.12)
⋆Tetra Pak/Alfa-Laval M.68 (IV.B.2.1)
Eridania/ISI M.62 (para.14)
⋆Aérospatiale-Alenia/de Havilland M.53 (paras 8–19)
Metallgesellschaft/Safic Alcan M.146 (para.14)
TNT/Canada Post M.102 (paras 20–29)
Eurocom/RSCG M.147 (paras 8–11)
Courtaulds/SNIA M.113 (para.9–14)
Torras/Sarrio M.166 (para.17)

[For the tables of case citations see Tables 5 to 8 and 12 at the back of the book.]

Generali/BCHA M.189 (para.15)
Accor/Wagon-Lits M.126 (para.25)
Nestlé/Perrier M.190 (paras 11–12)
Péchiney/VIAG M.198 (para.12)
Rhône-Poulenc/SNIA M.206 (paras 6.1–6.2)
Linde AG/Fiat M.256 (paras 10–17)
★Du Pont/ICI M.214 (paras 14–28)
Air France/Sabena M.157 (para.25)
Mannesmann/Hoesch M.222 (paras 42, 48–52, 55, 61–63)
British Airways/TAT M.259 (paras 19–20)
KNP/Bührmann Tetterode/VRG M.291 (paras 36–37)
Codan/Hafnia M.344 (para.7)
Rhône-Poulenc/SNIA M.355 (paras 17–18)
American Cyanamid/Shell M.354 (paras 11–16)
Synthomer/Yule Catto M.376 (paras 16–18)
Kali-Salz/MDK/Treuhand M.308 (paras 14, 22)
Mannesmann/Vallourec/Ilva M.315 (paras 18–20)
Rhône-Poulenc-SNIA/Nordfaser M.399 (paras 15–18)
ABB/Renault Automation M.409 (paras 13–16)
Newspaper Publishing M.423 (paras 13–14)
Unilever France/Ortiz Miko M.422 (paras 20–25)
CGP/GEC/KPR/KONE M.420 (para.15)
VIAG/Bayernwerk M.417 (paras 8–10)
Shell/Montecatini M.269 (paras 23–27)
Procter & Gamble/VP Schnickendanz M.430 (paras 14, 29–41)
Holderchim/Cedest M.460 (paras 11–15)
★Tractebel/Distrigaz M.493 (paras 22–23)
Vesuvius/Wülfrath M.472 (paras 18–20)
MSG Media Service M.469 (paras 20, 32–38)
Elf Atochem/Shell Chimie M.475 (paras 32–35)
AKZO Nobel/Monsanto M.523 (para.18)
Mercedes-Benz/Kässbohrer M.477 (paras 9–10)
Orkla/Volvo M.582 (paras 25, 32)
Crown Cork & Seal/Carnaud Metalbox M.655 (paras 12, 30)
Kimberley-Clark/Scott Paper M.623 (paras 45–47)
Thomson/Daimler-Benz M.744 (paras 18–21)
Saint Gobain/wacker Chemie/Nom M.774 (paras 24–97)
Coca-Cola/Amalgamated Beverages GB M.794 (paras 26–92)
Siemens/Elektrowatt M.913 (paras 26–28, 34–38)
Swedish Match/KAV M.997 (paras 14–15)
Caterpillar/Perkins Engine M.1094 (paras 11–14)
TKS/ITW Signode/Titan M.970 (paras 22–28)
Allianz/AGF M.1082 (para.20)
Schneider Electric/Legrand M.2283 (paras 178–192)
Tetra Laval/Sidel M.2416 (paras 40–71, 176–188)
Oracle/People Soft M.3216 (paras 62–86)
Bertelsmann/Springer M.3380 (paras 20–39)
Inco/Falconbridge M.4000 (paras 49–93, 129–154, 166–187)
Mittal/Arcelor M.4137 (paras 27–29, 52–57)

1.2.1.1. Product/Components

Schneider Electric/Legrand M.2283 (paras 124–177)
Honeywell/Novar M.3686 (paras 11–16)

1.2.2. Price

Digital/Kienzle M.57 (para.10)
VIAG/Continental Can M.81 (para.12)
Mannesmann/Boge M.134 (para.11)
★Aérospatiale-Alenia/de Havilland M.53
Metallgesellschaft/Safic Alcan M.146 (para.15)
Courtaulds/SNIA M.113 (para.13)
Nestlé/Perrier M.190 (paras 13, 16–17)
★Du Pont/ICI M.214 (paras 14, 23–24, 27–28)
Mannesmann/Hoesch M.222 (paras 44, 53)
KNP/Bührmann Tetterode/VRG M.291 (para.39)
Synthomer/Yule Catto M.376 (para.18)
Kali-Salz/MDK/Treuhand M.308 (paras 13, 16, 24)
Mannesmann/Vallourec/Ilva M.315 (paras 17–20, 29–32)
Rhône-Poulenc-SNIA/Nordfaser M.399 (para.16)
BMW/Rover M.416 (paras 10–13)
Medeol/Elosua M.431 (para.12)
BSN/Euralim M.445 (para.16)
Shell/Montecatini M.269 (para.25)
Procter & Gamble VP/Schnickendanz M.430 (paras 43, 49)
Holderchim/Cedest M.460 (paras 11–15)
Tractebel/Distrigaz M.493 (para.23)
Elf Atochem/Shell Chimie M.475 (paras 32, 36)
AKZO Nobel/Monsanto M.523 (para.18)
Svenska Cellulosa/PWA M.549 (para.14)
Orkla/Volvo M.582 (paras 26–27, 31)
Henkel/Schwarzkopf M.630 (para.10)
Repola/Kymmene M.646 (paras 11, 18)

[For the tables of case citations see Tables 5 to 8 and 12 at the back of the book.]

Crown Cork & Seal/Carnaud Metalbox M.655 (para.15)
★Gencor/Lonrho M.619 (paras 41–43, 46–60)
Saint Gobain/wacker Chemie/Nom M.774 (paras 29, 42–43, 95)
★Coca-Cola/Amalgamated Beverages GB M.794 (paras 26–33, 49–63)
Valinox/Timet M.917 (para.24)
Siemens/Elektrowatt M.913 (para.28)
Swedish Match/KAV M.997 (paras 14, 18)
TKS/ITW Signode/Titari M.970 (paras 26, 31–32)
Price Waterhouse/Coopers & Lybrand M.1016 (para.36)
Inco/Falconbridge M.4000 (paras 105–119, 193–194)

1.2.2.1. SSNIP Test

CVC/Lenzing M.2187 (paras 25–26, 36–37, 39–40, 62–68)
Oracle/People Soft M.3216 (paras 86–115)

1.2.3. Consumer preference

VIAG/Continental Can M.81 (para.12)
Courtaulds/SNIA M.113 (para.(c))
Du Pont/ICI M.214 (para.22)
British Airways/TAT M.259 (paras 21–22)
Allied Lyons/HWE-Pedro Domecq M.400 (paras 13–16)
Medeol/Elosua M.431 (para.12)
BSN/Euralim M.445 (paras 18, 23)
Procter & Gamble VP/Schnickendanz M.430 (paras 35–42)
Cardo/Thyssen M.818 (paras 13–17)
Coco-Cola/Amalgamated Beverages GB M.794 (para.26–92)
Swedish Match/KAV M.997 (paras 14–15)
CVC/Danone/Gerresheimer M.1539 (paras 9–13)
Volvo/Scania M.1672 (paras 25, 28, 227–228)

1.2.4. Supply-side substitutability/potential competition

Notice on market definition (para.42)
VIAG/Continental Can M.81 (para.13)
★Aérospatiale-Alenia/de Havilland M.53 (para.14)
Metallgesellschaft/Safic Alcan M.146 (para.14)
★Lucas/Eaton M.149 (paras 21–22)
Torras/Sarrio M.166 (paras 18–20)
Nestlé/Perrier M.190 (para.18)
Avesta/British Steel/NCC M.239 (paras 20–22)
Du Pont/ICI M.214 (para.31)
Air France/Sabena M.157 (para.26)
Mannesmann/Hoesch M.222 (para.66–69)
Waste Management/SAE M.283 (paras 12–16)
KNP/Bührmann Tetterode/VRG M.291 (para.34)
Rhône-Poulenc/SNIA M.355 (para.17)
Knorr-Bremse/Allied Signal M.337 (para.4)
★Kali-Salz/MDK/Treuhand M.308 (paras 14, 25–28)
Mannesmann/Vallourec/Ilva M.315 (paras 18, 20)
BSN/Euralim M.445 (para.16)
★GKN/Brambles/Leto Recycling M.448 (para.13)
Shell/Montecatini M.269 (paras 26–27)
Procter & Gamble VP/Schnickendanz M.430 (paras 43, 45)
★Electrolux/AEG M.458 (para.11)
Tractebel/Distrigaz M.493 (para.24)
Vesuvius/Wülfrath M.472 (para.21)
Elf Atochem/Shell Chimie M.475 (para.37)
AKZO Nobel/Monsanto M.523 (para.16)
Mercedes-Benz/Kässbohrer M.477 (para.21)
Svenska Cellulosa/PWA M.549 (para.14, 39)
Repola/Kymmene M.646 (paras 10, 16)
Minorco/Tilcon M.678 (paras 12–13)
Kimberley-Clark/Scott Paper M.623 (paras 11–15, 34–44)
BP Mobil M.727 (para.29)
Saint Gobain/wacker Chemie/Nom M.774 (paras 29, 43, 69)
Coco-Cola/Amalgamated Beverages GB M.794 (paras 26, 93)
Dupont/ICI M.984 (para.4)
Alcoa/Inespal M.1003 (paras 11–14)
Caterpillar/Perkins Engines M.1094 (paras 11–14)
Price Waterhouse/Coopers & Lybrand M.1016 (paras 41–48)
Candover/Cinven/Bertelsmann- Springer M.3197 (para.14)
Omya/J.M. Huber PCC M.3796 (para.143)
Inco/Falconbridge M.4000 (paras 155–162, 188–192)
Ineos/BP Dormagen M.4094 (paras 54–55)
★Glatfelter/Crompton assets M.4215 (paras 35–48, 105–114)
Mahle/Dana EPG M.4456 (paras 15–16)
Givaudan/Quest International M.4507 (paras 8–18)
★Alcoa/Orkla/Soft Alloy Extrusion M.4518 (para.18)

[For the tables of case citations see Tables 5 to 8 and 12 at the back of the book.]

1.2.5. Industry product classifications/internal company marketing classifications

Sanofi/Sterling Drugs M.72 (paras 21–24)
Accor/Wagon-Lits M.126 (para.21)
Procordia/Erbamont M.323 (paras 8–10)
BMW/Rover M.416 (paras 10–13)
CGP/GEC/KPR/Kone M.420 (para.15)
Medeol/Elosua M.431 (para.12)
BSN/Euralim M.445 (paras 18, 20–21, 23)
Rhône-Poulenc/Cooper M.427 (para.11)
La Roche/Syntex M.457 (para.6)
Sanofi/Kodak M.480 (para.10)
BMSC/UPSA M.464 (paras 10–11)
Mercedes-Benz/Kässbohrer M.477 (para.15)
Glaxo/Wellcome M.555 (paras 6–7)
Saint Gobain/wacker Chemie/Nom M.774 (para.16–46)
AT&T/Global Network M.1396 (paras 9–16)
Hoechst/Rhône Poulenc M.1378 (paras 10–24)
VNU/AC Nielsen M.2291 (para.11)
Inco/Falconbridge M.4000 (paras 139–143)
Toshiba/Westinghouse M.4153 (para.12)
Johnson & Johnson/Pfizer Consumer Healthcare M.4314 (para.8)

1.2.6. In-house production

Accor/Wagon-Lits M.126 (para.15)
AT&T/Global Network M.1396 (para.23)
CVC/Danone/Gerresheimer M.1569 (para.28)
⋆Alcoa/Reynolds M.1693 (para.13)
Schneider Electric/Legrand M.2283 (paras 525–529)
UCB/Solutia M.3060 (para.31)
Sanofi-Synthelabo/Aventis M.3354 (para.350)
Sonoco/Ahlstrom/JV M.3431 (para.84)
T-Systems/Gedas M.4108 (paras 15–19)
Endemol T–221/95 (para.107)
Schneider Electric T–310/01 (paras 268–296)
Ineos/BP Dormagen M.4094 (para.32)
Nemak/Hydro Castings M.4524 (para.23)

1.2.7. Similar or identical products, but different distribution channels/production processes

SITA-RPC/Scori M.295
Arvin/Sogefi M.360 (para.15)
Knorr-Bremsel/Allied Signal M.337 (paras 25–27)
⋆Pilkington/SIV M.358 (paras 18–19)
Unilever/Ortiz Miko M.422 (paras 20–25, 31)
Rhône-Poulenc/Cooper M.427 (paras 12–17)
MSG Media Service M.469 (paras 39–43)
Glaxo/Wellcome M.555 (para.8)
Orkla/Volvo M.582 (paras 29–30)
Henkel/Schwarzkopf M.630 (para.10)
Coca-Cola/Amalgamated Beverages GB M.794 (paras 26, 80–93)
Lyonnaise des Eaux/Suez M.916 (para.24)
Nestlé/San Pellegrino M.1065 (paras 12–16)
Danish Crown/Vestjyske Slagterier M.1313 (paras 36–42)
Linde/Aga M.1641 (paras 20–21)
Unilever/Amora-Maille M.1802 (paras 18–20)
Alcoa/Reynolds M.1693 (paras 14–17)
Dow Chemical/Union Carbide M.1671 (paras 69–95)
Metsä-Serla/Modo M.2020 (paras 13–20)
Siemens/Dematic/VDO/Sachs M.2059 (para.101)
Unilever/Bestfoods M.1990 (paras 9–11)
Nestlé/Ralston Purina M.2337 (paras 15–19)
Linde/Boc M.4141 (paras 24–33)
Gaz de France/Suez M.4180 (paras 70–86, 355–379, 688–695)

1.2.8. Relevant evidence

CVC/Lenzing M.2187 (paras 23–24)

1.2.8.1. Consumer surveys/views of competitors and customers

Notice on market definition (paras 33–34, 40–41)
⋆Tetra Pak/Alfa-Laval M.68 (para.IV.B.2)
Aérospatiale-Alenia/de Havilland M.53 (para.13)
Nestlé/Perrier M.190 (paras 10, 14)
Du Pont/ICI M.214 (para.22)
Costa Crociere/Chargeurs Accor M.334 (para.15)
Rhône-Poulenc/SNIA M.355 (paras 16, 18)
Procter & Gamble VP/Schnickendanz M.430 (paras 35, 46–47)
AKZO Nobel/Monsanto M.523 (paras 17–18)
Mercedes-Benz/Kässbohrer M.477 (para.15)
Svenska Cellulosa/PWA M.549 (para.15)
Repola/Kymmene M.646 (para.19)
Crown Cork & Seal/Carnaud Metalbox M.655 (paras 13, 20–21, 30)
Saint Gobain/wacker Chemie/Nom M.774 (paras 25, 54–84, 91)
⋆Coca-Cola/Amalgamated Beverages GB M.794 (paras 34–48, 68, 85–92)
Mannesmann/Vallourec M.906 (para.44, 49)
Nestlé/San Pellegrino M.1065 (para.8)
⋆TKS/ITW Signode/Titan M.970 (paras 34–39)
Price Waterhouse/Coopers & Lybrand M.1016 (para.36)

[For the tables of case citations see Tables 5 to 8 and 12 at the back of the book.]

Sanitec/Sphinx M.1578 (paras 19, 23–28)
Volvo/Scania M.1672 (paras 24–28)
Siemens/Va Tech M.3653 (paras 244–269)

1.2.8.2. "Conditions of competition"

★Magneti-Marelli/CEAC M.43 (para.10)
★Varta/Bosch M.12 (paras 13–16, 37)
Mannesmann/Boge M.134 (paras 10–13)
Metallgesellschaft/Safic Alcan M.146 (para.14)
Arvin/Sogefi M.365 (para.15)
Knorr-Bremse/Allied Signal M.337 (para.21)
★Pilkington/SIV M.358 (para.18)
Medeol/Elosua M.431 (para.12)
Orkla/Volvo M.582 (para.30)
★Mannesmann/Vallourec M.906 (para.45)
Lyonnaise des Eaux/Suez M.916 (paras 23–24)
TotalFina/Elf M.1628 (paras 172–175)

1.2.8.3. Historical evidence/studies on cross-elasticity

Notice on market definition (paras 38–39)
Chiquita, 101
Henkel/Nobel M.186 (paras 7–10)
Generali/BCHA M.189 (para.15)
Thorn EMI/Virgin Music M.202 (para.13)
Accor/Wagon-Lits M.126 (para.21)
Nestlé/Perrier M.190 (paras 13)
Du Pont/ICI M.214 (para.25–28)
★Kali-Salz/MDK/Treuhand M.308 (paras 25–28)
Newspaper Publishing M.423 (para.14)
Medeol/Elosua M.431 (para.12)
★Procter & Gamble VP/Schnickendanz M.430 (paras 48–71)
Elf Atochem/Shell Chimie M.475 (para.38)
Crown Cork & Seal/Carnaud Metalbox M.655 (paras 14, 20–24, 30)
Kimberley-Clark/Scott Paper M.623
★Gencor/Lonrho M.619 (paras 45–60)
Saint Gobain/wacker Chemie/Nom M.774 (paras 54–84)
★Coca-Cola/Amalgamated Beverages GB M.794 (paras 26–33, 49–63, 65–79)
Swedish Match/KAV M.997 (paras 14–18)
Nestlé/San Pellegrino M.1065 (para.8)
TKS/ITW Signode/Titan M.970 (paras 29–32)
CVC/Lenzing M.2187 (paras 72–80, 108–115)

1.2.8.4. Different producers only active on different product markets

Unilever/Ortiz Miko M.422 (para.24)

1.2.8.5. Switching costs

Notice on market definition (para.42)
★Crown Cork & Seal/Carnaud Metalbox M.655 (paras 19, 33)
Minorco/Tilcon M.678 (para.11)
Gencor/Lonrho M.619 (paras 25–32)
Exxon/DSM M.708 (para.11)
ICI/Unilever M.933 (para.18)
TKS/ITW Signode/Titan M.970 (para.33)
Allianz/AGF M.1082 (paras 20–21)
★Price Waterhouse/Coopers & Lybrand M.1016 (paras 37, 40, 112–113)
Exxon/Mobil M.1383 (paras 121–130)
Philips/Marconi Medical Systems M.2537 (paras 35–40)

1.2.9. Time frame in which substitution by new product likely to occur

Rütgers/Hüls Troisdorf M.401 (para.8)
Dow Chemical/Union Carbide M.1671 (para.64)

1.2.10. Chains of substitution

Notice on market definition (paras 57–58)
Dupont/ICI M.984 (para.40)
Promodes/Casino M.991 (para.14)
TotalFina/Elf M.1628 (paras 177–188)
Pirelli/BICC M.1882 (paras 16–19)

1.2.11. Imperfect substitutes

See under "Substantive test" B.2.10

1.2.12. Definition in other areas of EU law (anti-dumping)

★Saint Gobain/wacker Chemie/Nom M.774 (paras 43–49)

1.2.13. Products not yet at commercial stage (emerging markets)

Shell/Montecatini M.269 (paras 28–44)
Glaxo/Wellcome M.555 (para.28)
Rhône-Poulenc/Fisons M.632 (paras 55–58)
Ciba-Geigy/Sandoz M.737 (paras 42–46)
Sanofi/Synthelabo M.1397 (paras 41–43)
Hoechst/Rhône Poulenc M.1378 (paras 26–27)
Monsanto/Pharmacia & Upjohn M.1835 (paras 34, 46)
Vodafone Airtouch/Mannesmann M.1795 (paras 12–21)
Glaxo Wellcome/SmithKline Beecham M.1846 (paras 70–72)

[For the tables of case citations see Tables 5 to 8 and 12 at the back of the book.]

Pfizer/Warner Lambert M.1878 (paras 42–44)
France Telecom/Orange M.2016 (paras 14–16)
AOL/Time Warner M.1845 (para.26)
Vivendi/Canal+/Seagram M.2050 (paras 22–33)

2. Relevant geographic market

2.1. Definition of the term "relevant geographic market"

Notice on market definition (paras 2, 8, 10–13)
Eridania/ISI M.62
Swissair/Sabena M.616
(see also position under Article 82)

2.2. Relevant factors

2.2.1. Regulatory trade barriers (including taxes and anti-dumping duties)

Notice on market definition (para.50)
Elf/Ertoil M.63
⋆Sanofi/Sterling Drugs M.72 (paras 17–20)
⋆UAP/Transatlantic/Sunlife M.141 (para.21)
Alcatel/AEG Kabel M.147 (paras 14–17)
Courtaulds/SNIA M.113 (paras 15–16)
Torras/Sarrio M.166 (para.30)
Generali/BCHA M.189 (para.17b)
Accor/Wagon-Lits M.126 (para.25)
Elf Atochem/Rohm & Haas M.160 (para.16)
Du Pont/ICI M.214 (para.29)
Rhône-Poulenc Chimie/Lyonnaise des Eaux M.266 (paras 23–26)
Del Monte/Royal Foods/Anglo-American M.277 (para.26)
Waste Management/SAE M.283 (paras 17–25)
Fletcher Challenge/Methanex M.331 (paras 16–17)
GEHE AG/OCP S.A. M.328 (paras 7–9)
Procordia/Erbamont M.323 (paras 11–12)
KNP/Bührmann Tetterode/VRG M.291 (para.46)
Rhône-Poulenc/SNIA M.355 (paras 19–20)
American Cyanamid/Shell M.354 (paras 20–22)
Mannesmann/Vallourec/Ilva M.315 (paras 21, 23, 27)
Rhône-Poulenc-SNIA/Nordfaser M.399 (paras 19–20)
Rütgers/Hüls Troisdorf M.401 (para.16)
Unilever/Ortiz Miko M.422 (para.26)
Rhône-Poulenc/Cooper M.426 (para.18)
Allied Lyons/HWE-Pedro Domecq M.400 (paras 18–19)
VIAG/Bayerwerk M.417 (para.15)
La Roche/Syntex M.457 (paras 8–10)
Electrolux/AEG M.458 (para.16)
Elf Atochem/Rütgers M.442 (para.37)
Tractebel/Distrigaz M.493 (para.25)
BMSC/UPSA M.464 (paras 17–18)
American Home Products/American Cyanamid M.500 (para.12)
MSG Media Service M.469 (paras 46–47)
⋆Mercedes-Benz/Kässbohrer M.477 (paras 26, 37–38, 95–100)
Siemens/Italtel M.468 (para.20)
Glaxo/Wellcome M.555 (paras 15–18)
Swissair/Sabena M.616 (para.25–31)
RWE-DEA/Augusta M.612 (para.19)
Orkla/Volvo M.582 (paras 45–49)
ABB/Daimler Benz M.580 (para.28)
Ciba-Geigy/Sandoz M.737 (paras 47–49)
Saint Gobain/wacker Chemie/Nom M.774 (paras 121–123)
Mannesmann/Vallourec M.906 (para.78)
Swedish Match/KAV M.997 (para.25)
TKS/ITW Signode/Titan M.970 (para.48)
Axa/Gre M.1453 (para.11)
Areva/Urenco/ECT JV M.3099 (paras 72–74)
Toshiba/Westinghouse M.4153 (paras 39, 48)

2.2.2. Local specification requirements/differing national standards

⋆Renault/Volvo M.4 (para.17)
Magneti-Marelli/CEAC M.43 (para.16)
Varta/Bosch M.12 (paras 21–22)
Alcatel/AEG Kabel M.147 (paras 14–17)
Linde AG/Fiat M.256 (para.18)
Mannesmann/Hoesch M.222 (paras 74–75)
Kali-Salz/MDK/Treuhand M.308 (para.33)
Unilever/Ortiz Miko M.422 (para.26)
Electrolux/AEG M.458 (para.16)
Elf Atochem/Shell Chimie M.475 (para.43)
Mercedes-Benz/Kässbohrer M.477 (paras 24–26, 94–98)
Siemens/Italtel M.468 (paras 27–28, 32)
ABB/Daimler Benz M.580 (paras 28–36)
Ericsson/Ascom II M.676 (para.16)
Cardo/Thyssen M.818 (para.22)
Saint Gobain/wacker Chemie/Nom M.774 (paras 113–118)
Mannesmann/Vallourec M.906 (para.63)
⋆Siemens/Elektrowatt M.913 (paras 40, 43, 45–47, 51–53, 60–64)
Price Waterhouse/Coopers & Lybrand M.1016 (paras 55–56, 67)
EDF/London Electricity M.1346

Sanitec/Sphinx M.1578 (para.102–108)
Volvo/Scania M.1672 (paras 56–57, 243–244, 254–256)
Schneider Electric/Legrand M.2283 (paras 43–62, 200–202, 360–366, 387–388, 399–401)

2.2.3. National/Community procurement policies

★MBB/Aérospatiale M.17 (paras 10–12)
Alcatel/Telettra M.42 (paras 33–34)
Thomson/Pilkington M.86 (paras 21–24)
★Alcatel/AEG Kabel M.147 (paras 14–17)
GC/ENI/Nuovo Pignone M.440 (para.20)
Siemens/Italtel M.468 (paras 29, 34)
ABB/Daimler Benz M.580 (paras 31–36)
Siemens/Elektrowatt M.913 (paras 49, 58)
GEC Alsthom NV/AEG M.706 (para.11)
Preussag/Babcock/Celsius M.1709 (paras 42–47)

2.2.4. Adequate distribution facilities

Notice on market definition (para.50)
★Fiat/Ford/New Holland M.58 (paras 26–30)
Magneti-Marelli/CEAC M.43 (para.16)
Eridania/ISI M.62 (para.22)
Varta/Bosch M.12 (paras 28–30, 40)
Torras/Sarrio M.166 (para.33)
Generali/BCHA M.189 (para.17c)
Nestlé/Perrier M.190 (paras 31–32)
Fortis/La Caixa M.254 (para.6.3)
American Cyanamid/Shell M.354 (para.19)
Kali-Salz/MDK/Treuhand M.308 (paras 33, 41)
Mannesmann/Vallourec/Ilva M.315 (paras 26, 34–37)
Neste/Statoil M.361 (paras 19–25)
Unilever/Ortiz Miko M.422 (para.26)
★VIAG/Bayernwerk M.417 (para.11)
Procter & Gamble VP/Schnickendanz M.430 (paras 92–94, 98)
Tractebel/Distrigaz M.493 (paras 25, 28)
Orkla/Volvo M.582 (para.43)
Coca-Cola/Amalgamated Beverages GB M.794 (para.97)
Swedish Match/KAV M.997 (para.27)
American Home Products/Monsanto M.1229 (para.37)
Imetal/English China Clays M.1381 (para.47)
France T–68/94 (grounds 142, 149)

2.2.5. Need for locally-based service/just-in-time delivery

KNP/Bührmann Tetterode/VRG M.291 (paras 14–15)
IBM France/CGI M.336 (para.10)
Rhône-Poulenc/SNIA M.355
Rhône-Poulenc/SNIA/Nordfaser M.399
CGP/GEC/KPR/KONE M.420 (para.17)
Rhône-Poulenc/Caffaro M.427 (para.25)
Ingersoll-Rand/Man M.479 (para.20)
BHF/CCF M.508 (para.10)
British Steel/Svensk Stal/VSO M.503 (para.20)
MSG Media Service M.469 (para.53)
Mercedes-Benz/Kässbohrer M.477 (paras 33, 39, 88–90)
ABB/Daimler Benz M.580 (paras 24–25, 29)
Saint Gobain/wacker Chemie/Nom M.774 (para.120)
Lyonnaise des Eaux/Suez M.916 (para.28)
Siemens/Elektrowatt M.913 (paras 41, 50)
Price Waterhouse/Coopers & Lybrand M.1016 (para.62)
Dupont/Hoechst/Herberts M.1363
★Volvo/Scania M.1672 (paras 61–64, 241–242)
Siemens/Drägerwerk/JV M.2861 (paras 41–47)

2.2.6. Transport costs

Notice on market definition (para.50)
★VIAG/Continental Can M.81 (para.15)
Eridania/ISI M.62 (para.22)
Torras/Sarrio M.166 (para.33)
Elf Atochem/Rohm & Haas M.160 (para.16)
Péchiney/VIAG M.198 (para.14)
Du Pont/ICI M.214 (para.29)
Fletcher Challenge/Methanex M.331 (paras 16–17)
KNP/Bührmann Tetterode/VRG M.291 (para.44)
Synthomer/Yule Catto M.376 (paras 22–26)
Mannesmann/Vallourec/Ilva M.315 (paras 21, 23)
Rhône-Poulenc-SNIA/Nordfaser M.399 (para.19)
Kali-Salz/MDK/Treuhand M.308 (paras 33–34, 42)
Pilkington/SIV M.358 (paras 16, 23)
Rütgers/Hüls Troisdorf M.401 (para.14)
Shell/Montecatini M.269 (paras 46–48)
CGP/GEC/KPR/Kone M.420 (para.17)
Rhône-Poulenc/Caffaro M.427 (para.24)
Electrolux/AEG M.458 (para.6)
Holderchim/Cedest M.460 (paras 16, 28)
British Steel/Svensk Stal/VSO M.503 (para.20)
Shell/Atochem M.475 (para.44)
Orkla/Volvo M.582 (paras 43, 73–80)
Crown Cork & Seal/Carnaud Metalbox M.655 (paras 42, 50)

[For the tables of case citations see Tables 5 to 8 and 12 at the back of the book.]

Minorco/Tilcon M.678 (paras 20–22, 24–25)
Kimberley-Clark/Scott Paper M.623 (paras 63–68, 83)
Cardo/Thyssen M.818 (para.22)
Coca-Cola/Amalgamated Beverages GB M.794 (paras 97, 100)
Lyonnaise des Eaux/Suez M.916 (para.30)
Swedish Match/KAV M.997 (para.22)
Nestlé/San Pellegrino M.1065 (para.19)
British Steel/Europipe M.1014 (para.36)
TKS/ITW Signode/Titan M.970 (para.47)
Linde/Aga M.1641 (paras 24–26)
Industri Kapital (Nordkem)/Dyno M.1813 (paras 56–58, 73, 82–84)
⋆France T–68/94 (grounds 134, 141, 149)
Ineos/BP Dormagen M.4094 (paras 48–49)
Mittal/Arcelor M.4137 (paras 68–70)

2.2.7. Language/culture

Notice on market definition (para.46)
Otto/Grattan M.70 (para.10)
Redoute/Empire Stores M.80 (para.12)
IBM France/CGI M.336 (para.10)
MSG Media Service M.469 (paras 46–47)
Kirch/Richemont M.577 (para.17)
CLT/Disney/Super RTL M.566 (para.17)
RTL/Veronica Endemol M.553 (paras 25–29)
Seagram/Polygram M.1219 (para.15)
Recoletos/Unedisa M.1401

2.2.8. Consumer preferences

Notice on market definition (para.46)
Renault/Volvo M.4 (para.17)
⋆Magneti-Marelli/CEAC M.43
⋆Varta/Bosch M.12 (paras 25–27, 40)
Generali/BCHA M.189 (para.17a)
Nestlé/Perrier M.190 (paras 21–34)
Fortis/La Caixa M.254 (para.6.3)
Kali-Salz/MDK/Treuhand M.308 (paras 33–34)
Unilever/Ortiz Miko M.422 (para.26)
Medeol/Elosua M.431 (para.16)
BSN/Euralim M.445 (para.25)
⋆Procter & Gamble VP/Schnickendanz M.430 (para.78)
Electrolux/AEG M.458 (para.19)
Ingersoll Rand/MAN M.479 (para.20)
⋆Mercedes Benz/Kässbohrer M.477 (paras 35–36, 53, 82–87)
ABB/Daimler Benz M.580 (paras 23–28, 34)
Coca-Cola/Amalgamated Beverages GB M.794 (paras 97–99)
Promodes/Casino M.991 (para.25)
⋆Volvo/Scania M.1672 (paras 50–55, 239–240, 251–254)
Schneider Electric/Legrand M.2283 (paras 203–226)
Siemens/Drägerwerk/JV M.2861 (paras 59–65)

2.2.9. Potential entry

⋆Elf Aquitaine Thyssen/Minol AG M.235 (paras 11–14)
Procordia/Erbamont M.323 (paras 18, 20)
VIAG/Bayerwerk M.417 (para.15)
Procter & Gamble VP/Schnickendanz M.430 (paras 95–104, 175–181)
Tractebel/Distrigaz M.493 (para.40)
Vesuvius/Wülfrath M.472 (para.29)
AKZO Nobel/Monsanto M.523 (paras 40–42, 48)
⋆Mercedes Benz/Kässbohrer M.477 (paras 53, 79–100)
Siemens/Italtel M.468 (para.26)
RTL/Veronica/Endemol M.553 (paras 84–86)
⋆Saint Gobain/wacker Chemie/Nom M.774 (paras 188–219)
SCA/Metsä Tissue M.2097 (paras 58–59)

2.2.10. Need for secure supplies and thus local delivery

Rhône-Poulenc/SNIA M.355 (para.20)
Kali-Salz/MDK/Treuhand M.308 (paras 33–34)
Crown Cork & Seal/Carnaud Metalbox M.655 (para.43)
Saint Gobain/wacker Chemie/Nom M.774 (para.119)
Metsä-Serla/Modo M.2020 (paras 21–23)

2.2.11. Access to an essential facility

Nordic Satellite M.490 (paras 65–66, 71)
Swissair/Sabena M.616 (paras 31–37)

2.2.12. Chains of substitution

Notice on market definition (paras 57–58)
⋆Pilkington/SIV M.358 (para.16)
Tesco/ABF M.914 (para.12)
OBS! Danmark M.998 (paras 14–15)
Promodes/Catteau M.1085 (paras 13–19)

2.3. Relevant evidence

2.3.1. Price differences between neighbouring areas

ICI/Tioxide M.23 (para.12)
Mitsubishi/UCAR M.24 (para.10)
⋆Magneti-Marelli/CEAC M.43 (para.16)
⋆Varta/Bosch M.12 (para.18)

[For the tables of case citations see Tables 5 to 8 and 12 at the back of the book.]

Mannesmann/Boge M.134 (para.11)
Generali/BCHA M.189 (para.17b)
Solvay-Laporte/Interox M.197 (paras 26–29)
Fortis/La Caixa M.254 (para.6.3)
Del Monte/Royal Foods/Anglo-American M.277 (para.26)
KNP/Bührmann Tetterode/VRG M.291 (para.17)
Rhône-Poulenc/SNIA M.355 (paras 19–20)
Mannesmann/Vallourec/Ilva M.315 (paras 24, 35)
Rhône-Poulenc/SNIA/Nordfaser M.399 (paras 19–20)
Kali-Salz/MDK/Treuhand M.308 (para.43)
Rhône-Poulenc/Caffaro M.427 (para.24)
Procter & Gamble VP/Schnickendanz M.430 (paras 79–91)
Elf Atochem/Shell Chimie M.475 (para.42)
Mercedes-Benz/Kässbohrer M.477 (para.25)
ABB/Daimler Benz M.580 (para.40)
Crown Cork & Seal/Carnaud Metalbox M.655 (para.45)
Kimberley-Clark/Scott Paper M.623 (paras 72–81)
Dow/DuPont M.663 (para.30)
Saint Gobain/wacker Chemie/Nom M.774 (paras 125–130)
Swedish Match/KAV M.997 (para.24)
Nestlé/San Pellegrino M.1065 (para.18)
British Steel/Europipe M.1014 (para.35)
Neste/IVO M.931 (para.25)
Sanitec/Sphinx M.1578 (paras 79–88)
Volvo/Scania M.1672 (paras 38–49, 233, 246- 247, 250, 257–258)
Schneider Electric/Legrand M.2283 (paras 227–238, 269–284, 408–419, 462–472)
Siemens/Drägerwerk/JV M.2861 (paras 54–58)
Areva/Urenco/ETC JV M.3099 (paras 84–100)
Blackstone/Acetex M.3625 (paras 38–41)
★France T–68/94 (ground 148)
Inco/Falconbridge M.4000 (paras 218–220)
Ineos/BP Dormagen M.4094 (para.50)

2.3.2. Market share differences/similarities between neighbouring areas

★Magneti-Marelli/CEAC M.43 (para.16)
★Varta/Bosch M.12 (para.18)
Mannesmann/VDO M.164 (para.17)
Solvay-Laporte/Interox M.197 (paras 40–43)
Péchniney/VIAG M.198 (para.13)
Mannesmann/Hoesch M.222 (paras 72–73)
KNP/Bührmann Tetterode/VRG M.291 (para.43)
Knorr-Bremse/Allied Signal M.337 (para.31)
Rhône-Poulenc/SNIA/Nordfaser M.399 (para.19)
Unilever/Ortiz Miko M.422 (para.26)
Medeol/Elosua M.431 (para.16)
BSN/Euralim M.445 (para.25)
★Procter & Gamble VP/Schnickendanz M.430 (paras 16–17, 82–91)
Tractebel/Distrigaz M.493 (para.25)
MSG Media Service M.469 (paras 48, 50)
AKZO Nobel/Monsanto M.523 (para.20)
ABB/Daimler Benz M.580 (para.39)
Ericsson/Ascom II M.676 (para.16)
Coca-Cola/Amalgamated Beverages GB M.794 (para.98)
Promodes/Casino M.991 (para.25)
Siemens/Elektrowatt M.913 (para.49)
Nestlé/San Pellegrino M.1065 (para.18)
Schneider Electric/Legrand M.2283 (paras 286–292, 473–476)
Siemens/Drägerwerk/JV M.2861 (paras 36–40)
France T–68/94 (grounds 131–132, 137–138)

2.3.3. Significant trade flows between neighbouring areas

Notice on market definition (paras 45, 48–49)
Torras/Sarrio M.166 (paras 26–28)
Avesta/British Steel/NCC M.239 (para.24)
Rhône-Poulenc/SNIA M.355 (para.20)
Kali-Salz/MDK/Treuhand M.308 (paras 32–40)
Mannesman/Vallourec/Ilva M.315 (paras 21–23, 27, 33)
Rütgers/Hüls Troisdorf M.401 (para.15)
BSN/Euralim M.445 (para.25)
Shell/Montecatini M.269 (para.45)
Rhône-Poulenc/Caffaro M.427 (para.25)
Medeol/Elosua M.430 (para.16)
Elf Atochem/Rütgers M.442 (paras 35, 36, 41)
Vesuvius/Wülfrath M.472 (paras 23–24)
Elf Atochem/Shell Chimie M.475 (paras 41, 45)
AKZO Nobel/Monsanto M.523 (para.20)

[For the tables of case citations see Tables 5 to 8 and 12 at the back of the book.]

Mercedes Benz/Kässbohrer M.477 (para.30–32, 35, 53)
Orkla/Volvo M.582 (para.90)
ABB/Daimler Benz M.580 (paras 24, 38)
Repola/Kymmene M.646 (para.33)
Crown Cork & Seal/Carnaud Metalbox M.655 (paras 38, 50)
RWE-DEA/Augusta M.567 (para.19)
Ericsson/Ascom II M.676 (para.16)
Kimberley-Clark/Scott Paper M.623 (paras 61–68)
Norsk Hydro/Arnyca M.769 (paras 20–23)
Saint Gobain/wacker Chemie/Nom M.774 (paras 99–112)
Coca-Cola/Amalgamated Beverages GB M.794 (paras 102–103)
Mannesmann/Vallourec M.906 (para.62)
Swedish Match/KAV M.997 (paras 23, 28–29)
Nestlé/San Pellegrino M.1065 (para.19)
British Steel/Europipe M.1014 (para.34)
TKS/ITW Signode/Titan M.970 (para.49)
Neste/IVO M.931
Sanitec/Sphinx M.1578 (paras 47–69)
Volvo/Viag M.1673 (paras 22–31)
⋆Blackstone/Acetex M.3625 (paras 26–37)
France T–68/94 (grounds 129, 130, 139)

2.3.4. Homogeneous conditions of competition

⋆Magneti-Marelli/CEAC M.43 (para.16)
⋆Varta/Bosch M.12 (para.29)
Mannesmann/Boge M.134 (para.15)
Linde AG/Fiat M.256 (para.19)
Mannesmann/Hoesch M.222 (para.77)
Fletcher Challenge/Methanex M.331 (paras 16–17)
Costa Crociere/Chargeurs Accor M.334 (para.18)
Kali-Salz/MDK/Treuhand M.308 (para.41)
Mannesman/Vallourec/Ilva M.315 (paras 22–26)
Procter & Gamble VP/Schnickendanz M.430 (paras 95–104, 175–181)
Tractebel/Distrigaz M.493 (para.25)
ABB/Daimler Benz M.580 (para.23)
France T–68/94 (grounds 130–136)

2.3.5. Stability of market shares

Areva/Urenco/ETC JV M.3099 (paras 76–79)
Iberdrola/Scottish Power M.4517 (27–32)

2.3.6. Historical evidence on cross-elasticity

Notice on market definition (para.45)
Mannesmann/Vallourec/Ilva M.315 (paras 29–32, 35)
Svenska Cellulosa/PWA M.549 (para.37)
Saint Gobain/wacker Chemie/Nom M.774 (paras 126, 128–130)
Danish Crown/Vestjske Slagterier M.1313 (paras 62–64)

2.3.7. Consumer surveys/views of competitors and customers

Notice on market definition (para.47)
KNP/Bührmann Tetterode/VRG M.291 (para.15)
Kali-Salz/MDK/Treuhand M.308 (para.34)
Rütgers/Hüls Troisdorf M.401 (para.16)
Vesuvius/Wülfrath M.472 (para.24)
AKZO Nobel/Monsanto M.523 (para.20)
Orkla/Volvo M.582 (para.53)
ABB/Daimler Benz M.580 (para.36–37)
Crown Cork & Seal/Carnaud Metalbox M.655 (para.41)
Cardo/Thyssen M.818 (para.23)
Coca-Cola/Amalgamated Beverages GB M.794 (para.104)
Price Waterhouse/Coopers & Lybrand M.1016 (paras 59–61)
TPG/Technologistica M.1500 (paras 16–17)

2.3.8. Domestic supply exceeds domestic demand

Kali-Salz/MDK/Treuhand M.308 (paras 34–39)

2.3.9. Single EU brand/packaging

Nordic Capital/Mölnlycke Clinical/Kolmi M.1075 (para.15)
Sanitec/Sphinx M.1578 (paras 89–101, 109–111)
Unilever/Bestfoods M.1990 (paras 55–57)

2.3.10. Different distribution systems in different Member States

Sanitec/Sphinx M.1578 (paras 73–74)
Siemens/Dematic/VDO/Sachs M.2059 (para.126)
⋆France T–68/94 (grounds 142, 149)

2.3.11. Effect of liberalisation

Veba/Viag M.1673 (paras 34–41)
Verbund/EnergieAllianz M.2947 (paras 16–23, 103)
Gaz de France/Suez M.4180 (paras 155–160, 696–698)

MERGERS: SUBSTANTIVE ISSUES

[For the tables of case citations see Tables 5 to 8 and 12 at the back of the book.]

2.4. Examples of local markets

Promodes/Dirsa M.27 (para.8)
Promodes/BRMC M.242 (paras 9–13)
Ahold/Jeronimo Martins/Inovçao M.320 (paras 14, 17)
Delhaise/PG M.480 (paras 9–11)
Somerfield/115 Morrison Stores UK M.8
HMV/Ottakars UK M.7

2.5. Examples of regional markets

VIAG/Continental Can M.81 (paras 16–17)
Eridania/ISI M.62 (paras 22–25)
Promodes/BRMC M.242 (para.16)
Avesta/British Steel/NCC M.239 (para.125)
Procordia/Erbamont M.323 (paras 11–12)
Costa Crociere/Chargeurs Accor M.334 (para.17–19)
British Steel/Svensk Stal/VSO M.503 (paras 19–20)
Crown Cork & Seal/Carnaud Metalbox M.655 (paras 46–49)
OBS! Danmark M.998 (paras 14–15)
Lafarge/Redland M.1030 (paras 16–18)
Promodes/Catteau M.1085 (paras 13–19)
BP/E.ON M.2533 (paras 12–16)
Group 4 Falck/Securicor M.3396 (paras 39–47)
Owens Illinois/BSN Glasspack M.3397 (paras 17–26)
Sovion/HMG M.3650 (paras 17–44)
Sonoco/Ahlstrom/JV M.3431 (paras 50–68, 76–81)
Jefferson Smurfit/Kappa M.3935 (paras 23, 27)
Sovion/Südfleisch M.3968 (paras 16–36)

2.6. Examples of national markets

AG/Amev M.18 (para.12)
Fiat/Ford/New Holland M.58 (paras 16–18, 24–26, 30)
Otto/Grattan M.70 (para.10)
Alcatel/Telettra M.42 (paras 33–34)
Redoute/Empire Stores M.80 (para.12)
Usinor/ASD M.73 (para.8)
Sanofi/Sterling Drugs M.72 (para.17)
Thomson/Pilkington M.86 (paras 21–24)
UAP/Transatlantic/Sunlife M.141 (para.21)
TNT/Canada Post M.102 (paras 31–33)
Alcatel/AEG Kabel M.147 (paras 13–17)
Accor/Wagon-Lits M.126 (para.16)
Thomas Cook/LTU/West LB M.229 (paras 10, 13–15)
Matra/Cap Gemini Sogeti M.272 (para.14)
ABB/Daimler Benz M.580 (para.23–43)
Ciba-Geigy/Sandoz M.737 (paras 47–49)
Promodes/Casino M.991 (para.25)
OBS! Danmark M.998 (paras 14–15)
Price Waterhouse/Coopers & Lybrand M.1016 (paras 55–63)

2.7. Examples of Community/EEA markets

Fiat/Ford/New Holland M.58 (paras 16–18, 21–22)
Tetra Pak/Alfa-Laval M.68 (paras IV.B.2.3)
Mannesmann/Boge M.134 (paras 14–16)
Metallgesellschaft/Safic Alcan M.146 (paras 20–21)
Lucas/Eaton M.149 (para.35)
Alcatel/AEG Kabel M.147 (paras 13–17)
Courtaulds/SNIA M.113 (paras 15–16)
Du Pont/ICI M.214 (para.29)
Siemens/Va Tech M.3653 (paras 21–30)

2.8. Examples of world markets

MBB/Aérospatiale M.17 (para.18)
Aérospatiale-Alenia/de Havilland M.93 (para.20)
Metallgesellschaft/Safic Alcan M.146 (paras 17–19)
ERC/NRG Victory M.433
Gencor/Lonrho M.619 (paras 68–73)
Mederic/Urrpimmec/CRI/Munich Re M.949 (para.13)
Imetal/English China Clays M.1381 (paras 45–48)
Alcoa/Reynolds M.1693 (paras 18, 96)
Oracle/People Soft M.3216 (paras 173–176)
Blackstone/Acetex M.3625 (paras 26–82)

2.9. Examples of markets in evolution from national to Community-wide

Notice on market definition (para.32)
★Torras/Sarrio M.166 (paras 30–34, 38–40)
Henkel/Nobel M.186 (paras 11–13)
Generali/BCHA M.189 (para.18)
Eureko M.207 (para.16b)
ABB/Brel M.221 (paras 10–12)
★Mannesmann/Hoesch M.222 (paras 79–88)
KNP/Bührmann Tetterode/VRG M.291 (para.58)
Deutsche Bank/Banco de Madrid M.341 (para.8)
American Cyanamid/Shell M.354 (paras 20–22)
VIAG/Bayernwerk M.417 (para.15)
Tractebel/Distrigaz M.493 (para.26)
★Mercedes Benz/Kässbohrer M.477 (paras 79–100)

[For the tables of case citations see Tables 5 to 8 and 12 at the back of the book.]

★ABB/Daimler Benz M.580 (paras 31–36, 43)
PTT Post/TNT/GD Express M.843 (para.28)
★Mannesmann/Vallourec M.906 (paras 61–65)
Siemens/Elektrowatt M.913 (paras 44, 49–53)
Dicta in Corus/Arcelor UK M.9

2.10. Speed at which markets must evolve from national to EU to World

★ABB/Daimler Benz M.580 (para.43)

2.11. Consequence of market definition on the competition assessment

Schneider Electric T–310/01 (paras 163–164, 170–192)

B. SUBSTANTIVE ASSESSMENT

1. Definition

Article 2(3), Regulation 139/2004
Guidelines on horizontal mergers (paras 1–4)
★Continental Can 36 (para.3)
Renault/Volvo M.4
MSG Media Service M.469 (para.35)
CVC/Lenzing M.2187 (para.137)
United Brands 27/76 (grounds 63–65)
★Hoffman-La Roche 85/76 (grounds 38–41, 70–71)
Michelin 322/81 (grounds 57–59)
EDP T–87/05 (paras 44–55)
General Electric T–210/01 (paras 84–89)

1.1. Commission's burden of proof

France T–68/94 (paras 223–224)
Airtours T–342/99 (para.63)
Schneider Electric T–77/02 (paras 176–191)
Tetra Laval T–5/02 (para.312)
Commission v Tetra Laval C-12/03P (paras 38–39, 42–44)
General Electric T–210/01 (paras 60, 62–64, 253)
Impala T–464/04 (paras 284–285)
OFT and others v IBA Health Limited UK M.6
Unichem v OFT UK M.5
Celesio AG v OFT UK M.3

2. Non coordinated effects: Relevant factors

2.1. Market share

Notice on market definition (para.53)
Guidelines on horizontal mergers (paras 14–18, 27)
★Hoffman-La Roche 85/76 (grounds 38–41, 51, 57–58, 61–63)
Akzo III C-62/86 (grounds 60)
Alcatel/Telettra M.42 (para.37)
Magneti-Marelli/CEAC M.43 (para.16)
★Tetra Pak/Alfa-Laval M.68 (para.IV.B.3.2)
Varta/Bosch M.12 (paras 32–33)
Digital/Philips M.129 (para.18)
Mannesmann/Boge M.134 (paras 18–19, 27)
★Aérospatiale-Alenia/de Havilland M.53 (paras 28–31)
Lucas/Eaton M.149 (paras 36–37)
Mannesmann/VDO M.164 (paras 21, 27–28, 31)
Accor/Wagon-Lits M.126 (paras 17, 25)
★Du Pont/ICI M.214 (para.32)
Air France/Sabena M.157 (paras 29, 35)
Mannesmann/Hoesch M.222 (paras 91–94)
British Airways/Dan Air M.278 (para.10)
Rhône-Poulenc/SNIA M.355 (para.23)
American Cyanamid/Shell M.354 (paras 29–33)
★Kali-Salz/MDK/Treuhand M.308 (paras 46–49, 69)
SNECMA/TI M.368 (paras 23–25)
★Mannesmann/Vallourec/Ilva M.315 (paras 47–51)
Rhône-Poulenc-SNIA/Nordfaser M.399 (para.22)
Unilever/Ortiz Miko M.422 (para.33)
★Allied Lyons/HWE-Pedro Domecq M.400 (paras 27–31)
Medeol/Elosua M.431 (paras 18–20)
Shell/Montecatini M.269 (paras 53–54, 61–62, 103)
Procter & Gamble VP/Schnickendanz M.430 (paras 112–121)
Tractebel/Distrigaz M.493 (paras 34, 37–38)
Vesuvius/Wülfrath M.472 (paras 26–27)
MSG Media Service M.469 (paras 55–57, 75, 92)
Elf Atochem/Shell Chimie M.475 (paras 46–48)
★Mercedes-Benz/Kässbohrer M.477 (paras 48–49, 59, 61–65, 86–87)
Siemens/Italtel M.468 (paras 37–43)
Svenska Cellulosa/PWA M.549 (paras 34–35)
Nordic Satellite M.490 (paras 75–76)
RTL/Veronica/Endemol M.553 (paras 64, 67–80, 91–97)
Orkla/Volvo M.582 (para.60)
Henkel/Schwarzkopf M.630 (paras 18, 25)
ABB/Daimler Benz M.580 (paras 55–64, 71, 81)
Chase Manhattan/Chemical M.642 (paras 13–18)

MERGERS: SUBSTANTIVE ISSUES

[For the tables of case citations see Tables 5 to 8 and 12 at the back of the book.]

Crown Cork & Seal/Carnaud Metalbox M.655 (paras 55, 106–108, 111–112)
Kimberley-Clark/Scott Paper M.623 (paras 117–119, 124–127)
Siemens/Lagardere M.685 (para.22)
Ciba-Geigy/Sandoz M.737 (paras 135–141)
Zeneca/Vanderhave M.781 (para.20)
Baxter/Immuno M.821 (paras 15, 19–20, 24)
⋆Saint Gobain/wacker Chemie/Nom M.774 (paras 161, 170, 223, 240–243)
P&O/Royal Nedlloyd M.831 (paras 42–43, 48–101)
Coca-Cola/Amalgamated Beverages GB M.794 (paras 132–136)
Boeing/McDonnell Douglas M.877 (paras 28–37, 54–57)
Siemens/Elektrowatt M.913 (paras 82–93, 94–99, 116)
Credit Suisse First Boston/Barclays M.1068 (para.7)
Merrill Lynch/Mercury M.1067 (para.9)
TKS/ITW Signode/Titan M.970 (paras 55–70)
Price Waterhouse/Coopers & Lybrand M.1016 (paras 69, 84–94)
France T–68/94 (grounds 192–195)
GE T–210/01 (grounds 124–181)
Bombardier/Adtranz M.2139 (para. 40)
Inco/Falconbridge M.4000 (paras 234–236, 296–321, 436–447)
⋆Freeport-McMoran Copper & Gold/Phelps Dodge M.4505 (paras 24–29)
Orica/Dyno M.4151 (paras 60–61)

2.1.1. Absence of available market share data/alternative calculation

Accor/Blackstone/Colony/Vivendi M.1596 (para.33)
Exxon/Mobil M.1383 (paras 22–25, 334–341)
Allied Signal/Honeywell M.1601 (para.65)
Carrefour/Promodes M.1684 (paras 47–50)
Ocean Group/Exel (NFC) M.1895 (para.12)
Compagnie de Saint-Gobain/Raab Karcher M.1974 (para.14)
Scottish & Newcastle/Groupe Danone M.1925 (paras 14–17)
WPP Group/Young & Rubicam M.2000 (paras 25–27)
Tyco/Mallinckrodt M.2074 (para.15)
Masterfoods/Royal Canin M.2544 (paras 28–30)
Lagardère/Natexis/VUP M.2978 (paras 420–438, 514–523)
BT/AT&T JV15 (paras 106–110, 133–136)
Group 4 Falck/Securicor M.3396 (paras 98–121)
WPP/Grey M.3579 (paras 50–52, 58–61)
Verizon/MCI M.3752 (paras 27–32, 75)
Toshiba/Westinghouse M.4153 (paras 66–68)

2.2. Size and importance of competitors

Michelin 165 (paras 15, 17, 35)
United Brands 27/76 (grounds 109–121)
⋆Hoffman-La Roche 85/76 (grounds 48, 51, 58)
Renault/Volvo M.4 (para.14)
⋆Tetra Pak/Alfa-Laval M.68 (paras IV.B.3.3, B.3.4, C.3.2)
Varta/Bosch M.12 (paras 33–34, 45–50, 58–63)
Mannesmann/Boge M.134 (paras 20–28, 34–36)
⋆Aérospatiale-Alenia/de Havilland M.53 (paras 34–42)
Metallgesellschaft/Safic Alcan M.146 (paras 22, 24)
Mannesmann/VDO M.164 (paras 28, 31)
⋆Courtaulds/SNIA M.113 (paras 20–29)
Accor/Wagon-Lits M.126 (paras 17, 25)
⋆Du Pont/ICI M.214 (paras 32, 38–41)
British Airways/Dan Air M.278 (para.10)
KNP/Bührmann Tetterode/VRG M.291 (paras 20, 23, 49, 54, 58)
Costa Crociere/Chargeurs Accor M.334 (para.22)
Rhône-Poulenc/SNIA M.355 (para.23)
Mannesmann/Vallourec/Ilva M.315 (paras 97–124, 130–131)
Rhône-Poulenc-SNIA/Nordfaser M.399 (para.22)
Unilever/Ortiz Miko M.422 (para.33)
Allied Lyons/HWE-Pedro Domecq M.400 (para.38)
Medeol/Elosua M.431 (paras 18–20, 34–36)
BSN/Euralim M.445 (paras 31–37)
Shell/Montecatini M.269 (paras 72–84, 104)
Procter & Gamble VP/Schnickendanz M.430 (paras 148–150, 172–174)
Elf Atochem/Rütgers M.442 (paras 52–55)
Tractebel/Distrigaz M.493 (para.39)
Vesuvius/Wülfrath M.472 (para.27)
MSG Media Service M.469 (paras 55–57, 62, 65–68, 75, 92)
Elf Atochem/Shell Chimie M.475 (para.46)
Mercedes Benz/Kässbohrer M.477 (paras 69–78)

[For the tables of case citations see Tables 5 to 8 and 12 at the back of the book.]

Svenska Cellulosa/PWA M.549 (paras, 35–36)
Siemens/Italtel M.468 (paras 55–57)
Nordic Satellite M.490 (paras 77–95)
RTL/Veronica/Endemol M.553 (paras 47–68)
Orkla/Volvo M.582 (paras 61–64, 91–93)
Henkel/Schwarzkopf M.630 (paras 22, 30)
Crown Cork & Seal/Carnaud Metalbox M.655 (paras 56–59, 65–68)
Ciba-Geigy/Sandoz M.737 (paras 70–75)
Baxter/Immuno M.821 (paras 25–27)
Saint Gobain/wacker Chemie/Nom M.774 (paras 143–161, 171, 175–179)
Coca-Cola/Amalgamated Beverages GB M.794 (paras 142–146, 152–188)
Boeing/McDonnell Douglas M.877 (para.59)
Siemens/Elektrowatt M.913 (paras 84–88, 94–99)
Swedish Match/KAV M.997 (paras 39–40)
TKS/ITW Signode/Titan M.970 (paras 55–70)
★Price Waterhouse/Coopers & Lybrand M.1016 (paras 71–94)
Recoletos/Unedisa M.1401 (para.32)
France T–68/94 (grounds 186–191)
Inco/Falconbridge M.4000 (paras 237–269, 322–353, 448–464)

2.3. Acquisition of closest/maverick competitor

Guidelines on horizontal mergers (paras 28–30, 37–38)
Exxon/Mobil M.1383 (paras 219–224)
Volvo/Scania M.1672 (paras 80–82, 97, 107, 148, 188, 279, 289, 308)
Volvo/Renault VI M.1980 (paras 34, 37)
SCA/Metsä Tissue M.2097 (paras 147, 150)
Schneider Electric/Legrand M.2283 (paras 545–549, 679–685, 759–771)
CVC/Lenzing M.2187 (para.161)
Philips/Marconi Medical Systems M.2537 (paras 31–34)
Promatech/Sulzer M.2698 (para.75)
Siemens/Drägerwerk/JV M.2861 (paras 88–103, 123–142)
GE/Instrumentarium M.3083 (paras 243–248)
Johnson&Johnson/Guidant M.3687 (paras 265–272)
Adidas/Reebok M.3942 (paras 37–47)
Linde/Boc M.4141 (paras 189–192)
T-Mobile Austria/tele.ring M.3916 (paras 125–126)
Inco/Falconbridge M.4000 (paras 259–269, 293–296)
Gaz de France/Suez M.4180 (paras 161–174, 477–500)

2.4. Gap cases (unilateral effects)

Largardere/Natexis/VU M.1970 (paras 700–707)
Oracle/People Soft M.2046 (paras 187)
T-Mobile Austria/tele.ring M.3916 (paras 125–126)

2.5. HHI

Guidelines on horizontal mergers (paras 19–21)
Vivendi/FCC M.1365 (para.40)
Hutchison/RCPM/ECT JV55 (para.50)
Yamanouchi/Fujisawa M.3493 (para. 14)
Kesko/ICA JV M.3464 (paras 30,47)
Johnson & Johnson/Pfizer Consumer Healthcare M.4314 (para. 73)
T-Mobile Austria/tele.ring M.3916 (paras 44–48)
Inco/Falconbridge M.4000 (para 234)

2.6. Commercial advantages over competitors (including product range, access to essential facilities and vertical integration)

Vitamins 104 (paras 4, 6, 8, 21)
Michelin 165 (paras 13, 36)
British Plaster Board 299 (paras, 43, 120)
AT&T/NCR M.50 (paras 28–30)
Aérospatiale-Alenia/de Havilland M.53 (paras 32–33)
★Du Pont/ICI M.214 (paras 34–36, 41)
Mannesmann/Hoesch M.222 (para.95)
Procter & Gamble VP/Schnickendanz M.430 (paras 155–160)
MSG Media Service M.469 (paras 61, 63, 76–90, 93)
AKZO Nobel/Monsanto M.523 (paras 26–28)
★Nordic Satellite M.490 (paras 77–141)
RTL/Veronica/Endemol M.553 (paras 41–45, 66, 72)
Orkla/Volvo M.582 (paras 66, 96)
ABB/Daimler Benz M.580 (paras 65, 67)
★Crown Cork & Seal/Carnaud Metalbox M.655 (paras 77–141)
Kimberley-Clark/Scott Paper M.623 (paras 133–135, 133–138, 149–155, 170–171, 177, 200–205)
Cardo/Thyssen M.818 (paras 29–30)
Saint Gobain/wacker Chemie/Nom M.774 (paras 137–150)
Coca-Cola/Amalgamated Beverages GB M.794 (paras 137–150)
British Telecom/MCI (II) M.856 (paras 58–65, 74)

MERGERS: SUBSTANTIVE ISSUES

[For the tables of case citations see Tables 5 to 8 and 12 at the back of the book.]

★Boeing/McDonnell Douglas M.877 (paras 38–47, 61–71, 83–103, 105–112)
Siemens/Elektrowatt M.913 (paras 118–119)
★Bertelsmann/Kirch/Premiere M.993 (paras 31–42, 48–69, 78–98, 106–118)
★Deutsche Telekom/Beta Research M.1027 (paras 25–54)
Rewe/Meinl M.1221 (paras 31–55, 107–114)
Carrefour/Promodes M.1684 (paras 56–63)
Shell/BASF-Project Nicole M.1751 (paras 32–34, 53)
AOL/Time Warner M.1845 (paras 66–74, 81–85, 88–90)
Schneider Electric/Legrand M.2283 (paras 550–565, 628–641, 654–678, 725–732)
United Brands 27/76 (grounds 69–96)
GE T–210/01 (grounds 182–242)
Axalto/Gemplus M.3998 (paras 55–66)
Gaz de France/Suez M.4180 (paras 175–201)

2.7. Technical advantages over competitors

Michelin 165 (para.13)
Tetra Pak I 289 (para.44)
★Du Pont/ICI M.214 (para.33)
Shell/Montecatini M.269 (paras 65, 68, 111)
MSG Media Service M.469 (paras 61, 63)
Crown Cork & Seal/Carnaud Metalbox M.655 (para.61)
Kimberley-Clark/Scott Paper M.623 (paras 154–157)
Saint Gobain/wacker Chemie/Nom M.774 (paras 172–174)
Shell/BASF-Project Nicole M.1751 (paras 47–52)
Dow Chemical/Union Carbide M.1671 (paras 104–114, 135–136, 139–144)
Alcoa/Reynolds M.1693 (paras 49–51)
AOL/Time Warner M.1845 (paras 55–58, 60–64)
★General Electric/Honeywell M.2220 (paras 146–162)
De Beers/LVMH M.2333 (paras 48–53)
★United Brands 27/76 (grounds 82–83)

2.8. Financial advantages over competitors

Volvo/Procordia M.196 (para.12)
Boeing/McDonnel Douglas M.877 (paras 53, 72)
BP Amoco/Arco M.1532 (para.29)
Carrefour/Promodes M.1684 (paras 70–75)
★General Electric/Honeywell M.2220 (paras 107–120)
Deutsche Post/DHL (11) M.2908 (paras 29–38)
BSkyB/Kirch Pay-Tv JV37 (para.50)
GE T–210/01 (grounds 201, 228)

2.9. Statutory dominance or monopoly

★General Motors 84
★British Telecommunications 188 (paras 25–27)
★General Motors 26/75 (grounds 4–10)
Télémarketing v CLT 311/84 (ground 17)
British Leyland 226/84
Tractebel/Distrigaz M.493 (paras 30, 41)
Sanofi/Synthelabo M.1397; M.1397 (paras 57–59)
Telia/Telenor M.1439 (paras 8, 131, 171)
Seita/Tabacalera M.1735 (para.5)

2.10. Entry barriers

2.10.1. Basic concept

Alcatel/Telettra M.42 (paras 38–40)
★Tetra Pak/Alfa-Laval M.68 (paras IV.B.3.4)
Varta/Bosch M.12 (paras 31–40)
★Aérospatiale-Alenia/de Havilland M.53 (paras 53–63)
Lucas/Eaton M.149 (para.371)
★Courtaulds/SNIA M.113 (paras 22–29)
Mannesmann/VDO (paras 22, 28)
Accor/Wagon-Lits M.126 (paras 17, 25(2)(a))
★Elf Aquitaine Thyssen/Minol AG M.235 (paras 11–13)
★Mannesmann/Hoesch M.222 (paras 103–111)
Procordia/Erbamont M.323 (paras 18, 20)
Rhône-Poulenc/SNIA M.355 (paras 20, 26)
Mercedes Benz/Kässbohrer M.477 (paras 79–100)
Continental/Phoenix M.3436 (paras 19–37, 193–197)
Cementbouw Handel T–282/02 (grounds 216–226)
Inco/Falconbridge M.4000 (paras 383–394, 415–476)
Gaz de France/Suez M.4180 (paras 202–270, 500–615, 876–932)

2.10.2. Regulatory barriers

Eridania/ISI M.62 (para.14)
★Courtaulds/SNIA M.113 (paras 22–29)

Accor/Wagon-Lits M.126 (para.25)
Air France/Sabena M.157 (paras 26, 30, 52–54)
British Airways/TAT M.259 (paras 23–24)
Ahold/Jeronimo Martins/Inovçao M.320 (para.22)
Siemens/Italtel M.468 (paras 48–49)
Orkla/Volvo M.582 (paras 79, 106)
Tesco/ABF M.914 (para.34)
British Telecom/MCI (II) M.856 (paras 27–37)
TotalFina/Elf M.1628 (paras 207–210)
Gaz de France/Suez M.4180 (paras 899–907)

2.10.3. Risk/likely return on investment: saturated nature of market

Draeger/IBM/HMP M.101 (para.10)
Tetra Pak/Alfa-Laval M.68 (paras IV.3.4, IV.4)
⋆Aérospatiale-Alenia/de Havilland M.53 (paras 54–63)
TNT/Canada Post M.102 (para.43)
Accor/Wagon-Lits M.126 (para.17)
Procter & Gamble VP/Schnickendanz M.430 (paras 132–133)
MSG Media Service M.469 (para.60)
Svenska Cellulosa/PWA M.549 (para.40)
Kimberley-Clark/Scott Paper M.623 (paras 206–210)
Siemens/Elektrowatt M.913 (para.118)
Bertelsmann/Kirch/Premiere M.993 (paras 108–109)
Johnson & Johnson/Guidant M.3687 (paras 223–229)
Inco/Falconbridge M.4000 (paras 277–287, 383–394)

2.10.4. Capital requirements

⋆Procter & Gamble VP/Schnickendanz M.430 (paras 136–147)
MSG Media Service M.469 (paras 57–58, 60)
Nordic Satellite M.490 (paras 100, 104)
Saint Gobain/wacker Chemie/Nom M.774 (para.184)
Coca-Cola/Amalgamated Beverages GB M.794 (para.189)
British Telecom/MCI (II) M.856 (paras 70–75)
Boeing/McDonnell Douglas M.877 (para.49)
Linde/Aga M.1641 (paras 82–88)
Volvo/Scania M.1672 (paras 136–138, 141–142)
Alcoa/Reynolds M.1693 (paras 31–33, 38, 118)
SCA/Metsä Tissue M.2097 (paras 92–93)
Johnson & Johnson/Guidant M.3687 (paras 219–220)
Inco/Falconbridge M.4000 (paras 397–398)
Ineos/BP Dormagen M.4094 (para 151)
Linde/Boc M.4141 (paras 174–178)

2.10.5. Need for adequate distribution facilities

KNP/Bührmann Tetterode/VRG M.291 (para.27)
Allied Lyons/HWE-Pedro Domecq M.400 (para.36)
Procter & Gamble VP/Schnickendanz M.430 (para.135)
Orkla/Volvo M.582 (paras 65, 85–90)
Kimberley-Clark/Scott Paper M.623 (paras 213–223)
Coca-Cola/Amalgamated Beverages GB M.794 (paras 109–191)
Volvo/Scania M.1672 (paras 134–135, 197-199, 303–304)
Johnson & Johnson/Guidant M.3687 (paras 214–221)
Linde/Boc M.4141 (paras 174–178)

2.10.6. Entrenched consumer loyalty

KNP/Bührmann Tetterode/VRG M.291 (paras 26–29)
Rhône-Poulenc-SNIA/Nordfaser M.399 (para.22)
BSN/Euralim M.445 (paras 43–45)
Shell/Montecatini M.269 (para.65)
⋆Procter & Gamble VP/Schnickendanz M.430 (paras 125–131)
Svenska Cellulosa/PWA M.549 (para.38)
Kimberley-Clark/Scott Paper M.623 (paras 133–138, 149–155, 170–171, 177, 200–205)
British Telecom/MCI (II) M.856 (para.73)
Promodes/Catteau M.1085 (paras 22–26)
Promodes/S21/Gruppo GS M.1086 (paras 33–36)
Danish Crown/Vestjyske Slagterier M.1313 (paras 152–154, 160–170)
Carrefour/Promodes M.1684 (paras 64–65)
Unilever/Amora-Maille M.1802 (paras 49–52)
Volvo/Scania M.1672 (paras 100–104, 167-169, 177–185, 190–191, 287)
Siemens/Dematic/VDO/Sachs M.2059 (paras 71–72)
Schneider Electric/Legrand M.2283 (paras 489–510)
SEB/Moulinex M.2621 (paras 36–40)
ENI/EDP/GDP M.3440 (paras 489–493)
Linde/Boc M.4141 (paras 174–178)

[For the tables of case citations see Tables 5 to 8 and 12 at the back of the book.]

2.10.7. Previous entry provides evidence that entry barriers low

Costa Crociere/Chargeurs Accor M.334 (para.22)
American Cyanamid/Shell M.354 (paras 34–35)
Svenska Cellulosa/PWA M.549 (para.37)
British Telecom/MCI (II) M.856 (paras 72–73)

2.10.8. Time frame within which entry must be foreseeable

Nordic Satellite M.490 (paras 97–104, 111)
Alcoa/Reynolds M.1693 (paras 31–32, 38)
Johnson & Johnson/Guidant M.3687 (para. 222)

2.10.9. Reinforcement of entry barriers

EDF/Louis Dreyfus M.1557 (paras 45–47)
Allied Signal/Honeywell M.1601 (paras 99–103)
BSkyB/Kirch Pay-Tv JV37 (paras 76–80)
Newscorp/Telepiu M.2876 (paras 117–133)
Nokia/Siemens M.4297 (paras 107–117)

2.11. Imperfect substitutes

Sanofi/Sterling Drugs M.72 (paras 12, 24–25)
Courtauld/SNIA M.113 (para.26)
⋆Du Pont/ICI M.214 (paras 45–46)
Procter & Gamble VP/Schnickendanz M.430 (paras 161–165)
Bertelsmann/News International/Vox M.489 (paras 17–19)
Elf Atochem/Shell Chimie M.475 (paras 39, 50)
Mercedes Benz/Kässbohrer M.477 (paras 17–19)
Svenska Cellulosa/PWA M.549 (paras 40)
Glaxo/Wellcome M.555 (paras 30–31)
Ciba-Geigy/Sandoz M.737 (para.75)
P&O/Royal Nedlloyd M.831 (paras 28–30, 36)
Promodes/Casino M.991 (para.19)
Price Waterhouse/Coopers & Lybrand M.1016 (para.71)
TotalFina/Elf M.1628 (paras 250–272)
Linde/Aga M.1641 (paras 16–19)

2.12. Buying power of customers

Alcatel/Telettra M.42
VIAG/Continental Can M.81 (para.21)
Pechiney/Usinor-Saciler M.97 (para.30)
Mannesmann/Boge M.134 (paras 29–31)
Aérospatiale-Alenia/de Havilland M.53 (paras 43–50)
Metallgesellschaft/Safic Alcan M.146 (para.22)
Lucas/Eaton M.149 (para.37(d))
Accor/Wagon-Lits M.126 (para.17)
⋆Du Pont/ICI M.214 (paras 42–44)
Kingfisher/Darty M.300 (para.9)
KNP/Bührmann Tetterode/VRG M.291 (paras 22–24)
Knorr-Bremse/Allied Signal M.337 (para.39)
Rütgers/Hüls Troisdorf M.401 (paras 26–27)
Allied Lyons/HWE-Pedro Domecq M.400 (para.39)
BSN/Euralim M.445 (para.38)
Shell/Montecatini M.269 (paras 100–101)
Procter & Gamble VP/Schnickendanz M.430 (paras 166–171)
Electrolux/AEG M.458 (para.31)
Vesuvius/Wülfrath M.472 (para.28)
AKZO Nobel/Monsanto M.523 (paras 29–33, 47)
Svenska Cellulosa/PWA M.549 (para.41)
RTL/Veronica/Endemol M.553 (paras 81–83)
Orkla/Volvo M.582 (paras 69–77, 102)
Henkel/Schwarzkopf M.630 (para.27)
Crown Cork & Seal/Carnaud Metalbox M.655 (paras 70, 110)
Kimberley-Clark/Scott Paper M.623 (paras 185–189)
Ciba-Geigy/Sandoz M.737 (para.69)
Thomson/CSF/Finmeccanica M.767 (para.15)
Mannesmann/Vallourec M.906 (paras 87, 91, 104)
Boeing/McDonnell Douglas M.877 (para.47)
Siemens/Elektrowatt M.913 (paras 89, 115, 120)
TKS/ITW Signode/Titan M.970 (paras 73–74)
⋆Enso/Stora M.1225 (paras 84–97)
Danish Crown/Vestjyske Slagterier M.1313 (paras 171–172)
Tyco/Siemens M.1711 (para.15)
Sanitec/Sphinx M.1578 (paras 218–225)
TotalFina/Elf M.1628 (paras 91–101)
General Electric/Honeywell M.2220 (paras 445–458)
Usinor/Arbed/Aceralia M.2382 (paras 161–169)
Schneider Electric/Legrand M.2283 (paras 567–594)
Hutchison/RCPM/ECT JV55 (paras 114–130)
Procter & Gamble/Gillette M.3732 (paras 23–24)
France T–68/94 (grounds 196–197)
Linde/Spectra M.4091 (paras 64–67)
Ineos/BP Dormagen M.4094 (para.149)

[For the tables of case citations see Tables 5 to 8 and 12 at the back of the book.]

2.12.1. Monopsonist customer

General Dynamics/Alvis M.3418 (para.22)

2.13. Size and resources of alleged dominant firm (supply-side buying power)

Boeing/McDonnell Douglas M.877 (paras 72–82, 104–112)
Alcoa/Reynolds M.1693 (paras 39–45)

2.14. Views of customers/competitors; market research

KNP/Bührmann Tetterode/VRG M.291 (para.25)
Costa Crociere/Chargeurs/Accor M.334 (para.22)
Rhône-Poulenc/SNIA M.355 (para.20)
Knorr-Bremse/Allied Signal M.337 (para.41)
Rhône-Poulenc-SNIA/Nordfaser M.399 (para.22)
Unilever/Ortiz Miko M.422 (para.35)
Shell/Montecatini M.269 (paras 65, 69–71)
AKZO Nobel/Monsanto M.523 (para.39)
Mercedes Benz/Kässbohrer M.477 (paras 91–93)
Henkel/Schwarzkopf M.630 (paras 25–26)
Crown Cork & Seal/Carnaud Metalbox M.655 (paras 51–52, 66)
Kimberley-Clark/Scott Paper M.623 (paras 130–136, 190–196)
Baxter/Immuno M.821 (paras 22, 29)
PTT Post/TNT/GD Express M.843 (paras 39–42)
P&O/Royal Nedlloyd M.831 (paras 102–103)
Boeing/McDonnell Douglas M.877 (para.58)
Siemens/Elektrowatt M.913 (para.90)
Swedish Match/KAV M.997 (para.42)
Deutsche Telekom/Beta Research M.1027 (para.49)
Volvo/Scania M.1672 (paras 85–90, 261–263)
Industri Kapital (Nordkem)/Dyno M.1813 (paras 108–110)
Boeing/Hughes M.1879 (paras 84–88)

2.15. Econometric studies and statistical analysis

Volvo/Scania M.1672 (paras 72–75)
GE/Instrumentarium M.3083 (para.131)
Lagardère/Natexis/VUP M.2978 (para.700)
Oracle/People Soft M.3216 (paras 191–205)
Ineos/BP Dormagen M.4094 (paras 91–100)

2.16. Possibilities of switching suppliers

Guidelines on horizontal mergers (para.31)
KNP/Bührmann Tetterode/VRG M.291 (para.24)
Rhône-Poulenc/SNIA M.355 (paras 23, 26)
Rhône-Poulenc-SNIA/Nordfaser M.399 (para.22)
Shell/Montecatini M.269 (para.67)
Siemens/Italtel M.468 (paras 41–42)
Crown Cork & Seal/Carnaud Metalbox M.655 (paras 19, 33, 75–77)
Boeing/McDonnel Douglas M.877 (para.70)
Agfa Gevaert/Du Pont M.986 (paras 63–71)
Price Waterhouse/Coopers & Lybrand M.1016 (paras 37, 40)
Pirelli/BICC M.1882 (paras 24–27)
Siemens/Dematic/VDO/Sachs M.2059 (paras 71–72)
Philips/Marconi Medical Systems M.2537 (paras 35–40)
Magna/New Venture Gear M.3486 (paras 52–64)
Bertelsmann/Springer M.3178 (paras 140–153)
Ineos/BP Dormagen M.4094 (paras 145–154)

2.17. Multi-sourcing policy of customers/shrinkage effect

Dupont/ICI M.984 (para.30)
Volvo/Scania M.1672 (paras 113–131, 155, 193–194, 264–268, 305–306)
Veba/Viag M.1673 (paras 174–175)

2.18. Existence of spare capacity on the market/available alternative capacity

Guidelines on horizontal mergers (paras 32–35)
KNP/Bührmann Tetterode/VRG M.291 (paras 50, 54)
Rhône-Poulenc/SNIA M.355 (para.23)
★Mannesmann/Vallourec/Ilva M.315 (paras 39–43, 62–67)
Rhône-Poulenc-SNIA/Nordfaser M.399 (para.22)
Elf Atochem/Rütgers M.442 (pars. 56–59)
Elf Atochem/Shell Chimie M.475 (para.49)
AKZO Nobel/Monsanto M.523 (para.31)
Orkla/Volvo M.582 (paras 63–64)
Crown Cork & Seal/Carnaud Metalbox M.655 (paras 60, 67, 76–79, 113)
Swedish Match/KAV M.997 (para.40)
CVC/Lenzing M.2187 (paras 162–173)
★Bertelsmann/Springer M.3178 (paras 104–139)

[For the tables of case citations see Tables 5 to 8 and 12 at the back of the book.]

France T-68/94 (ground 238)
Ineos/BP Dormagen M.4094 (paras 80–90, 120, 141)
Mittal/Arcelor M.4137 (paras 112–113)
Orica/Dyno M.4151 (paras 64–65)
Glatfelter/Crompton assets M.4215 (paras 96–104)
Nemak/Hydro Castings M.4524 (para.22)

2.19. New capacities

★Alcoa/Reynolds M.1693 (paras 30–48, 121)
SCA/Metsä Tissue M.2097 (paras 187–191)
Ineos/BP Dormagen M.4094 (paras 101–109, 112)
Glatfelter/Crompton assets M.4215 (para.95)

2.20. Evidence of existing monopoly pricing

Kali-Salz/MDK/Treuhand M.308 (para.47)
Svenska Cellulosa/PWA M.549 (para.40)
Orkla/Volvo M.582 (paras 67, 100–101)

2.21. Ownership of essential infrastructure/raw materials forecloses competition

MSG Media Service M.469 (paras 61, 63, 76, 90, 93)
Saint Gobain/wacker Chemie/Nom M.774 (para.186)
British Telecom/MCI (II) M.856 (paras 38–57)
Bertelsmann/Kirch/Premiere M.993 (paras 31–42, 48–69, 78–98, 110–118)
★Deutsche Telekom/BetaResearch M.1027 (paras 25–54)
DHL/Deutsche Post M.1168
BP Amoco/Arco M.1532 (paras 56–69)
Telia/Telenor M.1439 (paras 287–298, 317, 351–358)
Allied Signal/Honeywell M.1601 (paras 101–103)
★TotalFina/Elf M.1628 (paras 56–90, 119–117, 129–153, 284–291)
Vodafone Airtouch/Mannesmann M.1795 (paras 44–48)
ENI/EDP/GDP M.3440 (para.380)

2.22. Removal of potential competition

Exxon/Mobil M.1383 (para.257)
Telia/Telenor M.1439 (paras 148–154, 215, 331)
Akzo Nobel/Hoechst Roussel Vet M.1681 (paras 69, 74, 82)
Air Liquide/BOC M.1630 (paras 196–222)
EADS M.1745 (paras 92–94)
★EDF/ENBW M.1853 (paras 54–74)
Veba/Viag M.1673 (para.144)
Grupo Villar MIR/ENBW/Hidroelectrica del Cantabrico M.2434 (paras 73–87)
Tetra Laval/Sidel M.2416 (paras 265, 325)
Südzucker/St Louis M.2530 (paras 80–125)
BSkyB/Kirch Pay-Tv JV37 (paras 52–72)
ENI/EDP/GDP M.3440 (paras 335–364)
★Johnson & Johnson/Guidant M.3687 (paras 104–139)
Tetra Laval T-5/02 (paras 312–333)
Commission v Tetra Laval T-12/03P (paras 125–133)
Linde/Boc M.4141 (paras 164–167)
Mittal/Arcelor M.4137 (paras 96–99)
Toshiba/Westinghouse M.4153 (paras 81–98)
Gaz de France/Suez M.4180 (paras 106, 141–142, 159, 161–163, 189, 367–391, 438–439, 447, 471–476)

2.23. Potential for retaliation

Air Liquide/BOC M.1630 (para.193)
EDF/ENBW M.1853 (paras 69–74)
Südzucker/St Louis M.2530 (paras 126–136)

2.24. Raising rival's costs

Guidelines on horizontal mergers (para.36)
Exxon/Mobil M.1383 (para.414)
★Telia/Telenor M.1439 (paras 155–159, 169, 191, 201, 223)
Alcan/Alusuisse M.1663 (paras 77–81)
MMS/Dasa/Astrium M.1636 (paras 60–65)
Alcoa/Reynolds M.1693 (para.28)
Alcan/Pechiney (II) M.3225 (paras 42–43)
ENI/EDP/GDP M.3440 (paras 411–428)
GE T-210/01 (grounds 299–305)

2.25. Effect of liberalisation

Telecom Eireann M.802 (paras 29–35)
British Telecom/MCI (II) M.856 (paras 32–37)
Electrabel/EPON M.1803 (paras 30–31)
Pirelli/BICC M.1882 (paras 59–61)
Framatome/Siemens/Cogema/JV M.1940 (paras 89–95)
EDP/Cajastur/Caser/Hidroelectrica del Cantabrico M.2340 (paras 13–14)

2.26. Products not yet at commercial stage/emerging markets

Hoechst/Rhône Poulenc M.1378 (paras 71–88)
Allied Signal/Honeywell M.1601 (paras 104–108)

[For the tables of case citations see Tables 5 to 8 and 12 at the back of the book.]

Monsanto/Pharmacia & Upjohn M.1835 (paras 92–94)
Vodafone Airtouch/Mannesmann M.1795 (para.33)
Reuters/Equant - Project Proton M.1875 (paras 22, 27–28)
Glaxo Wellcome/SmithKline Beecham M.1846 (paras 150–216)
Pfizer/Warner-Lambert M.1878 (paras 77–80)
France Telecom/Orange M.2016 (paras 36–41)
Siemens/Dematic/VDO/Sachs M.2059 (paras 148–154)
PSA/Vivendi/Wappi! M.2082 (paras 20–22)
AOL/Time Warner M.1845 (paras 46–59)
Vivendi/Canal+/Seagram M.2050 (paras 51–64)
GE/Instrumentarium M.3083 (paras 280–284)
BSkyB/Kirch Pay-Tv JV37 (paras 73–75)

2.27. Bidding markets

Matra/Aerospatiale M.1309 (para.37)
TPG/Technologistica M.1500 (paras 26–27)
Preussag/Babcock/Celsius M.1709 (paras 58–60, 68–73)
Dow Chemical/Union Carbide M.1671 (para.131)
Alcoa/Reynolds M.1693 (paras 52–56, 103–126)
EADS M.1745 (paras 144–154, 164–169)
Pirelli/BICC M.1882 (paras 77–79)
Valeo/Labinal M.2036 (para.26)
Alstom/Fiat Ferroviaria M.2069 (paras 26, 29–30)
Boeing/Hughes M.1879 (paras 33, 38, 42, 63–66)
Alcoa/British Aluminium M.2111 (para.13)
Smith & Nephew+Beiersdorf/JV M1453 (paras 21–22)
GE/Instrumentarium M.3083 (paras. 118–193)
Magna/New Venture Gear M.3486 (paras 38–43)
Siemens/Va Tech M.3653 (paras 38–42, 51–56)
GE T–210/01 (grounds 149–151)
Bombardier/Adtranz M.2139 (paras 39–42)
Gaz de France/Suez M.4180 (paras 980–997)
Alcatel/Lucent Technologies M.4214 (paras 39, 49, 55, 60)
Nokia/Siemens M.4297 (paras 83–87)

3. Vertical mergers

Draft Non-Horizontal merger Guidelines (paras 27–89)

3.1. Commission's burden of proof

GE CM 40 (grounds 296–297)

3.2. Vertical effects

Chiquita 101 (para.11.A.2)
United Brands 27/76 (grounds 69–96)
ICI/Tioxide M.23 (paras 15–18)
Cargill/Unilever M.26 (para.5)
⋆VIAG/Continental Can M.81 (paras 41–51)
VIAG/Brühl M.139 (paras 13–17)
Thorn EMI/Virgin Music M.202 (paras 62–66)
Shell/Montecatini M.269 (para.113)
⋆Tractebel/Distrigaz M.493 (paras 47–49)
British Steel/Svensk Stal/NSD M.503 (para.26)
⋆MSG Media Service M.469
⋆Siemens/Italtel M.468 (paras 58–67)
Nordic Satellite M.490 (paras 80–95, 105, 114–118, 126–131)
RTL/Veronica/Endemol M.553 (paras 45, 98–104)
Crown Cork & Seal/Carnaud Metalbox M.655 (paras 88–95)
Promodes/Catteau M.1085 (paras 21–26)
Caterpillar/Perkins Engines M.1094 (paras 32–37)
Promodes/S21/Gruppo GS M.1086 (paras 33–36)
Nestlé/Dalgety M.1127
⋆Deutsche Telekom/Beta Research M.1027 (paras 25–54)
Neste/IVO M.931
Alcatel/Thomson CSF-SCS M.1185 (paras 31–37)
NC/Canal+/CDPQ/Bank America M.1327
EDF/London Electricity M.1346
International Paper/Union Camp M.1391
Imetal/English China Clays M.1381 (paras 68–70, 78–79)
Matra/Aerospatiale M.1309 (paras 69–77)
British Aerospace/GEC Marconi M.1438 (paras 20–28)
Rhodia/Donau Chemie/Albright & Wilson M.1517 (paras 79–81)
EDF/South Western Electricity M.1471 (paras 27–38)
⋆Telia/Telenor M.1439 (paras 317–324, 359–362)
⋆Alcoa/Reynolds M.1693 (paras 98, 124–128)
Vivendi/Canal+/Seagram M.2050 (paras 39–67)
⋆Framatome/Siemens/Cogema/JV M.1940 (paras 59–69)
General Electric/Honeywell M.2220 (paras 107–120, 337–340, 342–348, 419–427)

MERGERS: SUBSTANTIVE ISSUES

[For the tables of case citations see Tables 5 to 8 and 12 at the back of the book.]

Cendant/Galileo M.2510 (paras 23–37)
Tetra Laval/Sidel M.2416 (paras 291–318)
GE/Instrumentarium M.3083 (paras 287–320)
Lagardère/Natexis/VUP M.2978 (paras 445–467, 527–543, 597–617, 708–733)
Syngenta CP/Advanta M.3465 (paras 85–101)
Verizon/MCI M.3752 (paras 80–97)
Thermo Electron/Fisher Scientific M.4242 (paras 87–106)
WLR/BST M.4389 (paras 26–38)
Lagardere/Sportfive M.4519 (paras 25–38)
Johnson & Johnson/Pfizer Consumer Healthcare M.4314 (paras 125–135)
Evraz/Highveld M.4494 (paras 94–131)
Ineos/BP Dormagen M.4094 (paras 167–209)
Gaz de France Suez M.4180 (paras 839–875)

4. Conglomerate mergers

Draft Non-Horizontal merger Guidelines (paras 90–119)
Tetra Laval/Sidel M.2416 (paras 311–318, 325–370)
Lagardère/Natexis/VUP M.2978 (paras 445–467, 527–543, 597–617, 650–651, 708–733)

4.1. Commission's burden of proof

Tetra Laval T–5/02 (grounds 148–162)
Commission v Tetra Laval T–12/03P (grounds 38–39, 42–44, 71–78)
GE T–210/01 (grounds 65–75, 331–364)

4.2. Bundling/portfolio effects

Matsushita/MCA M.37
AT&T/NCR M.50 (para.23–31)
⋆Tetra Pak/Alfa-Laval M.68
VIAG/Brühl M.139 (paras 18–20)
INFINT/EXOR M.187
RTL/Veronica/Endemol M.553 (paras 30, 45–47, 98)
Coca-Cola/Amalgamated Beverages GB M.794 (paras 208–209)
⋆Guiness Grand Metropolitan M.938 (paras 91–103)
Danish Crown/Vestjyske Slagterier M.1313 (paras 196–197)
Schneider/Lexel M.1434 (paras 16–21)
Akzo Nobel/Hoechst Roussel Vet M.1681 (paras 32, 40–42, 100–104)
Allied Signal/Honeywell M.1601 (paras 61–62, 72–73, 110–124)
Unilever/Amora-Maille M.1802 (paras 53–58)
⋆General Electric/Honeywell M.2220 (paras 276–282, 293–297, 349–406, 412–416)
SEB/Moulinex M.2621 (paras 45–47, 52, 60, 69)
Masterfoods/Royal Canin M.2544 (para.57)
⋆GE/Amersham M.3304 (paras 31–60)
Pernod Ricard/Allied Domeq M.3779 (paras 74–79)
⋆Procter & Gamble/Gillette M.3732 (paras 110–151)
Johnson & Johnson/Guidant M.3687 (paras 335–343)
Schneider Electric T–310/01 (grounds 234–262)
Babyliss T–114/02 (grounds 339–365)
GE T–210/01 (grounds 399–470)
Thule/Chaas Holdings/Advanced Accessory Systems/Valley M.4129 (paras 33–40)
Siemens/UGS Corporation M.4608 (paras 26–31)
Gaz de France/Suez M.4180 (paras 861–866, 1012–1017)

4.3. Leveraging

Tetra Laval T–5/02 (paras 146–309)
Commission v Tetra Laval T–12/03P (paras 71–89)
Gaz de France/Suez M.4180 (paras 1057–1066)
Hewlett Packard/Mercury Interactive M.4350 (paras 23–25)

4.4. Decrease of potential competition

Tetra Laval T–5/02 (paras 310–333)

5. Causality link between merger and dominance

Rewe/Meinl M.1221 (paras 62–69)

6. Co-ordinated effects/Oligopolistic or Joint dominance

6.1. Concept/burden of proof

Guidelines on horizontal mergers (paras 39–60)
European Sugar Industry 69
Flat Glass 300 (paras 78–79)

[For the tables of case citations see Tables 5 to 8 and 12 at the back of the book.]

Varta/Bosch M.12 (para.32)
Alcatel/AEG Kabel M.147 (paras 19–27)
★Nestlé/Perrier M.190 (paras 110–116)
Mannesmann/Vallourec/Ilva M.315 (paras 53, 55, 129)
★Price Waterhouse/Coopers & Lybrand M.1016 (paras 104–106)
Kali-Salz/MDK/Treuhand M.308
★Airtours/First Choice M.1524 (paras 52–56, 148–153)
Ernst & Young France/Andersen France M.2816 (paras 73–75)
★France T–68/94 (grounds 152–178)
★Gencor T–106/96 (grounds 123–157)
Airtours T–342/99 (paras 56–64)
★Impala T–464/04 (paras 245–254, 522–523)

6.2. Relevant factors

6.2.1. Significant market share in few hands

Thorn EMI/Virgin Music M.202 (paras 20–28)
Nestlé/Perrier M.190 (paras 38–48, 118)
Rhône-Poulenc/SNIA M.206 (para.7.2)
CCIE/GTE M.258 (para.23)
Harrisons & Crosfield/AKZO M.310 (paras 30–31, 34)
Kali-Salz/MDK/Treuhand M.308 (paras 51–53)
Pilkington/SIV M.358 (paras 25–28)
Mannesmann/Vallourec/Ilva M.315 (paras 53, 55)
Holderchim/Cedest M.460 (para.28)
Elf Atochem/Shell Chimie M.475 (para.51)
Henkel/Schwarzkopf M.630 (paras 28, 29)
ABB/Daimler Benz M.580 (paras 55–64, 71, 81)
Crown Cork & Seal/Carnaud Metalbox M.655 (para.98)
Cardo/Thyssen M.818 (para.31)
P&O/Royal Nedlloyd M.831 (paras 48–101)
★Price Waterhouse/Coopers & Lybrand M.1016 (paras 68, 84–96, 113)
Rhodia/Donau Chemie/Albright & Wilson M.1517 (paras 63, 69)
★Airtours/First Choice M.1524 (paras 72–73)
★Exxon/Mobil M.1383 (paras 466, 529–531)
Linde/Aga M.1641 (para.44)
France T–68/94 (grounds 192–195)
Gencor T–106/96 (grounds 195–216)
Linde/Boc M.4141 (para.181)

6.2.2. Remaining competitors few/weak

Henkel/Nobel M.186 (para.17)
Nestlé/Perrier M.190 (paras 49–56, 64–76, 119, 129)
Kali-Salz/MDK/Treuhand M.308 (paras 54–56)
★Mannesmann/Vallourec/Ilva M.315 (paras 97–124, 130–131)
Holderchim/Cedest M.460 (para.28)
Elf Atochem/Shell Chimie M.475 (para.51)
Henkel/Schwarzkopf M.630 (para.30)
ABB/Daimler Benz M.580 (paras 66, 68–70, 73–86, 101–137)
Unilever Diversey M.704 (paras 24–29)
Airtours/First Choice M.1524 (paras 75–86)
Veba/Viag M.1673 (paras 91–96)
France T–68/94 (grounds 186–191)
Linde/Boc M.4141 (paras 181–182)

6.2.3. HHI

Enso/Stora M.1225 (para.67)
Airtours/First Choice M.1524 (para.139)
Exxon/Mobil M.1383 (paras 256, 260)
TotalFina/Elf M.1628 (paras 199, 217)

6.2.4. High entry barriers

Thorn EMI/Virgin Music M.202 (paras 34–35)
Nestlé/Perrier M.190 (paras 90–107, 130)
CIE/GTE M.258 (para.25)
Knorr-Bremse/Allied Signal M.337 (para.45)
SNECMA/TI M.368 (para.37)
Mannesmann/Vallourec/Ilva M.315 (paras 116–124)
Gencor/Lonrho M.619 (paras 141, 154)
Price Waterhouse/Coopers & Lybrand M.1016 (para.96)
Airtours/First Choice M.1524 (paras 114–122)
Veba/Viag M.1673 (paras 110–114)
Grupo Villar MIR/ENBW/Hidroelectrica del cantabrico M.2434 (paras 49–66)
BP/E.ON M.2533 (paras 116–127)
★France T–68/94 (grounds 198–200)
Gencor T–106/96 (grounds 247–263)

6.2.5. Stagnant/mature markets (existence of over-capacity)

Henkel/Nobel M.186 (para.17)
Thorn EMI/Virgin Music M.202 (para.36)
Nestlé/Perrier M.190 (para.50)
CCIE/GTE M.258 (para.24)
Harrisons & Crosfield/AKZO M.310 (para.34)
Rhône-Poulenc/SNIA M.355 (para.24)
Pilkington/SIV M.358 (paras 30, 37)
Mannesmann/Vallourec/Ilva M.315 (para.55)
Rhône-Poulenc-SNIA/Nordfaser M.399 (para.24)
Crown Cork & Seal/Carnaud Metalbox M.655 (para.98)
Gencor/Lonrho M.619 (paras 152–153)
Price Waterhouse/Coopers & Lybrand M.1016 (para.98)

[For the tables of case citations see Tables 5 to 8 and 12 at the back of the book.]

Airtours/First Choice M.1524 (paras 92–97)
Exxon/Mobil M.1383 (paras 475, 532–535)
Veba/Viag M.1673 (paras 81–84)
France T–68/94 (ground 238)
Gencor T–106/96 (grounds 231–246)
Airtours T–342/99 (paras 123–133)

6.2.6. Little/innovation/product development (homogeneous product)

Guidelines on horizontal mergers (para.45)
Thorn EMI/Virgin Music M.202 (para.29)
Nestlé/Perrier M.190 (para.126)
Rhône-Poulenc/SNIA M.206 (para.7.2.2.)
CCIE/GTE M.258 (para.28)
Harrisons & Crosfield/AKZO M.310 (para.34)
Rhône-Poulenc/SNIA M.355 (para.24)
Knorr-Bremse/Allied Signal M.337 (para.45)
SNECMA/TI M.368 (para.37)
Rhône-Poulenc-SNIA/Nordfaser M.399 (para.24)
MercedesBenz/Kässbohrer M.477 (para.104)
ABB/Daimler Benz M.580 (para.91)
Crown Cork & Seal/Carnaud Metalbox M.655 (para.98)
Baxter/Immuno M.821 (para.30)
Cardo/Thyssen M.818 (para.33)
TRW/Magna M.872 (para.16)
ICI/Unilever M.933 (para.19)
Price Waterhouse/Coopers & Lybrand M.1016 (para.96)
Airtours/First Choice M.1524 (paras 88–91)
Linde/Aga M.1641 (para.45)
Veba/Viag M.1673 (para.71)
France T–68/94 (ground 240)
Impala T–464/04 (paras 460–462)

6.2.7. Transparent pricing patterns

Guidelines on horizontal mergers (para.47)
Nestlé/Perrier M.190 (paras 62, 121–122)
Rhône-Poulenc/SNIA M.355 (para.24)
Knorr-Bremse/Allied Signal M.337 (para.45)
Pilkington/SIV M.358 (para.36)
SNECMA/TI M.368 (para.37)
Mannesmann/Vallourec/Ilva M.315 (paras 80–95)
Rhône-Poulenc-SNIA/Nordfaser M.399 (para.24)
Elf Atochem/Shell Chimie M.475 (para.52)
AKZO Nobel/Monsanto M.523 (para.45)
ABB/Daimler Benz M.580 (para.89)
Crown Cork & Seal/Carnaud Metalbox M.655 (para.99)
Unilever/Diversey M.704 (para.22)
Gencor/Lonrho M.619 (paras 137–139, 141)
Cardo/Thyssen M.818 (para.33)
Agfa-Gevaert/Sterling M.1432 (paras 26–28)
Airtours/First Choice M.1524 (paras 102–113)
Exxon/Mobil M.1383 (para.474)
Veba/Viag M.1673 (paras 72–74)
Gencor T–106/96 (grounds 223–230)
⋆Impala T–464/04 (paras 278–459)

6.2.8. Bidding markets

Agfa-Gevaert/Sterling M.1432 (para.27)
Robert Bosch/Magnetti Marelli M.1491 (para.28)
CVC/Danone/Gerresheimer M.1539 (para.36)
BP Amoco/Arco M.1532 (para.36)
Castrol/Carless/JV M.1597 (para.34)
Pirelli/BICC M.1882 (para.82)
Alcoa/British Aluminium M.2111 (para.13)
Siemens/Va Tech M.3653 (paras 102–104)

6.2.9. Transparency on capacities, expansions

Norske Skog/Parenco/Walsum M.2499 (paras 82–85)
Airtours T–342/99 (paras 148–182)
Linde/Boc M.4141 (para. 185)

6.2.10. Symmetrical market structure/structural similarities between competitors/common interests

Guidelines on horizontal mergers (para.48)
Pilkington/SIV M.358 (paras 28, 41–42)
Nestlé/Perrier M.190 (para.125)
Rhône-Poulenc/SNIA M.206 (para.7.2.2.)
Mannesmann/Vallourec/Ilva M.315 (paras 57–59)
AKZO Nobel/Monsanto M.523 (para.47)
Mercedes Benz/Kässbohrer M.477 (para.104)
Gencor/Lonrho M.619 (paras 137–139, 182–185)
P&O/Royal Nedlloyd M.831 (paras 48–101)
⋆Airtours/First Choice M.1524 (paras 59–65, 99–101)
⋆Exxon/Mobil M.1383 (paras 476–478, 536-538, 626–629, 660–662, 750–751)
Veba/Viag M.1800 (paras 75–77)
Linde/Aga M.1641 (para.53)
Siemens/Dematic/VDO/Sachs M.2059 (paras 132–134)
Bosch/Rexroth M.2060 (para.79)
BP/E.ON M.2533 (paras 72–94)
Celanese/Degussa M.3056 (paras 44–46)
⋆France T–68/94 (grounds 205–239)
Gencor T–106/96 (grounds 217–222)

[For the tables of case citations see Tables 5 to 8 and 12 at the back of the book.]

E.ON/Prazla Plynarenska M.4238 (para.30)
Omya/J.M. Huber PCC M.3796 (paras 446–450

6.2.11. Structural/personal links between oligopolists

★Kali-Salz/MDK/Treuhand M.308 (paras 57–68)
Pilkington/SIV M.358 (paras 29, 37–40)
ABB/Daimler Benz M.580 (paras 95–96)
Gencor/Lonrho M.619 (paras 141, 155–158)
Cardo/Thyssen M.818 (para.34)
Price Waterhouse/Coopers & Lybrand M.1016 (paras 96, 101–106)
Danish Crown/Vestjyske Slagterier M.1313 (paras 177–179)
Vodafone/AirTouch M.1430 (para.28)
Rhodia/Donau Chemie/Albright & Wilson M.1517 (paras 54, 62, 65)
Airtours/First Choice M.1524 (paras 71, 143–144)
Veba/Viag M.1673 (paras 78–79)
Bosch/Rexroth M.2060 (paras 80–83)
Maersk/PONL M.3829 (paras 38–43, 56–61, 74–81, 86–92, 120–123, 130–135, 140–145)
TUI/CP Ships M.3863 (paras 28–33, 38–43)
★France T–68/94 (grounds 205- 239)
Gencor T–106/96 (grounds 264–284)

6.2.12. Evidence of existing price parallelism/structure of competition in the past

Guidelines on horizontal mergers (para.43)
Nestlé/Perrier M.190 (para.59)
Pilkington/SIV M.358 (paras 32–35)
ABB/Daimler Benz M.580 (paras 92–94)
Gencor/Lonrho M.619 (paras 160–177)
Price Waterhouse/Coopers & Lybrand M.1016 (paras 103–106, 113)
Airtours/First Choice M.1524 (paras 128–138)
Exxon/Mobil M.1383 (paras 243–244, 510-512, 539–553, 708–738)
Veba/Viag M.1673 (para.80)
Gencor T–106/96 (grounds 293–296)
Airtours T–342/99 (paras 80–120)
Impala T–464/04 (paras 252–254)

6.2.13. Buying power

Nestlé/Perrier M.190 (paras 77, 89)
Harrisons & Crosfield/AKZO M.310 (para.34)
Pilkington/SIV M.358 (para.56)
SNECMA/TI M.368 (para.37–38)
Mannesmann/Vallourec/Ilva M.315 (para.125)
★ABB/Daimler Benz M.580 (paras 101–137)
Unilever/Diversey M.704 (para.24)
Baxter/Immuno M.821 (para.30)
TRW/Magna M.872 (para.16)
Airtours/First Choice M.1524 (paras 124–126)
Veba/Viag M.1673 (paras 85–87)
Siemens/Dematic/VDO/Sachs M.2059 (paras 127–128 & 156)
France T–68/94 (grounds 196–197)
Orica/Dyno M.4151 (para.66)

6.2.14. Price-inelastic demand

Nestlé/Perrier M.190 (para.124)
Rhône-Poulenc/SNIA M.355 (para.24)
Mannesmann/Vallourec/Ilva M.315 (para.55)
Gencor/Lonrho M.619 (paras 141, 149)
Price Waterhouse/Coopers & Lybrand M.1016 (para.99)
Agfa-Gevaert/Sterling M.1432 (para.29)
Airtours/First Choice M.1524 (para.98)
Exxon/Mobil M.1383 (para.479)
Veba/Viag M.1673 (paras 83–84)
Celanese/Degussa M.3056 (paras 47–48)

6.2.15. Absence of potential competition

Exxon/Mobil M.1383 (paras 481–485, 562, 605–607, 670–679, 755–757)

6.2.16. Commercial advantages over competitors (including product range, access to essential facilities and vertical integration)

Veba/Viag M.1673 (paras 105–109, 115–119, 126–129)
★General Electric/Honeywell M.2220 (paras 121–145)
De Beers/LVMH M.2333 (paras 63–83)

6.2.17. Co-ordination mechanism

Norske Skog/Parenco/Walsum M.2499 (paras 131–132, 138)

6.2.18. Monitoring deviations

Guidelines on horizontal mergers (paras 49–51)

6.2.19. Retaliation mechanism

Guidelines on horizontal mergers (para.52–55)
★Airtours/First Choice M.1524 (paras 148–153)
Exxon/Mobil M.1383 (paras 487, 566–567)
TotalFina/Elf M.1628 (paras 218–219)

[For the tables of case citations see Tables 5 to 8 and 12 at the back of the book.]

Alcan/Alusuisse M.1663 (para.97)
Alcoa/British Aluminium M.2111 (para.14)
Outokumpu/Norzink M.2348 (paras 24–25)
Norske Skog/Parenco/Walsum M.2499 (paras 131–132, 138)
BP/E.ON M.2533 (paras 106–115)
Airtours T–342/99 (paras 183–207)
Impala T–464/04 (paras 463–474)
Linde/Boc M.4141 (paras 186–188)

6.2.20. Reaction of outsiders and clients

Guidelines on horizontal mergers (paras 56–57)
★Airtours/First Choice M.1524 (paras 77–86, 124–125)
★Airtours T–342/99 (paras 208–276)
LSG Lufthansa Service Holding/Gate Gourmet Switserland M.4170 (paras 45–48)
Impala T–464/04 (paras 383–387)

6.2.21. Strengthening of collective dominance

Sony/BMG M.3333 (paras. 60–154)
Impala T–464/04 (paras 243–481)

7. Significant impediment of competition

Aérospatiale-Alenia/de Havilland M.53
Procter & Gamble VP/Schnickendanz M.430 (para.182)
Mercedes Benz/Kässbohrer M.477 (paras 101–102)
RWE/Hidroelectrica del Cantabrico M.2353 (para.10)

8. Strengthening of an existing dominant position

Mannesmann/VDO M.164 (paras 29–30, 34–37)
VIAG/Bayernwerk M.417 (paras 12–15)
Tractebel/Distrigaz M.493 (paras 44–50)
AKZO Nobel/Monsanto M.523 (paras 37–42)
Glaxo/Wellcome M.555 (paras 26–33)
Gencor/Lonrho M.619 (paras 179–206)
Coca-Cola/Amalgamated Beverages GB M.794 (paras 196–212)
EDF/ENBW M.1853 (paras 51–89)
Babyliss T–114/02 (paras 318–327)

9. Creation/Strengthening of a dominant position of a third party

Exxon/Mobil M.1383 (paras 225–229)
★Newscorp/Telepiu M.2876 (paras 269–324)
France T–68/94 (para.171)

10. Significant part of the Common Market

VIAG/Bayernwerk M.417 (para.13)

C. EFFICIENCY DEFENCE (PROMOTING TECHNICAL/ECONOMIC PROGRESS, EFFICIENCIES)

Article 2(1)(b) and preamble 29, Regulation 139/2004
Guidelines on the assessment of horizontal mergers (paras 76–88)
AT&T/NCR M.50 (paras 28–30)
★Aérospatiale-Alenia/de Havilland M.53 (paras 65–71)
MSG Media Service M.469 (paras 100–101)
Nordic Satellite M.490 (para.150)
Gencor/Lonrho M.619 (paras 212–214)
Saint Gobain/wacker Chemie/Nom M.774 (paras 244–246)
★Bertelsmann/Kirch/Premiere M724 (paras 119–122)
Danish Crown/Vestjyske Slagterier M.1313 (para.198)
★Inco/Falconbridge M.4000 (paras 529–550)

D. FAILING-FIRM DEFENCE

Guidelines on the assessment of horizontal mergers (paras 89–91)
Kelt/American Express M.116
★Kali-Salz/MDK/Treuhand M.308 (paras 70–90)
Saint Gobain/wacker Chemie/Nom M.774 (paras 247–259)
★Bertelsmann/Kirch/Premiere M.993 (paras 69–76)
BASF/Eurodiol/Pantochim M.2314 (paras 135–163)
Sogecable/Canalsatelite Digital/Via Digital M.2845 (paras 110–117)
Newscorp/Telepiu M.2876 (paras 202–221)
France T–68/94

[For the tables of case citations see Tables 5 to 8 and 12 at the back of the book.]

E. MERGERS & STATE AIDS

Metronet/Infraco M.2694 (paras 63–70)
SNCF/Trenitalia /AFA M.3150 (para.15)
Deutsche Post/Exel M.3971 (paras 76–82)
RJB Mining T–156/98
★Iberdrola/Scottish Power M.4517 (38–47)

F. ANCILLARY RESTRAINTS

1. Concept

Articles 6(1)(b), 8(1) & 8(2), Regulation 139/2004
Notice on restrictions (paras 6–11)
Canal+ & Lagardère T–251/00

2. Trade mark licences

Notice on restrictions (paras 23–24)
Fiat/Ford/New Holland M.58 (paras 7–9)
Thomas Cook/LTU/West LB M.229 (paras 14–15)
Elf Atochem/Rohm & Haas M.160 (para.19)
Linde AG/Fiat M.256 (para.31)
British Airways/TAT M.259 (para.30)
Coca-Cola/Amalgamated Beverages GB M.794 (para.17)
RTL 7 M.878 (para.13)
★Recticel/Greiner M.835 (para.28)
Hagemeyer/ABB Asea Skandia M.990 (paras 13–14)
Gruner+Jahr/Financial Times/JV M.1455 (paras 37–40)
Cap Gemini/Ernst & Young M.1901 (para.21)

3. Patent/know-how licences

Notice on restrictions (paras 21–24, 42–44)
Thomson/Pilkington M.86 (para.14)
Elf Atochem/Rohm & Haas M.160 (para.19)
Avesta/British Steel/NCC M.239 (para.33)
Harrisons & Crosfield/AKZO M.310 (para.39)
BHF/CCF/Charterhouse M.319 (paras 17–20)
American Cyanamid/Shell M.354 (para.40)
UAP/Vinci M.384 (para.14)
SNECMA/TI M.368 (para.41)
Matra Marconi Space/British Aerospace M.437 (para.36)
Matra Marconi Space/Satcomms M.497 (paras 14, 17)
AKZO Nobel/Monsanto M.523 (paras 50–52)
Mederic/Urrpimmec/CRI/Munich Re M.949 (para.17)

4. Product/service supply agreement

Notice on restrictions (paras 25–31, 45)
SHV/Chevron 87
Reuter/BASF 107
BPCL/ICI 215
ENI-Montedison 256
Fiat/Ford/New Holland M.58 (paras 7–9)
Otto/Grattan M.70 (paras 5–6)
Digital/Philips M.129 (para.26)
Courtaulds/SNIA M.113 (paras 30–31)
Solvay-Laporte/Interox M.197 (para.51)
Thomas Cook/LTU/West LB M.229 (paras 14–15)
Elf Atochem/Rohm & Haas M.160 (para.19)
Rhône-Poulenc/SNIA M.206 (para.8.1)
Avesta/British Steel/NCC M.239 (para.32)
Rhône-Poulenc Chimie/Lyonnaise des Eaux M.266 (para.29)
British Airways/TAT M.259 (paras 28–29)
Matra/Cap Gemini Sogeti M.272 (para.19)
BHF/CCF/Charterhouse M.319 (paras 17–18)
American Cyanamid/Shell M.354 (para.39)
SNECMA/TI M.368 (paras 44–45)
ABB/Renault Automation M.409 (para.20)
Jefferson Smurfit/St Gobain M.499 (para.25)
AKZO Nobel/Monsanto M.523 (paras 50–52)
Saudi Aramco/MOH M.574 (para.22)
RWE-DEA/Augusta M.612 (paras 38–50)
★Thomas Cook/Sunworld M.785 (para.13)
Agrevo/Marubeni M.788 (paras 18–19)
British Gas Trading/Group 4 M.791 (para.23)
Telecom Eireann M.802 (para.40)
P&O/Royal Nedlloyd M.831 (para.109)
★BT/NS-Telfort M.855 (para.35)
Prudential/HSBC/Finnish Chemicals M.883 (para.21)
Valinox/Timet M.917 (paras 32–35, 17–18)
★Cable & Wireless/Maersk Data-Nautec M.951 (para.22)
★Philips/Lucent Technologies M.966 (para.17)
Hagemeyer/ABB Asea Skandia M.990 (para.15)
Albacom/BT/ENI/Mediaset M.975 (paras 32–33)
Dupont/ICI M.984 (para.55.4)
ALCOA/Inespal M.1003 (para.43)
BASF/Shell (II) M.1041 (paras 52–54, 58–60)
Eastman Kodak/Sun Chemical M.1042 (paras 40–42)
Swiss Life/Lloyd Continental M.1499 (paras 13–14)
Solvay/BASF M.1469 (paras 20–27)
Sasol/Condea M.2269 (paras 23–27)
Dow/Enichem Polyurethane M.2355 (paras 29–31)

MERGERS: SUBSTANTIVE ISSUES

[For the tables of case citations see Tables 5 to 8 and 12 at the back of the book.]

5. Exclusive/preferred status product/service supply agreement

Notice on restrictions (para.29)
Astrolink M.1564 (paras 48–50)
France Telecom/STI/SRD M.1679 (paras 21–23)
TXU Europe/EDF-London Investments JV36 (para.55)

6. Non-competition clause

Notice on restrictions (paras 13–20, 35–40)
Nicholas Frères Vitapro 4
SHV/Chevron 87
Reuter/BASF 107
⋆Nutricia 206
Mecaniver/PPG 225
ENI-Montedison 256
Quantel 357 (paras 41–42)
6th Comp. Rep. (paras 60–63)
Sedame/Precilec 11th Comp. Rep. (para.95)
Tyler/Linde 11th Comp. Rep. (para.96)
Allied/VIL 19th Comp. Rep. (para.41)
Remia 42/84
Fiat/Ford/New Holland M.58 (paras 8–9)
VIAG/Continental Can M.81 (para.52)
Sanofi/Sterling Drugs M.72 (point V)
Draeger/IBM/HMP M.101 (paras 12–20)
ELF/Enterprise M.88 (para.7)
Digital/Philips M.129 (para.25)
ABC/Générale des Eaux/Canal + W.H. Smith M.110 (para.14)
Thomson/Pilkington M.86 (para.14)
⋆TNT/Canada Post M.102 (paras 58–61)
Ingersoll Rand/Dresser M.121 (para.18)
Courtaulds/SNIA M.113 (para.32)
⋆Inchcape/IEP M.182 (para.16)
⋆Solvay-Laporte/Interox M.197 (paras 49–50)
Mondi/Frantschach M.210 (para.29)
Ericsson/Ascom M.236 (para.27)
Thomas Cook/LTU/West LB M.229 (paras 14–15)
Elf Atochem/Rohm & Haas M.160 (para.18)
Rhône-Poulenc/SNIA M.206 (para.8.2)
Ahold/Jeronimo Martins M.263 (para.15)
Rhône-Poulenc Chimie/Lyonnaise des Eaux M.266 (para.30)
British Airways/TAT M.259 (para.27)
Waste Management/SAE M.283 (para.28)
Tesco/Catteau M.301 (paras 10–15)
Volkswagen AG/VAG (UK) M.304
Sara Lee/BP Food Division M.299 (paras 15–16)
Matra/Cap Gemini Sogeti M.272 (para.19)
Harrisons & Crosfield/AKZO M.310 (para.38)
Aegon/Scottish Equitable M.349 (para.20)
BHF/CCF/Charterhouse M.319 (para.21)
American Cyanamid/Shell M.354 (para.38)
Synthomer/Yule Catto M.376 (para.34)
⋆Kali-Salz/MDK/Treuhand M.308 (paras 91–94)
SNECMA/TI M.368 (para.41)
ABB/Renault Automation M.409 (para.20)
Allied Lyons/HWE-Pedro Domecq M.400 (para.41)
GKN/Brambles/Leto Recycling M.448 (para.18)
Matra Marconi Space/British Aerospace M.437 (paras 34–35)
GE/CIGI M.465 (paras 17–18)
Jefferson Smurfitt/St Gobain M.499 (para.26)
Matra/Marconi Space/Satcoms M.497 (para.15)
General Re/Kölnische Ruck M.491 (paras 14–15)
UAP/Provincial M.512 (para.14)
Sappi/Warren M.526 (para.33)
Elf Atochem/Shell Chimie M.475 (para.53)
AKZO Nobel/Monsanto M.523 (paras 50–52)
⋆Hermes Europe/Railtel M.683 (paras 7–12)
Cardo/Thyssen M.818 (paras 40–41)
⋆KNP BT/Bunzl/Wilhelm Seiler M.884 (paras 15–20)
⋆RTL 7 M.878 (para.12)
⋆Birmingham International Airport M.786 (paras 21–30)
Tesco/ABF M.914 (paras 42–43)
⋆CLF CCB (Dexia)/San Paolo Crediop M.910 (paras 21–24)
⋆Mederic/Urrpimmec/CRI/Munich Re M.949 (para.16)
⋆Merck/Rhône-Poulenc-Merial M.885 (para.82)
⋆Thomson/Siemens/ATM M.953 (paras 28–29)
⋆Lear/Keiper M.937 (paras 19–29)
Ingersoll-Rand/Thermo King M.1011 (paras 19–21)
ALCOA/Inespal M.1003 (paras 41–47)
Suez Lyonnaise des Eaux/BFI M.1059 (paras 31–35)
⋆BASF/Shell (II) M.1041 (paras 45–49)
Stinnes/BTL M.1056 (paras 16–18)
Société Générale/Hambros Bank M.1096 (paras 16–17)
Kingfisher/Grosslabor M.1482 (paras 24–29)
Swiss Life/Lloyd Continental M.1499 (paras 11–12)
FNAC/Coin/JV M.1792 (paras 18–23)

[For the tables of case citations see Tables 5 to 8 and 12 at the back of the book.]

7. Obligation to maintain confidentiality

Notice on restrictions (paras 20, 41)
⋆Inchcape/IEP M.182 (para.17)
⋆Solvay-Laporte/Interox M.197 (para.50)
BTR/Pirelli M.253 (paras 28–32)
Matra Marconi Space/British Aerospace M.437 (para.35)
Sappi/Warren M.526 (para.33)
Swiss Bank/SG Warburg M.597 (para.29)

8. Loan agreements

CCIE/GTE M.258 (para.30)

9. R&D agreements

CCIE/GTE M.258 (para.31)
BASF/Shell (II) M.1041 (para.550)
Eastman Kodak/Sun Chemical M.1042 (paras 40–42)

10. Obligation not to solicit employees

Notice on restrictions (paras 20, 41)
BHF/CCF/Charterhouse M.319 (para.16)
Tesco/ABF M.914 (paras 42–43)
⋆Bacob Banque/Banque Paribus Belgique M.983 (paras 17–18)
ICI/Williams M.1167
Kingfisher/Grosslabor M.1482 (paras 28–29)

11. Customer limitation clause

Europe/Railtel M.683 (para.29)

12. Most-favoured customer arrangement

Astrolink M.1564 (paras 54–56)

13. Financial co-operation between parents

UAP/Vinci M.384 (para.17)

14. Transitional control of day-to-day business by parents

ABB Renault/Automation M.409 (para.20)

CHAPTER 4

PROCEDURE

1. Pre-notification guidance

Best practice guidelines on the conduct of merger control

2. Notification

Article 4, Regulation 139/2004
Articles 1–5, Regulation 802/2004
Torras/Sarrio M.166 (paras 2–3)
Air France/Sabena M.157 (para.21)
Rhône-Poulenc/SNIA M.355 (para.1)

2.1. Who must submit notification

Article 4(2), Regulation 802/2004

2.2. Information to be provided/consequence of incomplete notification

Articles 4 & 5, Regulation 802/2004
Cardo/Thyssen M.818 (para.2)
Mannesmann/Olivetti/Infostrada M.1025 (paras 2–3)
Nestlé/San Pellegrino M.1065 (para.1)
Caterpillar/Perkins Engines M.1094 (para.2)

2.3. Modification of notification

Kaysersberg T–290/94 (paras 124–134)

2.4. Withdrawal of notification (aborted concentration)

Consolidated Jurisdictional Notice (paras 117–122)
MCI T–310/00
DG Competition Information note on Art. 6 (1) c 2nd sentence of Regulation 139/2004 (abandonment of concentrations)

3. Suspension of the concentration

Articles 7 and 18(2), Regulation 139/2004
Gilette/Duracell M.836 (para.2)
Mannesmann/Vallourec M.906 (para.3)

4. Fact-finding

Articles 11–13, Regulation 139/2004
GE/Agfa/NDT M.3136 (para.3)
Siemens/Va Tech M.3653 (paras 47–50)
Endemol T–221/95 (paras 83–90)

5. Rights of defence and complainants

Article 18, Regulation 139/2004
Articles 11–17, Regulation 802/2004
Kaysersberg T–290/94 (paras 66–67, 98–123)
Endemol T–221/95 (paras 48–91)
Schneider Electric T–310/01 (paras 437–462)
EasyJet Airline Case T–177/04 (paras 30–42)

MERGERS: PROCEDURE

[For the tables of case citations see Tables 5 to 8 and 12 at the back of the book.]

5.1. Access to the file

Notice on access to the file
Article 18(3) Regulation 139/2004
Article 17–18 Regulation 802/2004
Siemens/Va Tech M.3653 (Report of Hearing Officer)
Endemol T–221/95 (paras 71–72)
Tetra Laval T–5/02 (paras 89–117)
GE T–210/01 (grounds 629–633, 649–687, 692–696, 700–713)

5.2. Hearing

Article 18 Regulation 139/2004
Article 11–16 Regulation 802/2004
Siemens/Va Tech M.3653 (Report of Hearing Officer)

6. Role of the Member States

6.1. Information provided to Member States

Article 19, Regulation 139/2004
Kaysersberg T–290/94 (paras 79–97)

6.2. Assistance of Member States during fact-finding procedure

Article 12, Regulation 139/2004

6.3. Advisory committee

Article 19(3–7), Regulation 139/2004
Kaysersberg T–290/94 (paras 79–97)

6.4. Referral of a case to a Member State

See above, Chapter 2, section E.

7. Co-operation with other anti-trust authorities

Article 24, Regulation 139/2004
Best practices on co-operation in merger cases (Co-operation between the European Union and the United States)
Boeing/McDonnell Douglas M.877 (paras 11–12)

7.1. International co-operation

See the European Commission website on international co-operation *http://ec.europa.eu/comm/competition/mergers/legislation/international_cooperation.html*

8. Types of decisions available to the Commission

8.1. Derogation of suspension

Article 7(4) Regulation 139/2004
BP/JV Dissolution M.1820 (para.2)
SEB/Moulinex M.2621 (para.9)

8.2. Clearance during phase 1: not falling under the Merger Regulation

Article 6.1(a), Regulation 139/2004.

8.3. Clearance during phase 1: simplified procedure

Notice on simplified procedure.
See Table 2 above, Chronological list of merger decisions (EC) — Simplified procedure — Reference

8.4. Clearance during phase 1: no serious risk of creating/strengthening dominance

Article 6.1(b), Regulation 139/2004

8.5. Clearance during phase 1: following commitments/undertakings

Article 6(2), Regulation 139/2004

8.6. Opening proceedings and a full investigation

Article 6.1(c), Regulation 139/2004

8.7. Second stage clearance

8.7.1. Without commitments/undertakings

Article 8(1), Regulation 139/2004

8.7.2. With commitments/undertakings

Article 8(2), Regulation 139/2004
Universal Music Group/BMG Music Publishing M.4404
JCI/Fiamm M.4381
Metso/Aker Kvaerner M.4187
Gaz de France/Suez M.4180
Inco/Falconbridge M.4000
T-Mobile Austria/Tele.Ring M.3916
Dong/Elsam/Energi E2 M.3868
Omya/J.M. Huber PCC M.3796

[For the tables of case citations see Tables 5 to 8 and 12 at the back of the book.]

E.ON/Mol M.3696
Jonson & Johnson/Guidant M.3687
Siemens/Va Tech M.3653
Continental/Phoenix M.3436
Sonoco/Ahlstrom/JV M.3431
Areva/Urenco/ETC JV M.3099
GE/Instrumentarium M.3083
Lagardere/Natexis/Vup M.2978
DSM/Roche Vitamins M.2972
Verbund/Energie M.2947
Daimler Chrysler/Deutsche Telekom/JV M.2903
Newscorp/Telepiu M.2876
Siemens/Drägerwerk/JV M.2861
ENBW/ENI/GVS M.2822
Promatech/Sulzer M.2698
Haniel/Cementbouw/JV M.2650
Haniel/Ytong M.2568
Bayer/Aventis Crop Science M.2547
BP/E.ON M.2533
Südzucker/Saint Louis M.2530
Grup Villar MIR/ENBW/Hidroelectrica Del Cantabrico M.2434
Mitsui/CVRD/CAEMI M.2420
Shell/Dea M.2389
Bombardier/Adtranz M.2139
Bosch/Rexroth M.2060
Metso/Svedala M.2033
The Post office/TPG/SPPL M.1915
EDF/ENBW M.1853
AOL/Time Warner M.1845
Industri Kapital/Dyno M.1813
Astra Zeneca/Novartis M.1806
Alcoa/Reynolds M.1693
Veba/Viag M.1673
Dow Chemical/Union Carbide M.1671
Alcan/Alusuisse M.1663
Linde/Aga M.1641
MMs/Dasa.Astrium M.1636
Air Liquide/BOC M.1630
Totalfina/ELF Aquitaine M.1628
Allied Signal/Honeywell M.1601
Sanitec/Sphinx M.1578
BP Amoco/Atlantic Richfield M.1532
Telia/Telenor M.1439
Exxon/Mobil M.1383
Danish Crown/Vestjyske Slagterier M.1313
Rewe/Meinl M.1221
Skanska/Scancem M.1157
Worldcom/MCI M.1069
Agfa-Gevaert/Du Pont M.986
Hoffmann-La Roche/Boehringer Mannheim M.950
Veba/Degussa M.942
Guinness/Grand Metropolitan M.938
Siemens/Elektrowatt M.913
Boeing/McDonnell Douglas M.877
British Telecom/MCI M.856
The Coca Cola Company/Carlsberg M.833
Anglo American Corporation/Lonrho M.754
Ciba-Geigy/Sandoz M.737
Kimberly-Clark/Scott Paper M.623
Crown Cork & Seal/Carnaudmetalbox M.603
Orkla/Volvo M.582
ABB/Daimler Benz M.580
RTL/Veronica/Endemol ("HMG") M.553
Procter & Gamble/VP Schickedanz M.430
Kali+Salz/MDK/Treuhand M.308
KNP/Bührmann Tetterode/VRG M.291
Shell/Montecatini M.269
DU PONT/ICI M.214
Nestle/Perrier M.190
Accor/Wagons-Lits M.126
Ceac/Magneti Marelli M.43
Alcatel/Telettra M.42
Varta/Bosch M.12

8.8. Prohibition

Article 8(3), Regulation 139/2004
Eni/Edp/Gdp M.3440
Tetra Laval/Sidel M.2416
Schneider/Legrand M.2283
General Electric/Honeywell M.2220
CVC/Lenzing M.2187
SCA/Metsä Tissue M.2097
MCI Worldcom/Sprint M.1741
Volvo/Scania M.1672
Airtours/First Choice M.1524
Deutche Telekom/Betaresearch M.1027
Bertelsmann/Kirch/Premiere M.993
Blokker/Toys "R" Us M.890
Kesko/Tuko M.784
Saint Gobain/Wacker Chemie/Nom M.774
Gencor/Lonrho M.619
RTL/veronica/Endemol M.553
Nordic Satelite Distribution M.490
MSG Media Service M.469
Aerospatiale/Alenia/De Havilland M.53

8.9. Separation orders and interim measures

Article 8(4), Regulation 139/2004
Blokker/Toys "R" Us M.890
Tetra Laval/Sidel M.2416
Tetra Laval T–80/02

[For the tables of case citations see Tables 5 to 8 and 12 at the back of the book.]

Schneider/Legrand M.2283
Schneider Electric T–77/02
Article 8(5), Regulation 139/2004

9. Time limits

9.1. Time limits for Commission decisions

Article 10, Regulation 139/2004

9.2. Consequence of failure to decide in stated time

Article 10(6), Regulation 139/2004
McCormick/CPC M.330

9.3. Calculating the time periods

Articles 7–10, Regulation 802/2004

9.4. Suspension of phase II deadline

Schneider Electric T–310/01 (grounds 74–113)

10. Revocation of decisions

Article 6(3–4), 8(5–6), Regulation 139/2004
Sanofi/Synthelabo M.1397 (paras 1–4)

11. Changes of transactions after authorisation

Consolidated Jurisdictional Notice (paras 122–123)

12. Fines

Articles 14–15, Regulation 139/2004
A.P. Moller (Art. 14 Proc.) M.969
Sanofi/Synthelabo M.1397
Deutsche Post/Trans-o-Flex [2001] L97/1
Mitsubishi Heavy Industries [2001] L4/31
BP/Erdölchemie (Art. 14 Proc) M.2345
TetraLaval/Sidel

CHAPTER 5

REMEDIES

Notice on remedies
Draft revised Notice on merger remedies

1. Concept

Notice on remedies (paras 4–12)
ARD T–158/00 (paras 199–211)

2. First phase undertakings

Notice on remedies (paras 1, 11, 33–38)

3. Second phase undertakings

Notice on remedies (paras 1, 11, 39–43)

4. Behavioural undertakings

Notice on remedies (para.9)
★Gencor/Lonrho M.619 (para.216)
General Electric/Honeywell M.2220 (paras 530–532)
★Gencor T–106/96 (grounds 292–329)
★EDP T–87/05 (paras 99–105)
Commission v Tetra Laval C–12/03P (paras 85–89)

5. Structural undertakings

Notice on remedies (paras 13–25, 46–60)
★Gencor T–106/96 (ground 319)

6. Type of undertaking (other than divestiture)

6.1. Separate management of assets

Boeing/McDonnell Douglas M.877 (para.115)

6.2. Prohibition/termination of exclusivity arrangements

Notice on remedies (para.27)
Fiat/Ford/New Holland M.58 (para.30)
TNT/Canada Post M.102 (paras 46–47)
Grand Met. Cinzano M.184
KNP/Bührmann Tetterode/VRG M.291 (para.166)
Boeing/McDonnell Douglas M.877 (para.116)
American Home Products/Monsanto M.1229
Rohm+Haas/Morton M.1467 (para.41)
BT/ESAT M.1838 (paras 31–32)
Newscorp/Telepiu M.2876 (paras 225, 229–238)
Orkla/Chips M.3658 (para.32)
Gencor T–106/96 (ground 319)

[For the tables of case citations see Tables 5 to 8 and 12 at the back of the book.]

6.3. Behaviour to suppliers/dealers

Boeing/McDonnell Douglas M.877 (para.119)
New Holland/Case M.1571 (paras 77, 81, 86)
Veba/Viag M.1673 (paras 216, 221–223)
AOL/Time Warner M.1845 (para.95)
Amer/Salomon M.3765 (paras 173–175)
Bombardier/Adtranz M.2139 (paras 93–100)

6.4. Offering access to essential infrastructures, licences, products to competitors and customers

Notice on remedies (paras 28–29)
Elf Aquitaine Thyssen/Minol M.235 (para.13)
Du Pont/ICI M.214 (paras 47–48)
Glaxo/Wellcome M.555 (para.29)
Swedish Match/KAV M.997 (para.42)
Bertelsmann/Kirch/Premiere M.993 (paras 124–129, 133–135, 143–153)
Deutsche Telekom/Beta Research M.1027 (paras 56–79)
Rhodia/Donau Chemie/Albright & Wilson M.1517 (paras 82–83)
Pakhoed/Van Ommeren M.1621 (para.30)
Allied Signal/Honeywell M.1601 (para.128)
Vodafone Airtouch/Mannesmann M.1795 (paras 58–60)
Alcoa/Reynolds M.1693 (para.135)
Vivendi/Canal+/Seagram M.2050 (paras 70, 77–79)
EDF/ENBW M.1853 (paras 93–104)
Shell/DEA M.2389 (paras 136, 140–147)
BP/E.ON M.2533 (paras 140–147)
Newscorp/Telepiu M.2876 (paras 225, 257)
BSkyB/Kirch Pay-Tv JV42 (para.94)
Daimler Chrysler/Deutsche Telecom M.2903 (para.68)
Procter & Gamble/Wella M.3149 (para.61)
GE/Instrumentarium M.3083 (paras 347–358)
Piaggio/Aprilia M.3570 (paras 63–64)
E.On/Mol M.3696 (paras 768–819)
Gencor T–106/96 (ground 319)
Axalto/Gemplus M.3998 (paras 82–90)
T-Mobile Austria/tele.ring M.3916 (paras 133–138)
Gaz de France/Suez M.4180 (paras 1189–1190)
Evraz/Highveld M.4494 (paras 147–151, 165–184)

6.5. Co-operation agreements with competitors

Varta/Bosch M.12 (paras 51–56)
Kali-Salz/MDK/Treuhand M.308 (paras 63–68)
Glaxo/Wellcome M.555 (para.29)
Bertelsmann/Kirch/Premiere M.993 (paras 126–153)
Deutsche Telekom/BetaResearch M.1027 (paras 56–79)
DHL/Deutsche Post M.1168
KLM/Alitalia JV19 (para.69)

6.6. IP licensing policy

Boeing/McDonnell Douglas M.877 (paras 117–118)
Bertelsmann/Kirch/Premiere M.993 (paras 128–131, 137–139)
Deutsche Telekom/BetaResearch M.1027 (paras 58–60, 64–65)
MMS/Dasa/Astrium M.1636 (paras 91–92)
Shell/BASF-Project Nicole M.1751 (para.55)
Dow Chemical/Union Carbide M.1671 (para.173)
Glaxo Wellcome/SmithKline Beecham M.1846 (paras 218, 220–222)
BASF/American Cyanamid M.1932 (para.96, 98–100)
SEB/Moulinex M.2621 (paras 129–134)
Reuters/Telerate M.3692 (paras 21–25)
Procter & Gamble/Gillette M.3732 (para.153)
Gencor T–106/96 (ground 319)
Babyliss T–114/02 (paras 191–196, 244–253)
★Royal Philips Electronics T–119/02 (paras 88–103, 112–129, 171–175)
Axalto/Gemplus M.3998 (paras 82–90)

6.7. Withdrawal of anti-dumping complaint

Saint Gobain/wacker Chemie/Nom M.774 (paras 260–264)

6.8. Maintenance of existing capacity/output levels

Gencor/Lonrho M.619 (paras 215–216)
★Gencor T–106/96 (grounds 321–327)

6.9. Unbundling

EDF/Louis Dreyfus M.1557 (para.48)
Telia/Telenor M.1439 (paras 381–382)
Wegener/PCM/JV M.3817 (para.68)

6.10 Structural limitation/increase of access

Vivendi/Canal +/Seagram M.2050 (paras 69, 72–74)
Grupo Villar MIR/ENBW/Hidroelectrica del cantabrico M.2434 (paras 129–132)

MERGERS: REMEDIES

[For the tables of case citations see Tables 5 to 8 and 12 at the back of the book.]

ENBW/EDP/Cajastur/Hidrocantanbrico M.2684 (paras 54–56)
Siemens/Drägerwerk M.2861 (para.156)

6.11. Removal of structural links/reallocation of voting rights

⋆Notice on remedies (paras 24–25)
RTL/Veronica/Endemol M.553 (paras 11–16)
Rohm+Haas/Morton M.1467 (para.41)
Vodafone/Air Touch M.1430 (para.31)
Rhodia/Donau Chemie/Albright & Wilson M.1517 (para.84)
AT&T/MediaOne M.1551 (para.14)
Hoechst/Rhône Poulenc M.1378 (paras 119, 125)
BP Amoco/Arco M.1532 (para.73)
Exxon/Mobil M.1383 (paras 835–836)
Mannesmann/Orange M.1760 (para.28–29)
TotalFina/Elf M.1628 (paras 321–322)
Alcoa/Reynolds M.1693 (paras 131, 133)
Veba/Viag M.1673 (paras 215, 217–220)
France Telecom/Orange M.2016 (para.47)
Volvo/Renault VI M.1980 (paras 44, 48, 51–53)
AOL/Time Warner M.1845 (para.95)
Nordbanken/Postgirot M.2567 (paras 58–63)
BP/E.ON M.2533 (paras 138–139)
Areva/Urenco/ETC JV M.3099 (paras 229–230)
E.On/Mol M.3696 (paras 762–767)
Linde/Boc M.4141 (para.250)
Gaz de France/Suez M.4180 (paras 1189–1190)

6.12. Corporate governance provisions

Wegener/PCM/JV M.3817 (para.69)
Siemens/Va Tech M.3653 (para. 491)
Toshiba/Westinghouse M.4153 (paras 108–119)

6.13. Legal separation

Telia/Sonera M.2803 (paras 119, 135–137)

6.14. Remedies related to prices and tariffs

Veba/Viag M.1673 (paras 221–223)
EnergieAllianz/Verbund M.2947 (paras 145, 153)
Alcatel/Finmeccanica/Alcatel Alenia Space & Telespazio M.3680 (para.118)

6.15. Withdrawal from airline routes/making new slots available and other measures

Air France/Sabena M.157 (paras 32, 36–38, 43–46, 50–51, 55–57)
British Airways/TAT M.259 (paras 25–26)
Swissair/Sabena M.616 (paras 42–48)
United Airlines/US Airways M.2041 (para.75)
Air France/KLM M.3280 (paras 158–169)
KLM/Alitalia JV19 (para.69)
Lufthansa/Swiss M.3770
Lufthansa/Eurowings M.3940

6.16. Termination of activity

Unilever/Amora-Maille M.1802 (paras 105–107)

6.17. Modification of parties' interest/assets acquired

Rewe/Meinl M.1221 (paras 118–120)
Framatome/Siemens/Cogema/JV M.1940 (para.98)

7. Divestiture

7.1. Sale of capacity/production facility

Nestlé/Perrier M.190 (paras 51–56)
Air France/Sabena M.157 (paras 32, 36–38, 43–46, 50–51, 55–57)
British Airways/TAT M.259 (paras 25–26)
British Telecom/MCI (II) M.856 (paras 76–80)
Pakhoed/Van Ommeren M.1621 (paras 29–30)
Alcan/Alusuisse M.1663 (paras 130–131, 140–144)
Shell/BASF-Project Nicole M.1751 (para.55)
Degussa/Laporte M.2277 (para.50, 54)
Owens Illinois/BSN Glasspack M.3397 (paras 43–46)
Sonoco/Ahlstrom/JV M.3431 (paras 106–112)
Renolit/Solvay M.3946 (para. 67)
Jefferson Smurfit/Kappa M.3935 (paras 31, 51, 65)
Inco/Falconbridge M.4000 (para 558)
Mittal/Arcelor M.4137 (paras 133–135, 148–176)
Evraz/Highveld M.4494 (paras 136–151)

7.2. Divestiture/sale of whole or part of an undertaking

Alcatel/Telettra M.42 (paras 44–46)
Magnetti-Marelli/CEAC M.43 (para.19)
Accor/Wagon-Lits M.126 (paras 29–31)
Nestlé/Perrier M.190 (paras 51–56)

[For the tables of case citations see Tables 5 to 8 and 12 at the back of the book.]

Du Pont/ICI M.214 (paras 47–48)
KNP/Bührmann Tetterode/VRG M.291 (para.166)
Shell/Montecatini M.269 (paras 6, 115–122)
Procter & Gamble VP/Schnickendanz M.430 (paras 186–189)
MSG Media Service M.469 (paras 94–99)
Nordic Satellite M.490 (paras 153–160)
RTL/Veronica/Endemol M.553 (paras 111–113)
Orkla/Volvo M.582 (para.123)
ABB/Daimler Benz M.580 (paras 139–147)
Repola/Kymmene M.646 (paras 54, 64–67)
Crown Cork & Seal/Carnaud Metalbox M.655 (paras 115–118)
Kimberley-Clark/Scott Paper M.623 (paras 223–240)
Shell/Montecatini M.269 (paras 1–21)
British Telecom/MCI (II) M.856 (paras 76–83)
Siemens/Elektrowatt M.913 (paras 112–136)
Bertelsmann/Kirch/Premiere M.993 (paras 128, 138, 147, 154)
Deutsche Telekom/Beta Research M.1027 (paras 57, 63, 71, 78)
Neste/IVO M.931
Akzo Nobel/Courtaulds M.1182
Exxon/Shell M.1137
Linde/Aga M.1641 (paras 91–94)
Alcoa/Reynolds M.1693 (para.137)
Siemens/Dematic/VDO/Sachs M.2059 (paras 79–80)
Bosch/Rexroth M.2060 (paras 85–95)
Orica/Dyno M.4151 (paras 76–79)
Linde/Boc M.4141 (paras 244–249)
Omya/J.M. Huber PCC M.3796 (paras 459–472)
Veolia/Cleanaway M.4318 (paras 40–45)
Thermo Electron/Fisher Scientific M.4242 (paras 107–110)
Johnson & Johnson/Pfizer Consumer Healthcare M.4314 (paras 138–142)
Evraz/Highveld M.4494 (paras 137–146, 152–161)
Somerfield v Competition Commission UK M.4
Stericycle and STG v Competition Commission UK M.1

7.3. Divestiture with pre-identified purchaser

Exxon/Shell M.1137 (para.31)
Dow Chemical/Union Carbide M.1671 (para.173)
Pfizer/Warner Lambert M.1878 (para.89)
Bosch/Rexroth M.2060 (paras 84–87, 92)
Masterfoods/Royal Canin M.2544 (paras 90, 100–102)
Verbund/EnergieAllianz M.2947 (para.143)
DSM/Roche M.2972 (paras 80–90)
★GE/Agfa NDT M.3136 (paras 47–53)
Sonoco/Ahlstrom/JV M.3431 (paras 106–112)
Continental/Phoenix M.3436 (paras 220, 227)
T-Mobile Austria/tele.ring M.3916 (paras 131–132)
Inco/Falconbridge M.4000 (paras 680–736)

7.4. Divestiture: suitable purchaser

★Petrolessence SG2R T–251/00 (paras 100–121)
Omya/J.M. Huber PCC M.3796 (paras 504–514)
Veolia/Cleanaway M.4318 (para.44)

7.5. Creation of a "new supplier" on the market

Du Pont/ICI M.214 (paras 47–48)
Gencor/Lonrho M.619 (paras 215–216)
Hoechst/Rhône Poulenc M.1378 (para.123)
★Gencor T–106/96 (grounds 319, 321–327)

8. Arbitration procedure

Alcatel/Thomson CSF-SCS M.1185 (para.40)
Matra/Aerospatiale M.1309 (para.76)
Lufthansa/Swiss M.3770

9. Combined undertakings (divestitures, sale of capacity, licences, etc.)

Notice on remedies (para.30)
Hoechst/Rhône Poulenc M.1378 (paras 120-121, 123–124)
Exxon/Mobil M.1383 (paras 828–862)
Akzo Nobel/Hoechst Roussel Vet M.1681 (paras 105–113)
Sanitec/Sphinx M.1578 (para.252)
Sara Lee/Courtaulds M.1892 (paras 43–45)
Unilever/Bestfoods M.1990 (paras 123–131, 176–177, 187)
Smith & Nephew + Beiersdorf/JV JV.54 (paras 91–92, 96–97, 100–101, 106)
KLM/Alitalia JV19 (paras 68–69)
Inco/Falconbridge M.4000 (paras 558–576)
Gaz de France/Suez M.4180 (paras 1137–1145)

10. Alternative acceptable undertakings

Notice on remedies (paras 22–23)
Axa/Gre M.1453 (paras 34–38)
Imetal/English China Clays M.1381 (paras 81–82, 86)

[For the tables of case citations see Tables 5 to 8 and 12 at the back of the book.]

Hoechst/Rhône Poulenc M.1378 (para.122)
Nestlé/Ralston Purina M.2337 (paras 61–63)
Exxon/Mobil M.1383 (para.841)
Telia/Telenor M.1439 (para.381)
New Holland/Case M.1571 (para.87)
TotalFina/Elf M.1628 (paras 334–335)
Dow Chemical/Union Carbide M.1671 (para.173)
Glaxo Wellcome/SmithKline Beecham M.1846 (para.219)
Veba/Viag M.1673 (paras 249–250)
Industri Kapital (Nordkem)/Dyno M.1813 (paras 132–133)
Alcan/Pechiney (II) M.3225 (paras 150–154)
Johnson & Johnson/Guidant M.3687 (paras 358–360)

11. Undertakings exceed competition problems

Siemens/Elektrowatt M.913 (para.134)
Sanitec/Sphinx M.1578 (para.255)
Unilever/Amora-Maille M.1802 (para.103)
Masterfoods/Royal Canin M.2544 (para.87)
Cementbouwe T–282/02 (grounds 307–311)

12. Evidence that undertakings restore competition

Exxon/Mobil M.1383 (paras 829, 832–833, 837, 845, 860)
Telia/Telenor M.1439 (paras 386–392)
Allied Signal/Honeywell M.1601 (paras 130–135)
TotalFina/Elf M.1628 (paras 323–333)
Dow Chemical/Union Carbide M.1671 (paras 175–194)
Veba/Viag M.1673 (paras 226–248, 253–255)
Unilever/Bestfoods M.1990 (paras 133–150, 178–186)
KLM/Alitalia JV19 (paras 71–72)
T-Mobile Austria/tele.ring M.3916 (paras 154–165)
Evraz/Highveld M.4494 (paras 165–184)

13. Insufficient/unacceptable undertakings

13.1. Concept, burden of proof

Notice on remedies (paras 31–32)
⋆EDP T–87/05 (paras 60–73, 80–81, 171–237)

13.2. Examples of insufficient/unacceptable undertakings

MSG Media Service M.469 (paras 94–99)
Nordic Satellite M.490 (paras 153–160)
Saint Gobain/wacker-Chemie/Nom M.774 (paras 260–264)
Airtours/First Choice M.1524 (paras 181–192)
Volvo/Scania M.1672 (paras 332–362)
SCA/Metsä Tissue M.2097 (paras 248–255)
General Electric/Honeywell M.2220 (paras 500–532, 546–562)
Schneider Electric/Legrand M.2283 (paras 788–850)
Tetra Laval/Sidel M.2416 (paras 423–451)
ENI/EDP/GDP M.3440 (paras 650–914)
Omya/J.M. Huber PCC M.3796 (para. 455–457)
Inco/Falconbridge M.4000 (paras 577–679)

14. Non-binding undertakings

Carrefour/Promodes M.1684 (para.135)
France Telecom/Orange M.2016 (para.35)
Boeing/Hughes M.1879 (para.102)
Celanese/Degussa M.3056 (para.79)

15. Procedural considerations (timing, subsequent review of commitments)

Notice on remedies (paras 10, 12, 46–60)
Article 10(1–2), Regulation 139/2004
Articles 19–20, Regulation 802/2004
Shell/Montecatini M.269 (paras 1–21)
Airtours/First Choice M.1524 (para.193)
Telia/Telenor M.1439 (paras 378–380)
TotalFina/Elf M.1628 (paras 341–345, 355–358)
Alcoa/Reynolds M.1693 (para.130)
Tyco/Mallinckrodt M.2074 (para.3)
⋆Hoechst/Rhône Poulenc M.1378
Kaysersberg SA T–290/94 (paras 135–146)
⋆Babyliss T–114/02 (paras 127–150, 162–182)
Royal Philips Electronics T–119/02 (paras 226–250)
ARD T–346/02 (paras 382–426)
EDP T–87/05 (paras 66–73)
Inco/Falconbridge M.4000 (paras 575–576)

[For the tables of case citations see Tables 5 to 8 and 12 at the back of the book.]

16. Implementation of the commitments (e.g. monitoring Trustee)

Axalto/Gemplus M.3998 (paras 82–92)

T-Mobile Austria/tele.ring M.3916 (paras 139–140)

Stericycle and STG v Competition Commission UK M.2

[For the tables of case citations see Tables 5 to 8 and 12 at the back of the book.]

BOOK THREE

NATIONAL DECISIONS

BOOK THREE—CONTENTS

USER GUIDE

Book Three is a new section of the Handbook and reports key National Decisions of almost all EC jurisdictions. National cases have been selected on the basis that they should be of relevance for a competition lawyer in another jurisdiction. The missing jurisdictions will be added in the future editions of the Handbook. This section follows the same general outline as Book I and Book II but, under the relevant subject headings, National Cases are presented with *unique identifiers* (e.g. for France: F1, F2, etc.). The cases may subsequently be traced by locating them in the corresponding Tables which give the relevant references to source them (including their web address).

Not all jurisdictions have the same standard of internet infrastructure available for accessing their key decisions and in some instances the cases reported have not been published on the internet. It may therefore take more time to trace the relevant decisions. The *e-Competitions* bulletin is in the process of commenting on all the cases that are included in this chapter. The text of most of these cases in their original languages with English summaries are available on the *e-Competitions* website *www.concurrences.com*.

e-Competitions is the first bulletin exclusively dedicated to the implementation of EU competition rules in the 27 Member States of the European Union. It is a twice-monthly electronic news bulletin and appears in English and on the internet only (*www.concurrences.com*). The bulletin exclusively deals with national competition laws.

e-Competitions is published by Transactive, a subsidiary of the Thomson/Sweet & Maxwell Group, in partnership with the Institute of Competition Law.

NATIONAL ABBREVIATIONS

BL	Belgium	I	Italy
BG	Bulgaria	LV	Latvia
CY	Cyprus	L	Luxembourg
CZ	Czech Republic	NL	The Netherlands
DK	Denmark	SK	Slovakia
EST	Estonia	ES	Spain
F	France	SE	Sweden
DE	Germany	PT	Portugal
H	Hungary	UK	United Kingdom
IE	Ireland		

NATIONAL CONTRIBUTORS

Belgium
Thomas Chellingsworth
Howrey LLP, Brussels

Bulgaria
Anton Petrov
Petko Kantchevski
DJINGOV, GOUGINSKI, KYUTCHUKOV & VELICHKOV

Cyprus
Eleana Spyris
ANDREAS NEOCLEOUS & CO

Czech Republic and Slovak Republik
Rudolf Rentsch
Martin Nedelka
Gleiss Lutz

Denmark
Kromann Reumert
Jens Munk Plum
Kromann Reumert

Estonia
Tanel Kalaus
Raidla & Partners

Finland
Ami Kayhko
Christian Wik
Roschier

France
Jacques Buhart
Dominique Brault
Lionel Lesur
Herbert Smith LLP

Germany
Petra Linsmeier
Gleiss Lutz

Hungary
Adam Mattyus
Eszter Ritter
Linklaters

Ireland
Pat O'Brien
Arthur Cox

Italy
Denis Fosselard
GIANNI, ORIGONI, GRIPPO & PARTNERS

Latvia and Lithuania
Dagnija Libane
Eriks Blumbergs
Law Firm of Glimstedt un partneri

Luxembourg
Vincent Wellens
Philippe-Emmanuel Partsch
Arendt & Medernach

The Nederlands
Rein Wesseling
Dennis van Kerkel
Stibbe

Poland
Michael Markowicz
Gliess Lutz

Portugal
Frederico Pereira Coutinho
GONÇALVES PEREIRA, CASTELO BRANCO & ASSOCIADOS, RL

Spain
Irene Moreno-Tapia
Maria Gonzalez Navarrete
CUATRECASAS

Sweden
Anna Elm
Advokatfirman Vinge KB

UK
James Quinney
Suzy Campbell
Herbert Smith

e-COMPETITIONS NATIONAL CONTRIBUTORS

Belgium
Alexandre Defossez
IEJE, Liège University
Jacques Derenne
Lovells LLP, Brussels
Dieter Gillis
KU, Leuven
Antoine Gosset-Grainville
Gide Loyrette Nouel, Brussels
Tarik Hennen

Bulgaria
Dessislava Fessenko
Ivan Gurov
Freshfields Bruckhaus Deringer, Paris

Cyprus
Antigoni Lykotrafiti
King's College, London
Kleopatra Koutra
University College, London

Czech Republic
Jana Jichova
University Paris I Panthéon-Sorbonne
Robert Pelikán
Linklaters, Prague
Jan Prevrátil
Court of First Instance, Luxembourg

Denmark
Jacob Borum
White & Case, Brussels
Alexandre Defossez
IEJE, Liège University

Estonia
Vaido Põldoja
Paul Varul, Tallinn

France
François Blanc
University Paris II Panthéon-Assas
Laura Castex
Gide Loyrette Nouel, Paris
Raphaël Chetrit
University Paris II Panthéon-Assas
Caroline Evrard
Freshfields Bruckhaus Deringer, Paris
Sylvie Grando
August & Debouzy, Paris
Jérôme Philippe
Freshfields Bruckhaus Deringer, Paris
Mathilde Masson
Freshfields Bruckhaus Deringer, Paris
Marie-Charlotte Rouzier
Montpellier Law Faculty
David Spector
CNRS, Paris

Germany
Dr Helmut Bergmann
Freshfields Bruckhaus Deringer, Berlin
Joerg Meinzenbach
Freie Universität, Berlin
Ken Mueller-Tautphaeus
Debevoise & Plimpton, Frankfurt
Thomas Lübbig
Freshfields Bruckhaus Deringer, Berlin
Dr Stefan Thomas
Johannes Gutenberg University, Mainz
Dr Frank Röhling
Freshfields Bruckhaus Deringer, Berlin

Hungary
Kõmíves Attila
White & Case, Budapest
Bálint Bassola
Hungarian NCA
Gábor Báthory
Europa College, Bruges
Alma Biró
Lovells, Budapest
Toth Csaba
Lovells, Budapest
Tünde Gönczöl
White & Case, Budapest
Anikó Kertész
Gide Loyrette Nouel, Brussels
Ákos Kovách
Gide Loyrette Nouel, Brussels

Ireland
Gary Dennis
Arendt & Medernach, Luxembourg
Orla Lynskey
Europa College, Bruges
Philippe-Emmanuel Partsch
Arendt & Medernach, Luxembourg

Italy
Pablo Ibáñez Colomo
European University Institute, Florence
Silvia d'Alberti
Allen & Overy, Roma
Lucio d'Amario
Allen & Overy, Roma
Michele Giannino
Paolisa Nebbia
Faculty of Law, Leicester
Isidoro Niola
Freshfields Bruckhaus Deringer, Rome
Silvio Nobili
Federico Perego
Studio Legale Bernardi, Milan

Tommaso Salonico
Freshfields Bruckhaus Deringer, Rome
Valerio Torti
University College, London
Luciano Vasques
Studio Legale Bernardi, Milan
Gian Luca Zampa
Freshfields Bruckhaus Deringer, Rome

Luxembourg
Gabriel Bleser
Allen & Overy, Luxembourg
hilippe-Emmanuel Partsch
Arendt & Medernach, Luxembourg
Vincent Wellens
Arendt & Medernach, Luxembourg

Malta
Silvio Meli
Maltese NCA

Netherlands
Tristan Baumé
Court of First Instance, Luxembourg
Katelijne Lafleur
Court of First Instance, Luxembourg
Marsela Maci
Queen Mary College, ICC, London
Sebastian Vos
Freshfields Bruckhaus Deringer, Brussels

Portugal
Joaquim Caimoto Duarte
Uría Menéndez, Lisbon
Jaime Folguera
Uría Menéndez, Madrid
Pablo Ibáñez Colomo
European University Institute, Florence
Miguel Gorjão-Henriques
Vieira de Almeida, Lisboa

Slovakia
Peter Oravec
Freshfields Bruckhaus Deringer, Bratislava
Andrej Soltys
Freshfields Bruckhaus Deringer, Bratislava

Spain
Margarita Fernandez
Freshfields Bruckhaus Deringer, Madrid
Jaime Folguera
Uría Menéndez, Madrid
Henar González Durántez
Uría Menéndez, Madrid
Pablo Ibáñez Colomo
European University Institute, Florence
Paloma Martínez-Lage
Martinez Lage & Asociados, Madrid
Aitor Montesa Lloreda
Court of First Instance, Luxembourg
Angel Givaja Sanz
Guarrigues, Brussels

Sweden
Anders Flood
Andreas Jasper

UK
Charles Balmain
White & Case, London
Alexandra Brown
Lovells LLP, London
Matthew Giles
Hogan & Hartson, Brussels
Suzanne Innes-Stubb
White & Case, Brussels
Alison Jones
King's College/Freshfields Bruckhaus Deringer, London
Jon Lawrence
Freshfields Bruckhaus Deringer, London
Liza Lovdahl Gormsen
King's College, London
Iva Philipova
White & Case, London
Alex Potter
Freshfields Bruckhaus Deringer, London
David Revelin
Ecole Normale Supérieure, Paris
Peter Turner-Kerr
Freshfields Bruckhaus Deringer, London
Elaine Whiteford
Freshfields Bruckhaus Deringer, London

PART I

CONDITIONS FOR THE APPLICATION OF BOTH ARTICLES 81 AND 82

CHAPTER 1

UNDERTAKINGS

1. Concept of undertaking

General health insurance company, (p.5) SK1
Deutscher Lotto- und Totoblock DE16
Aral—Koepfler L4 (paras 23–30)
NCC AB and others v SCA SE1
Banverket SE6
Bettercare v OFT UK13
Cools/CM Antwerpen BE1

2. Natural persons

3. Change of corporate structure

Economic Continuity Test—Railway company, (pp.3–5) SK4

4. Collective responsibility of the group

5. Intra-enterprise conspiracy doctrine

NCC AB and others v SCA SE1
Banverket SE6

6. Difference between undertakings and public bodies

International Gemmological Institute v Hoge Raad voor Diamant BE6
NCC AB and others v SCA SE1
Banverket SE6

CHAPTER 2

EFFECT ON TRADE BETWEEN MEMBER STATES

A. GUIDELINES ON THE EFFECT OF TRADE CONCEPT CONTAINED IN ARTICLES 81 AND 82 OF THE TREATY [2004] O.J. C101/8

Filigranbetondecken DE9

B. CASES ON DELIMITATION OF COMMUNITY COMPETENCE

Rock—Tanklux L9 (paras 59–61)

C. THE ASSESSMENT OF THE EFFECT ON TRADE

1. Direct, indirect, actual or potential effect

Norsk Hydro Olje AB and others v SCA SE4
Aktiebolaget Bil-Bengtsson and others v SCA SE8
Rock—Tanklux L9 (para.59)

2. Structural arguments

2.1. Agreement may affect the structure of competition in the Common Market

2.2. Elimination of a competitor

2.3. Involvement of a transnational company

[For the tables of case citations see Tables 16 and 17 at the back of the book.]

3. Cumulative effect of parallel agreements

3.1. Similar agreements concluded by the same and other companies

3.2. Similar agreements concluded by the same company

4. Consideration of the agreement as a whole

5. Export bans, a per se rule?

6. Use of raw material for a product/service that is exported

7. Product/service cross-border in nature

Rock —Tanklux L9 (para.61)

D. TYPES OF AGREEMENT THAT DO NOT NECESSARILY AFFECT TRADE BETWEEN MEMBER STATES

1. Minor importance: appreciability

Filigranbetondecken DE9
Cajas Rurales Jalón y Zaragoza ES1
Hardi International ES2

2. Trade with third states

2.1. Export to third states

2.2. Import from third states

2.3 Trade between third states

3. Export boosters: increasing trade

4. National cartels

Norsk Hydro Olje AB and others v SCA SE4

CHAPTER 3

WITHIN THE COMMON MARKET: EXTRA TERRITORIALITY

A. CASES

B. NOTICE OF OCTOBER 21, 1972 ON IMPORTS FROM JAPAN [1972] O.J. C111/13

CHAPTER 4

DEFINITION OF RELEVANT MARKET

Rock—Tanklux L9 (paras 44–45)

[For the tables of case citations see Tables 16 and 17 at the back of the book.]

PART II

ARTICLE 81(1), (2) AND (3)

CHAPTER 1

AGREEMENTS

A. DEFINITION OF AGREEMENT

Cyprus Telecommunications Authority/Lumiere TV Public Co. Ltd. CY1

1.1. Understanding

Norsk Hydro Olje AB and others v SCA SE4
Aktiebolaget Bil-Bengtsson and others v SCA SE8

1.2. Understanding may be tacit or express

Norsk Hydro Olje AB and others v SCA SE4
Argos v OFT (paras 666–669) UK8

2. Irrelevance of the form of the agreement

CPC Decision No.136/2006 BG6
Norsk Hydro Olje AB and others v SCA SE4
Aktiebolaget Bil-Bengtsson and others v SCA SE8

2.1. Written or oral

2.2. Gentleman's agreement

2.3. Meetings

Norsk Hydro Olje AB and others v SCA SE4
Aktiebolaget Bil-Bengtsson and others v SCA SE8
Adeptus Rt. and others H9 (para.106)

2.4. Unilateral conduct of a company in a contractual context

2.4.1. Sales conditions

2.4.2. Circular/recommendation/instruction

2.4.3. Refusal to sell in the framework of selective distribution agreements; termination or threat of termination of selective distribution agreements

2.4.4. Unilateral measures implementing upstream agreement

Texaco petrol stations NL1

2.4.5. Monitoring mechanism

2.5. Court settlement

3. Relation between restriction of competition and agreement

3.1. Causation

Mobile Operators NL9

3.2. Agreement continues to produce its effects after termination of agreement

4. Distinction between agreement and public authority decision

SAC Decision No.1700/2006 BG1
Consorzio industrie fiammiferi I4

5. Undertaking's liability for others' conduct in wider agreement

B. CONCERTED PRACTICE

1. Concept

Norsk Hydro Olje AB and others v SCA SE4
Pharmaceutical companies'cartel PT6

[For the tables of case citations see Tables 16 and 17 at the back of the book.]

1.1. Definition

Rifornimenti aeroportuali I1
Prezzi del latte per l'infanzia I2
Norsk Hydro Olje AB and others v SCA SE4
Argos v OFT (paras 761–762) UK8
Argos Limited v OFT/JJB Sports v OFT [2006] EWCA Civ 1318 (paras 126–145) UK33
JJB v OFT paras 657–660 UK7

1.2. Difference between concerted practice and agreement

Rifornimenti aeroportuali I1
Prezzi del latte per l'infanzia I2
Norsk Hydro Olje AB and others v SCA SE4

2. Evidence of a concerted practice

Rifornimenti aeroportuali I1
Prezzi del latte per l'infanzia I2
Norsk Hydro Olje AB and others v SCA SE4
Alterra Kft. and others H7 (para.34.3)
Pharmaceutical companies'cartel PT6

2.1. Similarity of behaviour

Norsk Hydro Olje AB and others v SCA SE4
Rifornimenti aeroportuali I1
Prezzi del latte per l'infanzia I2
Texaco petrol stations NL1
Mobile Operators NL9
Decision 05-D-65 F2

2.2. Exchange of information

Rifornimenti aeroportuali I1
Prezzi del latte per l'infanzia I2
Advertising agencies LV3 (para.5)
Norsk Hydro Olje AB and others v SCA SE4
Texaco petrol stations NL1
Mobile Operators NL9
Argos v OFT UK8
JJB v OFT (paras 657–660) UK7

2.3. Meetings

Eggs case LV1 (para.4)
Rifornimenti aeroportuali I1
Prezzi del latte per l'infanzia I2
Norsk Hydro Olje AB and others v SCA SE4
Texaco petrol stations NL1
Mobile Operators NL9
Decision 06-D-03 bis F3

2.4. Difference between concerted practice and market behaviour resulting from the structure of the relevant market

Norsk Hydro Olje AB and others v SCA SE4
Texaco petrol stations NL1

C. DECISIONS OF ASSOCIATIONS OF UNDERTAKINGS

1. Association of undertakings

Competition Authority v Beef Industry Development Society Limited and Barry Brothers (Carrigmore) Meats Limited IE3
Competition Authority v O'Regan & ors IE1, IE4
Assistancekåren Sverige AB and others v SCA SE
Portuguese Veterinary Medical Association PT1
Portuguese Medical Association PT3

2. Decision

VVS-Installatörerna v SCA SE3
Assistancekåren Sverige AB and others v SCA SE9

2.1. Definition of decision

VVS-Installatörerna v SCA SE3
Assistancekåren Sverige AB and others v SCA SE

2.2. Agreements with associations of undertakings

2.3. Agreements between associations of undertakings

2.4. No guilt through mere association

2.5. Distinction between a decision of an association of undertakings and a public authority decision

SAC Decision No.1700/2006 BG1

2.6. Advice/assistance in the context of a dispute

D. THE PREVENTION, RESTRICTION, OR DISTORTION OF COMPETITION

1. Concept

Keyvent AB and others v SCA SE5

[For the tables of case citations see Tables 16 and 17 at the back of the book.]

Aktiebolaget Bil-Bengtsson and others v SCA SE8

1.1. Interbrand or intrabrand competition

ICS Renting—Étoile L6 (paras 10–18)
Aktiebolaget Bil-Bengtsson and others v SCA SE

1.2. Competition between the parties and competition with third parties

Keyvent AB and others v SCA SE5

1.3. Actual and potential competition
Interpay NL8

1.4. Price or non-price competition

Norsk Hydro Olje AB and others v SCA SE4

1.5. State interference and competition

Lamesch—Oeko-Services L5 (para.34)

1.6. Interaction between upstream and downstream agreements

Consorzio industrie fiammiferi I4

2. Object and effect

CPC Decision No.136/2006 BG2
Norsk Hydro Olje AB and others v SCA SE4
Assistancekåren Sverige AB and others v SCA SE9

2.1. Object of restriction alone suffices/does not suffice

ICS Renting—Étoile L6 (para.18)
SAP and others H10 (paras 406–409)
Norsk Hydro Olje AB and others v SCA SE4
Modint NL7
Secon NL6
Schools: exchange of information on future fees UK26

2.2. Definition of the relevant market in Article 81

Competition Authority v O'Regan & ors IE1, IE4

3. Restriction must be appreciable

Rock—Tanklux L9 (paras 43–53)
Henkel and others H1 (para.18)
TDC 457/99, Hardi International ES2
Norsk Hydro Olje AB and others v SCA SE4
Aktiebolaget Bil-Bengtsson and others v SCA SE

3.1. Commission Notice of December 22, 2001 on agreements of minor importance which do not appreciably restrict competition under Article 81(1) of the Treaty establishing the European Community (de minimis) [2001] O.J. C368/13.

3.2. Cases regarding appreciability

Aktiebolaget Bil-Bengtsson and others v SCA SE
Secon NL6
Memorandum of Understanding on the Supply of Oil in Emergencies UK24

4. Rule of reason/ancillary restraints: assessing the restriction in the context of the relevant market

5. Facilitating market entry

CHAPTER 2

ARTICLE 81(2)

1. Concept of nullity

Wintergarten Feddersen L1 (para.25)
Univers du Cuir L2 (para.7)
Boliden Mineral AB v Fortum Värme SE2

2. Retroactive effect

Emond v Brasserie Haacht BE2

3. Severability of offending clauses

Wintergarten Feddersen L1 (paras 26–30)
Univers du Cuir L2 (paras 38–39)
James E McCabe Ltd v Scottish Courage Ltd [2006] EWHC 538 UK27
English Welsh & Scottish Railways Ltd v E.On UK Ltd and Office of Rail Regulation [2007] EWHC 599 (Comm) UK32

4. Effect of a Commission decision

[For the tables of case citations see Tables 16 and 17 at the back of the book.]

CHAPTER 3

ARTICLE 81(3)

Guidelines on the application of Article 81(3) of the Treaty [2004] O.J. C101/97

A. CONDITIONS FOR THE APPLICATION OF ARTICLE 81(3)

1. Contribution to the improvement, production or distribution of goods, or promoting technical progress

Lamesch—Oeko-Services L5 (para.35)

2. Allowing consumers a fair share of the resulting benefit

Lamesch—Oeko-Services L5 (para.35)

3. No imposition on the undertakings concerned of restrictions which are not indispensable to the attainment of these objectives

4. Not affording such undertakings the possibility of eliminating competition in respect of a substantial part of the products in question

B. ELEMENTS RELEVANT TO THE ASSESSMENT OF ARTICLE 81(3)

1. Balancing the pros and cons

2. Social considerations

Memorandum of Understanding on Supply of Oil in Emergencies UK24
Pool Reinsurance Company Limited UK19

3. Environmental considerations

Lamesch—Oeko-Services L5 (para.35)

4. Burden of proof

5. Unilateral behaviour extraneous to contractual terms

6. Advantage must be objective

7. Conditions are cumulative

8. Discretion of the Commission

9. Can an Article 82 abuse be exempted?

10. Contribution to other EC policies

11. An exemption is never extended per se

12. Relation with Article 82(2)

13. Ruinous competition

C. EXEMPTION BY CATEGORY

1. Delegation of the authority to adopt Regulations to the Commission

1.1. Council Regulation 19/65 of March 2, 1965 on application of Article 85(3) of the Treaty to certain categories of agreements and concerted practices J.O. 533/65; [1965] O.J. Spec. Ed. 35 as amended by Regulation 1/2003 O.J. L1/1

1.2. Council Regulation 2821/71 of December 20, 1971 on application of Article 85(3) of the Treaty to categories of agreements, decisions and concerted practices J.O. 46/71; [1971] O.J. Spec Ed. 1032 as amended by Regulation 1/2003 [2003] O.J. L1/1

2. Effect of a group exemption regulation

3. Withdrawal of the benefit of a group exemption regulation

[For the tables of case citations see Tables 16 and 17 at the back of the book.]

PART III

HORIZONTAL AGREEMENTS

CHAPTER 1

CARTELS

A. LIST OF CARTEL CASES

Lamesch—Oeko-Services L5
Rock—Tanklux L9
Portuguese Veterinary Medical Association PT1
Argos v OFT UK8
JJB Sports v OFT UK7
Apex Asphalt v OFT UK9
Schools: exchange of information on future fees UK26

B. SPECIFIC CLAUSES OR AGREEMENTS TYPICAL OF CARTEL SCHEMES

1. Production related schemes or clauses

1.1. Production quotas for existing capacity

1.2. Provisions regulating capacity

1.2.1. Prohibition of new capacity

1.2.2. Prohibition on sale of capacity outside cartel

1.2.3. Matching supply and demand

1.3. Clauses relating to the nature of the product

1.3.1. Common product range

1.3.2. Sharing of product ranges between competitors

1.4. Supply agreements

CPC Decision No.174/2006 BG3

1.4.1. Emergency supply agreements

Memorandum of Understanding on Supply of Oil in Emergencies UK24

1.4.2. Reciprocal supply arrangements

1.5. Production information exchange schemes

1.6. Compensation schemes

2. Market sharing schemes, agreements or clauses

Norsk Hydro Olje AB and others v SCA SE4
Keyvent AB and others v SCA SE5
Aktiebolaget Bil-Bengtsson and others v SCA SE8

2.1. Dividing territories between competitors

2.1.1. Between Member States

Insolvency agreement in the pharmaceutical sector DK4
Aktiebolaget Bil-Bengtsson and others v SCA SE8

2.1.2. Third country markets

2.2. Quotas

2.3. Dividing customers between competitors

Norsk Hydro Olje AB and others v SCA SE4
Keyvent AB and others v SCA SE5

2.4. Market and/or sales information exchange

[For the tables of case citations see Tables 16 and 17 at the back of the book.]

2.5. Compensation schemes

Keyvent AB and others v SCA SE5

3. Price agreements between competitors

VVS-Installatörerna v SCA SE3
Norsk Hydro Olje AB and others v SCA SE4
Keyvent AB and others v SCA SE5
Aktiebolaget Bil-Bengtsson and others v SCA SE8

3.1. Agreed minimum prices

Norsk Hydro Olje AB and others v SCA SE4
Portuguese Veterinary Medical Association PT1

3.1a. Agreed maximum prices

3.2. Agreed common prices

Norsk Hydro Olje AB and others v SCA SE4
Aktiebolaget Bil-Bengtsson and others v SCA SE8

3.3. Agreed recommended prices

VVS-Installatörerna v SCA SE3
Norsk Hydro Olje AB and others v SCA SE4
Argos v OFT UK8
JJB Sports v OFT UK7

3.4. Agreed price increase

Eggs case LV 1 (para.4)

3.5. Collective R.P.M.

Argos v OFT UK8
JJB Sports v OFT UK7

3.6. Common rebate/discount policy

Norsk Hydro Olje AB and others v SCA SE4
Aktiebolaget Bil-Bengtsson and others v SCA SE8
Texaco petrol stations NL4

3.7. Bidding agreements

Producers of gas-insulated switchgear R 059-070, 075-078/2007/01-08115/2007/310 CZ
AB Aegon and others H8 (paras 32–36
Keyvent AB and others v SCA SE5
Apex Asphalt and Paving Co v OFT UK9

3.8. Aligning prices in another's territory

3.9. Price information exchange agreements

VVS-Installatörerna v SCA SE3
Schools: Exchange of information on future fees UK26
JJB Sports v OFT UK7

4. Sales agreements

4.1. Common or joint sales

4.2. Common exports

4.3. Common sales policy

4.4. Common purchasing policy, purchasing cartels

4.5. Common sales conditions

4.6. Information exchange on sales conditions

Holcim Hungária and others H3 (para.46)
Decision 05-D-64 'Parisian luxury hotels' F1
Paris Cour of Appeal Parisian luxury hotels c/ decision 05-D-64 F4
Decision 05-D-65 F2
Paris Cour of Appeal Bouygues, SFR, Orange c/05-D-65 F5
French Supreme Court, Bouygues, SFR, Orange c/ CA F6

4.7. Mutual respect for distribution channels

4.8 Restrictions on advertising

5. Exclusionary practices

5.1. Collective exclusive dealing

5.2. Agreements intended to control the supply of a product

5.3. Predatory price-cutting agreements

5.4. Joint production with exclusive purchasing

5.5. Collective refusal to supply

5.6. Aggregate rebates

5.7. Patent pooling

5.8. Poaching of employees

5.9. Agreements preventing imports

CEZ S215 215/02-116/03-ORP CZ5

[For the tables of case citations see Tables 16 and 17 at the back of the book.]

6. Practices used by cartels to enforce agreements

6.1. Boycotting non-members

6.2. Fines on cartel members for breach of rules

Pannelli truciolati in legno I3

6.3. Moratoria

7. Crisis cartels

8. Minority acquisitions

9. Agreement to purchase or not to purchase third parties

10. Facilitating others' cartels

CHAPTER 2

CO-OPERATION AGREEMENTS

A. LIST OF CASES ON CO-OPERATION AGREEMENTS

Cyprus Telecommunications Authority (ATHK)/Lumiere TV Public Co. Ltd CY1

B. TEXT OF RELEVANT NOTICES

1. Co-operation agreements

1.1. Commission Notice Guidelines on the applicability of Article 81 of the EC Treaty to horizontal co-operation agreements [2001] O.J. C3/2

1.2. Cases on the interpretation of the Notice of July 29, 1968 on co-operation between enterprises [1968] O.J. C75/3, amended by corrigendum [1968] O.J. C84/14

2. Commission Notice of December 18, 1978 concerning its assessment of certain sub-contracting agreements in relation to Article 85(1) of the EEC Treaty [1979] O.J. C1/2

C. TYPES/CATEGORIES OF CO-OPERATION AGREEMENTS

1. Sharing of research and development (R&D) costs

See R&D agreements, Chapter 4.

2. Patent pools

3. Sharing of capacity

4. Building consortia

5. Uniform standards

6. Uniform sales conditions

7. Joint or common advertising

8. Adoption of common trademarks or quality marks

9. Joint sales

10. Inter-bank agreements

11. Buying groups

12. Exploitation/sharing of infrastructure

13. Collective lobbying

14. Shareholders' agreements

CHAPTER 3

SPECIALISATION AGREEMENTS

A. LIST OF CASES ON SPECIALISATION AGREEMENTS

B. COMMISSION REGULATION 2658/2000 OF NOVEMBER 29, 2000 ON THE APPLICATION OF ARTICLE 81(3) OF THE TREATY TO CATEGORIES OF SPECIALISATION AGREEMENTS [2000] O.J. L304/3

C. CASES ON THE INTERPRETATION OF THE REGULATION

[For the tables of case citations see Tables 16 and 17 at the back of the book.]

[For the tables of case citations see Tables 16 and 17 at the back of the book.]

5.6. Post-term use ban of jointly developed technology

5.7. Patent no-challenge clause

5.8. Obligation to inform the other party of patent infringement

6. Duration of the agreement

6.1. Between competitors

6.2. Between non-competitors

7. Royalty provisions

7.1. Obligation to pay royalties to the other party if contribution to R&D is unequal

7.2. Obligation to share royalties received from third parties

7.3. Profit-sharing through royalty payments

CHAPTER 5

TRADE ASSOCIATIONS

A. CASES ON TRADE ASSOCIATIONS

1. General list

Association of British Insurers v OFT UK11
Association of British Insurers (II) UK22

2. List of cases where a trade association was acting as a cartel

Eggs case LV1 (para.4)
VVS-Installatörerna v SCA SE3

B. STIPULATIONS COMMON TO TRADE ASSOCIATION AGREEMENTS

1. Rules regarding membership of associations

1.1. Objective criteria for membership

1.2. Limit on numbers of members

1.3. Provisions limiting withdrawal from association

2. Pricing obligations

SAC Decision No.1700/2006 BG1
The Society of Film Directors UK23

3. Agreement to purchase minimum percentages from domestic producers

4. Discriminatory conditions against non-members

Competition Authority v O'Regan & ors IE1, IE4

5. Industry organised distribution schemes

6. Collective exclusive dealing

7. Collective lobbying

CHAPTER 6

TRADE FAIR AND EXHIBITION AGREEMENTS

A. CASES ON TRADE FAIR AND EXHIBITION AGREEMENTS

B. STIPULATIONS COMMON TO EXHIBITION AGREEMENTS

1. Agreement not to exhibit at other exhibitions

2. Objective criteria for admittance

3. Discrimination against foreign exhibitors

[For the tables of case citations see Tables 16 and 17 at the back of the book.]

PART IV

VERTICAL AGREEMENTS

CHAPTER 1

LEGISLATION

A. COMMISSION REGULATION 2790/1999 OF DECEMBER 22, 1999 ON THE APPLICATION OF ARTICLE 81(3) OF THE TREATY TO CATEGORIES OF VERTICAL AGREEMENTS AND CONCERTED PRACTICES [1999] O.J. L336/21

Nestlé PT4

B. COMMISSION NOTICE GUIDELINES ON VERTICAL RESTRAINTS [2000] O.J. C291/1

CHAPTER 2

DISTRIBUTION AGREEMENTS

A. LIST OF CASES ON EXCLUSIVE DISTRIBUTION

TDC CEPSA 493/00 ES3
Wintergarten Feddersen L1
Univers du Cuir L2

B. LIST OF CASES ON NON-EXCLUSIVE DISTRIBUTION

ICS Renting—Étoile L6

C. CLAUSES COMMONLY STIPULATED IN DISTRIBUTION AGREEMENTS

1. Territorial restrictions

Tupperware R 17/2005–22148/2006/300 CZ3

1.1. Grant of an exclusive territory to the distributor

CPC Decision No.163/2006 BG4
Wintergarten Feddersen L1 (para.21)

1.2. No active sales policy outside agreed territory

1.3. Profit pass-over clause

1.4. Export ban on direct sales by distributor

1.4.1. Between Member States

1.4.2. Into the EC

1.4.3. Outside the EC

1.5. Export ban on indirect sales, i.e. export ban reimposed upon customers

2. Clauses relating to the product that the distributor may sell

2.1. Non-competition clause

Univers du Cuir L2 (para.40)

2.2. Minimum purchasing obligations

2.3. Exclusive purchasing requirements

Wintergarten Feddersen L1 (para.21)

2.4. Guaranteed after-sales service

2.5. Assembly and manufacture by distributor

2.6. Stocking requirement

3. Clauses related to the price of the product

VVS-Installatörerna v SCA SE3

3.1. Resale price maintenance

Hanzas maiznicas LV2 (paras 5–7)
Wintergarten Feddersen L1 (paras 21–23)

[For the tables of case citations see Tables 16 and 17 at the back of the book.]

Univers du Cuir L2 (paras 33–39)
VVS-Installatörerna v SCA SE3
Lladro Comercial UK20

3.2. Discriminatory pricing between different territories

3.3. Obligation to transmit recommended prices

4. Clauses relating to the customers to which the distributor may sell

5. Distribution agreements between competing manufacturers

5.1. Reciprocal

5.2. Non-reciprocal

CHAPTER 3

EXCLUSIVE PURCHASING AGREEMENTS

A. CASES ON EXCLUSIVE PURCHASING AGREEMENTS

Wintergarten Feddersen L1
Heineken—out of home agreements NL1

B. CLAUSES COMMONLY FIGURING IN EXCLUSIVE PURCHASING AGREEMENTS

1. Exclusivity

Wintergarten Feddersen L1 (para.21)
Heineken—out of home agreements NL1

2. Non-competition clause

Wintergarten Feddersen L1 (para.21)
Henkel and others H1 (para.18)

3. English clause

4. Purchasing or supply obligations

Wintergarten Feddersen L1 (para.21)

5. Resale price maintenance

Wintergarten Feddersen L1 (para.21)

CHAPTER 4

SELECTIVE DISTRIBUTION AGREEMENTS

A. CASES ON SELECTIVE DISTRIBUTION AGREEMENTS

B. COMMISSION REGULATION 1400/2002 OF JULY 31, 2002 ON THE APPLICATION OF ARTICLE 81(3) OF THE TREATY TO CATEGORIES OF VERTICAL AGREEMENTS AND CONCERTED PRACTICES IN THE MOTOR VEHICLE SECTOR [2002] O.J. L203/30

C. CASES ON THE INTERPRETATION OF REGULATIONS 123/85, 1475/95 AND 1400/2002

Citroen DE5
Bezugsbindung DE6
Qualitative Selektionn DE10
Kfz-Vertragshändler II DE11
5-Sterne-Premium-Paket DE15

D. THE ASSESSMENT OF SELECTIVE DISTRIBUTION AGREEMENTS

1. Nature of the product which justifies selective distribution

2. Selection of the dealer

2.1. Qualitative criteria (experience, professional qualifications, specialisation, after-sales service, shop opening hours)

2.2. Quantitative criteria

2.2.1. Related to population in allotted territory

2.2.2. Related to the turnover of the distributor

2.2.3. Stocking requirements

2.2.4. Minimum purchase obligation

3. Procedure for the authorisation of the dealer

3.1. Objective

[For the tables of case citations see Tables 16 and 17 at the back of the book.]

3.2. Not related to prices

3.2.1. Non-discriminatory application of the criteria

3.2.2. Refusal to supply

3.2.3. Impeding parallel trade in the framework of a selective distribution

3.3. No a priori exclusion of certain categories of shops

4. No rigidity in market

5. Requirement that system is tight ("Lückenlosigkeit")

E. FEATURES AND CLAUSES COMMON IN SELECTIVE DISTRIBUTION AGREEMENTS

1. Territorial restrictions

1.1. Exclusivity

1.2. No active sales policy outside agreed territory

1.3. Export bans

1.3.1. Between Member States

1.3.2. Outside the EC

1.4. Control of sales by principal

2. Clauses relating to the customer to whom the dealer may sell

2.1. Inherent restriction (horizontal sales only to other authorised dealers)

2.2. Separation of wholesale and retail level

2.3. Sales to specific types of customers

2.4. Preventing sales between authorised dealers

3. Clauses relating to the product which the dealer is authorised to sell

3.1. Exclusive purchase obligations imposed on the dealer

3.2. Non-competition clause

3.3. Guarantee and after-sales service

3.4. Obligation to sell product in specified packaging

3.5. Obligation not to sell incompatible products

4. Clauses relating to the prices of the contract products

4.1. Effect on prices resulting from selective distribution

4.2. Resale price maintenance

Lladro Comercial UK 20

CHAPTER 5

AGENCY AGREEMENTS

1. Cases on agency agreements

TDC 493/00 CEPSA ES3
Ara—Koepfler L4

CHAPTER 6

FRANCHISING AGREEMENTS

A. CASES ON FRANCHISING AGREEMENTS

Wintergarten Feddersen L1
Univers du Cuir L2

B. CLAUSES COMMONLY STIPULATED IN FRANCHISING AGREEMENTS

1. Clauses relating to the franchisee

1.1. Selection of the franchisee

1.2. Non-competition restraint of trade clauses

1.2.1. Obligation not to engage in competing activities during agreement

Wintergarten Feddersen L1 (para.21)

1.2.2. Post-term non-competition clause

Univers du Cuir L2 (paras 40–49)

1.3. Best endeavours clause

2. Licensing of know-how or trade marks

2.1. Grant of licence

2.2. Royalties

[For the tables of case citations see Tables 16 and 17 at the back of the book.]

2.3. Field of use restrictions

2.4. Grant back of improvements

2.5. Post-term use ban

3. Clauses promoting the uniformity of the franchise network

3.1. Regarding the decoration of the shop

3.2. Collective advertising provisions

3.3. Business methods

4. Territorial restrictions

4.1. Fixed location of retail outlet

4.2. Exclusivity in the contract territory

Wintergarten Feddersen L1 (para.21)

4.3. Obligation not to open a new outlet outside agreed territory

5. Clauses related to the product the franchisee is authorised to sell

5.1. Obligation not to sell competing products in authorised outlet

Wintergarten Feddersen L1 (para.21)

5.2. Purchase obligations on the franchisee

5.2.1. General

5.2.2. Obligation to purchase goods of defined quality

5.2.3. Exclusive purchasing

Wintergarten Feddersen L1 (para.21)

6. Clauses relating to the customers the franchisee may serve

6.1. Obligation not to sell outside the network

6.2. Restrictions on the franchisee regarding the customers to which it may sell

7. Recommended prices

Wintergarten Feddersen L1 (paras 21–23)
Univers du Cuir L2 (paras 33–39)

CHAPTER 7

AGREEMENTS PREVENTING PARALLEL TRADE

A. CASES ON AGREEMENTS PREVENTING PARALLEL TRADE

ICS Renting — Étoile L6

B. CLAUSES OR PRACTICES WHICH MAY HAVE THE OBJECT/EFFECT OF PREVENTING PARALLEL TRADE

1. General sales conditions

ICS Renting — Étoile L6 (para.4)

2. Circular sent by principal to distributors

3. Pressure exercised by principal on distributor

CPC Decision No.136/2006 BG2

4. Discriminatory trading conditions

4.1. Quality marks

4.2. On grounds of nationality

4.3. State of the product

4.4. Prices and rebates

NAT. DECISIONS: VERT. AGREEMENTS

[For the tables of case citations see Tables 16 and 17 at the back of the book.]

PART V

INDUSTRIAL AND INTELLECTUAL PROPERTY AGREEMENTS

CHAPTER 1

TECHNOLOGY TRANSFER AGREEMENTS

A. CASES ON LICENSING AGREEMENTS

B. LEGISLATION

1. **Text of Commission Regulation 772/2004 on the application of Article 81(3) of the Treaty to categories of technology transfer agreements [2004] O.J. L123/11**

2. **Guidelines on the application of Article 81 of the EC Treaty to technology transfer agreements [2004] C101/2**

C. CLAUSES COMMONLY STIPULATED IN TECHNOLOGY TRANSFER AGREEMENTS

1. Territorial provisions

1.1. Right to use the technology exclusively within an agreed territory

1.1.1. To manufacture the product

1.1.2. To exploit the product

1.2. Obligation not to pursue an active sales policy outside agreed territory

1.3. Obligation not to export outside agreed territory (passive sales)

1.3.1. Between Member States

1.3.2. To third countries

1.3.3. Into the Common Market

1.4. Limitation on site of manufacture

1.5. Grant of a non-exclusive licence authority for exclusive territory

1.6. Obligation to respect confidentiality

2. Clauses relating to the product that the licensee may sell

2.1. Non-competition clause

2.2. Obligation on licensee to restrict output

See Article 4(1)(b); Article 4(1)(c) i—ii, vi—vii; Article 4(2)(b) (iii—v) Regulation 772/2004

2.3. Quality norms

2.4. Purchase or supply obligations

2.4.1. Purchasing

2.4.2. Tying

2.5. Trade mark clauses

2.6. Best endeavours clause

3. Pricing restrictions on the licensee

4. Restrictions upon the customers which the licensee may serve

5. Clauses relating to the protection of the technology

5.1. Field of use restrictions

5.2. No-challenge clause

5.3. Guaranteed rights to any subsequent improvements

5.4. Restrictions on sub-licensing

5.5. Requirement that the know-how is unintentional and identified

[For the tables of case citations see Tables 16 and 17 at the back of the book.]

6. Royalties

6.1. Obligation to pay minimum royalties/produce minimum quantities

6.2. Obligation to pay royalties after expiration or invalidity of the patent

6.3. Most favoured licensee clause

6.4. Obligation to pay royalty even if patent not used

6.5. Obligation to pay royalties on a know-how if in the public domain

7. Clauses relating to the duration of the agreement, post-term provisions

7.1. Automatic extension of agreement

7.2. Post-term use restrictions

8. Patent dispute settlements

9. Patent pooling

CHAPTER 2

TRADE MARK AGREEMENTS

A. CASES ON TRADE MARK LICENSING AGREEMENTS

B. CASES ON TRADE MARK ASSIGNMENTS

C. CASES ON THE CREATION OF A JOINT TRADE MARK

D. TRADE MARK DELIMITATION AGREEMENTS

CPC Decision No.136/2006 BG2
SAC Decision No.1402/2007 BG5

E. CLAUSES COMMONLY FIGURING IN TRADE MARK LICENSING OR ASSIGNMENT AGREEMENTS

1. Territorial restrictions

1.1. Right to use the trade mark exclusively within an agreed territory

1.2. Export ban

1.3. Grant of exclusivity gives licensee ability to prevent parallel imports

CPC Decision No.136/2006 BG2

2. Trade mark no-challenge clause

3. Duration of the validity of the trade mark

4. Non-use clause

5. Between competitors

CHAPTER 3

COPYRIGHT AND DESIGN RIGHT AGREEMENTS

CPC Decision No.331/2006 BG6

A. CASES ON COPYRIGHT AGREEMENTS

B. CASES ON DESIGN RIGHT AGREEMENTS

C. CLAUSES TYPICALLY STIPULATED IN COPYRIGHT/DESIGN RIGHT AGREEMENTS

1. Territorial restrictions

1.1. Exclusivity

1.2. Export bans

2. No-challenge clause

3. Royalties

4. Non-competition restraint of trade clause

5. Improvements

6. Tying

7. Sub-licensing

[For the tables of case citations see Tables 16 and 17 at the back of the book.]

CHAPTER 4

BREEDERS' RIGHTS LICENSING AGREEMENTS

A. CASES ON BREEDERS' RIGHTS

B. CLAUSES COMMONLY FIGURING IN BREEDERS' RIGHTS AGREEMENTS

1. Territorial restrictions

1.1. Exclusivity

1.2. Export ban

2. Non-competition restraint of trade clause

3. Control of prices by licensor

4. No-challenge clause

5. Grant back of improvements

6. Purchasing obligations on licensee

7. Customer limitation clause

[For the tables of case citations see Tables 16 and 17 at the back of the book.]

PART VI

JOINT VENTURES

CHAPTER 1

LIST OF CASES ON JOINT VENTURE AGREEMENTS

CHAPTER 2

TYPES OF JOINT VENTURES

A. JOINT VENTURES UNDER THE MERGER REGULATION

B. JOINT VENTURES UNDER ARTICLE 81(1)

1. Joint R&D

2. Joint buying

3. Joint production

4. Joint sales

5. Co-ordination centres

6. Shareholders agreements

TPS 440

CHAPTER 3

PURPOSE OF THE CO-OPERATION

1. Market extension

2. Technological progress/transfer of technology

3. Restructuring operations

4. Market sharing

5. Rationalisation of production capacity

CHAPTER 4

LEGISLATION

1. Commission Regulation 2658/2000 on the application of Article 81(3) of the Treaty to categories of specialisation agreements [2000] O.J. L304/3

2. Commission Regulation 2659/2000 on the application of Article 81(3) of the Treaty to categories of research and development agreements [2000] O.J. L304/7

3. Commission Regulation 773/2004 on the application of Article 85(3) of the Treaty to certain categories of technology transfer agreements [2004] O.J. L123/11

4. Other information

23rd Comp. Rep. (paras 193–197)

CHAPTER 5

OPERATIONS/CLAUSES TYPICAL OF JOINT VENTURE AGREEMENTS

1. Restriction of competition which may result from the creation of the joint venture

1.1. Competition between the parent companies

1.1.1. Actual competition

1.1.2. Potential competition

Interpay NL8

1.1.3. Spill-over effect

Interpay NL8

[For the tables of case citations see Tables 16 and 17 at the back of the book.]

1.2. Effect of the joint venture on the competitive position of third parties

1.3. Restriction of future competition resulting from the joint venture agreements

1.3.1. Between parents and the joint venture

Nord-KS/Xella DE14

1.3.2. Between several joint ventures having a common parent company

1.4. Need to have joint control

2. Ancillary clauses which may restrict competition

2.1. Non-competition clauses

2.2. Co-ordination of investment policy

2.3. Post-termination provisions

2.4. Licensing and exchange of technical information

2.5. Joint price-fixing

2.6. Purchasing and supply obligations

2.7. Grant of exclusive distribution rights

2.8. Territorial restrictions

2.9. Trade mark related clauses

[For the tables of case citations see Tables 16 and 17 at the back of the book.]

PART VII

ARTICLE 82

CHAPTER 1

THE ESTABLISHMENT OF A DOMINANT POSITION

A. THE RELEVANT MARKET

1. The relevant product market

1.1. Definition of the term "relevant product market"

NCA/Cyprus Telecommunications Authority CY2
Rock—Tanklux L9 (paras 44–45)
Genzyme v OFT UK5
Aberdeen Journals v DGFT UK12

1.2. Relevant factors

1.2.1. Physical characteristics/end use

Coditel L4 (para.25)

1.2.2. Price

Latvijas pasts LV5 (para.3.4)
Coditel L4 (para.25)
Rock—Tanklux L9 (para.47)

1.2.3. Consumer preference

Coditel L4 (para.25)
Rock—Tanklux L9 (para.47)

1.2.4. Exclusion of in-house production

Rock—Tanklux L9 (para.47)

1.2.5. Existence of specialised producers

1.2.6. Specific distribution channels

Paris Cour of Appeal, Royal Canin c/ Décision 05-D-32 F8

1.2.7. Product represents small part of overall final product cost

1.2.8. Supply-side substitutability/potential competition

Coditel L4 (para.25)
Rock—Tanklux L9 (para.47)
MÁV Rt. H11 (para.314)

1.2.9. Relevant product market defined in light of product range of alleged dominant firm

1.2.10. Cellophane fallacy

1.3. Relevant evidence

1.3.1. Consumer surveys

1.3.2. Conditions of competition

Rock—Tanklux L9 (para.47)

1.3.3. Historical evidence on cross-elasticity

1.3.4. Definition given by defendant

Rock—Tanklux L9 (para.47)

1.3.5. Industry product classifications

1.3.6. One-way sustitutability

1.3.7. Dependence on competitors for input

Rock—Tanklux L9 (para.47)

1.4. Narrow definition of relevant product market

Rock—Tanklux L9 (para.47)

2. Relevant geographic market

Merk—principi attivi I1
ENI/Trans Tunisian Pipeline I11

2.1. Definition of the term "relevant geographic market"

Golden Telemedia Ltd./Cyprus Telecommunications Authority CY3
Rock—Tanklux L9 (paras 44–45)

NAT. DECISIONS: ARTICLE 82

[For the tables of case citations see Tables 16 and 17 at the back of the book.]

2.2. Relevant factors

2.2.1. Regulatory trade barriers

Rock—Tanklux L9 (para.48)

2.2.2. Local specification requirements/differing national standards

Rock—Tanklux L9 (para.48)

2.2.3. National procurement policies

2.2.4. Adequate distribution facilities/different distribution systems

Rock—Tanklux L9 (para.48)

2.2.5. Transport costs

Rock—Tanklux L9 (para.48)

2.2.6. Language

2.2.7. Consumer preferences

Rock—Tanklux L9 (para.48)

2.2.8. Need for secure/regular supplies or rapid after-sales service and thus locally based suppliers

2.2.9. Supply side substitutability; potential competition

Rock—Tanklux L9 (para.48)

2.2.10. Market defined on basis of geographic scope of alleged dominant firms' scope of activities

2.3. Relevant evidence

2.3.1. Price difference between neighbouring areas

2.3.2. Market share differences between neighbouring areas

2.3.3. Significant trade flows between neighbouring areas

3. A substantial part of the Common Market

3.1. Local/regional markets

3.2. National markets

3.3. Transport infrastructure/essential facilities

Tallinna Sadam 31–L EST1
Rock—Tanklux L9 (para.52)
Airport Bratislava, 2005/DZ/2/1/127 (pp.13, 18–22) SK2
Slovak Telekom, 2005/DZ/R/2/143 (pp.15–16) SK5

B. DOMINANCE

1. Definition of the term "dominant position"

Coditel L4 (para.21)
Nemzeti Autópálya Rt. H5 (paras 42–49)
Genzyme v OFT UK5
Napp v OFT UK15
JJ Burgess and Sons v OFT UK6

2. Relevant factors

B2 Bredband Holding/TeliaSonera AB SE7

2.1. Market share

Darbo S.A.S./ Sonae Industria SGPS S.A. CYM3
Comportamenti restrittivi sulla Borsa elettrica I10
Latvijas pasts LV5 (para.4)
Rock—Tanklux L9 (para.54)
B2 Bredband Holding/TeliaSonera AB SE7

2.2. Size and resources of the group

B2 Bredband Holding/TeliaSonera AB SE7

2.3. Size and importance of competitors

B2 Bredband Holding/TeliaSonera AB SE7

2.4. Commercial advantage over competitors

2.4.1. Product range

2.4.2. Established trade marks; customer loyalty

2.4.3. Vertical integration of firm

2.4.4. Extensive sales/service network

Latvijas pasts LV5 (para.5)

2.5. Technical advantages

2.5.1. General

[For the tables of case citations see Tables 16 and 17 at the back of the book.]

2.5.2. Patents

2.5.3. Know-how

2.5.4. Copyright

2.5a. Advantages of a regulatory nature

2.6. Dependence of consumers

2.7. Statutory dominance or monopoly

NCA/Cyprus Telecommunications Authority CY2
Lamesch—Oeko-Services L (para.39)

2.8. Supply side substitutability; entry barriers

B2 Bredband Holding/TeliaSonera AB SE
JJ Burgess and Sons V OFT UK6

2.8.1. Basic concept

2.8.2. Regulatory barriers

Rock—Tanklux L9 (para.48)
B2 Bredband Holding/TeliaSonera AB SE7
Genzyme v OFT UK5
Napp v OFT UK15

2.8.3. Financial risk (likely return on investment if market already mature or saturated)

2.8.4. High capital cost of entry

Coditel L4 (para.25)
Genzyme v OFT UK5

2.8.5. Marketing entry barriers

Mr. Alexis Philippides/Cyprus Telecommunications Authority CY4

2.8.6. Technical entry barriers

Coditel L4 (para.25)

2.8.7. Economies of scale

B2 Bredband Holding/TeliaSonera AB SE7

2.8.8. Historical evidence of past entry indicates entry barriers surmountable

2.8.9. Entry must be likely in the short term

2.8.10 Opinions of customers and competitors regarding possibility for new entry

2.8.11. High switching costs for customers

2.8.12. Network effects

2.9. Imperfect substitutes

Coditel L4 (para.25)
Rock—Tanklux L9 (para.48)

2.10. Countervailing buying power

2.11. Dominance in rapidly evolving markets

2.12. Superdominance

Napp v OFT UK15

3. Relevant evidence for determining dominance

B2 Bredband Holding/TeliaSonera AB SE7

3.1. Historical evidence of ability to maintain prices unilaterally

3.2. Ability to engage in abusive conduct (circular argument)

3.3. Ability to maintain market share over time

Napp v OFT UK15

3.4. Econometric studies provided by parties

B2 Bredband Holding/TeliaSonera AB SE7

4. Joint and collective dominance

5. Monopsonistic dominant position

Nemzeti Autópálya Rt. H5 (paras 31–33)

[For the tables of case citations see Tables 16 and 17 at the back of the book.]

CHAPTER 2

ABUSE OF A DOMINANT POSITION

A. CONCEPT OF AN ABUSE OF A DOMINANT POSITION

TS 9174/2003 Retevisión/Telefónica ES11
Coditel L4 (para.22)
UPC Magyarország Kft H2 (para.XIV)

B. EXAMPLES OF ABUSE

1. Unfair terms imposed on clients

Coditel L4 (paras 30–31)

2. Unfair or excessive prices

NCA/Cement market (04/04/2006) CY5
Tallinna Sadam 31–L EST1
Eesti Telefon 3–3–1–66–02 EST2 (paras 24–34)
UPC Magyarország Kft. H2 (para.XV)
Decision 06–D–34 F36
Coditel L4 (para.27)
Napp v OFT UK15
Albion Water v DG of Water Services UK1
Attheraces v British Horseracing Board [2007] EWCA Civ 38 UK31

3. Exclusive purchasing

BiljettDirekt Ticnet SE10
MÁV Rt. H11 (paras 311–312)
Decision 06-D-18 F7

4. Exclusive distribution systems

Bacardi exclusive distribution agreements UK21
Pernod Ricard SA v OFT UK10

5. Discriminatory pricing

SABAM v Production & Marketing BE3
NCA/Cyprus Telecommunications Authority (26/9/2006) CY2
RWE Transgas R 98/2006/01-05326/2007/300 CZ2
Tallinna Sadam 31-L EST1
Airport "Riga" case LV6 (paras 5–8)

6. Discriminatory conditions between different customers

Linde Technoplyn R 012/2003 CZ1
Comportamenti abusivi Telecom Italia I9
Enel Trade/Clienti idonei I8
Tallinna Sadam 31–L EST1

7. Discrimination on grounds of nationality

8. Discriminatory allocation of products during supply shortages

Tallinna Sadam 39–L EST3

9. Predatory pricing

TELE2 v Belgacom MEDE-V/M-05/0043 BE6
Decision 07-D-09 F38
TS 915/2002 Tabacos Canarias ES8
Comportamenti abusivi Telecom Italia I9
Lamesch—Oeko-Services L5 (para.37)
Aberdeen Journals v DGFT UK12
Napp Pharmaceuticals Holding Ltd v OFT UK15

10. Refusal to supply

TS 9710/1997, Telefónica/3c ES6
Floe Telecom v Ofcom UK2
Tallinna Sadam 39-L EST3
Rock—Tanklux L9 (paras 63–65)
Merck-principi attivi I5
Glaxo-principi attivi I6
Wrigley Hungária Kft. H4 (paras 31–32)
Soda-Club DE13

11. Refusal to do business with competition

Soda-Club DE13

12. Tying

CESKÝ TELECOM R 8/2005 CZ4
Lattelekom LV4 (para.14)

13. Rebates and discounts

SABAM v Production & Marketing BE3
Arla—rebates and marketing contribution DK3
Enel Trade/Clienti idonei I8
Comportamenti abusivi Telecom Italia I9
Latvijas pasts LV5
GESTIRETALHO PT5
Paris Cour of Appeal, Royal Canin c/ Décision 05-D-32 F8

14. Using dominance to move into or protect ancillary markets

[For the tables of case citations see Tables 16 and 17 at the back of the book.]

15. Actions preventing parallel trade

16. Refusal to disclose technical information, e.g. details of products

Computer Resource Management MEDE-V/M-03/0060 BE6

17. Abusive registration of a trade mark

18. Restricting intra-band competition

Mazda Motor DK 1

19. Abuse of intellectual/industrial property rights

Merck-principi attivi I5
Glaxo-principi attivi I6

19a. Abuse of intellectual/industrial property procedures

Lamesch—Oeko-Services L5 (paras 37–39)

19b. Misleading representations to regulatory authorities

19c. Misleading representations in legal proceedings

20. Acquisition

21. Pressure on dependent market players

22. Product swaps

23. Litigation and complaints

24. Abuse of collective or joint dominant position

25. Limiting production, markets or technical development

ENI/Trans Tunisian Pipeline I11
Gestione ed utilizzo della Capacità di rigassificazione I7

26. Long-term/indefinite duration contracts/excessive notice periods

E.ON/Ruhrgas DE 12

27. Margin squeeze/raising rivals' costs

TDC—margin squeeze DK 2
Comportamenti abusivi Telecom Italia I9
Genzyme v OFT UK5
Slovak Telecom, 2005/DZ/2/1/133 (pages 10, 24–26) SK3
Magyar Távközlési Rt. H6 (para.94–98)
Decision 04-D-48 F9 (paras 261–262)

28. Abusive tender procedures

Thiry v ASAF CONC-P/K-00/0011 BE4

29. Abuse of regulatory procedures

30. Exploiting legal uncertainty or legal loopholes

C. OBJECTIVE JUSTIFICATION

Coditel L4 (para.27)
Lamesch—Oeko-Services L5 (para.39)
Rock—Tanklux L9 (paras 63–65)
Superunie v Interpay NL2 (para.41)

[For the tables of case citations see Tables 16 and 17 at the back of the book.]

PART VIII

STATE INTERVENTION

CHAPTER 1

ARTICLE 86

1. **Cases on the interpretation of Article 86(1)**

2. **Article 86(2)**

Portuguese Medical Association PT3

2.1. Direct effect

2.2. Cases on the interpretation of Article 86(2).

See also Communication from the Commission—Services of general interest in Europe
Pool Reinsurance Company Limited UK19

3. **Article 86(3)**

CHAPTER 2

APPLICATION OF ARTICLE 86

A. GENERAL

1. **Communication from the Commission on services of general interest in Europe [2001] O.J. C17/4**

Portuguese Medical Association PT A3

2. **References**

Report to the Laeken European Council—Services of General Interest (COM (2001) 598—final, 17.10.2001)
Green Paper on Services of General Interest (COM (2003) 270 final, 21.5.2003)

B. TELECOMMUNICATIONS

1. **Commission Directive 2002/77 of September 16, 2002 on competition in the markets for electronic communication networks and services [2002] O.J. L249/21**

2. **Commission guidelines on market analysis and the assessment of significant market power under the Community regulatory framework for electronic communications networks and services [2002] O.J. C165/6**

3. **Notice on the application of the competition rules to access agreements in the telecommunications sector [1998] O.J. C265/2**

4. **Reference to old notice**

Commission Guidelines on the application of the EEC competition rules in the telecommunications sector ([1991] O.J. C233/2)

5. **Cases on previous Directives**

C. POSTAL SERVICES

1. **Notice on the application of the competition rules to the postal service and on the assessment of certain State measures relating to postal services [1998] O.J. C39/2**

2. **Cases on postal services**

[For the tables of case citations see Tables 16 and 17 at the back of the book.]

CHAPTER 3

STATE RESPONSIBILITY

A. STATE RESPONSIBILITY UNDER ARTICLES 3F AND 5 OF THE TREATY FOR FACILITATING OR ENCOURAGING BEHAVIOUR CONTRARY TO ARTICLES 81 AND 82

B. GOVERNMENTAL SILENCE, ENCOURAGEMENT OR APPROVAL IS NO EXCUSE FOR INFRINGING

ARTICLES 81 AND 82

[For the tables of case citations see Tables 16 and 17 at the back of the book.]

PART IX

SECTORAL APPLICATION OF EC COMPETITION RULES

CHAPTER 1

AGRICULTURE

A. COUNCIL REGULATION 26/62 APPLYING CERTAIN RULES OF COMPETITION TO PRODUCTION OF AND TRADE IN AGRICULTURAL PRODUCTS [1962] O.J. SPEC. ED. 129

B. CASES REGARDING AGRICULTURE AND COMPETITION

1. General cases

2. Cases in which Regulation 26/62 was applicable

3. Cases in which Regulation 26/62 was not applicable

CHAPTER 2

TRANSPORT

A. INLAND WATERWAYS, RAIL AND ROAD TRANSPORT

1. Legislation

Council Regulation 1017/68 of July 19, 1968 applying rules of competition to transport by rail, road and inland waterway [1968] O.J. Spec. Ed. 302, as amended by Regulation 1/2003 [2003] O.J. L1/1.

2. Cases on the interpretation and application of the Regulations

B. MARITIME TRANSPORT

1. Council Regulation 4056/86 of December 22, 1986 laying down detailed rules for the application of Articles 85 and 86 of the Treaty to maritime transport [1986] O.J. L378/4, as amended by Regulation 1/2003 [2003] O.J. L1/1

2. Council Regulation 479/92 of February 25, 1992 on the application of Article 85(3) of the Treaty to certain categories of agreements, decisions and concerted practices between liner shipping companies (consortia) [1992] O.J. L55/3, as amended by Regulation 1/2003 [2003] O.J. 11/1

3. Commission Regulation 823/2000 of April 19, 2000 on the applicability of Article 81(3) of the Treaty to certain categories of agreements, decisions and concerted practices between liner shipping companies (consortia) [2000] O.J. L100/24 as amended by Regulation 463/2004 [2004] O.J. L77/23

4. Cases

C. AIR TRANSPORT

1. Council Regulation 3976/87 of December 14, 1987 on the application of Article 85(3) of the Treaty to certain categories of agreements and concerted practices in the air transport sector [1987] O.J. L374/9 as amended by Regulation 2344/90 [1990] O.J. L217/15, Regulation 2411/92 [1992] O.J. L240/19 and Regulation 411/2004 [2004] O.J. L68/1

[For the tables of case citations see Tables 16 and 17 at the back of the book.]

2. Commission Regulation 1617/93 of June 25, 1993 on the application of Article 85(3) of the Treaty to certain categories of agreements, and concerted practices concerning joint planning and co-ordination of schedules, joint operations, consultations on passenger and cargo tariffs on scheduled air services and slot allocation at airports [1993] O.J. L155/18, as amended by Regulation 1523/96 [1996] O.J. L190/11, Regulation 1083/1999 [1999] O.J. L131/27, Regulation 1324/2001 [2001] O.J. L177/56 and the Act of Accession of Austria, Sweden and Finland [1994] O.J. C241/21 (adapted by Council Decision 95/1/EC, Euraton, ECSC [1995] O.J. L1/1), corrigendum in [1994] O.J. L15/20

3. Commission Regulation 1324/2001 of June 29, 2001 amending Regulation 1617/93 as regards consultations on passenger tariffs and slot allocation at airports [2001] O.J. L177/56

4. Notice concerning procedures for communications to the Commission pursuant to Articles 4 and 5 of Commission Regulation 1617/93 of June 25, 1993 on the application of Article 85(3) of the Treaty to certain categories of agreements and concerted practices concerning joint planning and co-ordination of schedules, joint operations, consultations on passenger and cargo tariffs on scheduled air services and slot allocation at airports [1993] O.J. C177/6

5. Cases

CHAPTER 3

FINANCIAL SERVICES

A. LEGISLATION

1. Council Regulation 1534/91 of May 31, 1991 on the application of Article 85(3) of the Treaty to certain categories of agreements, decisions and concerted practices in the insurance sector [1991] O.J. L143/1, as amended by Regulation 1/2003 [2003] O.J. L1/1

2. Commission Regulation 358/2003 of February 27, 2003 on the application of Article 85(3) of the Treaty to certain categories of agreements, decision and concerted practices in the insurance sector [2003] O.J. L53/8

3. Notice on the application of the EC competition rules to cross-border credit transfers [1995] O.J. C25/3

B. CASES

1. Banking

Link ATM Rules UK25
Mastercard v OFT UK4

2. Insurance

GISC rules UK28
Association of British Insurers v OFT UK11
Institute of Insurance Brokers/Association of British Travel Agents v OFT UK14
Pool Reinsurance Company Ltd UK19

CHAPTER 4

SPORTS

A. CASES

Cyprus Footballer's Union, Costas Malekos, Angelos Efthimiou/ Cyprus Football Federation CY6
Adidas-Salomon Ag v Drape & Ors [2006] EWHC 1318 UK28

[For the tables of case citations see Tables 16 and 17 at the back of the book.]

PART X

PROCEDURE AND REMEDIES

CHAPTER 1

PROCEDURAL LEGISLATION

A. RELEVANT PROVISIONS OF THE TREATY

1. **Article 83 (ex 87)**
2. **Cases on the interpretation of Article 83 (ex 87)**
3. **Articles 84–85 (ex 88–89)**
4. **Cases on the interpretation of Articles 84–85 (ex 88–89)**

B. RELEVANT LEGISLATIVE PROVISIONS

1. **Council Regulation 1/2003 of December 16, 2002 on the interpretation of the rules on competition laid down in Articles 81 and 82 of the Treaty [2003] O.J. L1/1 as amended by Regulation 411/2004 [2004] O.J. L68/1**
2. **Commission Regulation 773/2004 on the conduct of proceedings by the Commission pursuant to Articles 81 and 82 of the EC Treaty [2004] O.J. L123/18**
3. **Notice on informal guidance relating to novel questions concerning Articles 81 and 82 of the EC Treaty that arise in individual cases (guidance letters) [2004] O.J. C101/78**
4. **Notice on the handling of complaints by the Commission under Articles 81 and 82 of the EC Treaty [2004] O.J. C101/65**

CHAPTER 2

THE HANDLING OF A CASE

A. THE OPENING OF A FILE

1. Method of notification; what constitutes a valid notification (Former Regulation 17)

1.1. When is notification necessary (Former Regulation 17)

1.2. Conversion of notification (Former Regulation 17)

1.3. Effect of notification

1.3.1. Possibility of the grant of an exemption

1.3.2. Immunity from fines (Former Regulation 17)

1.3.3. Provisional validity for old agreements (Former Regulation 17)

2. Complaints

2.1. Method of lodging a complaint/locus standi

2.2. Rights and obligations of complainant

Pernod Ricard SA v OFT UK10

3. Ex-officio investigation

B. THE INVESTIGATION OF A CASE

1. By letter

1.1. Potential addressees of a letter pursuant to Article 8 Regulation 1/2003

1.2. Simple request for information

1.2.1. Text of a typical request for information letter sent pursuant to Article 18 of Regulation 1/2003

[For the tables of case citations see Tables 16 and 17 at the back of the book.]

1.2.2. Cases

1.3. Request for information by decision

1.4. Oral questions

2. By inspection

X—Inspection de la concurrence L7

2.1. Inspectors

2.1.1. National inspectors
2.1.2. Commission inspectors

Christakis Lazaridis, Byronas Tegerakis/NCA, Republic of Cyprus CY7

2.2. Powers of inspectors

2.3. Inspection without decision

2.3.1. Text of typical authorisation to investigate under Article 20 of Regulation 1/2003

2.3.2. Cases on inspections without decisions

2.4. Inspection with decision

2.4.1. Cases on inspections with decisions

3. Sectoral investigation

4. Co-operation with national authorities

5. Power to take statements

C. PROCEDURAL STEPS AND SAFEGUARDS

1. In relation to an infringement decision

1.1. Initiation of proceedings

1.2. Statement of objections

1.3. Access to file

1.3.1. Grant of access to all documents upon which the Commission relies

1.3.2. Text of Commission Notice on the internal rules of procedure for processing requests for access to the file in cases pursuant to Articles 85 and 86 of the EC Treaty, Articles 65 and 66 of the ECSC Treaty and Council Regulation 4064/89 [1997] O.J. C23/3

1.3.3. Text of Commission Notice on the rules for access to the Commission file in cases pursuant to Articles 81 and 82 of the EC Treaty, Articles 53, 54 and 57 of the EEA Agreement and Council Regulation 139/2004 [2005] O.J. C325/7

1.4. Reply to the statement of objections by the parties

1.4.1. In writing

1.4.2. Oral hearing

1.4.3. Notice on the internal rules of procedure for processing requests for access to the file in cases pursuant to Articles 85 and 86 of the EC Treaty, Articles 65 and 66 of the ECSC Treaty and Council Regulation 4064/89 [1997] O.J. C23/3

1.4.4. Role of the Hearing Officer

1.4.5. General considerations on the right to be heard

1.4.6. Minutes of the hearing

1.5. Advisory committee

2. Relating to a positive decision

2.1. Publication of Notice (Former Regulation 17)

2.2. Advisory committee

3. Relating to a rejection of a complaint

4. General procedural safeguards

X—Inspection de la concurrence L7

4.1. Legal professional privilege

SCC r 508/02 Pepsi-Cola/Coca-Cola ES5

4.2. Obligation of the Commission as to confidentiality

4.2.1. General obligation

4.2.2. Business secrets

4.2.3. Result of disclosure of business secrets or confidential information

4.3. Statement of position prior to a decision

4.4. Objective and impartial investigation

4.5. Duty to make a record of meetings

[For the tables of case citations see Tables 16 and 17 at the back of the book.]

D. INFORMAL STEPS OFTEN TAKEN BY THE COMMISSION

1. Negotiations and modifications of agreements

2. Informal settlement

2.1. Undertakings

Schools: Exchange of information on future fees UK26

3.1. Text of a typical comfort letter issued under Former Regulation 17

3.2. Cases on comfort letters

E. LENGTH OF PROCEDURE

F. COMMISSION DECISIONS

1. Administrative decisions

1a. Decisions of the Hearing Officer

2. Provisional decisions

2.1. Removal of immunity from fines (Former Regulation 17)

2.2. Interim measures

London Metal Exchange v OFT UK3

2.3. Rejecting request for interim measures

Areeba Ltd./Cyprus Telecommunications Authority CY8

3. Recommendation

4. Final decisions

4.1. Negative clearance (Former Article 2 Regulation 17)

4.2. Exemption (Former Article 8 Regulation 17)

4.2.1. Duration of exemption (Former Article 8 Regulation 17)

4.2.2. Conditions or obligations for exemption (Former Article 8 Regulation 17)

4.2.3. Renewal of exemption (Former Article 8 Regulation 17)

4.2.4. Revocation of exemption (Former Article 8 Regulation 17)

4.2.5. Effect of an exemption (Former Article 8 Regulation 17)

4.3. Prohibition

Article 7 Regulation 1/2003

4.3.1. Order to cease

4.3.2. Order to act

4.3.3. Neutral; obligation of parties to suggest remedy

4.3.3a. Monitoring mechanism

4.3.4. Date of commencement of prohibition

4.3.5. Effects in time

4.3.6. Findings of past infringements: Legitimate interest

4.4. Rejection of complaint

4.5. Commitment decisions

TV Eye UK17
Associated Newspapers UK16

5. Formal requirements regarding the form/content of decisions

5.1. Decisions must be reasoned

L.I.A. Soundech Car & Home Solution Ltd./Republic of Cyprus, NCA CY9

5.2. Burden and standard of proof

Napp Pharmaceuticals v Director General of Fair Trading UK15
Aberdeen Journals (2) v OFT UK12

5.3. Must contain only that which figured in the statement of objections

5.4. Obligation to take account of the defendant's views in the decision

5.5. Obligation to respect internal procedural and linguistic rules

5.6. Notification of decision

5.7. Withdrawal of decision

5.8. Publication of decision

[For the tables of case citations see Tables 16 and 17 at the back of the book.]

G. FINES AND PERIODIC PENALTY PAYMENTS

1. Fines for substantive infringements

Keyvent AB and others v SCA SE5

1.1 Requirements

1.1.1 Intentional infringement

1.1.2. Negligence

1.2. Relevant Legislation

1.2.1. Articles 23–26 of Regulation 1/2003

1.2.2. Guidelines on the method of setting fines imposed pursuant to Article 15(2) of Regulation 17 and Article 65(5) of the ECSC Treaty [1998] O.J. C9/3

1.2.3. Commission Notice on immunity from fines and reduction of fines in cartel cases [2002] O.J. C45/3

1.3. List of cases on the fining guidelines

1.4. List of cases on the leniency notice

Keyvent AB and others v SCA SE5

1.5. Factors taken into account

MTN International (Mauritius) Investcom/Areeba Limited CY M4
Keyvent AB and others v SCA SE5

1.5.1. Gravity

Decision 05–D–65 F2

1.5.2. Size and profitability of the undertaking

Keyvent AB and others v SCA SE5

1.5.3. Multi-product undertaking

1.5.4. Mark-up for deterrent effect

1.5.5. Size of the relevant geographic market

1.5.6. Size of the relevant product market

1.5.7. Duration

1.5.8. Effect/impact of infringement

1.5.9. Extent of culpability

1.5.10. Non-enforcement/non-implementation of agreement

1.5.11. Use of violence/physical force

1.5.12. Difficult market conditions

1.5.13. Co-operative or unco-operative attitude of the undertaking

1.5.13.1. Undertakings and modification of the agreements at the Commission's request

1.5.13.2. Introduction of a compliance programme

1.5.13.3. Active participation of company

1.5.13.4. Offering victims compensation

1.5.13.5. Unco-operative attitude

1.5.13.6. Disputing the facts for the first time on appeal

1.5.13.7. Dismissal of persons involved in infringement

1.5.14. State of the law

1.5.14.1. State of legal development

1.5.14.2. Well-documented infringement

1.5.14.3. Ignorance of the law, obtaining wrong legal opinion

TS 3895/2002 Expertos inmobiliarios ES9

1.5.15. Repeated infringement

TS 4777/2002 Telefónica/BT ES10

1.5.16. Continuation of infringement following clarification of the law

1.5.17. Continuation or cessation of the infringement following Commission action

1.5.17a. Cessation of the infringement prior to Commission action

1.5.18. Governmental pressure, encouragement or approval

1.5.18a. Acting under other participant's instructions

1.5.19. Additional profit from infringement

1.5.20. Non bis in idem (double jeopardy)

NAT. DECISIONS: PROCEDURE

[For the tables of case citations see Tables 16 and 17 at the back of the book.]

1.5.21. Sanctions imposed by other authorities

Decision 05-D-65 F2
French Supreme Court, Bouygues, SFR, Orange c/ CA F6

1.5.22. Duration of proceedings

1.5.23. The existence of sector-specific regulation

1.5.24. Non-discrimination; undertakings involved in the same infringement should be fined equally

1.5.25. Single fine for multiple infringements

AN 525/2000 Autoescuelas Alcalá ES7

1.6. No more than 10% of turnover

1.7. Limitation periods

TDC 457/99 Hardi International ES2

1.8. Recovery of fine/interest upon annulment/reduction

AN 162/2004 Astel/Telefónica ES12

2. Fines for infringement of procedural rules
X L8

3. Periodic penalty payments

X L8
Portuguese Veterinary Medical Association PT A2

CHAPTER 3

JUDICIAL REVIEW

A. JURISDICTION

1. Text of Article 220 (ex 164)

2. Article 229 (ex 172)

2.1. Text of Article 229 (ex 172)

2.2. Cases on the interpretation of Article 229 (ex 172)

3. Article 31 Regulation 1/2003

4. Competence of the Court of First Instance

B. TYPES OF PROCEDURE

1. Article 226 (ex 169)

1.1. Text of Article 226 (ex 169)

1.2. Cases on the interpretation of Article 226 (ex 169)

2. Article 230 (ex 173)

2.1. Text of Article 230 (ex 173)

2.2. Direct and individual concern

2.3. Challengeable acts

2.3.1. Challengeable steps

2.3.2. Interim decisions

2.3.3. Disclosure of confidential information

2.3.4. Rejection of a complaint

2.3.5. Absence of legal effect

2.3.6. Undertakings

2.3.7 Negative clearance

2.3.8. Comfort letters

2.3.9. Exemption

2.3.10. Decisions of the Hearing Officer

2.4. Limitation periods

2.5. Estoppel

2.6. Scope of judicial review

2.6a. Impact of admission of facts on standing

2.7. Article 233 (ex 176)

2.8. Relationship with Article 229

FNICGV T–252/03

3. Article 232 (ex 175)

[For the tables of case citations see Tables 16 and 17 at the back of the book.]

[For the tables of case citations see Tables 16 and 17 at the back of the book.]

NAT. DECISIONS: PROCEDURE

B. NATIONAL COURTS

1. Direct effect of Articles 81 and 82

Wintergarten Feddersen L1 (paras 20–30)
Univers du Cuir L2 (paras 30–49)
Lamesch—Oeko-Services L5 (para.42)
ICS Renting—Étoile L6 (para.18)
Tschechisches Bier DE4 (para.1b)

2. Conflict rules

2.1. General [See also Part II, Ch 1, 1 and Part XI, Ch 2, 2]

2.2. Provisional validity for old agreements

3. Co-operation between the Commission/National Competition Authorities and the courts of the EU Member States in the application of Articles 81 and 82 EC

3.1. Interpretation of Notice on the co-operation between the Commission and the courts of the EU Member States in the application of Articles 81 and 82 EC [2004] O.J. C101/54

3.2. Cases

Wintergarten Feddersen L1
Univers du Cuir L2
Aral—Koepfler L4
Lamesc—Oeko-Services L5
ICS Renting—Étoile L6
Provimi v Aventis [2003] EWHC 961 (Comm) UK29
Courage v Crehan UK30

3.3. Amicus curiae

4. Actions for damages for breach of competition rules

Provincial Audience of Girona 495/01 Hidroeléctrica del Emporda ES4

4.1. Standard of fault requirement

4.2. Causation and remoteness

Vitaminpreise Mainz DE1 (para.III)
Vitaminpreise Dortmund DE3

4.3. Damages

Wintergarten Feddersen L1 (para.13)

4.3.1. Calculation of damages

4.3.2. Mitigation and contributory negligence

4.3.3. Joint & several liability and contribution amongst defendants

4.3.4. Combination of damages for national and EC infringements

4.3.5. Interest

4.3.6. Passing-on defence

Vitaminpreise DE2 (para.1b)
Vitaminpreise Dortmund DE3

4.4. Applicable law/Private International Law issues

Wintergarten Feddersen L1 (para.14)
Regenerative Wärmeaustauscher DE6

4.5. National procedural rules limiting application of competition law

4.5.1. Standing

Courage v Crehan UK30

4.5.1.1 Collective claims, class actions

4.5.1.2 Direct purchasers

Wintergarten Feddersen L1 (para.14)

4.5.1.3 Indirect purchasers

Vitaminpreise Mainz DE1 (para.III)
Vitaminpreise Dortmund DE3
Selbstdurchschreibepapier DE8

4.5.2. Limitation/prescription

Paris Court of Appeal, DBS c/05–D–51 F10

4.5.3. Burden and standard of proof, rules of evidence

4.5.3.1 Burden of proof

Vitaminpreise DE M2 (paras 1a, 1c)
Vitaminpreise Dortmund DE3
Selbstdurchschreibepapier DE8

4.5.3.2. Standard of proof

Decision 06–D–03 bis F3

4.5.3.3. Inadmissible evidence

4.5.3.4. Discovery and production of evidence

4.5.3.5. In follow-on claims

4.5.3.5 Evidential value of NCA or Commission decision

[For the tables of case citations see Tables 16 and 17 at the back of the book.]

5. Civil actions other than actions for damages

5.1. Nullity

Wintergarten Feddersen L1
Univers du Cuir L2
ICS Renting—Étoile L6

5.2. Cease and desist actions

6. Criminal sanctions

6.1. Against individuals

Paris Court of Appeal STAL c/ 04–D–39 F11
S. 188 and 190 Enterprise Act 2002

6.2. Against undertakings

[For the tables of case citations see Tables 16 and 17 at the back of the book.]

PART XI

RELATIONS WITH OTHER AREAS OF LAW

CHAPTER 1

RELATIONS WITH OTHER EC LAWS

1. Anti-dumping law

2. Free circulation law

ICS Renting—Étoile L6 (para.13)

3. State aid

Lamesch—Oeko-Services L5 (paras 46–47)

4. Environmental law

Eesti Pandipakend 7–L EST4
Eesti Põlevkivi 40–L EST5
Lamesch—Oeko-Services L5 (para.35)

5. ECSC Treaty

6. Trade policy

7. Charter of Fundamental Rights

X—Inspection de la concurrence L7

CHAPTER 2

NATIONAL LAW

1. Supremacy of EC competition law over national law in general

Deutscher Lotto- und Totoblock DE16

2. Supremacy of EC law over national competition rules

3. National property law

4. National defence interests

5. National social security legislation

CHAPTER 3

INTERNATIONAL LAW

A. GENERAL

B. EUROPEAN CONVENTION ON HUMAN RIGHTS

1. Selected Articles

Article 6: Right to a Fair and Public Hearing

1. In the determination of his civil rights and obligations or of any criminal charge against him, everyone is entitled to a fair and public hearing within a reasonable time by an independent and impartial tribunal established by law. Judgment shall be pronounced publicly but the press and public may be excluded from all or part of the trial in the interest of morals, public order or national security in a democratic society, where the interests of juveniles or the protection of the private life of the parties so require, or to the extent strictly necessary in the opinion of the court in special circumstances where publicity would prejudice the interests of justice.

2. Everyone charged with a criminal offence shall be presumed innocent until proved guilty according to law.

3. Everyone charged with a criminal offence has the following minimum rights:
(a) to be informed promptly, in a language which he understands and in detail, of the nature and cause of the accusation against him;

[For the tables of case citations see Tables 16 and 17 at the back of the book.]

(b) to have adequate time and facilities for the preparation of his defence;

(c) to defend himself in person or through legal assistance of his own choosing or, if he has not sufficient means to pay for legal assistance, to be given it free when the interests of justice so require;

(d) to examine or have examined witnesses on his behalf under the same conditions as witnesses against him;

(e) to have the free assistance of an interpreter if he cannot understand or speak the language use d in court.

Article 7: Freedom From Retrospective Effect of Penal Legislation

1. **No one shall be held guilty of any criminal offence on account of any act or omission which did not constitute a criminal offence under national or international law at the time when it was committed. Nor shall a heavier penalty be imposed than the one that was applicable at the time the criminal offence was committed.**

2. **This Article shall not prejudice the trial and punishment of any person for any act or omission which, at the time when it was committed, was criminal according to the general principles of law recognised by civilised nations.**

Article 8: Right to Respect for Privacy

1. **Everyone has the right to respect for his private and family life, his home and his correspondence.**

2. **There shall be no interference by a public authority with the exercise of this right except such as in accordance with the law and is necessary in a democratic society in the interests of national security, public safety or the economic well-being of the country, for the prevention of disorder or crime, for the protection of health or morals, or for the protection of the rights and freedoms of others.**

Article 10: Freedom of Expression

1. **Everyone has the right to freedom of expression. This right shall include freedom to hold opinions and to receive and impart information and ideas without interference by public authority and regardless of frontiers. This Article shall not prevent States from requiring the licensing of broadcasting, television or cinema enterprises.**

2. **The exercise of these freedoms, since it carries with it duties and responsibilities, may be subject to such formalities, conditions, restrictions or penalties as are prescribed by law and are necessary in a democratic society, in the interests of national security, territorial integrity or public safety, for the prevention of disorder or crime, for the protection of health or morals, for the protection of the reputation or rights of others, for preventing the disclosure of information received in confidence, or for maintaining the authority and impartiality of the judiciary.**

Article 11: Freedom of Association and Assembly

1. **Everyone has the right to freedom of peaceful assembly and to freedom of association with others, including the right to form and to join trade-unions for the protection of his interests.**

2. **No restrictions shall be placed on the exercise of these rights other than such as prescribed by law and are necessary in a democratic society in the interests of national security or public safety, for the prevention of disorder or crime, for the protection of health or morals or for the protection of the rights and freedoms of others. This Article shall not prevent the imposition of lawful restrictions on the exercise of the administration of the State.**

2. Cases

2.1. Community cases

2.2. Strasbourg cases

[For the tables of case citations see Tables 16 and 17 at the back of the book.]

C. AGREEMENTS CONCLUDED BY THE COMMUNITY

1. Co-operation Agreements EC-USA

1.1. Agreements

1.1.1. First Agreement

1.1.2. Second Agreement

1.1.3. Exchange of interpretative letters

1.2. Comments

2.1. Decision of the Council and the Commission of April 1995 concerning the conclusion of the Agreement between the European Communities and the Government of the United States of America regarding the application of their competition laws 95/145/EC, ECSC, [1995] O.J. L95/45, [1995] O.J. L131/38

2.2. Decision of the Council and the Commission of May 29, 1998 concerning the conclusion of the Agreement between the European Communities and the Government of the United States of America on the application of positive comity principles in the enforcement of their competition laws 98/386/EC, ECSC [1998] O.J. L173/26

2.3. Agreement between the European Communities and the Government of the United States of America on the application of positive comity principles in the enforcement of their competition laws [1998] O.J. L173/28

2.4. Agreement between the European Communities and the Government of Canada regarding the application of their competition laws [1999] O.J. L175/50

2.5. Agreement between the EC and the Government of Japan on co-operation regarding anti-competitive activities

3. European Economic Area

3.1. Comments

3.2. Commission Regulation 3666/93 of December 15, 1993 amending Regulation 27 and Regulations 1629/69, 4260/88, 4261/88 and 2367/90 with a view to implementing the competition provisions laid down in the Agreement on the European Economic Area [1993] O.J. L336/1

3.3. Cases

[For the tables of case citations see Tables 16 and 17 at the back of the book.]

CHAPTER 1

LEGISLATION

CHAPTER 2

JURISDICTION: CASES AND REFERENCES

A. CONCENTRATION

1. Definition of the term "concentration" (control)

VP Market/Soldino Kaubandus 53-KO EST M1
Wõro Kommerts/Oskar LT 52-KO EST M5

2. Mergers

2.1. De jure merger

2.2. De facto merger

Sai/La Fondiaria I M3

2.2.1. Creation of a single economic unit

2.2.2. Common single management

2.2.3. Other factors

3. Acquisitions

3.1. Underlying concept: definition of the term "control"

Emilcarta/Agrifood Machinery I M1
National Geographic DE M6 (paras 14–23)
Csemege-Julius Meinl/Alfa H M1 (paras 13–19)
Renault S.A. H M2 (paras 15–17)
MOL/TVK H M5 (paras 50–55)

3.2. Sole control

3.2.1. Acquisition of majority of shares

LATTELEKOM/MICROLINK LV M1 (para.3)

3.2.2. Specific rights attached to minority shareholding

CPC Decision No.308/2005 BG M1

3.2.3. Majority of votes at shareholders' meetings

3.2.4. Contractual right to manage the company

Unión Radio/Antena 3 Radio ES M1

3.2.5. Sole shareholder with ability to veto strategic decisions

3.2.6. Economic dependency

Emilcarta/Agrifood Machinery I M1

3.3. Acquiring control via holding/management companies ("hidden control")

3.4. Acquisition of part of an undertaking

Maspex/Apenta H M8 (paras 10–12)

3.5. Acquisition of assets

Neste LV M2 (para.4)
Radiotelevisione italiana/Rami di azienda I M2

3.6. Passive acquisition

4. Joint ventures: joint control

4.1. Definition of joint control: joint strategic decision making

CPC Decision No.141/2005 BG M2
Holcim H M4 (paras 41–61)

4.2. Equality in voting/decision making

4.3. De jure veto rights over strategic decisions (usually by agreement)

Kinepolis Remedies BE M1

4.4. De facto veto rights over strategic decisions

CPC Decision No.308/2005 BG M1
Baucont H M6 (para.16)
MOL/Slovnaft H M3 (paras 33–36)
Sai/La Fondiaria I M3
Conseil d'Etat, France Antilles F M1

4.5. Joint exercise of voting rights by minority shareholders (through common interest, agreement or common mandated manager)

4.6. One parent company exercises day-to-day management of JV

[For the tables of case citations see Tables 16 and 17 at the back of the book.]

4.7. Both parents provide contribution to JV vital to its success

4.8. Joint control for an initial period only

MOL/Slovnaft H M3 (para.37)

4.9. Joint control following initial "running-in" period of sole control

4.10. Change in identity of parties sharing joint control in an existing JV

4.11. Change in quality of control

4.12. Financing and commercial agreements do not give control

4.13. Member State has right to determine behaviour on public service grounds ("Golden Share")

4.14. Other circumstances leading to joint control

Sai/La Fondiaria I M3

5. Possibility of "changing alliances" between parents

6. Asset swaps

7. Acquisitions by individuals and management buy-outs

8. Passage from joint to sole control ("demergers")

National Geographic II DE M8 (paras 23–28)

9. Internal restructuring by private companies

10. State-owned companies (restructuring/concentration)

AKK/UKE DE M4 (paras 5–7)

11. Option to purchase shares
CPC Decision No.308/2005 BG M1

12. Exceptions

12.1 Acquisition of shares by trading/investment companies

CPC Decision No.141/2005 BG M2

12.2. Liquidation, etc.

12.3. Rescue operations

B. COMMUNITY DIMENSION (TURNOVER)

1. Companies taken into account in calculation: definition of control for the purposes of turnover calculation

1.1. Mergers

1.2. Acquisition by a subsidiary of a group of companies

1.3. Acquisition of sole control

1.4. Acquisition of joint control

CPC Decision No.308/2005 BG M1

1.5. Acquisition of control by a JV ("lifting the veil")

1.6. Acquisition of part of an undertaking

1.7. Change from joint to sole control

1.8. Change in identity of parties sharing joint control in an existing JV

1.9. "Demergers" and the break-up of companies

1.10. Asset swaps

1.11. Acquisitions by individuals and management buy-outs

1.12. Acquisitions by state-owned companies

2. Turnover calculation

2.1. Underlying concept

2.2. Multiple notification test

2.3. "Net" turnover

2.3.1. Rebates and taxes

2.3.2. Intra-group turnover

2.3.3. State aid

2.3.4. Turnover generated under contracts to manage assets

2.3.5. Franchisees

[For the tables of case citations see Tables 16 and 17 at the back of the book.]

2.4. Which accounts to use?

2.5. Services (including airlines)

2.6. Staggered operations ("salami operations")

2.7. Timing of disposal of assets if excluded from turnover calculation

2.8. Group turnover

2.9. State-owned companies

2.10. Geographical allocation of turnover

2.11. Conversion into Euros

2.12. Special cases

2.12.1. Banks and other financial institutions

2.12.2. Leasing companies

2.12.3. Insurance companies

2.12.4. Financial holding companies

C. CONCENTRATIVE AND CO-OPERATIVE JOINT VENTURES

1. Autonomous Economic Entity

Ringier/Népszabadság/Sanoma/F-Log H M9 (para.42)

1.1. Full function JV (all assets necessary to carry out independent market role)

1.1.1. Own management (commercial policy)

1.1.2. Own resources

1.1.3. Need for JV to have access to market

1.1.4. Existence of purchase/supply agreements between parent and JV

1.1.4.1. During start-up period

1.1.4.2. Longer-term dependence relationship (no full-function JV)

1.1.4.3. Normal long-term commercial activities between parents and JV

1.1.4.4. Supply relationship of de minimis importance

1.1.4.5. JV as a trading company

1.1.4.6. Value added to JV to purchases from parents

1.1.5. JV exercises activities purely ancillary to those of parents

1.1.5.1. R&D JV

1.1.5.2. Production JV

1.1.5.3. Joint sales agency

1.2. Structural change must be permanent

1.2.1. Commitment of resources/sunk costs

1.2.2. Contingency clause on modification/ dissolution of JV

1.2.3. JV agreement specifies term of JV

1.2.3.1. JV constituted for a lengthy period

1.2.3.2. Possible prolongation after initial term

1.2.3.3. Short fixed period/single project JVs

1.3. Gradual transfer of business to JV

2. Co-ordination of competitive behaviour

2.1. Actual competition between parents

2.2. Potential competition between parents

2.3. Non-competition clause excludes competition between parents

2.4. Neighbouring market spill-over

2.5. Upstream/downstream market spillover

2.6. Actual/potential competition between parents and the JV

2.7. One parent company remains on the same market as the JV

2.8. Spill-over effects must be appreciable

3. Full-function JVs resulting in the co-ordination of competitive conduct (Article 81 and Merger Regulation)

3.1. Concept

3.2. Likelihood of co-ordination

3.2.1. JV will do business with third parties

[For the tables of case citations see Tables 16 and 17 at the back of the book.]

3.2.2. Low competition of parents in the past

3.2.3. Links between parents

3.2.4. Market shares

3.2.5. Size and importance of competitors

3.2.6. Size of the JV market/size of the parents' market

3.2.7. Buying power

3.2.8. Low barriers to entry

3.2.9. Non-transparent market

3.2.10. Innovation

3.2.11. Oligopolistic market

3.2.12. Examples of possible co-ordination

3.3. Appreciable restriction of competition

3.4. Effect on trade between Member States

3.5. Causality link

D. RESIDUAL APPLICABILITY OF ARTICLES 81 AND 82

1. Do Articles 81 and 82 still apply to concentrations?

2. List of cases relevant to Article 81(1)

3. List of cases relevant to Article 82

E. ARTICLE 9: REFERRAL TO A MEMBER STATE

1. Concept

Entremont et Unicopa, C2005–78

2. Accepted requests

2.1. Total referral

2.2. Partial referral

Aggregate Industries/Foster Yeoman UK M44

3. Rejected requests

EDF/London Electricity Case No.IV/M.1346

4. Cases in which request received and proceedings opened

5. Referral challenged before the CFI

F. ARTICLES 4(5) & 22: REFERRAL TO THE COMMISSION

1. Article 22

GEES/Unison Case No.IV/M.2738
Promatch//Sulzer Textil Case No.IV/M.2698

2. Pre-filing referral

G. LEGITIMATE INTERESTS

EDF/London Electricity Case No.IV/M.1346

H. ARTICLE 296: MILITARY PRODUCTS

I. RELATIONS WITH EEA

J. EXTRATERRITORIAL JURISDICTION

Sulzer/Kelmix DE M9 (paras 26–29)

A. RELEVANT MARKET

1. Relevant product market

Sonaecom/PT PT M3
TPS/CanalSat, C.2006–02 F M2

1.1. Definition of the term "relevant product market"

Celesios acquisition of Max Jenne and Tjellesen DK M3

1.2. Relevant factors

1.2.1. Physical characteristics/end use

1.2.1.1. Product/Components

1.2.2. Price

1.2.2.1. SSNIP Test

1.2.3. Consumer preference

[For the tables of case citations see Tables 16 and 17 at the back of the book.]

1.2.4. Supply-side substitutability/potential competition

Salcai/Utinsa ES M2
Ziekenhuis Hilversum-Ziekenhuis Gooi-Noord NL M5
Cegid/CCMX, C 2004–122 F M3
Conseil d'Etat, Fiducial (Cegid), 279180 F M4
French Competition Council, Cegid/CCMX, 05–A–24 F M5
Conseil d'Etat, Fiducial (Cegid), 279180 F M6

1.2.5. Industry product classifications/internal company marketing classifications

1.2.6. In-house production

1.2.7. Similar or identical products, but different distribution channels/production processes

1.2.8. Relevant evidence

1.2.8.1. Consumer surveys/views of competitors and customers

Ziekenhuis Hilversum-Ziekenhuis Gooi-Noord NL M5

1.2.8.2. "Conditions of competition"

Salcai/Utinsa ES M2

1.2.8.3. Historical evidence/studies on cross-elasticity

Ziekenhuis Hilversum-Ziekenhuis Gooi-Noord NL M5

1.2.8.4. Different producers only active on different product markets

1.2.8.5. Switching costs

1.2.9. Time frame in which substitution by new product likely to occur

1.2.10. Chains of substitution

1.2.11. Imperfect substitutes

1.2.12. Definition in other areas of EU law (anti-dumping)

1.2.13. Products not yet at commercial stage (emerging markets)

2. Relevant geographic market

2.1. Definition of the term "relevant geographic market"

2.2. Relevant factors

2.2.1. Regulatory trade barriers (including taxes and anti-dumping duties)

2.2.2. Local specification requirements/ differing national standards

2.2.3. National/Community procurement policies

2.2.4. Adequate distribution facilities

2.2.5. Need for locally-based service/just-in-time delivery

2.2.6. Transport costs

2.2.7. Language/culture

2.2.8. Consumer preferences

Ziekenhuis Hilversum-Ziekenhuis Gooi-Noord NL M5

2.2.9. Potential entry

2.2.10. Need for secure supplies and thus local delivery

2.2.11 Access to an essential facility

2.2.12. Chains of substitution

2.3. Relevant evidence

2.3.1. Price differences between neighbouring areas

2.3.2. Market share differences/similarities between neighbouring areas

2.3.3. Significant trade flows between neighbouring areas

2.3.4. Homogeneous conditions of competition

2.3.5. Stability of market shares

2.3.6. Historical evidence on cross-elasticity

Ziekenhuis Hilversum-Ziekenhuis Gooi-Noord NL M5

2.3.7. Consumer surveys/views of competitors and customers

Ziekenhuis Hilversum-Ziekenhuis Gooi-Noord NL M5

[For the tables of case citations see Tables 16 and 17 at the back of the book.]

2.3.8. Domestic supply exceeds domestic demand

2.3.9. Single EU brand/packaging

2.3.10. Different distribution systems in different Member States

2.3.11. Effect of liberalisation

2.4. Examples of local markets

Unión Radio/Antena 3 Radio ES M1
Somerfield/115 Morrison stores UK M19
HMV/Ottakers UK M15

2.5. Examples of regional markets

RWE/Saar Ferngas DE M10 (paras V.A.1.)

2.6. Examples of national markets

Prosegur/Blindados del Norte ES M3
Via Oeste (Brisa)—Auto-estradas do Oeste/Auto-estradas do Atlântico PT M2

2.7. Examples of Community/EEA markets

2.8. Examples of world markets

2.9. Examples of markets in evolution from national to Community-wide

Dicta in Corus/Arcelor UK M29

2.10. Speed at which markets must evolve from national to EU to World

2.11. Consequence of market definition on the competition assessment

Cegid/CCMX, C 2004–122 F M3

B. SUBSTANTIVE TEST

1. Definition

1.1. Commission's burden of proof

OFT and others v IBA Health Limited UK M6
Unichem v OFT UK M5
Celesio AG v OFT UK M3

2. Relevant factors

Swedish Meats ek. för./SLP Pärsons AB SE M2
Posten AB/Strålfors AB SE M3

2.1. Market share

2.1.1. Absence of available market share data/alternative calculation

2.2. Size and importance of competitors

2.3. Acquisition of closest/maverick competitor

Konnklijke Numico/Mellin I M4

2.4. HHI

LMT/ZetCOM LV M3 (para.6)
Konnklijke Numico/Mellin I M4

2.5. Commercial advantages over competitors (including product range, access to essential facilities and vertical integration)

2.6. Technical advantages over competitors
Posten AB/Strålfors AB SE M3

2.7. Financial advantages over competitors

2.8. Statutory dominance or monopoly
Posten AB/Strålfors AB SE M3

2.9. Supply-side substitutability: entry barriers

Posten AB/Strålfors AB SE M3

2.9.1. Basic concept

2.9.2. Regulatory barriers

2.9.3. Risk/likely return on investment: saturated nature of market

Coherent/Excel DE M7 (paras 145–146)

2.9.4. Capital requirements

Posten AB/Strålfors AB SE M3
Coherent/Excel DE M7 (paras 145–147)

2.9.5. Need for adequate distribution facilities

Posten AB/Strålfors AB SE M3

2.9.6. Entrenched consumer loyalty

2.9.7. Previous entry provides evidence that entry barriers low

Cegid/CCMX, C 2004–122 F M3
Conseil d'Etat, Fiducial (Cegid), 279180 F M4
French Competition Council, Cegid/CCMX, 05–A–24 F M5

[For the tables of case citations see Tables 16 and 17 at the back of the book.]

2.9.9. Reinforcement of entry barriers

2.10. Imperfect substitutes

Werner Söderström—Malmberg NL M1

2.11. Monopsonist customer

2.12. Size and resources of alleged dominant firm (supply-side buying power)

2.13. Views of customers/competitors; market research

Swedish Meats ek. för./SLP Pärsons AB SE M2

2.14. Econometric studies and statistical analysis

Sonaecom/PT PT M3
Werner Söderström—Malmberg NL M1
Nuon—Reliant Enery Europe NL M7

2.15. Possibilities of switching suppliers

2.16. Multi-sourcing policy of customers/shrinkage effect

2.17. Existence of spare capacity on the market/available alternative capacity

Swedish Meats ek. för./SLP Pärsons AB SE M2

2.18. New capacities

2.19. Evidence of existing monopoly pricing

2.20. Ownership of essential infrastructure/raw materials forecloses competition

Posten AB/Strålfors AB SE M3

2.21. Removal of potential competition

Stichting Evean Zorg—de Weerden NL M2 (paras 27–41)

2.22. Potential for retaliation

2.23. Raising rival's costs

Posten AB/Strålfors AB SE M3

2.24. Effect of liberalisation

2.25. Products not yet at commercial stage/emerging markets

French competition council, TPS/CanalSat, Opinion 06–A–13 F M7

2.26. Bidding markets

CIE/Ish DE M2 (paras 188–199)
HHvL-SWS NL M6 (paras 111–119)

3. Unilateral effects

4. Vertical mergers

Posten AB/Strålfors AB SE M3

4.1. Commission's burden of proof

4.2. Vertical effects

Posten AB/Strålfors AB SE M3
UPC-Canal+ NL M3
Cinven/Warburg Pincus-Essent Kabelcom NL M8

5. Conglomerate mergers

Springer/Pro7Sat1 DE M3 (para.2.3.2.1)

5.1. Commission's burden of proof

5.2. Bundling/portfolio effects

5.3. Leveraging

5.4. Decrease of potential competition

6. Causality link between merger and dominance

Stichting Evean Zorg—de Weerden NL M2 (paras 27–41)
KPN-Nozema Services NL M4 (paras 271–284)

C. CO-ORDINATED EFFECTS/OLIGOPOLISTIC OR JOINT DOMINANCE

1. Concept/burden of proof

2. Relevant factors

2.1. Significant market share in few hands

Salcai/Utinsa ES M2
Springer/Pro7Sat1 DE M3 (para.1.2.3)

[For the tables of case citations see Tables 16 and 17 at the back of the book.]

2.2. Remaining competitors few/weak

Springer/Pro7Sat1 DE M3 (para.1.2.3)

2.3. HHI

2.4. High entry barriers

2.5. Stagnant/mature markets (existence of over-capacity)

2.6. Little/innovation/product development (homogeneous product)

2.7. Transparent pricing patterns

Springer/Pro7Sat1 DE M3 (para.1.2.3.1.1)

2.8. Bidding markets

2.9. Transparency on capacities, expansions

2.10. Symmetrical market structure/structural similarities between competitors/common interests

Springer/Pro7Sat1 DE M3 (para.1.2.3.2)

2.11. Structural/personal links between oligopolists

E.ON/Eschwege DE M10 (paras II.1.b.bb.bbb.3)
Konnklijke Numico/Mellin I M4

2.12. Evidence of existing price parallelism/structure of competition in the past

2.13. Buying power

2.14. Price-inelastic demand

2.15. Absence of potential competition

E.ON/Eschwege DE M10 (paras II.1.b.bb.bbb.(3.))

2.16. Commercial advantages over competitors (including product range, access to essential facilities and vertical integration)

2.17. Co-ordination mechanism

2.18. Monitoring deviations

2.19. Retaliation mechanism

2.20. Reaction of outsiders and clients

2.21. Strengthening of collective dominance

D. SIGNIFICANT IMPEDIMENT OF COMPETITION

E. STRENGTHENING AN EXISTING DOMINANT POSITION

F. CREATION/STRENGTHENING A DOMINANT POSITION OF A THIRD PARTY

G. SIGNIFICANT PART OF THE COMMON MARKET

H. PROMOTING TECHNICAL/ECONOMIC PROGRESS

B.V. Tabora/Népszabadság/Ringier H M7 (para.113)

I. EFFICIENCY DEFENCE

French competition council, Seb/Moulinex, 02–A–07 F M8
Seb/Moulinex, C2002–2 F M9
Conseil d'Etat, Philips (Seb/Moulinex), 249262 F M10
French competition council, Seb/Moulinex, 04–A–16 F M11
Seb/Moulinex, C2004–40 F M12

J. FAILING-FIRM DEFENCE

RTL/n-tv DE M 5 (para.4)
French competition council, Seb/Moulinex, 02–A–07 F M8
Seb/Moulinex, C2002–2 F M9
Conseil d'Etat, Philips (Seb/Moulinex), 249262 F M10
French competition council, Seb/Moulinex, 04–A–16 F M11
Seb/Moulinex, C2004–40 F M12

K. MERGERS & STATE AIDS

[For the tables of case citations see Tables 16 and 17 at the back of the book.]

L. ANCILLARY RESTRAINTS

1. Concept

2. Trade mark licences

3. Patent/know-how licences

4. Product/service supply agreement

5. Exclusive/preferred status product/service supply agreement

6. Non-competition clause

7. Obligation to maintain confidentiality

8. Loan agreements

9. R&D agreements

10. Obligation not to solicit employees

11. Customer limitation clause

12. Most-favoured customer arrangement

13. Financial co-operation between parents

14. Transitional control of day-to-day business by parents

CHAPTER 3

PROCEDURE

1. Pre-notification guidance

Best practice guidelines on the conduct of merger control

2. Notification

2.1. Who must submit notification

2.2. Information to be provided/consequence of incomplete notification

Ansaldo Engineering S.p.A/Thomassen Turbine Systems BV CY M1
Lanitis Bros Public Ltd./Coca Cola Hellenic Bottling Co. S.A CY M2

2.3. Modification of notification

2.4. Withdrawal of notification (aborted concentration)

3. Suspension of the concentration

4. Fact-finding

5. Rights of defence and complainants

Akos Apteek—Konkurentsiamet 2–3/241/05 EST M7 (paras 10–11)

5.1. Access to the file

5.2. Hearing

Leggett & Platt DE M1 (paras 42–46)

6. Role of the Member States

6.1. Information provided to Member States

6.2. Assistance of Member States during fact-finding procedure

6.3. Advisory committee

6.4. Referral of a case to a Member State

Tesco 2006/FH/3/1/146 (pages 2–4) SK M1
Seb/Moulinex, C2002–2 F M9
Seb/Moulinex, C2004–40 F M12

7. Co-operation with other anti-trust authorities

8. Types of decisions available to the Commission

8.1. Derogation of suspension

8.2. Clearance during phase 1: not falling under the Merger Regulation

8.3. Clearance during phase 1: simplified procedure

Salcai/Utinsa ES M2

8.4. Clearance during phase 1: no serious risk of creating/strengthening dominance

8.5. Clearance during phase 1: following commitments/undertakings

8.6. Opening proceedings and a full investigation

8.7. Second stage clearance

[For the tables of case citations see Tables 16 and 17 at the back of the book.]

8.7.1. Without commitments/undertakings

8.7.2. With commitments/undertakings

Prosegur/Blindados del Norte ES M3

9. Time limits

9.1. Time limits for Commission decisions

9.2. Consequence of failure to decide in stated time

Salcai/Utinsa ES M2

9.3. Calculating the time periods

9.4. Suspension of phase II deadline

10. Revocation of decisions

11. Fines

CHAPTER 4

REMEDIES

1. Concept

2. First phase undertakings

Posten AB/Strålfors AB SE M3

3. Second phase undertakings

DONG Naturgas A/S/Nova Supply AB SE M1
Philip Morris/Amer 28–KO EST M2

4. Behavioural undertakings

DONG Naturgas A/S/Nova Supply AB SE M1
Posten AB/Strålfors AB SE M3
Barraqueiro/Arriva (ATMS) PT M1
A.Le Coq/Finelin 38–KO EST M3
A.Le Coq/Finelin 27–KO EST M4
TPS/CanalSat, C.2006–02 F M2

5. Structural undertakings

Philip Morris/Amer 28–KO EST M2
Elion Ettevõtted/MicroLink 47–KO EST M6

6. Type of undertaking other than divestiture)

6.1. Separate management of assets

6.2. Prohibition/termination of exclusivity arrangements

6.3. Behaviour to suppliers/dealers

6.4. Offering access to essential infrastructures, licences, products to competitors and customers

6.5. Co-operation agreements with competitors

6.6. IP licensing policy

6.7. Withdrawal of anti-dumping complaint

6.8. Maintenance of existing capacity/output levels

A.Le Coq/Finelin 38–KO EST M3
A.Le Coq/Finelin 27–KO EST M4

6.9. Unbundling

6.10 Structural limitation/increase of access

6.11. Removal of structural links/reallocation of voting rights

6.12. Corporate governance provisions

TV2 Sport DK M2

6.13. Legal separation

6.14. Remedies related to prices and tariffs

Post Danmark DK M1
Posten AB/Strålfors AB SE M3

6.15. Withdrawal from airline routes/making new slots available and other measures

6.16. Termination of activity

6.17. Modification of parties' interest/assets acquired

7. Divestiture

7.1. Sale of capacity/production facility

7.2. Divestiture/sale of whole or part of an undertaking

7.3. Divestiture with pre-identified purchaser

Philip Morris/Amer 28–KO EST M2

7.4. Divestiture: suitable purchaser

Elion Ettevõtted/MicroLink 47–KO EST M6

[For the tables of case citations see Tables 16 and 17 at the back of the book.]

7.5. Creation of a "new supplier" on the market

8. Arbitration procedure

9. Combined undertakings (divestitures, sale of capacity, licences, etc.)

10. Alternative acceptable undertakings

11. Undertakings exceed competition problems

Prosegur/Blindados del Norte ES M3
A.Le Coq/Finelin 27–KO EST M4

12. Evidence that undertakings restore competition

13. Insufficient/unacceptable undertakings

Barraqueiro/Arriva (ATMS) PT M1

13.1. Concept, burden of proof

13.2. Examples of insufficient/unacceptable undertakings

14. Non-binding undertakings

15. Procedural considerations (timing, subsequent review of commitments)

Belgacom—Vodafone Belgium—Belgacom Mobile CONC-C/C–06/0036 BE M2
Wõro Kommerts/Oskar LT 52–KO EST M5
Stericycle and STG v Competition Commission UK M2

NAT. DECISIONS: JURISDICTION

[For the tables of case citations see Tables 16 and 17 at the back of the book.]

BOOK FOUR

COAL & STEEL

BOOK FOUR—CONTENTS

Lists

USER GUIDE

Book Four is divided into four chapters and each case or judgment bears a *unique identifier* next to it, except for European court judgments, which uses its *official case number*. When an official case number is provided, users should be able to either move straight from the digest to an online search for the full text of the case/ judgment or in the case of unique identifiers, can consult the corresponding Tables to find its full reference.

BOOK FOUR

COAL AND STEEL

CHAPTER 1

RESTRICTIVE PRACTICES

A. TEXT OF ARTICLE 65 ECSC

Communication: Outlines of competition policy on the structures of the Iron and Steel Industry, p.15

Opinion: Amendment to Article 65 [1970] O.J. C30, CS14

1. Potential effect on competition

Wirtschaftsvereinigung Stahl CS112

B. DIRECT EFFECT

Banks v British Coal CS24
Hopkins v British Coal CS25

C. FORM OF PRACTICE WITHIN THE AMBIT OF THE TREATY

1. Binding agreements

German Rolled Steel CS84
NICIA CS100

2. Recommendations

German Rolled Steel CS84

3. Concerted practices

OKB I CS4
Präsident I CS8
Geitling I CS9
Geitling II CS10
Alloy Surcharge CS113
Thyssen Stahl v Commission CS31

4. Declarations of intent

Minerais Préréduits CS51

5. Associations of undertakings

German Scrap Cartel CS28
German Rolled Steel CS84
Stainless Steel Cartel CS106
NICIA CS100
Steel Beam Cartel CS110
Wirtschaftsvereinigung Stahl CS112
Sorema v HA (pp. 161–162) CS18

D. PROHIBITED PRACTICES

1. Cases

Walker/Champion CS58
Stork v HA CS8

1.1. Agreements fixing or determining prices

1.2. Uniform pricing method/joint prices

COBECHAR I CS2
COBECHAR II CS7
Präsident I CS8
Geitling I CS9
Geitling II CS10
Walzstahlkontor I CS16
Hoesch/Rheinstahl CS30
Danish Steel Distributors CS39
German Rolled Steel CS84
Stainless Steel Cartel CS106
Steel Beam Cartel CS110
Alloy Surcharge CS113

1.3. Circulation of price lists

German Rolled Steel CS84
Steel Beam Cartel CS110

COAL & STEEL: RESTRICTIVE PRACTICES

[For the tables of case citations see Tables 9, 10 and 12 at the back of the book.]

1.4. Uniform discounts

German Rolled Steel CS84

1.5. Setting maximum prices

German Scrap Cartel CS28

1.6. Most favoured customer clause

Ruhrkohle CS105
Stainless Steel Cartel CS106

1.7. Mutually co-ordinated prices

Ruhrkohle CS105

1.8. Common point based transport tariff

German Scrap Cartel CS28

1.9. Purchase quotas

German Scrap Cartel CS28

1.10. Information on producer prices

German Rolled Steel CS84
Steel Beam Cartel CS110

1.11. Price equalisation system

Scrap fund I CS1
Scrap fund II CS3
Präsident I CS8
Geitling I CS9
Geitling II CS10
Walzstahlkontor I CS16
Chamber of Coal Traders CS86
Worms v HA CS16

1.12. Equalisation system in event of market change

Thyssen/Krupp/Wuppermann CS29
Maxhütte/Klöckner I CS31
Dillinger/Arbed I CS32
Rötzel/Krupp CS61

1.13. Monitoring of orders

Steel Beam Cartel CS110

1.14. Monitoring of deliveries

Steel Beam Cartel CS110

1.15. Information on quantities

Wirtschaftsvereinigung Stahl CS112

2. Restricting or controlling production, technical development or investment

2.1. Agreement to stop/prohibit production

Walzstahlkontor I CS16
★Creusot/Loire CS23
Thyssen/Krupp/Wuppermann CS29
Hoesch/Rheinstahl CS30
Maxhütte/Klöckner I CS31
Dillinger/Arbed I CS32
Hoesch/Benteler CS35
Rötzel/Krupp CS61
Creusot-Loire/Ugine CS73
Cockerill/Klöckner CS77
Cockerill/Estel CS78
Irish Steel/Dunkerque CS80
Boël/Clabecq CS87
Arbed/Cockerill-Sambre CS95
Arbed/Unimétal CS103
Ruhrkohle CS105
Stainless Steel Cartel CS106

2.2. Co-ordination of production

Falck/Redaelli I CS21
Thyssen/Krupp/Wuppermann CS29
Maxhütte/Klöckner I CS31
Creusot-Loire/Ugine CS73
Falck/Redaelli II CS75
Stainless Steel Cartel CS106

2.3. Co-ordination of investment

Falck/Redaelli I CS21
Creusot/Loire CS23
Thyssen/Krupp/Wuppermann CS29
Hoesch/Rheinstahl CS30
Maxhütte/Klöckner I CS31
Dillinger/Arbed CS32
Minerais Préréduits CS51
Rötzel/Krupp CS61
COIMPRE CS69
Falck/Redaelli II CS75
Cockerill/Klöckner CS77
Cockerill/Estel CS78
Boël/Clabecq CS87
Arbed/Cockerill-Sambre CS95
Arbed/Unimétal CS103

2.4. Purchase of shareholding

Falck/Redaelli I CS21
Falck/Redaelli II CS75
Cockerill/Klöckner CS77
Cockerill/Estel CS78

2.5. Harmonisation of size or quality

Steel Beam Cartel CS110

[For the tables of case citations see Tables 9, 10 and 12 at the back of the book.]

3. Sharing markets, products, customers or sources of supply

3.1. Joint buying agreements

OKB I CS4
SOREMA CS11
Stahlring I CS17
Falck/Redaelli I CS21
Dillinger/Arbed I CS32
Danish Steel Distributors CS39
Steelmaking Supplies I CS40
Minerais Préréduits CS51
Walker/Champion CS58
Stahlring III CS65
Maier/Röchling CS67
COIMPRE CS69
Falck/Redaelli II CS75
Boël/Clabecq CS87
Steelmaking Supplies II CS96
NICIA CS100
Ruhrkohle CS105

3.2. Agreements to refrain from buying

Maier/Röchling CS67

3.3. Joint selling agreements

COBECHAR I CS2
Union Charbonnière CS5
COBECHAR II CS7
Präsident I CS8
Geitling I CS9
Geitling II CS10
Walzstahlkontor I CS16
Falck/Redaelli I CS21
Walzstahlkontor II CS22
Creusot/Loire CS23
Thyssen/Krupp/Wuppermann CS29
Hoesch/Rheinstahl CS30
Maxhütte/Klöckner I CS31
VCRO CS74
Falck/Redaelli II CS75
Boël/Clabecq CS87
Röchling/Possehl CS98
Saarlor V CS101
Ensidesa S.A./Aristrain CS108
Jahrhundertvertrag CS109
Geitling v HA CS4
Präsident v HA CS13
Geitling v HA CS15
Netherlands v HA CS19

3.4. Agreements to refrain from selling/market partitioning

Maier/Röchling CS67
Irish Steel/Dunkerque CS80
Röchling-Possehl CS98
Stainless Steel Cartel CS106
Steel Beam Cartel CS110

3.5. Exclusive purchasing/selling agreements

Walzstahlkontor I CS16
Hoesch/Rheinstahl CS30
Hoesch/Benteler CS35
Danish Steel Distributors CS39
Creusot-Loire/Ugine CS73
Ruhrkohle CS105

3.6. Product/know-how exchange agreements

Walker/Champion CS58
Boël/Clabecq CS87
Arbed/Unimétal CS103

3.7. Direct sales obligation

Präsident I CS8
Geitling I CS9
Geitling II CS10
Walzstahlkontor I CS16
Geitling v HA CS4
Präsident v HA CS13

3.8. Joint production

Creusot-Loire/Ugine CS73
Arbed/Cockerill-Sambre CS95

3.9. Allocation system in times of shortage

NICIA CS100

3.10. Co-ordination of transport

NICIA CS100

3.11. New undertaking joining cartel

Kempense CS20

3.12. Participation of third country producers

Steel Beam Cartel CS110

3.13. Accession of new Member States

Steel Beam Cartel CS110

3.14. Involvement of Commission

Steel Beam Cartel CS110

[For the tables of case citations see Tables 9, 10 and 12 at the back of the book.]

E. VOID AGREEMENTS

Article 65(4)
Stork v HA CS8

F. AUTHORISATION OF AGREEMENTS

Article 65(2)

1. Specialisation agreements

Walzstahlkontor I CS16
⋆Creusot/Loire CS23
Thyssen/Krupp/Wuppermann CS29
Hoesch/Rhienstahl CS30
Maxhütte/Klöckner I CS31
Dillinger/Arbed I CS32
Hoesch/Benteler CS35
Rötzel/Krupp CS61
Creusot-Loire/Ugine CS73
Cockerill/Klöckner CS77
Cockerill/Estel CS78
Irish Steel/Dunkerque CS80
Boël/Clabecq CS87
Arbed/Cockerill-Sambre CS95
Arbed/Unimétal CS103
Ensidesa S.A./Aristrain CS108
Jahrhundertvertrag CS109
21st Comp. Rep. (p.386)
22nd Comp. Rep. (pp.452–453)

2. Joint buying agreements

OKB I CS4
Stahlring I CS17
Falck/Redaelli I CS21
Dillinger/Arbed I CS32
Danish Steel Distributors CS39
Steelmaking Supplies I CS40
Minerais Préréduits CS51
Walker/Champion CS58
Stahlring III CS65
Maier/Röchling CS67
COIMPRE CS69
Falck/Redaelli II CS75
Boël/Clabecq CS87
Steelmaking Supplies II CS96
NICIA CS100
Ruhrkohle CS105

3. Joint selling agreements

COBECHAR I CS2
Union Charbonnière CS5
COBECHAR II CS7
Präsident I CS8
Geitling I CS9
Geitling II CS10
Walzstahlkontor I CS16
Kempense CS20
Falck/Redaelli I CS21
Walzstahlkontor II CS22
Thyssen/Krupp/Wuppermann CS29
Hoesch/Rheinstahl CS30
Maxhütte/Klöckner I CS31
VCRO CS74
Falck/Redaelli II CS75
Chamber of Coal Traders I CS86
Boël/Clabecq CS87
Saarlor V CS101
Arbed/Usinor-Sacilor CS107
Ensidesa S.A./Aristrain CS108
Jahrhundertvertrag CS109
22nd Comp. Rep. (p.453)
Geitling v HA (p.104) CS15
Netherlands v HA (pp.548–549) CS19

4. Formation of a jointly held undertaking

Präsident I CS8
Geitling I CS9
Geitling II CS10
⋆Creusot/Loire CS23
Danish Steel Distributors CS39
Röchling-Possehl CS98

5. Factors considered in assessing these agreements

5.1. Improvement in production or distribution

5.1.1. Efficient allocation of production

Walzstahlkontor I CS16
Falck/Redaelli I CS21
⋆Creusot/Loire CS23
Thyssen/Krupp/Wuppermann CS29
Hoesch/Rheinstahl CS30
Maxhütte/Klockner I CS31
Dillinger/Arbed I CS32
Hoesch/Benteler CS35
Creusot-Loire/Ugine CS73
Falck/Redaelli II CS75
Cockerill/Klöckner CS77
Cockerill/Estel CS78
Irish Steel/Dunkerque CS80
Boël/Clabecq CS87
Arbed/Cockerill-Sambre CS95
Arbed/Unimétal CS103

[For the tables of case citations see Tables 9, 10 and 12 at the back of the book.]

Arbed/Usinor-Sacilor CS107

5.1.2. Avoid duplication of investment

Hoesch/Benteler CS35
Rötzel/Krupp CS61

5.1.3. Reduce overcapacity

Arbed/Cockerill-Sambre CS95
Röchling-Possehl CS98
Arbed/Usinor-Sacilor CS107

5.1.4. Adjustment to structural decline

COBECHAR II CS7
Kempense CS20
Maier/Röchling CS67
Irish Steel/Dunkerque CS80
Boël/Clabecq CS87
Nold v Commission CS23

5.1.5. Injection of capital

Cockerill/Klöckner CS77
Cockerill/Estel CS78

5.1.6. Reduce overheads

Union Charbonnière CS5
Präsident I CS8
Geitling I CS9
Geitling II CS10
Walzstahlkontor I CS16
Falck/Redaelli I CS21
Thyssen/Krupp/Wuppermann CS29
Dillinger/Arbed I CS32
Danish Steel Distributors CS39
Minerais Préréduits CS51
COIMPRE CS69
VCRO CS74
Falck/Redaelli II CS75
Arbed/Usinor-Sacilor CS107

5.1.7. Ensure continuity of supply

Scrap fund I CS1
Scrap fund II CS3
Hoesch/Benteler CS35
Steelmaking Supplies I CS40
Walker/Champion CS58
Chamber of Coal Traders CS86
Steelmaking Supplies II CS96
NICIA CS100
Ruhrkohle CS105

5.1.8. Existence of Community crisis measures

UCRO CS74

Steel Beam Cartel CS110

5.1.9. Non-exclusive agreement

Minerais Préréduits CS51

5.2. Agreements essential and no more restrictive than necessary

COBECHAR I CS2
Präsident I CS8
Geitling I CS9
Geitling II CS10
★SOREMA CS11
Walzstahlkontor I CS16
Thyssen/Krupp/Wuppermann CS29
Hoesch/Rheinstahl CS30
Maxhütte/Klöckner I CS31
Dillinger/Arbed I CS32
Steelmaking Supplies I CS40
Rötzel/Krupp CS61
Boël/Clabecq CS87
Arbed/Cockerill-Sambre CS95
Steelmaking Supplies II CS96
Röchling-Possehl CS98
Arbed/Unimétal CS103
Arbed/Usinor-Sacilor CS107
Geitling v HA CS4
Eisen und Stahlindustrie v HA (p.286) CS6
Centre-Midi v HA (para.393) CS7
★*Knutange v HA* CS11

5.3. Power to determine prices, or control or restrict production or marketing

Opinion: *Amendment to Article 65* (p.260) CS14
Geitling v HA (para.102) CS15

5.3.1. Relevant market: whole Community

COBECHAR I CS2
Falck/Redaelli I CS21
Walzstahlkontor II CS22
★Creusot/Loire CS23
Thyssen/Krupp/Wuppermann CS29
Hoesch/Rheinstahl CS30
Maxhütte/Klöckner I CS31
Dillinger/Arbed I CS32
Danish Steel Distributors CS39
Rötzel/Krupp CS61
Creusot-Loire/Ugine CS73
Falck/Redaelli II CS75
Cockerill/Klöckner CS77
Cockerill/Estel CS78
Irish Steel/Dunkerque CS80
Boël/Clabecq CS87

[For the tables of case citations see Tables 9, 10 and 12 at the back of the book.]

Arbed/Unimétal CS103
Stainless Steel Cartel CS106
Arbed/Usinor-Sacilor CS107
Ensidesa S.A./Aristrain CS108
Steel Beam Cartel CS110
Geitling v HA (p.115) CS15
Netherlands v HA (p.650) CS19

5.3.2. Relevant market: whole or part of Member State

Walker/Champion CS58
NICIA CS100
Ruhrkohle CS105

5.3.3. Competition from outside Community

Walzstahlkontor II CS22
Chamber of Coal Traders CS86
Boël/Clabecq CS87
Arbed/Cockerill-Sambre CS95
Arbed/Unimétal CS103
Geitling v HA (p.104) CS15

5.3.4. Competition from alternative products

Minerais Préréduits CS51
COIMPRE CS69
Chamber of Coal Traders I CS86
NICIA CS100
Netherlands v HA (p.549) CS19

5.3.5. ***De minimis*****/small market share**

Union Charbonnière CS5
Kempense CS20
Falck/Redaelli I CS21
Thyssen/Krupp/Wuppermann CS29
Hoesch/Rheinstahl CS30
Maxhütte/Klöckner I CS31
Hoesch/Benteler CS35
Danish Steel Distributors CS39
Steelmaking Supplies I CS40
Walker/Champion CS58
Rötzel/Krupp CS61
Maier/Röchling CS67
Creusot-Loire/Ugine CS73
Falck/Redaelli II CS75
Steelmaking Supplies II CS96
Röchling-Possehl CS98
Ruhrkohle CS105

5.3.6. Group effect

Dillinger/Arbed I CS32
Röchling-Possehl CS98

5.3.7. Cumulative effect of agreements with other undertakings

Cockerill/Klöckner CS77
Cockerill/Estel CS78

5.3.8. Independence of the parties maintained

★Creusot/Loire CS23
Thyssen/Krupp/Wuppermann CS29
Hoesch/Rhienstahl CS30
Maxhütte/Klöckner I CS31
Dillinger/Arbed I CS32
Rötzel/Krupp CS61
Arbed/Cockerill-Sambre CS95
Arbed/Unimétal CS103

CHAPTER 2

CONCENTRATIONS

A. TEXT OF ARTICLE 66 ECSC

B. DIRECT EFFECT

Banks v British Coal CS24
Hopkins v British Coal CS25

C. CONCENTRATIONS SUBJECT TO PRIOR AUTHORISATION

Article 66 (1)
Decision No. 24–54 of May 6, 1954 laying down in implementation of Article 66(1) of the Treaty a regulation on what constitutes control of an undertaking.

1. Decisions applying Decision No. 24–54

★Creusot/Loire CS23
Thyssen/Rheinstahl CS38
GKN/Miles Druce CS41
BSC/Lye Trading CS43
Thyssen/SOLMER CS44
Gelsenberg CS45
Marcoke CS47
CLIF/Marine-Firminy CS48
Krupp/Stahlwerke CS49
IVECO CS50
EGAM/Vetrocoke CS52
Maxhütte/Klöckner II CS53
BSC/Walter Blume CS57
Framtek CS70
Arbed/Rodange CS71

[For the tables of case citations see Tables 9, 10 and 12 at the back of the book.]

Ruhrkohle/Brennstoffhandel CS72
Lange/Stinnes CS79
BSC/Dunlop & Ranken CS81
Hoogovens/Ijzerhandel CS85
Rogesa CS88
Eurocoal CS89
Zentralkokerei CS90
Usinor/Sacilor/Normandie CS92
UNICO CS94
Röchling-Possehl CS98
British Fuel CS102
Eschweiler/Ruhrkohle CS104
British Steel/Walker CS106

1.1. Acquisitions of under 25 per cent of share capital

Ruhrkohle/Brennstoffhandel CS72
British Fuel CS102
22nd Comp. Rep. (pp.452–453)

1.2. Acquisitions of over 25 per cent but under 50 per cent of share capital

GKN/Miles Druce CS41
Thyssen/SOLMER CS44
Arbed/Rodange CS71
UNICO CS94
20th Comp. Rep. (para.120)

1.3. Acquisitions of over 50 per cent of share capital

Thyssen/Rheinstahl CS38
BSC/Lye Trading CS43
Krupp/Stahlwerke CS49
⋆CLIF/Marine-Firminy CS48
EGAM/Vetrocoke CS52
BSC/Walter Blume CS57
Klöckner/Maxhütte IV CS63
Arbed/Rodange CS71
Lange/Stinnes CS79
BSC/Dunlop & Ranken CS81
Hoogovens/Ijzerhandel CS85
Eschweiler/Ruhrkohle CS104
British Steel/Walker CS106
22nd Comp. Rep. (p.452)

1.4. Creation of jointly held undertaking

Marcoke CS47
IVECO CS50
Framtek CS70
Rogesa CS88
Eurocoal CS89
Zentralkokerei CS90
Röchling-Possehl CS98
British Fuel CS102
22nd Comp. Rep. (p.452)

1.5. Contested or hostile bids

⋆CLIF/Marine-Firminy CS48
4th Comp. Rep. (paras 141–143)
Miles Druce v Commission I CS21
Miles Druce v Commission II CS22

1.6. Acquisition by the State

Gelsenberg CS45
⋆Usinor/Sacilor/Normandie CS92

D. CONDITIONS FOR AUTHORISATION

Article 66(2)
1st Comp. Rep. (paras 95–97)
3rd Comp. Rep. (paras 70–76)
4th Comp. Rep. (paras 120–143)
6th Comp. Rep. (paras 180–187)
13th Comp. Rep. (paras 158–164)
16th Comp. Rep. (paras 79–87)
17th Comp. Rep. (paras 87–96)
18th Comp. Rep. (paras 83–96)
20th Comp. Rep. (paras 116–144)
21st Comp. Rep. (pp.387–391)
22nd Comp. Rep. (pp.452–453)
25th Comp. Rep. (para.146)

1. Power to determine prices

BSC/Lye Trading CS43
Thyssen/SOLMER CS44
Marcoke CS47
CLIF/Marine-Firminy CS48
Krupp/Stahlwerke CS49
IVECO CS50
EGAM/Vetrocoke CS52
BSC/Walter Blume CS57
Framtel CS70
Arbed/Rodange CS71
Ruhrkohle/Brennstoffhandel CS72
Lange/Stinnes CS79
Rogesa CS88
Eurocoal CS89
Usinor/Sacilor/Normandie CS92
UNICO CS94
British Fuel CS102
Eschweiler/Ruhrkohle CS104
⋆British Steel/Walker CS106

2. Power to control or restrict production or distribution

BSC/Lye Trading CS43

[For the tables of case citations see Tables 9, 10 and 12 at the back of the book.]

Thyssen/SOLMER CS44
Gelsenberg CS45
Marcoke CS47
IVECO CS50
EGAM/Vetrocoke CS52
BSC/Walter Blume CS57
Framtek CS70
Lange/Stinnes CS79
Rogesa CS88
Eurocoal CS89
Usinor/Sacilor/Normandie CS92
Eschweiler/Ruhrkohle CS104
British Steel Walker CS106

3. Power to hinder effective competition

Thyssen/Rheinstahl CS38
GKN/Miles Druce CS41
BSC/Lye Trading CS43
Thyssen/SOLMER CS44
Gelsenberg CS45
Marcoke CS47
CLIF/Marine-Firminy CS48
Krupp/Stahlwerke CS49
IVECO CS50
EGAM/Vetrocoke CS52
BSC/Walter Blume CS57
Rogesa CS88
Eurocoal CS89
Usinor/Sacilor/Normandie CS92
Röchling-Possehl CS98
British Fuel CS102
★British Steel/Walker CS106

4. Establishing an artificially privileged position

Thyssen/Rheinstahl CS38
GKN/Miles Druce CS41
Thyssen/SOLMER CS44
CLIF/Marine-Firminy CS48
Krupp/Stahlwerke CS49
BSC/Walter Blume CS57
Klöckner/Maxhütte IV CS63
Framtek CS70
Lange/Stinnes CS79
BSC/Dunlop & Ranken CS81
Hoogovens/Ijzerhandel CS85
★Zentralkokerei CS90
UNICO CS94
Röchling-Possehl CS98
British Fuel CS102
Ruhrkohle CS104

E. ANALYSIS OF THE MARKET

1. Relevant geographical market: whole of Common Market

Thyssen/SOLMER CS44
Krupp/Stahlwerke CS49
Arbed/Rodange CS71
Lange/Stinnes CS79

2. Relevant geographical market: Member State

Thyssen/Rheinstahl CS38
GKN/Miles Druce CS41
BSC/Lye Trading CS43
BSC/Walter Blume CS57
Frantek CS70
BSC/Dunlop & Ranken CS81
Hoogovens/Ijzerhandel CS85
UNICO CS94
British Steel/Walker CS106

3. Competition from third countries

Thyssen/Rheinstahl CS38
Hoogovens/Ijzerhandel CS85
Ruhrkohle CS104
British Steel/Walker CS106

4. Competition from substitute products

EGAM/Vetrocoke CS52
Ruhrkohle/Brennstoffhandel CS72
British Fuel CS102

5. Small market share

GKN/Miles Druce CS41
Eurocoal CS89
UNICO CS94

6. Compatibility with EC rules on competition

1st Comp. Rep. (para.97)
13th Comp. Rep. (paras 160–164)
16th Comp. Rep. (paras 81 & 85)

F. EXEMPTION BY CATEGORY

1. Article 66(3)

1.1 Decision No. 25–67 of June 22, 1967 laying down in implementation of Article 66(3) of the Treaty a regulation concerning exemption from prior authorisation [1952–67] O.J. Spec. Ed. 186, as amended by [1978] O.J. L300/21 and [1991] O.J. L348/12

[For the tables of case citations see Tables 9, 10 and 12 at the back of the book.]

G. DOMINANT POSITION

Article 66(7)
NICIA CS100
Netherlands v HA CS3
Banks v British Coal CS24
Hopkins v British Coal CS25
Naloo v Commission CS28
Small Mines 21st Comp. Rep. (para. 107)
21st Comp. Rep. (page 386)

CHAPTER 3

STATE BEHAVIOUR

1. Article 67

CHAPTER 4

PROCEDURE

A. CONTROL BY COMMISSION

1. Exclusive control of Article 65

Article 65(4) second indent
Geitling v HA CS10

2. Exclusive power in concentrations

Article 66(1)

B. OBTAINING INFORMATION

1. In general

Text of Article 47
★Röchling-Burbach CS68

2. For the purposes of Article 65

Article 65(3)
Text of decision no. 1–65 of February 3, 1965 concerning notification of decisions on information to be obtained from or checks to be made on associations of undertakings for the purposes of application of Article 65 of the Treaty (not printed).
★Röchling-Burbach CS68

3. For the purposes of Article 66

Article 66(4)

C. RIGHTS OF THE DEFENCE

Text of Article 36

D. SECRECY

Text of Article 47(2)
Article 65(2)(5)

E. NOTIFICATION

1. Notification of agreements under Article 65

Article 65(2) & 4(2)
Stainless Steel Cartel CS106

2. Notification of concentrations

2.1. Obligatory notification

Article 66(1)

2.2. Failure to notify

2.2.1. Authorisation withheld

2.2.2. Authorisation with fine for failure to notify

Article 66(5)(1)

F. DECISIONS TAKEN BY THE COMMISSION

Article 14(2)
Article 15(1), (2) & (3)

1. Decisions pursuant to Article 65

1.1. Authorisation

Geitling v HA CS10

1.1.1. Conditional authorisation

Article 65(2)(3)

[For the tables of case citations see Tables 9, 10 and 12 at the back of the book.]

1.1.2. Conditions aiming to prevent discrimination between trading partners

COBECHAR I CS2
OKB I CS4
Union Charbonnière CS5
COBECHAR II CS7
Walzstahlkontor I CS16
NICIA CS100
SOREMA v HA CS20

1.1.3. Conditions preventing cross directorships or management

Präsident I CS8
Thyssen/Krupp/Wuppermann CS29
Hoesch/Rheinstahl CS30
Maxhütte/Klöckner I CS31
Dilliner/Arbed I CS32
Rötzel/Krupp CS61
Boël/Clabecq CS87

1.1.4. Other conditions to safeguard competition

OKB I CS4
Union Charbonnière CS5
Präsident I CS8
Walzstahlkontor I CS16
Thyssen/Krupp/Wuppermann CS29
Maxhütte/Klöckner I CS31
Dillinger/Arbed I CS32
Creusot-Loire/Ugine CS73
VCRO CS74
Cockerill/Klöckner CS77
Cockerill/Estel CS78
Arbed/Cockerill-Sambre CS95

1.1.5. Authorisation conditional upon existence of crisis measures

VCRO CS74

1.1.6. Conditions requiring submission of information

Walzstahlkontor I CS16
Stahlring I CS17
Falck/Redaelli I CS21
Creusot/Loire CS23
Danish Steel Distributors CS39
Maier/Röchling CS67
COIMPRE CS69
Falck/Redaelli II CS75
Chamber of Coal Traders I CS86
Arbed/Unimétal CS103

1.1.7. Temporary authorisation

Article 65(2)(3)
Union Charbonnière CS5
Stahlring III CS65

1.1.8. Revocation of authorisation

Article 65(2)(4)
SOREMA CS11
Geitling III CS12
Präsident II CS13
SOREMA v HA (p.339) CS20

1.2. Prohibition

Article 65(4)(2)
German Rolled Steel CS84
Stainless Steel Cartel CS106
Steel Beam Cartel CS110
Alloy Surcharge CS113

1.3. Fines

Article 65(5)
German Scrap Cartel CS28
Stainless Steel Cartel CS106
Steel Beam Cartel CS110
Alloy Surcharge CS113

1.3.1. Payment by instalments

Steel Beam Cartel CS110

1.4. Limitation periods

6th Comp. Rep. (paras 19–21)

1.5. Addresses of decision

Steel Beam Cartel CS110

2. Decisions pursuant to Article 66

2.1. Authorisation

2.1.1. Conditional authorisation

Article 66(2)(3)
Nold v Commission CS23

2.1.2. Conditions aiming to prevent discrimination between trading partners

Ruhrkohle CS37
British Fuel CS102
Nold v Commission CS23

2.1.3. Conditions preventing cross directorships or management

Thyssen/Rheinstahl CS38

[For the tables of case citations see Tables 9, 10 and 12 at the back of the book.]

Thyssen/SOLMER CS44
CLIF/Marine-Firminy CS48
Krupp/Stahlwerke CS49
Arbed/Rodange 6.6.78 CS71
Rogesa CS88
Usinor/Sacilor/Normandie CS92
17th Comp. Rep. (para.92)

2.1.4. Other conditions to safeguard competition

Ruhrkohle CS37
Thyssen/SOLMER CS44
CLIF/Marine-Firminy CS48
Krupp/Stahlwerke CS49
Arbed/Rodange CS71
Usinor/Sacilor/Normandie CS92
British Fuel CS102

2.1.5. Conditions requiring submission of information

British Fuel CS102
British Steel/Walker CS106

2.1.6. Authorisation with fines for failure to notify

Article 66(5)(1)

2.2. Prohibition

Article 66(5)(2)

2.2.1. Interim order

Article 66(5)(3)
⋆CLIF/Marine-Firminy CS48
4th Comp. Rep. (paras 141–143)

2.2.2. Divestiture order

Article 66(5)(2)

2.2.3. Executory measures

Article 66(5)(5)

2.3. Periodic penalty payments

Article 66(5)(4)

2.4. Fines

Article 66(6)
GKN/Miles Druce CS41

G. CHALLENGING DECISIONS BEFORE THE COURT OF JUSTICE

1. Exercise of control by the Court

1.1. In general

Text of Articles 33(1), (2) and 35(3) ECSC
Article 65(4) ECSC
Nold v HA CS5
Stork v HA CS8
Nold v HA CS9
Geitling v HA CS12
Schlieker v HA CS17
SOREMA v HA (pp. 161–162) CS18

1.2. In cases of concentrations

Article 66(5)(2) ECSC
Schlieker v HA CS17

2. Time limits

Text of Article 33(3) ECSC

3. Interim measures

Text of Article 39(3) ECSC
Geitling v HA CS10
SOREMA v HA CS20
Miles Druce v Commission I CS21
Miles Druce v Commission II CS22

4. Suspensory effect

4.1. In general

Text of Article 39(1) ECSC

4.2. In cases of interim measures

Text of Article 39(2) & (3) and Article 66(5)(3)
Nold v HA CS5
Aristrain v Commission CS27

5. Transmission of documents to Court

5.1. Access to file

Text of Article 23 of Statute (ECSC) of Court of Justice
NMH v Commission CS26
NMH Stahlwerke II CS29
NMH Stahlwerke III CS30

COAL & STEEL: RESTRICTIVE PRACTICES

[For the tables of case citations see Tables 9, 10 and 12 at the back of the book.]

TABLES

TABLES—CONTENTS

Lists and Tables

TABLE 1

CHRONOLOGICAL LIST OF COMMISSION DECISIONS (GENERAL COMPETITION RULES)

No.	NAME	DATE	O.J.[1]	C.M.L.R.[2]	TYPE OF DECISION	PRODUCT	SUBJECT
1.	Grosfillex/Fillestorf	11.03.64	J.O. 915/64	[1964] 237	Clearance	Plastics	Exclusive Distribution
2.	Convention Faience	13.05.64	J.O. 1167/64	—	Recommendation	China	Collective Exclusive
3.	Bendix/Mertens and Straet	01.06.64	J.O. 1426/64	[1964] 416	Clearance	Brakes	Non-exclusive Distribution
4.	Nicholas Frères Vitapro	30.07.64	J.O. 2287/64	[1964] 505	Clearance	Cosmetics	Non-competition
5.	Grundig/Consten	23.09.64	J.O. 2545/64	[1964] 489	Infringement 85	Consumer Electronics	Exclusive Distribution
6.	DECA	22.10.64	J.O. 2761/64	[1965] 50	Clearance	Construction	Bidding Agreement
7.	DRU/Blondel	08.07.65	J.O. 2194/65	[1965] 180	Exemption	Household Products	Exclusive Distribution
8.	Hummel/Isbecque	17.09.65	J.O. 2581/65	[1965] 242	Exemption	Agricultural Machines	Exclusive Distribution
9.	Maison Jallatte	17.12.65	J.O. 37/66	[1966] D1	Exemption	Shoes	Exclusive Distribution
10.	Transocean Marine Paint Association I	27.06.67	J.O. 163/10	[1967] D9	Exemption	Paint	Co-operation Agreement
11.	Eurogypsum	26.02.68	[1968] L57/9	[1968] D1	Clearance	Plaster	R&D Agreement
12.	Alliance des Constructeurs Français	17.07.68	[1968] L201/1	[1968] D23	Clearance	Machine Tools	Common Export Agency
13.	Socemas	17.07.68	[1968] L201/4	[1968] D28	Clearance	Foodstuffs	Buying Group
14.	ACEC/Berliet	17.07.68	[1968] L201/7	[1968] D35	Exemption	Heavy Vehicles	R&D Agreement
15.	Cobelaz	06.11.68	[1968] L276/13	[1968] D45	Clearance	Fertilisers	Sales Agency
16.	Cobelaz Cokes	06.11.68	[1968] L276/19	[1968] D68	Clearance	Fertilisers	Sales Agency
17.	Rieckerman	06.11.68	[1968] L276/25	[1968] D78	Clearance	Heating Equipment	Exclusive Distribution
18.	CFA	06.11.68	[1968] L276/29	[1968] D57	Clearance	Fertilisers	Sales Agency
19.	EMO I	13.03.69	[1969] L69/13	[1969] D1	Exemption	Machine Tools	Exhibition Agreements

[1] Official Journal of the European Communities.
[2] Common Market Law Reports.

Table 1

No.	NAME	DATE	O.J.	C.M.L.R.	TYPE OF DECISION	PRODUCT	SUBJECT
20.	Chaufourniers	05.05.69	[1969] L122/8	[1969] D15	Clearance	Cement	Production Cartel
21.	Christiani & Nielsen	18.06.69	[1969] L165/12	[1969] D36	Clearance	Construction	Intra-enterprise Co-operation
22.	VVVF	25.06.69	[1969] L168/22	[1970] D1	Clearance	Paint	Common Quality Standards
23.	SEIFA	30.06.69	[1969] L173/8	—	Clearance	Fertilisers	Sales Agency
24.	Quinine Cartel	16.07.69	[1969] L192/5	[1969] D41	Infringement 85	Quinine	Cartel
25.	Clima Chappée	22.07.69	[1969] L195/1	[1970] D7	Exemption	Air-conditioning	Specialisation
26.	Jaz/Peter I	22.07.69	[1969] L195/5	[1970] 129	Exemption	Clocks	Specialisation
27.	Dyestuffs	24.07.69	[1969] L195/11	[1969] D23	Infringement 85	Dyes	Cartel
28.	Pirelli/Dunlop	05.12.69	[1969] L323/21	—	Clearance	Tyres	Production Capacity Swap
29.	Kodak	30.06.70	[1970] L147/24	[1970] D19	Clearance	Photographic Equipment	Sales Conditions
30.	ASPA	30.06.70	[1970] L148/9	[1970] D25	Clearance	Toiletries	Collective Exclusive Dealing
31.	ASBL	29.06.70	[1970] L153/14	[1970] D31	Clearance	Welded Steel Tubes	Joint Promotion
32.	Julien/Van Katwijk	28.10.70	[1970] L242/18	[1970] D43	Infringement 85	Cardboard Tubes	Cartel
33.	Omega	28.10.70	[1970] L242/22	[1970] D49	Exemption	Watches	Selective Distribution
34.	Supexie	23.12.70	[1971] L10/12	[1971] D1	Clearance	Fertilisers	Sales Agency
35.	Ceramic Tiles	29.12.70	[1971] L10/15	[1971] D6	Infringement 85	Ceramic Tiles	Aggregate Rebates
36.	CICG	01.02.71	[1971] L34/13	[1971] D23	Article 11(5)	Tape Recorders	Royalty Collecting Agreement
37.	FN/CF	28.05.71	[1971] L134/6	—	Exemption	Shotgun Cartridges	Specialisation
38.	Gema I	02.06.71	[1971] L134/15	[1971] D35	Infringement 86	Copyright Royalties	Performing Rights Society
39.	Alba	18.06.71	[1971] L161/2	—	Article 11(5)	Beer	—
40.	Union des Brasseries	18.06.71	[1971] L161/6	—	Article 11(5)	Beer	—
41.	Maes	18.06.71	[1971] L161/10	—	Article 11(5)	Beer	—
42.	Asphaltoïd/Keller	02.07.71	[1971] L161/32	—	Article 11(5)	Bitumen	—
43.	Cematex I	24.09.71	[1971] L227/26	[1973] D135	Exemption	Textile Machinery	Exhibition Agreement
44.	SIAE	09.11.71	[1971] L254/15	[1972] D112	Article 11(5)	Copyright Royalties	Performing Rights Society

No.	NAME	DATE	O.J.	C.M.L.R.	TYPE OF DECISION	PRODUCT	SUBJECT
45.	Boehringer	25.11.71	[1971] L282/46	[1972] D121	Rejection of request	Quinine	Cartel
46.	Continental Can	09.12.71	[1972] L7/25	[1972] D11	Infringement 86	Containers	Acquisition
47.	VCH	16.12.71	[1972] L13/34	[1973] D16	Infringement 85	Cement	Cartel
48.	SAFCO	16.12.71	[1972] L13/44	[1972] D83	Clearance	Foodstuffs	Export Agency
49.	SOPELEM/Langen	20.12.71	[1972] L13/47	[1972] D77	Exemption	Optical Systems	Specialisation Agreement
50.	Burroughs/ Delplanque	22.12.71	[1972] L13/50	[1972] D67	Clearance	Carbon Paper	Patent Licence
51.	Burroughs/Geha	22.12.71	[1972] L13/53	[1972] D72	Clearance	Carbon Paper	Patent Licence
52.	Henkel/Colgate	23.12.71	[1972] L14/14	—	Exemption	Detergents	R&D Agreement
53.	NCH	23.12.71	[1972] L22/16	[1973] D257	Infringement 85	Cement	Sales Agency
54.	MAN/SAVIEM	17.01.72	[1972] L31/29	2 [1974] D123	Exemption	Heavy Vehicles	Specialisation
55.	Wild/Leitz	23.02.72	[1972] L61/27	[1972] D36	Clearance	Microscopes	Specialisation
56.	Davidson Rubber	09.06.72	[1972] L143/31	[1972] D52	Exemption	Car Seats	Patent Licence
57.	Raymond/Nagoya	09.06.72	[1972] L143/39	[1972] D45	Clearance	Car Components	Patent Licence
58.	Gema II	06.07.72	[1972] L166/22	[1972] D115	Addendum	Copyright Royalties	Performing Rights Society
59.	Thin Paper	26.07.72	[1972] L182/24	[1972] D94	Exemption	Thin Paper	Specialisation
60.	Central Heating	20.10.72	[1972] L264/22	[1972] D130	Infringement 85	Heating Equipment	Collective Exclusive Dealing
61.	Rodenstock	28.09.72	[1972] L267/17	[1973] D40	Article 11(5)	Glasses	Exclusive Distribution
62.	Misal	28.09.72	[1972] L267/20	[1973] D37	Article 11(5)	Various Products	Exclusive Distribution
63.	Pittsburgh Corning	23.11.72	[1972] L272/35	[1973] D2	Infringement 85	Glass	Preventing Parallel Trade
64.	Zoja/CSC-ICI	14.12.72	[1972] L299/51	[1973] D50	Infringement 86	Pharmaceuticals	Refusal to Supply
65.	Dutch Cement	18.12.72	[1972] L303/7	[1973] D149	Infringement 85	Cement	Cartel
66.	Cimbel	22.12.72	[1972] L303/24	[1973] D167	Infringement 85	Cement	Cartel
67.	GISA	22.12.72	[1972] L303/45	[1973] D125	Infringement 85	Sanitary Equipment	Collective Exclusive Dealing
68.	WEA/Filipacchi Music S.A.	22.12.72	[1972] L303/52	[1973] D43	Infringement 85	Records	Preventing Parallel Trade
69.	European Sugar Industry	02.01.73	[1973] L140/17	[1973] D65	Infringement 85/86	Sugar	Cartel

Table 1

No.	NAME	DATE	O.J.	C.M.L.R.	TYPE OF DECISION	PRODUCT	SUBJECT
70.	SCPA/Kali & Salz	11.05.73	[1973] L217/3	[1973] D219	Infringement 85	Fertilisers	Cartel
71.	Dupont de Nemours Germany	14.06.73	[1973] L194/27	[1973] D226	Clearance	Photographic Materials	Sales Conditions
72.	Heaters and Boilers	03.07.73	[1973] L217/34	[1973] D231	Infringement 85	Heating Equipment	Cartel
73.	Deutsche Philips	05.10.73	[1973] L293/40	[1973] D241	Infringement 85	Consumer Electronics	Preventing Parallel Trade
74.	Prym/Beka	08.10.73	[1973] L296/24	[1973] D250	Exemption	Needles	Exclusive Purchasing
75.	Transocean Marine Paint Association II	21.12.73	[1974] L19/18	1 [1974] D11	Exemption	Paint	Co-operation Agreement
76.	Kali & Salz/ Kalichemie	21.12.73	[1974] L19/22	1 [1974] D1	Infringement 85	Fertilisers	Exclusive Distribution
77.	IFTRA Glass	15.05.74	[1974] L160/1	2 [1974] D50	Infringement 85	Glass Containers	Cartel
78.	Belgian Wallpaper	23.07.74	[1974] L237/3	2 [1974] D102	Infringement 85	Wallpaper	Cartel
79.	Advocaat Zwarte Kip	24.07.74	[1974] L237/12	2 [1974] D79	Infringement 85	Alcoholic Drinks	Trademark Assignment
80.	FRUBO	25.07.74	[1974] L237/16	2 [1974] D89	Infringement 85	Fruit	Exclusionary Practice
81.	Franco-Japanese Ball-Bearings	29.11.74	[1974] L343/19	1 [1975] D8	Infringement 85	Ball Bearings	Cartel
82.	BMW	13.12.74	[1975] L29/1	1 [1975] D44	Exemption	Cars	Selective Distribution
83.	DuroDyne	19.12.74	[1975] L29/11	1 [1975] D62	Exemption	Heating/Air-conditioning	Exclusive Distribution
84.	General Motors	19.12.74	[1975] L29/14	1 [1975] D20	Infringement 86	Cars	Excessive Pricing
85.	Goodyear Italiana/ Euram	19.12.74	[1975] L38/10	1 [1975] D31	Exemption	Packaging Material	Exclusive Distribution
86.	Rank/SOPELEM	20.12.74	[1975] L29/20	1 [1975] D72	Exemption	Optical Equipment	Specialisation
87.	SHV/Chevron	20.12.74	[1975] L38/14	1 [1975] D68	Clearance	Petroleum	Joint Venture
88.	Tinned Mushrooms	08.01.75	[1975] L29/26	1 [1975] D83	Infringement 85	Mushrooms	Cartel
89.	Sirdar/Phildar	05.03.75	[1975] L125/27	1 [1975] D93	Article 15(6)	Wool	Trademark Delimitation
90.	Fireplaces	03.06.75	[1975] L159/22	2 [1975] D1	Infringement 85	Heating Equipment	Collective Exclusive Dealing
91.	Intergroup	14.07.75	[1975] L212/23	2 [1975] D14	Clearance	Foodstuffs	Buying Group
92.	IFTRA Aluminium	15.07.75	[1975] L228/3	2 [1975] D20	Infringement 85	Aluminium	Cartel

No.	NAME	DATE	O.J.	C.M.L.R.	TYPE OF DECISION	PRODUCT	SUBJECT
93.	UNIDI I	17.07.75	[1975] L228/14	2 [1975] D51	Exemption	Dental Equipment	Exhibition Agreement
94.	Kabelmetal/Luchaire	18.07.75	[1975] L222/34	2 [1975] D40	Exemption	Steel Components	Know-how/Patent Licence
95.	Bronbemaling	25.07.75	[1975] L249/27	2 [1975] D67	Article 15(6)	Drainage Equipment	Patent Pooling
96.	Transocean Marine Paint Association III	23.10.75	[1975] L286/24	2 [1975] D75	Exemption	Paint	Co-operation Agreement
97.	Bomée-Stichting	21.11.75	[1975] L329/30	1 [1976] D1	Infringement 85	Toiletries	Collective Exclusive Dealing
98.	AOIP/Beyrard	02.12.75	[1976] L6/8	1 [1976] D14	Infringement 85	Variable Resistors	Patent Licence
99.	SABA I	15.12.75	[1976] L28/19	1 [1976] D61	Exemption	Consumer Electronics	Selective Distribution
100.	Bayer/Gist-Brocades	15.12.75	[1976] L30/13	1 [1976] D98	Exemption	Pharmaceutical	Specialisation
101.	Chiquita	17.12.75	[1976] L95/1	1 [1976] D28	Infringement 86	Bananas	Refusal to Supply
102.	United Reprocessors	23.12.75	[1976] L51/7	2 [1976] D1	Exemption	Nuclear Waste	Joint Venture
103.	KEWA	23.12.75	[1976] L51/15	2 [1976] D15	Exemption	Nuclear Waste	Joint Venture
104.	Vitamins	09.06.76	[1976] L223/27	2 [1976] D25	Infringement 86	Vitamins	Exclusionary Practices
105.	CSV	25.06.76	[1976] L192/27	—	Article 11(5)	Fertilisers	Sales Agency
106.	Pabst & Richarz/ BNIA	26.07.76	[1976] L331/24	2 [1976] D63	Infringement 85	Alcoholic Drinks	Preventing Parallel Trade
107.	Reuter/BASF	26.07.76	[1976] L254/40	2 [1976] D44	Infringement 85	Base Chemicals	Non-Competition
108.	Miller	01.12.76	[1976] L357/40	1 [1977] D61	Infringement 85	Records	Preventing Parallel Trade
109.	Junghans	21.12.76	[1977] L30/10	1 [1977] D82	Exemption	Clocks	Selective Distribution
110.	Theal/Watts	21.12.76	[1977] L39/19	1 [1977] D44	Infringement 85	Record Cleaners	Preventing Parallel Trade
111.	Gerofabriek	22.12.76	[1977] L16/8	1 [1977] D35	Infringement 85	Cutlery	Resale Price Maintenance
112.	Vacuum Interrupters I	20.01.77	[1977] L48/32	1 [1977] D67	Exemption	Electrical Equipment	Joint Venture
113.	ABG/Oil Companies	19.04.77	[1977] L117/1	2 [1977] D1	Infringement 86	Petroleum	Refusal to Supply
114.	DeLaval/Stork I	25.07.77	[1977] L215/11	2 [1977] D69	Exemption	Heavy Machinery	Joint Venture

Table 1

No.	NAME	DATE	O.J.	C.M.L.R.	TYPE OF DECISION	PRODUCT	SUBJECT
115.	Cobelpa/VNP	08.09.77	[1977] L242/10	2 [1977] D28	Infringement 85	Paper	Information Exchange
116.	BPICA I	07.11.77	[1977] L299/18	2 [1977] D43	Exemption	Cars	Exhibition Agreement
117.	GEC/Weir Sodium Circulators	23.11.77	[1977] L327/26	1 [1978] D42	Exemption	Electrical Equipment	Joint Venture
118.	Centraal Bureau voor de Rijwielhandel	02.12.77	[1978] L20/18	2 [1978] 194	Infringement 85	Bicycles	Collective Exclusive Dealing
119.	Cauliflowers	02.12.77	[1978] L21/23	1 [1978] D66	Infringement 85	Foodstuffs	Exclusionary Practice
120.	German Blacksmiths	08.12.77	[1978] L10/32	1 [1978] D63	Article 14(3)	Forges	—
121.	Hugin/Liptons	08.12.77	[1978] L22/23	1 [1978] D19	Infringement 86	Cash Registers	Refusal to Supply
122.	Video Cassette Recorders	20.12.77	[1978] L47/42	2 [1978] 160	Infringement 85	Consumers Electronics	Patent Licence
123.	The Distillers Company	20.12.77	[1978] L50/16	1 [1978] 400	Infringement 85	Alcoholic Drinks	Preventing Parallel Trade
124.	Spices	21.12.77	[1978] L53/20	2 [1978] 116	Infringement 85	Foodstuffs	Exclusive Purchasing
125.	SOPELEM/Vickers I	21.12.77	[1978] L70/47	2 [1978] 146	Exemption	Microscopes	Specialisation
126.	BMW Belgium	23.12.77	[1978] L46/33	2 [1978] 126	Infringement 85	Cars	Selective Distribution
127.	Penney	23.12.77	[1978] L60/19	2 [1978] 100	Clearance	Textiles	Trademark Delimitation
128.	Jaz/Peter II	23.12.77	[1978] L61/17	2 [1978] 186	Exemption	Clocks	Specialisation
129.	Vegetable Parchment	23.12.77	[1978] L70/54	1 [1978] 534	Infringement 85	Paper	Information Exchange
130.	Campari	23.12.77	[1978] L70/69	2 [1978] 397	Exemption	Alcoholic Drinks	Trademark Licence
131.	RAI/Unitel	26.05.78	[1978] L157/39	3 [1978] 306	Article 11(5)	Performing Rights	Exclusive Licence
132.	SNPE/LEL	12.06.78	[1978] L191/41	2 [1978] 758	Article 15(6)	Explosive Engineering	Cartel
133.	FEDETAB	20.07.78	[1978] L224/29	3 [1978] 524	Infringement 85	Tobacco	Cartel
134.	CSV	20.07.78	[1978] L242/15	1 [1979] 11	Infringement 85	Fertilisers	Sales Agency
135.	Arthur Bell & Sons Ltd	28.07.78	[1978] L235/15	3 [1978] 298	Infringement 85	Alcoholic Drinks	Preventing Parallel Trade
136.	Teacher & Sons	28.07.78	[1978] L235/20	3 [1978] 290	Infringement 85	Alcoholic Drinks	Preventing Parallel Trade

No.	NAME	DATE	O.J.	C.M.L.R.	TYPE OF DECISION	PRODUCT	SUBJECT
137.	Maize Seeds	21.09.78	[1978] L286/23	3 [1978] 434	Infringement 85	Seeds	Breeders' rights Licence
138.	WANO	20.10.78	[1978] L322/26	1 [1979] 403	Infringement 85	Explosives	Joint Venture
139.	Zanussi	23.10.78	[1978] L322/26	1 [1979] 81	Clearance	Consumer Electronics	Guarantee
140.	EMO II	07.12.78	[1979] L11/16	1 [1979] 419	Exemption	Machine Tools	Exhibition Agreement
141.	Kawasaki	12.12.78	[1979] L16/9	1 [1979] 448	Infringement 85	Motor Cycles	Preventing Parallel Trade
142.	White Lead	12.12.78	[1979] L21/16	1 [1979] 464	Infringement 85	White Lead	Cartel
143.	Vaessen/Moris	10.01.79	[1979] L19/32	1 [1979] 511	Infringement 85	Machinery	Patent Licence
144.	Beecham/Parke Davis	17.01.79	[1979] L70/11	2 [1979] 157	Exemption	Pharmaceuticals	Research & Development
145.	Fides	31.01.79	[1979] L57/33	1 [1979] 650	Article 14(3)	Glass	Cartel
146.	AM & S Europe	06.07.79	[1979] L199/31	3 [1979] 376	Article 14(3)	Zinc	Cartel
147.	BP Kemi/DDSF	05.09.79	[1979] L286/32	3 [1979] 684	Infringement 85	Chemicals	Exclusive Purchasing
148.	Floral	28.11.79	[1980] L39/51	2 [1980] 285	Infringement 85	Fertilisers	Sales Agency
149.	Rennet	05.12.79	[1980] L51/19	2 [1980] 402	Infringement 85	Foodstuffs	Exclusive Purchasing
150.	Cane sugar Supply Agreements	07.12.79	[1980] L39/64	2 [1980] 559	Clearance	Sugar	Exclusive Purchasing
151.	Transocean Marine Paint Association IV	12.12.79	[1980] L39/73	1 [1980] 694	Exemption	Paint	Co-operation Agreement
152.	Pioneer	14.12.79	[1980] L60/21	1 [1980] 457	Infringement 85	Consumer Electronics	Preventing Parallel Trade
153.	Fabbrica Pisana	20.12.79	[1980] L75/30	2 [1980] 354	Article 15(1)	Glass	Incorrect Infomation
154.	Fabbrica Lastre	20.12.79	[1980] L75/35	2 [1980] 362	Article 15(1)	Glass	Incorrect Information
155.	Krups	17.04.80	[1980] L120/26	3 [1980] 274	Clearance	Consumer Electronics	Selective Distribution
156.	National Sulphuric Acid Association I	09.07.80	[1980] L260/25	3 [1980] 429	Exemption	Base Chemical	Buying Group
157.	Distillers-Victuallers	22.07.80	[1980] L233/43	3 [1980] 244	Clearance	Alcoholic Drinks	Sales Conditions
158.	IMA Rules	18.09.80	[1980] L318/1	2 [1981] 498	Infringement 85	Plywood	Exclusionary Practice
159.	Natursteinplatten	16.10.80	[1980] L318/32	2 [1981] 308	Clearance	Stones	Co-operation Agreement

Table 1

No.	NAME	DATE	O.J.	C.M.L.R.	TYPE OF DECISION	PRODUCT	SUBJECT
160.	Johnson & Johnson	25.11.80	[1980] L377/16	2 [1981] 287	Infringement 85	Para-pharmaceuticals	Preventing Parallel Trade
161.	Vacuum Interrupters II	11.12.80	[1980] L383/1	2 [1981] 217	Exemption	Electrical Machinery	Joint Venture
162.	Hennessy/Henkell	11.12.80	[1980] L383/11	1 [1981] 601	Infringement 85	Alcoholic Drinks	Exclusive Distribution
163.	Italian Cast Glass	17.12.80	[1980] L383/19	2 [1982] 61	Infringement 85	Glass	Cartel
164.	Italian Flat Glass	28.09.81	[1981] L326/32	3 [1982] 366	Infringement 85	Glass	Cartel
165.	Michelin	07.10.81	[1981] L353/33	1 [1982] 643	Infringement 86	Tyres	Rebate Scheme
166.	GVL	29.10.81	[1981] L370/49	1 [1982] 221	Infringement 86	Copyright	Performing Rights Society
167.	Comptoir d'Importation	17.11.81	[1982] L27/31	1 [1982] 440	Article 15(1)	Consumer Electronics	Incorrect Information
168.	Langenscheidt/ Hachette	17.11.81	[1982] L39/25	1 [1982] 181	Exemption	Books	Joint Venture
169.	VBBB/VBVB	25.11.81	[1982] L54/36	2 [1982] 344	Infringement 85	Books	Collective Resale Price Maintenance
170.	Telos	25.11.81	[1982] L58/19	1 [1982] 267	Article 15(1)	Cameras	Incorrect Information
171.	SOPELEM/Vickers II	26.11.81	[1981] L391/1	3 [1982] 443	Exemption	Microscopes	Specialisation
172.	Moët et Chandon (London) Ltd.	27.11.81	[1982] L94/7	2 [1982] 166	Infringement 85	Alcoholic Drinks	Preventing Parallel Trade
173.	Hasselblad	02.12.81	[1982] L161/18	2 [1982] 233	Infringement 85	Cameras	Preventing Parallel Trade
174.	Gema Statutes	04.12.81	[1982] L94/22	2 [1982] 482	Clearance	Copyright	Performing Rights Society
175.	Fire Insurance	09.12.81	[1982] L80/36	2 [1982] 159	Article 11(5)	Insurance	Request for Information
176.	National Panasonic (Belgium)	11.12.81	[1982] L113/3	2 [1982] 410	Article 15(1)	Consumer Electronics	Incorrect Information
177.	National Panasonic (France)	11.12.81	[1982] L211/32	3 [1982] 623	Article 15(1)	Consumer Electronics	Incorrect Information
178.	NAVEWA-ANSEAU	17.12.81	[1982] L167/39	2 [1982] 193	Infringement 85	Domestic Appliances	Preventing Parallel Trade
179.	AEG-Telefunken	06.01.82	[1982] L117/15	2 [1982] 386	Infringement 85	Consumer Electronics	Selective Distribution

No.	NAME	DATE	O.J.	C.M.L.R.	TYPE OF DECISION	PRODUCT	SUBJECT
180.	BPICA II	30.04.82	[1982] L156/16	2 [1983] 40	Exemption	Cars	Exhibition Agreement
181.	SSI	15.07.82	[1982] L232/1	3 [1982] 702	Infringement 85	Tobacco	Cartel
182.	Ford Werke-Interim Measures	18.08.82	[1982] L256/20	3 [1982] 267	Interim measures	Cars	Selective Distribution
183.	Fédération Chaussure de France	27.10.82	[1982] L319/12	1 [1983] 575	Article 15(1)	Shoes	Incorrect Information
184.	Amersham Buchler	29.10.82	[1982] L314/34	1 [1983] 619	Exemption	Nuclear Materials	Joint Venture
185.	NAVEWA-ANSEAU (Bosch)	04.11.82	[1982] L325/20	1 [1983] 470	Withdrawal of fine	Domestic Appliances	Preventing Parallel Trade
186.	National Panasonic	07.12.82	[1982] L354/28	1 [1983] 497	Infringement 85	Consumer Electronics	Preventing Parallel Trade
187.	Cafeteros de Colombia	10.12.82	[1982] L360/31	1 [1983] 703	Infringement 85	Coffee	Preventing Parallel Trade
188.	British Telecommunications	10.12.82	[1982] L360/36	1 [1983] 457	Infringement 86	Telecommunications	Exclusionary Practices
189.	Zinc	14.12.82	[1982] L362/40	2 [1983] 285	Infringement 85	Zinc	Cartel
190.	AROW/BNIC	15.12.82	[1982] L379/1	2 [1983] 240	Infringement 85	Alcoholic Drinks	Cartel
191.	Toltecs/Dorcet	15.12.82	[1982] L379/19	1 [1983] 412	Infringement 85	Tobacco	Trademark Delimitation
192.	Castrol	10.01.83	[1983] L114/26	3 [1983] 165	Article 11(5)	Petroleum Products	—
193.	Cematex II	24.05.83	[1983] L140/27	3 [1984] 69	Exemption	Textile Machinery	Exhibition Agreement
194.	Windsurfing International	11.07.83	[1983] L229/1	1 [1984] 1	Infringement 85	Leisure Articles	Patent Licence
195.	Vimpoltu	13.07.83	[1983] L200/44	3 [1983] 619	Infringement 85	Agricultural Machines	Cartel
196.	Rockwell/IVECO	13.07.83	[1983] L224/19	3 [1983] 709	Exemption	Vehicle Components	Joint Venture
197.	ECS/AKZO-Interim Measures	29.07.83	[1983] L252/13	3 [1983] 694	Interim measures 86	Chemicals	Predatory Pricing
198.	Cast-Iron & Steel Rolls	17.10.83	[1983] L317/1	1 [1984] 694	Infringement 85	Steel Products	Cartel
199.	Ford Werke AG	16.11.83	[1983] L327/31	1 [1984] 596	Infringement 85	Cars	Preventing Parallel Trade

TABLE 1

Table 1

No.	NAME	DATE	O.J.	C.M.L.R.	TYPE OF DECISION	PRODUCT	SUBJECT
200.	Murat	05.12.83	[1983] L348/20	1 [1984] 219	Clearance	Jewellery	Selective Distribution
201.	SMM&T	05.12.83	[1983] L376/1	1 [1984] 611	Exemption	Cars	Exhibition Agreement
202.	IPTC Belgium	05.12.83	[1983] L376/7	2 [1984] 131	Infringement 85	Domestic Appliances	Preventing Parallel Trade
203.	VW/MAN	05.12.83	[1983] L376/11	1 [1984] 621	Exemption	Heavy Vehicles	Specialisation
204.	Schlegel/CPIO	06.12.83	[1983] L351/20	2 [1984] 179	204—Exemption & Clearance	Vehicle Components	Exclusive Purchasing
205.	Carbon Gas Technologie	08.12.83	[1983] L376/17	2 [1984] 275	Exemption	Chemical Processes	R&D Agreement
206.	Nutricia	12.12.83	[1983] L376/22	2 [1984] 165	Infringement 85	Foodstuffs	Acquisition
207.	International Energy Agency	12.12.83	[1983] L376/30	2 [1984] 186	Exemption	Petroleum	Co-operation Agreement
208.	SABA II	21.12.83	[1983] L376/41	1 [1984] 676	Exemption	Consumer Electronics	Selective Distribution
209.	Nuovo-CEGAM	30.03.84	[1984] L99/29	2 [1984] 484	Exemption	Insurance	Co-operation Agreement
210.	IBM PC	18.04.84	[1984] L118/24	2 [1984] 342	Clearance	Computers	Selective Distribution
211.	Polistil/Arbois	16.05.84	[1984] L136/9	2 [1984] 594	Infringement 85	Toys	Preventing Parallel Trade
212.	British Leyland	02.07.84	[1984] L207/11	3 [1984] 92	Infringement 86	Cars	Preventing Parallel Trade
213.	Synthetic Fibres	04.07.84	[1984] L207/17	1 [1985] 787	Exemption	Textiles	Restructuring Agreement
214.	Carlsberg	12.07.84	[1984] L207/26	1 [1985] 735	Exemption	Beer	Distribution Agreement
215.	BPCL/ICI	19.07.84	[1984] L212/1	2 [1985] 330	Exemption	Base Chemicals	Restructuring Agreement
216.	Flat Glass (Benelux)	23.07.84	[1984] L212/13	2 [1985] 350	Infringement 85	Glass	Cartel
217.	Zinc Producer Group	06.08.84	[1984] L220/27	2 [1985] 108	Infringement 85	Zinc	Cartel
218.	Peroxide Products	23.11.84	[1985] L35/1	1 [1985] 481	Infringement 85	Chemicals	Cartel
219.	UNIDI II	23.11.84	[1984] L322/10	2 [1985] 38	Exemption	Dental Equipment	Exhibition Agreement
220.	Fire Insurance	05.12.84	[1985] L35/20	3 [1985] 246	Infringement 85	Insurance	Cartel

No.	NAME	DATE	O.J.	C.M.L.R.	TYPE OF DECISION	PRODUCT	SUBJECT
221.	Milchfoerderungs-fonds	07.12.84	[1985] L35/35	3 [1985] 101	Infringement 85	Milk	Export Subsidies
222.	Grohe Sales System	10.12.84	[1985] L19/17	4 [1988] 612	Infringement 85	Sanitary Equipment	Selective Distribution
223.	Ideal Standard Sales System	10.12.84	[1985] L20/38	4 [1988] 627	Infringement 85	Sanitary Equipment	Selective Distribution
224.	Uniform Eurochèques	10.12.84	[1985] L35/43	3 [1985] 434	Exemption	Banking	Co-operation Agreement
225.	Mecaniver/PPG	12.12.84	[1985] L35/54	3 [1985] 359	Clearance	Glass	Acquisition
226.	John Deere	14.12.84	[1985] L35/58	2 [1985] 554	Infringement 85	Agricultural Machines	Preventing Parallel Trade
227.	Woodpulp	19.12.84	[1985] L85/1	3 [1985] 474	Infringement 85	Woodpulp	Cartel
228.	Aluminium	19.12.84	[1985] L92/1	3 [1987] 813	Infringement 85	Aluminium	Cartel
229.	Olympic Airways	23.01.85	[1985] L46/51	1 [1985] 730	Article 11(5)	Airline Services	—
230.	Greek Insurance	24.04.85	[1985] L152/25	—	Infringement 90	Insurance	Discrimination
231.	EATE Levy	10.07.85	[1985] L219/35	4 [1988] 698	Infringement Reg. 1017/68	Waterway Transport	Cartel
232.	Grundig	10.07.85	[1985] L233/1	4 [1988] 865	Exemption	Consumer Electronics	Selective Distribution
233.	Velcro/Aplix	12.07.85	[1985] L233/22	4 [1989] 157	Infringement 85	Fasteners	Patent Licence
234.	Ivoclar	27.11.85	[1985] L369/1	4 [1988] 781	Exemption	Dental Equipment	Selective Distribution
235.	BP/Kellogg	02.12.85	[1985] L369/6	2 [1986] 619	Exemption	Chemicals	R&D Agreement
236.	Breeders' rights; roses	13.12.85	[1985] L369/9	4 [1988] 193	Infringement 85	Flowers	Breeders' Rights Licence
237.	Whisky and Gin	13.12.85	[1985] L369/19	2 [1986] 664	Exemption	Alcoholic Drinks	Exclusive Distribution
238.	London Sugar Market	13.12.85	[1985] L369/25	4 [1988] 138	Clearance	Sugar	Futures Market
239.	London Cocoa Market	13.12.85	[1985] L369/28	4 [1988] 143	Clearance	Cocoa	Futures Market
240.	London Coffee Market	13.12.85	[1985] L369/31	4 [1988] 155	Clearance	Coffee	Futures Market
241.	London Rubber Market	13.12.85	[1985] L369/34	4 [1988] 149	Clearance	Rubber	Futures Market
242.	ECS/AKZO	14.12.85	[1985] L374/1	3 [1986] 273	Infringement 86	Chemicals	Predatory Pricing

Table 1

No.	NAME	DATE	O.J.	C.M.L.R.	TYPE OF DECISION	PRODUCT	SUBJECT
243.	P&I Clubs	16.12.85	[1985] L376/2	4 [1989] 178	Exemption	Insurance	Co-operation Agreement
244.	Villeroy & Boch	16.12.85	[1985] L376/15	4 [1988] 461	Clearance	China	Selective Distribution
245.	Sperry New Holland	16.12.85	[1985] L376/21	4 [1988] 306	Infringement 85	Agricultural Machinery	Preventing Parallel Trade
246.	Siemens/Fanuc	18.12.85	[1985] L376/29	4 [1988] 945	Infringement 85	Electronic Machinery	Exclusive Distribution
247.	Polypropylene	23.04.86	[1986] L230/1	4 [1988] 347	Infringement 85	Base Chemicals	Cartel
248.	Roofing Felt	10.07.86	[1986] L232/15	4 [1991] 130	Infringement 85	Construction Materials	Cartel
249.	Optical Fibres	14.07.86	[1986] L236/30	—	Exemption	Optical Fibres	Joint Venture
250.	Peugeot	25.09.86	[1986] L295/19	4 [1989] 371	Infringement 85	Cars	Preventing Parallel Trade
251.	VIFKA	30.09.86	[1986] L291/46	—	Exemption	Office Equipment	Exhibition Agreement
252.	Irish Banks Standing Committee	30.09.86	[1986] L295/28	2 [1987] 601	Clearance	Banking	Co-operation Agreement
253.	Meldoc	26.11.86	[1986] L348/50	4 [1989] 853	Infringement 85	Milk	Cartel
254.	Fatty Acids	02.12.86	[1987] L3/17	4 [1989] 445	Infringement 85	Chemicals	Cartel
255.	IPEL	04.12.86	[1987] L3/27	4 [1989] 280	Clearance	Petroleum	Futures Market
256.	ENI/Montedison	04.12.86	[1987] L5/13	4 [1988] 444	Exemption	Base Chemicals	Restructuring Agreement
257.	London Grain Market	10.12.86	[1987] L19/22	4 [1989] 294	Clearance	Cereals	Futures Market
258.	London Potato Market	10.12.86	[1987] L19/26	4 [1989] 301	Clearance	Potatoes	Futures Market
259.	London Meat Exchange	10.12.86	[1987] L19/30	4 [1989] 308	Clearance	Meat	Futures Market
260.	GAFTA	10.12.86	[1987] L19/18	4 [1989] 287	Clearance	Soya Beans	Futures Market
261.	Belgian Banking Association	11.12.86	[1987] L7/27	4 [1989] 141	Exemption	Banking	Co-operation Agreement
262.	ABI	12.12.86	[1987] L43/51	4 [1989] 238	Exemption	Banking	Co-operation Agreement

No.	NAME	DATE	O.J.	C.M.L.R.	TYPE OF DECISION	PRODUCT	SUBJECT
263.	X/Open Group	15.12.86	[1987] L35/36	4 [1988] 542	Exemption	Computer Systems	Co-operation Agreement
264.	Boussois/Interpane	15.12.86	[1987] L50/30	4 [1988] 124	Exemption	Glass	Know-how Licence
265.	Yves Rocher	17.12.86	[1987] L8/49	4 [1988] 592	Exemption	Cosmetics	Franchising
266.	Pronuptia	17.12.86	[1987] L13/39	4 [1989] 355	Exemption	Textiles	Franchising
267.	Mitchell Cotts/ Sofiltra	17.12.86	[1987] L41/31	4 [1988] 111	Exemption	Air Filters	Joint Venture
268.	Canary Islands	22.06.87	[1987] L194/28	1 [1988] 331	Infringement 90	Transport	Discrimination
269.	Tipp-Ex	10.07.87	[1987] L222/1	4 [1989] 425	Infringement 85	Stationery	Preventing Parallel Trade
270.	Computerland	13.07.87	[1987] L222/12	4 [1989] 259	Exemption	Computers	Franchising
271.	BIFFEX	13.07.87	[1987] L222/24	4 [1989] 314	Clearance	Maritime Transport	Futures Market
272.	Sandoz	13.07.87	[1987] L222/28	4 [1989] 628	Infringement 85	Pharmaceuticals	Preventing Parallel Trade
273.	Boosey & Hawkes	29.07.87	[1987] L286/36	4 [1988] 67	Interim-Measures 86	Musical Instruments	Refusal to Supply
274.	International Dental Exhibition	18.09.87	[1987] L293/58	—	Exemption	Dental Equipment	Exhibition Agreement
275.	Fisher-Price	18.12.87	[1988] L49/19	4 [1989] 553	Infringement 85	Toys	Preventing Parallel Trade
276.	New Potatoes	18.12.87	[1988] L59/25	4 [1988] 790	Regulation 26/62	Potatoes	National Market Organisa- tion
277.	Konica	18.12.87	[1988] L78/34	4 [1988] 848	Infringement 85	Photographic Material	Preventing Parallel Trade
278.	ARG/Unipart	22.12.87	[1988] L45/34	4 [1988] 513	Exemption	Car Components	Exclusive Distribution
279.	Enichem/ICI	22.12.87	[1988] L50/18	4 [1989] 54	Exemption	Base Chemicals	Restructuring Agreement
280.	Olivetti/Canon	22.12.87	[1988] L52/51	4 [1989] 940	Exemption	Office Equipment	Joint Venture
281.	De Laval-Stork II	22.12.87	[1988] L59/32	4 [1988] 714	Exemption	Heavy Machinery	Joint Venture
282.	Hilti	22.12.87	[1988] L65/19	4 [1989] 677	Infringement 85	Tools	Tying
283.	Rich Products	22.12.87	[1988] L69/21	4 [1988] 527	Exemption	Foodstuffs	Know-how Licence
284.	BP/Bayer	05.05.88	[1988] L150/35	4 [1989] 24	Exemption	Base Chemicals	Restructuring Agreement

Table 1

No.	NAME	DATE	O.J.	C.M.L.R.	TYPE OF DECISION	PRODUCT	SUBJECT
285.	British Dental Trade Association	11.07.88	[1988] L233/15	4 [1989] 1021	Infringement 85	Dental equipment	Exhibition Agreement
286.	British Sugar	18.07.88	[1988] L284/41	4 [1990] 196	Infringement 86	Sugar	Predation
287.	IVECO/Ford	20.07.88	[1988] L230/39	4 [1989] 40	Exemption	Heavy Vehicles	Joint Venture
288.	VBA	26.07.88	[1988] L262/27	4 [1989] 500	Infringement 85	Flowers	Exclusionary Practice
289.	Tetra Pak I	26.07.88	[1988] L272/27	4 [1990] 47	Infringement 86	Packaging Machinery	Acquisition
290.	Continental/ Michelin	11.10.88	[1988] L305/33	4 [1989] 920	Exemption	Tyres	R&D Agreement
291.	BBC Brown Boveri	11.10.88	[1988] L301/68	4 [1989] 610	Exemption	Batteries	Joint Venture
292.	Delta Chemie	13.10.88	[1988] L309/34	4 [1989] 535	Exemption	Household Products	Know-how Licence
293.	Eurotunnel	24.10.88	[1988] L311/36	4 [1989] 419	Clearance	Construction	Building Consortium
294.	Hudson Bay	28.10.88	[1988] L316/43	4 [1989] 340	Infringement 85	Furs	Exclusionary Practices
295.	SABENA	04.11.88	[1988] L317/47	4 [1989] 662	Infringement 86	Computer Reservations	Exclusionary Practices
296.	ServiceMaster	14.11.88	[1988] L332/38	4 [1989] 581	Exemption	Cleaning Services	Franchising
297.	Transocean Marine Paint Association V	02.12.88	[1988] L351/40	4 [1989] 621	Exemption	Paint	Co-operation Agreement
298.	Charles Jourdan	02.12.88	[1989] L35/31	4 [1989] 591	Exemption	Luxury Products	Franchising
299.	British Plasterboard	05.12.88	[1989] L10/50	4 [1990] 464	Infringement 86	Building Materials	Exclusionary Practice
300.	Flat Glass	07.12.88	[1989] L33/44	4 [1990] 535	Infringement 85/86	Glass	Cartel
301.	Net Book Agreements	12.12.88	[1989] L22/12	4 [1989] 825	Infringement 85	Books	Collective RPM
302.	Uniform Eurochèques Manufacturing	19.12.88	[1989] L36/16	4 [1989] 907	Exemption	Manufacturing	Common Standards
303.	EMO III	20.12.88	[1989] L37/11	4 [1990] 231	Exemption	Machine Tools	Exhibition Agreement
304.	Decca	21.12.88	[1989] L43/27	4 [1990] 627	Infringement 85/86	Radar	Patent Licence
305.	PVC	21.12.88	[1989] L74/1	4 [1990] 345	Infringement 85	Base Chemicals	Cartel
306.	LdPE	21.12.88	[1989] L74/21	4 [1990] 382	Infringement 85	Base Chemicals	Cartel
307.	Magill	21.12.88	[1989] L78/43	4 [1989] 757	Infringement 86	TV Guides	Intellectual Property Rights

No.	NAME	DATE	O.J.	C.M.L.R.	TYPE OF DECISION	PRODUCT	SUBJECT
308.	National Sulphuric Acid Association II	09.06.89	[1989] L190/22	4 [1990] 612	Exemption	Base Chemicals	Buying Group
309.	UIP	12.07.89	[1989] L226/25	4 [1990] 749	Exemption	Cinema	Joint Venture
310.	Dutch Banking Association	19.07.89	[1989] L253/1	4 [1990] 768	Exemption	Banking	Co-operation Agreement
311.	Welded Steel Mesh	02.08.89	[1989] L260/1	4 [1991] 13	Infringement 85	Construction Materials	Cartel
312.	ARD	15.09.89	[1989] L284/36	4 [1990] 841	Exemption	Cinema	Purchasing Agreement
313.	Bayonox	13.12.89	[1990] L21/71	4 [1990] 930	Infringement 85	Animal feed	Preventing Parallel Trade
314.	APB	14.12.89	[1990] L18/35	4 [1990] 619	Clearance	Para-pharmaceuticals	Co-operation Agreement
315.	Sugar Beet	19.12.89	[1990] L31/35	4 [1991] 629	Infringement 85	Sugar Beet	Exclusionary practice
316.	Concordato	20.12.89	[1990] L15/27	4 [1991] 199	Exemption	Insurance	Co-operation Agreement
317.	TEKO	20.12.89	[1990] L13/34	4 [1990] 957	Exemption	Insurance	Co-operation Agreement
318.	Dutch express delivery	20.12.89	[1990] L10/47	4 [1990] 947	Article 90	Mail delivery	Monopolisation
319.	Alcatel/ANT	12.01.90	[1990] L32/19	4 [1991] 208	Exemption	Satellites	R&D Agreement
320.	Moosehead	23.03.90	[1990] L100/32	4 [1991] 391	Exemption	Beer	Trademark Licence
321.	Metaleurop	26.06.90	[1990] L179/41	4 [1991] 222	Clearance	Metal	Merger
322.	Odin	13.07.90	[1990] L209/15	4 [1991] 832	Clearance	Packaging Material	Joint Venture
323.	Konsortium ECR 900	27.07.90	[1990] L228/31	4 [1992] 54	Clearance	Telecommunications	R&D Agreement
324.	Spanish Courier services	01.08.90	[1990] L233/19	4 [1991] 560	Article 90	Mail delivery	Monopolisation
325.	GEC-Siemens/ Plessey	01.09.90	[1990] C239/2	4 [1992] 471	Article 6 Reg. 99/63	Electronics	Joint Take Over
326.	Cekacan	15.10.90	[1990] L299/64	4 [1992] 406	Exemption	Packaging Material	Joint Venture
327.	Bayer Dental	28.11.90	[1990] L351/46	4 [1992] 61	Infringement 85	Dental Equipment	Preventing Parallel Trade

Table 1

No.	NAME	DATE	O.J.	C.M.L.R.	TYPE OF DECISION	PRODUCT	SUBJECT
328.	KSB	12.12.90	[1991] L19/25	5 [1992] 55	Exemption	Machinery	R&D Agreements
329.	D'Ieteren	19.12.90	[1991] L20/42	4 [1992] 399	Clearance	Motoroil	Selective Distribution
329a.	Secrétama	19.12.90	[1991] L35/23	5 [1992] 76	Article 16 Reg. 4056/86	Maritime Transport	Incorrect Information
330.	Solvay/ICI	19.12.90	[1991] L152/1	4 [1994] 454	Infringement 85	Soda Ash	Cartel
331.	Solvay/CFK	19.12.90	[1991] L152/16	4 [1994] 482	Infringement 85	Soda Ash	Cartel
332.	Solvay	19.12.90	[1991] L152/21	4 [1994] 645	Infringement 86	Soda Ash	Tying
333.	ICI	19.12.90	[1991] L152/40	4 [1994] 645	Infringement 86	Soda Ash	Tying
333a.	ANSAC	19.12.90	[1991] L152/54	—	Infringement 85	Soda Ash	Joint Sales
334.	Vichy	11.01.91	[1991] L75/57	—	Article 15(6)	Cosmetics	Selective Distribution
335.	Ijsselcentrale	16.01.91	[1991] L28/32	5 [1992] 154	Infringement 85	Electricity	Collective Exclusive Dealing
336.	Sippa	15.02.91	[1991] L60/19	5 [1992] 528	Exemption	Paper	Exhibition Agreement
337.	Screensport/EBU	19.02.91	[1991] L63/32	5 [1992] 273	Infringement 85	Television	Joint Venture
338.	Baccarat	15.03.91	[1991] L97/16	5 [1992] 189	Article 16	Luxury Products	Penalty Payments
339.	Scottish Nuclear	30.04.91	[1991] L178/31	—	Exemption	Energy	Exclusive Purchasing
340.	Gosme/Martell	15.05.91	[1991] L185/23	5 [1992] 586	Prohibition	Alcoholic Drinks	Preventing Parallel Trade
341.	Viho/Toshiba	05.06.91	[1991] L287/39	5 [1992] 180	Prohibition	Photocopiers	Preventing Parallel Trade
342.	IATA Passengers	30.07.91	[1991] L258/18	5 [1992] 496	Exemption	Agency-Services	Similar Distribution systems
343.	IATA Cargo	30.07.91	[1991] L258/29	5 [1992] 496	Exemption	Agency-Services	Similar Distribution systems
344.	Eirpage	18.10.91	[1991] L306/22	4 [1993] 64	Exemption	Paging Services	Joint Venture
344a.	Eco System	04.12.91	[1992] L66/1	4 [1993] 42	Prohibition	Cars	Selective Distribution
345.	Yves Saint Laurent	16.12.91	[1992] L12/24	4 [1993] 120	Exemption	Cosmetics	Selective Distribution
346.	Assurpol	14.01.92	[1992] L37/16	4 [1993] 338	Exemption	Insurance	Co-operation Agreement
347.	U.K. Tractors	17.02.92	[1992] L68/19	4 [1993] 358	Prohibition	Tractors	Information Exchange
348.	Tetra Pak II	24.07.91	[1992] L72/1	4 [1992] 551	Infringement 86	Packing Materials	Exclusionary Practices

No.	NAME	DATE	O.J.	C.M.L.R.	TYPE OF DECISION	PRODUCT	SUBJECT
349.	Dutch Building Cartel	05.02.92	[1992] L92/1	5 [1993] 135	Infringement 85	Construction	Cartel
350.	British Midland	26.02.92	[1992] L96/34	4 [1993] 596	Infringement 85/86	Air Transport	Exclusionary Practice
351.	Newitt/Dunlop	18.03.92	[1992] L131/32	5 [1993] 352	Infringement 85	Tennis Balls	Preventing parallel trade
352.	Eurocheques; Helsinki	25.03.92	[1992] L95/50	5 [1993] 323	Infringement 85	Banking	Cartel
353.	French African Shipping	01.04.92	[1992] L134/1	5 [1993] 446	Infringement 85/86	Shipping	Cartel
354.	UKWAL	06.04.92	[1992] L121/45	5 [1993] 632	Article 19/ Regulation 4056/86	Shipping	Refusal to submit to investigation
355.	VIHO/Parker Pen	15.07.92	[1992] L233/27	5 [1993] 382	Infringement 85	Stationary	Export ban
356.	Parfums Givenchy	24.07.92	[1992] L236/11	5 [1993] 579	Exemption	Perfume	Selective Distribution
357.	Quantel	27.07.92	[1992] L235/9	5 [1993] 497	Infringement 85	Laser Products	Market Sharing
358.	Scottish Salmon	30.07.92	[1992] L246/37	5 [1993] 602	Infringement 85	Fish	Cartel
359.	CSM	07.10.92	[1992] L305/16	—	Article 15(1)/ Regulation 17	Sugar	Refusal to co-operate during investigation
360.	World Cup Football	27.10.92	[1992] L326/31	5 [1994] 253	Infringement 85	Sports	Exclusive Distribution
361.	Gillette	10.11.92	[1993] L116/21	5 [1993] 559	Infringement 85/86	Shaving equipment	Acquisition
362.	Railway Tickets	25.11.92	[1992] L366/47	—	Infringement 85	Travel agencies	Cartel
363.	Lloyd's Underwriters	04.12.92	[1993] L4/26	—	Negative Clearance	Insurance	Co-operation Agreement
364.	Ford Agricultural	15.12.92	[1993] L20/1	5 [1995] 89	Infringement 85	Tractors	Preventing Parallel Trade
365.	MEWAC	17.12.92	[1993] L20/6	5 [1994] 275	Article 19/ Regulation 4056/86	Shipping	Refusal to submit to investigation
366.	FIAT/Hitachi	21.12.92	[1993] L20/10	4 [1994] 571	Exemption	Earthmoving machines	Joint Venture
367.	Ford/Volkswagen	23.12.92	[1993] L20/14	5 [1993] 617	Exemption	Cars	Joint Venture
368.	Astra	23.12.92	[1993] L20/23	5 [1994] 226	Infringement 85	Satellite	Joint Venture
369.	Mars/Langnese	23.12.92	[1993] L183/19	4 [1994] 51	Infringement 85	Ice-cream	Exclusive Purchasing
369a.	Mars/Schöller	23.12.92	[1993] L183/1	4 [1994] 51	—	—	—

Table 1

No.	NAME	DATE	O.J.	C.M.L.R.	TYPE OF DECISION	PRODUCT	SUBJECT
370.	Jahrhundertvertrag	22.12.92	[1993] L50/14	—	Exemption	Energy	Exclusive Purchasing
371.	CEWAL	23.12.92	[1993] L34/20	5 [1995] 198	Infringement 85/86	Shipping	Cartel
372.	Combined Transport	24.02.93	[1993] L73/38 and L145/31	—	Exemption	Railway Transport	Tariff Structure
373.	UER	11.06.93	[1993] L179/23	4 [1995] 56	Exemption	Television	Joint Buying
374.	ZERA	22.06.93	[1993] L272/28	5 [1995] 320	Infringement 85	Plant Chemicals	Preventing Parallel Trade
375.	CNSD	30.06.93	[1993] L203/27	5 [1995] 495	Infringement 85	Customs Agents	Price-fixing
376.	Auditel	24.11.93	[1993] L306/50	5 [1995] 719	Infringement 85	Television	Exclusive Purchasing
377.	Sea Containers	23.12.93	[1994] L15/8	4 [1995] 84	Rejection of Interim Measures	Shipping	Market Access
378.	Grundig	21.12.93	[1994] L20/15	4 [1995] 658	Exemption	Consumer Electronics	Selective Distribution
379.	Rodby	21.12.93	[1994] L55/52	5 [1994] 457	Article 90	Shipping	Market Access
380.	International Energy Agency II	21.02.94	[1994] L68/35	—	Exemption 85	Oil	Co-operation Agreement
381.	HOV SVZ/MCN	29.03.94	[1994] L104/34	—	Articles 85 & 86	Railway Transport	Discriminatory Prices
382.	Stichting Kraanverhuur	13.04.94	[1994] L117/30	—	Article 15(6)/ Regulation 17	Cranes	Exclusionary Practices
383.	Stichting Baksteen	29.04.94	[1994] L131/15	4 [1995] 646	Exemption	Bricks	Cartel
384.	Exxon/Shell	18.05.94	[1994] L144/20	—	Exemption	Chemicals	Joint Venture
385.	Carton Board	13.07.94	[1994] L243/1	5 [1994] 547	Infringement 85	Carton board	Cartel
386.	BP/Bayer	06.06.94	[1994] L174/34	—	Exemption	Chemicals	Joint Venture
387.	BT/MCI	27.07.94	[1994] L223/36	5 [1995] 285	Exemption	Telecommunications	Joint Venture
388.	ACI	27.07.94	[1994] L224/28	—	Exemption	Transport	Joint Venture
389.	PVC II	27.07.94	[1994] L239/14	—	Infringement 85	Chemicals	Cartel
390.	Night Services	07.10.94	[1994] L259/20	5 [1995] 76	Exemption	Transport	Joint Venture
391.	AKZO	14.10.94	[1994] L294/31	—	Article 15(1)/ Regulation 17	Salt	Inspection
392.	Pasteur/Merck	06.10.94	[1994] L309/1	—	Exemption	Drugs	Joint Venture
393.	Olivetti/Digital	06.10.94	[1994] L309/24	—	Exemption	Computer Systems	Co-operation Agreement
393a.	Trans Atlantic	19.10.94	[1994] L376/1	—	Infringement 85	Transport	Cartel
394.	Cement	30.11.94	[1994] L343/1	4 [1995] 327	Infringement 85	Cement	Cartel

No.	NAME	DATE	O.J.	C.M.L.R.	TYPE OF DECISION	PRODUCT	SUBJECT
395.	Fujitsu AMD	12.12.94	[1994] L341/66	—	Exemption	Semi-Conductors	Joint Venture
396.	Eurotunnel	13.12.94	[1994] L354/66	4 [1995] 801	Exemption	Transport	Joint Venture
397.	IPSP	15.12.94	[1994] L354/75	—	Negative Clearance	Satellites	Joint Venture
398.	Asahi/St Gobain	16.12.94	[1994] L354/87	—	Exemption	Glass	R&D
399.	Far Eastern Freight	21.12.94	[1994] L378/17	—	Infringement 85	Transport	Cartel
400.	Philips/Osram	21.12.94	[1994] L378/37	4 [1996] 48	Exemption	Lamps	Joint Venture
401.	Tretorn	21.12.94	[1994] L378/45	—	Infringement 85	Tennis Balls	Preventing Parallel Trade
402.	COAPI	30.01.95	[1995] L122/37	5 [1995] 468	Infringement 85	Patent Protection	Price Fixing
403.	Brussels Airport	28.06.95	[1995] L216/8	4 [1996] 232	Article 90	Airport Facilities	Rebates
404.	PMI-DSV	31.01.95	[1995] L221/34	5 [1996] 320	Negative Clearance	Television	Exclusive Rights
405.	BASF/Accinauto	12.07.95	[1995] L272/16	4 [1996] 811	Infringement 85	Car paint	Preventing Parallel Trade
406.	Italian GSM	04.10.95	[1995] L280/49	4 [1996] 700	Article 90	Telecommunications	Discriminatory Levies
407.	Dutch Cranes	29.11.95	[1995] L312/79	4 [1996] 565	Infringement 85	Cranes	Exclusionary Practices
408.	Adalat	10.01.96	[1996] L201/1	5 [1996] 416	Infringement 85	Pharmaceuticals	Preventing Parallel Trade
409.	LH/SAS	16.01.96	[1996] L54/28	4 [1996] 845	Exemption	Air Transport	Co-operation Agreement
409a.	Fenex	05.06.96	[1996] L181/28	5 [1996] 332	Infringement	Freight forwarding	Common Recommended Prices
410.	BNP/Dresdner Bank	24.06.96	[1996] L188/37	5 [1996] 582	Exemption	Financial Services	Co-operation Agreement
411.	Atlas	17.07.96	[1996] L54/28 [1997] L47/8	4 [1997] 89	Exemption	Telecommunications	Joint Venture
412.	Phoenix	19.09.96	[1996] L239/57	4 [1997] 147	Exemption	Telecommunications	Joint Venture
413.	Ferry Services	30.10.96	[1997] L26/23	4 [1997] 789	Infringement 85	Sea Transport	Cartel
414.	Irish Telecom-munications	27.11.96	[1997] L41/8	—	Directive 90/388	Telecommunications	Implementation Period
415.	Novalliance	04.12.96	[1997] L47/11	4 [1997] 876	Infringement 85	Office equipment	Preventing Parallel Trade

Table 1

No.	NAME	DATE	O.J.	C.M.L.R.	TYPE OF DECISION	PRODUCT	SUBJECT
416.	Iridium	18.12.96	[1997] L16/87	4 [1997] 1065	Negative Clearance 85	Telecommunications	Consortium
417.	Spanish GSM	18.12.96	[1997] L76/19	—	Article 90	Telecommunications	Discriminatory Levies
417A.	Portuguese Telecommunications	12.02.97	[1997] L133/19	—	Directive 90/388	Telecommunications	Implementation Period
418.	Irish Sugar	14.05.97	[1997] L258/1	5 [1997] 666	Infringement 86	Sugar	Rebates
419.	Luxembourg Telecommunications	14.05.97	[1997] L234/7	—	Directive 90/388	Telecommunications	Implementation Period
420.	Spanish Telecommunications	10.06.97	[1997] L243/48	—	Directive 90/388	Telecommunications	Implementation Period
421.	Greek Telecommunications	18.06.97	[1997] L245/6	—	Directive 90/388	Telecommunications	Implementation Period
422.	VTM/VT4	26.06.97	[1997] L244/18	5 [1997] 18	Article 90	Television	Special Broadcasting Rights
423.	Italian Ports	21.10.97	[1997] L301/17	4 [1998] 73	Article 90	Ports	Special Rights
424.	Italian Pilots	21.10.97	[1997] L301/27	4 [1998] 91	Article 90	Ports	Special Rights
425.	Unisource	29.10.97	[1997] L318/1	4 [1998] 105	Exemption	Telecommunications	Joint Venture
426.	Uniworld	29.10.97	[1997] L318/24	4 [1998] 145	Exemption	Telecommunications	Joint Venture
427.	German Steel	26.11.97	[1997] L1/10	4 [1998] 450	Article 65 ECSC	Steel	Information Exchange
428.	Frankfurt Airport	14.01.98	[1998] L72/30	4 [1998] 779	Article 86	Airport	Tying
429.	VW-Audi	28.01.98	[1998] L124/60	5 [1998] 333	Infringement 85	Cars	Preventing Parallel Trade
430.	Alloy Surcharge	21.01.98	[1998] L100/55	4 [1998] 973	Article 65 ECSC	Steel	Cartel
431.	Van den Bergh Foods	11.03.98	[1998] L246/1	5 [1998] 530	Infringements 85 & 86	Ice-cream	Exclusive Purchasing
432.	Alpha Flight Services	11.06.98	[1998] L230/10	5 [1998] 611	Infringement 86	Airports	Discriminatory Prices
433.	Italian Tobacco	17.06.98	[1998] L252/47	5 [1998] 786	Infringement 86	Tobacco	Exclusionary Practices
434.	British Sugar II	14.10.98	[1999] L76/1	4 [1998] 1316	Infringement 85	Sugar	Price Fixing

No.	NAME	DATE	O.J.	C.M.L.R.	TYPE OF DECISION	PRODUCT	SUBJECT
435.	Pre-Insulated Pipe Cartel	21.10.98	[1999] L24/1	4 [1999] 402	Infringement 85	Pipes	Full Fledged Cartel
436.	Sicasov	14.12.98	[1999] L4/27	4 [1999] 192	Exemption	Breeder's rights	Licensing Agreements
437.	Portuguese Airports	10.02.99	[1999] L69/31	5 [1999] 103	Article 90	Airports	Discriminatory Pricing
438.	Finnish Airports	10.02.99	[1999] L69/24	5 [1999] 90	Infringement 86	Airports	Discriminatory Pricing
439.	Whitbread	24.02.99	[1999] L88/26	5 [1999] 118	Exemption	Beer	Lease Agreements
440.	TPS	03.03.99	[1999] L90/6	5 [1999] 168	Exemption	Television	Ancillary Restrictions
441.	TACA	16.09.99	[1999] L95/1	4 [1999] 1415	Infringements 85 & 86	Container transport	Cartel
443.	Greek Ferries	09.12.98	[1999] L109/24	5 [1999] 47	Infringement 81	Ferry Services	Price Fixing
444.	EPI	07.04.99	[1999] L106/14	5 [1999] 540	Exemption	Patent agents' servies	Regulations on Professional Discipline
445.	P&O Stena Line	26.01.99	[1999] L163/1	5 [1999] 682	Exemption	Ferry services	Joint Venture
446.	P&I Clubs	12.04.99	[1999] L125/12	5 [1999] 646	Negative clearance (Arts 81 & 82) and exemption	Marine insurance	Risk Pooling Agreement
447.	Bass	16.06.99	[1999] L186/1	5 [1999] 782	Exemption	Standard pub lease agreements	Exclusive Purchasing Agreement
448.	Scottish and Newcastle	16.06.99	[1999] L186/28	5 [1999] 831	Exemption	Standard pub lease agreements	Exclusive Purchasing Agreement
449.	Europe Asia Trade Agreements	30.04.99	[1999] L193/23	5 [1999] 1380	Non-exemption	Shippping	Supply Restrictions & Information Exchange
450.	CEGETEL+4	20.05.99	[1999] L218/14	4 [2000] 106	Negative clearance exemption	Telecommunications	Joint Venture
451.	Télécom Dévéloppement	27.07.99	[1999] L218/24	4 [2000] 124	Negative clearance	Telecommunications	Joint Venture
452.	NVB–GSA	08.09.99	[1999] L271/28	4 [2000] 137	Negative clearance	Banking	Co-operation Agreement
453.	Reims II	15.09.99	[1999] L275/17	4 [2000] 704	Exemption	Postal services	Co-operation Agreement, Price Fixing Agreement
454.	BIB/Open	15.09.99	[1999] L312/1	4 [2000] 901	Exemption	Digital interactive television	Joint Venture

Table 1

No.	NAME	DATE	O.J.	C.M.L.R.	TYPE OF DECISION	PRODUCT	SUBJECT
455.	Football tickets	20.07.99	[2000] L5/55	4 [2000] 963	Infringement 82	Football match tickets	Discrimination
456.	Virgin/BA	14.07.99	[2000] L30/1	4 [2000] 999	Article 82 infringement	Air transport/Travel agency	Rebates and Discounts
457.	FEG & TU	26.10.99	[2000] L39/1	4 [2000] 1208	Article 81 infringement	Electrical installation equipment	Collective Exclusive Dealing, Retail Price Maintenance
458.	Scottish & Newcastle II	14.12.99	[2000] L49/37	5 [2000] 75	Article 15(1)	Beer	Incorrect Information
459.	GEAE	14.09.99	[2000] L58/16	5 [2000] 49	Exemption	Aero-engines	Joint Venture
460.	Eurovision	10.05.00	[2000] L151/18	5 [2000] 650	Exemption	TV Sport Programmes	Co-operation Agreement
461.	CECED	24.01.00	[2000] L187/47	5 [2000] 635	Exemption	Domestic applicances	Common Quality Standard
462.	Spring & Inntrepreneur	29.06.00	[2000] L195/49	5 [2000] 948	Clearance	Standard pub lease agreements	Exclusive Purchasing Agreement
463.	Spanish Airports	26.07.00	[2000] L208/36	5 [2000] 967	Article 86 (ex 90)	Airport landing fees	Discriminatory Discounts
464.	FETTCSA	16.05.00	[2000] L268/1	5 [2000] 1011	Article 81 infringement	Shipping	No Discount Agreement, Discount Ban
465.	Amino Acids	07.06.00	[2000] L152/24	5 [2001] 10	Article 81 infringement	Synthetic Lysine	Price & Sales Volume Fixing, Exchange of Information
466.	Nathan Bricolux	05.07.00	[2001] L54/1	4 [2001] 33	Article 81 infringement	Educational material	Preventing Parallel Trade (Retail Price Maintenance)
467.	Opel Nederland	20.09.00	[2001] L59/1	4 [2001] 40	Article 81 infringement	Motor vehicles	Preventing Parallel Trade
468.	Italian Post	21.12.00	[2001] L63/59	5 [2001] 15	Article 86 (ex 90)	Postal services	Exclusive Rights
469.	Unisource	29.12.00	[2001] L52/31	—	Clearance	Telecommunications	Joint Venture
470.	Deutsche Post	20.03.01	[2001] L125/27	5 [2001] 3	Article 82 infringement	Parcel services	Fidelity Rebates & Predatory Pricing

No.	NAME	DATE	O.J.	C.M.L.R.	TYPE OF DECISION	PRODUCT	SUBJECT
471.	UEFA Broadcasting	19.04.01	[2001] L171/13	5 [2001] 17	Clearance	Broadcasting	Broadcasting Restrictions
472.	Duales	20.04.01	[2001] L166/1	5 [2001] 16	Article 82 infringement	Packaging recovery	Trade Mark Licence Agreement
473.	Glaxo Wellcome	08.05.01	[2001] L302/1	4 [2001] 11	Article 81 prohibition	Drugs	Geographical Price Discrimination
474.	Volkswagen	29.06.01	[2001] L262/14	5 [2001] 1309	Article 81 infringement	Cars	Retail Price Maintenance
475.	SAS/Maersk Air	18.07.01	[2001] L265/15	5 [2001] 31	Article 81 infringement	Air transport	Cartel
476.	Identrus	31.07.01	[2001] L249/12	5 [2001] 1294	Article 81 negative clearance	Electronic commerce	Co-operation
477.	VISA	09.08.01	[2001] L293/24	4 [2002] 4[3]	Article 81 negative clearance	Credit cards	Resale Conditions
478.	DSD	20.04.01	[2001] L166/1	5 [2002] 609	Article 82 infringement	Waste collection	License Conditions
479.	JCB	21.12.00	[2002] L69/1	4 [2002] 37	Article 81 infringement	Construction & earth moving equipment	Selective Distribution
480.	Eco Emballages	15.06.01	[2001] L233/37	5 [2001] 30	Clearance	Waste collection & recovery	Co-operation
481.	Michelin	20.06.01	[2002] L143/1	5 [2002] 8	Article 82 infringement	Tyres	Fidelity Rebates
482.	Graphite Electrodes	18.06.01	[2002] L100/1	5 [2002] 17	Article 81 infringement	Graphite electrodes	Cartel
483.	DPAG Cross-border mail	25.07.01	[2001] L331/40	4 [2002] 17	Article 82 infringement	Cross-border mailings	Discrimination
484.	DSD II	17.09.01	[2001] L319/1	4 [2002] 12	Clearance	Sales packaging, collection & recovery	Exclusive/Market Partitioning
485.	SNELPD	23.10.01	[2002] L120/19	—	Article 86 (ex 90)	Mail preparation	Scrutiny of Statutory Monopolist
486.	De Post/La Poste	05.12.01	[2002] L61/32	4 [2002] 36	Article 82 infringement	Mail services	Tying

[3] C.M.L.R. references from 2002 onwards are to the unique citation number.

Table 1

No.	NAME	DATE	O.J.	C.M.L.R.	TYPE OF DECISION	PRODUCT	SUBJECT
487.	Soda Ash	13.12.00	[2003] L10/1	—	Article 81 infringement	Soda ash	Cartel
488.	Soda Ash (Solvay)	13.12.00	[2003] L10/10	—	Article 82 infringement	Soda ash	Exclusionary Practices
489.	Soda Ash (ICI)	13.12.00	[2003] L10/33	—	Article 82 infringement	Soda ash	Exclusionary Practices
490.	Mercedes Benz	10.10.01	[2002] L257/1	4 [2003] 2	Article 81 infringement	Cars	Preventing Parallel Trade
491.	Vitamins	21.11.01	[2003] L6/1	4 [2003] 22	Article 81 infringement	Vitamins	Cartel
492.	Citric Acid	05.12.01	[2002] L239/18	5 [2002] 24	Article 81 infringement	Citric acid	Cartel
493.	Luxembourg Brewers	05.12.01	[2002] L253/21	5 [2002] 30	Article 81 infringement	Beer	Cartel
494.	German Bank Charges	11.12.01	[2003] L15/1	4 [2003] 18	Article 81 infringement	Currency exchange	Cartel
495.	AuA/LH	05.07.02	[2002] L242/25	4 [2003] 7	Exemption	Air transport	Joint Venture
496.	Visa II	24.07.02	[2002] L318/17	4 [2002] 8	Exemption	Credit cards	Pricing Agreement
497.	Industrial Gases	24.07.02	[2003] L84/1 and L123/49	5 [2003] 8	Article 81 infringement	Industrial & medical gases	Cartel
498.	IFPI Simulcasting	08.10.02	[2003] L107/58	5 [2003] 5	Exemption	Internet broadcasting	One-Stop Shop Authorisation
499.	Seamless Steel Tubes	08.12.99	[2003] L140/1	—	81 fines	Seamless Steel Tubes	Cartel
500.	Interbrew & Alken-Maes	07.08.03	[2003] L200/1	—	81 fines	Beer	Cartel
501.	Zinc Phosphate	11.12.01	[2003] L153/1	5 [2003] 14	81 fines	Zinc phosphate	Cartel
502.	Carbonless Paper	20.12.01	[2004] L115/1	—	81 fines	Carbonless Paper	Cartel
503.	Austrian Banks	11.06.02	[2004] L56/1	5 [2004] 10	81 fines	Banks	Cartel
504.	Methionine	02.07.02	[2003] L255/1	4 [2004] 20	81 fines	Animal feed	Cartel
505.	Ninentendo	30.10.02	[2003] L255/34	4 [2004] 8	81 fines	Video games	Preventing Parallel Trade
506.	Christies/Sotheby's	30.10.02	—	—	81 fines	Auction sales	Cartel
507.	Revised TACA	14.11.02	[2003] L26/53	4 [2003] 21	Exemption	Shipping	Liner Conferences

No.	NAME	DATE	O.J.	C.M.L.R.	TYPE OF DECISION	PRODUCT	SUBJECT
508.	Methyglucamine	27.11.02	[2004] L38/18	4 [2004] 30	81 fines	Chemicals	Cartel
509.	Food flavour enhancers	17.12.02	[2004] L75/1	5 [2004] 11	81 fines	Flavour enhancers	Cartel
510.	Speciality graphite	17.12.02	—	—	81 fines	Graphite products	Cartel
511.	Plasterboard	27.11.02	—	—	81 fines	Plasterboard	Cartel
512.	Concrete reinforcing bars	17.12.02	—	—	81 fines	Concrete reinforcing bars	Cartel
513.	French beef	02.04.03	[2003] L209/12	5 [2003] 18	81 fines	Beef	Cartel
514.	Network Sharing UK	30.04.03	[2003] L200/59	4 [2004] 25	Exemption	Mobile telephony	Network Sharing
515.	Deutsche Telekom	21.05.03	[2003] L163/9	4 [2004] 16	82 fines	Fixed telephony	Price Squeeze
516.	Wanadoo	16.07.03	—	5 [2005] 5	82 fines	Broadband internet	Predatory Pricing
517.	Yamaha	16.07.03	—	—	81 fines	Musical instruments	Selective Distribution
518.	German networking sharing	16.07.03	[2003] L75/32	—	Exemption	Mobile telephony	Network Sharing
519.	UEFA	23.07.03	[2003] L291/25	4 [2004] 9	Exemption	Football TV rights	Joint Selling
520.	NDC/IMS	13.08.03	[2003] L268/69	5 [2003] 15	Interim measures	Industry norms	Refusal to License
521.	Georg/Ferrovie	25.08.03	[2004] L111/17	4 [2004] 26	82 fines	Railways	Access Refusal
522.	Austrian Waste	17.10.03	[2004] L75/59	5 [2004] 22	Exemption	Packaging waste	Collection Scheme
523.	Reims II	23.10.03	[2004] L56/76	5 [2004] 2	Exemption	Postal services	Cross-border Mail Changes
524.	Organic peroxides	10.12.03	—	5 [2005] 14	81 fines	Chemicals	Cartel
525.	Carbon & Graphite products	03.12.03	[2004] L125/45	—	81 fines	Carbon & graphite	Cartel
526.	Industrial Copper Tubes	16.12.03	[2004] L125/50	—	81 fines	Copper tubes	Cartel
527.	Telenor/Canal+	29.12.03	—	—	Exemption	Pay TV	Exclusive Distribution
528.	Microsoft	24.03.04	—	4 [2005] 19	82 fines	Operating systems	Typing and Refusal to License
529.	Air France/Alitalia	07.04.02	07.04.04	—	Exemption	Airlines	Strategic Alliance
530.	Topps	26.05.04	—	—	81 fines	Pokémon cards	Preventing Parallel Trade

Table 1

No.	NAME	DATE	O.J.	C.M.L.R.	TYPE OF DECISION	PRODUCT	SUBJECT
531.	Clearstream	02.06.04	—	5 [2005] 22	82 fines	Securities clearing	Refusal to Supply, Price Discriminations
532.	Eurocontrol	12.02.04	—	—	Rejection of complaint	Air traffic control	Concept of Undertaking
533.	CIK-FIA	19.03.04	—	—	Rejection of complaint	Tyres	Private Tender Procedures
534.	IMAX	25.03.04	—	—	Rejection of complaint	Cinema projection systems	Excessive Pricing & Tying
535.	Belgian Architects	24.06.04	—	4 [2005] 10	81 fines	Architects' fees	Price Fixing
536.	Scandlines	23.07.04	—	4 [2006] 23	82 rejection of complaint	Port services	Excessive Pricing, Discrimination
537.	Sundbusserne	23.07.04	—	4 [2006] 22	82 rejection of complaint	Port services	Excessive Pricing, Discrimination
538.	Copper Tubes	03.09.04	—	4 [2006] 11	81 fines	Copper plumbing tubes	Cartel
539.	French Brewers	29.09.04	—	4 [2006] 12	81 fines	Beer	Market Sharing, Non-Acquisition Agreement
540.	Spanish Raw Tobacco	20.10.04	—	4 [2006] 16	81 fines	Tobacco	Cartel
541.	German Postal Law	20.10.04	—	4 [2006] 17	Article 86	Postal services	Discounts
542.	Needles	26.10.04	—	4 [2005] 14	81 fines	Needles	Cartel
543.	Choline chloride	09.12.04	—	4 [2005] 1	81 fines	Choline chloride	Cartel
544.	Bundesliga Broadcasting	19.01.05	[2005] L134/46	4 [2005] 26	9 commitments	Broadcasting rights	Joint Selling
545.	AstraZeneca	15.06.05	—	—	82 fines	Pharmaceuticals	Misleading Patent Offices, Product Withdrawal, Surrendering Marketing Authorisation
546.	CocaCola	22.06.05	[2005] L253/21	4 [2006] 27	9 commitments	Soft drinks	Exclusivity, Rebates, Tying

No.	NAME	DATE	O.J.	C.M.L.R.	TYPE OF DECISION	PRODUCT	SUBJECT
547.	Microsoft Monitoring Trustee	28.07.05	—	—	7 remedy enforcement	Software	Appointment of Monitoring Trustee
548.	European Cement Producers	28.09.05	—	—	81 rejection of complaint	Cement	Joint Standards
549.	Peugeot	05.10.05	—	—	81 fines	Cars	Preventing Parallel Trade
550.	Italian Raw Tobacco	20.10.05	—	4 [2006] 29	81 fines	Tobacco	Cartel
551.	FA Premier League	22.03.06	—	—	9 commitments	Broadcasting rights	Joint Selling
552.	Repsol	12.04.06	—	—	9 commitments	Petrol distribution	Exclusive Supply
553.	De Beers	22.02.06	—	5 [2006] 26	9 commitments	Diamonds	Distribution
554.	Methacrylates	31.05.06	—	—	81 fines	Methacrylates	Cartel
555.	Microsoft Penalty Payments	12.07.06	—	—	24 remedy	Software	Non-compliance with infringement decision
556.	Dutch Bitumen	13.09.06	—	—	81 fines	Bitumen	Cartel
557.	Alloy Surcharge Readoption	20.12.06	—	—	65 CS fines	Steel	Price fixing
558.	Gas Insulated Switchgear	24.01.07	—	—	81 fines	Switchgear	Cartel
559.	Dutch Brewers	18.04.07	—	—	81 fines	Beer	Cartel

TABLE 2

LIST OF CASES REPORTED IN COMPETITION REPORTS (GENERAL COMPETITION RULES)

NAME	SUBJECT	REP.	PARA.	REFERENCE
Sheet Glass	Market Sharing	1	4	III,1,B,2
	Common Prices			III,1,B,3
International Cable	Market Sharing	1	4	III,1,B,2
Cleaning Products	Market Sharing	1	4	III,1,B,2
Remington Rand	Trademark Assignment	1	64	V,4
Dutch Liquorice	Common Rebate Policy	2	34	III,1,B,3
				III,1,B,5
ADOX	Selective Distribution, Export Ban	2	43	IV,3,F,1
Tripoli Oil Agreements	Extra-territoriality	2	61	I,3,A
Dutch Cartridges	Collective RPM	3	55	III,1,B,3
	Information Exchange			
	Collective Exclusive Dealing			III,1,B,5
Eumaprint	Exhibition Agreement	3	57	III,6
Railway Rolling Stock	Article 86/Unfair Terms	3	68	VII,2,B
Dutch Record Agreement	Collective Exclusive Dealing	4	76	III,1,B,5
Belgian & Dutch Electrodes	Common Rebate Policy	4	78	III,1,B,3
Glass Industry	Common Rebate Policy	4	79	III,1,B,3
Dior & Lancôme	Selective Distribution	4	93	IV,3
Constructa	Guarantee	4	109	IV,1,F,2
				IV,3,F,3
SACEM & SABAM	Article 86/Unfair Terms	4	112	VII,1,C
Brazilian Coffee	Customer Limitation Clause	5	33	IV,1,F,4
IBC	Preventing Parallel Trade	5	33	IV,6,B,4
Safety Glass	Joint Sales	5	34	III,1,B,4
Lino Cartel	Common Prices	5	35	III,1,B,3
	Common Rebate Policy			
	Common Sales Conditions			III,1,B,4

Table 2

NAME	SUBJECT	REP.	PARA.	REFERENCE
Belgian Wood Cartel	Common Purchasing Policy	5	37	III,1,B,4
Fruit Agreements	Production Quota	5	38	III,1,B,1
Non Ferrous Metals	Information Exchange	5	39	III,1,B,2
Ship Chains	Agreed Recommended Prices	5	40	III,1,B,3
Dutch Design Institute	Design Right Licences	5	69	V,5
Leopold/ASF	Trademark Delimitation Agreement	5	70	V,4,D
Herbage Seed	Price Alignment	6	119	III,1,B,3
	Trade Association			III,5,A,2
	How to Complain			X,2,A,2
Dutch Transport Insurers	Collective Exclusive Dealing	6	120	III,1,B,5
	Trade Association			III,5,A,2
Sand Producers	Market Sharing	6	122	III,1,B,2
Nitrogeneous Fertilisers	Market Sharing	6	126	III,1,B,2
Beecham Pharma	Exclusive Distribution	6	129	IV
	Customer Limitation Clause			IV,1,F,4
	Removal Immunity from Fines			X,2,E,2
Paper Machine Wire	Information Exchange	6	134	III,1,B,2
				III,1,B,3
Peugeot/Zimmern	Patent Licensing	6	159	V,2
BBC	Copyright Licences	6	163	V,5
	How to Complain			X,2,A,2
The Old Man and the Sea	Copyright Licences	6	164	V,5
PME	Appreciability of Restriction	7	21	II,1,D,3
Zip Fasteners	Intra-enterprise Conspiracy	7	29	I,1,5
	Control			B2,2,C,1
Sarabex	Collective Exclusive Dealing	8	35	III,1,B,5
	Trade Association			III,5
Man-made Fibres	Crisis Cartel	8	42	III,1,B,7
	Settlement			X,2,D
Michelin	Merger Control	8	146	B2,2,D,3
Avebe/KSH	Merger Control	8	147	B2,2,D,3
PSA	How to Complain	8	149	X,2,A,2
	Merger Control	11	46	B2,2,D,3

NAME	SUBJECT	REP.	PARA.	REFERENCE
Dutch Pharmaceuticals	Collective RPM	8	81	III,1,B,3
	Collective Exclusive Dealing			III,1,B,5
	Trade Association			III,5
	Governmental Approval			VIII,2,B
Hachette	Article 86/Exclusive Distribution	8	114	VII,2,B
	Settlement			X,2,D
Pentacon	Patent Licensing	8	118	V,2
	No-challenge Clause			V,2,D,5
Clutch-type Disc Brakes	Patent Licensing	8	121	V,2
	National Courts			X,4,B,3
Bayer/Tanabe	Trademark Delimitation Agreement	8	125	V,4,D
Department Stores	Trade Associations	9	89	III,5
BP/Ruhrgas	Co-operation Agreement	9	94	III,2,A
	Merger Control			B2,2,D,3
ACC/Fabry	Patent Licensing/No-Challenge Clause	9	107	V,2,D,5
Zoller/Frölich	Patent Dispute Settlement	9	109	V,2,D,7
Fondasol	Patent Licensing/Export Ban	9	112	V,2,D,1
France/Suralmo	Patent Licensing/Field of Use	9	114	V,2,D,5
	No Sub-licensing			
English Football	Copyright Licences	9	116	V,5
Ernest Benn	Copyright Licences	9	118	V,5
Plant Royalty Bureau	Breeder's Right Licences	9	120	V,5
ITA-Tubi	Merger Control	9	126	B2,2,D,3
Vallourec	Merger Control	9	128	B2,2,D,3
Kaiser/Estel	Joint Venture	9	131	VI
	Merger Control			B2,2,C,1
				B2,2,D,3
Coats Patons	Merger Control	9	132	B2,2,D,3
Fichtel	Merger Control	9	132	B2,2,D,3
Boat Equipment	Article 86/Discrimination	10	19	VII,2,B
Moulinex	Guarantee	10	122	IV,1,F,2
				IV,3,F,3
Seita	Exclusive Distribution	10	124	IV

TABLE 2

Table 2

NAME	SUBJECT	REP.	PARA.	REFERENCE
	Article 86			VII,2,B
Preflex/Lipski	Patent Licensing/Post-term Royalties	10	126	V,2,D,6
Nodet/Gougis	Patent Licensing/Improvements	10	127	V,2,D,5
Bramley/Gilbert	Patent Licensing/Exclusive Purchasing	10	128	V,2,D,2
Cartoux/Terrapin	Know-how/Post-term Use Restriction	10	129	V,3,D,7
Poroton	Common Trademark	10	130	III,2,C,8
				V,4,C
Sterling Airways	Article 86/Unfair Prices	10	136	VII,2B
	Air Transport			IX,5,B
Winniger Domgarten	Trademark Delimitation Agreement	10	133	V,4,D
Pilkington/BSN	Settlement	10	152	X,2,D
	Merger Control			B2,2,D,3
Michelin/Kleber	Merger Control	10	156	B2,2,D,3
Baxter Tavenol	Merger Control	10	156	B2,2,D,3
Soda-Ash	Exclusive Purchasing	11	73	IV,2,A
Concast/Mannesmann	Patent Pooling	11	92	III,1,B,5
				III,2,C,2
IGR Stereo TV	Patent Pooling	11	94	III,1,B,5
				III,2,C,2
Tyler/Linde	Trademark Licensing	11	96	V,4
	Duration of Validity			V,4,D,3
Osram/Airam	Trademark Delimitation Agreement	11	97	V,4,D
	Article 86/Abusive Trademark Registration			VII,2,B
Stemra	Copyright Licences	11	98	V,5
Amicon/Fortia	Merger Control	11	112	B2,2,D,3
Woollen Fabrics	Agreed Prices Increases	12	71	III,1,B,3
	Settlement			X,2,C
Feldmühle/Stora	Common Sales Policy	12	73	III,1,B,4
	Joint Venture			VI
	Settlement			X,2,D
Matsushita	Guarantee	12	77	IV,1,F,2
				IV,3,F,3
Air-Forge	Production Quota	12	85	III,1,B,1

NAME	SUBJECT	REP.	PARA.	REFERENCE
	Market Sharing			III,1,B,2
	Joint Venture			VI,2,4
Spitzer/Van Hool	Patent Licensing	12	86	V,2
	No-competition Clause			V,2,D,2
	No-challenge Clause			V,2,D,5
	Royalties and Non-use			V,2,D,6
	Know-how Licensing			V,3
Nielson/Hordell	Copyright Licences	12	88	V,5
Eagle Star	Merger Control	12	103	B2,2,D,3
British Sugar/Berisford	Rejection of Complaint	12	104	X,2,C,3
				X,2,E,4
	Merger Control			B2,2,D,3
Zinc Producers	Crisis Cartel	13	56	III,1,B,7
Ford Germany	Guarantee	13	104	IV,1,F,2
				IV,3,F,3
	Preventing Parallel Trade			IV,6
Euglucon	Preventing Parallel Trade	13	107	IV,6
Knoll/Hille-Form	Copyright Licences	13	142	V,5
BIEM-IFPI	Preventing Parallel Trade	13	147	IV,6
	Copyright Licences			V,5
Polaroid	Article 86/Refusal to Supply	13	155	VII,2,B
British Bright Bar	Merger Control	13	160	B2,2,D,3
Dillingen	Merger Control	13	162	B2,2,D,3
British Steel	Merger Control	13	163	B2,2,D,3
Fagersta	Merger Control	13	164	B2,2,D,3
British Sugar/Napier Brown	Merger Control	13	165	B2,2,D,3
Maison des Bibliothèques	No Active Sales Outside Territory	14	68	IV,1,F,1
	Discriminatory Pricing			IV,1,F,3
Fiat	Guarantee	14	70	IV,1,F,2
	Selective Distribution and Parallel Trade			IV,3,E,3
Shell/AKZO	Joint Venture	14	85	VI,2,3
BBC/Grenfell/Holt	Joint Venture	14	86	VI
Roquette/National Starch	Joint Venture	14	87	VI,5,2

Table 2

NAME	SUBJECT	REP.	PARA.	REFERENCE
IGR	Patent Pooling	14	92	III,1,B,5
UNARCO	Patent Licensing/Post-term Royalties	14	93	V,2,D,6
IBM	Article 86/Tying	14	94	VII,2,B
	Settlements	16	75	
		17	85	X,2,D
		21	106	
Philip Morris	Settlement	14	98	X,2,D
	Merger Control			B2,2,D,2
Ashland Oil	Merger Control	14	109	B2,2,D,3
Stanton & Stavely	Merger Control	14	110	B2,2,D,3
Interlübcke	Selective Distribution	15	15	IV,3
	Resale Prices Maintenance			IV,3,F,4
Memrad	Selective Distribution	15	64	IV,3
Rodenstock	Selective Distribution	15	65	IV,3
Italian Spectacles	Resale Prices Maintenance	15	66	IV,3,F,4
Luxembourg Car Insurance	Discrimination Based upon Nationality	15	71	IV,6,B,4
	Financial Services			IX,6,B
VFA/SAVER	Specialisation Agreement	15	78	III,3,A
GEMA	Copyright Licences	15	81	V,5
	Article 86			VII,2,B
BB/TGWU	How to Complain	16	43	X,2,A,2
IBC	Customer Limitation Clause	16	54	IV,1,F,4
VEB/Shell	Collective RPM	16	55	III,1,B,3
				IV,1,F,3
	Rejection of Complaint			X,2,E,4
EBU	Common Prices	16	62	III,1,B,3
United Reprocessors	Joint Venture	16	69	VI
ICL/Fujitsu	Co-operation Agreement	16	72	III,2,A
	Know-how Licensing			V,3
	Design Right Licences			V,5
Instituto/IMC & Angus	Article 86/Exclusive Purchasing	16	76	VII,2,B
Distillers	Discriminatory Pricing between Territories	17	65	IV,1,F,3

NAME	SUBJECT	REP.	PARA.	REFERENCE
Sony	Guarantee	17	67	IV,1,F,2
Montedison/Hercules	Joint Venture	17	69	VI
Carnaud/Sofreb	Joint Venture	17	70	VI
	Settlement			X,2,D
	Merger Control			B2,2,D,2
Volvo	Article 86/Refusal to Supply	17	72	VII,2,B
PRB/Shell	Fourth Condition 85(3)	17	74	II,A,4
	Joint Venture			VI
Standardised Bottles	Rejection of Complaint	17	75	X,2,C,3
				X,2,E,4
Macron/Angus	Article 86/Predatory Pricing	17	81	VII,2,B
	Settlement			X,2,D
Olio Fiat	Selective Distribution/Exclusive Purchasing	17	84	IV,3,F,3
	Article 86/Tying			VII,2,B
London European/SABENA	Article 86/Refusal to Supply	17	86	VII,2,B
Nutrasweet	Cumulative Effect of Agreement on Trade	18	50	I,2,B,3
	Exclusive Purchasing			IV,2,A
Citroën	Regulation 123/85	18	56	IV,3,C
	Parallel Trade			IV,6
EMC/DSM	Joint Venture	18	58	VI
FIEC-CTETB	Co-operation Agreement	18	62	III,2,A
EWIS	Information Exchange	18	63	III,1,B,2
				III,1,B,3
				III,1,B,4
				III,2,A
Campari	Trademark Licensing	18	69	V,4
Irish Distillers	Bidding Agreement	18	80	III,1,B,3
	Joint Venture			VI
	Settlement			X,2,D
	Merger Control			B2,2,D,1
British Airways	Merger Control	18	81	B2,2,D,1
Finnpap	Common Sales Conditions	19	44	III,1,B,4
	Joint Venture			VI,2,4

Table 2

NAME	SUBJECT	REP.	PARA.	REFERENCE
AKZO	Guarantee and Parallel Trade	19	45	IV,1,F,2
				IV,6
	Settlement			X,2,D
Volkswagen	Selective Distribution and Parallel Trade	19	48	IV,3,E,3
Coca Cola	Article 86/Rebates	19	50	VII,2,B
	Settlement			X,2,D
Fluke/Philips	Distribution between Competitors	19	54	IV,1,F,5
IATA	Air Transport	19	58	IX,5,B
Syntex/Synthelabo	Trademark Delimitation Agreement	19	59	V,4,D
Pilkington/Covina	Patent Licensing	19	60	V,2
Filtrona/Tabacalera	Article 86/Tying	19	61	VII,2,B
Industrial gases	English Clause	19	62	IV,2,E,3
	Article 86/Exclusive Purchasing			VII,2,B
Gestetner & Xerox	Article 86/Market Share	19	63	VII,1,C
TWIL/Bridon	Merger Control	19	64	B2,2,C,1
Rhône Poulenc/Monsanto	Merger Control	19	67	B2,2,D,3
Consolidated Goldfields	Settlement	19	68	X,2,B
	Merger Control			B2,2,D,3
Carnaud/Metal Box	Merger Control	19	69	B2,2,D,2
Stena-Holder	Merger Control	19	70	B2,2,D,2
Irish Timber Importers	Collective Exclusive Dealing	20	98	III,1,B,5
Hershey/Herschi	Trademark Delimitation Agreement	20	111	V,4,D
Ford	Design Right Licences	20	112	V,5
Railway Companies	Regulation 1017/68	20	115	IX,3,B
Orptie	Buying Group	20	120	III,2,C,11
Flying German Officials	Article 90(3)	20	357	VIII,1,B,3
Danish PTT	Article 90(3)	20	358	VIII,1,B,3
Flying Belgian Officials	Article 90(3)	21	33	VIII,1,B,3
Elders/Grand Metropolitan	Exclusive Purchasing	21	68	IV,2,A
Campina	Regulation 26	21	83	IX,1,B
Dupont Merck	Joint Venture	21	85	VI,5,1

NAME	SUBJECT	REP.	PARA.	REFERENCE
Apollinaris/Schweppes	Joint Venture	21	87	VI,5,1
DHL International	Joint Venture	21	88	VI,5,1
KLM/Transavia	Merger Control	21	89	B2,2,D,2
Amadeus/Sabre	Computer Reservation Systems	21	93	IX,5,B
UK Small Mines (Naloo)	Article 86/Buying Power	21	107	VII,1,C
	Energy			VIII,1,B,4
France Telecom	Telecommunications	21	324	VIII,1,B,4
Transmediterranean	Article 90(3)	21	334	VIII,1,B,3
New Focus Health Care	Rejection of Complaint	21	p.333	X,2,E,4
	National Courts			X,4,B,3
Iqbal	Export to Third States	21	p.334	I,2,C,2
	Rejection of Complaint			X,2,E,4
BDO Binder	Co-operation Agreement	21	p.335	III,2,A
Mercury	Telecommunications	21	p.335	VIII,1,B,4
Halifax	Financial Services/Exclusive Purchasing	21	p.335	IX,6,B
Tepar	Financial Services	21	p.336	IX,6,B
Carlsberg/Courage	Distribution between Competitors	22	130	IV,1,F,5
Carlsberg/Tetley	Joint Venture	22	131	VI,5,1
SHG/EDF & NEC	Energy	22	142	VIII,1,B,4
Milk Marketing Board	Regulation 26	22	161	IX,1,B,1
Chiquita/Fyffes	Article 86/Trademark Abuse	22	168	VII,2,B
VOTOB	Competition and Environment	22	177	XI,1,4
Holyhead	Article 86/Maritime Transport	22	219	IX,4,B
	Interim Measures			X,2,E,2
GEC/Alstom-Fiat	Notification	22	p.415	X,2,A,1
British Sheep Breeders	Trade Associations	22	p.416	III,5,B,1
Infonet	Telecommunications	22	p.416	VIII,1B,4
DSB	Regulation 4056/86	22	p.418	IX,4,B
Center Parcs	Agency Agreements	22	p.420	IV,4
Philips Thomson Sagem	Joint Venture	23	215	VI,1
Alenia Honeywell	Joint Venture	23	216	VI,5,2.3

Table 2

NAME	SUBJECT	REP.	PARA.	REFERENCE
Intrax	Joint Venture	23	218	VI,5,1.2 and VIII,1,B,4.5
Pego	Exclusive Supply	23	222	VIII,B,4.7
DISMA	Joint Venture	23	223	VI,5,1.2
Texaco	Franchising	23	225	IV,2,C and IV,5,C
Sevel	Joint Venture	23	227	III,4,C
Rover	RPM	23	228	IV,1,F,3.1
FIAT	Selective Distribution	23	229	IV,3,C
EAC	Liner Conference	23	230	IX,4,B
Irish Club	Sea Transport	23	233	IX,4,B
IATA	Cargo Tariffs	23	238	IX,5,B
Sabre	Computer Reservation Systems	23	239	IX,5,B
Spa Monopole	Exclusionary Practices	23	240	XI,1,4
Cyclopore	Patent Licensing	23	241	V,2,A
Papeteries de Golbey	Joint Venture	23	244	VI,3,4
ISMA	Banking Agreement	23	p.453	IX,6,B.1
Acriss	Computer Reservation System	23	p.454	II,2,A
BP/Montedipe	Capacity Agreement	23	p.455	II,1,B,1.3.2
Enimont/Orkem	Specialisation Agreement	23	p.457	II,3,A
Abim Card	Co-operation Agreement	23	p.458	II,2,A
BSB	Copyright	23	p.459	V,5,C,1.1
BBC	Copyright	23	p.459	V,5,A
Philips/Matsushita	Patent Pooling	23	p.460	II,1,B,5.7
Microsoft	Exclusionary Practices	24	p.365, paras 197, 200, 206, 212	
Interbrew	Exclusive Licencing	24	p.351, paras 198, 201, 204, 209, 213	
Camelot	Joint Venture	24	p.346	
Proctor & Gamble/Finaf	Joint Venture	24	p.249	

NAME	SUBJECT	REP.	PARA.	REFERENCE
Lederle	Refund to Licence	24	p.353	
Cicra	Discounts	24	p.361	
UCB	Exclusive Supply Agreements	24	p.362	
Oliebranches	Co-operation Agreement	24	p.368	
Ducros/DHL	Co-operation Agreement	24	p.371	
Unilever/Mars	Exclusive Purchasing	25	p.137, para. 41	
Organon	Preventing Parallel Trade	25	p.142, paras 37, 38	
Morlaix	Essential Facilities	25	p.120, para. 43	
ATR/BAe	Joint Venture	25	p.128, paras 61, 62	
Gas Interconnector	Joint Venture	25	p.125, para. 82	
Pelikan/Kyocera	Exclusionary Practices	25	p.140, para. 87	
Vebacom	Telecommunication	25	para. 111	
Dresser/Ingersoll	Cartel with Minority Acquisitions	25	p.116	
Minidiscs	Patent Licensing	25	p.123	
Aspen	Joint Venture	25	p.123	
General Electric/BASF	Joint Venture	25	p.124	
Sovereign Exploration	Joint Venture	25	p.124	
Exxon/Hoechst	Research and Development	25	p.125	
ACE	Joint Venture	25	p.127	
Sevel	Joint Venture	25	p.127	
ETSI	Industry Standard	25	p.131	
Global Satellite	Consortia	25	p.132	
Premiair	Air Transport	25	p.134	
Sony Peda	Selective Distribution	25	p.135	
Chanel	Selective Distribution	25	p.136	

Table 2

NAME	SUBJECT	REP.	PARA.	REFERENCE
MD Foods	Exclusive Purchasing	25	p.136	
Postal Cases	Remail	25	p.141	
Channel Five Broadcasting	Joint venture	26	p.142	VI,4
BF Goodricht/Messier Bugatti	Joint venture	26	p.143	VI,2.5
Finnish Wood	Joint sales	26	p.144	III,B,4.3.
CEPI-Carton Board	Information exchange	26	p.145	III,B,1.5
IBOS	Data processing	26	p.146	IX,B,4.
Eurogiro	Data processing	26	p.147	IX,B,1.
Finansrädet	Data Processing	26	148	IX,B,1.
ISAB Energy	Exclusive Purchasing	26	152	VI,2,A, VII,B,1.4.7
REN Turboga	Exclusive Purchasing	26	153	VI,2,A, VII,B,1.4.7
Transgas	Exclusive Purchasing	26	154	VI,2,A, VII,B,1.4.7
British Gas	Co-operation Agreement	26	155	VIII,B,1.4.7
Europay	Travel Cheques	26	154	IX,B,1.
British Nuclear	Supply Agreements	26	156	IX,1.47
IPS/Péchiney	Article 86	26	157	VII,2,B,23
Interbrew	Article 86	26	159	VII,2,B,15
Annex/Vira	Article 86	26	160	VII,2,B,2
Pelika Ray	Article 86	26	161	VII,2,B,3
Aéroports de Paris	Discriminatory Slot Allocation	26	162	IX,B
Novo/Nordisk	Tying	26	162	VII,B,12
CSK/Gist Brocades	Exclusive Distribution	26	163	VII,B,4, IV,F,5.1
Atlanta Olympic Games	Exclusive Distribution	26	164	IV,A
IRI/Nielsen	Tying	26	164	VII,2,12, X,D,21
GEN (Global European Network)	Strategic Alliances	27	128	VIII,1,4.6/III,2.12
Carnival & Airtours	Joint Venture	27	129	VI,1
Michelin & Continental	Joint Venture	27	129	VI,1
Sanofi & Bristol-Myers-Squibb	Joint Venture	27	130	VI,1
Hydro Texaco Holdings A/A-Preem (formerly OK Petroleum AB)	Joint Venture	27	131	VI,1
Scandairy	Joint Venture	27	131	VI,1

NAME	SUBJECT	REP.	PARA.	REFERENCE
HFC Bank plc/Bristish Gas Trading Ltd	Joint Venture	27	131	VI,1
British Dental Trade Association	Exhibition Agreement	27	134	II,6,A
Joint Operational Service Agreement and West Coast/ Mediterranean Agreement	Shipping Consortia	27	134	IX,4,B
Consortia arrangements between Sea-Land, P&O Neddlloyd, Maersk and OOCL ("Vessel-Sharing Agreements")	Shipping Consortia	27	134	IX,4,B
New Carribean Service (NCS) and Eurosal III	Shipping Consortia	27	137	IX,4,B
EUROCAR	Joint R&D	27	138	III,4,A
Swedish Match Sverige AB and Skandivisk Tobakskompagni A/S	Exclusive Manufacturing and Sales License between Competitors	27	138	V,3,E,5
Britannia Gas Condensate Field	Joint Sales	27	139	VIII,1,4.7
The GSM MoU standard international roaming agreement	Roaming Agreement	27	139	VIII,1,4.6
Microsoft/Santa Cruz Operation	Licensing Conditions	27	140	V,2,A/V,2,C,6.4
Relais & Châteaux	De Minimis	27	141	II,1,3.2
TARGET	Agreement on Payment Systems	27	142	IX,B,1
SWIFT	Agreement on Payment Systems	27	143	IX,B,1
Sport 7/KNVB	Football Rights	27	145	V,4,A
1998 Football World Cup	Exclusive Distribution	27	146	IV,2,A
The Smart Case—MC Micro Compact	Motor Car Distribution	27	147	IV,4,C
Ford Service Outlet Agreement	Motor Car Distribution	27	147	IV,4,C
BWI	Franchising Agreement	27	148	IV,6,A
Video Games: Sega and Nintendo	Licensing Agreement	27	148	V,2,C,2.1
Banksys/Belgacom	Joint Product	27	149	IX,B,1
Guérin Automobiles/Volvo France	Rejection of Complaint	27	150	—
Guérin Automobiles/Nissan France	Rejection of Complaint	27	150	—

Table 2

NAME	SUBJECT	REP.	PARA.	REFERENCE
Electrabel/Mixed intercommunal electricity distribution companies in Belgium	Electricity Distribution	27	150	VIII,1,4.7
ITT/Belgacom	Excessive Pricing	27	152	VIII,2,B,2
Digital	Tying	27	153	VII,2,B,12
Agreement on the joint control of BBL	Shareholders' Agreement on Joint Control	27	154	III,2,C,14
Stainless Steel	Cartel	28	p.137	I,1,A,1,1.1
British Sugar	Cartel	28	p.138	I,1,A,1,1.1
Greek Ferries	Cartel	28	p.140	I,1,A,1,1.1
Pre-insulated pipes	Cartel	28	p.140	I,A,1,1.1
Volkswagen-Audi	Preventing Parallel Trade	28	p.141	I,1,A,1,1.2
Van den Bergh Foods	Ice-cream Distribution	28	p.142	I,1,A,1,1.2
Italian cigarettes	Article 82	28	p.143	I,1,A,1,1.3
AFS/ADP	Article 82	28	p.144	I,1,A,1,1.3
Frankfurt/Main	Article 82	28	p.145	I,1,A,1,1.3
TACA	Article 82	28	p.145	I,1,A,1,1.3
Finnair/Maersk	Joint Venture	28	p.146	I,1,A,2,2.1,a
Canon/Kodak	Co-operation Agreement	28	P. 147	I,1,A,2,2.1,b
Pripps/Tuborg	Licensing Agreement	28	p.148	I,1,A,2,2.1,b
P&O Stena Line	Joint Venture	28	p.149	I,1,A,2,2.1,b
BDB	Joint Venture	28	p.149	I,1,A,2,2.1,b
EUCAR	R&D Agreements	28	p.150	I,1,A,2,2.1,c
ACEA	Environmental Commitments	28	p.151	I,1,A,2,2.1,c
EACEM	Common Quality Commitments	28	p.152	I,1,A,2,2.1,c
Valpak	Packaging Recovery Scheme	28	p.152	I,1,A,2,2.1,c
Stack	Joint Venture	28	p.153	I,1,A,2,2.1,c
Inmarsat	Joint Venture	28	p.154	I,1,A,2,2.1,c
DHLI	Joint Venture	28	p.155	I,1,A,2,2.1,c
Verbändevereinbarung	Electricity Grid Access Tariffs	28	p.156	I,1,A,2,2.1,c
TÜV/Cenelec	Harmonisation of Technical Standards	28	p.159	I,1,A,2,2.1,c

NAME	SUBJECT	REP.	PARA.	REFERENCE
Sony	Licensing Agreement	28	p.159	I,1,A,2,2.2
Danish Tennis Federation	Sponsorship Agreements	28	p.160	I,1,A,2,2.2
Sicasov	Seed Production Contracts	28	p.160	I,1,A,2,2.2
NALOO	Rejection of Complaint	28	p.162	I,1,A,3
IFCO	Rejection of Complaint	28	p.165	I,1,A,3
EUDIM	Rejection of Complaint	28	p.165	I,1,A,3
Microleader/Microsoft	Rejection of Complaint	28	p.166	I,1,A,3
Greene King/Roberts	Rejection of Complaint	28	p.167	I,1,A,3
Tambue	Rejection of Complaint	28	p.167	I,1,A,3
Vickers/Rolls-Royce	Rejection of Complaint	28	p.168	I,1,A,4
IRE/Nordion	Article 82	28	p.169	I,1,A,5
SPEGNN	Article 86 (ex 90)	28	p.170	I,1,A,5
FEG+TU	Collective Exclusive Dealing	29	p.135	I,A,1,1.1
Seamless steel tubes	Market Sharing	29	p.137	I,1,A,1,1.1
Lee Cooper	Preventing Parallel Trade	29	p.138	I,1,A,1,1.2
Portuguese airports	Article 86 (ex 90)	29	p.138	I,1,A,1,1.2
Finnish airports	Article 82	29	p.139	I,1,A,1,1.2
Virgin/BA	Article 82	29	p.139	I,1,A,1,1.2
Football World Cup	Article 82	29	p.140	I,1,A,1,1.2
ESAT Telecom	Access Agreement	29	p.141	I,1,A,2,2.1,a
GlobalOne II	Joint Venture	29	p.141	I,1,A,2,2.1,a
Farland Network	Network Linking Agreements	29	p.142	I,1,A,2,2.1,a
Cégétel+4	Joint Venture	29	p.142	I,1,A,2,2.1,a
Télécom Développement	Co-operation Agreements	29	p.143	I,1,A,2,2.1,a
MetroHoldings	Joint Venture	29	p.144	I,1,A,2,2.1,a
Symbian II	Joint Venture	29	p.144	I,1,A,2,2.1,a
Télévision par Satellite	Joint Venture	29	p.144	I,1,A,2,2.1,a
BIB	Joint Venture	29	p.145	I,1,A,2,2.1,a
UIP	Joint Venture	29	p.148	I,1,A,2,2.1,a
Revised TACA	Liner Conference	29	p.150	I,1,A,2,2.1,a

Table 2

NAME	SUBJECT	REP.	PARA.	REFERENCE
VSA2/CSAV	Joint Liner Service	29	p.151	I,1,A,2,2.1,a
P&O Stena Line	Joint Venture	29	p.152	I,1,A,2,2.1,a
CIA	Joint Venture	29	p.153	I,1,A,2,2.1,a
Ecomet	Joint Venture	29	p.153	I,1,A,2,2.1,a
GE/Pratt & Whitney	Joint Venture	29	p.154	I,1,A,2,2.1,a
Yoplait/Vallo	Joint Venture	29	p.155	I,1,A,2,2.1,a
Tractors	Information Exchanges	29	p.156	I,1,A,2,2.1,a
Dutch banks	Joint Processing Agreement	29	p.158	I,1,A,2,2.1,a
EPI code of conduct	Restrictions on Advertising	29	p.159	I,1,A,2,2.1,a
JAMA	Environmental Commitments	29	p.160	I,1,A,2,2.1,a
IDS	Trade Fair	29	p.160	I,1,A,2.2
Belgian newspapers	Selective Distribution	29	p.161	I,1,A,2,2.2
Microsoft Internet Explorer	Licensing & Distribution Agreements	29	p.162	I,1,A,2,2.2
CTRL	Track Access Agreements	29	p.163	I,1,A,2,2.2
Eurotunnel	Usage Contract	29	p.163	I,1,A,2,2.2
UK Beer	Pub Lease Agreements	29	p.164	I,1,A,2,2.2
Dutch electricity grid	Grid Access Agreements	29	p.165	I,1,A,2,2.3
Irish Interconnector	Capacity Allocation	29	p.165	I,1,A,2,2.3
Lille/UEFA	UEFA Rules	29	p.l66	I,1,A,3
TF1/France 2&3	Rejection of Complaint	29	p.167	I,1,A,3
M5/EBU	Rejection of Complaint	29	p.167	I,1,A,3
CanalSatellite/TPS	Exclusive Retransmission Rights	29	p.168	I,1,A,3
Info-Lab/Ricoh	Essential Facilities	29	p.169	I,1,A,3
Lif	Price Freeze and Quota Agreement	29	p.170	I,1,A,4
Telecommunications	Telecoms Sector Investigation	29	p.170	I,1,A,5
Anheuser-Busch	Infringement of Procedural Rules	29	p.171	I,1,A,6
Lysine	Cartel	30	p.141	I.A.1.1
FETTCSA	Transport Tariffs	30	p.141	I.A.1.1
Opel	Preventing Parallel Trade	30	p.142	I.A.1.2
JCB	Preventing Parallel Trade	30	p.143	I.A.1.2

NAME	SUBJECT	REP.	PARA.	REFERENCE
Nathan	Preventing Parallel Trade	30	p.144	I.A.1.2
Jigsaw	Joint Venture	30	p.144	I.A.2.1.1
Ogilvy/Acxiom	Joint Venture	30	p.145	I.A.2.1.1
OM & SOM	Joint Venture	30	p.145	I.A.2.1.1
CECED	Common Energy Efficiency Policy	30	p.145	I.A.2.1.2
Eurovision	Broadcasting Rights	30	p.146	I.A.2.1.2
DVD	Patent Pooling	30	p.147	I.A.2.1.2
Biffpack	Packaging Waste Collection Scheme	30	p.148	I.A.2.1.2
BIAC + BSS	Airport Transit Area Pricing	30	p.149	I.A.2.2
Inntrepreneur & Spring	Pub Lease Agreements	30	p.149	I.A.2.2
Spanish landing fees	Article 82 – Discounts	30	p.150	I.A.2.3
I.W./Skandia	Insurance Terms	30	p.151	I.A.3
Elonex/Microsoft	Article 82	30	p.152	I.A.3
DSF/EBU	Broadcasting Rights Licensing	30	p.152	I.A.3
Telecinco/EBU	Broadcasting Rights Licensing	30	p.152	I.A.3
UEFA	Ticket Sales Arrangements	30	p.153	I.A.3
Gas Natural/Endesa	Article 82	30	p.154	I.A.4
Statkraft/Elsam	Interconnector Capacity Access	30	p.155	I.A.4
Telefonica/Sogecable/AVS II	Broadcasting Rights	30	p.156	I.A.4
Nintendo	Preventing Parallel Trade	30	p.157	I.A.4
Sun/Microsoft	Article 82	30	p.158	I.A.4
Bank Cards	Bank Card Rules	30	p.159	I.A.4
Air France/Sabre	Discrimination	30	p.159	I.A.5
SAS/Maersk Air	Market Sharing	31	p.171	I.A.1.1
Sun-Air/SAS/Maersk Air	Market Sharing	31	p.171	I.A.1.1
Graphite electrodes	Cartel	31	p.172	I.A.1.1
Sodium Gluconate	Cartel	31	p.173	I.A.1.1
Vitamins	Cartel	31	p.174	I.A.1.1
Citric Acid	Cartel	31	p.176	I.A.1.1
Belgian Breweries	Cartel	31	p.177	I.A.1.1

Table 2

NAME	SUBJECT	REP.	PARA.	REFERENCE
Luxembourg Breweries	Cartel	31	p.180	I.A.1.1
Zinc Phosphate	Cartel	31	p.182	I.A.1.1
Bank Charges – Germany	Price Fixing	31	p.183	I.A.1.1
Carbonless Paper	Cartel	31	p.184	I.A.1.1
GlaxoWellcome	Preventing Parallel Trade	31	p.185	I.A.1.2
Volkswagen	Retail Price Maintenance	31	p.186	I.A.1.2
DaimlerChrysler	Preventing Parallel Trade	31	p.187	I.A.1.2.
Deutsche Post AG I	Article 82	31	p.189	I.A.1.3
Duales I	Article 82	31	p.189	I.A.1.3
Michelin	Article 82	31	p.190	I.A.1.3
IMS Health	Article 82	31	p.191	I.A.1.3
Deutsche Post AG II	Article 82	31	p.193	I.A.1.3
De Post/La Poste	Article 82	31	p.193	I.A.1.3
La Poste (France)	Article 86	31	p.193	I.A.1.4
P&O Stena Line 2	Joint Venture	31	p.194	I.A.2.1
bmi British Midland	Joint Venture	31	p.194	I.A.2.1
Grand Alliance	Liner Shipping Consortia	31	p.196	I.A.2.1
UEFA	Broadcasting Regulations	31	p.197	I.A.2.1
Europe to Carribean	Linershipping Consortium	31	p.198	I.A.2.1
Intelsat	Restructuring (Public to Private)	31	p.198	I.A.2.1
Identrus	E-commerce Network	31	p.198	I.A.2.1
Pro Europe	Packaging Waste Recovery Scheme	31	p.198	I.A.2.1
IATA cargo tariffs	Tariff Conference	31	p.199	I.A.2.1
Returpack/Returglas	Packaging Waste Recovery Scheme	31	p.200	I.A.2.2
Yves Saint Laurent	Selective Distribution	31	p.200	I.A.2.2
Eco-Emballages	Packaging Waste Recovery Scheme	31	p.201	I.A.2.2
Visa International	Payment Systems	31	p.201	I.A.2.2
Duales II	Packaging Waste Recovery Scheme	31	p.202	I.A.2.2
Porsche	Selective & Exclusive Distribution	31	p.203	I.A.2.2
FIA	Conflict of Interests	31	p.203	I.A.2.2

NAME	SUBJECT	REP.	PARA.	REFERENCE
Bank Charges	Price Fixing	31	p.205	I.A.3
Corrib	Joint Marketing	31	p.206	I.A.3
Marathon	Gas Pipeline Access	31	p.207	I.A.3
UK/France Interconnector	Electricity Infrastructure Access	31	p.208	I.1.3
Austrian Banks	Cartel	32	39, 190–192	I.B.1.1.2, I.C.7
Methionine	Cartel	32	40–41	I.B.1.1.2
Industrial & Medical Gases	Cartel	32	42	I.B.1.1.2
Carlsberg & Heineken	Suspected cartel	32	43–45	I.B.1.1.2
Fine Art Auction Houses	Cartel	32	46–47	I.B.1.1.2
Methylglucamine	Cartel	32	48–49	I.B.1.1.2
Plasterboard	Cartel	32	50–52	I.B.1.1.2
Food Flavour Enhancers	Cartel	32	53–54	I.B.1.1.2
Specialty Graphite	Cartel	32	55	I.B.1.1.2
Concrete Reinforcing Bars	Cartel	32	56–60	I.B.1.1.2
Nintendo	Preventing parallel trade	32	61–66	I.B.1.2
IMS Health	Abuse of IP rights	32	68–69	I.B.2.1
Airline Alliances	Cooperation agreements	32	109–116	I.C.4.1.3, I.C.4.1.4
TACA	Liner conference	32	128–130	I.C.4.2.3
FS & Deutsche Bahn	Discrimination & exclusion of new entrant	32	133	I.C.4.3
IFPI ("Simulcasting")	Copyright collecting societies	32	147–150	I.C.5.3
Visa International	Multilateral interchange fee	32	187–189	I.C.7
French Beef	Price fixing & preventing imports	33	36–37	I.B.1.2
Sorbates	Cartel	33	38	I.B.1.2
Carbon & Graphite Products	Cartel	33	39	I.B.1.2
Organic Peroxides	Cartel	33	40–41	I.B.1.2
Industrial Copper Tubes	Cartel	33	42–43	I.B.1.2
BA/SN	Airline alliance	33	50–53	I.B.1.4
ARA, ARGEV, ARO	Packaging collection system	33	54–59	I.B.1.4
T–Mobile & O2	Network sharing	33	60–62, 118	I.B.1.4, I.C.3.3
Yamaha	Territorial restrictions & resale price maintenance	33	63–64	I.B.1.4

NAME	SUBJECT	REP.	PARA.	REFERENCE
Philips/Sony	Joint licensing	33	65–67	I.B.1.4
Reims II	Cross–border mail terminal dues	33	68–70	I.B.1.4
Deutsche Telekom	Network access, margin squeeze	33	71–73	I.B.2.1
Wanadoo Interactive	Predatory pricing	33	74–76, 120	I.B.2.1, I.C.3.3
IMS Health	Withdrawal of decision	33	77–79	I.B.2.1
GVG/FS	Essential facilities	33	80–85, 137	I.B.2.1, I.C.4.2
ENI/Gazprom	Gas supply	33	98	I.C.1
Dong/DUC	Gas supply, territorial sales restrictions	33	96 & 99	I.C.1
Incentive schemes for travel agents	Loyalty remuneration	33	132	I.C.4.1
Deep–sea car carriers	Price fixing	33	144–146	I.C.1.4.3
Audi	Car repairer network	33	155–157	I.C.5
Lubricants	Lubricant supply, non–compete clause	33	158	I.C.5

TABLE 3

LIST OF CFI JUDGMENTS (GENERAL COMPETITION RULES)

CASE No.	NAME	DATE	E.C.R.[1]	C.M.L.R.[2]	TYPE OF PROCEDURE	SUBJECT	PRODUCT/SERVICE
T–18/86 R	Dutch Cranes	04.06.96	—	5 [1996] 307	185	Interim Measures	Cranes
T–1/89	Rhône Poulenc	24.10.91	II [1991] 867	—	173	Cartel	Base Chemicals
T–2/89	Petrofina	24.10.91	II [1991] 1087	—	173	Cartel	Base Chemicals
T–3/89	Atochem	24.10.91	II [1991] 1177	—	173	Cartel	Base Chemicals
T–4/89	BASF	17.12.91	II [1991] 1523	—	173	Cartel	Base Chemicals
T–6/89	Enichem	17.12.91	II [1991] 1623	—	173	Cartel	Base Chemicals
T–7/89	Hercules	17.12.91	II [1991] 1711	4 [1992] 84	173	Cartel	Base Chemicals
T–8/89	DSM	17.12.91	II [1991] 1833	—	173	Cartel	Base Chemicals
T–9/89	Hüls	10.03.92	II [1992] 499	—	173	Cartel	Base Chemicals
T–10/89	Hoechst	10.03.92	II [1992] 629	—	173	Cartel	Base Chemicals
T–11/89	Shell	10.03.92	II [1992] 757	—	173	Cartel	Base Chemicals
T–12/89	Solvay	10.03.92	II [1992] 907	—	173	Cartel	Base Chemicals
T–13/89	ICI	10.03.92	II [1992] 1021	—	173	Cartel	Base Chemicals
T–14/89	Montedipe	10.03.92	II [1992] 1155	4 [1993] 110	173	Cartel	Base Chemicals
T–15/89	Linz	10.03.92	II [1992] 1275	—	173	Cartel	Base Chemicals
T–30/89	Hilti	12.12.91	II [1991] 1439	4 [1992] 16	173	Article 86	Tools
T–51/89	Tetra Pak	10.07.90	II [1990] 309	4 [1991] 334	173	Article 86	Packaging Material
T–55/89	Solomon	09.02.90	not published	—	175	—	Records
T–61/89	Danish Fur Breeders	02.07.92	II [1992] 1931	—	173	Cartel	Furs
T–64/89	Automec	10.07.90	II [1990] 367	4 [1991] 177	173	Letter DGIV	Cars
T–65/89	British Gypsum	01.04.93	II [1993] 389	5 [1993] 32	173	Article 86	Plaster Board
T–66/89	Publishers' Association	09.07.92	II [1992] 1995	5 [1993] 120	173	Collective RPM	Books
T–68, 77, 78/89	Flat Glass	10.03.92	II [1992] 1403	5 [1992] 302	173	Cartel	Flat Glass

[1] European Court Reports.
[2] Common Market Law Reports.

Table 3

CASE No.	NAME	DATE	E.C.R.	C.M.L.R.	TYPE OF PROCEDURE	SUBJECT	PRODUCT/SERVICE
T–69/89	RTE	10.07.91	II [1991] 485	4 [1991] 586	173	Article 86	TV Guides
T–70/89	BBC	10.07.91	II [1991] 535	4 [1991] 669	173	Article 86	TV Guides
T–76/89	ITV	10.07.91	II [1991] 575	4 [1991] 745	173	Article 86	TV Guides
T–79, 84–86, 89, 91, 92, 94, 96, 98, 102, 104/89	PVC	27.02.92	II [1992] 315	4 [1992] 357	173	Cartel	Base Chemicals
T–80/89	LDPE	06.04.95	II [1995] 729	—	173	Cartel	Chemicals
T–106/89	Norsk Hydro	19.06.90	not published	—	173	Cartel	Base Chemicals
T–113/89	Nefarma	13.12.90	II [1990] 797	—	173	Commission Letter	Pharmaceuticals
T–114/89	VNZ	13.12.90	II [1990] 827	—	173	Commission Letter	Pharmaceuticals
T–116/89	Prodifarma	13.12.90	II [1990] 843	—	173	Commission Letter	Pharmaceuticals
T–125/89	Filtrona	10.07.90	II [1990] 393	4 [1990] 832	173	Rejection Complaint	Cigarette Filters
T–131/89 R	Cosimex	06.12.89	II [1990] 1	4 [1992] 395	185	Interim Measures	Cosmetics
T–138/89	Dutch Banks	17.09.92	II [1992] 2195	5 [1993] 436	173	Negative Clearance	Banking
T–141/89	Tréfileurope	06.04.95	II [1995] 791	—	173	Cartel	Construction Materials
T–142/89	Gustave Boël	06.04.95	II [1995] 867	—	173	Cartel	Construction Materials
T–143/89	Ferriere Nord	06.04.95	II [1995] 917	—	173	Cartel	Construction Materials
T–144/89	Cockerill Sambre	06.04.95	II [1995] 947	—	173	Cartel	Construction Materials
T–145/89	Baustahlgewebe	06.04.95	II [1995] 987	—	173	Cartel	Construction Materials
T–147/89	Société Métallurgique de Normandie	06.04.95	II [1995] 1057	—	173	Cartel	Construction Materials
T–148/89	Tréfilunion	06.04.95	II [1995] 1063	—	173	Cartel	Construction Materials
T–149/89	Sotralentz	06.04.95	II [1995] 1127	—	173	Cartel	Construction Materials
T–150/89	Martinelli	06.04.95	II [1995] 1165	—	173	Cartel	Construction Materials

CASE No.	NAME	DATE	E.C.R.	C.M.L.R.	TYPE OF PROCEDURE	SUBJECT	PRODUCT/SERVICE
T–151/89	Société des Treillis et Panneaux Soudés	06.04.95	II [1995] 1191	—	173	Cartel	Construction Materials
T–152/89	Ilro	06.04.95	II [1995] 197	—	173	Cartel	Construction Materials
T–196/89Rev	Norsk Hydro	01.07.94	II [1994] 424	—	Rev.	Revision	Chemicals
T–3/90	Prodifarma	23.01.91	II [1991] 1	—	175	Commission Letter	Pharmaceuticals
T–12/90	Bayer	29.05.91	II [1991] 1219	4 [1993] 30	173	Limitation Periods	Animal Feed
T–23/90 R	Peugeot	21.05.90	II [1990] 195	4 [1990] 674	185	Interim Measures	Cars
T–23/90	Peugeot	12.07.91	II [1991] 653	4 [1990] 674	173	Interim Measures	Cars
T–24/90	Automec	18.09.92	II [1992] 2223	5 [1992] 431	173	Rejection of Complaint	Cars
T–28/90	Asia Motor France	18.09.92	II [1992] 2285	5 [1992] 431	175/173	Failure to Act	Cars
T–39/90 R	SEP	21.11.90	II [1990] 649	5 [1992] 27	185	Article 11, Regulation 17	Electricity
T–39/90	SEP	12.12.91	II [1991] 1497	5 [1992] 33	173	Article 11, Regulation 17	Electricity
T–44/90	La Cinq	24.01.92	II [1992] 1	4 [1992] 449	173	Interim Measures	Television
T–16/91	Rendo	18.11.92	II [1992] 2417	4 [1993] 110	173	Rejection of Complaint	Electricity
T–16/91RV	Rendo	12.12.96	II [1996] 1827	4 [1997] 453	173/119 RoP	Reasoning	Electricity
T–19/91 R	Vichy	07.06.91	II [1991] 265	—	185	Interim Measures	Cosmetics
T–19/91	Vichy	27.02.92	II [1992] 415	—	173	Article 15, paragraph 6, Regulation 17	Cosmetics
T–27/91	Sofacar	21.02.92	—	—	175	Competence CFI	Cars
T–30/91	Solvay	29.06.95	II [1995] 1775	5 [1996] 57	173	Cartel	Soda Ash
T–31/91	Solvay	29.06.95	II [1995] 1821	—	173	Cartel	Soda Ash
T–32/91	Solvay	29.06.95	II [1995] 1825	5 [1996] 91	173	Article 86	Soda Ash
T–36/91	ICI	29.06.95	II [1995] 1847	—	173	Cartel	Soda Ash
T–37/91	ICI	29.06.95	II [1995] 1901	—	173	Article 86	Soda Ash
T–42/91	PTT	21.06.91	II [1991] 273	—	173	Competence CFI	Courier Services
T–57/91	NALOO	24.09.96	II [1996] 1019	5 [1996] 672	33 ECSC	Rejection of Complaint	Coal
T–83/91	Tetra Pak II	06.10.94	II [1994] 755	4 [1997] 726	173	Article 86	Packaging Material
T–2/92	Rendo	29.03.92	not published	—	173	Rejection of Complaint	Energy
T–7/92	Asia Motor France II	29.06.93	—	4 [1994] 30	173	Rejection of Complaint	Cars

Table 3

CASE No.	NAME	DATE	E.C.R.	C.M.L.R.	TYPE OF PROCEDURE	SUBJECT	PRODUCT/SERVICE
T–9/92	Peugeot	22.04.93	II [1993] 493	5 [1995] 696	173	Regulation 123/85	Cars
T–10/92	Cement Industries	18.12.92	II [1992] 2667	4 [1992] 259	173	Access to File	Cement
T–10–15/92 R	Cement Industries	23.03.92	II [1992] 1571	4 [1993] 243	185	Interim Measures	Cement
T–19/92	Leclerc	12.12.96	II [1996] 1051	4 [1997] 995	173	Selective Distribution	Perfumes
T–24 & 28/92 R	Langnese Iglo	16.06.92	II [1992] 1839	—	185	Interim Measures	Ice-cream
T–29/92 R	Dutch Builders	16.07.92	II [1992] 1261	—	185	Interim Measures	Construction
T–29/92	SPO	21.02.95	II [1995] 289	—	173	Cartel	Construction
T–34/92	Fiat Agri	27.10.94	II [1994] 905	—	173	Info-exchange	Tractors
T–35/92	John Deere	27.10.94	II [1994] 957	—	173	Info-exchange	Tractors
T–36/92	SFEI	30.11.92	II [1992] 2479	4 [1993] 109	173	Rejection of Complaint	Courier Services
T–37/92	BEUC	18.05.94	II [1994] 285	4 [1995] 167	173	Procedure	Cars
T–38/92	All Weather Sports	28.04.94	II [1994] 211	4 [1995] 43	173	Parallel Trade	Tennis Balls
T–39 & 40/92	Europay	23.02.94	II [1994] 49	—	173	Cartel	Banking
T–43/92	Dunlop	07.07.94	II [1994] 441	—	173	Parallel Trade	Tennis Balls
T–46/92	Scottish Football Association	09.11.94	II [1994] 1039	—	173	Article 11, Regulation 17	Television
T–56/92	Koelman	29.11.93	II [1993] 1267	—	175	Complaint	Copyright
T–66/92	Herlitz	14.07.94	II [1994] 531	5 [1995] 458	173	Parallel Trade	Stationery
T–70 & 71/92	Florimex	14.05.97	II [1997] 693	5 [1997] 769	173	Rejection of complaint	Flowers
T–74/92	Ladbroke	13.05.93	II [1993] 535	—	175	Intervention	Horse Betting
T–74/92	Ladbroke	24.01.95	II [1995] 115	—	175	Rejection of Complaint	Bookmaking
T–77/92	Parker Pen	14.07.94	II [1994] 549	5 [1995] 435	173	Parallel Trade	Stationery
T–83/92	Zunis	28.10.93	II [1993] 1169	5 [1994] 154	173	Merger Control	Banking
T–87/92	Kruidvat	12.12.96	II [1996] 1931	4 [1997] 1046	173	Selective Distribution	Perfumes
T–88/92	Leclerc	12.12.96	II [1996] 1961	4 [1997] 352	173	Selective Distribution	Perfumes
T–96/92 R	Perrier's Employees	15.12.92	II [1992] 2579	4 [1993] 227	185	Interim Measures	Mineral Water
T–96/92	Perrier	27.04.95	II [1995] 1213	—	173	Merger Control	Drinking Water
T–102/92	Viho Europe	12.01.95	II [1995] 17	—	173	Intra-enterprise Conspiracy	Stationery
T–114/92	BEMIM	24.01.95	II [1995] 197	4 [1996] 305	173	Rejection of Complaint	Copyright
T–2/93	Air France	19.05.94	II [1994] 323	—	173	Merger Control	Air Transport

CASE No.	NAME	DATE	E.C.R.	C.M.L.R.	TYPE OF PROCEDURE	SUBJECT	PRODUCT/SERVICE
T-3/93	Air France	24.03.94	II [1994] 121	—	173	Merger Control	Air Transport
T-5/93	Tremblay	24.01.95	II [1995] 185	4 [1996] 305	173	Rejection of Complaint	Copyright
T-7/93	Langnese Iglo	08.06.95	II [1995] 1533	5 [1995] 602	173	Exclusive Purchasing	Ice-cream
T-9/93	Schöller	08.06.95	II [1995] 1611	5 [1995] 602	173	Exclusive Purchasing	Ice-cream
T-12/93 R	Vittel's Employees	02.04.93	II [1993] 449	—	185	Interim Measures	Mineral Water
T-12/93	Vittel	27.04.95	II [1995] 1247	—	173	Merger Control	Drinking Water
T-14/93	UICF	06.06.95	II [1995] 1503	5 [1996] 40	173	Regulation 17	Transport
T-17/93	Matra	15.07.94	II [1994] 595	—	173	Joint Venture	Cars
T-24/93 R	CMBT	13.05.93	II [1993] 543	—	185	Interim Measures	Maritime Transport
T-24-26 & 28/93	CMB a.o./v. Commission	08.10.96	II [1996] 1019	4 [1997] 273	173	Cartel	Maritime Transport
T-32/93	Ladbroke	27.10.94	II [1994] 1015	—	175	Procedure	Bookmaking
T-34/93	Société Générale	08.03.95	II [1995] 545	4 [1996] 665	173	Article 11 Reg. 17	Banking
T-504/93	Ladbroke	12.06.97	II [1997] 923	5 [1997] 309	173	Rejction of complaint	Betting
T-513/93	CNSD	30.03.00	II [2000] 1807	5 [2000] 614	230 (ex 173)	Price fixing	Custom Agents
T-528, 542, 543 & 546/93	Métropole	11.07.96	II [1996] 649	5 [1996] 386	173	Exemption	Television
T-543/93 R	Telecinco	14.12.93	II [1993] 1409	—	185	Interim Measures	Television
T-548/93	Ladbroke	18.09.95	II [1995] 2565	4 [1996] 549	173	Rejection of complaint	Bookmaking
T-575/93	Koelman	09.01.96	II [1996] 1	4 [1996] 636	173	Rejection of complaint	Copyright
T-789/93 R	Langnese	19.02.93	II [1993] 132	4 [1993] 299	185	Interim Measures	Ice-cream
T-77/94	VGB	14.05.97	II [1997] 759	5 [1997] 812	173	Rejection of complaint	Flowers
T-84/94	German Accountants	23.01.95	II [1995] 101	—	173	Complaint Article 90(3)	Auditing
T-88/94 R	SCPA	10.5.94 & 15.6.94	II [1994] 263	—	185	Merger Control	Fertilisers
T-134/94	NMH Stahlwerke	19.06.96	II [1996] 537	—	33 ECSC	Confidentiality	Steel Beams
T-141/94	Thyssen Stahl	11.03.99	II [1999] 347	5 [1999] 810	Article 33 ECSC	Cartel	Steel
T-186/94	Guérin Automobiles	27.06.95	II [1995] 1753	5 [1996] 685	173/175	Rejection of Complaint	Cars
T-229/94	Deutsche Bahn	22.10.97	II [1997] 1689	4 [1998] 220	173	Article 86	Rail Transport

TABLE 3

Table 3

CASE No.	NAME	DATE	E.C.R.	C.M.L.R.	TYPE OF PROCEDURE	SUBJECT	PRODUCT/SERVICE
T-235/94 R	Goldstein	27.02.96	—	5 [1996] 106	186	Interim Measures	Health Care
T-260/94	Air Inter	19.02.97	II [1997] 997	5 [1997] 851	173	Article 90(2)	Air transport
T-275/94	Cartes Bancaires	14.07.95	II [1995] 2169	5 [1995] 410	173	Fines	Banking
T-290/94	Kayserberg	27.11.97	II [1997] 2137	4 [1998] 336	173	Regulation 4064/89	Paper Products
T-295/94 R	Buchmann	21.12.94	II [1994] 1265	—	185	Suspension	Carton Board
T-295/94	Buchmann	14.05.98	II [1998] 813	—	173	Cartel	Carton Board
T-301/94 R	Laakmann Karton	21.12.94	II [1994] 1279	—	185	Suspension	Carton Board
T-304/94	Europa Carton	14.05.98	II [1998] 869	—	173	Cartel	Carton Board
T-305 e.s./94	PVC II	20.04.99	II [1999] 931	5 [1999] 303	173	Cartel	Base Chemicals
T-308/94 R	Cascades	17.02.95	II [1995] 265	—	185	Interim Measures	Carton Board
T-308/94	Cascades	14.05.98	II [1998] 925	—	173	Cartel	Carton Board
T-308/94	Cascades	28.02.02	II [2002] 813	4 [2002] 33	54S	Fine/corporate structure	Carton Board
T-309/94	Koninklijke KNP	14.05.98	II [1998] 1007	—	173	Cartel	Carton Board
T-310/94	Gruber & Weber	14.05.98	II [1998] 1043	—	173	Cartel	Carton Board
T-311/94	BPB de Eendracht	14.05.98	II [1998] 1129	—	173	Cartel	Carton Board
T-317/94	Moritz J. Weig	14.05.98	II [1998] 1235	—	173	Cartel	Carton Board
T-319/94	Fiskeby Board	14.05.98	II [1998] 1331	—	173	Cartel	Carton Board
T-327/94	SCA Holding	14.05.98	II [1998] 1373	5 [1998] 195	173	Cartel	Carton Board
T-334/94	Sarrió	14.05.98	II [1998] 1439	5 [1998] 195	173	Cartel	Carton Board
T-337/94	Enso-Gutzeit	14.05.98	II [1998] 1571	—	173	Cartel	Carton Board
T-338/94	Finnish Board Mills	14.05.98	II [1998] 1617	—	173	Cartel	Carton Board
T-339, 340, 341 & 342/94	Metsä-Serla	14.05.98	II [1998] 1727	—	173	Cartel	Carton Board
T-347/94	Mayr-Melnhof Kartongesellschaft	14.05.98	II [1998] 1751	—	173	Cartel	Carton Board
T-348/94	Enso Española	14.05.98	II [1998] 1875	—	173	Cartel	Carton Board
T-352/94	Mo och Domsjö	14.05.98	II [1998] 1989	—	173	Cartel	Carton Board
T-353/94 R	Postbank	05.12.94	II [1994] 1141	4 [1997] 62	185	Article 20, Regulation 17	Banking
T-353/94	Postbank	18.09.96	II [1996] 921	4 [1997] 33	173	Business Secrets	Banking
T-354/94	Stora Kopparbergs Bergslags	14.05.98	II [1998] 2111	—	173	Cartel	Carton Board

CASE No.	NAME	DATE	E.C.R.	C.M.L.R.	TYPE OF PROCEDURE	SUBJECT	PRODUCT/SERVICE
T-354/94	Stora Kopparbergs Bergslags II	28.02.02	II [2002] 843	5 [2002] 34	54S	Fine/corporate structure	Carton Board
T-369/94 & 85/95	DIR	19.02.98	II [1997] 357	—	173	Media programme	Film Industry
T-374, 375, 384 & 388/94	European Night Services	15.09.98	II [1998] 3141	5 [1998] 718	173	Exemption	Railways
T-387/94	Asia Motor France	18.09.96	II [1996] 961	5 [1996] 537	173	Rejection of Complaint	Cars
T-395/94 RII	Atlantic Container	22.11.95	II [1995] 595	5 [1997] 195	186	Interim Measures	Sea Transport
T-395/94 R	Atlantic Container	10.03.95	II [1995] 595	5 [1997] 181	185	Interim Measures	Transport
T-395/94	Atlantic Container Line	28.02.02	II [2002] 875	4 [2002] 28	230 (ex 173)	Article 81(3)	Intermodal Transport
T-5/95 R	Square d'Auvergne	16.02.95	II [1995] 255	—	185	Interim Measures	Real Estate
T-25, 26, 30, 32, 34, 39, 42, 46, 48, 50, 65, 68, 71, 87, 88, 103 and 104/95	Cement	15.03.00	II [2000] 491	5 [2000] 204	230 (ex 173)	Cartel	Cement
T-28/95	IECC	16.09.98	II [1998] 3597	—	175	Failure to act	Express Mail
T-49/95	Van Megen Sport	11.12.96	II [1996] 1799	4 [1997] 843	173	Proof of Infringement	Tennis Balls
T-77/95	UFEX	25.05.00	II [2000] 2167	4 [2001] 35	230 (ex 173	Rejection of complaint	Couriers
T-79 & 80/95 R	SNCF & BR	12.05.95	—	5 [1996] 26	185	Interim Measures	Railways
T-77/95	SFEI	15.01.97	II [1997] 1	5 [1997] 81	173	Rejection of Complaints	Courier Services
T-79 & 80/95	SNCF	22.10.96	II [1996] 1433	5 [1996] 26	173	Exemption	Rail Transport
T-86/95	Far Eastern Freight Conference	28.02.02	II [2001] 1011	4 [2002] 29	230 (ex 173)	Article 81 (ex 85)	Intermodal Transport
T-104/95 R	Halkidos	11.08.95	—	—	185	Interim Measures	Cement
T-106/95	FFSA	27.02.97	II [1997] 229	2 [1997] 78	173	Article 90	Insurance
T-110/95	IECC	16.09.98	II [1998] 3605	—	173	Rejection of complaint	Express Mail
T-133 & 204/95	IECC	16.09.98	II [1998] 3645	5 [1998] 992	173	Rejection of complaint	Express Mail
T-175/95	BASF	19.05.99	II [1999] 1581	4 [2000] 33	230 (ex 173)	Preventing parallel trade	Car Paint

Table 3

CASE No.	NAME	DATE	E.C.R.	C.M.L.R.	TYPE OF PROCEDURE	SUBJECT	PRODUCT/SERVICE
T–176/95	Accinauto	19.05.99	II [1999] 1635	4 [2000] 67	230 (ex 173)	Preventing parallel trade	Car Paint
T–189/95	SGA	13.12.99	II [1999] 3587	4 [2000] 7	230 (ex 173)	Rejection of complaint	Motor Vehicles
T–190/95 & 45/96	Sodima	13.12.99	II [1999] 3617	4 [2001] 8	230 (ex 173) + 232 (ex 175)	Failure to act	Motor Vehicles
T–195/95	Guérin	06.05.97	II [1997] 679	5 [1997] 219	173	Damages	Cars
T–195/95	Guérin	11.03.96	II [1997] 679	5 [1997] 212	175	Complaint	Cars
T–213/95 & 18/96	Dutch Cranes	22.10.97	II [1997] 1739	4 [1998] 259	173	Cartel	Cars
T–224/95	Tremblay	27.11.97	II [1997] 2215	4 [1998] 427	173	Rejection of complaint	Copyright
T–227/95	AssiDomän	10.07.97	II [1997] 1183	5 [1997] 364	173	Article 176	Woodpulp
T–235/95	Goldstein	16.03.98	II [1998] 523	5 [1996] 106	173	Interim measures	Doctors
T–9, 211/96	Européenne automobile	13.12.99	II [1999] 3639	4 [2001] 9	230 (ex 173)	Rejection of complaint	Motor Vehicles
T–17/96	TFI	03.06.99	II [1999] 1757	4 [2000] 678	232 (ex 175)	Failure to act	Broadcasting
T–38/96	Guérin	10.07.97	II [1997] 1223	5 [1997] 352	173/178	Rejection of complaint	Cars
T–41/96 R	Bayer	03.06.96	II [1996] 381	5 [1996] 290	185	Interim Measures	Pharmaceuticals
T–41/96	Adalat	26.10.00	II [2000] 3383	4 [2001] 126	230 (ex 173)	Concept of agreement	Pharmaceuticals
T–65/96	Kish Glass	30.03.00	II [2000] 1885	5 [2000] 229	230 (ex 173)	Rejection of complaint	Float Glass
T–83/96	Van der Wal	19.03.98	II [1998] 545	4 [1998] 954	173	Access to information	Legal Profession
T–87/96	Assicurazioni Generali	04.03.99	II [1999] 203	4 [2000] 312	173	Regulation 4064/89	Insurance
T–90/96	Peugeot	02.05.97	II [1997] 663	5 [1997] 261	173	Business secrets	Cars
T–102/96	Gencor	25.03.99	II [1999] 753	5 [1999] 971	173	Regulation 4064/89	Precious Metals
T–111/96	ITT Promedia	17.07.98	II [1998] 2937	5 [1998] 491	173	Rejection of complaint	Telephone Directories
T–117/96	Intertronic	19.02.97	II [1997] 141	4 [1998] 520	175	Rejection of complaint	Advertising
T–136/96	Peugeot	02.05.97	—	5 [1997] 261	173	Business secrets	Cars

CASE No.	NAME	DATE	E.C.R.	C.M.L.R.	TYPE OF PROCEDURE	SUBJECT	PRODUCT/SERVICE
T–185, 189 & 190/96	Riviera	21.01.99	II [1999] 93	5 [1999] 31	173	Rejection of complaint	Cars
T–5/97	Poudres Sphériques	30.11.00	II [2000] 3755	4 [2001] 28	230 (ex 173)	Article 82 (ex 86)	Primary calcium metal
T–9/97	Elf Autochem	09.06.97	II [1997] 909	5 [1997] 442	173	Investigation	Chemicals
T–18/97	Atlantic Container Line II	28.02.02	II [2002] 1125	4 [2002] 30	230 (ex 173)	Article 81	Shipping
T–83/97	Sateba	29.09.97	II [1997] 1523	4 [1998] 528	173	Public procurement	Construction Works
T–197 & 198/97	Weyl Beef	31.01.01	II [2001] 303	2 [2001] 22	230 (ex 173)	Rejection of complaint	Abattoirs
T–228/97	Irish Sugar	07.10.99	II [1999] 2969	5 [1999] 1300	232 (ex 175)	Discrimination & rebates 86	Sugar
T–241/97	Stork	17.02.00	II [2000] 309	5 [2001] 31	230 (ex 173)	Rejection of complaint	Plastic Bottles
T–266/97	VTM	08.07.99	II [1999] 2329	4 [2000] 1171	230 (ex 173)	Article 86(1) (ex 90(1))	Broadcasting
T–596/97	Dalmine	24.06.98	II [1998] 2383	—	173	Article 11(5), reg. 17	Steel
T–45 & 47/98	Krupp Thyssen Stainless	13.12.01	II [2001] 3757	—	65 ECSC	Cartel	Steel
T–48/98	Aceriuox	13.12.01	II [2001] 3859	—	65 ECSC	Cartel	Steel
T–62/98	Volkswagen	06.07.00	II [2000] 2707	5 [2000] 853	230 (ex 173)	Preventing parallel trade	Motor Vehicles
T–65/98 R	Van der Bergh Foods	07.07.98	II [1998] 2641	5 [1998] 475	185	Interim measures	Ice-cream
T–65/98	Van den Bergh Foods	23.10.03	II [2003] 4653	4 [2004] 7	230	Tying practices	Ice-cream
T–112/98	Mannesmann	20.02.01	II [2001] 729	5 [2001] 1	230 (ex 173)	Right to silence	Steel Pipes
T–127/98	UPS	09.09.99	II [1999] 2633	4 [2000] 94	232 (ex 175)	Failure to act	Parcel Service
T–128/98	Aéroports de Paris	12.12.00	II [2000] 3929	4 [2001] 38	230 (ex 173)	Article 82 (ex 86)	Airports
T–139/98	Italian Tobacco	22.11.01	II [2001] 3413	4 [2002] 10	230 (ex 173)	Article 82 (ex 86)	Cigarettes
T–154/98	Asia Motor France	26.10.00	II [2000] 3453	4 [2001] 6	230 (ex 173)	Rejection of complaint	Motor Vehicles

Table 3

CASE No.	NAME	DATE	E.C.R.	C.M.L.R.	TYPE OF PROCEDURE	SUBJECT	PRODUCT/SERVICE
T–191/98 R	DSR Senator	21.07.99	II [1999] 2533	—	242 (ex 185)	Interim measures	Shipping
T–191/98 R II	Cho Yang Shipping	28.06.00	II [2000] 2551	4 [2001] 31	242 (ex 185)	Suspension of obligation to pay fine	Shipping
T–191 e.a./98	Atlantic Container Line and others	30.09.03	II [2003] 3275	4 [2005] 20	230	Liner conference	Shipping
T–202, 204, 207/98	Tate & Lyle	12.07.01	5 [2001] 22	[2002] 25	230 (ex 173)	Article 81 (ex 85)	Sugar
T–9/99	HFB et al.	20.03.02	II [2002] 1487	—	230 (ex 173)	Cartel	Pipes
T–15/99	Brugg Rohrysteme	20.03.02	II [2002] 1613	—	230 (ex 173)	Cartel	Pipes
T–16/99	Lögstör Rör Deutschland	20.03.02	II [2002] 1633	—	230 (ex 173)	Cartel	Pipes
T–17/99	Ke Kelit	20.03.02	II [2002] 1647	—	230 (ex 173)	Cartel	Pipes
T–21/99	Dansk Rørindustri	20.03.02	II [2002] 1681	—	230 (ex 173)	Cartel	Pipes
T–23/99	LR AF 1998	20.03.02	II [2002] 1705	5 [2002] 10	230 (ex 173)	Cartel	Pipes
T–25/99	Roberts	05.07.01	5 [2001] 21	—	230 (ex 173)	Article 81	Beer
T–26/99	Trabisco	14.02.01	II [2001] 633	—	230 (ex 173)	Rejection of complaint	Motor Vehicles
T–28/99	Signa Tecnologie	20.03.02	II [2002] 1845	—	230 (ex 173)	Cartel	Pipes
T–31/99	ABB	20.03.02	II [2002] 1881	—	230 (ex 173)	Cartel	Pipes
T–54/99	Max Mobil	30.01.02	II [2002] 313	4 [2002] 32	230 (ex 173)	Rejection of complaint	Mobile Telephony
T–56/99	Marlines	11.12.03	II [2003] 5225	5 [2005] 28	230	Cartel	Shipping
T–59/99 R	Ventouris	20.07.99	II [1999] 2519	—	242 (ex 185)	Interim measures	Sea Transport

CASE No.	NAME	DATE	E.C.R.	C.M.L.R.	TYPE OF PROCEDURE	SUBJECT	PRODUCT/SERVICE
T–59/99	Ventouris	11.12.03	II [2003] 5257	5 [2005] 29	230	Cartel	Shipping
T–61/99	Adriatica di Navigazione	11.12.03	II [2003] 5549	—	230	Cartel	Shipping
T–62/99	Sodima	14.02.01	II [2001] 655	5 [2001] 36	230 (ex 173)	Rejection of complaint	Motor Vehicles
T–65/99	Strintzis Lines	11.12.03	II [2003] 5433	5 [2005] 31	230	Cartel	Shipping
T–66/99	Minoan Lines	11.12.03	II [2003] 5515	5 [2005] 32	230	Cartel	Shipping
T–95/99	Satellimages TV5	07.03.02	II [2002] 1425	4 [2002] 35	230 (ex 173)	Rejection of complaint	Broadcasting
T–112/99	Métropole Télévision	18.09.01	II [2001] 2459	5 [2001] 33	230 (ex 173)	Joint venture	Satellite Pay-TV
T–115/99	SEP	14.02.01	II [2001] 691	5 [2001] 14	230 (ex 173)	Rejection of complaint	Motor Vehicles
T–131/99	Shaw	21.03.02	II [2002] 2023	5 [2002] 3	230 (ex 173)	Article 81(3)	Standard Pub Lease Agreements
T–144/99 R	Patent Agents	14.04.00	II [2000] 2067	—	242 (ex 185)		Patent Agents
T–144/99	Patent Agents	28.03.01	II [2001] 1087	5 [2001] 2	230 (ex 173)		Patent Agents
T–175/99	UPS Europe	20.03.02	II [2002] 1915	5 [2002] 2	230 (ex 173)	Rejection of complaint	Postal Services
T–206/99	Métropole Télévision	21.03.01	II [2001] 1057	5 [2001] 33	230 (ex 173)	Rejection of complaint	Broadcasting
T–219/99	British Airways	17.12.03	II [2003] 5917	4 [2004] 19	230	82 rebates	Reservations Systems
T–231/99	Joynson	21.03.02	II [2002] 2085	5 [2002] 4	230 (ex 173)	Article 81(3)	Standard Pub Lease Agreements
T–319/99	FENIN	04.03.03	II [2003] 357	5 [2003] 2	230 (ex 173)	Rejection of complaint	Medical Goods & Equipment
T–5/00 R	FEG	14.12.00	II [2000] 4121	5 [2004] 19	242 (ex 185)	Interim measures	Electro-technical Installation Equipment
T–5 & 6/00	VEG & TU	16.12.03	II [2003] 5761	5 [2004] 20	230	Trade associations	Electronic Equipment
T–44/00	Mannesmannröhren-Werke	08.07.04	II [2004] 2223	—	230	Cartel	Steel Tubes
T–45/00	Conseil National	12.07.00	II [2000] 2927	—	230 (ex 173)	Locus standi	Motor Vehicles

TABLE 3

Table 3

CASE No.	NAME	DATE	E.C.R.	C.M.L.R.	TYPE OF PROCEDURE	SUBJECT	PRODUCT/SERVICE
T–48/00	Corus UK	08.07.04	II [2004] 2325	4 [2005] 3	230	Cartel	Steel Tubes
T–50/00	Dalmine	08.07.04	II [2004] 2395	4 [2005] 2	230	Cartel	Steel Tubes
T–52/00	Coe Clerici	17.06.03	II [2003] 2123	5 [2003] 11	230	Rejection complaint	Port Services
T–67e.s./00	JFE Engineering	08.07.04	II [2004] 2501	4 [2005] 2	230	Cartel	Steel Tubes
T–213/00	FETTCSA	19.03.03	II [2003] 913	5 [2003] 4	230 (ex 173)	Cartel	Shipping
T–220/00	Cheil Jedang	09.07.03	II [2003] 2473	—	203	Cartel	Lysine
T–223/00	Kyowa Hakko Kogyo and Kyowa Hakko Europe	09.07.03	II [2003] 2553	—	230	Cartel	Lysine
T–224/00	Archer Daniels Midland and Archer Daniel Midlands Ingredients	09.07.03	II [2003] 2597	5 [2003] 12	230	Cartel	Lysine
T–230/00	Daesang and Sewon Europe	09.07.03	II [2003] 2733	—	230	Cartel	Lysine
T–185, 216, 299, 300/00	Eurovision	10.08.02	II [2002] 3805	4 [2003] 14	230 (ex 173)	Joint purchasing	Television Rights
T–368/00	General Motors Nederland and Opel Nederland	21.10.03	II [2003] 4495	4 [2004] 23	230	Parallel trade	Cars
T–67/01	JCB Service	13.01.04	II [2004] 49	4 [2004] 24	230	Parallel trade	Earthmoving Equipment
T–151/01	Duales	24.05.07	—	5 [2007] 4	230	Waste collection	Abusive trade mark licensing
T–168/01	GlaxoSmithKline	27.09.06	—	5 [2006] 29	230	Preventing parallel trade	Medicines
T–184/01 R	IMS	26.10.01	II [2001] 3193	4 [2002] 2[3]	242–243	Abuse of IP rights	Pharmaceutical Sales Data
T–184/01	IMS	10.03.05	—	—	230	Withdrawal of decision	Pharmaceutical sales data
T–203/01	Michelin	30.09.03	II [2003] 4071	4 [2004] 18	230	82 rebates	Tyres
T–208/01	Volkswagen	03.12.03	II [2003] 5141	4 [2004] 14	230	Concept of agreement	Cars
T–213/01 & 23/02	Österreichische Postsparkasse	07.06.06	—	4 [2007] 14	230	Third Party Access to SO	Banking
T–236e.s./01	Tokai Carbon	29.04.04	II [2004] 1181	5 [2004] 29	230	Cartel	Graphite Electrodes

[3] C.M.L.R. references from 2002 are to the unique citation number.

CASE No.	NAME	DATE	E.C.R.	C.M.L.R.	TYPE OF PROCEDURE	SUBJECT	PRODUCT/SERVICE
T-241/01	SAS	18.07.05	—	5 [2005] 18	230	Cartel	Air transport
T-289/01	Duales II	24.05.07	—	5 [2007] 5	230	Waste collection	Access to facilities
T-314/01	Avebe	27.09.06	—	4 [2007] 1	230	Cartel	Sodium gluconate
T-322/01	Roquette Frères	27.09.06	—	—	230	Cartel	Sodium gluconate
T-325/01	DaimlerChrysler	15.09.05	—	4 [2007] 15	230	Agency, RPM	Motor vehicles
T-329/01	Archer Daniels Midland	27.09.06	—	4 [2007] 2	230	Cartel	Sodium gluconate
T-330/01	Akzo Nobel	27.09.06	—	4 [2007] 3	230	Cartel	Sodium gluconate
T-15/02	BASF	15.03.06	—	5 [2006] 2	230	Cartel	Vitamins
T-22 &23/02	Sumitomo	06.10.05	—	4 [2006] 3	230	Cartel	Vitamins
T-26/02	Daiichi	15.03.06	—	5 [2006] 3	230	Cartel	Vitamins
T-28/02	First Data	17.10.05	—	4 [2006] 4	230	No acquiring without issuing	Payment Cards
T-33/02	Britannia Alloys	29.11.05	—	4 [2006] 18	230	Cartel	Zinc Phosphates
T-38/02	Danone	29.10.05	—	4 [2006] 25	230	Cartel	Beer
T-43/02	Jugnbunzlauer	27.09.06	—	—	230	Cartel	Citric acid
T-44, 54, 56, 60 & 61/02	Dresdner Bank	27.09.06	—	—	122(4)	Cartel	Currency exchange
T-44/02	Dresdner Bank	14.10.04	—	4 [2007] 13	230	Cartel	Currency exchange
T-48/02	Brouwerij Haacht	06.12.05	—	4 [2006] 13	230	Cartel	Beer
T-49e.s./02	Luxembourg Brewers	27.07.05	—	4 [2006] 8	230	Cartel	Beer
T-52/02	SNCZ	29.11.05	—	4 [2006] 19	230	Cartel	Zinc Phosphates
T-54/02	Vereins- und Westbank	14.10.04	—	—	230	Cartel	Currency exchange
T-56/02	Bayerische Hypo- und Vereinsbank	14.10.04	II [2004] 3495	5 [2004] 29	230	Cartel	Currency exchange
T-59/02	Archer Daniels Midland	27.09.06	—	5 [2006] 28	230	Cartel	Citric acid
T-60/02	Deutsche Verkehrsbank	14.10.04	—	—	230	Cartel	Currency exchange
T-61/02	Commmerzbank	14.10.04	—	—	230	Cartel	Currency exchange
T-62/02	Union Pigments	29.11.05	—	4 [2006] 20	230	Cartel	Zinc Phosphates
T-64/02	Heubach	29.11.05	—	4 [2006] 21	230	Cartel	Zinc Phosphates
T-109, 118, 122, 125–126, 128–129, 132 & 136/02	Carbonless Paper	26.04.07	—	5 [2007] 2	230	Cartel	Carbonless paper
T-135/02	Greencore Group	14.12.05	—	4 [2006] 10	230	Interest on Refunded Fines	Sugar

CASE No.	NAME	DATE	E.C.R.	C.M.L.R.	TYPE OF PROCEDURE	SUBJECT	PRODUCT/SERVICE
T–193/02	Piau	26.01.05	—	5 [2005] 2	230	Rejection of complaint	Football
T–259–264 & 271/02	Austrian Banks	20.04.07	—	—	230	Cartel	Financial services
T–279/02	Degussa	05.04.06	—	—	230	Cartel	Methionine
T–303/02	Westfalen Gassen	05.12.06	—	4 [2007] 9	230	Cartel	Industrial & medical gases
T–304/02	Hoek Loos	04.07.06	—	5 [2006] 8	230	Cartel	Industrial & medical gases
T–313/02	Meca-Medina	30.09.04	II [2004] 3291	3 [2004] 60	230	Rejection of complaint	Swimming/doping
T–398/02 R	Linea	27.03.03	II [2003] 1139	5 [2005] 9	242 & 243	Suspension	Shipping
T–28/03	Holcim (Germany)	21.04.05	—	5 [2005] 3	235 & 288	Reimbursement of bank guarantee charges	Cement
T–71e.s./03	Specialty Graphite	15.06.05	—	5 [2005] 13	230	Cartel	Specialty graphites
T–86/03	Holcim (France)	04.05.05	—	—	233 & 288	Reimbursement of interests on fine	Cement
T–125 & 253/03 R	Akzo Nobel	30.10.03	II [2003] 4771	4 [2004] 15	242 & 243	Legal privilege	Chemicals
T–198/03 R	Bank Austria	07.11.03	II [2003] 4879	5 [2006] 9	242 & 243	Suspension	Banks
T–198/03	Bank Austria II	30.05.06	—	5 [2006] 10	230	Confidentiality/Publication of Decisions	Banking
T–204/03	Haladjian Frères	27.09.06	—	4 [2007] 27	230	Rejection of complaint	Spare parts
T–217/03	French Beef	21.01.04	II [2004] 271	5 [2005] 12	242 & 243	Interim measures	Beef
T–217 & 245/03	French Beef	31.12.06	—	—	230	Beef	Preventing imports
T–252/03	FNICGV	09.11.04	II [2004] 3795	4 [2005] 13	230	Time-limit for appeal	Beef
T–328/03	O2 (Germany)	02.05.06	—	5 [2006] 5	230	Network Sharing	Mobile Telephony
T–340/03	France Télécom	30.01.07	—	4 [2007] 21	230	Internet access	Predatory pricing
T–410/03	Hoechst	16.12.04	II [2004] 4451	—	230	Leave to intervene	Sorbates
T–104/04	Degussa	22.11.05	—	—	230	Cartel	Organic Peroxides
T–120/04	Peróxidos Orgánicos	16.11.06	—	4 [2007] 4	230	Cartel	Organic peroxides
T–153/04	Ferriere Nord	27.09.06	—	5 [2006] 24	230	Collection of fines	Steel mesh
T–155/04	SELEX	12.12.06	—	4 [2007] 10	230	Rejection of complaint	Air traffic control
T–201/04	Microsoft	22.12.04	II [2004] 4463	4 [2005] 5	242	Tying & refusal to license	Software
T–338/04	Centro Europa 7	16.02.06	—	—	230	Rejection of Complaint	Broadcasting
T–339/04	France Télécom	08.03.07	—	—	230	Internet access	Inspection decision

CASE No.	NAME	DATE	E.C.R.	C.M.L.R.	TYPE OF PROCEDURE	SUBJECT	PRODUCT/SERVICE
T–340/04	France Télécom	08.03.07	—	—	230	Internet access	Inspection decision
T–384/06	IBP	28.03.07	—	4 [2007] 24	242	Copper and alloy fittings	Fine/bank guarantee
T–12/07	Polimeri Europe	03.05.07	—	—	243	Synthetic rubber	Use of SO by complainant

TABLE 4

LIST OF EUROPEAN COURT JUDGMENTS (GENERAL COMPETITION RULES)

CASE No.	NAME	DATE	E.C.R.[1]	C.M.L.R.[2]	TYPE OF PROCEDURE	SUBJECT	PRODUCT/SERVICE
13/61	Bosch v De Geus	06.04.62	[1962] 45	[1962] 1	177	Provisional Validity	Domestic Appliances
6/64	Costa v ENEL	15.07.64	[1964] 585	[1964] 425	177	Supremacy EEC Treaty	Electricity
56 & 58/64	Consten & Grundig	13.07.66	[1966] 299	[1966] 418	173	Exclusive Distribution	Consumer Electronics
32/65	Italy v Council	13.07.66	[1966] 389	[1969] 39	173	Regulation 19/65	Distribution
56/65	LTM v MBU	30.06.66	[1966] 235	[1966] 357	177	Exclusive Distribution	Machinery
8–11/66	Cimenteries	15.03.67	[1967] 75	[1967] 77	173	Article 15(6) Letter	Cement
23/67	De Haecht v Wilkin I	12.12.67	[1967] 407	[1968] 26	177	Exclusive Purchase	Brewery Contracts
24/67	Parke, Davis v Centrafarm	29.02.68	[1968] 55	[1968] 47	177	Patent Rights	Pharmaceuticals
14/68	Walt Wilhelm	13.02.69	[1969] 1	[1969] 100	177	Supremacy EEC Treaty	Dyestuffs
5/69	Völk v Vervaecke	09.07.69	[1969] 295	[1969] 273	177	De minimis	Domestic Appliances
10/69	Portelange v Smith Corona	09.07.69	[1969] 309	1 [1974] 397	177	Provisional Validity	Typewriters
41/69	ACF Chemiefarma	15.07.70	[1970] 661	—	173	Cartel	Quinine
43/69	Bilger v Jehle	18.03.70	[1970] 127	1 [1974] 382	177	Article 4 Regulation 17/62	Beer
44/69	Buchler & Co.	15.07.70	[1970] 733	—	173	Cartel	Quinine
45/69	Boehringer	15.07.70	[1970] 769	—	173	Cartel	Quinine
48/69	ICI	14.07.72	[1972] 619	[1972] 557	173	Cartel (Price)	Dyestuffs
49/69	BASF	14.07.72	[1972] 713	[1972] 557	173	Cartel (Price)	Dyestuffs
51/69	Bayer	14.07.72	[1972] 745	[1972] 557	173	Cartel (Price)	Dyestuffs
52/69	Ciba-Geigy	14.07.72	[1972] 787	[1972] 557	173	Cartel (Price)	Dyestuffs
53/69	Sandoz	14.07.72	[1972] 845	[1972] 557	173	Cartel (Price)	Dyestuffs
54/69	Francolor	14.07.72	[1972] 851	[1972] 557	173	Cartel (Price)	Dyestuffs
55/69	Cassella	14.07.72	[1972] 887	[1972] 557	173	Cartel (Price)	Dyestuffs

[1] European Court Reports.
[2] Common Market Law Reports.

Table 4

CASE No.	NAME	DATE	E.C.R.	C.M.L.R.	TYPE OF PROCEDURE	SUBJECT	PRODUCT/SERVICE
56/69	Hoechst	14.07.72	[1972] 927	[1972] 557	173	Cartel (Price)	Dyestuffs
57/69	ACNA	14.07.72	[1972] 933	[1972] 557	173	Cartel (Price)	Dyestuffs
1/70	Parfums Rochas v Bitsch	30.06.70	[1970] 515	[1971] 104	177	Provisional Validity	Cosmetics
40/70	Sirena v Eda	18.02.71	[1971] 69	[1971] 260	177	Trade Marks	Cosmetics
78/70	Deutsche Grammophon v Metro	08.06.71	[1971] 487	[1971] 631	177	Copyright	Records
1/71	Cadillon v Höss	06.05.71	[1971] 351	[1971] 420	177	Exclusive Distribution	Building Tools
8/71	Komponistenverband	13.07.71	[1971] 705	[1973] 902	175	Right to be Heard	Performing Rights
10/71	Muller	14.07.71	[1971] 723	—	177	Article 90(2)	Dredging
22/71	Béguelin v GL	25.11.71	[1971] 949	[1972] 81	177	Exclusive Distribution	Lighters
6/72	Continental Can	21.02.73	[1973] 215	[1973] 199	173	Merger 86	Cans
7/72	Boehringer	14.12.72	[1972] 1281	[1973] 864	173	Non bis in idem	Quinine
8/72	Cement Dealers	17.10.72	[1972] 977	[1973] 7	173	Cartel (National)	Cement
48/72	De Haecht v Wilkin II	06.02.73	[1973] 77	[1973] 287	177	Conflict Rules	Brewery Contract
6 & 7/73	ICI & CSC	06.03.74	[1974] 223	1 [1974] 309	173	Refusal to Deal 86	Pharmaceuticals
40–48, 50, 54–56, 111, 113 & 114/73	Suiker Unie	16.12.75	[1975] 1663	1 [1976] 295	173	Market Sharing	Sugar
41, 43 & 44/73	Générale Sucrière	09.03.77	[1977] 445	—	173	Currency of Fine	Sugar
127/73	BRT v SABAM I	30.01.74	[1974] 51	2 [1974] 238	177	Conflict rules	Performing Rights
127/73	BRT v SABAM II	27.03.74	[1974] 313	2 [1974] 238	177	Copyright 86	Performing Rights
155/73	Sacchi	30.04.74	[1974] 409	2 [1974] 177	177	Public Monopoly	TV Advertising
192/73	Van Zuylen v Hag	03.07.74	[1974] 731	2 [1974] 127	177	Trade Marks	Coffee
8/74	Dassonville	11.07.74	[1974] 837	2 [1974] 436	177	Exclusive Distribution	Whisky
12/74	Germany	20.02.75	[1975] 181	1 [1975] 340	169	Origin Specification	Sekt
15/74	Centrafarm & De Peijper v Sterling Drug	31.10.74	[1974] 1147	2 [1974] 480	177	Patent Rights	Pharmaceuticals
16/74	Centrafarm & De Peijper v Winthrop	31.10.74	[1974] 1183	2 [1974] 480	177	Trade Marks	Pharmaceuticals
17/74	Transocean Marine Paint Association	23.10.74	[1974] 1063	2 [1974] 459	173	Hearing	Marine Paints
19 & 20/74	Kali & Salz	14.05.75	[1975] 499	2 [1975] 154	173	Cartel (Distribution)	Fertilisers
71/74	Frubo	15.05.75	[1975] 563	2 [1975] 123	173	Exclusionary Practices	Fruit

CASE No.	NAME	DATE	E.C.R.	C.M.L.R.	TYPE OF PROCEDURE	SUBJECT	PRODUCT/SERVICE
73/74	Papiers Peints	26.11.75	[1975] 1491	1 [1976] 589	173	Cartel (Price)	Wallpaper
25/75	Van Vliet v Dalle Crode	01.10.75	[1975] 1103	2 [1975] 549	177	Exclusive Distribution	Paint Brushes
26/75	General Motors	13.11.75	[1975] 1367	1 [1976] 95	173	Excessive Pricing 86	Cars
51/75	EMI-CBS	15.06.76	[1976] 811	2 [1976] 235	177	Trade Mark Rights	Records
63/75	Fonderies Roubaix v Fonderies Roux	03.02.76	[1976] 111	1 [1976] 538	177	Exclusive Distribution	Foundries
86/75	EMI-CBS	15.06.76	[1976] 871	2 [1976] 235	177	Trade Mark Rights	Records
96/75	EMI-CBS	15.06.76	[1976] 913	2 [1976] 235	177	Trade Mark Rights	Records
119/75	Terrapin v Terranova	22.06.76	[1976] 1039	2 [1976] 482	177	Trade Mark Rights	Building Materials
26/76	Metro	25.10.77	[1977] 1875	2 [1978] 1	173	Selective Distribution	Consumer Electronics
27/76	United Brands	14.02.78	[1978] 207	1 [1978] 429	173	Excessive Pricing 86	Bananas
47/76	De Norre v Concordia	01.02.77	[1977] 65	1 [1977] 378	177	Exclusive Purchasing	Brewery Contracts
85/76	Hoffmann-La Roche	13.02.79	[1979] 461	3 [1979] 211	173	Exclusionary Practices 86	Vitamins
90/76	Van Ameyde v UCI	09.06.77	[1977] 1091	2 [1977] 478	177	Article 90(1)	Insurance
107/76	Hoffmann-La Roche v Centrafarm	24.05.77	[1977] 957	2 [1977] 334	177	Trade Mark Rights	Pharmaceuticals
13/77	GB-INNO v ATAB	16.11.77	[1977] 2115	1 [1978] 283	177	State Responsibility	Tobacco
19/77	Miller	01.02.78	[1978] 131	2 [1978] 334	173	Export Ban	Records
28/77	Tepea	20.06.78	[1978] 1391	3 [1978] 392	177	Trade Mark Licence	Record Cleaners
59/77	De Bloos v Bouyer	14.12.77	[1977] 2359	1 [1978] 511	177	Provisional Validity	Agricultural Machines
77/77	Benzine & Petroleum BV	29.06.78	[1978] 1513	3 [1978] 174	173	Refusal to Deal 86	Petrol
102/77	Hoffmann-La Roche v Centrafarm	23.05.78	[1978] 1139	3 [1978] 217	177	Trade Mark Rights	Pharmaceuticals
3/78	Centrafarm v AHP	10.10.78	[1978] 1823	1 [1979] 326	177	Trade Mark Rights	Pharmaceuticals
22/78	Hugin	31.05.79	[1979] 1869	3 [1979] 345	173	Refusal to Deal 86	Cash Registers
30/78	Distillers	10.07.80	[1980] 2229	3 [1980] 121	173	Notification	Alcoholic Drinks
32, 36–82/78	BMW Belgium	12.07.79	[1979] 2435	1 [1980] 370	173	Export Ban	Cars
125/78	GEMA	18.10.79	[1979] 3173	2 [1980] 177	175	Copyright	Performing Rights
209–215, 218/78	FEDETAB	29.10.80	[1980] 3125	3 [1981] 134	173	Cartel	Tobacco
253/78, 1–3/79	Procureur v Guerlain	10.07.80	[1980] 2327	2 [1981] 99	177	Comfort Letter	Perfumes
258/78	Nungesser	08.06.82	[1982] 2015	1 [1983] 278	173	Breeders' Rights	Maize Seeds
22/79	Greenwich v SACEM	25.10.79	[1979] 3275	1 [1980] 629	177	Copyright 86	Performing Rights

TABLE 4

Table 4

CASE No.	NAME	DATE	E.C.R.	C.M.L.R.	TYPE OF PROCEDURE	SUBJECT	PRODUCT/SERVICE
37/79	Anne Marty v Estée Lauder	10.07.80	[1980] 2481	2 [1981] 143	177	Comfort Letter	Perfumes
52/79	Debauve	18.03.80	[1980] 833	2 [1981] 362	177	Monopoly	Cable TV
62/79	Coditel v Ciné Vog	18.03.80	[1980] 881	2 [1981] 362	177	Copyright	Cable TV
99/79	Lancôme v Etos	10.07.80	[1980] 2511	2 [1981] 164	177	Selective Distribution	Cosmetics
106/79	Boekhandels v Eldi Records	20.03.80	[1980] 1137	3 [1980] 719	177	Notification	Records
136/79	National Panasonic	26.06.80	[1980] 2033	3 [1980] 169	173	Inspection	Consumer Electronics
155/79	AM&S	18.05.82	[1982] 1575	2 [1982] 264	173	Legal Professional Privilege	Zinc
730/79	Philip Morris	17.09.80	[1980] 2671	2 [1981] 321	173	State Aids	Tobacco
792/79R	Camera Care	17.01.80	[1980] 119	1 [1980] 334	173	Interim Measures	Cameras
31/80	L'Oréal v De Nieuwe AMCK	11.12.80	[1980] 3775	2 [1981] 235	177	Selective Distribution	Cosmetics
55 & 57/80	Membran/K-Tel v GEMA	20.01.81	[1981] 147	2 [1981] 44	177	Copyright	Records
58/80	Dansk Supermarked v Imerco	22.01.81	[1981] 181	3 [1981] 590	177	Copyright & Trade Mark	China
61/80	Stremsel	25.03.81	[1981] 851	1 [1982] 240	173	Exclusive Purchasing	Rennet
100–103/80	Pioneer	07.06.83	[1983] 1825	3 [1983] 221	173	Export Ban	Consumer Electronics
113/80	Ireland	17.06.80	[1980] 1625	1 [1982] 706	169	Origin Specification	Souvenirs
126/80	Salonia v Poidomani & Baglieri	16.06.81	[1981] 1563	1 [1982] 64	177	Selective Distribution	Newspapers
172/80	Zuechner v Bayerische Vereinsbank	14.07.81	[1981] 2021	1 [1982] 313	177	Concerted Practice	Banking
187/80	Merck & Co v Stephar	14.07.81	[1981] 2063	3 [1981] 463	177	Patent Rights	Pharmaceuticals
188–190/80	France	06.07.82	[1982] 2545	3 [1982] 144	173	Article 90(3)	Public Undertakings
270/80	Polydor v Harlequin Record Shops	09.02.82	[1982] 329	1 [1982] 677	177	Copyright	Records
1/81	Pfizer v Eurim-Pharm	03.12.81	[1981] 2913	1 [1982] 406	177	Trade Mark Rights	Chemicals
6/81	IDG v Beele	02.03.82	[1982] 707	3 [1982] 102	177	Counterfeit	Building Materials
60/81	IBM	11.11.81	[1981] 2639	3 [1981] 635	173	Statement of Objections	Computers
144/81	Keurkoop v Nancy Kean Gifts	14.09.82	[1982] 2853	2 [1983] 47	177	Design Rights	Leatherwear
210/81	Demo Schmidt	11.10.83	[1983] 3045	1 [1984] 63	173	Complaint/Select Distribution	Consumer Electronics
246/81	Lord Bethell	10.06.82	[1982] 2277	3 [1982] 300	175	Locus standi	Transport
262/81	Coditel v Cine-Vog	06.10.82	[1982] 3381	1 [1983] 49	177	Copyright	Cable TV

CASE No.	NAME	DATE	E.C.R.	C.M.L.R.	TYPE OF PROCEDURE	SUBJECT	PRODUCT/SERVICE
322/81	Michelin	09.11.83	[1983] 3461	1 [1985] 282	173	Discounts 86	Tyres
7/82	GVL	02.03.83	[1983] 483	3 [1983] 645	173	Copyright 86	Performing Rights
43 & 63/82	VBVB & VBBB	17.01.84	[1984] 19	1 [1985] 27	173	Collective RPM	Books
86/82	Hasselblad	21.02.84	[1984] 883	1 [1984] 559	173	Preventing Parallel Trade	Cameras
96–102, 104, 105, 108 & 110/82	NAVEWA	08.11.83	[1983] 3369	3 [1984] 276	173	Preventing Parallel Trade	Domestic Appliances
107/82	AEG	25.10.83	[1983] 3151	3 [1984] 325	173	Selective Distribution	Electrical Goods
172/82	Inter-Huiles	10.03.83	[1983] 555	3 [1983] 485	177	Article 90	Waste Collection
177 & 178/82	Van der Haar v Kaveka	05.04.84	[1984] 1797	2 [1985] 566	177	Pricing Legislation	Tobacco
181/82	Roussel v Netherlands	29.11.83	[1983] 3849	1 [1985] 834	177	Pricing Legislation	Pharmaceuticals
228 & 229/82	Ford	28.02.84	[1984] 1129	1 [1984] 649	173	Interim Measures	Cars
238/82	Duphar	07.02.84	[1984] 523	1 [1985] 256	177	Drug Reimbursement Scheme	Pharmaceuticals
240–242, 261, 262, 268 & 269/82	SSI	10.12.85	[1985] 3831	3 [1987] 661	173	Cartel	Tobacco
260/82	NSO	10.12.85	[1985] 3801	4 [1988] 755	173	Cartel	Tobacco
319/82	Ciments et Bétons v Kerpen	14.12.83	[1983] 4173	1 [1985] 511	177	Resale Prohibition	Cement
16/83	Prantl	13.03.84	[1984] 1299	2 [1985] 238	177	Design Rights	Bottles
29 & 30/83	Zinc Producers	28.03.84	[1984] 1679	1 [1985] 688	173	Cartel	Zinc
35/83	BAT	30.01.85	[1985] 363	2 [1985] 470	173	Trade Marks	Cigarettes
41/83	Italy	20.03.85	[1985] 873	2 [1985] 368	173	Refusal to Supply 86	Telecommunications
123/83	BNIC v Clair	30.01.85	[1985] 391	2 [1985] 430	177	Price Fixing	Alcoholic Drinks
145/83	Stanley Adams	07.11.85	[1985] 3539	1 [1986] 506	215	Confidentiality	—
170/83	Hydrotherm v Andreoli	12.07.84	[1984] 2999	3 [1985] 224	177	Regulation 67/67	Heating Equipment
177/83	Kohl v Ringelhahn	06.11.84	[1984] 3651	3 [1985] 340	177	Logo	Pharmaceutical Equipment
193/83	Windsurfing	25.02.86	[1986] 611	3 [1986] 489	173	Patent Licences	Leisure Products
229/83	Leclerc	10.01.85	[1985] 1	2 [1985] 286	177	State Responsibility	Books
231/83	Cullet v Leclerc	29.01.85	[1985] 305	2 [1985] 524	177	State Responsibility	Petroleum Products
243/83	AMP v Binon	03.07.85	[1985] 2015	3 [1985] 800	177	Selective Distribution	Newspapers

TABLE 4

Table 4

CASE No.	NAME	DATE	E.C.R.	C.M.L.R.	TYPE OF PROCEDURE	SUBJECT	PRODUCT/SERVICE
289/83	GAARM	13.12.84	[1984] 4295	3 [1986] 15	215	Failure to Act	New Potatoes
298/83	CICCE	28.03.85	[1985] 1105	1 [1986] 486	173	Duties of a Complainant	Cinema
299/83	St. Herblain v Syndicat des Libraires	11.07.85	[1985] 2515	—	177	State Responsibility	Books
19/84	Pharmon v Hoechst	09.07.85	[1985] 2281	3 [1985] 775	177	Patent Rights	Pharmaceuticals
25 & 26/84	Ford	17.09.85	[1985] 2725	3 [1985] 528	173	Preventing Parallel Trade	Cars
42/84	Remia	11.07.85	[1985] 2545	1 [1987] 1	173	Acquisition	Foodstuffs
60 & 61/84	Cinéthèque	11.07.85	[1985] 2605	1 [1986] 365	177	Copyright	Video cassettes
75/84	Metro	22.10.86	[1986] 3021	1 [1987] 118	173	Selective Distribution	Radios
142 & 156/84	BAT & Philip Morris	17.11.87	[1987] 4487	4 [1988] 24	173	Minority Share Acquisition	Cigarettes
161/84	Pronuptia v Schillgalis	28.01.86	[1986] 353	1 [1986] 414	177	Franchising	Wedding Dresses
182/84	Miro	26.11.85	[1985] 3731	3 [1986] 545	177	Product denomination	Cinema
209–213/84	Nouvelles Frontières	30.04.86	[1986] 1425	3 [1986] 173	177	State Responsibility	Air Transport
226/84	British Leyland	11.11.86	[1986] 3263	1 [1987] 185	173	Preventing Parallel Trade 86	Cars
311/84	Télémarketing v CLT	03.10.85	[1985] 3261	2 [1986] 558	177	Tying 86	TV Advertising
5/85	AKZO	23.09.86	[1986] 2585	3 [1987] 716	173	Investigations	Chemicals
31/85	ETA v DKI	10.12.85	[1985] 3933	2 [1986] 674	177	Guarantee	Watches
43/85	ANCIDES	09.07.87	[1987] 3131	4 [1988] 821	173	Exhibition Agreement	Dental Equipment
45/85	Fire Insurance	27.01.87	[1987] 405	4 [1988] 264	173	Cartel	Fire Insurance
53/85	AKZO	24.06.86	[1986] 1965	1 [1987] 231	173	Business Secrets	Chemicals
89, 104, 114, 116, 117, 125–129/85	Woodpulp	27.09.88	[1988] 5193	4 [1988] 901	173	Extraterritoriality	Woodpulp
89/85	Woodpulp	31.03.93	I [1993] 1307	4 [1993] 407	173	Cartel	Woodpulp
118/85	Italy	16.06.87	[1987] 2599	3 [1988] 255	169	Article 90	State aids
179/85	Germany	04.12.86	[1986] 3879	1 [1988] 135	169	Product Specification	Bottles
218/85	Cerafel v Le Campion	25.11.86	[1986] 3513	1 [1988] 83	177	National Market Organisation	Vegetables
272/85	ANTIB	20.05.87	[1987] 2201	4 [1988] 677	173	Cartel	River Transport

CASE No.	NAME	DATE	E.C.R.	C.M.L.R.	TYPE OF PROCEDURE	SUBJECT	PRODUCT/SERVICE
311/85	Vlaamse Reisbureaus	01.10.87	[1987] 3801	4 [1989] 213	177	State Responsibility	Travel Agents
352/85	Bond van Adverteerders	26.04.88	[1988] 2085	3 [1989] 113	177	Monopoly	Cable TV
355/85	Procureur v Cognet	23.10.86	[1986] 3231	3 [1987] 942	177	State Responsibility	—
402/85	Basset v SACEM	09.04.87	[1987] 1747	3 [1987] 173	177	Copyright 86	Performing Rights
434/85	Allen & Hanburys v Generics	03.03.88	[1988] 1245	1 [1988] 701	177	Licence of Right	Pharmaceuticals
10/86	VAG v Magne	18.12.86	[1986] 4071	4 [1988] 98	177	Regulation 123/85	Cars
C–62/86	AKZO	03.07.91	I [1991] 3359	5 [1993] 215	177	Predatory Pricing 86	Chemicals
65/86	Bayer v Süllhöfer	27.09.88	[1988] 5249	4 [1990] 182	177	Patent Licence	Chemicals
66/86	Ahmed Saeed v Zentrale	11.04.89	[1989] 803	4 [1990] 102	177	Price Fixing	Air Transport
136/86	BNIC/Aubert	03.12.87	[1987] 4789	4 [1988] 331	177	Production Quotas	Spirits
158/86	Warner Brothers v Christiansen	17.05.88	[1988] 2605	3 [1990] 684	177	Copyright	Performing Rights
246/86	Belasco	11.07.89	[1989] 2117	4 [1991] 96	173	Cartel	Construction Machines
247/86	Alsatel v Novasam	05.10.88	[1988] 5987	4 [1990] 434	177	Article 86	Telephones
267/86	Van Eycke v Aspa	21.09.88	[1988] 4769	4 [1990] 330	177	State Responsibility	Banking
C–270/86	Cholay	12.12.90	I [1990] 4687	—	177	Copyright	Performing Rights
27/87	Louis Erauw v La Hesbignonne	19.04.88	[1988] 1919	4 [1988] 576	177	Breeders' Rights	Seeds
30/87	Bodson v Pompes Funèbres	04.05.88	[1988] 2479	4 [1989] 984	177	Articles 90 and 86	Undertakers
35/87	Thetford Corp. v Fiamma	30.06.88	[1988] 3585	3 [1988] 549	177	Patent Rights	Toilets
46/87R	Hoechst	26.03.87	[1987] 1549	4 [1988] 430	186	Investigation	Chemicals
46/87, 227/88	Hoechst	21.09.89	[1989] 2859	4 [1991] 410	173	Investigation	Base Chemicals
53/87	Maxicar v Renault	05.10.88	[1988] 6039	4 [1990] 265	177	Patent Rights 86	Car Parts
85/87R	Dow	28.10.87	[1987] 4367	4 [1988] 439	186	Investigation	Chemicals
85/87	Dow Benelux	17.10.89	[1989] 3137	4 [1991] 410	173	Investigation	Base Chemicals
97–99/87	Dow Iberica	17.10.89	[1989] 3165	4 [1991] 410	173	Investigation	Base Chemicals
212/87	UNILEC v Larroche	22.09.88	[1988] 5075	1 [1990] 592	177	National Market Organisation	Fruit & Vegetables
226/87	Greece	30.06.88	[1988] 3611	3 [1989] 569	169	Article 90	Insurance
238/87	Volvo v Veng	05.10.88	[1988] 6211	4 [1989] 122	177	Patent Rights 86	Car Parts
254/87	Syndicat v Leclerc Aigle	14.07.88	[1988] 4457	4 [1990] 37	177	State Responsibility	Books
266 & 267/87	Royal Pharmaceutical Society	18.05.89	[1989] 1295	2 [1989] 751	177	Drug Prescription Rules	Drugs

TABLE 4

Table 4

CASE No.	NAME	DATE	E.C.R.	C.M.L.R.	TYPE OF PROCEDURE	SUBJECT	PRODUCT/SERVICE
C–277/87	Sandoz	11.01.90	I [1990] 45	—	173	Preventing Parallel Trade	Pharmaceuticals
C–279/87	Tipp-Ex	08.02.90	I [1990] 261	—	173	Preventing Parallel Trade	Stationary
320/87	Ottung v Klee	12.05.89	[1989] 1177	4 [1990] 915	177	—	Brewery Machines
341/87	EMI v Patricia	24.01.89	[1989] 79	2 [1989] 413	177	Copyright	Records
374/87	Orkem	18.10.89	[1989] 3283	4 [1991] 502	173	Information	Base Chemicals
395/87	Ministère Public v Tournier	13.07.89	[1989] 2521	4 [1991] 248	177	Excessive Pricing 86	Copyright
C–18/88	RTT v GB-Inno	13.12.91	I [1991] 5941	—	177	Article 90	Telecommunication
C–27/88	Solvay	18.10.89	[1989] 3355	4 [1991] 502	173	Information	Base Chemicals
C–110, 241 & 242/88	Lucazeau v SACEM	13.07.89	[1989] 2811	4 [1991] 248	177	Excessive Pricing 86	Copyright
C–202/88	France	19.03.91	I [1991] 1223	5 [1992] 552	173	Article 90	Telecommunications
C–10/89	CNL-Sucal v Hag	17.10.90	I [1990] 3711	3 [1990] 571	177	Trade Marks	Coffee
C–56/89R	Publishers Association	13.06.89	[1989] 1693	4 [1989] 816	186	Cartel	Books
76, 77 & 91/89R	RTE & BBC	11.05.89	[1989] 1141	4 [1989] 749	186	Copyright 86	TV Guide
C–234/89	Delimitis v Henninger Bräu	28.02.91	I [1991] 935	5 [1992] 210	177	Exclusive Purchasing	Beer
C–235/89	Italy	18.02.92	I [1992] 777	2 [1992] 709	169	Compulsory Licensing	Patents
C–238/89	Pall v Dahlhausen	13.12.90	I [1990] 4824	—	177	Trade Mark law	Filters
C–260/89	ERT v DEP	18.06.91	I [1991] 2925	4 [1994] 540	177	Article 90	Television
C–332/89	Marchandise	28.02.91	I [1991] 1627	3 [1993] 746	177	Opening Hours	Retail Business
C–339/89	Ahlstrom v Sulzer	24.01.91	I [1991] 107	—	177	Product Liability	Ship Engines
C–347/89	Bayern v Eurim-Pharm	16.04.91	I [1991] 1747	1 [1993] 616	177	Drug Registration	Pharmaceuticals
C–353/89	Netherlands	25.07.91	I [1991] 4069	—	169	Television Monopoly	Television
C–358/89	Extramet v Council	11.06.92	I [1992] 3813	2 [1993] 619	173	Dumping	Phosphate
C–30/90	U.K.	18.02.92	I [1992] 829	2 [1992] 709	169	Compulsory Licensing	Patents
C–41/90	Höfner v Macrotron	23.04.91	I [1991] 1979	4 [1993] 306	177	Article 90	Recruitment Services
C–46/90 & C–93/91	Lagauche	27.10.93	I [1993] 5267	—	177	Article 90	Telecoms
C–47/90	Delhaize v Promalvin	09.06.92	I [1992] 3669	—	177	Designation of Origin	Wine
C–48 & 66/90	Netherlands	12.02.92	I [1992] 565	5 [1993] 316	173	Article 90	Courier Services
C–66/90	PTT	04.06.91	I [1991] 2723	5 [1993] 316	173	Competence CFI	Courier Services
C–72/90	Asia Motors	23.05.90	I [1990] 2182	—	175/178	Competence of the Court	Cars

CASE No.	NAME	DATE	E.C.R.	C.M.L.R.	TYPE OF PROCEDURE	SUBJECT	PRODUCT/SERVICE
C–179/90	Merci v Siderurgica	10.12.91	I [1991] 5009	4 [1994] 422	177	Article 90	Port Activities
C–191/90	Generics v Smith Kline	27.10.92	I [1992] 5335	1 [1993] 89	177	Licences of Right	Pharmaceuticals
C–271/90	Spain	17.11.92	I [1992] 5833	4 [1993] 110	173	Article 90	Telecommunications
C–320–322/90	Telemarsicabruzzo	26.01.93	I [1993] 393	4 [1993] 227	177	Admissibility	Television
C–2/91	Meng	17.11.93	I [1993] 5751	—	177	State Responsibility	Insurance
C–3/91	Exportur v LOR SA	10.11.92	I [1992] 5529	—	177	Designation of Origin	Sweets
C–60/91	Batista Morais	19.03.92	I [1992] 2085	2 [1992] 533	177	State Interference	Driver's Licence
C–67/91	Spanish Banks	16.07.92	I [1992] 4785	—	177	Relations with National Authorities	Banking
C–69/91	Decoster	27.10.93	I [1993] 5335	—	177	Article 90	Telecoms
C–92/91	Taillandier	27.10.93	I [1993] 5383	—	177	Article 90	Telecoms
C–117/91	Bosman	04.10.91	I [1991] 4837	3 [1990] 938	173/178	Rejection of Complaint	Football
C–159–160/91	Poucet	17.02.93	I [1993] 637	4 [1993] 401	177	Concept of Undertaking	Social Security
C–185/91	Reiff	17.11.93	I [1993] 5801	5 [1995] 145	177	State Responsibility	Road Transport
C–195/91P	Bayer	15.12.94	I [1994] 5619	4 [1996] 32	49S	Notification of Decision	Animal Feed
C–225/91	Matra	15.06.93	I [1993] 3203	—	173	Article 92	Cars
C–241/91P	RTE	06.04.95	I [1995] 797	4 [1995] 718	49S	Article 86	Copyright
C–245/91	Ohra	17.11.93	I [1993] 5851	—	177	State Responsibility	Insurance
C–317/91	Deutsche Renault v Audi	30.11.93	I [1993] 6227	1 [1995] 461	177	Trade Marks	Cars
C–320/91	Corbeau	19.05.93	I [1993] 2533	4 [1995] 621	177	Article 90	Remailing
C–325/91	France	16.06.93	I [1993] 3283	—	173	Article 90	State Aids
C–327/91	France	09.08.94	I [1994] 3641	5 [1994] 517	173	E.C./U.S. Agreement	—
C–36/92P	SEP	19.05.94	I [1994] 1911	—	49S	Article 11, Regulation 17	Electricity
C–39/92	Petrogal	10.11.93	I [1993] 5659	—	177	Regulation 1984/83	Petrol
C–49/92P	Anic	08.07.99	I [1999] 4125	4 [2001] 17	49S	Cartel	Polypropylene
C–51/92P	Hercules	08.07.99	I [1999] 4235	5 [1999] 976	49S	Cartel	Polypropylene
C–53/92P	Hilti	02.03.94	I [1994] 667	4 [1994] 614	173(2)	Article 86	Tools
C–60/92	Otto	10.11.93	I [1993] 5683	—	177	Confidentiality	Mail Ordering
C–80/92	Belgium	24.03.94	I [1994] 1019	—	169	Admission Procedure	Telecommunications
C–92 & 326/92	Phil Collins	20.10.93	I [1993] 5145	3 [1993] 773	177	Industrial Property	Records
C–93/92	CMC Motorrad	13.10.93	I [1993] 5009	—	177	Free Circulation	Motorcycles

Table 4

CASE No.	NAME	DATE	E.C.R.	C.M.L.R.	TYPE OF PROCEDURE	SUBJECT	PRODUCT/SERVICE
C–128/92	Banks v British Coal	13.04.94	I [1994] 1209	5 [1994] 30	177	ECSC	Coal
C–134/92	Mörlins	17.11.93	I [1993] 6017	—	177	National competition law	Agriculture
C–137/92P	PVC	15.06.94	I [1994] 255	—	49S	Non-existence	Chemicals
C–157/92	Banchero	19.03.93	I [1993] 1086	5 [1993] 401	177	Admissibility	Tobacco
C–199/92	Hüls	08.07.99	I [1999] 4287	5 [1999] 1016	49S	Cartel	Polypropylene
C–200/92P	ICI	08.07.99	I [1999] 4399	5 [1999] 1110	49S	Cartel	Polypropylene
C–227/92P	Hoechst	08.07.99	I [1999] 4443	—	49S	Cartel	Polypropylene
C–234/92P	Shell	08.07.99	I [1999] 4561	5 [1999] 1142	49S	Cartel	Polypropylene
C–235/92P	Montecatini	08.07.99	I [1999] 4539	4 [2001] 18	49S	Cartel	Polypropylene
C–245/92P	Chemie Linz	08.07.99	I [1999] 4643	—	49S	Cartel	Polypropylene
C–250/92	Gøttrup-Klim v DLG	15.12.94	I [1994] 5641	4 [1996] 191	177	Buying Group	Agricultural Products
C–350/92	Spain	13.07.95	I [1995] 1985	1 [1996] 415	173	Patents	Pharmaceuticals
C–360/92P	Publishers' Association	17.01.95	I [1995] 23	5 [1995] 33	49S	Collective RPM	Books
C–364/92	SAT v Eurocontrol	19.01.94	I [1994] 43	5 [1994] 208	177	Concept of Undertaking	Air Traffic Control
C–376/92	Metro v Cartier	13.01.94	I [1994] 15	5 [1994] 331	177	Selective Distribution	Watches
C–379/92	Mateo Peralta	14.07.94	I [1994] 3453	—	177	State Interference	Maritime Transport
C–386/92	Monin	26.04.93	I [1993] 2049	—	177	Admissibility	Cars
C–387/92	Banco de Credito v Valencia	15.03.94	I [1994] 877	3 [1994] 473	177	Article 90	Banking
C–393/92	Almelo v Ysselmij	27.04.94	I [1994] 1477	—	177	Exclusive Purchasing	Electricity
C–401 & 402/92	Tankstation't Heukske	02.06.94	I [1994] 2199	—	177	State Interference	Petrol
C–5/93	DSM	08.07.99	I [1999] 4695	—	49S	Cartel	Polypropylene
C–9/93	IHT v Ideal-Standard	22.06.94	I [1994] 2789	3 [1994] 857	177	Trade Marks	Sanitary equipment
C–18/93	Corsica Ferries	17.05.94	I [1994] 1783	—	177	Article 90	Shipping Pilots
C–19/93	Rendo	19.10.95	I [1995] 3319	4 [1997] 392	49S	Rejection of Complaint	Electricity
C–39/93P	SFEI	16.06.94	I [1994] 2681	—	49S	Rejection of Complaints	Courier Services
C–55/93	Van Schaik	05.10.94	I [1994] 4837	—	177	State Interference	Car Maintenance
C–70/93	BMW	24.10.95	I [1995] 3439	4 [1996] 478	177	Regulation 123/85	Leasing
C–153/93	Delta Schiffahrt	09.06.94	I [1994] 2517	4 [1996] 21	177	State Interference	Inland Waterways
C–266/93	Volkswagen	24.10.95	I [1995] 3477	4 [1996] 505	177	Regulation 123/85	Leasing
C–310/93	BPB	06.04.95	I [1995] 865	4 [1995] 718	49S	Article 86	Plasterboard

CASE No.	NAME	DATE	E.C.R.	C.M.L.R.	TYPE OF PROCEDURE	SUBJECT	PRODUCT/SERVICE
C–314/93	Rouffeteau	12.07.94	I [1994] 3275	—	177	Directive 88/301	Telecommunications
C–319/93, C–40 & 224/94	Dijkstra	12.12.95	I [1995] 4471	5 [1996] 178	177	Regulation 26/62	Agriculture
C–322/93P	Peugeot	16.06.94	I [1994] 2727	—	49S	Regulation 123/85	Cars
C–323/93	La Crespelle	05.10.94	I [1994] 5077	—	177	Article 90	Artificial Insemination
C–334/93	Bonapharma	23.02.95	I [1995] 319	2 [1996] 308	177	Parallel Trade	Pharmaceuticals
C–378/93	La Pyramide	09.08.94	I [1994] 3999	—	177	Admissibility	Copyright
C–387/93	Banchero	14.12.95	I [1995] 4663	1 [1996] 829	177	Exclusive rights	Tobacco
C–399/93	Oude Luttikhuis	12.12.95	I [1995] 4515	5 [1996] 178	177	Regulation 26/62	Agriculture
C–412/93	Leclerc-Siplec	09.02.95	I [1995] 179	3 [1995] 3	177	State Interference	Advertising
C–427, 429 & 436/93	Bristol-Myers Squibb	11.07.96	I [1996] 3457	1 [1997] 1151	177	Trade Marks	Pharmaceuticals
C–428/93	Monin II	16.05.94	I [1994] 1707	—	177	Admissibility	Cars
C–430 & 431/93	Van Schijndel	14.12.95	I [1995] 4705	1 [1996] 801	177	Application of Article 85 by National Court	Insurance
C–458/93	Saddik	23.03.95	I [1995] 511	3 [1995] 318	177	Exclusive Rights	Tobacco
C–470/93	Mars	06.07.95	I [1995] 1923	3 [1995] 1	177	RPM	Chocolate
C–480/93P	Zunis Holding	11.01.96	I [1996] 1	5 [1996] 219	49S	Merger Control	Banking
C–18/94	Hopkins	02.05.96	I [1996] 2281	4 [1996] 745	177	Scope E.C. Treaty	Coal
C–68/94	France	31.03.98	I [1998] 1453	4 [1998] 829	173	Regulation 4064/89	Potash
C–71–73/94	Eurim-Pharma	11.07.96	I [1996] 3603	1 [1997] 1222	177	Trade Marks	Pharmaceuticals
C–91/94	Tranchant	09.11.95	I [1995] 3911	4 [1997] 74	177	Directive 88/301	Telecommunications
C–96/94	Spediporto	05.10.95	I [1995] 2883	4 [1996] 613	177	State Responsibility	Road Transport
C–134/94	Esso Española	30.11.95	I [1995] 4223	5 [1996] 154	177	State Responsibility	Petrol
C–140–142/94	DIPA	15.10.95	I [1995] 3257	4 [1996] 157	177	State Responsibility	Retail
C–160/94	Spain	23.10.97	I [1997] 5851	2 [1998] 373	169	Exclusive rights	Electricity
C–167/94	Gomis	07.04.95	I [1995] 1023	2 [1996] 129	177	Criminal Law	Tobacco
C–226/94	Grand Garage Albigeois	15.02.96	I [1996] 651	4 [1996] 778	177	Regulation 123/85	Cars
C–232/94	MPA Pharma	11.07.96	I [1996] 3671	—	177	Trade Marks	Pharmaceuticals
C–244/94	French Insurance	16.11.95	I [1995] 4022	4 [1996] 536	177	Concept of Undertaking	Insurance

Table 4

CASE No.	NAME	DATE	E.C.R.	C.M.L.R.	TYPE OF PROCEDURE	SUBJECT	PRODUCT/SERVICE
C–309/94	Nissan France	15.02.96	I [1996] 677	4 [1996] 778	177	Regulation 123/85	Cars
C–313/94	Graffione	26.11.96	I [1996] 6039	1 [1997] 925	177	Trade Marks	Paper Tissue
C–333/94P	Tetra Pak	14.11.96	I [1996] 5951	4 [1997] 662	49S	Article 86	Packaging Material
C–7/95P	John Deere	28.05.98	I [1998] 3111	5 [1998] 311	495	Information exchange	Tractors
C–8/95P	New Holland Ford	28.05.98	I [1998] 3175	5 [1998] 311	495	Information exchange	Tractors
C–70/95	Sodemare	17.06.97	I [1997] 3395	4 [1998] 667	177	State responsibility	Social Security
C–73/95P	Viho	24.10.96	I [1996] 5457	4 [1997] 419	49S	Intra-enterprise Conspiracy	Stationery
C–91/95P	Tremblay	24.10.96	I [1996] 5547	4 [1997] 211	49S	Rejection of Complaints	Copyright
C–107/95P	German Accountants	20.02.97	I [1997] 947	5 [1997] 432	49S	Article 90(3)	Auditing
C–128/95	Fontaine	20.02.97	I [1997] 967	5 [1997] 39	177	Selective Distribution	Cars
C–137/95P	SPO	25.03.96	I [1996] 1611	—	49S	Cartel	Construction
C–149/95P(R)	Atlantic Container	19.07.95	I [1995] 2165	5 [1997] 167	50S	Interim Measures	Transport
C–157/95	Netherlands	23.10.97	I [1997] 5699	2 [1998] 373	169	Exclusive rights	Electricity
C–158/95	Italy	23.10.97	I [1997] 5789	2 [1998] 373	169	Exclusive rights	Electricity
C–159/95	France	23.10.97	I [1997] 5815	2 [1998] 373	169	Exclusive rights	Electricity
C–185/95P	Baustahlgewebe	17.12.98	I [1998] 8417	4 [1999] 1203	495	Length of procedure	Welded Steel
C–219/95P	Ferriere Nord	17.07.97	I [1997] 4414	5 [1997] 575	49S	Cartel	Welded Steel Mesh
C–222/95	Van der Woude	21.09.00	I [2000] 7111	4 [2001] 2	234 (ex 177)	Scope of Articles 81, 82 & 86	Health Insurance
C–242/95	GT-Link v DSB	17.07.97	I [1997] 4449	5 [1997] 601	177	Article 86	Maritime Transport
C–251/95	Sabel v Puma	11.11.97	I [1997] 6161	1 [1998] 445	177	Trademarks	Sportswear
C–264/95P	UIC	11.03.97	I [1997] 1287	5 [1997] 49	495	Regulation 1017/68	Railway Tickets
C–267 & 268/95	Merck II	05.12.96	I [1996] 6285	1 [1997] 383	177	Patents	Pharmaceuticals
C–279/95P	Lagnese-Iglo	01.10.98	I [1998] 5609	5 [1998] 933	495	Exclusive purchasing	Ice-cream
C–282/95P	Guérin	18.03.97	I [1997] 503	5 [1997] 447	495	Rejection of Complaint	Cars
C–286/95P	ICI	06.04.00	I [2000] 2341	5 [2000] 413	49S	Authentication of decisions	Soda Ash
C–287 & 288/95P	Solvay	06.04.00	I [2000] 2391	5 [2000] 454	49S	Authentication of decisions	Soda Ash
C–316/95	Generics v SKF	09.07.97	I [1997] 3929	1 [1997] 1	177	Free circulation	Pharmaceuticals

CASE No.	NAME	DATE	E.C.R.	C.M.L.R.	TYPE OF PROCEDURE	SUBJECT	PRODUCT/SERVICE
C–337/95	Dior v Evora	04.11.97	I [1997] 6013	1 [1998] 737	177	Trademarks	Perfumes
C–343/95	Dieglo Cali	18.03.97	I [1997] 547	5 [1997] 484	177	Article 86	Maritime Port
C–349/95	Loenders-loot	11.11.97	I [1997] 6227	1 [1998] 1015	177	Trademarks	Alcoholic Beverages
C–352/95	Phytheron	20.03.97	I [1997] 729	—	177	Trade Marks	Chemicals
C–359/95P	Ladbroke	11.11.97	I [1997] 6265	4 [1998] 27	495	Rejection of complaints	Betting
C–35/96	Italie	18.06.98	I [1998] 3851	5 [1998] 889	169	State responsibility	Custom Agents
C–39/96	KVBB v Free Record Shop	24.04.97	I [1997] 2303	5 [1997] 521	177	Provisional validity	Records
C–41/96	VAG v SYD-Consult	05.06.97	I [1997] 3123	5 [1997] 537	177	Selective distribution	Cars
C–55/96	Job Centre	11.12.97	I [1997] 7119	4 [1998] 708	177	Exclusive rights	Recruitment Services
C–59/96P	Koelman	16.09.97	I [1997] 4809	—	49S	Rejection of complaints	Copyright
C–67/96	Albany	21.09.99	I [1999] 5751	4 [2000] 446	234 (ex 177)	Article 86 (ex 90)	Pension Funds
C–148/96P	Goldstein	11.07.96	I [1996] 3383	5 [1997] 27	49S	Interim Measures	Health Care
C–163/96	Raso	12.02.98	I [1998] 533	4 [1998] 737	177	Exclusive Rights	Recruitment Services
C–203/96	Chemische Afvalstoffen Dusseldorp	25.06.98	I [1998] 4075	3 [1998] 873	177	State interference	Waste Management
C–215 & 216/96	Carlo Bagnasco	21.01.99	I [1999] 135	4 [1999] 624	177	Inter-bank agreement	Banking
C–230/96	Cabour v Arnor	30.04.98	I [1998] 2055	5 [1998] 679	177	Selective distribution	Cars
C–266/96	Corsica Ferries France	18.06.98	I [1998] 3949	5 [1999] 402	177	State interference	Maritime Transport
C–268/96P(R)	Dutch Cranes	14.10.96	I [1996] 4971	5 [1997] 157	49S	Interim Measures	Cranes
C–306/96	Javico v Yves Saint-Laurent	28.04.98	I [1998] 1997	5 [1998] 172	177	Trade with third states	Perfumes
C–355/96	Silhouette International Schmied	16.05.98	I [1998] 4799	2 [1998] 953	177	Trade mark	Sun Glasses
C–395 & 396/96P	CMB	16.03.00	I [2000] 1365	4 [2000] 1076	49S	Articles 81 & 82	Shipping
C–401/96P	Somaco	07.05.98	I [1998] 2587	4 [1999] 35	495	Rejection of Complaint	Cars
C–7/97	Oscar Bronner	26.11.98	I [1998] 7791	4 [1999] 112	177	Essential facilities	Newspapers
C–38/97	Autotransporti Librandi	01.10.98	I [1998] 5955	5 [1998] 966	177	State responsibility	Transport
C–61/97	Foreningen af Danske Videogramdistributører	22.09.98	I [1998] 5171	1 [1999] 1297	177	Copy Rights	Videocassettes
C–63/97	BMW	23.02.99	I [1999] 905	1 [1999] 1099	177	Trademark	Cars
C–70/97P	Kruidvat	17.11.98	I [1998] 7183	4 [1999] 68	495	Admissibility	Perfumes
C–78/97P	Goldstein	16.03.97	—	4 [1997] 627	495	Interim Measures	Medical Services

Table 4

CASE No.	NAME	DATE	E.C.R.	C.M.L.R.	TYPE OF PROCEDURE	SUBJECT	PRODUCT/SERVICE
C–115 & 117/97	Brentjens	21.09.99	I [1999] 6025	4 [2000] 566	234 (ex 177)	Article 86 (ex 90)	Pension Funds
C–119/97P	Ufex	04.03.99	I [1999] 1341	4 [2000] 268	492	Rejection of Complaint	Courier Services
C–126/97	Eco Swiss	01.06.99	I [1999] 3055	5 [2000] 816	234 (ex 177)	National procedures	Watches & Clocks
C–147 & 148/97	Deutsche Post	10.02.00	I [2000] 825	4 [2000] 838	234 (ex 177)	Article 86 (ex 90)	Postal Services
C–219/97	Drijvende Bokken	21.09.99	I [1999] 6121	4 [2000] 599	234 (ex 177)	Article 86 (ex 90)	Pension Funds
C–265/97P	Florimex	30.03.00	—	5 [2001] 34	49S	Rejection of complaint	Flowers
C–266/97	VBA & VGB	30.03.00	—	5 [2001] 34	49S	Rejection of complaint	Flowers
C–310/97	AssiDomän	14.09.99	I [1999] 5363	5 [1999] 1253	49S	Article 233 (ex 176)	Woodpulp
C–436/97P	Deutsche Bahn	27.04.99	I [1999] 2387	5 [1999] 776	49S	Appeal on points of law only	Rail Transport
C–22/98	Becu	16.09.99	I [1999] 5665	4 [2001] 26	234 (ex 177)	Article 86 (ex 90)	Ports
C–59/98	Luxembourg	25.02.99	I [1999] 1181	—	—	—	—
C–153/98P	Guérin	05.03.99	I [1999] 1441	—	49S	Time Limit for Appeal	Motor Vehicles
C–154/98P	Guérin	05.03.99	I [1999] 1451	—	49S	Time Limit for Appeal	Motor Vehicles
C–174 & 189/98	Van der Wal	11.01.00	I [2000] 1	1 [2002] 16[3]	49S	Access to information	Legal Profession
C–180–184/98	Pavlov	12.09.00	I [2000] 6451	4 [2001] 1	234 (ex 177)	Article 86 (ex 90)	Pension Funds
C–219/98	Sarrió	16.11.00	I [2000] 9991	—	49S	Cartel	Cardboard
C–238, 244, 245, 247, 250, 254/99P	PVC II	15.10.02	I [2002] 8375	4 [2003] 10	49S	Cartel	PVC
C–248/98P	KNP BT	16.11.00	I [2000] 9641	—	49S	Cartel	Cardboard
C–279/98P	Cascades	16.11.00	I [2000] 9693	—	49S	Cartel	Cardboard
C–280/98P	Moritz Weig	16.11.00	I [2000] 9757	—	49S	Cartel	Cardboard
C–282/98P	Enso Española	16.11.00	I [2000] 9817	—	49S	Cartel	Cardboard
C–283/98P	Mo och Domsjö	16.11.00	I [2000] 9855	4 [2001] 11	49S	Cartel	Cardboard

[3] C.M.L.R. references from 2002 are to the unique citation number.

CASE No.	NAME	DATE	E.C.R.	C.M.L.R.	TYPE OF PROCEDURE	SUBJECT	PRODUCT/SERVICE
C–286/98	Stora Kopparbergs Bergslags	16.11.00	I [2000] 9925	4 [2001] 12	49S	Cartel	Cardboard
C–294/98P	Metsa Serla Oyj	16.11.00	I [2000] 10065	—	49S	Cartel	Cardboard
C–297/98	SCA Holding	16.11.00	I [2000] 10101	4 [2001] 13	49S	Cartel	Cardboard
C–298/98P	Metsa Serla (Finnboard)	16.11.00	I [2000] 10157	—	49S	Cartel	Cardboard
C–344/98	Masterfoods	14.12.00	I [2000] 11369	4 [2001] 14	234 (ex 177)	National enforcement of EU law	Ice-cream
C–449/98P	IECC	17.05.01	I [2000] 3875	5 [2001] 7	49S	Rejection of complaint	Postal Services
C–450/98P	IECC	17.05.01	I [2000] 3947	5 [2001] 8	49S	Rejection of complaint	Postal Services
C–35/99	Arduino	19.02.02	I [2002] 1529	4 [2002] 25	234 (ex 177)	Article 81	Lawyers' Fees
C–163/99	Portugal	29.03.01	I [2000] 2613	4 [2002] 31	230 (ex 173)	Article 86 (ex 90)	Landing Fees
C–214/99	Neste	07.12.00	I [2000] 11121	4 [2001] 27	234 (ex 177)	Exclusive purchasing agreement	Petrol
C–221/99	Conte	29.11.01	I [2001] 9359	4 [2002] 8	234 (ex 177)	Article 81	Architects' Services
C–302 & 308/99P	TF1	12.07.01	I [2001] 5603	—	49S	Failure to act	Broadcasting
C–309/99	Wouters	19.02.02	I [2002] 1577	4 [2002] 27	234 (ex 177)	Articles 81, 82 & 86	Lawyers' Fees
C–340/99	TNT/Traco	17.05.01	I [2000] 4109	4 [2002] 13	234 (ex 177)	Article 86 (ex 90)	Postal Services
C–364/99P(R)	DSR Senator Lines	14.12.99	I [1999] 8733	4 [2000] 600	50S	Article 242 (ex 185)	Shipping
C–453/99	Courage	20.09.01	I [2001] 6297	5 [2001] 28	234 (ex 177)	Action for damages	Pub Lease Agreement
C–475/99	Glöckner	25.10.01	I [2001] 8086	4 [2002] 21	234 (ex 177)	Article 86 (ex 90)	Ambulance Services
C–44/00	Sodima	13.12.00	I [2000] 11231	4 [2001] 8	49S	Distribution agreement	Motor Vehicles
C–94/00	Roquette Frères/DGCCRFC	22.10.02	I [2002] 9011	4 [2003] 1	234 (ex 177)	Powers of investigation	Sodium Glucomate
C–137/00	Milk Marque	09.09.03	I [2003] 7975	4 [2004] 6	234	National competition law	Agriculture
C–204e.s./00P	Aarlborg Portland	07.01.04	I [2004] 123	4 [2004] 13	49S	Cartel	Cement
C–218/00	Cisal di Battistello	22.01.02	I [2002] 691	4 [2002] 24	234 (ex 177)	Articles 81, 82 & 86	Social Insurance

Table 4

CASE No.	NAME	DATE	E.C.R.	C.M.L.R.	TYPE OF PROCEDURE	SUBJECT	PRODUCT/SERVICE
C–338/00P	Volkswagen	18.09.03	I [2003] 9189	4 [2004] 7	49S	Parallel trade	Cars
C–361/00P(R)	Cho Yang Shipping	15.12.00	I [2000] 11657	4 [2001] 32	50S	Suspension of payment of fine	Shipping
C–2 & 3/01P	Bayer	06.01.04	I [2004] 23	4 [2004] 13	49S	Concept of agreement	Pharmaceuticals
C–34–38/01	Enirisorse	27.11.03	I [2003] 14243	1 [2004] 10	234	86	Port Services
C–82/01P	Aéroports de Paris	24.10.02	I [2002] 9297	4 [2003] 12	49S	Article 86	Airports
C–198/01	Consorzio Industrie Fiammiferi	09.09.03	I [2003] 8055	5 [2003] 16	234	State liability	Matches
C–207/01	Altair Chimica	11.09.03	I [2003] 8875	5 [2003] 17	234	82	Electricity
C–264 e.a./01	AOK-Bundesverband	16.03.04	I [2004] 2493	4 [2004] 22	234	Concept of undertaking	Insurance
C–359/01P	British Sugar	29.04.04	I [2004] 4933	5 [2004] 8	49S	Cartel	Sugar
C–418/01	IMS Health	29.04.04	I [2004] 5039	4 [2004] 28	234	82 and licensing	Industry Standards
C–57/02P	Acerinox	14.07.05	—	5 [2005] 15	49S	Article 65 ECSC	Steel
C–65 & 73/02P	ThyssenKrupp Stainless	14.07.05	—	5 [2005] 16	49S	Article 65 ECSC	Steel
C–141/02P	T-Mobile Austria	22.02.05	—	4 [2005] 12	49S	Article 86	Mobile telephony
C–189 e.a./02P	Dansk Rørindustri	28.06.05	—	5 [2005] 17	49S	Cartel	Pre-insulated pipes
C–438/02	Hanner	31.05.05	—	2 [2005] 42	234	Article 86	Medicines
C–470/02P	European Broadcasting Union	27.09.04	—	—	49S	Article 81(3)	Sports broadcasting rights
C–53/03	Syfait	31.05.05	—	5 [2005] 1	234	82 refusal to supply	Pharmaceuticals
C–123/03P	Greencore	09.12.04	I [2004] 11647	4 [2005] 1	56 (ex 49)S	Reimbursement of interest on fine	Sugar
C–134/03	Viacom	17.02.05	—	1 [2006] 47	234	Articles 82 & 86	Bill-posting services
C–205/03	FENIN	11.07.06	—	5 [2006] 7	56S	Concept of undertaking	Medical goods & equipment
C–231/03	Coname	21.07.05	—	1 [2006] 2	234	Scope of Article 81	Gas distribution
C–236/03P	CMA CGM	28.10.04	—	4 [2005] 7	56 (ex 49) S	Limitation periods	Maritime transport
C–250/03	Mauri	17.02.05	—	4 [2005] 11	234	Articles 81 & 82	Legal profession
C–397/03	Archer Daniels Midland	18.05.06	—	5 [2006] 4	56S	Cartel	Lysine
C–551/03P	General Motors	06.04.06	—	5 [2006] 1	56S	Preventing Parallel Trade	Cars
C–7/04	Akzo Nobel	27.09.04	I [2004] 8739	5 [2004] 24	57S	Legal privilege	—
C–74/04	Volkswagen	13.07.06	—	—	56S	Resale price maintenance	Motor vehicles

CASE No.	NAME	DATE	E.C.R.	C.M.L.R.	TYPE OF PROCEDURE	SUBJECT	PRODUCT/SERVICE
C–95/04	British Airways	15.03.07	—	4 [2007] 22	56S	82 rebates & bonuses	Reservation systems
C–95 & 202/04	Cipolla v Fazari	05.12.06	—	4 [2007] 8	234	Fee scales	Legal services
C–105/04	FEG	21.09.06	—	5 [2006] 22	56S	Trade association	Electrical goods & equipment
C–110/04P	Strintzis Lines	30.03.06	—	—	56S	Price Fixing	Ferry Services
C–111/04P	Adriatica di Navigazione	16.02.06	—	—	56S	Price Fixing	Ferry Services
C–112/04P	Marlines	15.09.05	—	—	56S	Price Fixing	Ferry Services
C–113/04	Technische Unie	21.09.06	—	—	56S	Trade association	Electrical goods & equipment
C–121/04P	Minoan Lines	17.11.05	—	—	56S	Price Fixing	Ferry Services
C–125/05	VW-Audi Dealers	07.09.06	—	4 [2007] 25	234	Selective distribution	Motor vehicles
C–167/04	JCB Service	21.09.06	—	5 [2006] 23	56s	Preventing parallel trade	Earthmoving equipment
C–289/04	Showa Denko	29.06.06	—	5 [2006] 14	56S	Cartel	Graphite electrodes
C–295 & 298/04	Italian Insurers	13.07.06	—	5 [2006] 17	234	Actions for damages	Insurance
C–301/04	Graphite Electrodes	29.06.06	—	5 [2006] 15	56S	Cartel	Graphite electrodes
C–308/04	SGL Carbon	29.06.06	—	5 [2005] 16	56S	Cartel	Graphite electrodes
C–403 & 405/04	Sumitomo & Nippon Steel	25.01.07	—	4 [2007] 16	56S	Cartel	Seamless steel tubes
C–407/04	Dalmine	25.01.07	—	—	56S	Cartel	Seamless steel tubes
C–411/04	Salzgitter Mannesmann	25.01.07	—	4 [2007] 17	56S	Cartel	Seamless steel tubes
C–519/04	Meca-Medina	18.07.06	—	5 [2006] 18	56S	Rejection of complaint	Sport/anti-doping rules
C–125/05	VW-Audi Dealers	07.09.06	—	4 [2007] 25	234	Selective distribution	Motor vehicles
C–217/05	CEEES v CEPSA	14.12.06	—	4 [2007] 5	234	Agency agreements	Petrol
C–238/05	Asnef-Equifax	23.11.06	—	4 [2007] 6	234	Exchange of information	Financial services
C–282/05	Holcim	19.04.07	—	4 [2007] 26	56S	Bank guarantee charges	Cement
C–328/05	SGL Carbon	10.05.07	—	5 [2007] 1	56S	Cartel	Specialty graphites
C–376–377/05	Brunsteiner & Hilgert	30.11.06	—	4 [2007] 7	234	Selective distribution	Motor vehicles
C–76/06	Britannia Alloys	07.06.07	—	5 [2007] 3	56S	Cartel	Zinc phosphate
C–273/06	Petschenig v Toyota	26.01.07	—	—	234	Selective distribution	Motor vehicles

TABLE 5

LIST OF MERGER DECISIONS

MERGER No.	NAME	DATE	O.J.[1]	C.M.L.R.[2]	TYPE OF DECISION	PRODUCT SECTOR
M.4	Renault/Volvo	07.11.90	—	4 [1991] 297 (D)[3]	Clearance Art.6(1)(b)	Vehicles
M.9	Fiat/Ford New Holland	08.02.91	—	—	Clearance Art.6(1)(b)	Agricultural Machinery
M.10	CONAGRA/IDEA	30.05.91	—	5 [1992] M19 (D)	Clearance Art.6(1)(b)	Slaughter of Animals/ Meat Products
M.12	Varta/Bosch	31.07.91	[1991] L320/26	5 [1992] M1 (D)	With conditions and obligations Art.8(2)	Batteries
M.17	MBB/Aerospatiale	25.02.91	—	4 [1992] M70 (D)	Clearance Art.6(1)(b)	Helicopters
M.18	AG/AMEV	21.11.90	—	4 [1991] 847 (D)	Clearance Art.6(1)(b)	Insurance
M.21	BNP/Dresdner Bank	04.02.91	—	—	Clearance Art.6(1)(b)	Banking
M.23	ICI/Tioxide	28.11.90	—	4 [1991] 792 (D)	Art. 6(1)(a)	Chemicals
M.24	Mitsubishi/UCAR	04.01.91	—	4 [1992] M50 (D)	Clearance Art.6(1)(b)	Graphite & Carbon Electrodes
M.25	Arjomari/Wiggins Teape	10.12.90	—	4 [1992] 854 (D)	Clearance Art.6(1)(b)	Paper And Pulp
M.26	Cargill/Unilever	20.12.90	—	4 [1992] M55 (D)	Clearance Art.6(1)(b)	Agricultural Merchanting
M.27	Promodes/Dirsa	17.12.90	—	5 [1992] M25 (D)	Clearance Art.6(1)(b)	Retailing
M.37	Matsushita/MCA	10.01.91	—	4 [1992] M36 (D)	Clearance Art.6(1)(b)	Films, Consumer Electronics
M.42	Alcatel/Telettra	12.04.91	[1991] L122/48	4 [1991] 778 (D)	Clearance Art.8(2)	Batteries
M.43	CEAC/Magneti-Marelli	29.05.91	[1991] L222/38	4 [1992] M61 (D)	With conditions and obligations Art.8(2)	Batteries
M.50	AT&T/NCR	18.01.91	—	4 [1992] M41 (D)	Clearance Art.6(1)(b)	Computers

[1] Phase II decisions published by the Official Journal of the European Communities.
[2] C.M.L.R. references relate to the volume and page number for full text decisions reported up to the end of 2001. Thereafter, they are to the unique reference allotted to the report of each decision. Press release references relate to the volume and page number up to the end of 2001. Thereafter, the unique number beginning with "IS" is used.
[3] ("D") indicates reporting of full text of the decision.

Table 5

MERGER No.	NAME	DATE	O.J.	C.M.L.R.	TYPE OF DECISION	PRODUCT SECTOR
M.53	Aérospatiale-Alenia/de Havilland	02.10.91	[1991] L334/42	4 [1992] M2	Prohibition Art.8(3)	Turboprop Aircraft
M.57	Digital/Kienzle	22.02.91	—	4 [1992] M99 (D)	Clearance Art.6(1)(b)	Computers
M.58	Baxter/Nestlé/Salvia	06.02.91	—	5 [1992] M33 (D)	Art. 6(1)(a)	Clinical Nutrition
M.62	Eridania/ISI	30.07.91	—	—	Clearance Art.6(1)(b)	Sugar
M.63	Elf/Ertoil	29.04.91	—	—	Clearance Art.6(1)(b)	Petrol, Lubricants
M.65	Asko/Omni	21.02.91	—	5 [1992] M30 (D)	Clearance Art.6(1)(b)	Personal and Other Services
M.68	Tetra Pak/Alfa-Laval	19.07.91	[1991] L290/35	4 [1992] M81	Without conditions and obligations Art.8(2)	Packaging Machines — Food Processing Machines
M.69	Kyowa/Saitama	07.03.91	—	4 [1992] 105 (D)	Clearance Art.6(1)(b)	Banking
M.70	Otto/Grattan	21.03.91	—	5 [1992] M49 (D)	Clearance Art.6(1)(b)	Mail Order
M.72	Sanofi/Sterling Drugs	10.06.91	—	—	Clearance Art.6(1)(b)	Pharmaceuticals
M.73	Usinor/ASD	29.04.91	—	—	Clearance Art.6(1)(b)	Coal & steel
M.76	Lyonnaise des Eaux/Brochier	11.07.91	—	—	Clearance Art.6(1)(b)	Pipeline Construction
M.80	Redoute/Empire Stores	25.04.91	—	5 [1992] M39 (D)	Clearance Art.6(1)(b)	Retail/Mail Order
M.81	VIAG/Continental Can	06.06.91	—	—	Clearance Art.6(1)(b)	Packaging
M.82	Asko/Jacobs/ADIA	16.05.91	—	4 [1993] M14 (D)	Clearance Art.6(1)(b)	Personnel Services
M.85	ELF/Occidental	13.06.91	—	4 [1993] M9 (D)	Clearance Art.6(1)(b)	Petroleum Products
M.86	Thomson/Pilkington	23.10.91	—	—	Clearance Art.6(1)(b)	Optronics
M.88	ELF/Enterprise	24.07.91	—	5 [1992] M66 (D)	Art. 6(1)(a)	Petroleum Products
M.90	BSN/Nestlé/Cokoladovni	17.02.92	—	—	Art. 6(1)(a)	Confectionery Products
M.92	RVI/VBC/HEULIEZ	03.06.91	—	5 [1992] M63 (D)	Clearance Art.6(1)(b)	Buses and Coaches
M.93	Apollinaris/Schweppes	24.06.91	—	4 [1992] M78 (D)	Clearance Art.6(1)(b)	Soft Drinks
M.97	Pechiney-Usinor/Sacilor	24.06.91	—	—	Clearance Art.6(1)(b)	Mechanical Parts
M.98	ELF/BC/CEPSA	18.06.91	—	—	Clearance Art.6(1)(b)	Petroleum Products
M.99	Nissan/Richard Nissan	28.06.91	—	5 [1992] M46 (D)	Clearance Art.6(1)(b)	Automobile Distribution
M.101	Draeger/IBM/HMP	28.06.91	—	—	Clearance Art.6(1)(b)	Hospital Data Management Systems
M.102	TNT/Canada Post	02.12.91	—	—	Clearance Art.6(1)(b)	Express Mail Services
M.105	ICL/Nokia Data	17.07.91	—	—	Clearance Art.6(1)(b)	Computers
M.110	ABC/Générale des Eaux/Canal & W.H. Smith	10.09.91	—	4 [1993] M1 (D)	Clearance Art.6(1)(b)	Television

MERGER No.	NAME	DATE	O.J.	C.M.L.R.	TYPE OF DECISION	PRODUCT SECTOR
M.111	BP/Petromed	29.07.91	—	4 [1992] M71 (D)	Clearance Art.6(1)(b)	Petroleum Products
M.112	EDS/SD-Scicon	17.07.91	—	4 [1993] M77 (D)	Clearance Art.6(1)(b)	High-tech Services
M.113	Courtaulds/SNIA	19.12.91	—	—	Clearance Art.6(1)(b)	Acetate Yarn
M.116	Kelt/American Express	20.08.91	—	—	Clearance Art.6(1)(b)	Petroleum Products
M.117	Koipe-Tabacalera/Elosua	28.07.92	—	—	Art. 6(1)(a)	Oils and Fats
M.119	Metallgesellschaft/Dynamit Nobel	14.10.91	—	—	Clearance Art.6(1)(b)	Mining Metal Ores
M.121	Ingersoll Rand/Dresser	18.12.91	—	5 [1993] M67 (D)	Clearance Art.6(1)(b)	Industrial Pumps
M.122	Paribas/MTH	17.10.91	—	—	Clearance Art.6(1)(b)	Machinery Wholesaling
M.124	BNP/Dresdner (Czechoslovakia)	26.08.91	—	5 [1993] M38 (D)	Clearance Art.6(1)(b)	Banking
M.126	Accor/Wagons-Lits	28.04.92	[1992] L204/1	5 [1993] M13 (D)	With conditions and obligations Art.8(2)	Hotels and Restaurants
M.129	Digital/Philips	02.09.91	—	4 [1994] M4 (D)	Clearance Art.6(1)(b)	Computers
M.130	Delta Airlines/Pan Am	13.09.91	—	5 [1992] M56 (D)	Clearance Art.6(1)(b)	Air Transport
M.133	Ericsson/Kolbe	22.01.92	—	4 [1992] 346 (IP)	Clearance Art.6(1)(b)	Telecommunications Equipment
M.134	Mannesmann/Boge	23.09.91	—	4 [1992] 11 (IP)[4]	Clearance Art.6(1)(b)	Shock Absorbers
M.137	Bank America/Security Pacific	24.10.91	—	—	Clearance Art.6(1)(b)	Banking
M.138	CAMPSA	19.12.91	—	—	Clearance Art.6(1)(b)	Petroleum Distribution
M.139	VIAG/Brühl	19.12.91	—	4 [1992] 342 (IP)	Clearance Art.6(1)(b)	Metal Casting
M.141	UAP/Transatlantic/Sunlife	11.11.91	—	—	Clearance Art.6(1)(b)	Insurance
M.146	Metallgesellschaft/Safic Alcan	08.11.91	—	—	Clearance Art.6(1)(b)	Rubber and Latex
M.147	Eurocom/RSCG	18.12.91	—	—	Clearance Art.6(1)(b)	Advertising
M.149	Lucas/Eaton	09.12.91	—	—	Clearance Art.6(1)(b)	Heavy Duty Braking Systems
M.152	Volvo/Atlas	14.01.92	—	4 [1992] 345 (IP)	Clearance Art.6(1)(b)	Hydraulic Pumps
M.156	Cereol/Continentale Italiana	27.11.91	—	4 [1992] 346 (IP)	Art. 6(1)(a)	Oils and Fats
M.157	Air France/Sabena	05.10.92	—	5 [1994] M1 (D)	Clearance Art.6(1)(b)	Air Transport
M.159	Mediobanca/Generali	19.12.91	—	4 [1994] M1 (D)	Clearance Art.6(1)(a)	Banking
M.160	Elf Atochem/Rohm & Haas	28.07.92	—	—	Clearance Art.6(1)(b)	Chemicals

[4] "(IP)" indicates reporting of Commission press release.

Table 5

MERGER No.	NAME	DATE	O.J.	C.M.L.R.	TYPE OF DECISION	PRODUCT SECTOR
M.162	James River/Rayne	13.02.92	—	4 [1992] 342 (IP)	Clearance Art.6(1)(b)	Tissue Paper
M.164	Mannesman/VDO	13.12.91	—	—	Clearance Art.6(1)(b)	Car Parts
M.165	Alcatel/AEG Kabel	18.12.91	—	—	Clearance Art.6(1)(b)	Cables and Wires
M.166	Torras/Sarrio	24.02.92	—	4 [1992] 341 (IP)	Clearance Art.6(1)(b)	Printing Papers
M.167	Gambogi/Cogei	19.12.91	—	—	Clearance Art.6(1)(b)	Construction
M.168	Flachglas/VEGLA/JVC	13.04.92	—	4 [1992] 543 (IP)	Art. 6(1)(a)	Recycling
M.176	Sunrise	13.01.92	—	—	Art. 6(1)(a)	Television
M.178	Saab/Ericsson Space	13.01.92	—	4 [1992] 345 (IP)	Clearance Art.6(1)(b)	Space Equipment
M.179	Spar/Dansk Supermarket	03.02.92	—	4 [1992] 348 (IP)	Clearance Art.6(1)(b)	Retailing
M.180	Tarmac/Steetley	12.02.92	—	4 [1992] 343 (IP)	Clearance Art.6(1)(b)	Building Materials
M.182	Inchcape/IEP	21.01.92	—	4 [1994] M11 (D)	Clearance Art.6(1)(b)	Vehicle Distribution
M.183	Schweizer Rück/ELVIA	14.01.92	—	4 [1992] 348 (IP)	Clearance Art.6(1)(b)	Insurance
M.184	Grand Met./Cinzano	07.02.92	—	4 [1992] 349 (IP)	Clearance Art.6(1)(b)	Alcoholic Beverages
M.186	Henkel/Nobel	23.03.92	—	4 [1992] 442 (IP)	Clearance Art.6(1)(b)	Detergents
M.187	INFINT/EXOR	02.03.92	—	—	Clearance Art.6(1)(b)	Mineral Water
M.188	Herba/IRR	28.04.92	—	—	Art. 6(1)(a)	Rice Merchanting
M.189	Generali/BCHA	06.04.92	—	—	Clearance Art.6(1)(b)	Insurance
M.190	Nestlé/Perrier	22.07.92	[1992] L356/1	4 [1993] M17	With conditions and obligations Art.8(2)	Mineral Water
M.192	Banesto/Totta	14.04.92	—	4 [1992] 542 (IP)	Clearance Art.6(1)(b)	Banking
M.196	Volvo/Procordia	11.10.93	—	4 [1994] 24 (IP)	Clearance Art.6(1)(b)	Food, Beverages, Pharmaceuticals
M.197	Solvay-Laporte/Interox	30.04.92	—	—	Clearance Art.6(1)(b)	Chemicals
M.198	Péchiney/VIAG	10.08.92	—	—	Clearance Art.6(1)(b)	Precious and Non-ferrous Metals
M.202	Thorn EMI/Virgin Music	27.04.92	—	4 [1992] 541 (IP)	Clearance Art.6(1)(b)	Music Publishing
M.206	Rhône-Poulenc/SNIA	10.08.92	—	—	Clearance Art.6(1)(b)	Chemicals
M.207	Eureko	27.04.92	—	4 [1992] 543 (IP)	Art. 6(1)(a)	Insurance
M.210	Mondi/Frantschach	12.05.92	—	—	Clearance Art.6(1)(b)	Pulp Paper
M.213	Hong Kong & Shanghai Bank/ Midland Bank	21.05.92	—	—	Clearance Art.6(1)(b)	Banking
M.214	Du Pont/ICI	30.09.92	[1993] L7/13	5 [1993] M41 (D)	With conditions and obligations Art.8(2)	Nylon Fibres

MERGER No.	NAME	DATE	O.J.	C.M.L.R.	TYPE OF DECISION	PRODUCT SECTOR
M.216	CEA Industrie/France Telecom/ SGS-Thomson	22.02.93	—	—	Clearance Art.6(1)(b)	Semi-conductors
M.218	Eucom/Digital	18.05.92	—	—	Clearance Art.6(1)(b)	Freight Management
M.220	Bibby/Finanzauto	29.06.92	—	5 [1993] M11 (D)	Clearance Art.6(1)(b)	Earth Moving
M.221	ABB/Brel	26.05.92	—	—	Clearance Art.6(1)(b)	Railway Rolling Stock
M.222	Mannesmann/Hoesch	12.11.92	[1992] L114/34	—	Without conditions and obligations Art.8(2)	Steel Tubes
M.224	Volvo/Lex I	21.05.92	—	—	Clearance Art.6(1)(b)	Vehicles
M.229	Thomas Cook/LTU/West LB	14.07.92	—	—	Clearance Art.6(1)(b)	Travel Agency
M.232	Pepsico/General Mills	05.08.92	—	—	Clearance Art.6(1)(b)	Snack Foods
M.234	GECC/Avis	15.07.92	—	—	Clearance Art.6(1)(b)	Vehicle Fleet Leasing
M.235	Elf Aquitaine Thyssen/Minol AG	10.08.92	—	—	Clearance Art.6(1)(b)	Petroleum Refining and Retailing
M.236	Ericsson/Ascom	08.07.92	—	5 [1992] 117 (IP)	Clearance Art.6(1)(b)	Cables and Wires
M.237	Dasa/Fokker	10.05.93	—	—	Clearance Art.6(1)(b)	Aircraft
M.238	Siemens/Philips	23.12.92	—	—	Clearance Art.6(1)(b)	Cables
M.239	Avesta/British Steel/NCC	04.09.92	—	—	Clearance Art.6(1)(b)	Iron and Steel
M.241	Eurocard/Eurocheque-Europay	13.07.92	—	—	Art. 6(1)(a)	Banking
M.242	Promodes/BRMC	13.07.92	—	—	Clearance Art.6(1)(b)	Wholesaling and Retailing
M.249	Northern Telecom/Matra Communication	10.08.92	—	—	Clearance Art.6(1)(b)	Telecommunications Equipment
M.251	Allianz/DKV	10.09.92	—	—	Clearance Art.6(1)(b)	Insurance
M.253	BTR/Pirelli	17.08.92	—	—	Clearance Art.6(1)(b)	Car Parts
M.254	Fortis/La Caixa	05.11.92	—	—	Clearance Art.6(1)(b)	Insurance
M.256	Linde AG/Fiat	28.09.92	—	—	Clearance Art.6(1)(b)	Materials Handling Equipment
M.258	CCIE/GTE	25.09.92	—	—	Clearance Art.6(1)(b)	Lighting Products
M.259	British Airways/TAT	27.11.92	—	4 [1993] 10 (IP)	Clearance Art.6(1)(b)	Air Transport
M.261	Volvo/Lex II	03.09.92	—	—	Clearance Art.6(1)(b)	Vehicles
M.263	Ahold/Jeronimo Martins	29.09.92	—	—	Clearance Art.6(1)(b)	Wholesaling
M.265	VTG/BPTL	12.10.92	—	—	Art. 6(1)(a)	Transport

Table 5

MERGER No.	NAME	DATE	O.J.	C.M.L.R.	TYPE OF DECISION	PRODUCT SECTOR
M.266	Rhône Poulenc Chimie/ Lyonnaise de Eaux	26.11.92	—	—	Clearance Art.6(1)(b)	Waste
M.269	Shell/Montecatini	24.04.96	[1996] L294/10	4 [1996] 741 (IP)	Art. 8(2) without conditions and obligations	Thermoplastics
M.269	Shell/Montecatini	08.06.94	[1994] L332/48	—	With conditions and obligations Art.8(2)	Chemicals
M.272	Matra/Cap Gemini Sogeti	17.03.93	—	—	Clearance Art.6(1)(b)	Military Equipment
M.277	Del Monte/Royal Foods/ Anglo-American	09.12.92	—	4 [1993] 236 (IP)	Clearance Art.6(1)(b)	Canned Food
M.278	British Airways/Dan Air	17.02.93	—	5 [1993] M61 (D)	Clearance Art.6(1)(b)	Air Transport
M.283	Waste Management/SAE	21.12.92	—	—	Clearance Art.6(1)(b)	Waste
M.284	Hoechst/Wacker	10.05.93	—	—	Clearance Art.6(1)(b)	Chemicals
M.285	Pasteur Merieux/Merck	05.07.93	—	5 [1993] 206 (IP)	Art. 6(1)(a)	Vaccines
M.286	Zürich/MMI	02.04.93	—	5 [1993] 14 (IP)	Clearance Art.6(1)(b)	Insurance
M.289	Pepsico/KAS	21.12.92	—	4 [1993] 236 (IP)	Clearance Art.6(1)(b)	Non-alcoholic Drink
M.290	Sextant/BGT-VDO	21.12.92	—	4 [1993] 237 (IP)	Clearance Art.6(1)(b)	Aeroplane Parts
M.291	KNP/Bührmann Tetterode/VRG	04.05.93	[1993] L217/35	5 [1993] 116 (IP)	With conditions and obligations Art.8(2)	Paper
M.292	Ericsson/Hewlett Packard	12.03.93	—	5 [1993] 403 (IP)	Clearance Art.6(1)(b)	Telecommunications Equipment
M.293	Philips/Thomson/SAGEM	18.01.93	—	—	Art. 6(1)(a)	Liquid Crystal Displays
M.295	SITA-RPC/Scori	19.03.93	—	—	Clearance Art.6(1)(b)	Waste
M.296	Credit Lyonnais/BFG Bank	11.01.93	—	—	Clearance Art.6(1)(b)	Banking
M.299	Sara Lee/BP Food Division	08.02.93	—	—	Clearance Art.6(1)(b)	Packaged Meat
M.300	Kingfisher/Darty	22.03.93	—	4 [1993] 403 (IP)	Clearance Art.6(1)(b)	Retailing
M.301	Tesco/Catteau	04.02.93	—	4 [1993] 402 (IP)	Clearance Art.6(1)(b)	Retailing
M.304	Volkswagen AG/VAG (UK)	04.02.93	—	4 [1993] 402 (IP)	Clearance Art.6(1)(b)	Car Parts
M.308	Kali+Salz/MDK/Treuhand	09.07.98	—	5 [1998] 292 (IP)	Clearance Art.6(1)(b) without undertakings	Potash and Rock Salt
M.308	Kali-Salz/MDK/Treuhandi	14.12.93	[1994] L186/38	4 [1994] 526 (IP)	With conditions and obligations Article 8(2)	Fertiliser: Potash

MERGER No.	NAME	DATE	O.J.	C.M.L.R.	TYPE OF DECISION	PRODUCT SECTOR
M.310	Harrisons & Crosfield/AKZO	29.04.93	—	4 [1993] 114 (IP)	Clearance Art.6(1)(b)	Chemicals
M.312	Sanofi/Yves St-Laurent	15.03.93	—	—	Clearance Art.6(1)(b)	Perfumes and Cosmetics
M.315	Mannesmann/Vallourec/Ilva	31.01.94	[1994] L102/15	4 [1994] 529 (IP)	Without condition and obligation Article 8(2)	Stainless Steel Tubes
M.317	Degussa/Ciba-Geigy	05.04.93	—	—	Clearance Art.6(1)(b)	Paints
M.318	Thomson/Shorts	14.04.93	—	5 [1993] 15 (IP)	Clearance Art.6(1)(b)	Military Equipment
M.319	BHF/CCF/Charterhouse	30.08.93	—	5 [1993] 207 (IP)	Clearance Art.6(1)(b)	Financial Services
M.320	Ahold/Jeronimo Martins/ Inovaçao	19.04.93	—	5 [1993] 16 (IP)	Clearance Art.6(1)(b)	Wholesaling
M.322	Alcan/Inespal/Palco	14.04.93	—	5 [1993] 16 (IP)	Clearance Art.6(1)(b)	Aluminium Cans
M.323	Procordia/Erbamont	29.04.93	—	5 [1993] 115 (IP)	Clearance Art.6(1)(b)	Pharmaceuticals
M.326	Toyota/Walter Frey	01.07.93	—	5 [1993] 205 (IP)	Clearance Art.6(1)(b)	Automobile Distribution
M.328	GEHE AG/OCP S.A.	05.04.93	—	5 [1993] 15 (IP)	Clearance Art.6(1)(b)	Pharmaceutical Wholesaling
M.330	McCormick/CPC	29.10.93	—	5 [1993] 535 (IP)	Article 9	Herbs, Spices
M.331	Fletcher Challenge/Methanex	31.03.93	—	—	Clearance Art.6(1)(b)	Chemicals
M.334	Costa Crociere/Chargeurs Accor	19.07.93	—	5 [1993] 206 (IP)	Clearance Art.6(1)(b)	Tour Operator
M.335	Schweiz. Kreditanst./Schweiz. Volksbank	29.04.93	—	—	Clearance Art.6(1)(b)	Banking
M.336	IBM France/CGI	19.05.93	—	—	Clearance Art.6(1)(b)	Computer Services
M.337	Allied Signal Knorr-Bremse	15.10.93	—	4 [1994] 24 (IP)	Clearance Art.6(1)(b)	Heavy Duty Braking Systems
M.341	Deutsche Bank/Banco de Madrid	28.05.93	—	—	Clearance Art.6(1)(b)	Banking
M.342	CGER Fortis	15.11.93	—	5 [1993] 534 (IP)	Clearance Art.6(1)(b)	Insurance and Banking
M.343	Société Générale de Belgique/Générale de Banque	03.08.93	—	—	Clearance Art.6(1)(b)	Banking
M.344	Hafnia/Codan	28.05.93	—	5 [1993] 17 (IP)	Clearance Art.6(1)(b)	Insurance
M.346	JCSAT/SAJAC	30.06.93	—	—	Clearance Art.6(1)(b)	Satellites
M.349	Aegon/Scottish Equitable	25.06.93	—	5 [1993] 117 (IP)	Clearance Art.6(1)(b)	Insurance
M.350	West LB/Thomas Cook	30.06.93	—	5 [1993] 309 (IP)	Clearance Art.6(1)(b)	Travel Agency
M.353	British Telecom/MCI	13.09.93	—	5 [1993] 310 (IP)	Clearance Art.6(1)(b)	Telecommunications Services

Table 5

MERGER No.	NAME	DATE	O.J.	C.M.L.R.	TYPE OF DECISION	PRODUCT SECTOR
M.354	American Cyanamid/Shell	01.10.93	—	4 [1994] 23 (IP)	Clearance Art.6(1)(b)	Agrochemicals
M.355	Rhône Poulenc/SNIA	08.09.93	—	—	Clearance Art.6(1)(b)	Nylon Textile Fibres
M.357	Commerzbank/CCR	09.08.93	—	5 [1993] 310 (IP)	Clearance Art.6(1)(b)	Financial Services
M.358	Pilkington/SIV	21.12.93	[1994] L158/24	4 [1994] 405 (IP)	With conditions and obligations Article 8(2)	Flat Glass
M.360	Arvin/Sogefi	23.09.93	—	5 [1993] 432 (IP)	Clearance Art.6(1)(b)	Car Parts
M.361	Neste/Statoil	17.02.94	—	4 [1994] 532 (IP)	Clearance Art.6(1)(b)	Polyolefins
M.362	Nestlé/Italger	15.09.93	—	5 [1993] 311 (IP)	Clearance Art.6(1)(b)	Confectionary
M.363	Continental/Kalico/DG Bank/ Benecke	29.11.93	—	4 [1994] 25 (IP)	Clearance Art.6(1)(b)	Plastic Foils and Car Parts
M.365	Thyssen/Balzer	30.09.93	—	5 [1993] 432	Clearance Art.6(1)(b)	Steel Products
M.366	Alcatel/STC	13.09.93	—	5 [1993] 311 (IP)	Clearance Art.6(1)(b)	Telecommunications Equipment
M.368	SNECMA/TI	17.01.94	—	—	Clearance Art.6(1)(b)	Aircraft Landing Gear
M.376	Synthomer/Yule Catto	22.10.93	—	5 [1993] 533 (IP)	Clearance Art.6(1)(b)	Chemicals: Synthetic Rubber
M.382	Philips/Grundig	03.12.93	—	—	Clearance Art.6(1)(b)	Consumer Electronics
M.384	UAP/Vinci	01.12.93	—	—	Clearance Art.6(1)(b)	Insurance
M.390	AKZO/Nobel Industries	10.01.94	—	—	Clearance Art.6(1)(b)	Chemicals
M.391	BAI/Banca Popolare de Lecco	20.12.93	—	4 [1994] 405	Clearance Art.6(1)(b)	Banking
M.392	Hoechst/Schering	22.12.93	—	—	Clearance Art.6(1)(b)	Agrochemicals
M.394	Mannesmann/RWE/Deutsche Bank	22.12.93	—	4 [1994] 528 (IP)	Clearance Art.6(1)(b)	Telecoms
M.395	CWB/Goldman Sachs/Tarkett	21.02.94	—	4 [1994] 533 (IP)	Clearance Art.6(1)(b)	Floor Coverings
M.397	Ford/Hertz	07.03.94	—	—	Art. 6(1)(a)	Car Rental
M.399	Rhône-Poulenc-SNIA/Nordfaser	03.02.94	—	—	Clearance Art.6(1)(b)	Nylon Fibres
M.400	Allied Lyons/HWE-Pedro Domecq	28.04.94	—	—	Clearance Art.6(1)(b)	Alcoholic Beverages
M.401	Rütgers/Hüls Troisdorf	02.03.94	—	4 [1994] 604 (IP)	Clearance Art.6(1)(b)	Laminants
M.402	Powergen/NRG/Morrison Knudsen/MIB	27.06.94	—	—	Clearance Art.6(1)(b)	Coal
M.403	AGF/La Unin y el Fenix	25.04.94	—	—	Clearance Art.6(1)(b)	Insurance
M.404	Generali/Central Hispano-Generali	09.02.94	—	—	Clearance Art.6(1)(b)	Insurance

MERGER No.	NAME	DATE	O.J.	C.M.L.R.	TYPE OF DECISION	PRODUCT SECTOR
M.406	Philips/Hoechst	11.03.94	—	4 [1994] 606 (IP)	Clearance Art.6(1)(b)	Optical Discs
M.408	RWE/Mannesmann	28.02.94	—	4 [1994] 604 (IP)	Clearance Art.6(1)(b)	Mobile network for data transmission
M.409	ABB/Renault Automation	09.03.94	—	4 [1994] 605 (IP)	Clearance Art.6(1)(b)	Robotics
M.410	Kirch/Richemont/Telepiu	02.08.94	—	—	Clearance Art.6(1)(b)	Pay TV
M.416	BMW/Rover	14.03.94	—	—	Clearance Art.6(1)(b)	Motor Vehicles
M.417	VIAG/Bayernwerk	05.05.94	—	5 [1994] 22 (IP)	Clearance Art.6(1)(B)	Energy
M.420	CGP/GEC/KPR/KONE	14.04.94	—	—	Clearance Art.6(1)(b)	Mobile Cranes
M.422	Unilever France/Ortiz Miko	15.03.94	—	—	Clearance Art.6(1)(b)	Ice-cream
M.423	Newspaper Publishing	14.03.94	—	—	Clearance Art.6(1)(b)	Newspaper Publishing
M.425	BS/BT	28.03.94	—	4 [1994] 607 (IP)	Art. 6(1)(a)	Telecommunications Services
M.426	Rhône-Poulenc/Cooper	18.04.94	—	—	Clearance Art.6(1)(b)	Pharmaceutical Distribution
M.427	Rhône-Poulenc/Caffaro	17.06.94	—	—	Clearance Art.6(1)(b)	Thermo-plastics
M.429	Winterthur/DBV	30.05.94	—	5 [1994] 24 (IP)	Clearance Art.6(1)(b)	Insurance
M.430	Procter & Gamble/VP Schickendanz	21.06.94	[1994] L354/32	5 [1994] 146 (IP)	With conditions and obligations Art.8(2)	Paper Products
M.431	Medeol/Elosua	06.06.94	—	5 [1994] 150 (IP)	Clearance Art.6(1)(b)	Olive Oil
M.433	ERC/NRG Victory	27.05.94	—	5 [1994] 24 (IP)	Clearance Art.6(1)(b)	Life Reinsurance
M.437	Matra Marconi Space/British Aerospace	23.08.94	—	—	Clearance Art.6(1)(b)	Satellites
M.439	Hüls-Phenolchemie	06.05.94	—	5 [1994] 23 (IP)	Clearance Art.6(1)(b)	Chemicals
M.440	GE/ENI/Nuovo Pignone	06.05.94	—	5 [1994] 22 (IP)	Clearance Art.6(1)(b)	Gas Turbines
M.441	Daimler Benz/RWE	20.06.94	—	5 [1994] 26 (IP)	Clearance Art.6(1)(b)	Solar Cells
M.442	ELF Atochem/Rütgers	27.07.94	—	—	Clearance Art.6(1)(b)	Chemical and Oil Products
M.444	Sidmar/Klöckner	30.05.94	—	5 [1994] 25 (IP)	Clearance Art.6(1)(B)	Steel
M.445	BSN/Euralim	07.06.94	—	—	Clearance Art.6(1)(b)	Prepared Foodstuffs
M.447	Schneider/AEG	01.08.94	—	—	Clearance Art.6(1)(b)	Electronic Equipment
M.448	GKN/Brambles/Leto Recycling	07.06.94	—	5 [1994] 150 (IP)	Clearance Art.6(1)(b)	Waste Management Services

Table 5

MERGER No.	NAME	DATE	O.J.	C.M.L.R.	TYPE OF DECISION	PRODUCT SECTOR
M.450	AGF/ASSUBEL	27.06.94	—	—	Clearance Art.6(1)(b)	Assurance
M.452	Avesta II	09.06.94	—	—	Clearance Art.6(1)(b)	Steel
M.455	Banco de Santander/Banesto	13.06.94	—	—	Clearance Art.6(1)(b)	Banking
M.457	La Roche/Syntex	20.06.94	—	5 [1994] 27 (IP)	Clearance Art.6(1)(b)	Pharmaceuticals
M.458	Electrolux/AEG	21.06.94	—	—	Clearance Art.6(1)(b)	Domestic Appliances
M.459	CINVEN/CIE/BP Nutrition	29.09.94	—	5 [1994] 324 (IP)	Clearance Art.6(1)(b)	Nutrition Products
M.460	Holdercim/Cedest	06.07.94	—	—	Clearance Art.6(1)(b)	Cement Construction Products
M.464	BMSC/UPSA	06.09.94	—	—	Clearance Art.6(1)(b)	Pharmaceuticals
M.465	GE/CIGI	29.08.94	—	—	Clearance Art.6(1)(b)	Insurance
M.466	Tractebel/Synatom	30.06.94	—	—	Clearance Art.6(1)(b)	Services To Nuclear Industry
M.468	Siemens/Italtel	17.02.95	[1995] L66/27	—	Without conditions and obligations Art.8(2)	Telecommunications
M.469	MSG Media Service	09.11.94	[1994] L364/1	5 [1994] 499 (IP)	Prohibition Art.8(3)	Pay TV Services
M.470	Gencor/Shell Kudu	29.08.94	—	—	Clearance Art.6(1)(b)	Metals
M.471	Delhaize/P.G.	22.08.94	—	—	Clearance Art.6(1)(b)	Supermarkets
M.472	Vesuvius/Wülfrath	05.09.94	—	—	Clearance Art.6(1)(b)	Refractory Product
M.473	PWT/Minemet	20.07.94	—	—	Clearance Art.6(1)(b)	Metal Distribution
M.475	ELF Atochem/Shell Chimie	22.12.94	—	4 [1995] 314 (IP)	Clearance Art.6(1)(b)	Chemicals
M.477	Mercedes Benz/Kässbohrer	14.02.95	[1995] L211/1	4 [1995] 600 (IP)	Without conditions and obligations Art. 8(2)	Buses
M.478	Voith/Sulzer II	29.07.94	—	—	Clearance Art.6(1)(b)	Paper Machinery
M.479	MAN Ingersoll-Rand	28.07.94	—	—	Clearance Art.6(1)(a) and 6(1)(b)	Compressors
M.480	Sanofi/Kodak	12.08.94	—	—	Clearance Art.6(1)(b)	Pharmaceuticals
M.484	Thyssen Stahl/Krupp/Riva/Falck/Acciaiter	21.12.94	[1995] L251/13	—	Without conditions and obligations Art.8(2)	Steel Products
M.485	Rheinelektra/Cofira/Dekra	26.09.94	—	—	Clearance Art.6(1)(b)	Telecommunications Services
M.486	Holdercim/Origny-Desvroise	05.08.94	—	—	Clearance Art.6(1)(b)	Construction Materials

MERGER No.	NAME	DATE	O.J.	C.M.L.R.	TYPE OF DECISION	PRODUCT SECTOR
M.489	Bertelsmann/News International/Vox	06.09.94	—	—	Clearance Art.6(1)(b)	TV
M.490	Nordic Satellite	19.07.95	[1996] L53/20	5 [1995] 258 (IP)	Clearance Art.8(3)	TV Distribution via Satellite
M.491	General Re/Kölnische Rück	24.10.94	—	5 [1994] 503 (IP)	Clearance Art.6(1)(b)	Re-insurance
M.492	Klöckner/Computer 2496	05.09.94	—	—	Clearance Art.6(1)(b)	Computer Products
M.493	Tractebel/Distrigaz	01.09.94	—	—	Clearance Art.6(1)(b)	Gas Distribution
M.495	Behringwerke AG/Armour Pharma	03.04.95	—	4 [1995] 609 (IP)	Clearance Art.6(1)(b)	Pharmaceuticals
M.496	Marconi/Finmeccanica	05.09.94	—	—	Clearance Art.6(1)(b)	Radio Products
M.497	Matra-Marconi Space/Satcoms	14.10.94	—	—	Clearance Art.6(1)(b)	Microwave Communication Systems
M.498	Commercial Union/Groupe Victoire	12.09.94	—	—	Clearance Art.6(1)(b)	Insurance
M.499	Jefferson Smurfitt/St Gobain	19.09.94	—	—	Clearance Art.6(1)(b)	Packaging
M.500	American Home Products/American Cyanamid	19.09.94	—	—	Clearance Art.6(1)(b)	Pharmaceuticals
M.502	VAG/SAB	19.09.94	—	—	Clearance Art.6(1)(b)	Cars
M.503	British Steel/Svensk Stal/NSD	07.11.94	—	5 [1994] 505 (IP)	Clearance Art.6(1)(b)	Steel Distribution
M.504	Avesta III	20.10.94	—	5 [1994] 503 (IP)	Clearance Art.6(1)(b)	Stainless Steel
M.505	Shell Monteshell	16.12.94	—	4 [1995] 160 (IP)	Clearance Art.6(1)(b)	Petroleum Derivatives
M.508	BHF/CCF	28.10.94	—	5 [1994] 504 (IP)	Clearance Art.6(1)(b)	Banking
M.511	Texaco/Norsk Hydro	09.01.95	—	4 [1995] 313 (IP)	Clearance Art.6(1)(b)	Distribution Of Fuels
M.512	UAP/Provincial	07.11.94	—	5 [1994] 504 (IP)	Clearance Art.6(1)(b)	Insurance
M.513	Rhône-Poulenc/Ambiente	07.11.94	—	—	Clearance Art.6(1)(b)	Chemicals
M.517	KKR/Borden	24.11.94	—	5 [1994] 316 (IP)	Clearance Art.6(1)(b)	Food and Packaging Products
M.518	Winterthur/Schweizer Rück	14.03.95	—	4 [1995] 605 (IP)	Clearance Art.6(1)(b)	Insurance
M.519	Ericsson/Raychem	21.11.94	—	5 [1994] 506 (IP)	Clearance Art.6(1)(b)	Fibre Optic Products
M.520	Direct Line/Bankinter	12.01.95	—	4 [1995] 318 (IP)	Clearance Art.6(1)(b)	Insurance
M.521	VIAG/Sanofi	21.12.94	—	4 [1995] 160 (IP)	Clearance Art.6(1)(b)	Chemicals
M.522	Scandinavian Project	28.11.94	—	4 [1995] 34 (IP)	Clearance Art.6(1)(b)	Vegetable Oils
M.523	AKZO Nobel/Monsanto	19.01.95	—	4 [1995] 315 (IP)	Clearance Art.6(1)(b)	Rubber Chemicals
M.525	VOX	21.12.94	—	4 [1995] 161 (IP)	Clearance Art.6(1)(B)	TV

Table 5

MERGER No.	NAME	DATE	O.J.	C.M.L.R.	TYPE OF DECISION	PRODUCT SECTOR
M.526	Sappi/Warren	28.11.94	—	4 [1995] 35 (IP)	Clearance Art.6(1)(B)	Paper
M.527	Thomson/Deutsche Aerospace AG	02.12.94	—	4 [1995] 160 (IP)	Clearance Art.6(1)(b)	Military Equipment
M.528	British Aerospace/VSEL	24.11.94	—	—	Clearance Art.6(1)(b)	Oil and Gas Products
M.529	GEC/VSEL	07.12.94	—	—	Clearance Art.6(1)(b)	Defence Equipment
M.531	Recticel/Cww-Cerko	03.02.95	—	4 [1995] 319 (IP)	Clearance Art.6(1)(b)	Sound Absorption Material
M.532	Cable and Wireless/ Schlumberger	22.12.94	—	4 [1995] 161 (IP)	Clearance Art.6(1)(b)	Communications Services
M.533	TWD/AKZO Nobel/Kuagtextil	10.02.95	—	—	Clearance Art.6(1)(b)	Textile Filaments
M.534	Bayer/Hoechst GV Textilfarbstoffe	21.12.94	—	4 [1995] 317 (IP)	Clearance Art.6(1)(b)	Dyestuffs for Textiles
M.535	Mannesmann Demag/Delaval Stork	21.12.94	—	4 [1995] 313 (IP)	Clearance Art.6(1)(b)	Compressors/Turbines and Pumps
M.536	Torrington/Ingersoll	28.03.95	—	4 [1995] 609 (IP)	Clearance Art.6(1)(b)	Vehicle Parts
M.537	Sidmar/Klöckner	09.01.95	—	4 [1995] 314 (IP)	Clearance Art.6(1)(b)	Steel Products
M.538	OMNITEL	27.03.95	—	4 [1995] 613 (IP)	Art. 6(1)(a)	Telecommunications
M.539	Allianz/Elvia	03.04.95	—	4 [1995] 611 (IP)	Clearance Art.6(1)(b)	Insurance
M.540	CEGELEC/AEG	20.02.95	—	4 [1995] 319 (IP)	Clearance Art.6(1)(b)	Electrical Engineering
M.542	Babcock/Siemens/BS Railcare	30.06.95	—	5 [1995] 133 (IP)	Clearance Art.6(1)(b)	Rail Transport
M.543	Zürich Insurance CY/Banco di Napoli	22.02.95	—	—	Clearance Art.6(1)(b)	Life Insurance
M.544	Unisource/Telefonica	06.11.95	—	—	Art. 6(1)(a)	Telecommunications
M.548	Nokia OY/SP Tyres	14.03.95	—	4 [1995] 605 (IP)	Clearance Art.6(1)(B)	Tyres
M.549	Svenska Cellulosa/PWA	20.02.95	—	4 [1995] 317 (IP)	Clearance Art.6(1)(b)	Paper and Packaging
M.550	Union Carbide/Enichem	13.03.95	—	4 [1995] 602 (IP)	Clearance Art.6(1)(b)	Chemicals
M.551	ATR/BAe	25.07.95	—	—	Art. 6(1)(a)	Aerospace
M.553	RLT/Veronica/Endemol	17.07.96	[1998] L294/14	5 [1996] 256 (IP)	Art. 8(2) with conditions and obligations	TV
M.553	RTL/Veronica/Endemol	20.09.95	[1996] L134/32	—	Clearance Art.8(3)	TV
M.554	Dalgety/Quaker Oats	13.03.95	—	4 [1995] 604 (IP)	Clearance Art.6(1)(b)	Pet Food
M.555	Glaxo plc/Wellcome plc	28.02.95	—	4 [1995] 321 (IP)	Clearance Art.6(1)(b)	Pharmaceuticals
M.556	Zeneca/Vanderhave	09.04.96	—	4 [1996] 734 (IP)	Clearance Art.6(1)(B)	Seeds
M.557	Toepfer/Champagne Cereales	06.04.95	—	—	Clearance Art.6(1)(b)	Cereals Trading
M.558	La Rinascente/Cedis Migliarini	15.03.95	—	4 [1995] 606 (IP)	Clearance Art.6(1)(b)	Food Distribution

MERGER No.	NAME	DATE	O.J.	C.M.L.R.	TYPE OF DECISION	PRODUCT SECTOR
M.560	EDS/Lufthansa	11.05.95	—	—	Clearance Art.6(1)(b)	It Services
M.561	Securicor Datatrak	20.03.95	—	4 [1995] 607 (IP)	Clearance Art.6(1)(b)	Vehicle Tracking Services
M.563	British Steel/UES	17.03.95	—	4 [1995] 605 (IP)	Clearance Art.6(1)(B)	Steel
M.564	Havas/American Express	06.04.95	—	—	Clearance Art.6(1)(b)	Travel Services
M.565	Solvay/Wienerberger	24.04.95	—	—	Clearance Art.6(1)(b)	Plastic Pipes
M.566	CLT/Disney/Super RTL	17.05.95	—	4 [1995] 711 (IP)	Clearance Art.6(1)(b)	Broadcasting
M.567	Lyonnaise des eaux/Northumbrian Water	21.12.95	—	4 [1996] 145 (IP)	Acquisition	Water
M.568	Edison-EDF/ISE	08.06.95	—	5 [1995] 23 (IP)	Clearance Art.6(1)(b)	Electricity Generation
M.570	Telenordic/BT/TeleDanmark/Telenor	24.04.95	—	4 [1995] 710 (IP)	Clearance Art.6(1)(b)	Telecommunications
M.571	CGI/Dassault	24.03.95	—	4 [1995] 608 (IP)	Clearance Art.6(1)(b)	Military Software
M.572	GEHE/AAH	03.04.95	—	—	Clearance Art.6(1)(b)	Pharmaceutical Wholesaling
M.573	ING/Barings	11.04.95	—	—	Clearance Art.6(1)(b)	Banking
M.574	Saudi Aramco/MOH	23.05.95	—	5 [1995] 23 (IP)	Clearance Art.6(1)(b)	Oil Refining/Distribution
M.575	Volvo/VME	11.04.95	—	—	Clearance Art.6(1)(b)	Earthmoving Equipment
M.576	Ferruzzi Finanziaria/Fondiaria	09.06.95	—	5 [1995] 24 (IP)	Clearance Art.6(1)(b)	Insurance
M.577	GE/Power Controls	28.04.95	—	—	Clearance Art.6(1)(b)	Electrical Equipment
M.578	Hoogovens/Klöckner	11.04.95	—	—	Art. 6(1)(a)	Steel Distribution
M.579	Blockbuster Burda	27.04.95	—	—	Clearance Art.6(1)(b)	Video Rental
M.580	ABB/Daimler-Benz	18.10.95	[1997] L11/1	5 [1995] 577 (IP)	Art. 8(2) with conditions and obligations	Railway Equipment
M.581	Frantschach/Bischof & Klein	28.08.95	—	5 [1995] 266 (IP)	Clearance Art.6(1)(b)	Packaging
M.582	Orkla/Volvo	20.09.95	[1996] L66/17	5 [1995] 388 (IP)	Clearance Art.8(2) with conditions	Drinks
M.583	Inchcape/Gestetner	01.06.95	—	5 [1995] 24 (IP)	Clearance Art.6(1)(b)	Office Machines
M.584	Kirch/Richemont	05.05.95	—	—	Clearance Art.6(1)(b)	Broadcasting
M.585	VAI/Davy	07.07.95	—	5 [1995] 135 (IP)	Clearance Art.6(1)(b)	Engineering/construction services
M.586	Generali/Comit/Flemings	15.06.95	—	—	Clearance Art.6(1)(b)	Pension Funds
M.587	Hoechst/Marion Merrell Dow	22.06.95	—	5 [1995] 134 (IP)	Clearance Art.6(1)(b)	Pharmaceuticals
M.588	Ingersoll Rand/Clark Equipment	15.05.95	—	5 [1995] 27 (IP)	Clearance Art.6(1)(b)	Construction Equipment

Table 5

MERGER No.	NAME	DATE	O.J.	C.M.L.R.	TYPE OF DECISION	PRODUCT SECTOR
M.589	Seagram/MCA	29.05.95	—	4 [1995] 712 (IP)	Clearance Art.6(1)(b)	Entertainment/Publishing
M.591	Dow Buna	04.07.95	—	5 [1995] 131 (IP)	Clearance Art.6(1)(b)	Chemicals
M.593	Volvo/Henlys	27.06.95	—	5 [1995] 131 (IP)	Clearance Art.6(1)(b)	Coach/Bus Manufacture
M.595	British Telecom/Viag	22.12.95	—	—	Clearance Art.6(1)(b)	Telecommunications
M.596	Mitsubishi Bank/Bank of Tokyo	17.07.95	—	5 [1995] 260 (IP)	Clearance Art.6(1)(b)	Banking
M.597	Swiss Bank/S.G. Warburg	28.06.95	—	5 [1995] 132 (IP)	Clearance Art.6(1)(b)	Banking
M.598	Daimler Benz/Carl Zeiss	27.06.95	—	5 [1995] 134 (IP)	Clearance Art.6(1)(b)	Optical
M.599	Noranda Forest/Glunz	08.09.95	—	5 [1995] 387 (IP)	Clearance Art.6(1)(b)	Wood Products
M.600	Employers Reins. Corp/Frankona Rück	30.06.95	—	5 [1995] 133 (IP)	Clearance Art.6(1)(b)	Insurance
M.601	Employers Reins. Corp/Aachener Rück	30.06.95	—	5 [1995] 133 (IP)	Clearance Art.6(1)(b)	Insurance
M.603	Crown Cork & Seal/Carnaud Metalbox	14.11.95	[1996] L75/38	4 [1996] 9 (IP)	Art. 8(2) with conditions and obligations	Packaging
M.604	Albacom	15.09.95	—	5 [1995] 388 (IP)	Art. 6(1)(a)	Telecommunications
M.605	Hoechst/Klöckner-Werke	23.05.96	—	5 [1996] 15 (IP)	Clearance Art.6(1)(b)	Plastic Products
M.606	Generali/Comit	26.07.95	—	5 [1995] 260 (IP)	Clearance Art.6(1)(b)	Pension Services
M.611	Dresdner Bank/Kleinworth Benson	28.07.95	—	5 [1995] 262 (IP)	Clearance Art.6(1)(b)	Banking
M.612	RWE-DEA/Augusta	27.07.95	—	5 [1995] 261 (IP)	Clearance Art.6(1)(b)	Chemicals
M.613	Jefferson Smurfit/Munksjo	31.07.95	—	5 [1995] 261 (IP)	Clearance Art.6(1)(b)	Paper Products
M.614	Generali/France Vie	21.08.95	—	5 [1995] 265 (IP)	Clearance Art.6(1)(b)	Insurance
M.615	Rhône-Poulenc/Engelhard	23.10.95	—	5 [1995] 582 (IP)	Clearance Art.6(1)(b)	Recycling Catalogues
M.616	Swissair/Sabena	20.07.95	—	—	Clearance Art.6(1)(b)	Air Transport
M.617	Credit Loc. de France/Hypth. Bank Berlin	10.08.95	—	5 [1995] 266 (IP)	Clearance Art.6(1)(b)	Banking
M.618	Cable & Wireless/Vebacom	16.08.95	—	5 [1995] 263 (IP)	Clearance Art.6(1)(b)	Telecommunications Service
M.619	Gencor/Lonhro	24.04.96	[1997] L11/30	5 [1996] 1076 (D)	Prohibition Art.8(3)	Platinum
M.620	Thomson/Teneo/Indra	22.08.95	—	5 [1995] 264 (IP)	Clearance Art.6(1)(b)	Defence/Electronics
M.621	Bayer Landesbank/Bank für Arbeit	21.12.95	—	—	Clearance Art.6(1)(b)	Banking
M.622	Ricoh/Gestetner	12.09.95	—	—	Clearance Art.6(1)(b)	Office Equipment
M.623	Kimberley-Clark/Scott Paper	16.01.96	[1996] L183/1	4 [1996] 461 (IP)	Art. 8(2) with conditions and obligations	Paper Products

MERGER No.	NAME	DATE	O.J.	C.M.L.R.	TYPE OF DECISION	PRODUCT SECTOR
M.625	Nordic Capital/Transpool	23.08.95	—	5 [1995] 237 (IP)	Clearance Art.6(1)(b)	Travel Service
M.627	UAP/Sunlife	21.08.95	—	5 [1995] 264 (IP)	Clearance Art.6(1)(b)	Insurance
M.628	Generale/Credit Lyonnais NL	25.09.95	—	5 [1995] 390 (IP)	Clearance Art.6(1)(b)	Banking
M.630	Henkel/Schwarzkopf	18.10.95	—	—	Clearance Art.6(1)(b)	Cosmetics
M.631	Upjohn/Pharmacia	28.09.95	—	5 [1995] 390 (IP)	Clearance Art.6(1)(b)	Pharmaceuticals
M.632	Rhône-Poulenc/Fisons	21.09.95	—	5 [1995] 389 (IP)	Clearance Art.6(1)(b)	Pharmaceuticals
M.639	Montedison/Vernes/SCI	08.12.95	—	4 [1996] 180 (IP)	Clearance Art.6(1)(b)	Agro-food
M.640	KNP/Société Générale	03.10.95	—	5 [1995] 391 (IP)	Clearance Art.6(1)(b)	Computer Distribution
M.642	Chase Manhattan/Chemical	26.10.95	—	5 [1995] 580 (IP)	Clearance Art.6(1)(b)	Banking
M.643	CGER/SNCI	23.10.95	—	5 [1995] 583 (IP)	Clearance Art.6(1)(b)	Financial Services
M.644	Swiss Life/INCA	25.10.95	—	5 [1995] 582 (IP)	Clearance Art.6(1)(b)	Insurance
M.646	Repola/Kymmene	30.10.95	—	5 [1995] 581 (IP)	Clearance Art.6(1)(b)	Newsprint Paper
M.648	McDermott/ETPM	27.11.95	—	4 [1996] 148 (IP)	Clearance Art.6(1)(b)	Marine Construction Services
M.650	SBG/Rentenanstalt	20.12.95	—	—	Art. 6(1)(a)	Banking
M.651	AT&T/Philips	05.02.96	—	4 [1996] 463 (IP)	Clearance Art.6(1)(b)	Telecommunications Equipment
M.655	Canal+/UFA/MDO	13.11.95	—	4 [1996] 144 (IP)	Clearance Art.6(1)(B)	TV
M.656	Seagate/Conner	17.11.95	—	4 [1996] 16 (IP)	Clearance Art.6(1)(b)	Computer Disk Drives
M.657	Röhm/Ciba-Geigy	22.12.95	—	—	Clearance Art.6(1)(b)	Chemicals
M.659	GE Capital/Sovac	17.11.95	—	—	Clearance Art.6(1)(b)	Financial Services
M.660	RTZ/CRA	07.12.95	—	4 [1996] 144 (IP)	Clearance Art.6(1)(b)	Mining Metals
M.661	Stragab/Bank of Austria	15.01.96	—	—	Art. 6(1)(a)	Road Construction
M.662	Leisure Plan	21.12.95	—	—	Clearance Art.6(1)(b)	Travel Services
M.663	Dow/Dupont	21.02.96	—	4 [1996] 464 (IP)	Clearance Art.6(1)(b)	Thermoplastics
M.664	GRS Holding	11.12.95	—	—	Clearance Art.6(1)(b)	Leasing
M.665	Havas/GPE Cité	29.11.95	—	4 [1996] 149 (IP)	Clearance Art.6(1)(b)	Publishing
M.666	Johnson Controls/Roth	05.12.95	—	4 [1996] 145 (IP)	Clearance Art.6(1)(b)	Car Parts
M.668	Philips/Origin	22.12.95	—	—	Clearance Art.6(1)(b)	Computer Services
M.669	Charterhouse/Porterbrook	11.12.95	—	—	Clearance Art.6(1)(b)	Railway Rolling Stock
M.670	Elsag Bailey/Hartmann & Brown	20.12.95	—	4 [1996] 147 (IP)	Clearance Art.6(1)(b)	Process Control Equipment

Table 5

MERGER No.	NAME	DATE	O.J.	C.M.L.R.	TYPE OF DECISION	PRODUCT SECTOR
M.672	BP/Sonatrach	12.02.96	—	—	Clearance Art.6(1)(b)	Natural Gas
M.673	Channel Five	22.12.95	—	—	Art. 6(1)(a)	TV Broadcasting
M.674	Demag/Komatsu	21.12.95	—	4 [1996] 146 (IP)	Clearance Art.6(1)(b)	Excavators
M.675	Alumix/Alcoa	21.12.95	—	4 [1996] 147 (IP)	Clearance Art.6(1)(b)	Aluminium
M.676	Ericsson/Ascom II	22.12.95	—	4 [1996] 465 (IP)	Clearance Art.6(1)(b)	Paging Systems
M.677	Skanska Fastigheter	08.01.96	—	—	Clearance Art.6(1)(b)	Hotel
M.678	Minorco/Tilcon	22.12.95	—	—	Clearance Art.6(1)(b)	Building Materials
M.681	Bank of Scotland/Bank of Ireland	05.02.96	—	—	Art. 6(1)(a)	Banking
M.683	Hermes Europe/Railtel	05.03.96	—	4 [1996] 730 (IP)	Clearance Art.6(1)(b)	Telecommunications
M.685	Siemens/Lagardere	08.02.96	—	—	Clearance Art.6(1)(b)	Transport Systems
M.686	Nokia/Autoliv	05.02.96	—	—	Clearance Art.6(1)(b)	Airbag Control Systems
M.689	ADSB/Belgacom	29.02.96	—	—	Clearance Art.6(1)(b)	Telecommunications Services
M.692	Elektrowatt/Landis & GYR	12.02.96	—	—	Clearance Art.6(1)(b)	Building Control
M.694	SKF/INA/WPB	19.02.96	—	4 [1996] 463 (IP)	Clearance Art.6(1)(b)	Ball Bearings
M.697	Lockheed Martin/Loral	27.03.96	—	4 [1996] 732 (IP)	Clearance Art.6(1)(b)	Defence Products
M.698	NAW/Saltano	26.02.96	—	—	Clearance Art.6(1)(b)	Airport Equipment
M.699	Tomkins/Gates	04.03.96	—	—	Clearance Art.6(1)(b)	Rubber Components
M.700	Emerson/Caterpillar	31.05.96	—	5 [1996] 15 (IP)	Clearance Art.6(1)(b)	Generators
M.702	Starck/Wienerberger	01.03.96	—	4 [1996] 730 (IP)	Clearance Art.6(1)(b)	Corundum
M.704	Unilver/Diversey	20.03.96	—	4 [1996] 738 (IP)	Clearance Art.6(1)(b)	Detergents
M.705	Deutsche Telekom/SAP-S	29.03.96	—	4 [1996] 733 (IP)	Clearance Art.6(1)(b)	Software
M.706	GEC Alsthom NV/AEG	03.09.96	—	5 [1996] 521 (IP)	Clearance Art.6(1)(b)	Power transmission/ distribution equipment
M.707	Toro/Banca di Roma	05.03.96	—	—	Clearance Art.6(1)(b)	Insurance
M.708	Exxon/DSM	13.06.96	—	5 [1996] 134 (IP)	Clearance Art.6(1)(b)	Thermoplastics
M.710	BHF/CCF	02.05.96	—	4 [1996] 736 (IP)	Clearance Art.6(1)(b)	Aeroplane Leasing
M.711	Generali/Unicredito	25.03.96	—	—	Clearance Art.6(1)(a)	Insurance
M.713	RWE/Thyssens	25.11.96	—	4 [1997] 23 (IP)	Art. 9(4) Referral	Electricity, gas, stream, hot water
M.714	Preussag/Ecco	14.03.96	—	4 [1996] 737 (IP)	Clearance Art.6(1)(b)	Heating Boilers

MERGER No.	NAME	DATE	O.J.	C.M.L.R.	TYPE OF DECISION	PRODUCT SECTOR
M.716	GEHE/Lloyds Chemists	22.03.96	—	—	Art. 9.4(a) referral to Member State	Pharmaceuticals
M.717	Viacom/Bear Sterns	25.03.96	—	4 [1996] 739 (IP)	Clearance Art.6(1)(b)	Broadcasting
M.718	Phoenix/Comifar	20.03.96	—	—	Clearance Art.6(1)(b)	Pharmaceutical Wholesaling
M.719	Röhm/Röhm and Haas	28.06.96	—	5 [1996] 137 (IP)	Clearance Art.6(1)(b)	Lubricating Oil
M.720	Cereol/Aceprosa	07.06.96	—	5 [1996] 16 (IP)	Clearance Art.6(1)(b)	Oil Seeds
M.721	Textron/Valois	20.03.96	—	4 [1996] 731 (IP)	Clearance Art.6(1)(b)	Car Parts
M.722	Teneo/Merrill Lynch/Bankers Trust	15.04.96	—	—	Art. 6(1)(a)	Air Transport Services
M.723	Norsk Alcoa/Elkem	06.08.97	—	5 [1997] 276 (IP)	Clearance Art.6(1)(b)	Aluminium
M.724	GEC/Thomson-CSF II	15.05.96	—	5 [1996] 13 (IP)	Clearance Art.6(1)(b)	Military Products
M.726	Bosch/Allied Signal	09.04.96	—	4 [1996] 733 (IP)	Clearance Art.6(1)(b)	Brakes, Abs Systems
M.727	BP/Mobil	07.08.96	—	5 [1996] 263 (IP)	Clearance Art.6(1)(b)	Oil Refining
M.729	GEC Alsthom/Tarmac	18.04.96	—	4 [1996] 735 (IP)	Clearance Art.6(1)(b)	Railway Infrastructure Services
M.730	IP/Reuters	05.07.96	—	5 [1996] 259 (IP)	Clearance Art.6(1)(b)	On-line Advertising Systems
M.731	Kvaerner/Trafalgar	15.04.96	—	4 [1996] 739 (IP)	Clearance Art.6(1)(b)	Oil Rigs
M.732	Nordic Capital/Euroc	18.04.96	—	4 [1996] 35 (IP)	Clearance Art.6(1)(b)	Building Products
M.733	Frantschach/B+	08.05.96	—	5 [1996] 17 (IP)	Clearance Art.6(1)(b)	Packaging
M.734	Melitta/Dow	25.07.96	—	5 [1996] 261 (IP)	Clearance Art.6(1)(b)	Packaging Products
M.735	BPB/Isover	03.07.96	—	5 [1996] 269 (IP)	Art. 6(1)(a)	Building Materials
M.736	CCB/CLF	08.08.96	—	—	Clearance Art.6(1)(b)	Banking
M.737	Ciba-Geigy/Sandoz	17.07.96	[1997] L201/1	5 [1996] 257 (IP)	Art. 8(2) with conditions and obligations	Pharmaceuticals
M.738	NatWest/Schroder/Sheffield	24.04.96	—	4 [1996] 736 (IP)	Clearance Art.6(1)(b)	Steel Products
M.740	Krupp II	02.05.96	—	4 [1996] 737 (IP)	Clearance Art.6(1)(b)	Steel Products
M.741	Ford/Mazda	24.05.96	—	5 [1996] 14 (IP)	Clearance Art.6(1)(B)	Cars
M.742	Toro/Nuova Tirrena	22.05.95	—	5 [1996] 15 (IP)	Clearance Art.6(1)(b)	Insurance
M.744	Thomson/Daimler-Benz	21.05.96	—	5 [1996] 13 (IP)	Clearance Art.6(1)(b)	Micro-chips
M.745	Bayernwerk/Gaz de France	01.07.96	—	5 [1996] 138 (IP)	Clearance Art.6(1)(b)	Oil/Gas Exploration
M.747	Chevron/British Gas	25.07.96	—	—	Clearance Art.6(1)(b)	Gas Distribution

Table 5

MERGER No.	NAME	DATE	O.J.	C.M.L.R.	TYPE OF DECISION	PRODUCT SECTOR
M.748	CGEA/NSC	21.05.96	—	5 [1996] 14 (IP)	Clearance Art.6(1)(b)	Railway
M.750	IFIL/Worms/Saint Louis	25.07.96	—	5 [1996] 261 (IP)	Clearance Art.6(1)(b)	Agro-food
M.751	Bayer/Hüls-Newco	03.07.96	—	5 [1996] 138 (IP)	Clearance Art.6(1)(B)	Latex
M.754	Anglo American Corporation/Lonrho	23.04.97	[1998] 149/21	4 [1997] 377 (IP)	Art. 8(2) Prohibition	Precious Metals
M.755	Creditanstalt/Koramic	18.06.96	—	5 [1996] 135 (IP)	Clearance Art.6(1)(b)	Building Materials
M.756	Credit Agricol/Banque Indosuez	28.06.96	—	5 [1996] 138 (IP)	Clearance Art.6(1)(b)	Financial Services
M.757	Hoechst/3M	18.07.96	—	5 [1996] 259 (IP)	Clearance Art.6(1)(b)	Plastics
M.758	Sara Lee/Aoste	25.06.96	—	5 [1996] 136 (IP)	Clearance Art.6(1)(b)	Processed Meat Products
M.759	Sun Alliance/Royal Insurance	18.06.96	—	5 [1996] 136 (IP)	Clearance Art.6(1)(b)	Insurance
M.760	Klöckner/Arus	20.08.96	—	5 [1996] 371 (IP)	Clearance Art.6(1)(b)	Stockholding/distribution: steel products
M.762	Cegelec/AEG (II)	03.09.96	—	—	Clearance Art.6(1)(b)	Automation Systems, Software
M.764	Saint Gobain/Poliet	04.07.96	—	—	Clearance Art.6(1)(b)	Building Materials
M.765	ADIA/ECCO	24.06.96	—	5 [1996] 136 (IP)	Clearance Art.6(1)(b)	Relocation Service
M.767	Thomson/CSF/Finmeccanica	29.07.96	—	5 [1996] 262 (IP)	Clearance Art.6(1)(b)	Military Products
M.768	Lucas/Varity	11.07.96	—	5 [1996] 255 (IP)	Clearance Art.6(1)(b)	Car Parts
M.769	Norsk Hydro/Arnyca	29.07.96	—	—	Clearance Art.6(1)(b)	Fertilisers
M.771	AMB/Rodutch	11.07.96	—	5 [1996] 255 (IP)	Clearance Art.6(1)(b)	Insurance
M.773	Westinghouse/Equipos Nucleares	18.12.96	—	4 [1997] 198 (IP)	Clearance Art.6(1)(b)	Power Plant Services
M.774	Saint Gobain/Wacker Chemie/Nom	04.12.96	[1997] L247/1	4 [1997] 25 (IP)	Art. 8(1) Prohibition	Chemicals (Silicon Carbide)
M.775	Hong Kong Aero Empire Services	01.07.96	—	—	Clearance Art.6(1)(b)	Aero-engineering Services
M.777	AGF/Camat	27.08.96	—	5 [1996] 377 (IP)	Art. 6(1)(a)	Insurance
M.779	Bertelsmann/CLT	07.10.96	—	5 [1996] 525 (IP)	Clearance Art.6(1)(b)	TV and Radio
M.781	Schering/Gehe-Jenapharm	13.09.96	—	5 [1996] 522 (IP)	Clearance Art.6(1)(b)	Pharmaceutical Products
M.782	Swissair/Allders	17.07.96	—	5 [1996] 259 (IP)	Clearance Art.6(1)(b)	Duty-free Retailing
M.784	Kesko/Tuko	20.11.96	[1997] L110/53	4 [1997] 24 (IP)	Art. 8(3) Prohibition	Retailing
M.785	Thomas Cook/Sunworld	07.08.96	—	—	Clearance Art.6(1)(b)	Tourism Services
M.786	Birmingham International Airport	25.03.97	—	4 [1997] 831 (IP)	Clearance Art.6(1)(b)	Airport Operation

MERGER No.	NAME	DATE	O.J.	C.M.L.R.	TYPE OF DECISION	PRODUCT SECTOR
M.787	PTT Post/TNT	22.07.96	—	5 [1996] 260 (IP)	Clearance Art.6(1)(b)	Express Mail Services
M.788	Agrevo/Marubeni	03.09.96	—	5 [1996] 521 (IP)	Clearance Art.6(1)(b)	Agricultural/horticultural distribution
M.789	Enderley/S.B.E.	15.07.96	—	5 [1996] 260 (IP)	Clearance Art.6(1)(b)	Micro Switches
M.791	British Gas Trading/Group 4	07.10.96	—	5 [1996] 526 (IP)	Clearance Art.6(1)(b)	Meter Reading Services
M.792	Temic/Leica-AD JV	30.09.96	—	5 [1996] 524 (IP)	Clearance Art.6(1)(b)	Automotive Equipment
M.794	Coca-Cola/Amalgamated Beverages GB	22.01.97	[1997] L218/15	4 [1997] 368 (IP)	Art. 8(1) Prohibition	Soft Drinks
M.796	Infraleuna	23.08.96	—	5 [1996] 373 (IP)	Clearance Art.6(1)(b)	Infrastructure and local services
M.797	Grantrail	22.08.96	—	5 [1996] 373 (IP)	Clearance Art.6(1)(b)	Railway Infrastructure
M.798	General Electric/Compunet	19.08.96	—	5 [1996] 372 (IP)	Clearance Art.6(1)(b)	Computers
M.800	Siemens/Sommer Allibert Industrie	14.08.96	—	5 [1996] 372 (IP)	Clearance Art.6(1)(b)	Car Parts (Cockpits)
M.802	Telecom Eireann	18.12.96	—	4 [1997] 199 (IP)	Clearance Art.6(1)(b)	Telecommunications
M.803	REWE/Billa	27.08.96	—	5 [1996] 373 (IP)	Clearance Art.6(1)(b)	Food Retail
M.804	Auchan/Pao de Aucar	27.08.96	—	5 [1996] 374 (IP)	Clearance Art.6(1)(b)	Consumer Retailing
M.806	British Airways/TAT (II)	26.08.96	—	5 [1996] 375 (IP)	Clearance Art.6(1)(b)	Air Transport
M.808	Bayernwerk/Isarwerke	25.11.96	—	4 [1997] 23 (IP)	Art. 9(4) Referral	Electricity, gas, stream, hot water
M.810	N-TV	16.09.96	—	5 [1996] 523 (IP)	Clearance Art.6(1)(b)	TV Broadcasting
M.811	Creditantstalt-Bankverein/Treibacher	30.08.96	—	5 [1996] 375 (IP)	Clearance Art.6(1)(b)	Non-metallic Mineral Products
M.812	Allianz/Vereinte	11.11.96	—	5 [1996] 663 (IP)	Clearance Art.6(1)(b)	Insurance
M.813	Allianz/Hermes	27.09.96	—	5 [1996] 524 (IP)	Clearance Art.6(1)(b)	Insurance & Pension Funding
M.816	CGEA/SET	07.10.96	—	5 [1996] 524 (IP)	Clearance Art.6(1)(b)	Rail Transport
M.818	Cardo/Thyssen	02.12.96	—	4 [1997] 20 (IP)	Clearance Art.6(1)(b)	Railways
M.820	British Aerospace/Lagardere SCA	23.09.96	—	5 [1996] 523 (IP)	Clearance Art.6(1)(b)	Precision optical engineering; electronics
M.821	Baxter/Immuno	09.10.96	—	5 [1996] 917 (IP)	Clearance Art.6(1)(b)	Pharmaceutical Products
M.823	John Deere Capital/Lombard	07.10.96	—	5 [1996] 527 (IP)	Clearance Art.6(1)(b)	Fertilisers
M.826	ESPN/Star	11.11.96	—	5 [1996] 664 (IP)	Clearance Art.6(1)(b)	Sports TV Broadcasting
M.827	DBKOM	23.10.96	—	5 [1996] 658 (IP)	Clearance Art.6(1)(b)	Telecommunications

Table 5

MERGER No.	NAME	DATE	O.J.	C.M.L.R.	TYPE OF DECISION	PRODUCT SECTOR
M.828	Schweizer Re/M&G Re	30.10.96	—	5 [1996] 661 (IP)	Clearance Art.6(1)(b)	Insurance & Pension Funding
M.829	Thyssen/Böhler Uddeholm	14.10.96	—	5 [1996] 658 (IP)	Clearance Art.6(1)(b)	—
M.831	P&O/Royal Nedlloyd	19.12.96	—	—	Clearance Art.6(1)(b)	Shipping
M.832	Norsk Hydro/Enichem Agricolturaterni (II)	25.10.96	—	5 [1996] 659 (IP)	Clearance Art.6(1)(b)	Fertilisers
M.833	The Coca-Cola Company/Carlsberg A/S	11.09.97	—	5 [1997] 564 (IP)	Art. 8(2) with conditions and obligations	Drinks
M.834	Metallgesellschaft/Safic-Alcon (II)	21.11.96	—	4 [1997] 19 (IP)	Clearance Art.6(1)(b)	Trading/distribution metals/chemicals
M.835	Recticel/Greiner	19.03.97	—	4 [1997] 830 (IP)	Clearance Art.6(1)(b)	Polyester Foams
M.836	Gillette/Duracell	08.11.96	—	5 [1996] 662 (IP)	Clearance Art.6(1)(b)	Batteries
M.839	Promodes/Garosci	16.12.96	—	—	Clearance Art.6(1)(b)	Wholesaling and Retailing
M.843	PTT Post/TNT/GD Express	08.11.96	—	5 [1996] 661 (IP)	Clearance Art.6(1)(b)	Postal Services
M.845	BASF/Hoechst	17.06.97	—	5 [1997] 143 (IP)	Clearance Art.6(1)(b)	Polypropylene
M.846	Philips/Hewlett-Packard	17.02.97	—	4 [1997] 373 (IP)	Clearance Art.6(1)(b)	Led Components
M.848	Ahold/C.S.C.	02.12.96	—	4 [1997] 20 (IP)	Clearance Art.6(1)(b)	Supermarket Retailing
M.849	ELG Haniel/Jewometaal	25.11.96	—	4 [1997] 19 (IP)	Clearance Art.6(1)(b)	Basic Metals
M.850	Fortis/Meespierson	06.02.97	—	4 [1997] 371 (IP)	Clearance Art.6(1)(b)	Banking
M.853	Bell Cabelmedia/Cable & Wireless/ Videotron	11.12.96	—	4 [1997] 196 (IP)	Clearance Art.6(1)(b)	Telecommuncations/Pay TV
M.855	BT/NS-Telfort	20.12.96	—	—	Clearance Art.6(1)(b)	Telecommunications
M.856	British Telecom/MCI (II)	14.05.97	[1997] L336/1	5 [1997] 17 (IP)	Art. 8(2) with conditions and obligations	Telecommunications
M.857	British Airways/Air Liberte	28.02.97	—	4 [1997] 650 (IP)	Clearance Art.6(1)(b)	Air Transports
M.859	Generali/Prime	18.12.96	—	4 [1997] 367 (IP)	Clearance Art.6(1)(b)	Insurance & Pension Funding
M.861	Textron/Kautex	18.12.96	—	4 [1997] 198 (IP)	Clearance Art.6(1)(b)	Plastic Products
M.862	AXA/UAP	20.12.96	—	4 [1997] 200 (IP)	Clearance Art.6(1)(b)	Insurance
M.865	Cable & Wireless/NYNEX/Bell Canada	11.12.96	—	4 [1997] 196 (IP)	Clearance Art.6(1)(b)	Telecommunications
M.866	Cereol/Ösat-Ölmühle	02.04.97	—	4 [1997] 831 (IP)	Clearance Art.6(1)(b)	Agricultural Food Oils

MERGER No.	NAME	DATE	O.J.	C.M.L.R.	TYPE OF DECISION	PRODUCT SECTOR
M.867	Wagons-Lits/Carlson	07.03.97	—	4 [1997] 651 (IP)	Clearance Art.6(1)(b)	Business Travel Services
M.868	GKN/Brambles/Mabeg	20.12.96	—	4 [1997] 199 (IP)	Clearance Art.6(1)(b)	Waste Management Senses
M.869	BGT/EHG-AIM	26.02.97	—	4 [1997] 649 (IP)	Clearance Art.6(1)(b)	Defence Technology
M.871	UPM-Kymmene/Finnpap	21.02.97	—	4 [1997] 649 (IP)	Clearance Art.6(1)(b)	Paper Marketing Association
M.872	TRW/Magna	28.01.97	—	4 [1997] 370 (IP)	Clearance Art.6(1)(b)	Automotive/Space/ Defence Components
M.873	Bank Austria/Creditanstalt	11.03.97	—	4 [1997] 651 (IP)	Clearance Art.6(1)(b)	Banking
M.874	AMEC/Financiere Spie Batignolles/Spie Batignolle	06.02.97	—	4 [1997] 370 (IP)	Clearance Art.6(1)(b)	Construction/Project Management
M.875	DBV/Gothaer/GPM	17.02.97	—	4 [1997] 374 (IP)	Clearance Art.6(1)(b)	Insurance
M.876	Telia/Ericsson	20.02.97	—	4 [1997] 648 (IP)	Clearance Art.6(1)(b)	Telecommunications & IT Services
M.877	Boeing/McDonnell Douglas	30.07.97	[1997] L336/16	5 [1997] 270 (IP)	Art. 8(2) with conditions and obligations	Commercial Jets
M.878	RTL 7	14.02.97	—	4 [1997] 374 (IP)	Clearance Art.6(1)(b)	TV Broadcasting
M.879	Vendex (Vedior)/BIS	20.02.97	—	4 [1997] 648 (IP)	Clearance Art.6(1)(b)	Employment Services
M.880	Schweizer Re/Uniorias	07.02.97	—	4 [1997] 372 (IP)	Clearance Art.6(1)(b)	Reinsurance
M.882	ADM/Grace	20.02.97	—	4 [1997] 648 (IP)	Clearance Art.6(1)(b)	Cocoa & Chocolate Products
M.883	Prudential/HSBC/Finnish Chemicals	13.02.97	—	4 [1997] 372 (IP)	Clearance Art.6(1)(b)	Chemicals
M.884	KNP BT/Bunzl/Wilhelm Seiler	14.02.97	—	4 [1997] 373 (IP)	Clearance Art.6(1)(b)	Paper Merchanting
M.885	Merck/Rhone-Poulen-Merial	02.07.97	—	—	Clearance Art.6(1)(b)	Animal Health Genetics
M.886	MRW/MHP	22.04.97	—	4 [1997] 978 (IP)	Clearance Art.6(1)(b)	Steel Pipes
M.887	Castle Tower/TDF/Candover/Berkshire-HSCo	27.02.97	—	4 [1997] 650 (IP)	Clearance Art.6(1)(b)	TV Broadcasting
M.890	Blokker/Toys "R" Us (II)	26.06.97	[1998] L316/1	5 [1997] 148 (IP)	Art. 8(3)–(4) prohibition and divestiture	Toy Retailing
M.891	Deutsche Bank/Commerzbank/J.M. Voith	23.04.97	—	4 [1997] 979 (IP)	Clearance Art.6(1)(b)	Machinery
M.894	Rheinmetall/British Aerospace/STN Atlas	24.04.97	—	4 [1997] 987 (IP)	Clearance Art.6(1)(b)	Defence & Simulation Technology

Table 5

MERGER No.	NAME	DATE	O.J.	C.M.L.R.	TYPE OF DECISION	PRODUCT SECTOR
M.896	Tenneco/KNP BT	30.04.97	—	4 [1997] 980 (IP)	Clearance Art.6(1)(b)	Packaging/Car Parts
M.897	Stinnes/Haniel Reederei	11.08.97	—	5 [1997] 284 (IP)	Clearance Art.6(1)(a)	Cargo Shipping
M.900	BT/Tele DK/SBB/Migros/UBS	16.04.97	—	4 [1997] 978 (IP)	Clearance Art.6(1)(b)	Telecommunications
M.901	Go-Ahead/VIA/Thameslink	24.04.97	—	4 [1997] 979 (IP)	Clearance Art.6(1)(b)	Railways
M.902	Warner Bros./Lusomundo/Sogecable	12.05.97	—	5 [1997] 19 (IP)	Clearance Art.6(1)(b)	Multiplex Cinemas
M.904	RSB/Tenex/Fuel Logistic	02.04.97	—	4 [1997] 834 (IP)	Art. 6(1)(a)	Transportation of Nuclear Products
M.906	Mannesmann/Vallourec	03.06.97	—	5 [1997] 20 (IP)	Clearance Art.6(1)(b)	Steel Tubes
M.907	Agos Itafinco	12.05.97	—	5 [1997] 17 (IP)	Clearance Art.6(1)(b)	Banking
M.908	PTA/STET/Mobilkom	11.06.97	—	—	Clearance Art.6(1)(b)	Mobile Telephony & Paging
M.909	Worms/Saint-Louis	04.06.97	—	5 [1997] 22 (IP)	Clearance Art.6(1)(b)	Paper Production and Distribution
M.910	CLF CCB (Dexia)/San Paolo/Crediop	27.06.97	—	5 [1997] 145 (IP)	Clearance Art.6(1)(b)	Retailing
M.911	Clariant/Hoechst	10.06.97	—	5 [1997] 22 (IP)	Clearance Art.6(1)(b)	Specialty Chemicals
M.912	Siemens/HUF	29.04.97	—	4 [1997] 980 (IP)	Clearance Art.6(1)(b)	Locking Systems
M.913	Siemens/Elektrowatt	18.11.97	[1997] L88/1	4 [2000] 1255 (D)[5]	Art. 8(2) with conditions and obligations	Electricity and Control Apparatus
M.914	Tesco/ABF	05.05.97	—	4 [1997] 981 (IP)	Clearance Art.6(1)(b)	Retailing
M.915	Tyco/ADT	02.06.97	—	5 [1997] 21 (IP)	Clearance Art.6(1)(b)	Fire/Security Systems
M.916	Lyonnaise des Eaux/Suez	05.06.97	—	—	Clearance Art.6(1)(b)	Waste Disposal
M.917	Valinox/Timet	12.06.97	—	—	Clearance Art.6(1)(b)	Specialist Welded Tubes
M.918	Klockner/ODS	05.08.97	—	5 [1997] 275 (IP)	Clearance Art.6(1)(b)	Distribution Of Steel Products
M.919	Abeille Vie/Viagere/Sinafer	12.06.97	—	5 [1997] 142 (IP)	Clearance Art.6(1)(b)	Insurance
M.920	Samsung/AST	26.05.97	—	5 [1997] 22 (IP)	Clearance Art.6(1)(b)	Personal Computers
M.922	VIAG/Goldschmidt	26.06.97	—	—	Clearance Art.6(1)(b)	Chemicals
M.923	Deutsche Bank/Dresdner Bank/ESG	23.06.97	—	—	Clearance Art.6(1)(b)	Software
M.926	Messer Griesheim/Hydrogas	23.10.97	—	5 [1997] 763 (IP)	Clearance Art.6(1)(b)	Industrial Gases

[5] "(D)" indicates report of full text of Commission decision.

MERGER No.	NAME	DATE	O.J.	C.M.L.R.	TYPE OF DECISION	PRODUCT SECTOR
M.927	STET/GET/Union Fenosa	20.08.97	—	5 [1997] 426 (IP)	Clearance Art.6(1)(b)	Telecommunications
M.929	DIA/BEBA/Immobilien/Deutschbau	23.06.97	—	—	Clearance Art.6(1)(b)	Property Letting
M.930	Ferrostall/DSD	26.06.97	—	5 [1997] 146 (IP)	Clearance Art.6(1)(b)	Building
M.931	Neste/Ivo	02.06.98	—	—	Clearance Art.6(1)(b) with undertakings	Energy
M.932	SEHB/VIAG/PE-Bewag	25.07.97	—	5 [1997] 285 (IP)	Art. 9(4) Referral	Electricity
M.933	ICI/Unilever	23.06.97	—	5 [1997] 145 (IP)	Clearance Art.6(1)(b)	Speciality Chemicals
M.934	Auchan/Leroy Merlin/IFIL/La Rinascente	16.06.97	—	5 [1997] 142 (IP)	Clearance Art.6(1)(b)	Retailing
M.936	Siebe/APV	16.06.97	—	5 [1997] 143 (IP)	Clearance Art.6(1)(b)	Industrial Process Control Equipment
M.937	Lear/Keiper	22.07.97	—	5 [1997] 269 (IP)	Clearance Art.6(1)(b)	Car Seats
M.938	Guinness/Grand Metropolitan	15.10.97	[1998] L288/24	5 [1997] 760 (IP)	Art. 8(2) with conditions and obligations	Spirits
M.939	Bank America/General Electric/ Cableuropa	19.06.97	—	5 [1997] 144 (IP)	Clearance Art.6(1)(b)	Cable TV Services
M.940	UBS/Mister Minit	09.07.97	—	5 [1997] 147 (IP)	Art. 6(1)(a)	Franchising: Shoe Repairs/Key Cutting
M.941	ADMI/Acatos & Hutcheson-Soya Mainz	11.08.97	—	5 [1997] 277 (IP)	Clearance Art.6(1)(b)	Soya Products
M.942	VEBA/Degussa	03.12.97	[1998] L201/102	4 [1998] 19 (IP)	Art. 8(2) with conditions and obligations	Chemicals
M.943	CGEA/EVS/DEGV	02.07.97	—	—	Clearance Art.6(1)(b)	Rail Transport
M.945	Matra BAE Dynamics/DASA/LFK	27.01.98	—	—	Clearance Art.6(1)(b)	Defence Systems
M.946	Intermarche/Spar	30.06.97	—	—	Clearance Art.6(1)(b)	Food Distribution and Retailing
M.949	Mederic/Urrpimmec/CRI/Munich Re	02.07.97	—	—	Clearance Art.6(1)(b)	Reinsurance
M.950	Hoffmann-La Roche/Boehringer Mannheim	04.02.98	[1998] L234/14	4 [2000] 735	Art. 8(2) with conditions and obligations	Pharmaceuticals
M.951	Cable & Wireless/Maersk Data-Nautec	10.07.97	—	5 [1997] 146 (IP)	Clearance Art.6(1)(b)	Telecommunicatios/It Services
M.953	Thomson/Siemens/ATM	18.07.97	—	5 [1997] 269 (IP)	Clearance Art.6(1)(b)	Air Transport Management Systems

Table 5

MERGER No.	NAME	DATE	O.J.	C.M.L.R.	TYPE OF DECISION	PRODUCT SECTOR
M.954	Bain/Hoechst-Dade Behring	02.09.97	—	5 [1997] 428 (IP)	Clearance Art.6(1)(b)	Medical Diagnostic Analysis Equipment
M.957	L'Oreal/Procasa/Cosmetique Iberica/ Albesa	19.09.97	—	5 [1997] 568 (IP)	Clearance Art.6(1)(b)	Cosmetics/Perfumes
M.958	Watt AG (II)	04.12.97	—	—	Clearance Art.6(1)(b)	Electricity
M.960	Frantschach/MMP/Celulozy Swiecie	26.09.97	—	5 [1997] 569 (IP)	Clearance Art.6(1)(B)	Paper
M.961	Frantschach/Bischof + Klein/F + B Verpackungen	26.09.97	—	5 [1997] 569 (IP)	Clearance Art.6(1)(b)	Industrial Bags
M.962	Daimler Benz/Deutsche Telekom-Telematik	31.07.97	—	5 [1997] 274 (IP)	Clearance Art.6(1)(b)	Telematics
M.963	Compaq/Tandem	11.08.97	—	5 [1997] 276 (IP)	Clearance Art.6(1)(b)	Computers
M.966	Philips/Lucent Technologies	20.08.97	—	5 [1997] 426 (IP)	Clearance Art.6(1)(b)	Telecommunications Hardware
M.967	KLM/Air UK	22.09.97	—	—	Clearance Art.6(1)(b)	Air Transport
M.968	Lufthansa Cityline/Bombardier/EBJS	26.08.97	—	5 [1997] 427 (IP)	Clearance Art.6(1)(b)	Air Travel
M.969	A.P. Moller (Art. 14 Proc.)	12.10.98	—	5 [1998] 392 (IP)	Art. 8(4) (absence of notification) Fines pursuant to Art.14	—
M.970	TKS/ITW Signode/Titan	06.05.98	[1998] L316/33	4 [1998] 824 (IP)	Clearance Art.8(2) without undertakings	Steel and Plastic Strapping
M.971	Klöckner/Comercial de Laminados	26.08.97	—	5 [1997] 427 (IP)	Clearance Art.6(1)(b)	Steel Stockholding
M.972	Bertelsmann/Burda/Springer-Hos MM	15.09.97	—	—	Clearance Art.6(1)(b)	Medical Information
M.973	Bertelsmann/Burda-Hos Lifeline	15.09.97	—	5 [1997] 567 (IP)	Clearance Art.6(1)(b)	Health Information
M.975	Albacom/BT/ENI/Mediaset	13.11.97	—	4 [1998] 14 (IP)	Clearance Art.6(1)(b)	Telecommunications
M.976	Banco Santander/San Paolo/ Finconsumo	15.09.97	—	5 [1997] 567 (IP)	Clearance Art.6(1)(b)	Banking
M.977	Fujitsu/Amdahl	08.09.97	—	—	Clearance Art.6(1)(b)	Computers
M.979	Preussag/Voest Alpine	01.10.97	—	5 [1997] 572 (IP)	Art. 6(1)(a)	Metals
M.980	Arbed/Aceralia	18.11.97	—	4 [1998] 20 (IP)	Clearance	Coal and Steel
M.981	Fortis/ASLK-CGER	02.10.97	—	5 [1997] 569 (IP)	Clearance Art.6(1)(b)	Banking/Insurance
M.983	Bacob Banque/Banque Paribas Belgique	22.09.97	—	5 [1997] 568 (IP)	Clearance Art.6(1)(b)	Banking
M.984	Dupont/ICI	02.10.97	—	5 [1997] 758 (IP)	Clearance Art.6(1)(b)	Plastics/Chemicals

MERGER No.	NAME	DATE	O.J.	C.M.L.R.	TYPE OF DECISION	PRODUCT SECTOR
M.985	Credit Suisse/Winterthur	15.10.97	—	5 [1997] 761 (IP)	Clearance Art.6(1)(b)	Banking/Insurance
M.986	AGFA-Gevaert/Du Pont	11.02.98	[1998] L211/22	4 [1998] 486 (IP)	Art. 8(2) with conditions and obligations	Graphic Art Offset Printing Products
M.987	Adtranz/Siemens/Thyssen-Transrapid INT	09.03.98	—	4 [1998] 650 (IP)	Clearance Art.6(1)(b)	Railways Technology
M.988	Maersk DFDS Travel	04.11.97	—	4 [1998] 12 (IP)	Clearance Art.6(1)(b)	Travel Agency
M.990	Hagemeyer/ABB Asea Skandia	07.10.97	—	5 [1997] 759 (IP)	Clearance Art.6(1)(b)	Wholesaling of Electrical Products
M.991	Promodes/Casino	30.10.97	—	5 [1997] 766 (IP)	Clearance Art.6(1)(b)	Retail Distribution
M.993	Bertelsmann/Kirch/Premiere	27.05.98	[1999] L53/1	4 [1994] 700 (D)	Prohibition Art.8(3)	Pay Television
M.994	Dupont/Hitachi	24.10.97	—	5 [1997] 762 (IP)	Clearance Art.6(1)(b)	Hi-tech Plastics
M.997	Swedish Match/KAV	18.12.97	—	4 [1998] 206 (IP)	Clearance Art.6(1)(b)	Matches
M.998	OBS! Danmark	10.11.97	—	4 [1998] 13 (IP)	Clearance Art.6(1)(b)	Hypermarket Retailing
M.999	CLT-UFA/Havas Intermediation	26.02.98	—	4 [1998] 492 (IP)	Clearance Art.6(1)(b)	Media/Advertising Services
M.1001	Preussag/Hapag-Lloyd	10.11.97	—	4 [1998] 21 (IP)	Clearance Art.6(1)(B)	Travel
M.1003	ALCOA/Inespal	24.10.97	—	5 [1997] 763 (IP)	Clearance Art.6(1)(b)	Aluminium
M.1004	Blohm+Voss/Lisnave	18.06.98	—	—	Clearance Art.6(1)(b) without undertakings	Ship Repair and Conversion of Ships and Offshore Units
M.1005	Maersk Data/Den Danske Bank-DM Data	15.01.98	—	4 [1998] 408 (IP)	Clearance Art.6(1)(b)	Office Machinery, Computers
M.1006	UPM-Kymmene/April	11.06.98	—	5 [1998] 151 (IP)	Clearance Art.6(1)(b) without undertakings	Chemical Pulp and Fine Paper
M.1007	Shell/Montell	23.10.97	—	5 [1997] 762 (IP)	Clearance Art.6(1)(b)	Plastics
M.1009	Georg Fischer/DISA	10.03.98	—	4 [1998] 649 (IP)	Clearance Art.6(1)(b)	Foundry Equipment
M.1011	Ingersoll-Rand/Thermo King	24.10.97	—	5 [1997] 762 (IP)	Clearance Art.6(1)(b)	Temperature Control Equipment (Vehicles)
M.1013	Shell UK/Gulf Oil (Great Britain)	28.11.97	—	4 [1998] 18 (IP)	Clearance Art.6(1)(b)	Petrol Refining
M.1014	British Steel/Europipe	26.02.98	—	4 [1998] 490 (IP)	Clearance Art.6(1)(b)	Steel Pipe
M.1015	Cummins/Wärtsilä	17.11.97	—	—	Clearance Art.6(1)(b)	Diesel Engines

MERGER No.	NAME	DATE	O.J.	C.M.L.R.	TYPE OF DECISION	PRODUCT SECTOR
M.1016	Price Waterhouse/Coopers & Lybrand	20.05.98	[1999] L50/27	4 [1999] 665 (D)	Art. 8(2) without conditions and obligations	Audit and Accounting Services
M.1017	Hannover RE/Skandia	03.11.97	—	4 [1998] 12 (IP)	Clearance Art.6(1)(b)	Insurance & Reinsurance
M.1018	GE Capital/Woodchester	07.11.97	—	4 [1998] 13 (IP)	Clearance Art.6(1)(b)	Financial Services
M.1019	Preussag/TUI	10.11.97	—	4 [1998] 21 (IP)	Clearance Art.6(1)(B)	Travel
M.1020	GE Capital/Sea Containers	28.04.98	—	4 [1998] 822 (IP)	Clearance Art.6(1)(b) without undertakings	Marine Container Operating
M.1021	CNN/Sogelfa-CIM	01.12.97	—	—	Clearance Art.6(1)(b)	Fuel Storage
M.1022	Cable I Televisio de Catalunya (CTC)	28.01.98	—	4 [1998] 411 (IP)	Clearance Art.6(1)(b)	Telecommunications
M.1023	IFIL/Worms & Cie	27.11.97	—	4 [1998] 18 (IP)	Clearance Art.6(1)(b)	Maritime Transport/ Paper/Sugar
M.1025	Mannesmann/Olivetti/Infostrada	15.01.98	—	4 [1998] 407 (IP)	Clearance Art.6(1)(b)	Telecommunications Services
M.1026	Nordic Capital/Apax Industri	06.11.97	—	—	Clearance Art.6(1)(b)	Furniture
M.1027	Deutsche Telekom/Betaresearch	27.05.98	[1999] L53/31	4 [1999] 700 (D)	Prohibition Art.8(3)	Technical Services for Pay Television, Cable Television Networks
M.1029	Merita/Nordbanken	10.12.97	—	4 [1998] 206 (IP)	Clearance Art.6(1)(b)	Banking
M.1030	Lafarge/Redland	16.12.97	—	4 [1998] 218 (IP)	Clearance Art.6(1)(b)	Building Materials
M.1031	Jardine/Appleyard	20.11.97	—	4 [1998] 17 (IP)	Clearance Art.6(1)(b)	Vehicle Sales/Servicing
M.1033	AXA-UAP/AXA Aurora	23.12.97	—	4 [1998] 214 (IP)	Clearance Art.6(1)(b)	Insurance
M.1035	Hochtief/AER Rianta/Düsseldorf Airport	22.12.97	—	4 [1998] 210 (IP)	Clearance Art.6(1)(b)	Airport Operation
M.1036	Chrysler/Distributors/BeNeLux and Germany)	22.12.97	—	4 [1998] 208 (IP)	Clearance Art.6(1)(b)	Automobile Distribution
M.1037	Nomura/Blueslate	17.11.97	—	4 [1998] 15 (IP)	Clearance Art.6(1)(b)	Bookmaking (Betting)
M.1041	BASF/Shell (II)	23.12.97	—	4 [1998] 215 (IP)	Clearance Art.6(1)(b)	Polyethylene
M.1042	Eastman Kodak/Sun Chemical	15.01.98	—	4 [1998] 40 (IP)	Clearance Art.6(1)(b)	Graphic Art Products and Services
M.1043	BAT/Zürich	16.02.98	—	4 [1998] 488 (IP)	Clearance Art.6(1)(b)	Insurance and Tobacco
M.1045	DFO/Scandlines	29.01.98	—	—	Clearance Art.6(1)(b)	Ferry Services
M.1046	Ameritech/Tele Danmark	05.12.97	—	4 [1998] 206 (IP)	Clearance Art.6(1)(b)	Telecommunications

MERGER No.	NAME	DATE	O.J.	C.M.L.R.	TYPE OF DECISION	PRODUCT SECTOR
M.1049	AKZO/PLV-EPL	04.12.97	—	—	Clearance Art.6(1)(b)	Paper Costing Systems
M.1053	Mannesmann/Philips	12.02.98	—	4 [1998] 486 (IP)	Clearance Art.6(1)(b)	Electronic Equipment
M.1054	LGV/BTR	11.12.97	—	—	Clearance Art.6(1)(b)	Polymers/Building Materials
M.1055	Cegetel/Vodafone-SFR	19.12.97	—	4 [1998] 206 (IP)	Clearance Art.6(1)(b)	Mobile Telecommunications
M.1056	Stinnes/BTL	04.02.98	—	4 [1998] 415 (IP)	Clearance Art.6(1)(b)	Transport Logistic Services
M.1057	Terra/ICI	19.12.97	—	4 [1998] 206 (IP)	Clearance Art.6(1)(b)	Fertilisers
M.1058	Unichem/Alliance Sante	22.12.97	—	4 [1998] 211 (IP)	Clearance Art.6(1)(b)	Pharmaceutical Wholesaling
M.1059	Suez Lyonnaise des Eaux/BFI	19.12.97	—	4 [1998] 209 (IP)	Clearance Art.6(1)(b)	Waste Collection and Treatment
M.1060	Vendex/Bijenkorf	26.05.98	—	—	Clearance Art.6(1)(b) and partial referral (MS only req. partial referral)	Non-food Retail
M.1061	ING/BBL	22.01.98	—	4 [1998] 411 (IP)	Clearance Art.6(1)(b)	Financial Services
M.1062	Alpitour/Francorosso	04.02.98	—	4 [1998] 414 (IP)	Clearance Art.6(1)(b)	Travel Tour Services
M.1063	Metro/Makro	22.12.97	—	4 [1998] 214 (IP)	Clearance Art.6(1)(b)	Wholesale Trade
M.1064	Bombardier/Deutsche Waggonbau	29.01.98	—	4 [1998] 411 (IP)	Clearance Art.6(1)(b)	Railway Vehicles
M.1065	Nestlé/San Pellegrino	16.02.98	—	4 [1998] 489 (IP)	Clearance Art.6(1)(b)	Mineral Water and Soft Drinks
M.1067	Merrill Lynch/Mercury	22.12.97	—	4 [1998] 213 (IP)	Clearance Art.6(1)(b)	Financial Services
M.1068	Credit Suisse First Boston/Barclays	19.12.97	—	4 [1998] 210 (IP)	Clearance Art.6(1)(b)	Financial Services
M.1069	Worldcom/MCI (II)	08.07.98	[1999] L116/1	5 [1999] 876 (D)	Clearance Art.8(2) without undertakings	Telecommunications
M.1070	SPAR/Pfannkuch	15.01.98	—	—	Clearance Art.6(1)(b)	Wholesale, Retail
M.1071	SPAR/PRO	15.01.98	—	4 [1998] 406 (IP)	Clearance Art.6(1)(b)	Wholesale, Retail
M.1072	Bertelsmann/Burda/Futurekids	29.01.98	—	—	Clearance Art.6(1)(b)	Adult and Other Education
M.1073	Metallgesellschaft/Klöckner Chemiehandel	29.01.98	—	—	Clearance Art.6(1)(b)	Chemicals, Fuels

Table 5

MERGER No.	NAME	DATE	O.J.	C.M.L.R.	TYPE OF DECISION	PRODUCT SECTOR
M.1075	Nordic Capital/Mölnlycke Clinical/Kolmi	20.01.98	—	4 [1998] 409 (IP)	Clearance Art.6(1)(b)	Surgical Products
M.1076	Aceralia/Aristrain	15.01.98	—	4 [1998] 406 (IP)	Clearance	Basic Iron & Steel
M.1078	BP/Hüls	13.02.98	—	4 [1998] 487 (IP)	Clearance Art.6(1)(b)	Platics (Polystyrene)
M.1079	Deutag/Ilbau/Sächsische Asphaltmischwerke	02.04.98	—	4 [1998] 657 (IP)	Art. 6(1)(a)	Bituminous Products
M.1080	Thyssen/Krupp	02.06.98	—	5 [1998] 161 (IP)	Clearance Art.6(1)(b) without undertakings	Steel, Automotive Parts, Industrial Products, Engineering and Trade
M.1081	Dow Jones/NBC-CNBC Europe	22.01.98	—	4 [1998] 410 (IP)	Clearance Art.6(1)(b)	Satellite TV
M.1082	Allianz/AGF	08.05.98	—	5 [1998] 22 (IP)	Clearance Art.6(1)(b) with undertakings	Insurance
M.1083	Rhône-Poulenc/Novalis/Nyltech	15.04.98	—	4 [1998] 820 (IP)	Clearance Art.6(1)(b) without undertakings	Polyamides
M.1085	Promodes/Catteau	06.02.98	—	4 [1998] 416 (IP)	Art. 6(1)(b)	Food Hypermarkets
M.1086	Promodes/S21/Gruppo GS	10.03.98	—	4 [1998] 656 (IP)	Clearance Art.6(1)(b)	Supermarkets/ Hypermarkets
M.1087	Promodes/Simago	06.02.98	—	4 [1998] 416 (IP)	Clearance Art.6(1)(b)	Food Supermarkets/ Hypermarkets
M.1088	Thomson Corporation/Fritidsresor	04.02.98	—	4 [1998] 414 (IP)	Clearance Art.6(1)(b)	Travel Tour Services
M.1089	Paribas Belgique/Paribas Nederland	26.01.98	—	—	Clearance Art.6(1)(b)	Banking
M.1090	GRE/PPP	16.02.98	—	4 [1998] 487 (IP)	Clearance Art.6(1)(b)	Medical Insurance
M.1091	Cableuropa/Spainco/CTC	28.01.98	—	4 [1998] 411 (IP)	Clearance Art.6(1)(b)	Pay-tv/ Telecommunications
M.1093	ECIA/Bertrand Faure	28.01.98	—	—	Clearance Art.6(1)(b)	Automobile Seats
M.1094	Caterpillar/Perkins Engines	23.02.98	—	4 [1998] 496 (IP)	Clearance Art.6(1)(b)	Diesel Engines
M.1095	NEC/Bull/PBN	06.02.98	—	—	Art. 6(1)(a)	Computers
M.1096	Société Générale/Hambros Bank	06.02.98	—	4 [1998] 415 (IP)	Clearance Art.6(1)(b)	Banking
M.1097	Wacker/Air Products	04.08.98	—	5 [1998] 301 (IP)	Clearance Art.6(1)(b) without undertakings	Dispersions, Powders and Resins
M.1098	Generalis/AMB/Athena	23.04.98	—	4 [1998] 822 (IP)	Clearance Art.6(1)(b) without undertakings	Insurance
M.1099	Otto Versand/Actebis	26.02.98	—	4 [1998] 491 (IP)	Clearance Art.6(1)(b)	Computer Wholesale
M.1100	CGEA/Linjebuss	16.02.98	—	4 [1998] 489 (IP)	Clearance Art.6(1)(b)	Public Transport

MERGER No.	NAME	DATE	O.J.	C.M.L.R.	TYPE OF DECISION	PRODUCT SECTOR
M.1101	Hermes/Sampo/FGB-FCIC	19.05.98	—	5 [1998] 19 (IP)	Clearance Art.6(1)(b) without undertakings	Credit Insurance and Reinsurance
M.1102	BBL/American Express	29.04.98	—	—	Clearance Art.6(1)(b) without undertakings	Travel Services
M.1105	Tengelmann/Gruppo PAM	10.03.98	—	4 [1998] 649 (IP)	Clearance Art.6(1)(b)	Retail Sales
M.1106	Bayerische Vereinsbank/FGH Bank	04.03.98	—	4 [1998] 492 (IP)	Clearance Art.6(1)(b)	Banking
M.1107	EDFI/ESTAG	17.03.98	—	4 [1998] 651 (IP)	Clearance Art.6(1)(b)	Electricity, Gas and Heat
M.1108	SBG/SBV	04.03.98	—	4 [1998] 492 (IP)	Clearance Art.6(1)(b)	Banking
M.1109	Owens-Illinois/BTR Packaging	21.04.98	—	4 [1998] 820 (IP)	Clearance Art.6(1)(b) with undertakings	Glass Containers
M.1110	VAW/Reynolds Metals	19.05.98	—	5 [1998] 16 (IP)	Clearance Art.6(1)(b) without undertakings	Aluminium
M.1112	Advent International/EMI/WH Smith	24.03.98	—	4 [1998] 653 (IP)	Clearance Art.6(1)(b)	Recorded Music and Book Retailing
M.1113	NORTEL/NORWEB	18.03.98	—	4 [1998] 652 (IP)	Clearance Art.6(1)(b)	Telecommunications, Digital Power Line Products
M.1114	SAP/Heidelberger	23.11.98	—	4 [1999] 20 (IP)	Clearance Art.6(1)(b) without undertakings	Business Activities
M.1117	Pinault/Guilbert	10.03.98	—	4 [1998] 649 (IP)	Clearance Art.6(1)(b)	Office Furniture
M.1120	Compaq/Digital	23.03.98	—	4 [1998] 652 (IP)	Clearance Art.6(1)(b)	Computer Hardware
M.1121	Alcatel/Thomas SA-Thomson CSF	25.05.98	—	5 [1998] 15 (IP)	Clearance Art.6(1)(b) without undertakings	Defence Electronics and Air Traffic Control Systems
M.1122	Kredietbank/Cera Bank	18.05.98	—	5 [1998] 14 (IP)	Clearance Art.6(1)(b) without undertakings	Banking and Insurance
M.1124	Maersk Air/LFV Holdings	06.07.98	—	5 [1998] 159 (IP)	Clearance Art.6(1)(b) without undertakings	Groundhandling Services
M.1125	Cereol/Sofiproteol-Saipol	10.03.98	—	4 [1998] 650 (IP)	Clearance Art.6(1)(b)	Agricultural Oil Production
M.1126	Cargil/Vandemoortele	20.07.98	—	5 [1998] 298 (IP)	Clearance Art.6(1)(b) without undertakings	Oilseed Crushing and Refining

Table 5

MERGER No.	NAME	DATE	O.J.	C.M.L.R.	TYPE OF DECISION	PRODUCT SECTOR
M.1127	Nestlé/Dalgety	02.04.98	—	4 [1998] 655 (IP)	Clearance Art.6(1)(b) without undertakings	Pet Food and Accessories
M.1129	Commercial Union/Berlinische Lebensversicherung AGM	30.06.98	—	5 [1998] 158 (IP)	Clearance Art.6(1)(b) without undertakings	Insurance
M.1131	AGF/Royal	23.04.98	—	4 [1998] 821 (IP)	Clearance Art.6(1)(b) without undertakings	Insurance
M.1132	BT/ESB	19.05.98	—	5 [1998] 18 (IP)	Clearance Art.6(1)(b) without undertakings	Telecommunications Services
M.1133	Bass plc/Saison Holdings BV	23.03.98	—	4 [1998] 653 (IP)	Clearance Art.6(1)(b)	Hotel Services
M.1134	Tarmac/Bovis	24.03.98	—	—	Clearance Art.6(1)(b)	General Plant Hire and Consumables Sale
M.1135	Elf/Texaco/Antifreeze JV	18.08.98	—	5 [1998] 467 (IP)	Clearance Art.6(1)(b) without undertakings	Antifreeze and Coolants
M.1137	Exxon/Shell	08.07.98	—	5 [1998] 160 (IP)	Clearance Art.6(1)(b) without undertakings	Lubricants and Fuel Additives
M.1138	Royal Bank of Canada/Bank of Montreal	02.04.98	—	—	Clearance Art.6(1)(b) without undertakings	Banking and Financial Services
M.1139	DLJ/FM/Holdings	28.04.98	—	—	Clearance Art.6(1)(b) without undertakings	Laminates, surfacing products, banking
M.1140	Haliburton/Dresser	06.07.98	—	5 [1998] 165 (IP)	Clearance Art.6(1)(b) without undertakings	Oilfield Services
M.1142	Commercial Union/General Accident I	06.05.98	—	5 [1998] 11 (IP)	Clearance Art.6(1)(b) without undertakings	Insurance
M.1143	DSM/Koninklijke Gist-Brocades	07.05.98	—	5 [1998] 11 (IP)	Clearance Art.6(1)(b) without undertakings	Antibiotics
M.1144	Winterthur/ARAG	14.04.98	—	4 [1998] 820 (IP)	Clearance Art.6(1)(b) without undertakings	Insurance
M.1146	SHV Energy/Thyssen Klöckner Recycling	19.05.98	—	—	Clearance Art.6(1)(b) without undertakings	Scrap Metal
M.1148	STET/GET/Madrid Cable	28.05.98	—	—	Clearance Art.6(1)(b) without undertakings	Telecommunications
M.1150	Schweizer Rück/NCM	26.06.98	—	5 [1998] 157 (IP)	Clearance Art.6(1)(b) without undertakings	Del Credere

MERGER No.	NAME	DATE	O.J.	C.M.L.R.	TYPE OF DECISION	PRODUCT SECTOR
M.1153	Krauss-Maffei/Wegmann	19.06.98	—	5 [1998] 167 (IP)	Clearance Art.6(1)(b) and partial referral (MS only req. partial referral)	Simulation Technology
M.1154	Mc Dermott/ETPM	04.06.98	—	5 [1998] 148 (IP)	Clearance Art.6(1)(b) without undertakings	Offshore Oil and Gas Services
M.1155	Cendant Corporation/NPC	24.04.98	—	—	Clearance Art.6(1)(b) without undertakings	Membership, Travel and Real Estate Services
M.1157	Skanska/Scancem	11.11.98	[1997] L183/1	5 [2000] 686 (D)	Clearance Art.6(1)(b) with undertakings	Mineral Products
M.1158	Elf Atochem/Atohaas	25.05.98	—	5 [1998] 20 (IP)	Clearance Art.6(1)(b) without undertakings	Organic Glass
M.1159	Snecma/Messier Dowty	18.06.98	—	—	Clearance Art.6(1)(b) without undertakings	Landing Gear and Overhaul Services
M.1160	GKN/Brambles/SKP	26.05.98	—	—	Clearance Art.6(1)(b) without undertakings	Waste Management Services
M.1161	Alcoa/Alumax	28.05.98	—	5 [1998] 149 (IP)	Clearance Art.6(1)(b) without undertakings	Aluminium
M.1162	GE/Bayer	11.06.98	—	5 [1998] 155 (IP)	Clearance Art.6(1)(b) without undertakings	Silicones
M.1163	Borealis/IPIC/OMV/PCD	24.07.98	—	5 [1998] 299 (IP)	Clearance Art.6(1)(b) without undertakings	Polyolefins
M.1164	GEC Alsthom/Cegelec	15.05.98	—	5 [1998] 12 (IP)	Clearance Art.6(1)(b) without undertakings	Power Generation, Transmission and Distribution, Transport, Industrial Processes
M.1165	Lufthansa/Menzies/LCC	30.06.98	—	5 [1998] 157 (IP)	Clearance Art.6(1)(b) without undertakings	Airport Cargo Handling
M.1167	ICI/Williams I	29.04.98	—	4 [1998] 824 (IP)	Clearance Art.6(1)(b) without undertakings	Decorative Coatings
M.1168	DHL/Deutsche Post	26.06.98	—	5 [1998] 156 (IP)	Clearance Art.6(1)(b) without undertakings	Expedited Transport Industry
M.1169	EDFI/Graninge	25.05.98	—	5 [1998] 21 (IP)	Clearance Art.6(1)(b) without undertakings	Electricity Sector
M.1170	Dan Transport/Inter Forward	25.05.98	—	5 [1998] 148 (IP)	Clearance Art.6(1)(b) without undertakings	Road Forwarding Services

MERGER No.	NAME	DATE	O.J.	C.M.L.R.	TYPE OF DECISION	PRODUCT SECTOR
M.1171	PTA/Telecom Italia/Telekom Austria	16.12.98	—	4 [1999] 179 (IP)	Clearance Art.6(1)(b) without undertakings	Telecommunications
M.1172	Fortis AG/Generale Bank	24.06.98	—	5 [1998] 155 (IP)	Clearance Art.6(1)(b) without undertakings	Banking and Insurance
M.1174	RWE-DEA/Hüls	11.06.98	—	5 [1998] 150 (IP)	Clearance Art.6(1)(b) without undertakings	Surfactants and Fats
M.1175	Magna/Steyr	28.05.98	—	5 [1998] 20 (IP)	Clearance Art.6(1)(b) without undertakings	Motor Vehicle Parts
M.1177	Belgacom/Tele Danmark/Tulip	19.05.98	—	5 [1998] 16 (IP)	Clearance Art.6(1)(b) without undertakings	Mobile Telephony
M.1178	Koch/Euro Splitter & J. Aron	14.05.98	—	—	Clearance Art.6(1)(b) without undertakings	Oil Refining and Oil Products
M.1179	Tech Data/Computer 2000	03.06.98	—	5 [1998] 149 (IP)	Clearance Art.6(1)(b) without undertakings	Wholesale IT Distribution
M.1182	Akzo Nobel/Courtaulds	30.06.98	—	5 [1998] 163 (IP)	Clearance Art.6(1)(b) with undertakings	Coatings
M.1184	Travelers/Citicorp	23.06.98	—	5 [1998] 154 (IP)	Clearance Art.6(1)(b) without undertakings	Banking and Financial Services
M.1185	Alcatel/Thomson CSF-SCS	04.06.98	—	5 [1998] 162 (IP)	Clearance Art.6(1)(b) with undertakings	Satellites
M.1186	GEAL/CREA/CGE	18.06.98	—	5 [1998] 155 (IP)	Clearance Art.6(1)(b) without undertakings	Water Supply
M.1188	Kingfisher/Wegert/Promarkt	18.06.98	—	—	Clearance Art.6(1)(b) without undertakings	Electrical Retailing
M.1189	Teksid/Norsk Hydro Produksjon/ Meridian	17.07.98	—	5 [1998] 297 (IP)	Clearance Art.6(1)(b) without undertakings	Automotive Components
M.1190	Amoco/Repsol/Iberdrola/Ente Vasco De La Energi	11.08.98	—	5 [1998] 465 (IP)	Clearance Art.6(1)(b) without undertakings	Electricity and Regasification
M.1192	CHS Electronic/Métrologie International	23.06.98	—	5 [1998] 154 (IP)	Clearance Art.6(1)(b) without undertakings	Wholesale IT products distribution
M.1193	AXA/Royale Belge	12.06.98	—	5 [1998] 152 (IP)	Clearance Art.6(1)(b) without undertakings	Insurance
M.1194	SGB/Fortis AG	24.06.98	—	5 [1998] 155 (IP)	Clearance Art.6(1)(b) without undertakings	Banking and Insurance

MERGER No.	NAME	DATE	O.J.	C.M.L.R.	TYPE OF DECISION	PRODUCT SECTOR
M.1195	Siebe/Eurotherm	11.06.98	—	—	Clearance Art.6(1)(b) without undertakings	Industrial Process Controls
M.1196	Johnson Controls/Becker	24.06.98	—	5 [1998] 156 (IP)	Clearance Art.6(1)(b) without undertakings	Automotive Interior Trimmings
M.1198	BAe/Saab	03.07.98	—	—	Clearance Art.6(1)(b) without undertakings	Combat Jets and Guided Weapons
M.1199	UTA Telekom AG/Swisscom	13.07.98	—	5 [1998] 295 (IP)	Clearance Art.6(1)(b) without undertakings	Telecommunications
M.1200	Arco/Union Texas	15.06.98	—	—	Clearance Art.6(1)(b) without undertakings	Crude Oil and Natural Gas
M.1201	Dupont/Merck I	23.06.98	—	5 [1998] 153 (IP)	Clearance Art.6(1)(b) without undertakings	Pharmaceutical Products, Chemicals and Energy
M.1202	Renault/Iveco	22.10.98	—	—	Clearance Art.6(1)(b) without undertakings	Buses and Coaches
M.1203	Usinor/Finarvedi (See ECSC.1282)	29.09.98	—	5 [1998] 670 (IP)	Clearance Art.6(1)(b) without undertakings	Steel Products
M.1204	Daimler-Benz/Chrysler	22.07.98	—	5 [1998] 296 (IP)	Clearance Art.6(1)(b) without undertakings	Pasenger Cars
M.1206	Drum Holdings/Natwest Equity/CVC	19.06.98	—	—	Clearance Art.6(1)(b) without undertakings	Storage Drums, Investment Banking
M.1207	Dana/Echlin	06.07.98	—	5 [1998] 160 (IP)	Clearance Art.6(1)(b) without undertakings	Automotive Components
M.1208	Jefferson Smurfit/Stone Containers	08.07.98	—	—	Clearance Art.6(1)(b) without undertakings	Corrugated Case
M.1211	Magneti Marelli/Telespazio	02.07.98	—	5 [1998] 159 (IP)	Clearance Art.6(1)(b) without undertakings	Infomobility
M.1218	Packaging International BV/NV Koninklijke KNP BT	03.07.98	—	5 [1998] 159 (IP)	Clearance Art.6(1)(b) without undertakings	Packaging
M.1219	Seagram/Polygram	21.09.98	—	5 [1998] 661 (IP)	Clearance Art.6(1)(b) without undertakings	Recorded Music and Films
M.1220	Alliance Unichem/Unifarma	23.07.98	—	5 [1998] 306 (IP)	Art. 9(4) total referral	Wholesale Of Pharmaceuticals
M.1221	Rewe/MEINL	03.02.99	[1999] L274/1	5 [2000] 256 (D)	Clearance Art.8(2) with undertakings	Food Retail and Procurement

MERGER No.	NAME	DATE	O.J.	C.M.L.R.	TYPE OF DECISION	PRODUCT SECTOR
M.1223	Tyco International/US Surgical Corp.	07.08.98	—	5 [1998] 304 (IP)	Clearance Art.6(1)(b) without undertakings	Wound Closure Products
M.1224	TPM/Wood Group	20.07.98	—	5 [1998] 297 (IP)	Clearance Art.6(1)(b) without undertakings	Gas Turbine Overhaul and Repair
M.1225	Enso/Stora	25.11.98	[1999] L254/9	4 [2000] 372 (D)	Art. 8(2) without undertakings	Paper and Board
M.1226	GEC/GPTH	27.07.98	—	—	Clearance Art.6(1)(b) without undertakings	Telecommunications equipment and systems
M.1227	Cargill/Vandemoortele-JV	20.07.98	—	5 [1998] 298 (IP)	Clearance Art.6(1)(b) without undertakings	Seed Oil Packing and Marketing
M.1229	American Home Products/Monsanto	28.09.98	—	5 [1998] 664 (IP)	Clearance Art.6(1)(b) with undertakings	Pharmaceutical, Agrochemical and Industrial Weed Control Products
M.1230	Glaverbel/PPG	07.08.98	—	5 [1998] 463 (IP)	Clearance Art.6(1)(b) without undertakings	Float Glass
M.1231	Ivo/Stockholm Energi	05.08.98	—	5 [1998] 303 (IP)	Clearance Art.6(1)(b) without undertakings	Electricity
M.1232	Ingram/Macrotron	17.07.98	—	5 [1998] 296 (IP)	Clearance Art.6(1)(b) without undertakings	Wholesale Hardware and Software Distribution
M.1235	New Holland/Orenstein & Koppel	18.12.98	—	4 [1999] 181 (IP)	Clearance Art.6(1)(b) without undertakings	Construction Machinery
M.1239	Rwe-Dea/Fuchs Petrolub	11.08.98	—	5 [1998] 465 (IP)	Clearance Art.6(1)(b) without undertakings	Lubricants and Antifreeze
M.1242	Paribas/Ecureuil-Vie/ICD	31.08.98	—	5 [1998] 472 (IP)	Clearance Art.6(1)(b) without undertakings	Commercial Property Letting
M.1243	Alliance Unichem plc/Safa Galenica SA	27.07.98	—	5 [1998] 299 (IP)	Clearance Art.6(1)(b) without undertakings	Wholesale Of Pharmaceuticals
M.1244	Bank America/Nationsbank	21.08.98	—	—	Clearance Art.6(1)(b) without undertakings	Banking
M.1245	Valeo/ITT Industries	30.07.98	—	5 [1998] 300 (IP)	Clearance Art.6(1)(b) without undertakings	Electrical Automotive Parts
M.1248	Kingfisher/BUT	21.08.98	—	5 [1998] 468 (IP)	Clearance Art.6(1)(b) without undertakings	Electrical Retailing

MERGER No.	NAME	DATE	O.J.	C.M.L.R.	TYPE OF DECISION	PRODUCT SECTOR
M.1251	Particitel International/Cableuropa	30.07.98	—	5 [1998] 301 (IP)	Clearance Art.6(1)(b) without undertakings	Pay television, telecommunications
M.1252	AT&T/TCI	04.12.98	—	4 [1999] 26 (IP)	Clearance Art.6(1)(b) without undertakings	Telecommunications
M.1253	Paribas/JDC/Gerflor	27.08.98	—	5 [1998] 471 (IP)	Clearance Art.6(1)(b) without undertakings	Floor Coverings
M.1254	Dexia/Argentaria/Credito Local	28.10.98	—	5 [1998] 879 (IP)	Clearance Art.6(1)(b) without undertakings	Banking
M.1255	Flughafen Berlin	21.05.99	—	5 [1999] 15 (IP)	Clearance Art.6(1)(b) Without undertakings	Airport Management
M.1256	Ok Ekonomisk Förening/Kuwait Petroleum Sverige AB	21.12.98	—	—	Clearance Art.6(1)(b) without undertakings	Fuels, lubricants, car-related services
M.1257	CHS Electronics/CHS Far East	18.08.98	—	—	Clearance Art.6(1)(b) without undertakings	Wholesale Hardware and Software Distribution
M.1258	GEC Marconi/Alenia	28.08.98	—	—	Clearance Art.6(1)(b) without undertakings	Electronic Systems
M.1259	Voest Alpine Stahl/Vossloh:VAE	06.10.98	—	5 [1998] 472 (IP)	Clearance Art.6(1)(b) without undertakings	Raills and Points
M.1260	Edon/Rova/Reco	24.08.98	—	5 [1998] 470 (IP)	Clearance Art.6(1)(b) without undertakings	Ldpe Recycling
M.1262	Cebeco/Plukon	24.09.98	—	5 [1998] 664 (IP)	Clearance Art.6(1)(b) without undertakings	Poultry
M.1263	Nortel/Bay	21.08.98	—	5 [1998] 468 (IP)	Clearance Art.6(1)(b) without undertakings	Data Networking
M.1265	CHS/Vobis	21.08.98	—	—	Clearance Art.6(1)(b) without undertakings	Wholesale Hardware and Software Distribution
M.1269	LSG/Onexcorp/Sky Chefs/Caterair	09.11.98	—	4 [1999] 15 (IP)	Clearance Art.6(1)(b) without undertakings	In-flight Catering Services
M.1270	KNP BT/Allium	03.09.98	—	5 [1998] 473 (IP)	Clearance Art.6(1)(b) without undertakings	Computer Product Distribution
M.1271	Pirelli/Siemens	30.09.98	—	5 [1998] 666 (IP)	Clearance Art.6(1)(b) without undertakings	Power Cables
M.1273	Credit Suisse/Nikko/MSA	14.08.98	—	5 [1998] 466 (IP)	Clearance Art.6(1)(b) without undertakings	Motorway Services

Table 5

MERGER No.	NAME	DATE	O.J.	C.M.L.R.	TYPE OF DECISION	PRODUCT SECTOR
M.1275	Havas/Bertelsmann/Doyma	27.08.98	—	5 [1998] 470 (IP)	Clearance Art.6(1)(b) without undertakings	Medical Publishing
M.1276	NEC/PBN I	03.09.98	—	—	Clearance Art.6(1)(b) without undertakings	Personal Computers
M.1279	CDE/La Hénin	03.09.98	—	—	Clearance Art.6(1)(b) without undertakings	Banking
M.1280	KKR/Willis Corroon	24.08.98	—	5 [1998] 469 (IP)	Clearance Art.6(1)(b) without undertakings	Insurance
M.1282	Retevisión Móvil	30.10.98	—	5 [1998] 882 (IP)	Clearance Art.6(1)(b) without undertakings	Mobile Telephony
M.1283	Volkswagen/Rolls-Royce/Cosworth	24.08.98	—	—	Clearance Art.6(1)(b) without undertakings	Passenger Cars and Car Engines
M.1286	Johnson & Johnson/Depuy	28.10.98	—	5 [1998] 880 (IP)	Clearance Art.6(1)(b) with undertakings	Orthopaedic Industry
M.1287	Elenac/Hoechst	24.11.98	—	4 [1999] 23 (IP)	Clearance Art.6(1)(b) without undertakings	Polyethylene and Pe-technology
M.1289	Harbert Management/DB/Bankers Trust/SPP/Öhma	31.08.98	—	5 [1998] 472 (IP)	Clearance Art.6(1)(b) without undertakings	Real Estate
M.1291	Bosch/ZF Friedrichshafen	14.09.98	—	5 [1998] 473 (IP)	Clearance Art.6(1)(b) without undertakings	Steering Mechanisms
M.1292	Continental/ITT	18.09.98	—	5 [1998] 662 (IP)	Clearance Art.6(1)(b) without undertakings	Break Mechanisms
M.1293	BP/Amoco	11.12.98	—	4 [1999] 176 (IP)	Clearance Art.6(1)(b) without undertakings	Petrochemicals
M.1296	Norske Skog/Abitibi/Hansol	14.09.98	—	5 [1998] 473 (IP)	Clearance Art.6(1)(b) without undertakings	Magazine Paper
M.1297	La Rinascente/Colmark	28.09.98	—	5 [1998] 663 (IP)	Clearance Art.6(1)(b) without undertakings	Consumer Goods Retail
M.1298	Kodak/Imation	23.10.98	—	5 [1998] 878 (IP)	Clearance Art.6(1)(b) without undertakings	Medical Imaging
M.1300	Allied Signal/AMP	18.09.98	—	5 [1998] 660 (IP)	Clearance Art.6(1)(b) without undertakings	Connectors and Cables
M.1301	Texaco/Chevron	30.10.98	—	5 [1998] 881 (IP)	Clearance Art.6(1)(b) without undertakings	Marine Lubricants and Residual Fuels

MERGER No.	NAME	DATE	O.J.	C.M.L.R.	TYPE OF DECISION	PRODUCT SECTOR
M.1303	ADEG/EDEKA	09.11.98	—	4 [1999] 15 (IP)	Clearance Art.6(1)(b) without undertakings	Foodstuffs Retail
M.1304	Hercules/Betzdearborn	05.10.98	—	5 [1998] 472 (IP)	Clearance Art.6(1)(b) without undertakings	Sizing and Creping Agents
M.1305	Eurostar	09.12.98	—	4 [1999] 175 (IP)	Clearance Art.6(1)(b) without undertakings	Passenger Travel
M.1306	Berkshire Hathaway/General Re	18.09.98	—	5 [1998] 660 (IP)	Clearance Art.6(1)(b) without undertakings	Reinsurance
M.1307	Marsh & McLennan/Sedgwick	23.10.98	—	5 [1998] 877 (IP)	Clearance Art.6(1)(b) without undertakings	Insurance, Human Resources Consulting
M.1308	Wolseley/Hall	30.09.98	—	5 [1998] 666 (IP)	Clearance Art.6(1)(b) without undertakings	Building Materials Distribution
M.1309	Matra/Areospatiale	28.04.99	—	4 [1999] 1183 (IP)	Clearance Art.6(1)(b) With undertakings	Military Products, Satellites
M.1313	Danish Crown/Vestjyske Slagterier	09.03.99	[2000] L20/1	5 [2000] 296 (D)	Clearance Art.8(2) with undertakings	Slaughterhouses
M.1314	Framatome/Berg Electronics	08.10.98	—	5 [1998] 876 (IP)	Clearance Art.6(1)(b) without undertakings	Electrical Connectors
M.1315	ENW/Eastern	15.10.98	—	—	Art. 6(1)(a)	Gas Supply
M.1318	Constructor/Dexion	30.10.98	—	5 [1998] 881 (IP)	Clearance Art.6(1)(b) without undertakings	Pallet Racks and Shelving
M.1319	Smurfit Condat/CVC	23.10.98	—	—	Clearance Art.6(1)(b) without undertakings	Paper
M.1320	LGV/Dorana/Emtec	07.12.98	—	—	Clearance Art.6(1)(b) without undertakings	Tapes, Data Storage, Pensions
M.1325	Bayer/Chiron Diagnostics	17.11.98	—	4 [1999] 19 (IP)	Clearance Art.6(1)(b) without undertakings	Diagnostic Analysis
M.1326	Toyota/Daihatsu	06.11.98	—	—	Clearance Art.6(1)(b) without undertakings	Passenger Cars
M.1327	NC/Canal+/CDPQ/Bank America	03.12.98	—	—	Clearance Art.6(1)(b) without undertakings	Cable Television Networks
M.1329	Usinor/Cockerill	04.02.99	—	4 [1999] 383 (IP)	Clearance Art.6(1)(b) with undertakings	Metal Products

MERGER No.	NAME	DATE	O.J.	C.M.L.R.	TYPE OF DECISION	PRODUCT SECTOR
M.1330	Pechiney/Samancor	26.01.99	—	4 [1999] 376 (IP)	Clearance Art.6(1)(b) without undertakings	Silicon Metal
M.1331	ING/BHF	16.11.98	—	4 [1999] 18 (IP)	Clearance Art.6(1)(b) without undertakings	Banking
M.1332	Thomson/Lucas	21.12.98	—	4 [1999] 180 (IP)	Clearance Art.6(1)(b) without undertakings	Cruise Control Systems
M.1333	Kingfisher/Castorama	17.12.98	—	4 [1999] 370 (IP)	Clearance Art.6(1)(b) without undertakings	Duy Products
M.1334	Volvo Aero/ABB/Turbogen	17.11.98	—	4 [1999] 18 (IP)	Clearance Art.6(1)(b) without undertakings	Turbogenerators
M.1335	Dana/Glacier Vandervell	11.12.98	—	4 [1999] 177 (IP)	Clearance Art.6(1)(b) without undertakings	Automotive Components
M.1336	Deutsche Bank/Vianova	09.12.98	—	—	Clearance Art.6(1)(b) without undertakings	Synthetic Resins
M.1337	Koch Industries/Saba/Hoechst	24.11.98	—	4 [1999] 23 (IP)	Clearance Art.6(1)(b) without undertakings	Polyester
M.1338	Teksid/Renault	15.03.99	—	4 [1999] 799 (IP)	Clearance Art.6(1)(b) without undertakings	Automotive Components
M.1339	ABB/Elsaq Bailey	16.12.98	—	4 [1999] 179 (IP)	Clearance Art.6(1)(b) with undertakings	Process Control Systems
M.1340	BNP/Dresdner Bank-Austrian JV	21.12.98	—	—	Clearance Art.6(1)(b) without undertakings	Banking
M.1341	Westdeutsche Landesbank/Carlson/ Thomas Cook	08.03.99	—	4 [1999] 608 (IP)	Clearance Art.6(1)(b) without undertakings	Travel Services
M.1342	Knorr-Bremse/Bosch	14.12.98	—	4 [1999] 177 (IP)	Clearance Art.6(1)(b) without undertakings	Breaking Systems
M.1346	EDF/London Electricity	27.01.99	—	4 [1999] 374 (IP)	Clearance Art.6(1)(b) without undertakings	Electricity
M.1347	Deutsche Post/Securicor	23.02.99	—	4 [1999] 600 (IP)	Clearance Art.6(1)(b) without undertakings	Parcel and Freight Delivery, Logistics
M.1348	Archer Daniels Midland Company/ Alfred C. Toepfer International GmbH/ In Trade N.V.	09.11.99	—	4 [2000] 19 (IP)	Clearance Art.6(1)(b) Without undertakings	Trading of Agricultural Commodities

MERGER No.	NAME	DATE	O.J.	C.M.L.R.	TYPE OF DECISION	PRODUCT SECTOR
M.1349	CVC Capital Partners/Dynoplast	08.03.99	—	4 [1999] 609 (IP)	Clearance Art.6(1)(b) without undertakings	Industrial Containers
M.1354	SAir Group/LTU	21.12.98	—	—	Clearance Art.6(1)(b) without undertakings	Air Transport
M.1355	Newell/Rubbermaid	13.01.99	—	4 [1999] 372 (IP)	Clearance Art.6(1)(b) without undertakings	Home Storage Systems
M.1356	Metsä-Serla/UK Paper	09.12.98	—	4 [1999] 174 (IP)	Clearance Art.6(1)(b) without undertakings	Pulp and Paper
M.1357	Nordic Capital/Hilding Anders	04.02.99	—	4 [1999] 385 (IP)	Clearance Art.6(1)(b) without undertakings	Beds
M.1358	Philips/Lucent/Technologies	06.01.99	—	4 [1999] 371 (IP)	Clearance Art.6(1)(b) without undertakings	Communication Terminal Devices
M.1359	Royale Belge/Anhyp	27.11.98	—	4 [1999] 24 (IP)	Clearance Art.6(1)(b) without undertakings	Banking
M.1360	AKZO Nobel/Glaverfin/Eijkelkamp	13.01.99	—	4 [1999] 373 (IP)	Clearance Art.6(1)(b) without undertakings	Decorative Coatings and Float Glass
M.1361	Rast-Und Tankstätten AG	07.12.98	—	4 [1999] 174 (IP)	Clearance Art.6(1)(b) without undertakings	Motorway Services
M.1362	BAY WA AG/RWA	03.06.99	—	5 [1999] 24 (IP)	Clearance Art.6(1)(b) Without undertakings	Agricultural Materials
M.1363	Dupont/Hoechst/Herberts	05.02.99	—	4 [1999] 386 (IP)	Clearance Art.6(1)(b) without undertakings	Industrial and Automotive Coatings
M.1365	FCC/Vivendi	04.03.99	—	4 [1999] 606 (IP)	Clearance Art.6(1)(b) without undertakings	Construction, Water Distribution, Waste Management
M.1366	Paribas/CDC/Beaufour	09.12.98	—	4 [1999] 182 (IP)	Clearance Art.6(1)(b) without undertakings	Pharmaceuticals, Banking
M.1367	Inchcape Holdings Hellas/EFG Eurobank	11.02.99	—	4 [1999] 388 (IP)	Clearance Art.6(1)(b) without undertakings	Consumer Financing
M.1368	Ford/ZF	21.12.98	—	—	Clearance Art.6(1)(b) without undertakings	Automatic Transmissions
M.1369	Thyssen Handel/Mannesmann Handel	07.04.99	—	4 [1999] 807 (IP)	Clearance Art.6(1)(b) Without undertakings	Steel Industry, Energy, Chemical
M.1370	Peugeot/Credipar	22.12.98	—	—	Clearance Art.6(1)(b) without undertakings	Vehicle Financing

MERGER No.	NAME	DATE	O.J.	C.M.L.R.	TYPE OF DECISION	PRODUCT SECTOR
M.1371	La Poste/Denkhaus	26.02.99	—	4 [1999] 604 (IP)	Clearance Art.6(1)(b) without undertakings	Parcel Distribution
M.1372	Hugh Baird/Scottish & Newcastle	18.12.98	—	4 [1999] 181 (IP)	Clearance Art.6(1)(b) without undertakings	Malt
M.1375	Volkswagen/Ford/Autoeuropa	02.02.99	—	4 [1999] 381 (IP)	Clearance Art.6(1)(b) without undertakings	Passenger Cars
M.1376	Cargill/Continental Grain M.1376	03.02.99	—	4 [1999] 382 (IP)	Clearance Art.6(1)(b) without undertakings	Grains and Oilseeds
M.1377	Bertelsmann/Wissenschaftsverlag Springer	15.02.99	—	4 [1999] 389 (IP)	Clearance Art.6(1)(b) without undertakings	Professional Publishing
M.1378	Hoechst/Rhône Poulenc	09.08.99	—	5 [1999] 758 (IP)	Clearance Art.6(1)(b) With undertakings	Pharmaceuticals, Plant Protection
M.1378	Hoechst/Rhône — Poulenc	30.01.04	—	4 [2004] IS49	Review of Commitments	Pharmaceuticals
M.1379	Valmet/Rauma	08.02.99	—	—	Clearance Art.6(1)(b) without undertakings	Machinery, Control Systems
M.1380	Siebe/BTR	13.01.99	—	4 [1999] 371 (IP)	Clearance Art.6(1)(b) without undertakings	Valves, Sensors, Servos
M.1381	Imetal/English China Clays	26.04.99	—	4 [1999] 1194 (IP)	Clearance Art.6(1)(b) With undertakings	Refractory products, kaolin, clays
M.1382	TYCO/AMP	03.02.99	—	4 [1999] 381 (IP)	Clearance Art.6(1)(b) without undertakings	Printed Circuit Boards
M.1383	Exxon/Mobil	29.09.99	[2004] L103/1	5 [1999] 959 (IP)	Art. 8(2) With undertakings	Petroleum Products
M.1384	Deutsche Bank/Bankers Trust	22.04.99	—	4 [1999] 1179 (IP)	Clearance Art.6(1)(b) Without undertakings	Banking
M.1387	Lufthansa/Menzies/Sigma AT Manchester	13.01.99	—	4 [1999] 372 (IP)	Clearance Art.6(1)(b) without undertakings	Passenger and Aircraft Handling
M.1391	International Paper/Union Camp	05.02.99	—	4 [1999] 387 (IP)	Clearance Art.6(1)(b) without undertakings	Speciality Chemicals
M.1394	Alba/Otto	26.01.99	—	4 [1999] 376 (IP)	Clearance Art.6(1)(b) without undertakings	Scrap
M.1396	AT&T/Global Network	22.04.99	—	4 [1999] 1180 (IP)	Clearance Art.6(1)(b) Without undertakings	Telecommunications

MERGER No.	NAME	DATE	O.J.	C.M.L.R.	TYPE OF DECISION	PRODUCT SECTOR
M.1397	Sanofi/Synthelabo	15.03.99	—	4 [1999] 798 (IP)	Clearance Art.6(1)(b) without undertakings	Pharmaceuticals
	Sanofi-Synthelabo	17.05.99	[2000] L95/34	5 [1999] 13 (IP)	Clearance Art.6(1)(b) With undertakings	Pharmaceuticals, Beauty Sector
M.1398	Deutsche Bank/Credit Lyonnais Belgium	03.02.99	—	—	Clearance Art.6(1)(b) without undertakings	Banking
M.1400	Rexam/PLM	01.02.99	—	4 [1999] 377 (IP)	Clearance Art.6(1)(b) without undertakings	Plastic Cups and Containers
M.1401	Recoletos/Unedisa	01.02.99	—	4 [1999] 377 (IP)	Clearance Art.6(1)(b) without undertakings	Newspaper and Magazine Publishing
M.1402	Gaz de France/Bewag/Gasag	20.01.99	—	4 [1999] 374 (IP)	Clearance Art.6(1)(b) without undertakings	Gas and Heating
M.1403	Astra/Zeneca	26.02.99	—	4 [1999] 602 (IP)	Clearance Art.6(1)(b) with undertakings	Pharmaceutical Products
M.1404	General Electric/Alstom	01.06.99	—	5 [1999] 22 (IP)	Clearance Art.6(1)(b) Without undertakings	Gas Turbines
M.1405	TNT Post Group/Jet Services	15.02.99	—	4 [1999] 390 (IP)	Clearance Art.6(1)(b) without undertakings	Express Delivery Services
M.1406	Hyundai/KIA	17.03.99	—	4 [1999] 800 (IP)	Clearance Art.6(1)(b) without undertakings	Cars
M.1407	Bertelsmann/Mondadori	22.04.99	—	5 [2000] 592 (IP)	Clearance Art.6(1)(b) Without undertakings	Books—Multimedia
M.1408	Halifax/Cetelem	26.02.99	—	4 [1999] 603 (IP)	Clearance Art.6(1)(b) without undertakings	Consumer Credit
M.1409	Fyffes/Capespan	27.04.99	—	4 [1999] 1182 (IP)	Clearance Art.6(1)(b) Without undertakings	Food Products
M.1410	Deutsche Post/Danzas	17.02.99	—	4 [1999] 391 (IP)	Clearance Art.6(1)(b) without undertakings	Express Delivery Services
M.1411	Deutsche Bank/Coral	03.02.99	—	4 [1999] 382 (IP)	Clearance Art.6(1)(b) without undertakings	Betting
M.1413	Thomson-CSF/Racal Electronics	15.03.99	—	5 [2000] 179 (IP)	Clearance Art.6(1)(b) without undertakings	Military Communications
M.1415	BAT/Rothmans	17.03.99	—	4 [1999] 800 (IP)	Clearance Art.6(1)(b) without undertakings	Tobacco

MERGER No.	NAME	DATE	O.J.	C.M.L.R.	TYPE OF DECISION	PRODUCT SECTOR
M.1418	SCA Packaging/Rexam	11.02.99	—	4 [1999] 388 (IP)	Clearance Art.6(1)(b) without undertakings	Corrugated Cases and Board
M.1419	Groupe Cofinoga/BNP	19.02.99	—	4 [1999] 600 (IP)	Clearance Art.6(1)(b) without undertakings	Retailer Storecards
M.1420	BASF/Svalöf Weibull	03.03.99	—	4 [1999] 607 (IP)	Clearance Art.6(1)(b) without undertakings	Seeds and Plants
M.1423	CRH/Ibstock	01.03.99	—	4 [1999] 605 (IP)	Clearance Art.6(1)(b) without undertakings	Bricks
M.1430	Vodafone/Air Touch	21.05.99	—	—	Clearance Art.6(1)(b) With undertakings	Telecommunications
M.1432	Afga-Gevaert/Sterling	15.04.99	—	4 [1999] 1174 (IP)	Clearance Art.6(1)(b) Without undertakings	Films and Processing Equipment
M.1433	Carrier Corporation/Toshiba	25.03.99	—	4 [1999] 801 (IP)	Clearance Art.6(1)(b) without undertakings	Air-conditioning
M.1434	Schneider/Lexel	03.06.99	—	5 [1999] 23 (IP)	Clearance Art.6(1)(b) Without undertakings	Electrical distribution equipment
M.1435	Ford/Jardine	23.02.99	—	—	Clearance Art.6(1)(b) without undertakings	Vehicle Retail
M.1437	CVC/WMO-Wavin	26.02.99	—	4 [1999] 604 (IP)	Clearance Art.6(1)(b) without undertakings	Plastic Pipes and Fittings
M.1438	British Aerospace/GEC Marconi	25.06.99	—	5 [1999] 286 (IP)	Clearance Art.6(1)(b) Without undertakings	Aircrafts, Civil Simulation and Training
M.1439	Telia/Telenor	13.10.99	[2001] L40/1	4 [2001] 36 (D)	Clearance Art.6(1)(b) Without undertakings	Television, Telecommun
M.1440	Lucent Technologies/Ascend Communications	06.04.99	—	4 [1999] 807 (IP)	Clearance Art.6(1)(b) without undertakings	Communications Networks
M.1442	MMP/AFP	03.03.99	—	4 [1999] 606 (IP)	Clearance Art.6(1)(b) without undertakings	Corrugated Board and Cases
M.1446	Daimler Chrysler/Adtranz-ABB Daimler Benz Transport	15.03.99	—	4 [1999] 799 (IP)	Clearance Art.6(1)(b) without undertakings	Railway Technology
M.1448	MAN Roland/Omnigraph (II)	05.05.99	—	4 [1999] 1187 (IP)	Clearance Art.6(1)(b) Without undertakings	Press and Printing Products
M.1449	Sabena/Snecma	29.04.99	—	4 [1999] 1185 (IP)	Clearance Art.6(1)(b) Without undertakings	Aircraft Repair and Maintenance

MERGER No.	NAME	DATE	O.J.	C.M.L.R.	TYPE OF DECISION	PRODUCT SECTOR
M.1450	SMS/Mannesmann Demag	08.04.99	—	4 [1999] 808 (IP)	Clearance Art.6(1)(b) Without undertakings	Steel Industry
M.1452	Ford/Volvo	26.03.99	—	4 [1999] 804 (IP)	Clearance Art.6(1)(b) without undertakings	Passenger Cars
M.1453	Axa/Gre	08.04.99	—	4 [1999] 807 (IP)	Clearance Art.6(1)(b) With undertakings	Asset Management and Insurance
M.1455	Gruner+Jahr/Financial Times/JV	20.04.99	—	4 [1999] 1175 (IP)	Clearance Art.6(1)(b) Without undertakings	Newspaper and Advertising
M.1456	Dura/Adwest	11.03.99	—	4 [1999] 614 (IP)	Clearance Art.6(1)(b) without undertakings	Automotive Components
M.1459	Bertelsmann/Havas/Bol	06.05.99	—	4 [1999] 1189 (IP)	Clearance Art.6(1)(b) Without undertakings	Internet Services
M.1460	Lafarge/Titan	03.03.99	—	4 [1999] 608 (IP)	Clearance Art.6(1)(b) without undertakings	Cement
M.1461	Rabobank-Beeck/Homann	06.04.99	—	4 [1999] 809 (IP)	Art. 9(4)(a) Total referral	Deli Food
M.1462	TRW/Lucas Varity	11.03.99	—	4 [1999] 613 (IP)	Clearance Art.6(1)(b) without undertakings	Automotive, Space and Defence
M.1464	Total/Petrofina (II)	26.03.99	—	4 [1999] 802 (IP)	Clearance Art.6(1)(b) without undertakings	Oil and Gas
M.1465	Deutsche Telekom/Max Mobil	22.04.99	—	4 [1999] 1176 (IP)	Clearance Art.6(1)(b) Without undertakings	Telecommunications
M.1466	Eaton Corporation/Aeroquip-Vickers	31.03.99	—	4 [1999] 805 (IP)	Clearance Art.6(1)(b) without undertakings	Aerospace and Automotive
M.1467	Rohm+Haas/Morton	19.04.99	—	4 [1999] 1195 (IP)	Clearance Art.6(1)(b) With undertakings	Chemicals
M.1469	Solvay/BASF	02.06.99	—	5 [1999] 22 (IP)	Clearance Art.6(1)(b) Without undertakings	Chemicals
M.1470	Goodyear/Sumitomo	23.07.99	—	5 [1999] 596 (IP)	Clearance Art.6(11(b) Without undertakings	Tyres
M.1471	Statoil/ICA	14.07.99	—	5 [1999] 590 (IP)	Clearance Art.6(1)(b) Without undertakings	Retail in Petrol Stations
M.1474	Maersk/Safmarine	07.05.99	—	4 [1999] 1191 (IP)	Clearance Art.6(1)(b) Without undertakings	Shipping

TABLE 5

Table 5

MERGER No.	NAME	DATE	O.J.	C.M.L.R.	TYPE OF DECISION	PRODUCT SECTOR
M.1476	Adecco/Delphi	26.03.99	—	—	Clearance Art.6(1)(b) without undertakings	Temporary Employment Services
M.1477	Metallgeselschaft/GEA	07.04.99	—	4 [1999] 805 (IP)	Clearance Art.6(1)(b) Without undertakings	Steel Industry
M.1479	Thomson/Banco Zaragozano/Caja Madrid/Indra	05.05.99	—	4 [1999] 1191 (IP)	Clearance Art.6(1)(b) Without undertakings	Information and Control Systems
M.1481	Denso/Magneti Marelli	26.04.99	—	4 [1999] 1182 (IP)	Clearance Art.6(1)(b) Without undertakings	Car Parts
M.1482	Kingfisher/Grosslabor	12.04.99	—	4 [1999] 1174 (IP)	Clearance Art.6(1)(b) Without undertakings	Electrical Retailing
M.1484	Alstom/ABB	02.06.99	—	5 [1999] 20 (IP)	Clearance Art.6(1)(b) Without undertakings	Turbines
M.1485	Carlyle/Honsel	28.04.99	—	4 [1999] 1186 (IP)	Clearance Art.6(1)(b) Without undertakings	Car Parts
M.1487	Johnson & Son/Melitta/Cofresco	06.05.99	—	4 [1999] 1189 (IP)	Clearance Art.6(1)(b) Without undertakings	Household Goods, Plastic Packing Goods
M.1488	William Hill/Cinven/CVC	26.03.99	—	4 [1999] 804 (IP)	Clearance Art.6(1)(b) without undertakings	Bookmaking
M.1489	Yit/Valmet/Rauma	06.05.99	—	4 [1999] 1192 (IP)	Clearance Art.6(1)(b) Without undertakings	Machinery For Paper
M.1491	Robert Bosh/Magnetti Marelli	25.05.99	—	5 [1999] 17 (IP)	Clearance Art.6(1)(b) Without undertakings	Car Parts
M.1492	Hyundai Electronics/LG Semicon	23.06.99	—	5 [1999] 285 (IP)	Clearance Art.6(1)(b) Without undertakings	Semiconductors
M.1493	United Technologies /Sundstrand	25.05.99	—	5 [1999] 17 (IP)	Clearance Art.6(1)(b) Without undertakings	Industrial and aerospace products
M.1494	Marine-Wendel/SairGroup/AOM	03.08.99	—	5 [1999] 604 (IP)	Clearance Art.6(1)(b) Without undertakings	Air Transport
M.1496	Olivetti/Telecom Italia	22.04.99	—	4 [1999] 1177 (IP)	Clearance Art.6(1)(b) Without undertakings	Computer Services
M.1497	Novartis/Maisadour	30.06.99	—	5 [1999] 291 (IP)	Clearance Art.6(1)(b) Without undertakings	Seeds
M.1498	Aegon/Transamerica	07.06.99	—	5 [1999] 24 (IP)	Clearance Art.6(1)(b) Without undertakings	Insurance

MERGER No.	NAME	DATE	O.J.	C.M.L.R.	TYPE OF DECISION	PRODUCT SECTOR
M.1499	Swiss Life/Lloyd Continental	20.04.99	—	4 [1999] 1176 (IP)	Clearance Art.6(1)(b) Without undertakings	Insurance
M.1500	TPG/Technologistica	11.05.99	—	5 [1999] 12 (IP)	Clearance Art.6(1)(b) Without undertakings	Contracts Logistic Services
M.1501	GKN Westland/Agusta/JV	22.11.00	—	—	Clearance Art.6(1)(b) Without undertakings	Helicopters
M.1502	Kuoni/First Choice	06.05.99	—	4 [1999] 1190 (IP)	Clearance Art.6(1)(b) Without undertakings	Travel Services
M.1504	NSR/VSN/CMI/Igoplus	02.08.99	—	5 [1999] 755 (IP)	Clearance Art.6(1)(b) Without undertakings	Train and Bus Transport
M.1506	Singapore Airlines/Rolls-Royce	10.05.99	—	4 [1999] 1193 (IP)	Clearance Art.6(1)(b) Without undertakings	Aircraft Repair
M.1509	Ispat/Unimetal	22.06.99	—	5 [1999] 284 (IP)	Clearance Art.6(1)(b) Without undertakings	Steel Products
M.1510	BT/AT&T/Japan Telecom	19.07.99	—	—	Clearance Art.6(1)(b) Without undertakings	Telecommunications
M.1512	Dupont/PioneerHi-Bred International	21.06.99	—	5 [1999] 283 (IP)	Clearance Art.6(1)(b) Without undertakings	Seeds
M.1513	Deutsche Post/Danzas/Nedlloyd	01.07.99	—	5 [1999] 292 (IP)	Clearance Art.6(1)(b) Without undertakings	Freight Forwarding, Mail and Parcel Services
M.1514	Vivendi/US Filter	29.04.99	—	4 [1999] 1184 (IP)	Clearance Art.6(1)(b) Without undertakings	Water Treatment Systems
M.1516	Thomson-CSF/Eurocopter	10.06.99	—	5 [1999] 279 (IP)	Clearance Art.6(1)(b) Without undertakings	Helicopter Driving Simulators
M.1517	Rhodia/Donau Chemie/Albright & Wilson	13.07.99	—	—	Clearance Art.6(2) With undertakings	Chemicals
M.1518	Lear/United Technologies	29.04.99	—	4 [1999] 1186 (IP)	Clearance Art.6(1)(b) Without undertakings	Car Parts
M.1519	Renault/Nissan	12.05.99	—	5 [1999] 13 (IP)	Clearance Art.6(1)(b) Without undertakings	Vehicles
M.1521	UBS/Valfond	19.05.99	—	5 [1999] 14 (IP)	Clearance Art.6(1)(b) Without undertakings	Ferrous Castings
M.1522	CSME/MSCA/Rrock	11.06.99	—	5 [1999] 301 (IP)	Art. 9(4)(a) Total referral	Mining

Table 5

MERGER No.	NAME	DATE	O.J.	C.M.L.R.	TYPE OF DECISION	PRODUCT SECTOR
M.1524	Airtours/First Choice	22.09.99	[2000] L93/1	5 [2000] 494 (D)	Prohibition, Art.8(3)	Travel Services
M.1526	Ford/Kwik-Fit	31.05.99	—	5 [1999] 18 (IP)	Clearance Art.6(1)(b) Without undertakings	Repair and Maintenance of Vehicles
M.1527	Otto Versand/Freemans	16.06.99	—	5 [1999] 281 (IP)	Clearance Art.6(1)(b) Without undertakings	Retail (Non-food), Home Shopping
M.1529	Havas Advertising/Media Planning	10.06.99	—	5 [1999] 278 (IP)	Clearance Art.6(1)(b) Without undertakings	Media Buying
M.1532	BP Amoco/Arco	29.09.99	[2001] L18/l	4 [2001] 19 (D)	Clearance Art.8(2) With undertakings	Petroleum Products
M.1533	Artemis/Sanofi Beauté	21.06.99	—	5 [1999] 282 (IP)	Clearance Art.6(1)(b) Without undertakings	Luxury Products
M.1534	Pinault-Printemps-Redoute/Gucci	22.07.99	—	5 [1999] 594 (IP)	Clearance Art.6(1)(b) Without undertakings	Luxury Products
M.1536	Wind/Enel STC	29.06.99	—	5 [1999] 289 (IP)	Clearance Art.6(1)(b) Without undertakings	Telecommunications
M.1538	Dupont/Sabanci	24.11.99	—	4 [2000] 215 (IP)	Clearance Art.6(1)(b) Without undertakings	Chemicals
M.1539	CVC/Danone/Gerresheimer	05.07.99	—	5 [1999] 294 (IP)	Clearance Art.6(1)(b) Without undertakings	Beverage Packaging
M.1541	Kingfisher/Asda	15.06.99	—	5 [1999] 280 (IP)	Clearance Art.6(1)(b) Without undertakings	Retail (Non-food)
M.1547	Lufthansa/Amadeus/Start	02.08.99	—	5 [1999] 600 (IP)	Clearance Art.6(1)(b) Without undertakings	Data Transmission Services For Travel Services
M.1549	Deutsche Post/ASG	08.07.99	—	5 [1999] 295 (IP)	Clearance Art.6(1)(b) Without undertakings	Freight Forwarding, Parcel
M.1551	AT&T/MediaOne	23.07.99	—	5 [1999] 597 (IP)	Clearance Art.6(21(b) With undertakings	Telecommunications
M.1552	Babcock Borsig/AE Energietechnik	30.06.99	—	5 [1999] 290 (IP)	Clearance Art.6(1)(b) Without undertakings	Machinery
M.1553	France Telecom/Editel/Lince	30.07.99	—	5 [1999] 599 (IP)	Clearance Art.6(1)(b) Without undertakings	Telecommunications
M.1555	Heineken/Cruzcampo	17.08.99	—	5 [1999] 771 (IP)	Art. 9(4)(A)Total Referral	Beverages
M.1556	Mo Och Domsjö/SCA	23.07.99	—	5 [1999] 598 (IP)	Clearance Art.6(1)(b) Without undertakings	Paper Products

MERGER No.	NAME	DATE	O.J.	C.M.L.R.	TYPE OF DECISION	PRODUCT SECTOR
M.1557	EDF/Louis Dreyfus	28.09.99	—	5 [1999] 966 (IP)	Clearance Art.6(1)(b) Without undertakings	Electricity, Gas
M.1558	Cinven/Investcorp/Zeneca Chemicals	25.06.99	—	5 [1999] 286 (IP)	Clearance Art.6(1)(b) Without undertakings	Chemicals
M.1559	STN Atlas Marine Electronics/SAIT Radio Holland	08.09.99	—	5 [1999] 951 (IP)	Clearance Art.6(1)(b) Without undertakings	Maritime Electronic Equipment
M.1560	TI GroupiWalbro	11.06.99	—	5 [1999] 279 (IP)	Clearance Art.6(1)(b) Without undertakings	Car Parts
M.1561	Getronics/Wang	15.06.99	—	5 [1999] 281 (IP)	Clearance Art.6(1)(b) Without undertakings	Information Technology
M.1562	Heidelberger Zement/Scancem	12.07.99	—	5 [1999] 589 (IP)	Clearance Art.6(1)(b) Without undertakings	Concrete, Building Materials
M.1563	Ford/Plastic Omnium	28.06.99	—	5 [1999] 289 (IP)	Clearance Art.6(1)(b) Without undertakings	Car Parts
M.1564	Astrolink	25.06.99	—	5 [1999] 287 (IP)	Clearance Art.6(1)(b) Without undertakings	Telecommunications
M.1567	Lucchini/Ascometal	21.06.99	—	5 [1999] 284 (IP)	Clearance Art.6(1)(b) Without undertakings	Steel Bars
M.1569	Gränges/Norsk Hydro	05.07.99	—	—	Clearance Art.6(1)(b) Without undertakings	Car Parts
M.1571	New Holland/Case	28.10.99	—	4 [2000] 14 (IP)	Clearance Art.6(1)(b) With undertakings	Tractors, Harvesters, Excavators
M.1572	Iss/Abilis	05.07.99	—	—	Clearance Art.6(1)(b) Without undertakings	Cleaning Services
M.1573	Norsk Hydro/Saga	05.07.99	—	—	Clearance Art.6(1)(b) Without undertakings	Exploration, Production of Oil, Gas
M.1574	Kirch/Mediaset	03.08.99	—	5 [1999] 602 (IP)	Clearance Art.6(1)(b) Without undertakings	Television
M.1575	Thyssen Krupp VDM Evidal/KME Schmöle	22.10.99	—	4 [2000] 12 (IP)	Clearance Art.6(1)(b) Without undertakings	Electric Domestic Appliances
M.1578	Sanitec/Sphinx	01.12.99	[2000] L294/1	4 [2001] 15 (D)	Art. 8(2) With undertakings	Bathroom Products
M.1580	CAI/Platinum	28.06.99	—	5 [1999] 288 (IP)	Clearance Art.6(1)(b) Without undertakings	Information Technology

MERGER No.	NAME	DATE	O.J.	C.M.L.R.	TYPE OF DECISION	PRODUCT SECTOR
M.1581	AT&T/Unisource/Aucs	08.07.99	—	5 [1999] 294 (IP)	Clearance Art.6(1)(b) Without undertakings	Telecommunications
M.1585	DFDS/FLS	14.07.99	—	—	Clearance Art.6(1)(b) Without undertakings	Freight Forwarding, Travel Agency Services
M.1587	Dana/GKN	04.11.99	—	—	Clearance Art.6(1)(b) Without undertakings	Car parts
M.1588	Tyco/Raychem	20.07.99	—	5 [1999] 595 (IP)	Clearance Art.6(1)(b) Without undertakings	Computer Touch Screens
M.1589	Meritor/ZF Friedrichshafen	02.08.99	—	5 [1999] 755 (IP)	Clearance Art.6(1)(b) Without undertakings	Car Parts
M.1590	HSBC/RNYC/SAFRA	30.06.99	—	5 [1999] 292 (IP)	Clearance Art.6(1)(b) Without undertakings	Banking
M.1592	Toyota Motor/Toyota Denmark	23.07.99	—	—	Clearance Art.6(1)(b) Without undertakings	Cars
M.1593	STS/Teerbau	09.08.99	—	5 [1999] 757 (IP)	Clearance Art.6(1)(b) Without undertakings	Road Construction
M.1594	Preussag/Babcock Borsig	17.08.99	—	5 [1999] 762 (IP)	Clearance Art.6(1)(b) Without undertakings	Waste Treatment, Energy
M.1595	British Steel/Hoogovens	15.07.99	—	5 [1999] 590 (IP)	Clearance Art.6(1)(b) Without undertakings	Steel Products
M.1596	Accor/Blackstone/Colony/Vivendi	08.09.99	—	5 [1999] 950 (IP)	Clearance Art.6(1)(b) Without undertakings	Hotels
M.1597	Castrol/Carless/JV	14.10.99	—	5 [1999] 1245 (IP)	Clearance Art.6(1)(b) Without undertakings	Electrical Oils
M.1598	Hicks, Muse, Tate & Furst Investment Partners/Hillsdown Holdings	30.07.99	—	5 [1999] 599 (IP)	Clearance Art.6(1)(b) Without undertakings	Canned Food
M.1599	Dupont/Teijin	24.11.99	—	4 [2000] 215 (IP)	Clearance Art.6(1)(b) Without undertakings	Films
M.1601	Allied Signal/Honeywell	01.12.99	[2001] L152/1	5 [2001] 23(D)	Art. 8(2) With undertakings	Aircraft Components
M.1603	General Motors Acceptance Corporation/AAS	22.07.99	—	5 [1999] 593 (IP)	Clearance Art.6(1)(b) Without undertakings	Vehicle Hire and Leasing
M.1606	EDF/South Western Electricity	19.07.99	—	5 [1999] 592 (IP)	Clearance Art.6(1)(b) Without undertakings	Electricity

MERGER No.	NAME	DATE	O.J.	C.M.L.R.	TYPE OF DECISION	PRODUCT SECTOR
M.1612	Wal-Mart/Asda	23.07.99	—	5 [1999] 595 (IP)	Clearance Art.6(1)(b) Without undertakings	Retail
M.1615	HSBC/Lindengruppen/CIH	09.08.99	—	—	Clearance Art.6(1)(b) Without undertakings	Manufacturing
M.1616	Antonio de Sommer Champalimaud/ Banco Santander Central Hispanoamericano	03.08.99	—	5 [1999] 601 (IP)	Clearance Art.6(1)(b) Without undertakings	Banking, Insurance
M.1617	Royal & Sun Alliance/Trygg Hansa	26.08.99	—	5 [1999] 766 (IP)	Clearance Art.6(1)(b) Without undertakings	Insurance
M.1618	Bank of New York/Royal Bank of Scotland Trust Bank	25.08.99	—	5 [1999] 766 (IP)	Clearance Art.6(1)(b) Without undertakings	Banking, Financial Services
M.1621	Pakhoed/Van Ommeren	10.09.99	—	5 [1999] 950 (IP)	Clearance Art.6(1)(b) With undertakings	Storage, Shipping
M.1623	Allied Signal/MTU	20.09.99	—	5 [1999] 955 (IP)	Clearance Art.6(1)(b) Without undertakings	Gas Turbines
M.1626	Sair Group/SAA	15.11.99	—	4 [2000] 10 (IP)	Clearance Art.6(1)(b) Without undertakings	Air Transport
M.1627	CU Italia/Bance delle Marche/JV	13.09.99	—	5 [1999] 954 (IP)	Clearance Art.6(1)(b) Without undertakings	Insurance
M.1628	TotalFina/Elf	09.02.00	[2001] L143/1	5 [2001] 18 (D)	Art.8(2) With Undertakings	Petroleum
M.1629	Knorr Bremse/Mannesmann	20.08.99	—	5 [1999] 763 (IP)	Clearance Art.6(1)(b) Without undertakings	Car Parts
M.1630	Air Liquide/BOC	18.01.00	[2004] L92/1	4 [2000] 246 (IP)	Art. 8(2) With conditions and obligations	Industrial Gases
M.1631	Suez-Lyonnaise/Nalco	20.08.99	—	5 [1999] 764 (IP)	Clearance Art.6(1)(b) Without undertakings	Water Treatment Systems
M.1632	Reckitt+ Coleman/Benckiser	03.09.99	—	5 [1999] 768 (IP)	Clearance Art.6(1)(b) Without undertakings	Cleaning Products
M.1633	RWE Umwelt/Vivendi/Berliner Wasserbetriebe	13.09.99	—	5 [1999] 952 (IP)	Clearance Art.6(1)(b) Without undertakings	Water Distribution
M.1636	MMS/Dasa/Astrium	21.03.00	[2003] L314/1	4 [2000] 820 (IP)	Art. 8 (2) With conditions and obligations	Satellites, Launch Services, Space Systems

Table 5

MERGER No.	NAME	DATE	O.J.	C.M.L.R.	TYPE OF DECISION	PRODUCT SECTOR
M.1637	DB Investments/SPP/Öhman	11.08.99	—	5 [1999] 760 (IP)	Clearance Art.6(1)(b) Without undertakings	Real Estate
M.1640	Acelaria/Ucin	26.08.99	—	5 [1999] 765 (IP)	Clearance Art.6(1)(b) Without undertakings	Building Products
M.1641	Linde/Aga	09.02.00	[2002] L120/1	4 [2000] 437 (IP)	Clearance Art.6(1)(b) With undertakings	Industrial Gases
M.1643	IBM/Sequent	23.09.99	—	5 [1999] 956 (IP)	Clearance Art.6(1)(b) Without undertakings	Information Technology
M.1644	Wienerberger/DSCB/Steinzeug	17.09.99	—	5 [1999] 954 (IP)	Clearance Art.6(1)(b) Without undertakings	Water Treatment
M.1649	GEFCO/KN/ELAN	30.09.99	—	5 [1999] 963 (IP)	Clearance Art.6(1)(b) Without undertakings	Road Freight Forwarding
M.1650	ACEA/Telefonica	01.12.99	—	4 [2000] 218 (IP)	Clearance Art.6(1)(b) Without undertakings	Telecommunications
M.1651	Maersk/Sea-Land	06.10.99	—	5 [1999] 1241 (IP)	Clearance Art.6(1)(b) Without undertakings	Shipping
M.1652	D'Ieteren/PGSI	17.11.99	—	—	Clearance Art.6(1)(b) Without undertakings	Car Parts
M.1653	Buhrmann/Corporate Express	08.09.99	—	5 [1999] 952 (IP)	Clearance Art.6(1)(b) Without undertakings	Distribution of Office Products
M.1654	Telexis/EDS	30.09.99	—	5 [1999] 963 (IP)	Clearance Art.6(1)(b) Without undertakings	Telecommunications
M.1656	Huhtamäki Oy/Packaging Industries Van Leer	23.09.99	—	5 [1999] 956 (IP)	Clearance Art.6(1)(b) Without undertakings	Packaging
M.1659	Preussen Elektra/EZH	30.09.99	—	—	Clearance Art.6(1)(b) Without undertakings	Electricity
M.1660	Bank of New York/Royal Bank of Scotland/RBSI Security Services	26.08.99	—	5 [1999] 767 (IP)	Clearance Art.6(1)(b) Without undertakings	Financial Services
M.1661	Credit Lyonnais/Allianz-Euler/JV	26.08.99	—	5 [1999] 768 (IP)	Clearance Art.6(1)(b) Without undertakings	Invoicing
M.1663	Alcan/Alusuisse	14.03.00	[2002] L90/1	5 [2002] 13 (D)	Art. 8(2) With conditions and obligations	Aluminium
M.1667	BBL/BT/ISP-Belgium	17.11.99	—	—	Clearance Art.6(1)(b) Without undertakings	Internet

MERGER No.	NAME	DATE	O.J.	C.M.L.R.	TYPE OF DECISION	PRODUCT SECTOR
M.1669	Deutsche Telekom/One2One	27.09.99	—	5 [1999] 957 (IP)	Clearance Art.6(1)(b) Without undertakings	Telecommunications
M.1670	Geril/FCC Construccion	10.09.99	—	5 [1999] 953 (IP)	Clearance Art.6(1)(b) Without undertakings	Waste Treatment
M.1671	Dow Chemical/Union Carbide	03.05.00	[2001] L245/1	4 [2000] 1072 (IP)	Art. 8(2) With conditions and obligations	Chemicals
M.1672	Volvo/Scania	15.03.00	[2001] L143/74	5 [2001] 11 (D)	Prohibition, Art.8(3)	Trucks, Buses
M.1673	Veba/Viag	13.06.00	(2001] L188/1	5 [2000] 211 (D)	Art.8 (2) With conditions and obligations undertakings	Electricity, Chemicals, Gas
M.1674	Maersk/ECT	27.09.99	—	5 [1999] 958 (IP)	Clearance Art.6(1)(b) Without undertakings	Shipping
M.1675	Ducros/Hero France	13.12.99	—	4 [2000] 225 (IP)	Clearance Art.6(1)(b) Without undertakings	Food Products
M.1677	BT/LGT Telecom	08.11.99	—	4 [2000] 16 (IP)	Clearance Art.6(1)(b) Without undertakings	Telecommunications
M.1679	FranceTelecom/STI/SRD	21.10.99	—	—	Clearance Art.6(1)(b) Without undertakings	Telecommunications
M.1681	Akzo Nobel/Hoechst Roussel Vet	22.11.99	—	—	Clearance Art.6(1)(b) With undertakings	Pharmaceuticals
M.1682	Ashland/Superfos	23.09.99	—	5 [1999] 955 (IP)	Clearance Art.6(1)(b) Without undertakings	Chemicals
M.1683	The Coca-Cola Company/Kar-Tess Group (Hellenic Bottling)	07.02.00	—	4 [2000] 435 (IP)	Clearance Art.6(1)(b) With undertakings	Soft Drinks
M.1684	Carrefour/Promodes	25.01.00	—	—	Clearance Art.6(1)(b) With undertakings	Retail
M.1686	DaimlerChrysler Services/MB Automobilvertriebsgesellschaft	15.09.99	—	—	ClearanceArt.6(1)(b) Without undertakings	Cars
M.1687	Adecco/Olsten	28.10.99	—	4 [2000] 15 (IP)	Clearance Art.6(1)(b) Without undertakings	Temporary Work
M.1689	Nestlé/Pillsburg/Häagen-Dazs US	06.10.99	—	5 [1999] 1241 (IP)	Clearance Art.6(1)(b) Without undertakings	Food Products

MERGER No.	NAME	DATE	O.J.	C.M.L.R.	TYPE OF DECISION	PRODUCT SECTOR
M.1691	Aegon/Guardian Life	28.09.99	—	5 [1999] 957 (IP)	Clearance Art.6(1)(b) Without undertakings	Insurance
M.1693	Alcoa/Reynolds	03.05.00	[2002] L58/25	5 [2002] 9 (D)	Art. 8(2) With conditions and obligations	Aluminium
M.1694	EMC/Data General	06.10.99	—	5 [1999] 1242 (IP)	Clearance Art.6(1)(b) Without undertakings	Information Technology
M.1698	RWA/Nordsee/Cerny	20.10.99	—	4 [2000] 11 (IP)	Clearance Art.6(1)(b) Without undertakings	Wholesale Trade
M.1699	TPG Bacchus/Bally	30.09.99	—	5 [1999] 967 (IP)	Clearance Art.6(1)(b) Without undertakings	Shoes, Clothing
M.1700	AVNET/Eurotronics	03.12.99	—	4 [2000] 221 (IP)	Clearance Art.6(1)(b) Without undertakings	Wholesale of Electronic Components
M.1701	Gruner+ Jahr/Dekra/Faircar	24.11.99	—	4 [2000] 214 (IP)	Clearance Art.6(1)(b) Without undertakings	Internet
M.1702	Vedior/Select Appointments	18.10.99	—	5 [1999] 1246 (IP)	Clearance Art.6(1)(b) Without undertakings	Temporary Employment Services
M.1707	Gilde Buy-Out Fund/Synbra	20.10.99	—	5 [1999] 1246 (IP)	Clearance Art.6(1)(b) With undertakings	Plastics
M.1708	Tapis Saint-Maclou/Allied Carpets Group	21.10.99	—	4 [2000] 12 (IP)	Clearance Art.6(1)(b) Without undertakings	Carpets
M.1709	Preussag/Babcock/Celsius	19.01.00	—	—	Clearance Art.6(1)(b) Without undertakings	Submarines
M.1710	Industri Kapital 1997 Ltd (Marmorandum)/Neste Chemicals Oy	29.11.99	—	4 [2000] 216 (IP)	Clearance Art.6(1)(b) Without undertakings	Insulation Materials, N-butanol
M.1711	Tyco/Siemens	16.11.99	—	4 [2000] 10 (IP)	Clearance Art.6(1)(b) Without undertakings	Connectors & Sensors
M.1712	Generali-INA	12.01.00	—	4 [2000] 244 (IP)	Clearance Art.6(1)(b) Without undertakings	Insurance
M.1714	Föreningssparbanken/Fi-Holding/Fih	21.10.99	—	4 [2000] 13 (IP)	Clearance Art.6(1)(b) Without undertakings	Financial Services
M.1716	Gehe/Herba	12.01.00	—	4 [2000] 238 (IP)	Clearance Art.6(1)(b) Without undertakings	Pharmaceuticals
M.1717	Siemens/Italtel	15.12.99	—	4 [2000] 227 (IP)	Clearance Art.6(1)(b) Without undertakings	Telecommunications

MERGER No.	NAME	DATE	O.J.	C.M.L.R.	TYPE OF DECISION	PRODUCT SECTOR
M.1719	Delta Lloyd Verzekeringsgroep/Nuts Ohra	10.11.99	—	4 [2000] 9 (IP)	Clearance Art.6(1)(b) Without undertakings	Insurance, Banking
M.1720	Fortum/Elektrizitätswerk Wesertal	05.01.00	—	—	Clearance Art.6(1)(b) Without undertakings	Electricity, Energy
M.1723	Illinois Tool Works/Premark	17.11.99	—	—	Clearance Art.6(1)(b) Without undertakings	Film Wrapping, Adhesives
M.1728	CVC/Torraspapel	03.12.99	—	4 [2000] 223 (IP)	Clearance Art.6(1)(b) Without undertakings	Paper Products
M.1735	Seita/Tabacalera	03.12.99	—	4 [2000] 221 (IP)	Clearance Art.6(1)(b) Without undertakings	Tobacco Products
M.1736	UIAG/Carlyle/Andritz	17.11.99	—	—	Clearance Art.6(1)(b) Without undertakings	Machinery
M.1739	Iveco/Fraikin	03.12.99	—	4 [2000] 220 (IP)	Clearance Art.6(1)(b) Without undertakings	Trucks
M.1740	Heinz/United Biscuits Frozen and Chilled Food	06.12.99	—	4 [2000] 223 (IP)	Clearance Art.6(1)(b) Without undertakings	Food Products
M.1741	MCI Worldcom/Sprint	28.06.00	[2003] L300/1	5 [2000] 198 (IP)	Prohibition Art.8(3)	Telecommunications, Internet
M.1742	Sun Chemical/Coates Brothers	22.12.99	—	4 [2000] 234 (IP)	Clearance Art.6(1)(b) Without undertakings	Printing Inks
M.1744	UPM-Kymene/Stora Enso/Metsäliitto/JV	03.12.99	—	4 [2000] 222 (IP)	Clearance Art.6(1)(b) Without undertakings	Ship Building and Repairing
M.1745	EADS	11.05.00	—	—	Clearance Art.6(1)(b) With undertakings	Aircrafts, Helicopters, Space, Weapons
M.1747	Telekom Austria/Libro	28.02.00	—	4 [2000] 650 (IP)	Clearance Art.6(1)(b) Without undertakings	Telecommunications, Internet
M.1748	Industri Kapital Limited/Superfos	24.11.99	—	4 [2000] 214 (IP)	Clearance Art.6(1)(b) With undertakings	Chemicals
M.1751	Shell/BASF/JV—Project Nicole	29.03.00	—	4 [2000] 1065 (IP)	Clearance Art.6(1)(b) With undertakings	Chemicals
M.1754	Morgan Grenfell/Piaggio	01.12.99	—	4 [2000] 219 (IP)	Clearance Art.6(1)(b) Without undertakings	Two-Wheeled Motor Vehicles
M.1755	CVC/Acordis	20.12.99	—	4 [2000] 231 (IP)	Clearance Art.6(1)(b) Without undertakings	Industrial Fibres

Table 5

MERGER No.	NAME	DATE	O.J.	C.M.L.R.	TYPE OF DECISION	PRODUCT SECTOR
M.1759	RMC/Rugby	15.12.99	—	4 [2000] 226 (IP)	Clearance Art.6(1)(b) Without undertakings	Cement, Concrete
M.1760	Mannesmann/Orange	20.12.99	—	4 [2000] 232 (IP)	Clearance Art.6(1)(b) With undertakings	Telecommunications
M.1761	Toyota Motor/Toyota Franco	30.11.99	—	4 [2000] 219 (IP)	Clearance Art.6(1)(b) Without undertakings	Cars
M.1763	Solutia Inc./Viking Resins Group Holdings B.V.	17.12.99	—	4 [2000] 228 (IP)	Clearance Art.6(1)(b) Without undertakings	Chemicals (Resins)
M.1764	Skandinavista Enskilda Banken/BFG Bank	10.12.99	—	4 [2000] 224 (IP)	Clearance Art.6(1)(b) Without undertakings	Banking, Financial Service
M.1765	KKR Associates/Siemens Nixdorf Retail and Banking Systems	17.12.99	—	4 [2000] 227 (IP)	Clearance Art.6(1)(b) Without undertakings	Banking Systems
M.1767	AT&T/1BM/Intesa	20.12.99	—	4 [2000] 231 (IP)	Clearance Art.6(1)(b) Without undertakings	Telecommunications
M.1768	Schoyen/Goldman Sachs/Swebus	10.12.99	—	4 [2000] 224 (IP)	Clearance Art.6(1)(b) Without undertakings	Buses and Coaches
M.1771	Sedgwick Noble Lowndes/Woolwich	17.12.99	—	4 [2000] 227 (IP)	Clearance Art.6(1)(b) Without undertakings	Financial Services
M.1772	Continental Teves/ADC Automotive Distance Control	10.01.00	—	—	Clearance Art.6(1)(b) Without undertakings	Car Parts
M.1773	Nordic Capital III Ltd/Trelleborg International B.V.	20.12.99	—	4 [2000] 230 (IP)	Clearance Art.6(1)(b) Without undertakings	Electrical Product Wholesale
M.1774	Deutsche BP/DaimlerChrysler AG/ Union-Tank Eckstein	21.02.00	—	—	Clearance Art.6(1)(b) Without undertakings	Tank and Service Cards
M.1775	Ingersoll-Rand/Dresser-Rand/Ingersoll-Dresser Pump	22.12.99	—	4 [2000] 235 (IP)	Clearance Art.6(1)(b) Without undertakings	Machinery and Equipment
M.1777	CGU/Hibernian	18.01.00	—	—	Clearance Art.6(1)(b) Without undertakings	Lnsurance
M.1778	Freudenberg/PhoeniX/JV	26.01.00	—	4 [2000] 427 (IP)	Clearance Art.6(1)(b) Without undertakings	Car Parts
M.1779	Anglo American/Tarmac	13.01.00	—	4 [2000] 253 (IP)	Art. 9(4)(A) Total Referral	Construction
M.1780	LVMH/Prada/Fendi	25.05.00	—	5 [2000] 20 (IP)	Clearance Art.6(1)(b) Without undertakings	Luxury Goods

MERGER No.	NAME	DATE	O.J.	C.M.L.R.	TYPE OF DECISION	PRODUCT SECTOR
M.1781	Electrolux/Ericsson	20.12.99	—	4 [2000] 233 (IP)	Clearance Art.6(1)(b) Without undertakings	Telecommunications
M.1783	ZF Gotha/Graziano Trasmissioni/JV	04.09.00	—	5 [2000] 590 (IP)	Clearance Art.6(1)(b) Without undertakings	Trucks Parts
M.1784	Delphi Automotive Systems/Lucas Diesel	05.01.00	—	—	Clearance Art.6(1)(b) Without undertakings	Car Parts
M.1786	General Electric/Thomson-CSF	02.02.00	—	4 [2000] 428 (IP)	Clearance Art.6(1)(b) Without undertakings	Flight Simulators
M.1787	Deutsche Bahn/NS Groep/JV Service Stores	17.12.99	—	4 [2000] 229 (IP)	Clearance Art.6(1)(b) Without undertakings	Stores In Railway Stations
M.1789	INA/Luk	22.12.99	—	4 [2000] 236 (IP)	Clearance Art.6(1)(b) Without undertakings	Car and Engine Parts
M.1790	Deutsche Bank/BHS/Pago	20.12.99	—	4 [2000] 230 (IP)	Clearance Art.6(1)(b) Without undertakings	Internet Services
M.1791	UBS Capital/Vencap/Stiga	20.12.99	—	4 [2000] 234 (IP)	Clearance Art.6(1)(b) Without undertakings	Garden Equipment
M.1792	Ahlström/Capman/Folding Carton Partners	17.01.00	—	4 [2000] 238 (IP)	Clearance Art.6(1)(b) Without undertakings	Packaging
M.1793	Voith/Siemens/JV	03.04.00	—	4 [2000] 1050 (IP)	Clearance Art.6(1)(b) Without undertakings	Hydraulic Engineering
M.1794	Deutsche Post/Air Express International (DP/AEI)	07.02.00	—	4 [2000] 434 (IP)	Clearance Art.6(1)(b) Without undertakings	Parcel and Express Delivery
M.1795	Vodafone Airtouch/Mannesmann	12.04.00	—	4 [2000] 1069 (IP)	Clearance Art.6(1)(b) With undertakings	Telecommunications
M.1796	Bayer/Lyondell	21.02.00	—	4 [2000] 648 (IP)	Clearance Art.6(1)(b) Without undertakings	Chemicals
M.1797	Saab/Celsius	04.02.00	—	4 [2000] 431 (IP)	Clearance Ant. 6(1)(b) Without undertakings	Military Products
M.1799	BSCH/Banco Totta y CPP/A. Champalimaud	11.01.00	—	4 [2000] 236 (IP)	Clearance Art.6(1)(b) Without undertakings	Banking
M.1800	Marconi/Bosch Public Network	19.01.00	—	—	Clearance Art.6(1)(b) Without undertakings	Telecommunications Equipment
M.1801	Neusiedler/American Israeli Paper Mills/JV	11.02.00	—	4 [2000] 442 (IP)	Clearance Art.6(1)(b) With undertakings	Paper

Table 5

MERGER No.	NAME	DATE	O.J.	C.M.L.R.	TYPE OF DECISION	PRODUCT SECTOR
M.1802	Unilever/Amora-Maille	08.03.00	—	4 [2000] 653 (IP)	Clearance Art.6(1)(b) With undertakings	Food
M.1803	Electrabel/EPON	07.02.00	—	4 [2000] 432 (IP)	Clearance Art.6(1)(b) Without undertakings	Electricity
M.1806	Astra Zeneca/Novartis	26.07.00	[2004] L110/1	—	Art. 8(2) With conditions and obligations	Crop Protection Products
M.1807	FNAC/COIN/CV	14.01.00	—	—	Clearance Art.6(1)(b) Without undertakings	Retail (Non-food)
M.1810	VW/Europcar	18.02.00	—	4 [2000] 647(IP)	Clearance Art.6(1)(b) Without undertakings	Car Leasing
M.1812	Telefonica/Terra/Amadeus	27.04.00	—	4 [2000] 1058 (IP)	Clearance Art.6(1)(b) Without undertakings	Internet Services
M.1813	Industri Kapital (Nordkem)/Dyno	12.07.00	[2001] L154/41	—	Clearance Art.8(2) With undertakings	Resins
M.1814	Bayer/Röhm/Makroform	17.04.00	—	4 [2000] 1056 (IP)	Clearance Art.6(1)(b) Without undertakings	Synthetic Materials
M.1816	Churchill Insurance Group/NIG Holdings	02.02.00	—	—	Clearance Art.6(1)(b) Without undertakings	Insurance
M.1817	BellSouth/Vodafone (E-Plus)	26.01.00	—	4 [2000] 427 (IP)	Clearance Art.6(1)(b) Without undertakings	Telecommunications
M.1820	BP/JV Dissolution	02.02.00	—	—	Clearance Art.6(1)(b) Without undertakings	Fuel
M.1821	BellSouth/VAT (E-Plus)	31.01.00	—	4 [2000] 444 (IP)	Art. 6(1)(A)	Telecommunications
M.1822	Mobil/JV-Dissolution	02.02.00	—	—	Clearance Art.6(1)(b) Without undertakings	Fuel & Lubricants
M.1825	Suzuki Motor/Suzuki KG/Fafin	03.02.00	—	4 [2000] 430 (IP)	Clearance Art.6(11(b) Without undertakings	Car Distribution
M.1826	KBC Bank/KBCPD/KBPDBV	31.03.00	—	4 [2000] 1048 (IP)	Clearance Art.6(1)(b) Without undertakings	Financial Services
M.1827	Hanson/Pioneer	24.03.00	—	—	Art. 9(4) Total referral	Concrete, Mineral Products
M.1830	Finalrealm/United Biscuits	03.02.00	—	4 [2000] 430 (IP)	Clearance Art.6(1)(b) Without undertakings	Food Products

MERGER No.	NAME	DATE	O.J.	C.M.L.R.	TYPE OF DECISION	PRODUCT SECTOR
M.1831	Deutsche Bank/CIBA	06.03.00	—	—	Clearance Art.6(1)(b) Without undertakings	Coating Systems, Composites, Adhesives, Photopolymers, etc.
M.1832	Ahold/ICA Förbundet/Canica	06.04.00	—	4 [2000] 1052 (IP)	Clearance Art.6(1)(b) Without undertakings	Retail
M.1835	Monsanto/Pharmacia & Upjohn	30.03.00	—	4 [2000] 1066 (IP)	Clearance Art.6(1)(b) With undertakings	Pharmaceuticals
M.1836	Siemens/Bosch Telecom	28.04.00	—	4 [2000] 1060 (IP)	Clearance Art.6(1)(b) Without undertakings	Electrical Equipment
M.1838	BT/ESAT	27.03.00	—	4 [2000] 823 (IP)	Clearance Art.6(1)(b) With undertakings	Telecommunications
M.1839	Halbergerhütte/Bopp & Reuter/ Muffenrohr	04.07.00	—	5 [2000] 190 (IP)	Clearance Art.6(1)(b) Without undertakings	Construction Materials
M.1840	KKR/Bosch Telekom Private Networks	29.02.00	—	4 [2000] 651 (IP)	Clearance Art.6(1)(b) Without undertakings	Telecommunications
M.1841	Celestina/IBM (EMS)	25.02.00	—	4 [2000] 649 (IP)	Clearance Art.6(1)(b) Without undertakings	Electronics Manufacturing Services, Servers
M.1842	Vattenfall/HEW	20.03.00	—	4 [2000] 818 (IP)	Clearance Art.6(1)(b) Without undertakings	Heat, Gas, Waste
M.1845	AOL/Time Warner	11.10.00	[2001] L268/28	4 [2002] 13 (D)	Clearance Art.8(2) With undertakings	Internet, Music
M.1846	Glaxo Wellcome/SmithKline Beecham	08.05.00	—	5 [2000] 25 (IP)	Clearance Art.6(1)(b) With undertakings	Pharmaceuticals
M.1847	GM/Saab	28.02.00	—	—	Clearance Art.6(1)(b) Without undertakings	Cars
M.1848	Schroder Ventures European Fiund/ Takko Modemarkt	08.03.00	—	—	Clearance Art.6(1)(b) Without undertakings	Textile Retail
M.1849	Solectron/Ericsson	29.02.00	—	4 [2000] 652 (IP)	Clearance Art.6(1)(b) Without undertakings	Telecommunication Components
M.1853	EDF/ENBW	07.02.01	[2002] L59/1	4 [2001] 1520 (IP)	Clearance Art.8(2) With undertakings	Electricity
M.1854	Emerson Electric/Ericsson Energy Systems	15.03.00	—	4 [2000] 817 (IP)	Clearance Art.6(1)(b) Without undertakings	Power Systems, Climate Systems, Power Supplies

Table 5

MERGER No.	NAME	DATE	O.J.	C.M.L.R.	TYPE OF DECISION	PRODUCT SECTOR
M.1855	Singapore Airlines/Virgin Atlantic	23.03.00	—	—	Clearance Art.6(1)(b) Without undertakings	Air Transport
M.1856	Citigroup/Schroders	29.03.00	—	4 [2000] 1047 (IP)	Clearance Art.6(1)(b) Without undertakings	Banking
M.1858	Thomson-CSF/Racal (II)	15.06.00	—	5 [2000] 179 (IP)	Clearance Art.6(1)(b) Without undertakings	Electronic Defence Systems
M.1859	ENI/Galp	29.06.00	—	5 [2000] 186 (IP)	Clearance Art.6(1)(b) Without undertakings	Retail Sale of Diesel, Fuels, Gasoline
M.1861	Man/Erf	29.02.00	—	4 [2000] 652 (IP)	Clearance Art.6(1)(b) Without undertakings	Trucks
M.1863	Vodafone/BT/Airtel/JV	18.12.00	—	4 [2001] 1522 (IP)	Clearance Art.6(1)(b) Without undertakings	Telecommunications, Internet
M.1865	France Telecom/Global One	24.03.00	—	4 [2000] 1514 (IP)	Clearance Art.6(1)(b) Without undertakings	Telecommunications
M.1866	Preussag/Hebel	29.03.00	—	4 [2000] 1064 (IP)	Clearance Art.6(1)(b) Without undertakings	Construction
M.1867	Volvo/Telia/Ericsson Wireless Car	27.03.00	—	—	Clearance Art.6(1)(b) Without undertakings	Telecommunications, Internet
M.1869	CVC/BTR Siebe Automotive Sealing Systems	06.03.00	—	—	Clearance Art.6(1)(b) Without undertakings	Car Parts
M.1870	ZF/Brembo/DFI	07.03.00	—	—	Clearance Art.6(1)(b) Without undertakings	Car Parts
M.1871	Arrow Electronics/Tekelec	13.04.00	—	4 [2000] 1055 (IP)	Clearance Art.6(1)(b) Without undertakings	Electronic Components
M.1873	Compagnie de Saint-Gobain/Meyer International	23.03.00	—	4 [2000] 822 (IP)	Clearance Art.6(1)(b) Without undertakings	Building Materials
M.1874	Lafarge/Blue Circle	07.04.00	—	4 [2000] 1052 (IP)	Clearance Art.6(1)(b) With undertakings	Cement, Concrete
M.1875	Reuters/Equant-Project Proton	17.04.00	—	4 [2000] 1057 (IP)	Clearance Art.6(1)(b) Without undertakings	Ip Financial Services
M.1876	Kohlberg Kravis & Roberts/Wassall/ Zumtobel	13.04.00	—	—	Clearance Art.6(1)(b) Without undertakings	Light Fittings
M.1877	Boskalis/HBG	04.07.00	—	5 [2000] 189 (IP)	Clearance Art.6(1)(b) Without undertakings	Dredging

MERGER No.	NAME	DATE	O.J.	C.M.L.R.	TYPE OF DECISION	PRODUCT SECTOR
M.1878	Pfizer/Warner-Lambert	22.05.00	—	5 [2000] 18 (IP)	Clearance Art.6(1)(b) With undertakings	Pharmaceuticals
M.1879	Boeing/Hughes	27.09.00	—	5 [2000] 801 (IP)	Clearance Art.8(2) Without undertakings	Satellites, Launch Services
M.1880	Minnesota Mining and Manufacturing/ Quante	3 1.03.00	—	4 [2000] 1048 (IP)	Clearance Art.6(1)(b) Without undertakings	Telecommunications
M.1882	Pirelli/BICC	19.07.00	[2003] L70/35	5 [2000] 393 (IP)	Art. 8(2) Without undertakings	Wiring, Power Cable
M.1883	NEC/Mitsubishi	03.04.00	—	4 [2000] 1049 (IP)	Clearance Art.6(1)(b) Without undertakings	Pc Monitors
M.1884	Mondi/Frantschach/Assidomän	31.07.00	—	5 [2000] 400 (IP)	Clearance Art.6(1)(b) Without undertakings	Packaging
M.1885	Babcock Borsig/VA Technologie/Pipe Tec	31.03.00	—	4 [2000] 1049 (IP)	Clearance Art.6(1)(b) Without undertakings	Pipelines Construction
M.1886	CGU/Norwich Union	13.04.00	—	4 [2000] 1055 (IP)	Clearance Art.6(1)(b) Without undertakings	Insurance
M.1887	Credit Suisse First Boston/Gala Group	13.04.00	—	—	Clearance Art.6(1)(b) Without undertakings	Games
M.1889	CLT-UFA/Canal+/Vox	21.03.00	—	4 [2000] 821 (IP)	Clearance Art.6(1)(b) Without undertakings	Television
M.1891	BP Amoco/Castrol	18.05.00	—	5 [2000] 15 (IP)	Clearance Art.6(1)(b) Without undertakings	Lubricants
M.1892	Sara Lee/Courtaulds	08.05.00	—	5 [2000] 27 (IP)	Clearance Art.6(1)(b) With undertakings	Hosiery, Underwear
M.1893	Butler Capital/CDC/Axa/Finauto/ Autodistribution/Finelist	10.04.00	—	—	Clearance Art.6(1)(b) Without undertakings	Car Parts
M.1895	Ocean Group/Exel (NFC)	03.05.00	—	4 [2000] 1061 (IP)	Clearance Art.6(1)(b) Without undertakings	Contract Logistics
M.1898	TUI Group/GTT Holding	31.05.00	—	5 [2000] 24 (IP)	Clearance Art.6(1)(b) Without undertakings	Package Tours, Travel
M.1900	Solvay/Plastic Omnium	28.06.00	—	5 [2000] 185 (IP)	Clearance Art.6(1)(b) Without undertakings	Car Parts
M.1901	Cap Gemini/Ernst & Young	17.05.00	—	—	Clearance Art.6(1)(b) Without undertakings	Information Technology Services

Table 5

MERGER No.	NAME	DATE	O.J.	C.M.L.R.	TYPE OF DECISION	PRODUCT SECTOR
M.1902	Telia/Commerzbank/FNH	27.04.00	—	4 [2000] 1059 (IP)	Clearance Art.6(1)(b) Without undertakings	Investments In Telecommunications
M.1904	Carrefour/Gruppo GS	06.04.00	—	4 [2000] 1051 (IP)	Clearance Art.6(1)(b) Without undertakings	Retail
M.1907	Woco/Michelin	28.04.00	—	—	Clearance Art.6(1)(b) Without undertakings	Car Parts
M.1908	Alcatel/Newbridge Networks	19.05.00	—	5 [2000] 17 (IP)	Clearance Art.6(1)(b) Without undertakings	Telecommunications Network Equipment
M.1909	Alstom/ABB Alstom Power	05.05.00	—	—	Clearance Art.6(1)(b) Without undertakings	Power Generation
M.1910	Meritanordbanken/Unidanmark	10.04.00	—	4 [2000] 1053 (IP)	Clearance Art.6(1)(b) Without undertakings	Financial Services
M.1911	Dow/BSL	27.04.00	—	4 [2000] 1059 (IP)	Clearance Art.6(1)(b) Without undertakings	Chemicals
M.1913	Lufthansa/Menzies/LGS/JV	29.08.00	—	5 [2000] 587 (IP)	Clearance Art.6(1)(b) Without undertakings	Groundhandling Services
M.1915	The Post Office/TPG/SPPL	13.03.01	[2004] L82/1	—	Clearance Art.8(2) With undertakings	Post Activities
M.1916	RTL Newmedia/Primus-Online	20.06.00	—	—	Clearance Art.6(1)(b) Without undertakings	Internet Services
M.1919	Alcoa/Cordant	19.05.00	—	5 [2000] 16 (IP)	Clearance Art.6(1)(b) Without undertakings	Aluminium
M.1920	Nabisco/United Biscuits	05.05.00	—	4 [2000] 1062 (IP)	Clearance Art.6(1)(b) With undertakings	Food
M.1922	Siemens/Bosch/Atecs	11.08.00	—	5 [2000] 581 (IP)	Clearance Art.6(1)(b) Without undertakings	Steam Turbines
M.1925	Scottish & Newcastle/Groupe Danone	11.07.00	—	—	Clearance Art.6(1)(b) Without undertakings	Beers
M.1926	Telefonica/Tyco/JV	11.08.00	—	5 [2000] 580 (IP)	Clearance Art.6(1)(b) Without undertakings	Undersea Cables
M.1929	Magneti Marelli/Seima	29.05.00	—	5 [2000] 22 (IP)	Clearance Art.6(1)(b) Without undertakings	Car Parts
M.1930	Ahlstrom/Andritz	30.05.00	—	5 [2000] 22 (IP)	Clearance Art.6(1)(b) Without undertakings	Equipment, Engineering For Pulping Sector

MERGER No.	NAME	DATE	O.J.	C.M.L.R.	TYPE OF DECISION	PRODUCT SECTOR
M.1932	BASF/American Cyanamid	30.06.00	—	5 [2000] 194 (IP)	Clearance Art.6(1)(b) With undertakings	Crop Protection Products
M.1933	Citigroup/Flender	20.06.00	—	—	Clearance Art.6(1)(b) Without undertakings	Power Transmission Equipment
M.1935	Rabobank/Gilde/Norit	05.05.00	—	—	Clearance Art.6(1)(b) Without undertakings	Water Treatment
M.1936	Siemens Business Services/Lufthansa Systems Synavion	06.07.00	—	—	Clearance Art.6(1)(b) Without undertakings	Edp Services For Airports
M.1937	Skandia Life/Diligentia	11.05.00	—	5 [2000] 14 (IP)	Clearance Art.6(1)(b) Without undertakings	Real Estate
M.1938	BT/Telefort	21.06.00	—	5 [2000] 181 (IP)	Clearance Art.6(1)(b) Without undertakings	Telecommunications
M.1939	Rexam/American National Can	19.07.00	—	5 [2000] 403 (IP)	Clearance Art.6(1)(b) With undertakings	Beverage Cans
M.1940	Framatome/Siemens/Cogema	06.12.00	[2001] L289/8	4 [2002] 18 (D)	Clearance Art.8(2) With undertakings	Nuclear
M.1943	Telefonica/Endemol	11.07.00	—	—	Clearance Art.6(1)(b) Without undertakings	TV Programmes, Television, Pay-TV
M.1944	HSBC/CCF	30.05.00	—	5 [2000] 23 (IP)	Clearance Art.6(1)(b) Without undertakings	Banking, Insurance
M.1946	Bellsouth/SBC/JV	26.05.00	—	5 [2000] 20 (IP)	Clearance Art.6(1)(b) Without undertakings	Telecommunications
M.1947	ABN Amro Lease Holding/Dial Group	15.06.00	—	5 [2000] 180 (IP)	Clearance Art.6(1)(b) Without undertakings	Car Leasing
M.1948	Techpack International/Valois	30.05.00	—	5 [2000] 23 (IP)	Clearance Art.6(1)(b) Without undertakings	Packaging
M.1949	Western Power Distribution/Hyder	14.07.00	—	5 [2000] 391 (IP)	Clearance Art.6(1)(b) Without undertakings	Electricity
M.1950	Toyoda Automatic Loom Works/BT Industries	15.06.00	—	5 [2000] 180 (IP)	Clearance Art.6(1)(b) Without undertakings	Warehouse Equipment
M.1951	BT/Japan Telecont/Vodafone Airtouch/JV	01.09.00	—	5 [2000] 591 (IP)	Clearance Art.6(1)(b) Without undertakings	Telecommunications
M.1952	RWE/Iberdrola/Tarragona Power JV	21.08.00	—	5 [2000] 581 (IP)	Clearance Art.6(1)(b) Without undertakings	Electricity

Table 5

MERGER No.	NAME	DATE	O.J.	C.M.L.R.	TYPE OF DECISION	PRODUCT SECTOR
M.1954	ACS/Sonera Vivendi/Xfera	31.07.00	—	5 [2000] 401 (IP)	Clearance Art.6(1)(b) Without undertakings	Telecommunications
M.1956	Ford/Autonova	24.05.00	—	5 [2000] 19 (IP)	Clearance Art.6(1)(b) Without undertakings	Car Assembler
M.1957	Viag Interkom/Telenor Media	14.06.00	—	5 [2000] 178 (IP)	Clearance Art.6(1)(b) Without undertakings	Telecommunications
M.1958	Bertelsmann/GBL/Pearson TV	29.06.00	—	5 [2000] 186 (IP)	Clearance Art.6(1)(b) Without undertakings	Television
M.1959	Meritor/Arvin	31.05.00	—	5 [2000] 177 (IP)	Clearance Art.6(1)(b) Without undertakings	Car Parts
M.1960	Carrefour/Marinopoulos	26.05.00	—	5 [2000] 21 (IP)	Clearance Art.6(1)(b) Without undertakings	Retail
M.1961	NHS (San Paolo-IMI)/MWCR (Schroders)	19.05.00	—	5 [2000] 17 (IP)	Clearance Art.6(1)(b) Without undertakings	Cash Registers
M.1964	Planet Internet/Fortis Bank/Mine JV	10.07.00	—	—	Clearance Art.6(1)(b) Without undertakings	Internet Services
M.1966	Philips/Chevron	29.06.00	—	5 [2000] 185 (IP)	Clearance Art.6(1)(b) Without undertakings	Chemicals
M.1968	Solectron/Nortel	31.05.00	—	5 [2000] 25 (IP)	Clearance Art.6(1)(b) Without undertakings	Printed Circuit Boards
M.1969	UTC/Honeywell/i2/My Aircraft.com	04.08.00	—	5 [2000] 575 (IP)	Clearance Art.6(1)(b) Without undertakings	Internet Services
M.1970	Johnson & Johnson/Mercury Assets Management/Agora Healthcare Services	08.06.00	—	—	Clearance Art.6(1)(b) Without undertakings	Information Technology
M.1972	Granada/Compass	29.06.00	—	5 [2000] 187 (IP)	Clearance Art.6(1)(b) Without undertakings	Food Service, Catering
M.1973	Telecom Italia/Endesa/Union Fenosa	12.09.00	—	5 [2000] 795 (IP)	Clearance Art.6(1)(b) Without undertakings	Telecommunications
M.1974	Compagnie de Saint-Gobain/Raab Karcher	22.06.00	—	5 [2000] 181 (IP)	Clearance Art.6(1)(b) Without undertakings	Building Products
M.1975	Deutsche Bank/Eurobank/Lamda Development/JV	15.06.00	—	5 [2000] 178 (IP)	Clearance Art.6(1)(b) Without undertakings	Real Estate

MERGER No.	NAME	DATE	O.J.	C.M.L.R.	TYPE OF DECISION	PRODUCT SECTOR
M.1976	Shell/Halliburton/Well Dynamics JV	15.03.01	—	4 [2001] 151 (IP)	Clearance Art.6(1)(b) Without undertakings	Completion Products
M.1978	Telecom Italia/News Television/Stream	29.06.00	—	5 [2000] 188 (IP)	Clearance Art.6(1)(b) Without undertakings	Television/Broadcasting Rights
M.1979	CDC/Banco Urquijo/JV	04.08.00	—	5 [2000] 578 (IP)	Clearance Art.6(1)(b) Without undertakings	Custodian Services
M.1980	Volvo/Renault VI	01.09.00	—	5 [2000] 597 (IP)	Clearance Art.6(1)(b) With undertakings	Trucks, Buses
M.1982	Telia/Oracle/Drutt	11.09.00	—	5 [2000] 793 (IP)	Clearance Art.6(1)(b) Without undertakings	Internet
M.1987	Basf/Bayer/Hoeschst/Dystar	05.09.00	—	5 [2000] 792 (IP)	Clearance Art.6(1)(b) Without undertakings	Paints
M.1989	Winterthur/Colonial	09.06.00	—	5 [2000] 177 (IP)	Clearance Art.6(1)(b) Without undertakings	Insurance
M.1990	Unilever/Bestfoods	28.09.00	—	5 [2000] 807 (IP)	Clearance Art.6(1)(b) With undertakings	Food Products
M.1993	Rhodia/Raisio/JV	20.0700	—	5 [2000] 395 (IP)	Clearance Art.6(1)(b) Without undertakings	Latices
M.1994	Andersen Consulting/BT/JV	28.07.00	—	5 [2000] 399 (IP)	Clearance Art.6(1)(b) Without undertakings	Human Resources Services
M.1996	SCA/Graninge/JV	05.07.00	—	—	Clearance Art.6(1)(b) Without undertakings	Timber and Forest Fuel
M.1997	Schroders/Liberty International Pension	28.06.00	—	5 [2000] 184 (IP)	Clearance Art.6(1)(b) Without undertakings	Financial Services
M.1998	Ford/Landrover	29.06.00	—	5 [2000] 187 (IP)	Clearance Art.6(1)(b) Without undertakings	Cars
M.2000	WPP Group/Young & Rubicam	24.08.00	—	5 [2000] 584 (IP)	Clearance Art.6(1)(b) Without undertakings	Media Buying, Marketing Communications Services
M.2002	Preussag/Thomson	26.07.00	—	5 [2000] 397 (IP)	Clearance Art.6(1)(b) With undertakings	Travel Services
M.2003	Carlyle/Gruppo Riello	27.06.00	—	5 [2000] 183 (IP)	Clearance Art.6(1)(b) Without undertakings	Heating Equipment

Table 5

MERGER No.	NAME	DATE	O.J.	C.M.L.R.	TYPE OF DECISION	PRODUCT SECTOR
M.2004	Investcorp/Chase Capital Investments	27.06.00	—	5 [2000] 183 (IP)	Clearance Art.6(1)(b) Without undertakings	Packaging
M.2006	Enron/MG	04.07.00	—	5 [2000] 189 (IP)	Clearance Art.6(1)(b) Without undertakings	Metal Trading
M.2008	AOM/Air Liberté/Air Littoral	27.07.00	—	5 [2000] 398 (IP)	Clearance Art.6(1)(b) Without undertakings	Air Transport
M.2011	Delta Selections/Arla Food Helas	21.08.00	—	5 [2000] 583 (IP)	Clearance Art.6(1)(b) Without undertakings	Food Products
M.2012	CGNU/Aseval	20.07.00	—	5 [2000] 395 (IP)	Clearance Art.6(1)(b) Without undertakings	Insurance
M.2015	TotalFina/Saarberg/MMH	31.08.00	—	5 [2000] 590 (IP)	Clearance Art.6(1)(b) Without undertakings	Petroleum Products
M.2016	France Telecom/Orange	11.08.00	—	5 [2000] 580 (IP)	Clearance Art.6(1)(b) With undertakings	Telecommunications
M.2020	Metsä Serla/Modo	04.08.00	—	5 [2000] 576 (IP)	Clearance Art.6(1)(b) With undertakings	Paper Products
M.2021	Snecma/Labinal	25.08.00	—	5 [2000] 586 (IP)	Clearance Art.6(1)(b) Without undertakings	Avionics
M.2023	Brambles/Ermewa/JV	04.08.00	—	5 [2000] 574 (IP)	Clearance Art.6(1)(b) Without undertakings	Tank Containers
M.2024	Invensys/Baan	07.07.00	—	—	Clearance Art.6(1)(b) Without undertakings	Information Technology
M.2025	GE Capital/BTPS/MEPC	27.07.00	—	5 [2000] 398 (IP)	Clearance Art.6(1)(b) Without undertakings	Real Estate
M.2026	Clear Channel Communications/SFX Entertainment	14.07.00	—	5 [2000] 392 (IP)	Clearance Art.6(1)(b) Without undertakings	Event Promotions
M.2027	Deutsche Bank/SAP/JV	13.07.00	—	5 [2000] 391 (IP)	Clearance Art.6(1)(b) Without undertakings	Internet Services
M.2028	ABB/Bilfinger/MVV Energie/JV	25.07.00	—	5 [2000] 396 (IP)	Clearance Ant. 6(1)(b) Without undertakings	Water Treatment
M.2029	Tate & Lyle/Amylum	11.08.00	—	5 [2000] 579 (IP)	Clearance Art.6(1)(b) Without undertakings	Sweeteners, Starch, Animal Feed
M.2032	SCA Packaging/Metsä Corrugated	25.08.00	—	5 [2000] 593 (IP)	Clearance Art.6(1)(b) With undertakings	Corrugated Board

MERGER No.	NAME	DATE	O.J.	C.M.L.R.	TYPE OF DECISION	PRODUCT SECTOR
M.2033	Metso/Svedala	24.01.01	[2004] L88/1	—	Art. 8(2) With conditions and obligations	Machinery
M.2034	Hagemeyer/WF Electrical	17.07.00	—	5 [2000] 392 (IP)	Clearance Art.6(1)(b) Without undertakings	Electrical Components
M.2035	Doughty Hanson/Rank Hovis McDougall	24.08.00	—	5 [2000] 585 (IP)	Clearance Art.6(1)(b) Without undertakings	Food Cans
M.2036	Valeo/Labinal	04.08.00	—	5 [2000] 574 (IP)	Clearance Art.6(1)(b) Without undertakings	Car Parts
M.2037	BNP Paribas/PHH	28.07.00	—	5 [2000] 400 (IP)	Clearance Art.6(1)(b) Without undertakings	Car Management Services
M.2041	United Airlines/US Airways	12.01.01	—	4 [2001] 1510 (IP)	Clearance Art.6(1)(b) With undertakings	Air Transport
M.2044	Interbrew/Bass	22.08.00	—	5 [2000] 594 (IP)	Art. 9(4) total referral without undertakings	Beers, Flavoured Alcoholic Beverages
M.2045	Salzgitter/Mannesmannröhren- Werke	05.09.00	—	5 [2000] 807 (IP)	Clearance Art.6(1)(b) Without undertakings	Steel Tubes
M.2046	Valeo/Robert Bosh/JV	28.07.00	—	5 [2000] 399 (IP)	Clearance Art.6(1)(b) Without undertakings	Car Parts
M.2047	Bayerische Hypo- und Vereinsbank/ Ixos/Mannesman/Memiq	04.08.00	—	5 [2000] 575 (IP)	Clearance Art.6(1)(b) Without undertakings	Internet Services
M.2048	Alcatel/Thomson Multimedia/JV	26.10.00	—	5 [2000] 1001 (IP)	Clearance Art.6(1)(b) Without undertakings	Interactive Video Networks
M.2050	Vivendi/Canal+/Seagram	13.10.00	—	5 [2000] 1007 (IP)	Clearance Art.6(1)(b) With undertakings	Internet, Music, Pay-TV
M.2051	Nordic Capital/Hiag/Nybron/Bauwerk	04.08.00	—	5 [2000] 577 (IP)	Clearance Art.6(1)(b) Without undertakings	Wooden Floors
M.2052	Industri Kapital/Alfa Laval Holding	11.08.00	—	5 [2000] 579 (IP)	Clearance Art.6(1)(b) Without undertakings	Processing Equipment
M.2053	Telenor/Bell South/Sonofon	04.08.00	—	5 [2000] 577 (IP)	Clearance Art.6(1)(b) Without undertakings	Telecommunications
M.2056	Sonera Systems/ICL Invia/Data-Info/JV	21.08.00	—	5 [2000] 583 (IP)	Clearance Art.6(1)(b) Without undertakings	Telecommunications

Table 5

MERGER No.	NAME	DATE	O.J.	C.M.L.R.	TYPE OF DECISION	PRODUCT SECTOR
M.2057	Randstad/VNU/JV	30.08.00	—	5 [2000] 589 (IP)	Clearance Art.6(1)(b) Without undertakings	Internet Services, Online Recruitment
M.2059	Siemens/Dematic/VDO/Sachs	29.08.00	—	5 [2000] 595 (IP)	Clearance Art.6(1)(b) With undertakings	Automation
M.2060	Bosch/Rexroth	13.12.00	[2004] L43/1	—	Clearance Art.8(2) With undertakings	Hydraulic Pumps, Valves
M.2061	Airbus	18.10.00	—	—	Clearance Art.6(1)(b) Without undertakings	Aircraft
M.2062	Rio Tinto/North	01.08.00	—	5 [2000] 402 (IP)	Clearance Art.6(1)(b) Without undertakings	Metals
M.2063	Sei/Mitsubishi Electric/JV	21.08.00	—	5 [2000] 584 (IP)	Clearance Art.6(1)(b) Without undertakings	Facility Management Services
M.2066	Dana/Getrag	07.11.00	—	5 [2000] 1005 (IP)	Clearance Art.6(1)(b) Without undertakings	Car Parts
M.2069	Alstom/Fiat Ferroviaria	18.09.00	—	—	Clearance Art.6(1)(b) Without undertakings	Railway Rolling Stock
M.2071	Riva/Sam	29.08.00	—	5 [2000] 588 (IP)	Clearance Art.6(1)(b) Without undertakings	Steel Products
M.2072	Phillip Morris/Nabisco	16.10.00	—	5 [2000] 998 (IP)	Clearance Art.6(1)(b) Without undertakings	Food Products
M.2074	Tyco/Mallinckrodt	28.09.00	—	5 [2000] 804 (IP)	Clearance Art.6(1)(b) Without undertakings	Medical Devices
M.2075	Newhouse/Jupiter/Scudder/M&G/JV	01.09.00	—	—	Clearance Art.6(1)(b) Without undertakings	Internet Services
M.2076	Ifil/Alpitour	07.09.00	—	5 [2000] 795 (IP)	Clearance Art.6(1)(b) Without undertakings	Travel
M.2077	Clayton Dubilier & Rice/Italtel	01.09.00	—	5 [2000] 591 (IP)	Clearance Art.6(1)(b) Without undertakings	Pay-TV Technical Services
M.2078	UBS Capital/Heiploeg Shellfish International	21.08.00	—	5 [2000] 582 (IP)	Clearance Art.6(1)(b) Without undertakings	Fishing Processing and Wholesale
M.2079	Raytheon/Thales/JV	30.03.01	—	4 [2001] 1521 (IP)	Clearance Art.6(1)(b) Without undertakings	Battlefield Systems, Radars
M.2082	PSA/Vivendi/Wappil!	22.09.00	—	5 [2000] 801 (IP)	Clearance Art.6(1)(b) Without undertakings	Internet Services

MERGER No.	NAME	DATE	O.J.	C.M.L.R.	TYPE OF DECISION	PRODUCT SECTOR
M.2084	CSM/European Bakery Supplies Business	28.09.00	—	5 [2000] 804 (IP)	Clearance Art.6(1)(b) Without undertakings	Bakery Supplies
M.2086	Deutsche Bank/Hamburigsche Immobilien Handlung/DLI	28.08.00	—	5 [2000] 587 (IP)	Clearance Art.6(1)(b) Without undertakings	Real Estate
M.2087	Feu Vert/Carrefour/Autocenter Delauto	11.09.00	—	5 [2000] 792 (IP)	Clearance Art.6(1)(b) Without undertakings	Car Repair
M.2091	HSBC Private Equity Investments/BBA Friction Materials	21.08.00	—	5 [2000] 583 (IP)	Clearance Art.6(1)(b) Without undertakings	Car Parts
M.2092	Repsol Quimica/Borealis/JV	19.12.00	—	4 [2001] 1524 (IP)	Clearance Art.6(1)(b) Without undertakings	Chemicals
M.2093	Airtours/Frosch Touristik	29.08.00	—	5 [2000] 587 (IP)	Clearance Art.6(1)(b) Without undertakings	Travel
M.2094	HT-Troplast/Kömmerling	28.09.00	—	4 [2000] 803 (IP)	Clearance Art.6(1)(b) Without undertakings	Parts For Doors and Windows
M.2095	Sextant/Diehl	29.08.00	—	5 [2000] 589 (IP)	Clearance Art.6(1)(b) Without undertakings	Avionics
M.2096	Bayer/Deutsche Telekom/Infrasev/JV	06.10.00	—	—	Clearance Art.6(1)(b) Without undertakings	Internet Services
M.2097	SCA/Metsä Tissue	31.01.01	[2002] L57/1	4 [2002] 38 (D)	Prohibition Art.8(3)	Tissue Paper Products
M.2099	Hutchison/NTT Docomo/KPN Mobile/JV	05.09.00	—	5 [2000] 593 (IP)	Clearance Art.6(1)(b) Without undertakings	Telecommunications
M.2101	General Mills/Pillsbury/Diageo	13.10.00	—	5 [2000] 998 (IP)	Clearance Art.6(1)(b) Without undertakings	Food Products
M.2102	Magneti Marelli/Magneti Marelli Automotive Lighting Business	26.10.00	—	5 [2000] 1001 (IP)	Clearance Art.6(1)(b) Without undertakings	Car Parts
M.2104	MIG/Carlyle/Eutectic and Castolin	12.09.00	—	5 [2000] 796 (IP)	Clearance Art.6(1)(b) Without undertakings	Welding Consumables
M.2107	TXU Germany/Stadtwerkke Kiel	29.09.00	—	—	Clearance Art.6(1)(b) Without undertakings	Electricity
M.2110	Deutsche Bank/SEI/JV	25.09.00	—	5 [2000] 797 (IP)	Clearance Art.6(1)(b) Without undertakings	Real Estate
M.2111	Alcoa/British Aluminium	27.10.00	—	5 [2000] 1002 (IP)	Clearance Art.6(1)(b) Without undertakings	Aluminium

Table 5

MERGER No.	NAME	DATE	O.J.	C.M.L.R.	TYPE OF DECISION	PRODUCT SECTOR
M.2114	Sanpaolo/Schroders/Omega/CEG/JV	11.09.00	—	5 [2000] 794 (IP)	Clearance Art.6(1)(b) Without undertakings	Electronic Scales
M.2115	Carrefour/GB	28.09.00	—	5 [2000] 805 (IP)	Clearance Art.6(1)(b) Without undertakings	Retail
M.2116	Flextronics/Italdata	25.09.00	—	5 [2000] 798 (IP)	Clearance Art.6(1)(b) Without undertakings	Electronic Manufacturing Services
M.2118	Telenor/Procuritas/ISAB/Newco	25.09.00	—	5 [2000] 800 (IP)	Clearance Art.6(1)(b) Without undertakings	Electrical Installations
M.2119	E.ON/ACP/Schmalbach – Lubeca	24.08.00	—	5 [2000] 585 (IP)	Clearance Art.6(1)(b) Without undertakings	Packaging
M.2120	Toyota Motor Corporation/Toyota GB	01.09.00	—	5 [2000] 592 (IP)	Clearance Art.6(1)(b) Without undertakings	Cars
M.2122	BAT/Cap Gemini/Ciberion	11.09.00	—	5 [2000] 794 (IP)	Clearance Art.6(1)(b) Without undertakings	Information Technology
M.2125	Hypo Vereinsbank/Bank Austria	14.11.00	—	—	Clearance Art.6(1)(b) Without undertakings	Banking
M.2127	Daimler Chrysler/Detroit Diesel Corporation	09.10.00	—	5 [2000] 997 (IP)	Clearance Art.6(1)(b) Without undertakings	Diesel Engines
M.2128	ABB Lummus/Engelhard/Equistar/ Novolen	25.09.00	—	5 [2000] 797 (IP)	Clearance Art.6(1)(b) Without undertakings	Chemicals (Pp) Technology
M.2131	BCP/Interamericain/Novabank/JV	15.09.00	—	5 [2000] 796 (IP)	Clearance Art.6(1)(b) Without undertakings	Banking
M.2133	Hicks/Bearstearns/Johns Manville	25.09.00	—	5 [2000] 798 (IP)	Clearance Art.6(1)(b) Without undertakings	Insulation Materials
M.2134	Avnet/Veba Electronics	18.10.00	—	5 [2000] 999 (IP)	Clearance Art.6(1)(b) Without undertakings	Electronic Systems
M.2136	Schroder Ventures/Memec	25.09.00	—	5 [2000] 799 (IP)	Clearance Art.6(1)(b) Without undertakings	Electronic Components
M.2137	SLDE/NTL/MSCP/NOOS	16.10.00	—	—	Clearance Art.6(1)(b) Without undertakings	Internet, Telephony, Pay-TV
M.2138	SAP/Siemens/JV	02.10.00	—	5 [2000] 806 (IP)	Clearance Art.6(1)(b) Without undertakings	Internet Services

MERGER No.	NAME	DATE	O.J.	C.M.L.R.	TYPE OF DECISION	PRODUCT SECTOR
M.2139	Bombardier/Adtranz	03.04.01	[2002] L69/50	5 [2002] 12	Clearance Art.8(2) With conditions and obligations	Trains, People Movers
M.2140	Bawag/PSK	07.11.00	—	5 [2000] 1006 (IP)	Clearance Art.6(1)(b) Without undertakings	Banking
M.2143	BT/Viag Intercom	19.02.01	—	4 [2001] 158 (IP)	Clearance Art.6(1)(b) Without undertakings	Telecommunications
M.2147	VNU/Hearst/Stratosfera	25.09.00	—	5 [2000] 800 (IP)	Clearance Art.6(1)(b) Without undertakings	Publishing
M.2152	Scottish & Newcastle/JV/Centralcer	22.11.00	—	—	Clearance Art.6(1)(b) Without undertakings	Beers
M.2154	C3D/Rhone/Go-Ahead	20.10.00	—	5 [2000] 1008 (IP)	Clearance Art.6(1)(b) Without undertakings Art. 9(4) partial referral	Buses, Services To Airports, Rail Transport
M.2156	Rewe/Sair Group/LTU	20.12.00	—	4 [2001] 1525 (IP)	Clearance Art.6(1)(b) Without undertakings	Air Transport
M.2158	Crédit Suisse Group/Donaldson, Lufkin & Jenrette	09.10.00	—	5 [2000] 997 (IP)	Clearance Art.6(1)(b) Without undertakings	Banking
M.2159	Creditanstalt/Lufthansa Airplus Service karten/AUA Beteilingungen/Airplus	08.12.00	—	4 [2001] 1515 (IP)	Clearance Art.6(1)(b) Without undertakings	Credit Cards
M.2161	Ahold/Superdiplo	23.10.00	—	5 [2000] 1000 (IP)	Clearance Art.6(1)(b) Without undertakings	Retailing
M.2168	Snecma/Hurel-Dubois	14.11.00	—	—	Clearance Art.6(1)(b) Without undertakings	Aircraft Components
M.2172	Babcock Borsig/MG Technologies/SAP Markets/ec4ec	07.11.00	—	5 [2000] 1005 (IP)	Clearance Art.6(1)(b) Without undertakings	Internet Services
M.2175	Dow Chemical/Gurit-Essex	08.12.00	—	4 [2001] 1516 (IP)	Clearance Art.6(1)(b) Without undertakings	Chemicals
M.2176	K+S/Solvay/JV	10.01.02	—	4 [2002] IS70	Clearance Art.6(1)(b) Without undertakings	Production of Salt
M.2179	Compart/Falck (II)	03.11.00	—	5 [2000] 1003 (IP)	Clearance Art.6(1)(b) Without undertakings	Electricity, Water
M.2180	Outokumpu/Avesta Sheffield	04.12.00	—	4 [2001] 1518 (IP)	Clearance Art.6(1)(b) Without undertakings	Steel Products

MERGER No.	NAME	DATE	O.J.	C.M.L.R.	TYPE OF DECISION	PRODUCT SECTOR
M.2183	Smiths Industries/Ti Group	28.11.00	—	4 [2001] 1515 (IP)	Clearance Art.6(1)(b) Without undertakings	Aircrafts Components, Hose Systems
M.2186	Preussag/Nouvelles Frontières	14.11.00	—	—	Clearance Art.6(1)(b) Without undertakings	Package Holidays
M.2187	CVC/Lenzing	17.10.01	[2004] L82/20	—	Article 8(3) – Prohibition	Fibres and Yarns
M.2190	LSG/OFSI	01.06.01	—	5 [2001] 1529 (IP)	Clearance Art.6(1)(b) Without undertakings	Catering
M.2192	SmithKline Beecham/Block Drug	11.01.01	—	4 [2001] 154 (IP)	Clearance Art.6(1)(b) Without undertakings	Toothpastes, Toothbrushes, Pharmaceuticals
M.2193	Alliance Unichem/Interpharm	07.12.00	—	4 2001] 1512 (IP)	Clearance Art.6(1)(b) Without undertakings	Pharmaceuticals
M.2195	Cap Gemini/Vodafone/JV	29.11.00	—	4 [2001] 1516 (IP)	Clearance Art.6(1)(b) Without undertakings	IT Services
M.2196	Enron/Bergmann/Hutzler	07.12.00	—	4 [2001] 1514 (IP)	Clearance Art.6(1)(b) Without undertakings	Non-ferrous Metals
M.2197	Hilton/Accor/Forte/Travel Services/JV	16.02.01	—	4 [2001] 159 (IP)	Clearance Art.6(1)(b) Without undertakings	Travel Agency, Computerised Reservation Systems Hotel Accommodation
M.2198	EL.FI/Moulinex	08.12.00	—	4 [2001] 1517 (IP)	Clearance Art.6(1)(b) Without undertakings	Home Appliances
M.2199	Quantum/Maxtor	08.12.00	—	4 [2001] 1517 (IP)	Clearance Art.6(1)(b) Without undertakings	Hard Disk Drives
M.2200	Deutsche Bank/DBG/Varta	07.12.00	—	4 [2001] 1513(IP)	Clearance Art.6(1)(b) Without undertakings	Batteries, Torches
M.2201	MAN/Auwärter	20.06.01	[2002] L116/35	—	Clearance Art.8(2) Without undertakings	Buses
M.2202	Stinnes/HCI	04.12.00	—	4 [2001] 1519 (IP)	Clearance Art.6(1)(b) Without undertakings	Chemicals Distribution
M.2208	Chevron/Texaco	28.02.01	—	4 [2001] 1513 (IP)	Clearance Art.6(1)(b) Without undertakings	Oil, Gas
M.2209	EDF/Group/Cottam Power Station	29.11.00	—	4 [2001] 1517 (IP)	Clearance Art.6(1)(b) Without undertakings	Electricity

MERGER No.	NAME	DATE	O.J.	C.M.L.R.	TYPE OF DECISION	PRODUCT SECTOR
M.2210	Georg Fischer/West LB/Krupp Werner & Pfleiderer	15.12.00	—	4 [2001] 1520 (IP)	Clearance Art.6(1)(b) Without undertakings	Industrial Machinery
M.2211	Universal Studios Networks/De Facto 829 (NTL)/Studio Channel Limited	20.12.00	—	4 [2001] 157(IP)	Clearance Art.6(1)(b) Without undertakings	Films, Pay-TV
M.2216	Enel/Wind/Infostrada	19.01.01	—	4 [2001] 1515 (IP)	Clearance Art.6(1)(b) Without undertakings	Telecommunications
M.2218	Thomas Cook Holdings/British Airways JV	30.04.01	—	4 [2001] 1511 (IP)	Clearance Art.6(1)(b) Without undertakings	Package Holidays
M.2220	General Electric/Honeywell	03.07.01	[2004] L48/1	—	Art. 8(3)—Prohibition	Aircraft Engines
M.2222	UGC/Liberty Media	24.04.01	—	4 [2001] 159 (IP)	Clearance Art.6(1)(b) Without undertakings	Internet, Pay-TV
M.2223	Getronics/Hagemeyer/JV	02.04.01	—	4 [2001] 1524 (IP)	Clearance Art.6(1)(b) Without undertakings	Information Technology
M.2224	Siemens/Demag Krauss – Maffei	20.12.00	—	4 [2001] 1527 (IP)	Clearance Art.6(1)(b) Without undertakings	Industrial Machinery
M.2225	Fortis/ASR	13.12.00	—	4 [2001] 1519 (IP)	Clearance Art.6(1)(b) Without undertakings	Banking, Insurance
M.2227	Goldman Sachs/Messer Griesheim	20.03.01	—	4 [2001] 1513 (IP)	Clearance Art.6(1)(b) Without undertakings	Industrial Gases
M.2228	C&N/Thomas Cook	09.02.01	—	4 [2001] 156 (IP)	Clearance Art.6(1)(b) Without undertakings	Travel
M.2230	Sanmina/Siemens/Inboard Leiterplattentechnologie	21.12.00	—	4 [2001] 1527 (IP)	Clearance Art.6(1)(b) Without undertakings	Paper Products
M.2231	Huntsman International/Albright & Wilson Surfactants Europe	30.03.01	—	4 [2001] 1523 (IP)	Clearance Art.6(1)(b) Without undertakings	Chemicals
M.2234	Metsäliitto Osuuskunta/Vapo Oy/JV	08.02.01	—	5 [2002] 11 (D)	Clearance Art.6(1)(b) Art. 9(4) referral without undertakings	Wood-based Fuels
M.2235	Corus Group/Cogifer/JV	19.12.00	—	4 [2001] 1523 (IP)	Clearance Art.6(1)(b) Without undertakings	Railway Track Components
M.2240	CVC/Mascotech	20.03.01	—	4 [2001] 1512 (IP)	Clearance Art.6(1)(b) Without undertakings	Car Parts
M.2241	Peugeot/Sommer Allibert	20.12.00	—	4 [2001] 1526 (IP)	Clearance Art.6(1)(b) Without undertakings	Car Parts

Table 5

MERGER No.	NAME	DATE	O.J.	C.M.L.R.	TYPE OF DECISION	PRODUCT SECTOR
M.2243	Stora Enso/Assidomän/JV	22.12.00	—	4 [2001] 1529 (IP)	Clearance Art.6(1)(b) Without undertakings	Paper Products
M.2244	Royal Vopak/Ellis & Everard	16.01.01	—	4 [2001] 156 (IP)	Clearance Art.6(1)(b) Without undertakings	Chemicals
M.2245	Metsä Serla/Zanders	15.12.00	—	4 [2001] 1521 (IP)	Clearance Art.6(1)(b) Without undertakings	Paper Products
M.2250	Du Pont/Air Products Chemicals/JV	22.12.00	—	—	Clearance Art.6(1)(b) Without undertakings	Abrasive Products
M.2254	Aviapartner/Maersk/Novia	11.01.01	—	4 [2001] 155 (IP)	Clearance Art.6(1)(b) Without undertakings	Ground Handling Services
M.2256	Philips/Agilent Health Care Solutions	02.03.01	—	4 [2001] 1517 (IP)	Clearance Art.6(1)(b) Without undertakings	Healthcare Equipment
M.2257	France Telecom/Equant	21.03.01	—	4 [2001] 1514 (IP)	Clearance Art.6(1)(b) Without undertakings	Telecommunications
M.2260	Hitachi/LG Electronics/JV	14.09.01	—	5 [2001] 1043 (IP)	Clearance Art.6(1)(b) Without undertakings	Odd Drives
M.2262	Flughafen Berlin (II)	05.02.01	—	4 [2001] 159 (IP)	Clearance Art.6(1)(b) Without undertakings	Airport Management
M.2263	Philips/LG Electronics/JV	09.04.01	—	4 [2001] 1532 (IP)	Clearance Art.6(1)(b) Without undertakings	Cathode Ray Tubes
M.2265	Ricoh/Lanier Worldwide	24.01.01	—	4 [2001] 157(IP)	Clearance Art.6(1)(b) Without undertakings	Photocopiers
M.2268	Pernod Ricard/Diageo/Seagram Spirits	08.05.01	—	4 [2001] 1515 (IP)	Clearance Art.6(1)(b) With undertakings	Spirits and Wines
M.2269	Sasol/Condea	30.01.01	—	4 [2001] 158 (IP)	Clearance Art.6(1)(b) Without undertakings	Chemicals
M.2271	Cargill/Agribrands	19.02.01	—	4 [2001] 1510 (IP)	Clearance Art.6(1)(b) Without undertakings	Animal Feed
M.2275	Pepsico/Quaker	27.03.01	—	4 [2001] 1518 (IP)	Clearance Art.6(1)(b) Without undertakings	Food Products
M.2276	The Coca-Cola Company/Nestlé/JV	27.09.01	—	5 [2001] 1050 (IP)	Clearance Art.6(1)(b) Without undertakings	Non-alcoholic Beverages
M.2277	Degussa/Laporte	12.03.01	—	4 [2001] 158 (IP)	Clearance Art.6(1)(b) With undertakings	Chemicals

MERGER No.	NAME	DATE	O.J.	C.M.L.R.	TYPE OF DECISION	PRODUCT SECTOR
M.2282	BT/Esat Digifone	16.03.01	—	4 [2001] 1510 (IP)	Clearance Art.6(1)(b) Without undertakings	Telecommunications
M.2283	Schneider Electric/Legrand	10.10.01	[2004] L101/1 and [2004] L101/34	—	Art. 8(3) – prohibition	Electrical Equipment
	Schneider Electric/Legrand	30.01.02	—	4 [2002] IS78	Art.8(4) Effective competition restored	
M.2286	Buhrmann/Samas Office Supplies	11.04.01	—	—	Clearance Art.6(1)(b) With undertakings	Office Supplies
M.2291	VNU/AC Nielsen	12.02.01	—	4 [2001] 157 (IP)	Clearance Art.6(1)(b) Without undertakings	Marketing Data Services
M.2294	Etexgroup/Glynwed Pipe Systems	28.02.01	—	4 [2001] 1512 (IP)	Clearance Art.6(1)(b) Without undertakings	Pipe Systems
M.2297	BP Chemicals/Solvay (PP)	29.10.01	—	5 [2001] 1223 (IP)	Clearance Art.6(1)(b) Without undertakings	Chemicals
M.2299	BP Chemicals/Solvay/HDPE JV	29.10.01	—	—	Clearance Art.6(1)(b) Without undertakings	Chemicals
M.2300	YLE/TDF/Digita	26.06.01	—	5 [2001] 1518 (IP)	Clearance Art.6(1)(b) With undertakings	Radio Transmission
M.2302	Heinz/CSM	23.02.01	—	4 [2001] 1511 (IP)	Clearance Art.6(1)(b) Without undertakings	Food Products
M.2305	Vodafone Group PLC/Eircell	02.03.01	—	4 [2001] 1518 (IP)	Clearance Art.6(1)(b) Without undertakings	Telecommunications
M.2308	Northrop Grumman/Litton Industries	23.03.01	—	4 [2001] 1516 (IP)	Clearance Art.6(1)(b) Without undertakings	Military Products
M.2312	Abbott/BASF	28.02.01	—	4 [2001] 1514 (IP)	Clearance Art.6(1)(b) Without undertakings	Pharmaceuticals
M.2313	Teka/Finatlantis/Holdivat	06.04.01	—	4 [2001] 1530 (IP)	Clearance Art.6(1)(b) Without undertakings	Stainless Steel Beverage Containers
M.2314	BASF/Eurodiol/Pantochim	11.07.01	[2002] L132/45	5 [2001] 223 (IP)	Clearance Art.8(2) Without conditions and obligations	Chemical Products
M.2315	The Airline Group/Nats	14.05.01	—	5 [2001] 1521 (IP)	Clearance Art.6(1)(b) Without undertakings	Airport Services, Air Traffic Services
M.2317	Lafarge/Blue Circle (II)	01.03.01	—	4 [2001] 1516 (IP)	Clearance Art.6(1)(b) Without undertakings	Cement, Concrete

Table 5

MERGER No.	NAME	DATE	O.J.	C.M.L.R.	TYPE OF DECISION	PRODUCT SECTOR
M.2330	Cargill/Banks	09.03.01	—	4 [2001] 156 (IP)	Clearance Art.6(1)(b) Without undertakings	Trading of Agricultural Commodities
M.2333	De Beers/LVMH	25.07.01	[2003] L29/40	—	Clearance Art.8(2) without conditions and obligations	Diamond Jewellery
M.2334	DMData/Kommunedata/e-Boks JV	30.03.01	—	4 [2001] 1522 (IP)	Clearance Art.6(1)(b) Without undertakings	Internet Services
M.2335	Michel Mineralölhandel/Thyssen-Elf Oil	28.02.01	—	4 [2001] 1515 (IP)	Clearance Art.6(1)(b) Without undertakings	Heating Oils
M.2337	Nestlé/Ralston Purina	27.07.01	—	—	Clearance Art.6(1)(b) With undertakings	Pet Food
M.2340	EDP/Cajastur/Caser/Hidroelectrica del Cantabrico	05.03.01	—	4 [2001] 1519 (IP)	Clearance Art.6(1)(b) Without undertakings	Electricity
M.2343	Toro Assicurazioni/Lloyd Italico	15.03.01	—	4 [2001] 159 (IP)	Clearance Art.6(1)(b) Without undertakings	Insurance
M.2345	Deutsche BP/Erdölchemie	26.04.01	—	—	Clearance Art.6(1)(b) Without undertakings	Chemicals
M.2348	Outokumpu/Norzink	27.03.01	—	—	Clearance Art.6(1)(b) Without undertakings	Zinc Production
M.2349	E.ON/Sydkraft	09.04.01	—	4 [2001] 1531 (IP)	Clearance Art.6(1)(b) Without undertakings	Electricity
M.2350	Campbell/ECBB	02.04.01	—	4 [2001] 1526 (IP)	Clearance Art.6(1)(b) Without undertakings	Food
M.2353	RWE/Hidroelectrica del Cantabrico	19.03.01	—	4 [2001] 1511 (IP)	Clearance Art.6(1)(b) Without undertakings	Electricity
M.2355	Dow/Enichem Polyurethane	06.04.01	—	5 [2001] 32 (D)	Clearance Art.6(1)(b) Without undertakings	Chemicals
M.2358	Flextronics/Ericsson	06.04.01	—	—	Clearance Art.6(1)(b) Without undertakings	Electronic Manufacturing Services
M.2362	Dalkia Holding/Clemessy	23.08.01	—	5 [2001] 815 (IP)	Clearance Art.6(1)(b) Without undertakings	Electricity and Control Apparatus
M.2365	Schlumberger/Sema	05.04.01	—	4 [2001] 1528 (IP)	Clearance Art.6(1)(b) Without undertakings	Information Technology
M.2366	Denso/MMC	27.03.01	—	4 [2001] 1517 (IP)	Clearance Art.6(1)(b) Without undertakings	Car Parts

MERGER No.	NAME	DATE	O.J.	C.M.L.R.	TYPE OF DECISION	PRODUCT SECTOR
M.2367	Siemens/E.On/Shell/SSG	27.03.01	—	4 [2001] 1520 (IP)	Clearance Art.6(1)(b) Without undertakings	Photovoltaïcs
M.2369	CNH/FHE	26.06.01	—	5 [2001] 1516 (IP)	Clearance Art.6(1)(b) Without undertakings	Construction Equipment
M.2370	Thales/Airsys-ATM	21.05.01	—	5 [2001] 1524 (IP)	Clearance Art.6(1)(b) Without undertakings	Telecommunications Products
M.2373	Compass/Selecta	08.05.01	—	4 [2001] 1514 (IP)	Clearance Art.6(1)(b) Without undertakings	Food Products
M.2374	Telenor/Ergogroup/DNB/Accenture/JV	02.05.01	—	4 [2001] 1513 (IP)	Clearance Art.6(1)(b) Without undertakings	Internet Services
M.2375	PAI+UGI/ElfAntargaz	21.03.01	—	4 [2001] 1515 (IP)	Clearance Art.6(1)(b) Without undertakings	Liquid Petroleum Gases
M.2382	Usinor/Arbed/Aceralia	19.07.01	—	5 [2001] 575 (IP)	Clearance Art.6(1)(b) Without undertakings	Construction Products
M.2384	Ratos/3iGroup/Atle	02.04.01	—	4 [2001] 1525 (IP)	Clearance Art.6(1)(b) Without undertakings	Water, Heating and Plumbing Products
M.2386	MEI/Philips	29.05.01	—	5 [2001] 1527 (IP)	Clearance Art.6(1)(b) Without undertakings	Batteries
M.2387	Heineken/Bayerische Brauholding	12.07.01	—	5 [2001] 565 (IP)	Clearance Art.6(1)(b) Without undertakings	Beers
M.2389	Shell/DEA	20.12.01	[2003] L15/35	4 [2002] IS56	Clearance Art.8(2) with conditions and obligations	Chemicals
M.2391	CVC/Cinven/Assidomän	10.05.01	—	5 [2001] 1520 (IP)	Clearance Art.6(1)(b) Without undertakings	Corrugated Case Materials, Packaging
M.2393	Skanska Sverige/Posten/Hooc	13.06.01	—	5 [2001] 159 (IP)	Clearance Art.6(1)(b) Without undertakings	Fairs, Showrooms
M.2396	Industri Kapital/Perstrop (II)	11.05.01	—	5 [2001] 1522 (IP)	Clearance Art.6(1)(b) With undertakings	Chemicals
M.2397	BC Funds/Sanitec	06.06.01	—	5 [2001] 1531 (IP)	Clearance Art.6(1)(b) Without undertakings	Bathroom Products
M.2398	Linde/Jungheinrich/JV	25.04.01	—	4 [2001] 1510 (IP)	Clearance Art.6(1)(b) Without undertakings	Internet Services
M.2399	Friesland Coberco/Nutricia	08.08.01	—	5 [2001] 812 (IP)	Clearance Art.6(1)(b) Without undertakings	Dairy Drinks

Table 5

MERGER No.	NAME	DATE	O.J.	C.M.L.R.	TYPE OF DECISION	PRODUCT SECTOR
M.2400	Dexia/Artesia	14.06.01	—	5 [2001] 1511 (IP)	Clearance Art.6(1)(b) Without undertakings	Banking, Insurance
M.2401	Industri Kapital/Telia Enterprise	29.05.01	—	5 [2001] 1526 (IP)	Clearance Art.6(1)(b) Without undertakings	Telecommunications
M.2402	Creditanstalt/RZB/JV	02.07.01	—	5 [2001] 217 (IP)	Clearance Art.6(1)(b) Without undertakings	Financial Intermediation
M.2403	Schneider/Thomson Multimedia/JV	13.06.01	—	5 [2001] 159 (IP)	Clearance Art.6(1)(b) Without undertakings	Internet Communications Products
M.2404	Elkem/Sapa	26.06.01	—	5 [2001] 1519 (IP)	Clearance Art.6(1)(b) Without undertakings	Aluminium
M.2411	Autologic/TNT/Wallenius/CAT JV	27.06.01	—	—	Clearance Art.6(1)(b) Without undertakings	Logistics Services
M.2413	BHP/Billiton	14.06.01	—	5 [2001] 1510 (IP)	Clearance Art.6(1)(b) Without undertakings	Copper Mining
M.2415	Interpublic/True North	21.06.01	—	5 [2001] 1515 (IP)	Clearance Art.6(1)(b) Without undertakings	Marketing Communications
M.2416	Tetra Laval/Sidel	30.10.01	[2004] L38/1 and [2004] L43/13	—	Article 8(3) – prohibition	Liquid Packaging and Equipment
M.2418	ORF/Netway/Adworx	21.05.01	—	5 [2001] 1525 (IP)	Clearance Art.6(1)(b) Without undertakings	Technical Services For Internet Advertising
M.2420	Mitsui/CVRD/CAEMI	30.10.01	[2004] L92/50	—	Clearance Art.8(2) with conditions and obligations	Mining of Metal Ores
M.2421	Continental/Temic	11.06.01	—	5 [2001] 1533 (IP)	Clearance Art.6(1)(b) Without undertakings	Car Parts
M.2422	Hapag-Lloyd/Hamburger Hafen-und Lagerhaus/HHLA-CTA	22.08.01	—	—	Clearance Art.6(1)(b) Without undertakings	Cargo Handling
M.2425	COOP NORDEN	26.07.01	—	5 [2001] 571 (IP)	Clearance Art.6(1)(b) Without undertakings	Procurement, Wholesale, Retail Daily Consumer Goods
M.2431	Allianz/Dresdner	19.07.01	—	5 [2001] 566 (IP)	Clearance Art.6(1)(b) With undertakings	Bank, Insurance
M.2432	Angelini/Phoenix/JV	06.07.01	—	5 [2001] 221 (IP)	Clearance Art.6(1)(b) Without undertakings	Distribution of Pharmaceuticals

MERGER No.	NAME	DATE	O.J.	C.M.L.R.	TYPE OF DECISION	PRODUCT SECTOR
M.2434	Grupo Villar MIR/ENBW/Hidroelectrica Del Cantabrico	26.09.01	[2004] L48/86	—	Clearance Art.8(2) With conditions and obligations	Electricity
M.2435	EDS/Systematics	11.05.01	—	5 [2001] 1523 (IP)	Clearance Art.6(1)(b) Without undertakings	Information Technology
M.2437	NEC/Toshiba	05.06.01	—	5 [2001] 1530 (IP)	Clearance Art.6(1)(b) Without undertakings	Space Industry
M.2438	SES/Stork/Fokker Space	24.07.01	—	5 [2001] 568 (IP)	Clearance Art.6(1)(b) Without undertakings	Space Industry
M.2439	Hitachi/ST MICROELECTRONICS/ SUPER HJV	03.07.01	—	5 [2001] 219 (IP)	Clearance Art.6(1)(b) Without undertakings	Computer Related Activities
M.2440	Siemens/Yazaki/JV	06.08.01	—	5 [2001] 812 (IP)	Clearance Art.6(1)(b) Without undertakings	Car Parts
M.2441	Amcor/Danisco/Ahlstrom	11.06.01	—	5 [2001] 1534 (IP)	Clearance Art.6(1)(b) Without undertakings	Packaging
M.2443	E.ON/Powergen	23.11.01	—	4 [2002] IS19	Clearance Art.6(1)(b) Without undertakings	Electricity
M.2447	Fabricom/GTI	09.08.01	—	5 [2001] 813 (IP)	Clearance Art.6(1)(b) Without undertakings	Electromechanical Systems
M.2451	Hilton/Scandics	31.05.01	—	5 [2001] 1528 (IP)	Clearance Art.6(1)(b) Without undertakings	Hotels
M.2456	Preussag/Tui Belgium	02.08.01	—	5 [2001] 572 (IP)	Clearance Art.6(1)(b) Without undertakings	Travel, Package Tours
M.2460	IBM/Informix	19.06.01	—	5 [2001] 1513 (IP)	Clearance Art.6(1)(b) Without undertakings	Systems Software Packages
M.2461	OM GROUP/DMC2	05.07.01	—	5 [2001] 221 (IP)	Clearance Art.6(1)(b) Without undertakings	Metal Products
M.2463	Speedy Tomato	14.06.01	—	5 [2001] I512 (IP)	Clearance Art.6(1)(b) Without undertakings	Internet Services
M.2465	CVC/Amstelland	16.07.01	—	5 [2001] 565 (IP)	Clearance Art.6(1)(b) Without undertakings	Building Materials, Concrete
M.2466	Sodexho/Abela (II)	08.06.01	—	5 [2001] 1532 (IP)	Clearance Art.6(1)(b) Without undertakings	Food Service
M.2468	Seat Pagine Gialle/Eniro	27.06.01	—	—	Clearance Art.6(1)(b) Without undertakings	Telephone Directories

Table 5

MERGER No.	NAME	DATE	O.J.	C.M.L.R.	TYPE OF DECISION	PRODUCT SECTOR
M.2469	Vodafone/Airtel	26.06.01	—	5 [2001] 1517 (IP)	Clearance Art.6(1)(b) Without undertakings	Telecommunications, Internet
M.2471	Accenture/Lagardere/JV	26.07.01	—	5 [2001] 570 (IP)	Clearance Art.6(1)(b) Without undertakings	Consulting for Interactive TV
M.2473	Finnforest/Moelven Industrier	18.07.01	—	5 [2001] 566 (IP)	Clearance Art.6(1)(b) Without undertakings	Wood Procurement, Modular Building
M.2478	IBM Italia/Business Solutions/JV	29.06.01	—	5 [2001] 1521 (IP)	Clearance Art.6(1)(b) Without undertakings	Information Technology
M.2479	Flextronics/Alcatel	29.06.01	—	5 [2001] 1520 (IP)	Clearance Art.6(1)(b) Without undertakings	Mobile Handsets Manufacturing
M.2481	Balli/Klockner	27.09.01	—	5 [2001] 1051 (IP)	Clearance Art.6(1)(b) Without undertakings	Steel Trading, Aluminium
M.2483	Group Canal+/RTL/GJCD/JV	13.11.01	—	4 [2002] IS13	Clearance Art.6(1)(b) Without undertakings	Trading of Sport TV Rights
M.2485	Verbund/Estag	14.12.01	—	4 [2002] IS49	Clearance Art.6(1)(b) Without undertakings	Electricity
M.2487	Bertelsmann/Arnoldo Mondadori	23.08.01	—	5 [2001] 815 (IP)	Clearance Art.6(1)(b) Without undertakings	Books
M.2488	Alcatel/Alcatel Space	06.07.01	—	5 [2001] 222 (IP)	Clearance Art.6(1)(b) Without undertakings	Satellites
M.2491	Sampo/Storebrand	27.07.01	—	—	Clearance Art.6(1)(b) Without undertakings	Banking, Insurance
M.2493	Norske Skog/Abitibi/Papco	03.07.01	—	5 [2001] 220 (IP)	Clearance Art.6(1)(b) Without undertakings	Newsprint Paper
M.2495	Haniel/Fels	21.02.02	[2003] L103/36	4 [2002] IS84	Clearance Art.8(2) without conditions and obligations Art. 9 partial referral	Mineral Products
M.2498	UPM-KYMMENE/HAINDL	21.11.01	[2002] L233/38	5 [2002] (D)	Clearance Art.8(2) without conditions and obligations	Paper Product
M.2499	Norske Skog/Parenco/Walsum	21.11.01	[2002] L233/38	—	Clearance Art.8(2) without conditions and obligations	Paper Product

MERGER No.	NAME	DATE	O.J.	C.M.L.R.	TYPE OF DECISION	PRODUCT SECTOR
M.2502	Cargill/Cerestar	18.01.02	—	4 [2002] IS76	Clearance Art.6(1)(b) Without undertakings	Starch and Sweeteners
M.2503	HBG/Ballast Nedam/Baggeren JV	03.08.01	—	5 [2001] 573 (IP)	Clearance Art.6(1)(b) Without undertakings	Dredging
M.2504	Cadbury Schweppes/Pernod Ricard	29.10.01	—	5 [2001] 1225 (IP)	Clearance Art.6(1)(b) Without undertakings	Soft Drinks
M.2505	Tyco/CR Bard	04.10.01	—	5 [2001] 1054 (IP)	Clearance Art.6(1)(b) Without undertakings	Medical Devices
M.2510	Cendant/Galileo	24.09.01	—	5 [2001] 1047 (IP)	Clearance Art.6(1)(b) Without undertakings	Gds/Car Rental
M.2513	RWE/Kärntner Energie Holding	02.08.01	—	5 [2001] 572 (IP)	Clearance Art.6(1)(b) Without undertakings	Electricity
M.2514	Mazda MotorCorporation/MCL	27.07.01	—	—	Clearance Art.6(1)(b) Without undertakings	Car Distribution
M.2517	Bristol Myers Squibb/Du Pont	09.08.01	—	5 [2001] 814 (IP)	Clearance Art.6(1)(b) Without undertakings	Pharmaceuticals
M.2522	SCA HygieneProducts/Cartoinvest	21.03.02	—	4 [2002] IS133	Clearance Art.6(1)(b) Without undertakings	Tissue Products
M.2524	HYDRO/SQM/Rotem/JV	05.12.01	—	4 [2002] IS25	Clearance Art.6(1)(b) Without undertakings	Fertilisers
M.2529	JCD/RCS/Publitransport	14.09.01	—	5 [2001] 1043 (IP)	Clearance Art.6(1)(b) Without undertakings	Outdoor Advertising
M.2530	Südzucker/Saint-Louis	20.12.01	(2003] L103/1	4 [2002] IS55	Clearance Art.8(2) with conditions and obligations	Sugar
M.2532	FIAT/ITALENENERGIA/MONTEDISON	28.08.01	—	5 [2001] 816 (IP)	Clearance Art.6(1)(b) Without undertakings	Electricity
M.2533	BP/E.ON	20.12.01	[2002] L276/31	5 [2002] (D)	Clearance Art.8(2) with conditions and obligations Art. 9 partial referral	Chemicals
M.2535	Sogefi/Filtrauto	29.10.01	—	5 [2001] 1224 (IP)	Clearance Art.6(1)(b) Without undertakings	Car Parts
M.2536	Fabricom/Sulzer	09.08.01	—	—	Clearance Art.6(1)(b) Without undertakings	Electromechanical Systems

MERGER No.	NAME	DATE	O.J.	C.M.L.R.	TYPE OF DECISION	PRODUCT SECTOR
M.2537	Philips/Marconi Medical Systems	17.10.01	—	—	Clearance Art.6(1)(b) Without undertakings	Medical Machines
M.2540	Fidis/SEI/JV	04.09.01	—	5 [2001] 819 (IP)	Clearance Art.6(1)(b) Without undertakings	Car Rental
M.2542	Schmalbach-Lubeca/Rexam	28.09.01	—	5 [2001] 1053 (IP)	Clearance Art.6(1)(b) Without undertakings	Beverage Cans
M.2544	Masterfoods/Royal Canin	15.02.02	—	4 [2002] IS96	Clearance Art.6(1)(b) with undertakings	Pet Food
M.2547	Bayer/Aventis Crop Science	17.04.02	[2004] L107/1	4 [2002] IS138	Clearance Art.8(2) with conditions and obligations	Pesticides
M.2550	Mezzo/Muzzik	06.12.01	—	—	Clearance Art.6(1)(b) Without undertakings	Thematic TV Chains
M.2552	Norske Skog/Peterson	01.10.01	—	5 [2001] 1052 (IP)	Clearance Art.6(1)(b) Without undertakings	Greaseproof Paper
M.2558	Havas/Tempus	04.09.0 1	—	5 [2001] 818 (IP)	Clearance Art.6(1)(b) Without undertakings	Media Buying, Marketing Communication Services
M.2565	PPC/Wind/JV	28.11.01	—	4 [2002] IS21	Clearance Art.6(1)(b) Without undertakings	Telecommunication, Internet
M.2567	Nordbanken/Postgirot	08.11.01	—	5 [2001] 1228 (IP)	Clearance Art.6(1)(b) with undertakings	Financial Intermediation
M.2568	Haniel/Ytong	09.04.02	[2003] L111/1	4 [2002] IS135	Clearance Art.8(2) with conditions and obligations Art.9(4) partial referral	Concrete
M.2569	Interbrew/Beck's	26.10.01	—	5 [2001] 1222 (IP)	Clearance Art.6(1)(b) Without undertakings	Beers
M.2572	Time/IPC	12.10.01	—	5 [2001] 1219 (IP)	Clearance Art.6(1)(b) Without undertakings	Magazines Publishing
M.2573	A&C/Grossfarma	30.08.01	—	5 [2001] 817 (IP)	Clearance Art.6(1)(b) Without undertakings	Distribution of Pharmaceuticals
M.2574	Pirelli/Edizione/Olivetti/Telecom Italia	20.09.01	—	5 [2001] 1045 (IP)	Clearance Art.6(1)(b) With undertakings	Telecommunications
M.2576	Telefonica/Ericsson/JV	28.09.01	—	5 [2001] 1052 (IP)	Clearance Art.6(1)(b) Without undertakings	Mobile Telephony

MERGER No.	NAME	DATE	O.J.	C.M.L.R.	TYPE OF DECISION	PRODUCT SECTOR
M.2577	GE Capital/Heller Financial	23.10.01	—	5 [2001] 1220 (IP)	Clearance Art.6(1)(b) Without undertakings	Factoring, Equipment Finance, Private Equity Investment
M.2578	Banco Santander Central Hispanico/ AKB	12.11.01	—	4 [2002] IS115[5]	Clearance Art.6(1)(b) Without undertakings	Bank
M.2584	Tyco/Sensormatic	01.10.01	—	5 [2001] 1051 (IP)	Clearance Art.6(1)(b) Without undertakings	Electronic Security Systems
M.2586	CE/Yorkshire Electric	17.09.01	—	5 [2001] 1044 (IP)	Clearance Art.6(1)(b) Without undertakings	Electricity
M.2588	Rheinbraun Brennstoff/SSM COAL	17.09.01	—	5 [2001] 1045 (IP)	Clearance Art.6(1)(b) Without undertakings	Trading of Fuel Grade Petroleum Coke
M.2596	RMC/UMA JV	12.03.03	—	—	Clearance Art.6(1)(b) Without undertakings	Aggregates
M.2597	Vopak/Van der Sluijs	25.02.02	—	4 [2002] IS87	Clearance Art.6(1)(b) Without undertakings	Inland Tanker Shipping
M.2598	TDC/CMG/MIGWAYJV	04.10.01	—	5 [2001] 1053 (IP)	Clearance Art.6(1)(b) Without undertakings	Telecommunication Sms
M.2601	WPP/TEMPUS	22.10.01	—	5 [2001] 1219 (IP)	Clearance Art.6(1)(b) Without undertakings	Media Buying
M.2602	Gerling/NCM	11.12.01	—	4 [2002] IS48	Clearance Art.6(1)(b) with undertakings	Insurance, Acquisition Raising Rival Costs
M.2603	ZF Friedrichshafen/Mannesmann Sachs	19.11.01	—	4 [2002] IS15	Clearance Art.6(1)(b) Without undertakings	Car Parts
M.2604	ICA AHOLD/Dansk Supermarked	13.11.01	—	4 [2002] IS12	Clearance Art.6(1)(b) Without undertakings	Daily Consumer Goods
M.2608	INA/FAG	18.10.01	—	5 [2001] 1221 (IP)	Clearance Art.6(1)(b) Without undertakings	Bearings
M.2609	HP/COMPAQ	31.01.02	—	4 [2002] IS74	Clearance Art.6(1)(b) Without undertakings	Computing Hardware, Software, Printers
M.2611	Schroder Ventures/Goldman Sachs/ Cognis	22.10.01	—	5 [2001] 1221 (IP)	Clearance Art.6(1)(b) Without undertakings	Leather Chemicals

[5] Press release references relate to unique reference number beginning with "IS".

MERGER No.	NAME	DATE	O.J.	C.M.L.R.	TYPE OF DECISION	PRODUCT SECTOR
M.2620	Enel/Viesgo	20.11.01	—	4 [2002] IS16	Clearance Art.6(1)(b) Without undertakings	Electricity
M.2621	SEB/Moulinex	08.01.02	—	4 [2002] IS57	Clearance Art.6(1)(b) with undertakings Art. 9 partial referral	Electrical Household Appliances
	SEB/Moulinex	11.11.03	[2005] L138/18	4 [2004] IS7	Art.8(2) with conditions and obligations	
M.2627	Otto Versand/Sabre/Travelocity JV	19.12.01	—	4 [2002] IS52	Clearance Art.6(1)(b) Without undertakings	Internet Travel Agency, GDS
M.2628	Koch/Kosa	12.11.01	—	4 [2002] IS9	Clearance Art.6(1)(b) Without undertakings	Polyesters
M.2629	Flextronics/Xerox	12.11.01	—	4 [2002] IS10	Clearance Art.6(1)(b) Without undertakings	Electronic Manufacturing Services
M.2632	Deutsche Bahn/ECT International/ United Depots/JV	11.02.02	—	4 [2002] IS83	Clearance Art.6(1)(b) Without undertakings	Container Transport
M.2635	DMVII	28.11.01	—	4 [2002] IS22	Clearance Art.6(1)(b) Without undertakings	Steel Tubes
M.2638	3i/Consors/100 World	10.12.01	—	—	Clearance Art.6(1)(A)	Computers
M.2639	Compass/Restorama/Rail Gourmet/ Gourmet Nova	26.02.02	—	4 [2002] IS99	Clearance Art.6(1)(b) Without undertakings Art. 9 partial referral	Food Service
M.2640	Nestlé/Schöller	25.02.02	—	4 [2002] IS86	Clearance Art.6(1)(b) Without undertakings	Ice-cream
M.2642	BT/Concert	17.12.01	—	—	Clearance Art.6(1)(b) Without undertakings	Telecommunication
M.2643	Blackstone/CDPQ/DETEKS BW	23.11.01	—	4 [2002] IS20	Clearance Art.6(1)(b) Without undertakings	Television, Telecommunication, Internet
M.2645	Saab/WM-DATA AB/SAAB CARAN JV	06.12.01	—	—	Clearance Art.6(1)(b) Without undertakings	Consulting Services
M.2648	KPNQWEST/EBONE/GTS	16.01.02	—	4 [2002] IS72	Clearance Art.6(1)(b) Without undertakings	Carrier's Carrier Services — Telecommunications — Internet
M.2650	Haniel/Cementbouw/JV (CVK)	26.06.02	[2003] L282/1	—	Art. 8(2) with conditions and obligations	Wall Building Materials

MERGER No.	NAME	DATE	O.J.	C.M.L.R.	TYPE OF DECISION	PRODUCT SECTOR
M.2652	Blackstone/CDPQ/DETEKS NRW	23.11.01	—	4 [2002] IS20	Clearance Art.6(1)(b) Without undertakings	Television, Telecommunication, Internet
M.2654	Flextronics Network Services/Telaris Södra	17.12.01	—	4 [2002] IS50	Clearance Art.6(1)(b) Without undertakings	Design of Telecom Network, PABX
M.2657	Robert Bosch/Buderus	10.07.03	—	5 [2003] IS70	Clearance Art.6(1)b without undertakings	Heating Appliances
M.2659	Fortum/Birka Energi	10.01.02	—	4 [2002] IS71	Clearance Art.6(1)(b) Without undertakings	Electricity
M.2662	Danish Crown/Steff-Houlberg	14.02.02	—	4 [2002] IS98	Clearance Art.6(1)(b) Without undertakings	Meat Food
M.2665	Johnson Professional Holdings/ Diverseylever	04.03.02	—	4 [2002] IS89	Clearance Art.6(1)(b) Without undertakings	Cleaning Products
M.2669	VTG/Warburg/Brambles European Rail Division	19.03.02	—	4 [2002] IS131	Clearance Art.6(1)(b) Without undertakings	Rail Logistics Business
M.2672	SAS/Spanair	05.03.02	—	4 [2002] IS93	Clearance Art.6(1)(b) Without undertakings	Air Transport
M.2675	EDF/TXU Europe/West Burton Power Station	20.12.01	—	4 [2002] IS53	Clearance Art.6(1)(b) Without undertakings	Electricity
M.2676	Sampo/Varma Sampo/IF Holding	18.12.01	—	4 [2002] IS54	Clearance Art.6(1)(b) Without undertakings	Insurance
M.2679	EDF/TXU Europe/24 Seven	20.12.01	—	4 [2002] IS53	Clearance Art.6(1)(b) Without undertakings	Electricity
M.2681	Conoco/Philips Petroleum	06.03.02	—	4 [2002] IS94	Clearance Art.6(1)(b) Without undertakings	Oil and Gas
M.2683	Aker Maritime/Kvaerner (II)	23.01.02	—	4 [2002] IS77	Clearance Art.6(1)(b) Without undertakings Art. 9 partial referral	Oil and Gas
M.2684	EnBW/EDP/Cajastur/Hidrocantabrico	19.03.02	—	4 [2002] IS130	Clearance Art.6(1)(b) with undertakings	Electricity
M.2688	ODS/IHC Holland/Metalix JV	20.03.02	—	4 [2002] IS132	Clearance Art.6(1)(b) Without undertakings	Steel Products
M.2690	Solvay/Montedison-Ausimont	09.04.02	—	4 [2002] IS136	Clearance Art.6(1)(b) with undertakings	Chemicals

MERGER No.	NAME	DATE	O.J.	C.M.L.R.	TYPE OF DECISION	PRODUCT SECTOR
M.2691	TUI/Nouveltes Frontières	26.08.02	—	5 [2002] IS116	Clearance Art.6(1)(b) Without undertakings	Package Holidays
M.2693	ADM/ACTI	11.02.02	—	4 [2002] IS82	Clearance Art.6(1)(b) Without undertakings	Oil Trading
M.2694	Metronet/Infraco	21.06.02	—	5 [2002] IS63	Clearance Art.6(1)(b) Without undertakings	Metro Vehicles
M.2696	TMD/MENETA/MAST	25.01.02	—	4 [2002] IS73	Clearance Art.6(1)(b) Without undertakings	Car Parts
M.2698	Promatech/Sulzer Textil	24.07.02	[2004] L79/27	5 [2002] IS93	Art. 8(2) with conditions and obligations	Textile Wearings
M.2701	Vattenfall/Bewag	04.02.02	—	4 [2002] IS75	Clearance Art.6(1)(b) Without undertakings	Electricity
M.2702	Norsk Hydro/VAW	04.03.02	—	4 [2002] IS91	Clearance Art.6(1)(b) Without undertakings	Aluminium
M.2703	Merloni/GE/GDA JV	04.03.02	—	4 [2002] IS88	Clearance Art.6(1)(b) Without undertakings	Electric Household Appliances
M.2704	Elyo/Cofathec/Climespace	05.03.02	—	4 [2002] IS92	Clearance Art.6(1)(b) Without undertakings	Cooling and Ventilation Equipment
M.2705	Enersys/Invensys (ESB)	04.03.02	—	4 [2002] IS90	Clearance Art.6(1)(b) Without undertakings	Energy Storage Products
M.2706	Carnival Corporation/P&O Princess	24.07.02	[2003] L248/1	5 [2002] IS94	Art. 8(2) Without Conditions	Cruises
M.2707	Wienerberger/Hanson	18.04.02	—	4 [2002] IS142	Clearance Art.6(1)(b) Without undertakings	Bricks
M.2712	Electrabel/Total Finaelf/Photovoltech	18.04.02	—	—	—	—
M.2722	Autologic/TNT/Wallenius/Wilhemsen/ CAT JV	25.02.02	—	4 [2002] IS85	Clearance Art.6(1)(b) Without undertakings	Cargo Handling, Logistic Services
M.2723	RTL/Prosiebensat.I/VG Media	21.05.02	—	5 [2002] IS25	Clearance Art.6(1)(b) Without undertakings	TV and Video Activities
M.2724	Royal Bank Private Equity/CINVEN/ Ambion Brick	13.03.02	—	4 [2002] IS129	Clearance Art.6(1)(b) Without undertakings	Bricks
M.2726	KPN/E-Plus	07.03.02	—	4 [2002] IS95	Clearance Art.6(1)(b) Without undertakings	Telecommunications
M.2730	Connex/DNVBVG/JV	24.04.02	—	4 [2002] IS12	Art. 9(4) total referral	Buses

MERGER No.	NAME	DATE	O.J.	C.M.L.R.	TYPE OF DECISION	PRODUCT SECTOR
M.2735	Totalfinaelf Deutschland/MMH/TSG/ EMB	17.04.02	—	4 [2002] IS141	Clearance Art.6(1)(b) Without undertakings	Mineral Products
M.2737	Royal Bank Private Equity/CINVEN/ Chelwood Group	13.03.02	—	4 [2002] IS129	Clearance Art.6(1)(b) Without undertakings	Bricks
M.2738	Gees/Unison	17.04.02	—	4 [2002] IS140	Clearance Art.6(1)(b) Without undertakings	Aircraft Components
M.2740	Scottish & Newcastle/Hartwall	04.04.02	—	4 [2002] IS134	Clearance Art.6(1)(b) Without undertakings	Beers
M.2744	RWE Gas/Lattice International/JV	07.08.02	—	5 [2002] IS112	Clearance Art.6(1)(b) Without undertakings	Gas Logistic Services
M.2745	Shell/Enterprise Oil	07.05.02	—	4 [2002] IS149	Clearance Art.6(1)(b) Without undertakings	Oil and Gas
M.2747	Ondeo – Thames Water/Water Portal	26.06.02	—	5 [2002] IS67	Clearance Art.6(1)(b) Without undertakings	Water-related Products and Services
M.2751	Dragabos/HUG	09.04.02	—	4 [2002] IS137	Clearance Art.6(1)(b) Without undertakings	Construction and Dredging Services
M.2760	Nehlsen/Rethmann/SWB/ Bremerhavener Entsorgungsgesellschaft	30.05.02	—	5 [2002] IS31	Art. 9(4) Total Referral	Waste Disposal
M.2761	BP/Veba Oel	01.07.02	—	5 [2002] IS71	Clearance Art.6(1)(b) with undertakings	Petroleum Products Petrochemicals
M.2763	Toray/Murata/Teijin	06.12.02	—	4 [2003] IS38	Clearance Art.6(1)(b) Without undertakings	Machinery
M.2766	Vivendi Universal/Hachette/ Multithematiques	03.05.02	—	4 [2002] IS147	Clearance Art.6(1)(b) Without undertakings	TV Chains
M.2768	Generali/Banca Intesa/JV	15.12.03	—	4 [2004] IS25	Clearance Art.6(1)b without undertakings	Insurance
M.2772	HDW/Ferrostaal/Hellenic Shipyard	25.04.02	—	4 [2002] IS144	Clearance Art.6(1)(b) Without undertakings	Military Vessels
M.2773	Nestlé/L'Oreal/Inneov	26.07.02	—	5 [2002] IS97	Clearance Art.6(1)(b) Without undertakings	Food Supplement For Cosmetic Purposes
M.2777	Cinven Limited/Angel Street Holdings	08.05.02	—	5 [2002] IS23	Clearance Art.6(1)(b) Without undertakings	"Managed" Pubs
M.2779	Imperial Tobacco/Reemtsma Cigarettenfabriken	08.05.02	—	5 [2002] IS22	Clearance Art.6(1)(b) with undertakings	Cigarettes

MERGER No.	NAME	DATE	O.J.	C.M.L.R.	TYPE OF DECISION	PRODUCT SECTOR
M.2780	GE Wind Turbines/Enron	30.04.02	—	4 [2002] IS145	Clearance Art.6(1)(b) Without undertakings	Electricity
M.2781	Northrop Grumman/TRW	16.10.02	—	5 [2002] IS146	Clearance Art.6(1)(b) Without undertakings	Military Products
M.2785	Publicis/BCom3	18.06.02	—	5 [2002] IS60	Clearance Art.6(1)(b) Without undertakings	Media Buying Marketing Services
M.2791	Gaz de France/Ruhrgas/Slovensky	06.06.02	—	5 [2002] IS30	Clearance Art.6(1)(b) Without undertakings	Gas
M.2792	Edison/Edipower/Eurogen	03.05.02	—	4 [2002] IS148	Clearance Art.6(1)(b) Without undertakings	Electricity
M.2793	DMT/EPC/Saar Montan	01.07.02	—	5 [2002] IS72	Clearance Art.6(1)(b) Without undertakings	Surface drillings Underground Mining Services Explosives
M.2794	Amadeus/GGL/JV	21.05.02	—	5 [2002] IS26	Clearance Art.6(1)(b) Without undertakings	Travel Agency, Gds
M.2796	Siemens/Aerolas/JV	11.06.02	—	5 [2002] IS57	Clearance Art.6(1)(b) Without undertakings	Airbearings
M.2801	RWE/Innogy	17.05.02	—	5 [2002] IS24	Clearance Art.6(1)(b) Without undertakings	Electricity
M.2803	Telia/Sonera	10.07.02	—	5 [2002] IS100	Clearance Art.6(1)(b) with undertakings	Telephony Services Internet
M.2804	Vendex KBB/Brico Belgium	18.06.02	—	5 [2002] IS62	Clearance Art.6(1)(b) Without undertakings	DIY Products
M.2805	Natexis Banques Populaires/Coface	01.07.02	—	5 [2002] IS73	Clearance Art.6(1)(b) Without undertakings	Insurance – Financing
M.2806	Sabic/DSM Petrochemicals	18.06.02	—	5 [2002] IS6l	Clearance Art.6(1)(b) Without undertakings	Petrochemicals Chemicals
M.2810	Deloitte &Touche/Andersen (UK)	01.07.02	—	5 [2002] IS69	Clearance Art.6(1)(b) Without undertakings	Audit
M.2813	Carlton + Thomson/Circuit A,RMBI, RMBC	21.06.02	—	5 [2002] IS65	Clearance Art.6(1)(b) Without undertakings	Cinema Screen Advertising Services
M.2815	Sanmina – SCI/Hewlett Packard	28.05.02	—	5 [2002] IS27	Clearance Art.6(1)(b) Without undertakings	Electronic Manufacturing Services, Computers
M.2816	Ernst & Young France/Andersen France	05.09.02	—	5 [2002] IS124	Clearance Art.6(1)(b) Without undertakings	Audit, Tax and Other Services

MERGER No.	NAME	DATE	O.J.	C.M.L.R.	TYPE OF DECISION	PRODUCT SECTOR
M.2817	Barilla/BPL/Kamps	25.06.02	—	5 [2002] IS64	Clearance Art.6(1)(b) with undertakings	Bread, Bread Substitutes
M.2819	Canal de Isabel II/Hidrocantabrico/JV	14.06.02	—	5 [2002] IS58	Clearance Art.6(1)(b) Without undertakings	Electricity
M.2820	Stmicroelectronics/Alcatel Microelectronics	24.06.02	—	5 [2002] IS66	Clearance Art.6(1)(b) Without undertakings	Semiconductor Devices
M.2821	Hitachi/IBM Harddisk Business	02.08.02	—	5 [2002] IS98	Clearance Art.6(1)(b) Without undertakings	Hard Disk Drives
M.2822	ENBW/ENI/GVS	17.12.02	[2003] L248/51	4 [2003] IS43	Clearance Art.8(2) with conditions and obligations	Gas
M.2823	Bank One Corporation/Howaldtswerke – Deutsche Werft AG (HDW)	30.05.02	—	5 [2002] IS28	Clearance Art.6(1)(b) Without undertakings	Submarine, Vessels
M.2824	Ernst & Young/Andersen Germany	27.08.02	—	5 [2002] IS117	Clearance Art.6(1)(b) Without undertakings	Audit
M.2825	Fortis AG SA/Bernheim – Comofi SA	09.07.02	—	5 [2002] IS76	Clearance Art.6(1)(b) Without undertakings	Real Estate Car Parking
M.2826	Alsen/E.ON/JV	14.08.02	—	5 [2002] IS113	Clearance Art.6(1)(b) Without undertakings	Mineral Construction Materials
M.2830	Lufthansa Cargo/Air France Finance/ British Airways/Global Freight Exchange/JV	25.10.02	—	5 [2002] IS158	Clearance Art.6(1)(b) Without undertakings	Trading Platform Services
M.2831	DSV/TNT Logistics/DSV Logistics	27.06.02	—	5 [2002] IS68	Clearance Art.6(1)(b) Without undertakings	Contract Logistics
M.2832	General Motors/Daewoo Motors	22.07.02	—	5 [2002] IS92	Clearance Art.6(1)(b) Without undertakings	Cars
M.2834	Alchemy/Compair	17.0602	—	5 [2002] IS59	Clearance Art.6(1)(b) Without undertakings	Air and Gas Compressors
M.2838	P&O Stena Line (Holding) Limited	07.08.02	—	5 [2002] IS111	Clearance Art.6(1)(b) Without undertakings	Ferry Transport Services
M.2840	Danapak/Teich/JV	30.08.02	—	5 [2002] IS119	Clearance Art.6(1)(b) Without undertakings	Flexible Packaging
M.2842	Saipem/Bouygues Offshore	02.07.02	—	5 [2002] IS74	Clearance Art.6(1)(b) Without undertakings	Offshore and Onshore Construction Subsea Pipelaying

Table 5

MERGER No.	NAME	DATE	O.J.	C.M.L.R.	TYPE OF DECISION	PRODUCT SECTOR
M.2843	Amcor/Schmalbach - Lubeca	28.06.02	—	5 [2002] IS70	Clearance Art.6(1)(b) Without undertakings	Packaging
M.2844	Linde/Komatsu/Komatsu Forklift	19.12.02	—	4 [2003] IS50	Clearance Art.6(1)(b) Without undertakings	Material Handling Equipment
M.2845	Sogecable/Canalsatélite Digital/Via Digital	14.08.02	—	—	Art. 9(4) total referral	Pay-TV TV Rights Telecommunication
M.2851	Intracom/Siemens/STI	10.02.03	—	4 [2003] IS81	Clearance Art.6(1)(b) Without undertakings	Telecom Equipment
M.2854	RAG/Degussa	18.11.02	—	4 [2003] IS27	Clearance Art.6(1)(b) with undertakings	Chemicals
M.2857	ECS/IEH	23.12.02	—	—	Art 9(4) Total Referral	Electricity
M.2859	Deutsche Bahn Cargo/Contship Italia/ JV	15.07.02	—	5 [2002] IS9l	Clearance Art.6(1)(b) Without undertakings	Intermodal Transport Services
M.2861	Siemens/Drägerwerk/JV	30.04.03	[2003] L291/1	5 [2004] 16	Art. 8(2) with conditions and obligations	Medical Devices
M.2863	Morgan Stanley/Olivetti/Telecom Italia/ Tiglio	30.08.02	—	5 [2002] IS120	Clearance Art.6(1)(b) Without undertakings	Real Estate
M.2867	UPM-Kymmene Corporation/Morgan Adhesives Company	16.10.02	—	5 [2002] IS155	Clearance Art.6(1)(b) Without undertakings	Self-adhesive Labelstock
M.2868	Linde/Sonatrach/JV	19.12.02	—	4 [2003] IS48	Clearance Art.6(1)(b) Without undertakings	Helium
M.2871	Air Liquide/BOC/Japan Air Gases	10.10.02	—	5 [2002] IS148	Clearance Art.6(1)(b) Without undertakings	Industrial Gases
M.2874	Starcore LLC	27.09.02	—	—	Clearance Art.6(1)(b) Without undertakings	Microcomponents Licensing
M.2876	Newscorp/Telepiu	02.04.03	[2004] L110/73	5 [2004] 30	Art.8(2) with conditions and obligations	Pay-TV, Acquisition of TV Rights
M.2877	Karlsberg/Brau Holding International/ Karlsberg International	27.08.02	—	5 [2002] IS118	Clearance Art.6(1)(b) Without undertakings	Brewing and Beer
M.2879	3* Wallenius Lines AB/Wilhelmsen ASA/Hyundai Merchant Marine	29.11.02	—	4 [2003] IS28	Clearance Art.6(1)(b) with undertakings	Deep Sea Transportation of Vehicles
M.2880	Legal & General Ventures/IWP (UK) Holdings	03.09.02	—	5 [2002] IS123	Clearance Art.6(1)(b) Without undertakings	Charcoal, Ignition Products Fire Logs

MERGER No.	NAME	DATE	O.J.	C.M.L.R.	TYPE OF DECISION	PRODUCT SECTOR
M.2881	Koninklijke BAM NBM/HBG	03.09.02	—	5 [2002] IS126	Clearance Art.6(1)(b) Without undertakings Art. 9(4) partial referral	Construction
M.2882	Terex/Demag	16.08.02	—	5 [2002] IS114	Clearance Art.6(1)(b) Without undertakings	Cranes
M.2883	Bertelsmann/Zomba	02.09.02	—	5 [2002] IS121	Clearance Art.6(1)(b) Without undertakings	Music
M.2886	Bunge/Cereol	20.09.02	—	5 [2002] IS135	Clearance Art.6(1)(b) Without undertakings	Oilseed Meal
M.2890	EDF/Seeboard	25.07.02	—	—	Clearance Art.6(1)(b) Without undertakings	Electricity, Gas
M.2891	CD & R Fund VI Limited/Brake Bros PLC	25.07.02	—	5 [2002] IS95	Clearance Art.6(1)(b) Without undertakings	Wholesale Food Distribution
M.2892	Goodrich/TRW Aeronautical Systems Group	23.08.02	—	5 [2002] IS115	Clearance Art.6(1)(b) Without undertakings	Aerospace Components
M.2897	Sita Sverige AB/Sydkraft Ecoplus	14.10.02	—	5 [2002] IS153	Clearance Art.6(1)(b) Without undertakings	Waste Management
M.2898	Leroy Merlin/Brico	13.12.02	—	—	Clearance Art.6(1)(b) Without undertakings Art. 9(4) partial referral	DIY
M.2901	Magna/Donnelly	16.09.02	—	5 [2002] IS132	Clearance Art.6(1)(b) Without undertakings	Car Parts
M.2903	Daimler Chrysler/Deutsche Telekom/JV	30.04.03	[2003] L300/62	5 [2004] 3	Art. 8(2) with conditions and obligations	Collection of Road Tolls Telematics Systems
M.2905	Deutsche Bahn/Stinnes	17.09.02	—	5 [2002] IS133	Clearance Art.6(1)(b) Without undertakings	Logistics
M.2907	Bank Austria/RZB/Erste Bank/JV	20.09.02	—	5 [2002] IS134	Clearance Art.6(1)(b) Without undertakings	Financial Services
M.2908	Deutsche Post/DHL (II)	21.10.02	—	5 [2002] IS157	Clearance Art.6(1)(b) Without undertakings	Mail, Parcel Freight Delivery Services INTL Services
M.2917	Wendel – KKR/Legrand	14.10.02	—	5 [2002] IS152	Clearance Art.6(1)(b) Without undertakings	Lighting
M.2922	Pfizer/Pharmacia	27.02.03	—	4 [2003] IS105	Clearance Art.6(1)(b) with undertakings	Pharmaceuticals

Table 5

MERGER No.	NAME	DATE	O.J.	C.M.L.R.	TYPE OF DECISION	PRODUCT SECTOR
M.2924	EADS/Astrium	20.12.02	—	4 [2003] IS56	Clearance Art.6(1)(b) Without undertakings	Satellites
M.2925	Charterhouse/CDC/Télédiffusion de France SA	15.11.02	—	4 [2003] IS25	Clearance Art.6(1)(b) Without undertakings	Site Research and Hosting For Mobile Telephony
M.2926	EQT/H&R/Dragoco	16.09.02	—	5 [2002] IS131	Clearance Art.6(1)(b) Without undertakings	Flavour & Fragrance Cosmetic Ingredients
M.2928	Alcoa/Fairchild	14.10.02	—	5 [2002] IS150	Clearance Art.6(1)(b) Without undertakings	Aluminium
M.2930	KKR/Demag Holding/Siemens Business	09.09.02	—	5 [2002] IS129	Clearance Art.6(1)(b) Without undertakings	Data Network Management
M.2931	Finmeccanica/Marconi Mobile Holdings	31.10.02	—	4 [2003] IS23	Clearance Art.6(1)(b) Without undertakings	Military Communication Systems
M.2938	SNPE/MBDA/JV	30.10.02	—	—	Clearance Art.6(1)(b) Without undertakings	Military Products
M.2939	JCI/Bosch/VB Autobatterien JV	18.10.02	—	5 [2002] IS156	Clearance Art.6(1)(b) Without undertakings	Oem/Oes
M.2940	TPG Advisors III/Goldman Sachs/Bain Capital Investors/Burger King	11.10.02	—	5 [2002] IS149	Clearance Art.6(1)(b) Without undertakings	Quick Service Restaurants
M.2941	CNP/Taittinger	16.10.02	—	5 [2002] IS154	Clearance Art.6(1)(b) Without undertakings	Wines
M.2946	IBM/PWC Consulting	23.09.02	—	5 [2002] IS136	Clearance Art.6(1)(b) Without undertakings	IT Services
M.2947	Verbund/Energie Allianz	11.06.03	[2004] L92/91	—	Art. 8(2) with conditions and obligations	Electricity
M.2948	CVC/Kwik-Fit	02.10.02	—	5 [2002] IS138	Clearance Art.6(1)(b) Without undertakings	Car Repair
M.2951	A.S. Watson/Kruidvat	27.09.02	—	5 [2002] IS137	Clearance Art.6(1)(b) Without undertakings	Health and Beauty Products
M.2956	CVC/Pai Europe/Provimi	28.10.02	—	4 [2003] IS22	Clearance Art.6(1)(b) Without undertakings	Animal Feed Vitamins
M.2958	Wind/BLU	12.09.02	—	5 [2002] IS130	Clearance Art.6(1)(b) Without undertakings	Mobile Telephony

MERGER No.	NAME	DATE	O.J.	C.M.L.R.	TYPE OF DECISION	PRODUCT SECTOR
M.2960	Keolis/AB Storstockholms Lokaltrafik/ Busslink	04.12.02	—	4 [2003] IS37	Clearance Art.6(1)(b) Without undertakings	Railways and Bus Services
M.2965	Staples/Guilbert	14.10.02	—	5 [2002] IS151	Clearance Art.6(1)(b) Without undertakings	Office Supplies
M.2966	ENBW/Laufenburg	19.12.02	—	4 [2003] IS52	Clearance Art.6(1)(b) Without undertakings	Electricity
M.2968	Jabil/Philips (Contract Manufacturing Services) INTL	21.10.02	—	5 [2002] IS147	Clearance Art.6(1)(b) Without undertakings	Oem/Ems
M.2970	GE/ABB Structured Finance	05.11.02	—	4 [2003] IS24	Clearance Art.6(1)(b) Without undertakings	Financial Services
M.2972	DSM/Roche Vitamins	23.07.03	[2004] L82/73	—	Clearance Art.8.2 with conditions and obligations	Additives For Humans and Animals
M.2977	Compass/Onama SPA	15.11.02	—	4 [2003] IS26	Clearance Art.6(1)(b) Without undertakings	Food Service
M.2978	Lagardère/Natexis/VUP	07.01.04	[2004] L125/54	—	Art 8(2) with conditions and obligations Art.9 partial referral	Books Distribution
M.2980	Cargill/AOP	19.12.02	—	4 [2003] IS49	Clearance Art.6(1)(b) Without undertakings	Seed Oils
M.2982	Lazard/Intesabci/JV	04.02.03	—	4 [2003] IS78	Clearance Art.6(1)(b) Without undertakings	Investment Banking Services
M.2992	Brenntag/Biesterfeld/JV	20.12.02	—	4 [2003] IS54	Clearance Art.6(1)(b) Without undertakings	Commodity Chemicals
M.2993	Carlyle Group/Qinetiq	16.01.03	—	4 [2003] IS70	Clearance Art.6(1)(b) Without undertakings	Defense-related Consultancy
M.2996	RTL/CNN/Time Warner/N-TV	05.11.02	—	—	Clearance Art.6(1)(b) Without undertakings	Free-access TV
M.2997	Accor/Ebertz/Dorint	23.12.02	—	4 [2003] IS53	Clearance Art.6(1)(b) Without undertakings	Hotels
M.3001	Celanese/Clariant Emulsion Business	16.12.02	—	4 [2003] IS40	Clearance Art.6(1)(b) Without undertakings	Chemicals
M.3003	Electrabel/Energia Italiana/Interpower	23.12.02	—	4 [2003] IS61	Art. 6(1)A	Electricity
M.3004	Bravida/Semco/Prenad/ Totalinstallatören/Backlunds	13.12.02	—	4 [2003] IS41	Clearance Art.6(1)(b) Without undertakings	Electrical & Sanitary Installations

Table 5

MERGER No.	NAME	DATE	O.J.	C.M.L.R.	TYPE OF DECISION	PRODUCT SECTOR
M.3007	E.ON/TXU Europe Group	18.12.02	—	4 [2003] IS45	Clearance Art.6(1)(b) Without undertakings	Electricity, Gas
M.3011	Timken/Torrington	23.01.03	—	4 [2003] IS72	Clearance Art.6(1)(b) Without undertakings	Bearings
M.3013	Carlyle Group/EDSCHA	16.12.02	—	4 [2003] IS42	Clearance Art.6(1)(b) Without undertakings	Car Parts
M.3014	Logica/CMG	09.12.02	—	4 [2003] IS39	Clearance Art.6(1)(b) Without undertakings	IT Services
M.3024	Bain Capital/Rhodia	19.12.02	—	4 [2003] IS47	Clearance Art.6(1)(b) Without undertakings	Chemical Products
M.3025	Bain Capital/Dor Chemical/Trespaphan	17.12.02	—	4 [2003] IS44	Clearance Art.6(1)(b) Without undertakings	Packaging
M.3027	State Street Corporation/Deutsche Bank Global Securities	16.01.03	—	4 [2003] IS71	Clearance Art.6(1)(b) Without undertakings	Financial Intermediation
M.3029	Société Générale/AIHL Europe	10.02.03	—	4 [2003] IS80	Clearance Art.6(1)(b) without undertakings	Fleet Leasing
M.3030	Eaton/Delta	23.01.03	—	4 [2003] IS73	Clearance Art.6(1)(b) Without undertakings	Electrical Machinery
M.3032	Interbrew/Brauergilde	19.12.02	—	4 [2003] IS46	Clearance Art.6(1)(b) Without undertakings	Beer
M.3035	Berkshire Hathaway Converium/Gaum/ JV	28.02.03	—	4 [2003] IS104	Clearance Art.6(1)(b) Without undertakings	Insurance
M.3039	Soprol/Cereol/Lesieur	30.01.03	—	4 [2003] IS76	Clearance Art.6(1)(b) Without undertakings	Oils and Fats
M.3042	Sony/Philips/Intertrust	20.12.02	—	4 [2003] IS55	Clearance Art.6(1)(b) Without undertakings	Digital Right Management
M.3044	ADM/PURA	03.04.03	—	—	Clearance Art.6(1)(b) Without undertakings	Oils and Fats
M.3045	Masco/Hansgrohe	19.12.02	—	4 [2003] IS51	Clearance Art.6(1)(b) Without undertakings	Sanitary Saps and Products
M.3048	Suomen Rehu/Kemira Agro Oy/ Hankkija-Maatalous Oy/Movere Oy	30.01.03	—	4 [2003] IS75	Clearance Art.6(1)(b) Without undertakings	Transport Logistics
M.3049	Alcan/FlexPac	24.02.03	—	4 [2003] IS101	Clearance Art.6(1)(b) Without undertakings	Packaging

MERGER No.	NAME	DATE	O.J.	C.M.L.R.	TYPE OF DECISION	PRODUCT SECTOR
M.3052	ENI/Fortum Gas	23.01.03	—	4 [2003] IS74	Clearance Art.6(1)(b) Without undertakings	Oil and Gas
M.3056	Celanese/Degussa/European Oxo Chemicals	11.06.03	[2004] L38/47	—	Art. 8(2) without conditions	Chemical Products
M.3057	CVC/REE/Iberdrola	07.01.03	—	4 [2003] IS68	Clearance Art.6(1)(b) Without undertakings	Electricity
M.3060	UCB/Solutia	31.01.03	—	4 [2003] IS77	Clearance Art.6(1)(b) Without undertakings	Coating Resins
M.3062	IBM/Rational	20.02.03	—	4 [2003] IS100	Clearance Art.6(1)(b) with undertakings	Software
M.3063	De Agostini/Holding di Partecipazioni/ RCS Diffusione JV	12.05.03	—	4 [2003] IS141	Clearance Art.6(1)(b) Without undertakings	Distribution To Kiosks
M.3064	Ahlström Capital/Capman/Nordkalk	10.02.03	—	4 [2003] IS79	Clearance Art.6(1)(b) Without undertakings	Limestone-based Products, Kaolin, Glass Fibre Products
M.3067	Intesa/Capitalia/IMI Investimenti/ Unicredito/Fidis Retail	25.04.03	—	—	Clearance Art.6(1)(b) Without undertakings	Consumer Credit
M.3068	Ascott Group/Goldman Sachs/Oriville	13.02.03	—	4 [2003] IS98	Clearance Art.6(1)(b) Without undertakings	Hotels
M.3071	Carnival Corporation/P&O Princess (II)	10.02.03	—	—	Clearance Art.6(1)(b) Without undertakings	Cruises
M.3075	ECS/Intercommunale IVEKA	13.02.03	—	—	Art. (9) Total Referral	Electricity
M.3076	ECS/Intercommunale IGAO	13.02.03	—	—	Art. (9) Total Referral	Electricity
M.3077	ECS/Intercommunale Intergem	13.02.03	—	—	Art. (9) Total Referral	Electricity
M.3078	ECS/Intercommunale Gasel West	13.02.03	—	—	Art. (9) Total Referral	Electricity
M.3079	ECS/Intercommunale IMEWO	13.02.03	—	—	Art. (9) Total Referral	Electricity
M.3080	ECS/Intercommunale Iverlek	13.02.03	—	—	Art. (9) Total Referral	Electricity
M.3081	Michelin/Viborg	07.03.03	—	4 [2003] IS99	Clearance Art.6(1)(b) Without undertakings	Tyres
M.3082	Pon/Nimbus/Geveke	24.02.03	—	4 [2003] IS102	Clearance Art.6(1)(b) Without undertakings	Industrial Equipment
M.3083	GE/Instrumentarium	02.09.03	[2004] L109/1	—	Art. 8(2) with conditions and obligations	Medical Equipment

Table 5

MERGER No.	NAME	DATE	O.J.	C.M.L.R.	TYPE OF DECISION	PRODUCT SECTOR
M.3084	Siemens/Sequa/JV	28.02.03	—	—	Clearance Art.6(1)(b) Without undertakings	Power Generation Services
M.3086	Gaz de France/Preussag Energie	25.04.03	—	4 [2003] IS135	Clearance Art.6(1)(b) Without undertakings	Crude Oil and Gas
M.3090	Volkswagen/Offset/Crescent/Leaseplan JV	29.06.04	—	5 [2004] IS29	Clearance Art.6(1)b without undertakings	Car rental, full fleet leasing
M.3091	Konica/Minolta	11.07.03	—	5 [2003] IS72	Clearance Art.6(1)b with undertakings	Photo-copiers, Cameras, Photo Meters
M.3096	TotalFinaElf/Mobil Gas	28.02.03	—	4 [2003] IS103	Clearance Art.6(1)(b) Without undertakings	Gas
M.3097	Maersk Data/Eurogate IT/Global Transport Solutions JV	12.03.03	—	4 [2003] IS117	Clearance Art.6(1)(b) Without undertakings	Software Applications For Transport
M.3099	Areva/Urenco/ETC JV	06.10.04	—	5 [2004] IS74	Art.8(2) with conditions and obligations	Nuclear energy
M.3101	Accor/Hilton/Six Continents/JV	16.05.03	—	5 [2003] IS17	Clearance Art.6(1)(b) Without undertakings	Hotel Accommodation
M.3107	Tech Data Corporation/Azlan Group	24.03.03	—	4 [2003] IS118	Clearance Art.6(1)(b) Without undertakings	IT Products and Services
M.3108	Office Depot/Guilbert	23.05.03	—	5 [2003] IS18	Clearance Art.6(1)(b) Without undertakings	Office Supplies
M.3109	Candover/Cinven/Gala	14.03.03	—	4 [2003] IS115	Clearance Art.6(1)(b) Without undertakings	Gambling Machines
M.3110	OMV/BP (Southern Germany Package)	11.06.03	—	5 [2003] IS26	Clearance Art.6(1)b without undertakings	Extraction of petroleum, gas manufacture of petroleum and chemicals
M.3113	GE/Jenbacher	14.04.03	—	4 [2003] IS134	Clearance Art.6(1)(b) Without undertakings	Gas Turbines
M.3125	Huntsman/Matlinpatterson/Vantico	19.06.03	—	5 [2003] IS39	Clearance Art.6(1)b without undertakings	Chemical Products Electrical Equipment
M.3130	Arla Foods/Express Dairies	10.06.03	—	5 [2003] IS48	Clearance Art.6(1)b without undertakings and Art.9 Partial referral	Dairy Products
M.3134	Arcelor/Umicore/Duology JV	04.07.03	—	5 [2003] IS44	Clearance Art.6(1)b without undertakings	Mon, Steel and Ferro Alloys
M.3136	GE/AGFA NDT	05.12.03	—	4 [2004] IS19	Clearance Art.6(1)b with undertakings	Testing Equipment

MERGER No.	NAME	DATE	O.J.	C.M.L.R.	TYPE OF DECISION	PRODUCT SECTOR
M.3141	Cementbouw/Enci/JV	01.08.03	—	5 [2003] IS83	Clearance Art.6(1)b without undertakings	Aggregates, Ready-mixed Concrete
M.3142	CVC/Danske Traelast	12.05.03	—	4 [2003] IS140	Clearance Art.6(1)(b) Without undertakings	Building Materials
M.3146	Smith & Nephew/Centerpulse	27.05.03	—	5 [2003] IS20	Clearance Art.6(1)(b) Without undertakings	Hip and Knee Implants
M.3148	Siemens/Alstom Gas and Steam Turbines	10.07.03	—	5 [2003] IS71	Clearance Art.6(1)b without undertakings	Turbines
M.3149	Procter & Gamble/Wella	30.07.03	—	5 [2003] IS81	Clearance Art.6(1)b with undertakings	Hair Care Products
M.3150	SNCF/Trenitalia/AFA	04.08.03	—	5 [2003] IS95	Clearance Art.6(1)b without undertakings	Rail Transport
M.3151	Thyssenkrupp/Sofedit	27.05.03	—	5 [2003] IS21	Clearance Art.6(1)(b) Without undertakings	Car Parts
M.3155	Deutsche Post/Securicor	19.06.03	—	5 [2003] IS38	Clearance Art.6(1)b without undertakings	Postal Services
M.3156	EADS/Astrium (II)	26.05.03	—	5 [2003] IS19	Clearance Art.6(1)(b) Without undertakings	Satellites
M.3159	Rheinmetall/STN Atlas	25.07.03	—	5 [2003] IS77	Clearance Art.6(1)b without undertakings	Electronic Systems
M.3161	CVRD/Caemi	18.07.03	—	5 [2003] IS74	Clearance Art.6(1)b with undertakings	Production of Iron Ore
M.3169	Bridgepoint Capital/Permira/Holmes Place	01.07.03	—	5 [2003] IS41	Clearance Art.6(1)b without undertakings	Fitness Clubs
M.3170	Sapa/Remi Claeys Aluminium	17.06.03	—	5 [2003] IS37	Clearance Art.6(1)b without undertakings	Aluminium
M.3171	Computer Sciences Corporation/Royal Mail Business Systems	27.05.03	—	5 [2003] IS23	Clearance Art.6(1)b without undertakings	IT Services, Outsourcing
M.3172	Ferrovial/Amey	27.05.03	—	5 [2003] IS22	Clearance Art.6(1)(b) Without undertakings	Railway Management and Maintenance Services
M.3173	E.On/Fortum Burghausen/Smaland/Edenderry	13.06.03	—	5 [2003] IS36	Clearance Art.6(1)b without undertakings	Electricity Generation
M.3175	Best Agrifund/Dumeco	02.07.03	—	5 [2003] IS42	Clearance Art.6(1)b without undertakings	Abattoir By-products

Table 5

MERGER No.	NAME	DATE	O.J.	C.M.L.R.	TYPE OF DECISION	PRODUCT SECTOR
M.3177	BASF/Glon-Sanders/JV	29.07.03	—	5 [2003] IS80	Clearance Art.6(1)b without undertakings	Feed Additives
M.3178	Bertelsmann/Springer	03.05.05	—	—	Clearance, Art.8 without conditions	Rotogravure printing
M.3182	Scottish & Newcastle/HP Bulmer	30.06.03	—	5 [2003] IS40	Clearance Art.6(1)b without undertakings	Cider and Beer
M.3184	Wolseley/Pinault Bois & Materiaux	03.07.03	—		Clearance Art.6(1)b without undertakings	Distribution of Building Materials
M.3188	ADM/VDBO	31.07.03	—	5 [2003] IS82	Clearance Art.6(1)b without undertakings	Edible Oils and Fats
M.3191	Philip Morris/Papastratos	02.10.03	—	5 [2003] IS110	Clearance Art.6(1)b without undertakings	Cigarettes
M.3192	Thyssenkrupp/HSP Hoesch/JV	03.07.03	—	5 [2003] IS43	Clearance Art.6(1)b without undertakings	Sheet Piling, Construction Equipment
M.3195	Heineken/BBAG	18.07.03	—	5 [2003] IS73	Clearance Art.6(1)b without undertakings	Beer
M.3196	Belgium CA — Agricaisse — Lanbokas/ Credit Agricole	20.08.03	—	5 [2003] IS98	Clearance Art.6(1)b without undertakings	Bank, Financial Services
M.3197	Candover/Cinven/Bertelsmann-Springer	29.07.03	—	5 [2003] IS78	Clearance Art.6(1)b with undertakings	Academic publishing, professional medical publishing
M.3198	VW-Audi/VW-Audi Vertriebszentren	29.07.03	—	5 [2003] IS79	Clearance Art.6(1)b without undertakings	Distribution of Car Parts
M.3205	SNPE/Saab/Patria/JV (Eurenco)	02.10.03	—	5 [2003] IS109	Clearance Art.6(1)b without undertakings	Explosives
M.3209	WPP/Cordiant	25.07.03	—	5 [2003] IS76	Clearance Art.6(1)b without undertakings	Marketing Communication Services, Media Buying
M.3210	EDF/EDFT	26.08.03	—	5 [2003] IS99	Clearance Art.6(1)b without undertakings	Electricity
M.3213	Umicore/OMG Precious Metal Group	29.07.03	—		Clearance Art.6(1)b without undertakings	Metal Recycling, Catalysts
M.3216	Oracle/Peoplesoft	26.10.04	[2005] L218/6	5 [2004] IS93	Art. 8(2) without conditions	Business software

MERGER No.	NAME	DATE	O.J.	C.M.L.R.	TYPE OF DECISION	PRODUCT SECTOR
M.3217	Carlyle/Finmeccanica/Avio	18.08.03	—	5 [2003] IS97	Clearance Art.6(1)b without undertakings	Aircraft Components
M.3225	Alcan/Pechiney (II)	29.09.03	—	5 [2003] IS107	Clearance Art.6(1)b with undertakings	Aluminium
M.3227	Paperlinx/Buhrmann Paper Merchanting Division	10.10.03	—	5 [2003] IS111	Clearance Art.6(1)b without undertakings	Distribution of Paper
M.3230	Statoil/BP/Sonatrach/In Salah JV	19.12.03	—	4 [2004] IS29	Clearance 61b without undertakings	Oil and Gas
M.3232	Trelleborg/Smiths (PSS Division)	19.09.03	—	5 [2003] IS106	Clearance Art.6(1)b without undertakings	Pipe Seals
M.3235	Teijin/Zeon/JV	12.08.03	—	5 [2003] IS96	Clearance Art.6(1)b without undertakings	Polymers
M.3245	Vodafone/Singlepoint	16.09.03	—	5 [2003] IS101	Clearance Art.6(1)b without undertakings	Mobile Telecommunications
M.3248	BAT/Tabacchi Italiani	23.10.03	—	5 [2003] IS122	Art. 9 Total Referral	Tobacco
M.3254	Vidacaixa/Swisslife Espana	03.11.03	—	5 [2003] IS120	Clearance Art.6(1)b without undertakings	Insurance
M.3259	CRH/CVC/Cementbouw	29.09.03	—	5 [2003] IS108	Clearance Art.6(1)b without undertakings	Ready-mixed Concrete
M.3267	CRH/Cementbouw	29.09.03	—	5 [2003] IS108	Clearance Art.6(1)b without undertakings	Building Materials
M.3268	Sydkraft/Graninge	30.10.03	—	5 [2003] IS119	Clearance Art.6(1)b without undertakings	Electricity
M.3271	Kabel Deutschland/ISH	07.06.04	—	5 [2004] IS15	Art. 9 Total referral	Operation of broadband cable
M.3273	First/Keolis/TPE JV	08.12.03	—	4 [2004] IS21	Clearance Art.6(1)b without undertakings	Rail Transport
M.3275	Shell España/Cepsa/SIS JV	23.11.04	—	—	Art.9 Total referral	Sale of automotive fuel
M.3276	Anglo American/Kumba Resources	03.12.03	—	4 [2004] IS18	Clearance Art.6(1)b without undertakings	Zircon, Titanium, Dioxide Feedstock
M.3280	Air France/KLM	11.02.04	—	4 [2004] IS47	Clearance Art.6(1)b with undertakings	Air Transport
M.3284	Outokumpu/Boliden	08.12.03	—	4 [2004] IS20	Clearance Art.6(1)b without undertakings	Sanitary Tubes, Industrial Tubes, Sulphuric Acid

Table 5

MERGER No.	NAME	DATE	O.J.	C.M.L.R.	TYPE OF DECISION	PRODUCT SECTOR
M.3287	Agco/Valtra	12.12.03	—	4 [2004] IS24	Clearance Art.6(1)b without undertakings	Tractors
M.3288	TNK-BP/Sibneft/Slavneft JV	19.12.03	—	4 [2004] IS34	Clearance Art.6(1)b without undertakings	Oil and Gas
M.3289	Interbrew/Spaten-Fanziskaner	19.12.03	—	4 [2004] IS33	Clearance Art.6(1)b without undertakings	Beer
M.3291	Preem/Skandinaviska Raffinaderi	01.12.03	—	4 [2004] IS17	Clearance Art.6(1)b without undertakings	Oil Refined Products
M.3293	Shell/BEB	20.11.03	—	4 [2004] IS8	Clearance Art.6(1)b without undertakings	Natural Gas
M.3294	Exxonmobil/BEB	20.11.03	—	4 [2004] IS8	Clearance Art.6(1)b without undertakings	Natural Gas
M.3296	Areva/Alstom T&D	19.12.03	—	4 [2004] IS31	Clearance Art.6(1)b without undertakings	Electrical Power
M.3297	Norsk Hydro/Duke Energy	19.12.03	—	4 [2004] IS32	Clearance Art.6(1)b without undertakings	Gas Supply
M.3304	GE/Amersham	21.01.04	—	4 [2004] IS42	Clearance Art.6(1)b without undertakings	Diagnostic Imaging
M.3306	E.On/Midlands	16.12.03	—	4 [2004] IS28	Clearance Art.6(1)b without undertakings	Electricity
M.3311	Van Oord/BHD/Bagger Holding	11.12.03	—	4 [2004] IS23	Clearance Art.6(1)b without undertakings	Dredging
M.3313	CRH/Samse/Doras	10.12.03	—	4 [2004] IS22	Clearance Art.6(1)b without undertakings	Building Materials
M.3314	Air Liquide/Messer Targets	15.03.04	—	4 [2004] IS76	Clearance Art.6(1)b with undertakings	Industrial and Medical Gases
M.3316	Celestica/MSL	18.12.03	—	4 [2004] IS30	Clearance Art.6(1)b without undertakings	Electronic Manufacturing Services
M.3318	ECS/Sibelga	19.12.03	—	4 [2004] IS37	Art. 9 Total Referral	Electricity, Gas
M.3322	Polestar/Prisa/Inversiones Ibersuizas/JV	15.12.03	—	4 [2004] IS26	Clearance Art.6(1)b without undertakings	Printing and Reproduction of Recorded Media
M.3326	LNM/PHS	05.02.04	—	4 [2004] IS46	Clearance Art.6(1)b without undertakings	Steel

MERGER No.	NAME	DATE	O.J.	C.M.L.R.	TYPE OF DECISION	PRODUCT SECTOR
M.3329	Tchibo/Beiersdorf	16.12.03	—	4 [2004] IS27	Clearance Art.6(1)b without undertakings	Cosmetic, medical and personal healthcare products
M.3330	RTL/M6	12.03.04	—	4 [2004] IS75	Clearance Art.6(1)b without undertakings	Television
M.3333	Sony/BMG	19.07.04	—	5 [2004] IS39	Clearance Art.8(2) without conditions	Recorded and on-line music
M.3333	Sony/BMG (4064)	01.03.07	—	—	Art.6(1)(c)	Entertainment
M.3334	Arcelor/Thyssenkrupp/Steel24–7	16.02.04	—	4 [2004] IS59	Clearance Art.6(1)B Without Undertakings	B2b
M.3337	Best Agrifund/Nordfleisch	19.03.04	—	4 [2004] IS79	Clearance Art.6(1)b without undertakings	Purchase of cattle for slaughtering — sale of meat
M.3341	Koch/Invista	21.01.04	—	4 [2004] IS43	Clearance Art.6(1)b without undertakings	Man-made Fibres
M.3344	Bain Capital/Interfer/Brenntag	21.01.04	—	4 [2004] IS44	Clearance Art.6(1)b without undertakings	Processing and Trade of Chemical Products
M.3347	Schneider Electric/MGE — UPS	05.02.04	—	4 [2004] IS45	Clearance Art.6(1)b without undertakings	Electrical Apparatus
M.3349	Toshiba/Samsung/JV	02.03.04	—	4 [2004] IS60	Clearance Art.6(1)b without undertakings	Cd-drives, Dvd-drives
M.3351	Arvin Meritor/Volvo (Assets)	01.10.04	—	5 [2004] IS72	Clearance Art.6(1)b without undertakings	Driven and non-driven axles
M.3352	VW/Hahn + Lang	16.02.04	—	4 [2004] IS58	Clearance Art.6(1)b without undertakings	Car Dealer
M.3354	Sanofi-Synthelabo/Aventis	26.04.04	—	4 [2004] IS105	Clearance Art.6(1)b with undertakings	Pharmaceuticals
M.3355	Apollo/JP Morgan/Primacom	15.06.04	—	5 [2004] IS24	Clearance Art.6(1)b without undertakings	TV and radio transmission
M.3365	Vidacaixa/Santander Central Hispano Prevision	09.03.04	—	4 [2004] IS61	Clearance Art.6(1)b without undertakings	Insurance
M.3370	BNP Paribas/ARI	09.03.04	—	4 [2004] IS62	Clearance Art.6(1)b without undertakings	Real Estate
M.3372	Carlsberg/Holsten	16.03.04	—	4 [2004] IS77	Clearance Art.6(1)b without undertakings	Beer

Table 5

MERGER No.	NAME	DATE	O.J.	C.M.L.R.	TYPE OF DECISION	PRODUCT SECTOR
M.3373	Accor/colony/Desseigne-Barriere/JV	04.06.04	—	5 [2004] IS14	Clearance Art.6(1)b without undertakings and Art.9 partial referral	Casinos, Hotels
M.3374	SR Technics/FLS Aerospace	14.04.04	—	4 [2004] IS84	Clearance Art.6(1)b without undertakings	Aircraft Repair & Maintenance
M.3375	Statoil/SDS	01.07.04	—	5 [2004] IS30	Clearance Art.6(1)b without undertakings	Retail and non-retail of petroleum products
M.3376	Dillinger Hüttenwerke/Saarstahl/ Cokerie De Carling	17.03.04	—	4 [2004] IS78	Clearance Art.6(1)b without undertakings	Carbon Core
M.3379	P&O/Royal Nedlloyd/P&O Nedlloyd	29.03.04	—	4 [2004] IS81	Clearance Art.6(1)b without undertakings	Ferry Port Services
M.3380	UTC/Linde Kältetechnik	12.07.04	—	5 [2004] IS32	Clearance Art.6(1)b without undertakings	Refrigeration business
M.3381	Alba/Beko/Grundig	29.04.04	—	4 [2004] IS108	Clearance Art.6(1)b without undertakings	Consumer electronics products (TV, DVD-players, etc.)
M.3382	Iberia/Cobra Instalaciones/Serpista JV	05.05.04	—		Clearance Art.6(1)b without undertakings	Repair, Ground Handling Equipment
M.3385	Cargill/BCA	01.04.04	—	4 [2004] IS83	Clearance Art.6(1)b without undertakings	Agricultural Merchanting
M.3387	BC Funds/Baxi	11.03.04	—	4 [2004] IS63	Clearance Art.6(1)b without undertakings	Showers
M.3388	Ford Motor Company Ltd/Polar Motor Group Ltd	30.04.04	—	4 [2004] IS109	Clearance Art.6(1)b without undertakings	Sale of Vehicles
M.3394	Johnson & Johnson/Johnson & Johnson MSD Europe	29.03.04	—	4 [2004] IS82	Clearance Art.6(1)b without undertakings	Pharmaceuticals
M.3395	Sampo/IF Skadeförsäkring	28.04.04	—	4 [2004] IS107	Clearance Art.6(1)b without undertakings	Insurance
M.3396	Group 4 Falck/Securicor	28.05.04	—	5 [2004] IS11	Clearance Art.6(1)b with undertakings	Cash and Guarding Services
M.3397	Owens-Illinois/BSN Glasspack	09.06.04	—	5 [2004] IS12	Clearance Art.6(1)b with undertakings	Glass packaging
M.3398	Hewlett Packard/Triaton	26.03.04	—	4 [2004] IS80	Clearance Art.6(1)b without undertakings	IT Services
M.3401	Danish Crown/Flagship Foods	17.06.04	—	5 [2004] IS26	Clearance Art.6(1)b without undertakings	Sale of pig meat

MERGER No.	NAME	DATE	O.J.	C.M.L.R.	TYPE OF DECISION	PRODUCT SECTOR
M.3407	Saint Gobain/Dahl	28.04.04	—	4 [2004] IS106	Clearance Art.6(1)b without undertakings	Distribution of Building Materials
M.3410	Total/Gaz de France	08.10.04	—	5 [2004] IS76	Clearance Art.6(1)b with undertakings	Gas
M.3411	UPC/Noos	17.05.04	—	5 [2004] IS9	Clearance Art.6(1)b without undertakings	Retail Distribution of Pay-TV
M.3415	CRH/Semapa/Secil JV	28.05.04	—	—	Clearance Art.6(1)b without undertakings	Cement and Other Building Materials
M.3418	General Dynamics/Alvis	26.05.04	—	5 [2004] IS10	Clearance Art.6(1)b without undertakings	Combat Vehicles
M.3419	Adecco/Manpower/Vediorbis/JV	05.11.04	—	—	Clearance Art.6(1)b without undertakings	Labour recruitment
M.3420	GIMD/Socpresse	16.06.04	—	5 [2004] IS25	Clearance Art.6(1)b with undertakings	Media buying
M.3424	Ciba/Raisio Chemicals	26.05.04	—		Clearance Art.6(1)b without undertakings	Paper Chemicals
M.3431	Sonoco/Ahlstrom/JV	06.10.04	—	5 [2004] IS75	Clearance Art.6(1)b with undertakings	Coreboard, cores
M.3433	Hella/Behr/Plastic Omnium/JV	13.05.04	—	5 [2004] IS8	Clearance Art.6(1)b without undertakings	Car Parts
M.3435	Lyondell/Millennium	10.06.04	—	5 [2004] IS13	Clearance Art.6(1)b without undertakings	Acetic acid
M.3436	Continental/Phoenix	26.10.04	—	5 [2004] IS92	Art. 8(2) with conditions and onligations	Car parts
M.3437	KKR/Vendex	15.06.04	—	5 [2004] IS23	Clearance Art.6(1)b without undertakings	Retail
M.3439	Agfa-Gevaert/Lastra	09.08.04	—	5 [2004] IS43	Clearance Art.6(1)b without undertakings	Pre-press equipment and chemicals, printing plates
M.3440	ENI/EDP/GDP	09.12.04	—	—	Art.8(3) Prohibition	Electricity & gas
M.3446	Uniqa/Mannheimer	28.06.04	—	5 [2004] IS27	Clearance Art.6(1)b without undertakings	Insurance
M.3448	EDP/Hidroelectrica del Cantabrico	09.09.04	—	5 [2004] IS52	Clearance Art.6(1)b without undertakings	Electricity and gas
M.3454	KKR/Dynamit Nobel	07.07.04	—	5 [2004] IS31	Clearance Art.6(1)b without undertakings	Commodity and specialty chemicals

Table 5

MERGER No.	NAME	DATE	O.J.	C.M.L.R.	TYPE OF DECISION	PRODUCT SECTOR
M.3459	Seiko Epson/Sanyo/Sanyo Epson Imaging Devices JV	22.09.04	—	5 [2004] IS69	Clearance Art.6(1)b without undertakings	LCD panels
M.3464	Kesko/ICA/JV	15.11.04	—	—	Clearance Art.6(1)b without undertakings	Retail of consumer goods
M.3465	Syngenta CP/Advanta	17.08.04	—	5 [2004] IS49	Clearance Art.6(1)b with undertakings	Seeds
M.3467	Dow Chemicals/Pic/White Sands	28.06.04	—	5 [2004] IS28	Clearance Art.6(1)b without undertakings	Ethylene glycols
M.3476	Cargill/Seara	28.10.04	—	5 [2004] IS95	Clearance Art.6(1)b without undertakings	Supply of chicken meat
M.3483	Voestalpine AG/Nedcon Groep N.V	10.08.04	—	5 [2004] IS44	Clearance Art.6(1)b without undertakings	Storage systems
M.3486	Magna/New Venture Gear	24.09.04	—	5 [2004] IS71	Clearance Art.6(1)b without undertakings	All-wheel drive systems, transfer cases
M.3491	BAE Systems/Alvis	10.08.04	—	5 [2004] IS45	Clearance Art.6(1)b without undertakings	Combat vehicles
M.3492	Exel/Tibbet & Britten	03.08.04	—	5 [2004] IS42	Clearance Art.6(1)b without undertakings	Freight logistics services
M.3493	Yamanouchi/Fujisawa	18.08.04	—	5 [2004] IS50	Clearance Art.6(1)b without undertakings	Pharmaceuticals
M.3496	TNT Forwarding Holding/Wilson Logistics	02.08.04	—	5 [2004] IS41	Clearance Art.6(1)b without undertakings	Sale of motor fuel, petroleum products
M.3506	Fox Paine/Advanta	20.08.04	—	—	Clearance Art.6(1)b without undertakings	Seeds
M.3511	Wiener Börse/ Budapest Stock	22.03.05	—	—	Clearance Art.6(1)b without undertakings	Securities listing & trading services
M.3512	VNU/WPP/JV	15.09.04	—	5 [2004] IS57	Clearance Art.6(1)b without undertakings	TV audience measurement
M.3516	Repsol YPF/Shell Portugal	13.09.04	—	5 [2004] IS55	Clearance Art.6(1)b without undertakings	Fuels, bitumen
M.3517	CVC/Permira/AA	27.08.04	—	5 [2004] IS51	Clearance Art.6(1)b without undertakings	Road assistance services
M.3522	Danish Crown/HK/Sokolow	13.09.04	—	5 [2004] IS54	Clearance Art.6(1)b without undertakings	Sale of meat
M.3530	Teliasonera/Orange DK	24.09.04	—	5 [2004] IS70	Clearance Art.6(1)b without undertakings	Mobile telephony
M.3535	Van Drie/Schils	08.12.04	—	—	Clearance Art.6(1)b without undertakings	Whey, skimmed milk products, calves

MERGER No.	NAME	DATE	O.J.	C.M.L.R.	TYPE OF DECISION	PRODUCT SECTOR
M.3542	Sony Pictures/Walt Disney/ODG/ Movieco	10.11.04	—	—	Clearance Art.6(1)b without undertakings	Agency, technical & marketing services in pay-TV
M.3543	PKN Orlen/Unipetrol	20.04.05	—	—	Clearance Art.6(1)b without undertakings	Sale of refined oil products, bitumen, lubricating petroleum oils
M.3544	Bayer Healthcare/Roche (OTC Business)	19.11.04	—	—	Clearance Art.6(1)b with undertakings	Pharmaceuticals (OTC)
M.3547	Banco Santander/Abbey National	15.09.04	—	5 [2004] IS56	Clearance Art.6(1)b without undertakings	Banking
M.3550	Midewa/Stadtwerke Halle/Fernwasser Sachsen-Anhalt	19.10.04	—	5 [2004] IS91	Clearance Art.6(1)b without undertakings	Water purification and supply
M.3553	Logista/Etinera/Terzia	04.10.04	—	5 [2004] IS73	Clearance Art.6(1)b without undertakings	Tobacco distribution
M.3554	Serco/Nedrailways/Northern Rail	16.09.04	—	5 [2004] IS58	Clearance Art.6(1)b without undertakings	Passenger rail services
M.3555	Hewlett - Packard/Synstar	09.09.04	—	5 [2004] IS53	Clearance Art.6(1)b without undertakings	IT services
M.3556	Fortis/BCP	19.01.05	—	—	Clearance Art.6(1)b without undertakings	Insurance
M.3558	Cytec/UCB-Surface Specialties	17.12.04	—	—	Clearance Art.6(1)b with undertakings	Specialty chemicals
M.3561	DT/Eurotel	15.12.04	—	—	Clearance Art.6(1)b without undertakings	Mobile telecommunications services
M.3564	CVC/Ani Printing Inks	28.10.04	—	5 [2004] IS94	Clearance Art.6(1)b without undertakings	Inks
M.3569	Wendel/Bureau Veritas	28.10.04	—	—	Clearance Art.6(1)b without undertakings	Certification services
M.3570	Piaggio/Aprilia	22.11.04	—	—	Clearance Art.6(1)b with undertakings	Motorbikes
M.3571	IBM/Maerskdata/Dmdata	18.11.04	—	—	Clearance Art.6(1)b without undertakings	IT services
M.3572	Cemex/RMC	08.12.04	—	—	Clearance Art.6(1)b without undertakings	Cement, concrete, mortar, aggregates
M.3576	ECT/PONL/Euromax	22.12.04	—	—	Clearance Art.6(1)b without undertakings	Container terminal services,liner shipping

Table 5

MERGER No.	NAME	DATE	O.J.	C.M.L.R.	TYPE OF DECISION	PRODUCT SECTOR
M.3578	BP/Nova Chemicals JV	01.07.05	—	—	Clearance Art.6(1)b without undertakings	Polystyrenes
M.3579	WPP/Grey	24.01.05	—	—	Clearance Art.6(1)b without undertakings	Marketing communication services, media buying
M.3583	Flextronics/Nortel	28.10.04	—	5 [2004] IS96	Clearance Art.6(1)b without undertakings	Electronic products
M.3589	Körber/Winkler + Dünnebier	30.11.04	—	—	Clearance Art.6(1)b without undertakings	Paper product machinery
M.3590	Fiat/Magneti Marelli	17.11.04	—	—	Clearance Art.6(1)b without undertakings	Electronic components for cars
M.3593	Apollo/Bakelite	11.04.05	—	—	Clearance Art.6(1)b with undertakings	Resins
M.3595	Sony/MGM	30.03.05	—	—	Clearance Art.6(1)b without undertakings	Acquisition of motion pictures for theatrical release, home entertainment, TV licensing
M.3596	Thyssenkrupp/Howaldswerke-Deutsche Werft	10.12.04	—	—	Clearance Art.6(1)b without undertakings	Shipbuilding activities
M.3603	UPS/Menlo	10.12.04	—	—	Clearance Art.6(1)b without undertakings	Freight forwarding business
M.3605	Sovion/HMG	21.12.04	—	—	Clearance Art.6(1)b without undertakings	Processing of pigs
M.3609	Cinven/FTC-NCN	04.03.05	—	—	Clearance Art.6(1)b without undertakings	Distribution of Pay-TV
M.3612	Henkel/Sovereign	22.12.04	—	—	Clearance Art.6(1)b without undertakings	Industrial adhesives
M.3621	Sagem/Snecma	22.12.04	—	—	Clearance Art.6(1)b without undertakings	Aircraft components & systems
M.3622	Valeo/Engel	09.02.05	—	—	Clearance Art.6(1)b without undertakings	Car parts
M.3625	Blackstone/Acetex	13.07.05	—	—	Clearance, Art.8 without conditions	Commodity chemicals
M.3641	BT/Infonet	25.01.05	—	—	Clearance Art.6(1)b without undertakings	Global telecommunications services

MERGER No.	NAME	DATE	O.J.	C.M.L.R.	TYPE OF DECISION	PRODUCT SECTOR
M.3643	Sephora/El Corte Ingles	09.03.05	—	—	Clearance Art.6(1)b without undertakings	Retail sale of cosmetics
M.3648	Gruner + Jarh/MPS	08.04.05	—	—	Clearance Art.6(1)b without undertakings	Publishing of magazines
M.3649	Finmeccanica/BAES Avionics and Communications	14.03.05	—	—	Clearance Art.6(1)b without undertakings	Helicopters & naval surface vessels
M.3653	Siemens/Va Tech	13.07.05	—	—	Clearance Art.8 with conditions	Turbines & generators
M.3657	Airbus Financial Services/Sita BV	27.01.05	—	—	Clearance Art.6(1)b without undertakings	In-flight passengers' communications services
M.3658	Orkla/Chips	03.03.05	—	—	Clearance Art.6(1)b with undertakings	Snacks, frozen ready meals
M.3664	Repsol/Butano/Shell Gas	02.03.05	—	—	Clearance Art.6(1)b without undertakings	Gas
M.3665	Enel/Slovenske Elektrarne	26.04.05	—	—	Clearance Art.6(1)b without undertakings	Electricity
M.3669	Blackstone (TBG CareCo)/NHP	01.02.05	—	4 [2005] IS25	Clearance Art.6(1)b without undertakings Art(9), partial referral.	Care home services
M.3670	EQT Group/Karl Zeiss/Sola	03.03.05	—	—	Clearance Art.6(1)b without undertakings	Optical lenses
M.3674	IESY Repository/ISH	14.02.05	—	4 [2005] IS26	Art.9, total referral	Cable network
M.3680	Alcatel/Finmeccanica/Alcatel Alenia Space & Telespazio	28.04.05	—	—	Clearance Art.6(1)b with undertakings	Launchers & space transportation, satellites
M.3686	Honeywell/Novar	30.03.05	—	—	Clearance Art.6(1)b with undertakings	Building security systems
M.3687	Johnson & Johnson/Guidant	25.08.05	—	—	Clearance Art.6(1)b with undertakings	Medical devices
M.3688	UTC/Kidde	18.03.05	—	—	Clearance Art.6(1)b without undertakings	Fire extinguishers, gaseous fire suppression systems
M.3692	Reuters/Telerate	23.05.05	—	—	Clearance Art.6(1)b with undertakings	Sale of market data
M.3693	TPV/Philips (Monitors)	05.08.05	—	—	Clearance Art.6(1)b without undertakings	Computer monitors
M.3695	BT/Radianz	22.04.05	—	—	Clearance Art.6(1)b without undertakings	Extranet services, global telecommunication services

MERGER No.	NAME	DATE	O.J.	C.M.L.R.	TYPE OF DECISION	PRODUCT SECTOR
M.3696	E.On/Mol	21.12.05	—	4 [2006] IS29	Art.8(2) with conditions and obligations	Electricity, gas
M.3697	Symantec/Veritas	15.03.05	—	—	Clearance Art.6(1)b without undertakings	Security & storage software
M.3699	EQT/Smurfit Munksjö	16.02.05	—	—	Clearance Art.6(1)b without undertakings	Value-added paper products
M.3713	Holcim/Aggregate Industries	14.03.05	—	—	Clearance Art.6(1)b without undertakings	Cement, aggregates, concrete
M.3716	AS Watson/Marionnaud	07.04.05	—	—	Clearance Art.6(1)b without undertakings	Retail sale of beauty products
M.3720	BAES/AMS	14.03.05	—	—	Clearance Art.6(1)b without undertakings	Avionics
M.3721	Stora Enso/Scaldia/Pdf	07.04.05	—	—	Clearance Art.6(1)b without undertakings	Paper merchanting, fine paper
M.3722	Nutreco/Stolt-Nielsen/MarineHarvest JV	12.04.05	—	—	Clearance Art.6(1)b without undertakings	Fish farming activities
M.3725	Cargill/Pagnan	22.03.05	—	—	Clearance Art.6(1)b without undertakings	Trading of agricultural commodities
M.3728	Autogrill/Altadis/Aldeasa	23.03.05	—	—	Clearance Art.6(1)b without undertakings	Retail services at airports, concession food services
M.3729	EDF/AEM/Edison	12.08.05	—	—	Clearance Art.6(1)b without undertakings	Electricity
M.3730	Lukoil/Teboil/Suomen Pertrooli	17.03.05	—	—	Clearance Art.6(1)b without undertakings	Oil and lubricants
M.3732	Procter & Gamble/Gillette	15.07.05	—	—	Clearance Art.6(1)b with undertakings	Toothbrushes & other oral care products
M.3733	DOW/DDE	26.04.05	—	—	Clearance Art.6(1)b without undertakings	Elastomers
M.3740	Barclays/Föreningssparbanken/JV	02.06.05	—	—	Clearance Art.6(1)b without undertakings	Payment cards
M.3746	Tetra Laval/SIG	25.07.05	—	—	Clearance Art.6(1)b without undertakings	PET and HDPE filling machines
M.3747	Rautaruukki/Wärtsilä/SKF/JV	03.05.05	—	—	Clearance Art.6(1)b without undertakings	Steel
M.3751	Novartis/Hexal	27.05.05	—	—	Clearance Art.6(1)b with undertakings	Pharmaceuticals

MERGER No.	NAME	DATE	O.J.	C.M.L.R.	TYPE OF DECISION	PRODUCT SECTOR
M.3752	Verizon/MCI	07.10.05	—	—	Clearance Art.6(1)b without undertakings	Internet connectivity Global telecommunications services
M.3753	Kodak/Creo	03.05.05	—	—	Clearance Art.6(1)b without undertakings	Sale of digital printing plates
M.3754	Strabag/Dywidag	23.06.05	—	—	Clearance Art.6(1)b without undertakings Art.9, partial referral	Building & civil engineering
M.3762	Apax/Travelex	16.06.05	—	—	Clearance Art.6(1)b without undertakings	VAT refund services
M.3764	Belgacom/Swisscom	19.05.05	—	—	Clearance Art.6(1)b without undertakings	International telecommunications carrier services
M.3765	Amer/Salomon	12.10.05	—	5 [2005] IS29	Clearance Art.6(1)b with undertakings	Winter sport hard goods
M.3767	BHP/WMC	26.04.05	—	—	Clearance Art.6(1)b without undertakings	Nickel, copper, uranium
M.3770	Lufthansa/Swiss	04.07.05	—	—	Clearance Art.6(1)b with undertakings	Air transport services
M.3772	Aviva/Rac	03.05.05	—	—	Clearance Art.6(1)b without undertakings	Insurance
M.3776	Vodafone/Oskar Mobile	25.05.05	—	—	Clearance Art.6(1)b without undertakings	Telecommunication services
M.3778	Böhler-Uddeholm/Buderus	30.06.05	—	—	Clearance Art.6(1)b without undertakings	Specialty steel
M.3779	Pernod/Ricard	24.06.05	—	—	Clearance Art.6(1)b with undertakings	Spirits and wines
M.3781	Crédit Agricole/Caisse d'Epargne/JV	14.06.05	—	—	Clearance Art.6(1)b without undertakings	Custody services
M.3783	TPG/British Vita	06.06.05	—	—	Clearance Art.6(1)b without undertakings	Synthetic elastomers, polymers
M.3786	BPI/Euler Hermes/Cosec	29.03.06	—	—	Clearance Art.6(1)b without undertakings	Credit insurance

Table 5

MERGER No.	NAME	DATE	O.J.	C.M.L.R.	TYPE OF DECISION	PRODUCT SECTOR
M.3789	JohnsonControls/Robert Bosch/ Delphi SLI	29.06.05	—	—	Clearance Art.6(1)b without undertakings	OEM/OES batteries
M.3796	OMYA/J.M. Huber PCC	19.07.06	[2005] C199	—	Art.8(2) with conditions and obligations	Non-metallic mineral products
M.3798	NYK/Lauritzen Cool/Lau CoolJV	19.08.05	—	—	Clearance Art.6(1)b without undertakings	Reefer transport services
M.3803	EADS/Nokia	28.07.05	—	—	Clearance Art.6(1)b without undertakings	Professional Mobile Radios
M.3804	Continental/Xtra print	04.07.05	—	—	Clearance Art.6(1)b without undertakings	Printing blankets
M.3805	Crompton/Great Lakes	15.06.05	—	—	Clearance Art.6(1)b without undertakings	Antioxydants, light stabilisers
M.3806	Telefonica/Cesky Telecom	10.06.05	—	—	Clearance Art.6(1)b without undertakings	Telecommunications, roaming services
M.3809	Siemens/Flender	29.06.05	—	—	Clearance Art.6(1)b without undertakings	Electric motors, wind generators, gear units
M.3813	FortuneBrands/Allied Domecq	10.06.05	—	—	Clearance Art.6(1)b without undertakings	Spirits
M.3816	Apax/Mölnlycke	15.06.05	—	—	Clearance Art.6(1)b without undertakings	Surgical products, wound care products
M.3817	Wegener/PCM/JV	07.07.05	—	—	Clearance Art.6(1)b with undertakings	Daily newspapers
M.3819	Daimler/Crysler/MAV	03.06.05	—	—	Clearance Art.6(1)b without undertakings	Vehicle distribution
M.3820	Avnet/Memec	24.06.05	—	—	Clearance Art.6(1)b without undertakings	Distribution of electronic components
M.3821	Rheinmetall/Diehl/AIM	19.08.05	—	—	Clearance Art.6(1)b without undertakings	Infrared components
M.3822	StoraEnso/Schneidersöhne Papier	25.07.05	—	—	Clearance Art.6(1)b without undertakings	Paper merchanting, fine paper
M.3823	MAG Ferrovial Aeropuertos/Exeter Airports	08.08.05	—	—	Art. 9 Total referral	Provision of airport infrastructure
M.3829	Maerks/PONL	29.07.05	—	—	Clearance Art.6(1)b with undertakings	Liner shipping, terminal services

MERGER No.	NAME	DATE	O.J.	C.M.L.R.	TYPE OF DECISION	PRODUCT SECTOR
M.3836	Goldman Sachs/PirelliCavi E Sistema Energia/Pirelli Cavi E Sistemi Telecom	05.07.05	—	—	Clearance Art.6(1)b without undertakings	Energy & telecommunication cables
M.3838	Avid/Pinnacle	04.08.05	—	—	Clearance Art.6(1)b without undertakings	Digital video products
M.3845	PAI/Chr. Hansen	18.07.05	—	—	Clearance Art.6(1)b without undertakings	Cultures for food production
M.3848	Sea-Invest/Emo-Ekom	18.08.06	[2006] C055	—	Art.8(1)	Cargo
M.3853	Solvay/Fournier	18.07.05	—	—	Clearance Art.6(1)b without undertakings	Pharmaceuticals
M.3856	Boeing/Lockheed Martin/United Launch Alliance JV	09.08.05	—	—	Clearance Art.6(1)b without undertakings	Launch services
M.3858	Lehman Brothers/SCG/Starwood/Le Meridien	20.07.05	—	—	Clearance Art.6(1)b without undertakings	Hotels
M.3863	TUI/CP Ships	12.10.05	—	5 [2005] IS28	Clearance Art.6(1)b with undertakings	Liner shipping Cargo handling and storage Freight forwarding
M.3864	Fimag/Züblin	14.10.05	—	—	Clearance Art.6(1)b without undertakings Art.9, partial referral	Asphalt
M.3865	Trinecke/VVT	21.09.05	—	—	Clearance Art.6(1)b without undertakings	Steel products
M.3866	Sun/Storagetek	26.08.05	—	—	Clearance Art.6(1)b without undertakings	Storage solutions
M.3867	Vattenfall/Elsam&E2 Assets	22.12.05	—	—	Clearance Art.6(1)b without undertakings	Electricity
M.3868	Dong/Elsam/Energi E2	14.03.06	—	4 [2006] IS57	Art.8(2) with conditions and obligations	Electricity, gaz
M.3874	CVC/Ruhrgas Industries	01.09.05	—	—	Clearance Art.6(1)b without undertakings	Meters
M.3876	Diester Industrie/Bunge/JV	30.09.05	—	—	Clearance Art.6(1)b without undertakings	Bio-diesel fuel
M.3883	GDF/Centrica/SPE	07.09.05	—	—	Clearance Art.6(1)b without undertakings	Electricity, gas

Table 5

MERGER No.	NAME	DATE	O.J.	C.M.L.R.	TYPE OF DECISION	PRODUCT SECTOR
M.3884	ADM Poland/Cefetra/BTZ	14.10.05	—	—	Clearance Art.6(1)b without undertakings	Cargo handling and storage
M.3886	Aster 2/Flint Inks	25.08.05	—	—	Clearance Art.6(1)b without undertakings	Inks
M.3894	Unicredito/HVB	18.10.05	—	4 [2006] IS40	Clearance Art.6(1)b without undertakings	Banking
M.3902	HeidelbergCement/De Hoop Terneuzen/Mermans Breton/JV	19.09.05	—	—	Clearance Art.6(1)b without undertakings	Concrete products
M.3905	Tesco/Carrefour	22.12.05	—	4 [2006] IS31	Clearance Art.6(1)b without undertakings Art.9, partial referral	Sale of daily consumer goods
M.3910	Rockwood/Süd-Chemie	13.12.05	—	—	Clearance Art.6(1)b without undertakings	Chemicals
M.3911	BenQ/Siemens Mobile	07.09.05	—	—	Clearance Art.6(1)b without undertakings	Mobile telephones
M.3914	Tele2/Versatel	07.09.05	—	—	Clearance Art.6(1)b without undertakings	Telephony services Internet access
M.3916	T-Mobile/tele.ring	26.04.06	—	4 [2006] IS12	Art.8(2) with conditions and obligations	Mobile telephony services
M.3920	France Télécom/Amena	24.10.05	—	—	Clearance Art.6(1)b without undertakings	Telecommunications services
M.3925	UPS/Lynx	23.09.05	—	—	Clearance Art.6(1)b without undertakings	Mail services Freight services
M.3928	Teva/Ivax	24.11.05	—	—	Clearance Art.6(1)b without undertakings	Pharmaceuticals
M.3930	LBO/Wheelabrator Allevard	29.09.05	—	—	Clearance Art.6(1)b without undertakings	Metallic abrasives Diamond tools
M.3935	Jefferson Smurfit/Kappa	10.11.05	—	5 [2005] IS30	Clearance Art.6(1)b with undertakings	Recovered paper Corrugated products
M.3939	Electra/CVC/CPI	27.09.05	—	—	Clearance Art.6(1)b without undertakings	Book manufacturing
M.3940	Lufthansa/Eurowings	22.12.05	—	4 [2006] IS30	Clearance Art.6(1)b with undertakings	Air transport
M.3942	Adidas/Reebok	24.01.06	—	—	Clearance Art.6(1)b without undertakings	Athletic footwear

MERGER No.	NAME	DATE	O.J.	C.M.L.R.	TYPE OF DECISION	PRODUCT SECTOR
M.3943	Saint-Gobain/BPB	09.11.05	—	—	Clearance Art.6(1)b without undertakings	Distribution of building materials
M.3944	BEHR/Hella/JV	24.11.05	—	—	Clearance Art.6(1)b without undertakings	Car parts
M.3946	Renolit/Solvay	22.02.06	—	—	Clearance Art.6(1)b with undertakings	Industrial foils
M.3968	Sovion/Südfleisch	21.12.05	—	—	Clearance Art.6(1)b without undertakings	Purchase of pigs and cattle for slaughtering, Sale of meat
M.3969	Société Générale/Ford Lease-Business Partner	22.11.05	—	—	Clearance Art.6(1)b without undertakings	Fleet leasing and management services
M.3971	Deutsche Post/Exel	24.11.05	—	—	Clearance Art.6(1)b without undertakings	Freight forwarding Contract logistics
M.3972	TRW Automotive/Dalphi Metal Espana	12.10.05	—	—	Clearance Art.6(1)b without undertakings	Car parts
M.3973	CMA CGM/Delmas	01.12.05	—	—	Clearance Art.6(1)b without undertakings	Liner shipping Cargo handling and storage
M.3975	Cargill/Degussa Food Ingredients	29.03.06	—	—	Art.8 without conditions and obligations	Food ingredients
M.3978	Oracle/Siebel	22.12.05	—	—	Clearance Art.6(1)b without undertakings	Enterprise application software
M.3981	Fives-Lilles/Landis	08.12.05	—	—	Clearance Art.6(1)b without undertakings	Engine components
M.3985	EADS/BAES/FNM/NLFK	07.02.06	—	—	Clearance Art.6(1)b without undertakings	Guided weapons
M.3987	FIDIS/Leasys	24.11.05	—	—	Clearance Art.6(1)b without undertakings	Fleet leasing and management services
M.3995	Belgacom/Telindus	01.12.05	—	—	Clearance Art.6(1)b without undertakings	IT Services
M.3998	Axalto/Gemplus	19.05.06	—	—	Clearance Art.6(1)b with undertakings	Smart cards
M.4000	Inco/Falconbridge	04.07.06	[2006] C020	5 [2006] IS11	Art.8(2) with conditions and obligations	Basic metals

Table 5

MERGER No.	NAME	DATE	O.J.	C.M.L.R.	TYPE OF DECISION	PRODUCT SECTOR
M.4002	OMV/Aral CR	21.12.05	—	—	Clearance Art.6(1)b without undertakings	Sale of fuel
M.4003	Ericsson/Marconi	20.12.05	—	—	Clearance Art.6(1)b without undertakings	Telecommunication equipment
M.4005	Ineos/Innovene	09.12.05	—	—	Clearance Art.6(1)b without undertakings	Chemicals
M.4007	Reckitt Benckiser/Boots Healthcare International	06.01.06	—	—	Clearance Art.6(1)b without undertakings	Pharmaceuticals
M.4010	Frenesius/Helios	08.12.05	—	—	Clearance Art.6(1)b without undertakings	Hospital services
M.4028	Flaga/Progas/JV	26.01.06	—	—	Clearance Art.6(1)b without undertakings	Sale of LPG
M.4034	Telenor/Vodafone Sverige	22.12.05	—	—	Clearance Art.6(1)b without undertakings	Mobile telecommunications
M.4035	Telefonica/O2	10.01.06	—	—	Clearance Art.6(1)b with undertakings	Retail telecommunication services
M.4036	TPG IV/Apax/Q-Telecommunications	13.01.06	—	—	Clearance Art.6(1)b without undertakings	Retail telecommunication services
M.4041	Basell/Société du Craqueur de l'Aubette	22.12.05	—	—	Clearance Art.6(1)b without undertakings	Chemicals
M.4042	Toepfer/InVivo/Soulès	22.12.05	—	—	Clearance Art.6(1)b without undertakings	Feedstuffs
M.4043	Plastal Group/Dynamit Nobel Kunstsoff GmbH	22.12.05	—	—	Clearance Art.6(1)b without undertakings	Thermoplastic products
M.4045	Deutsche Bahn/Bax Global	22.12.05	—	—	Clearance Art.6(1)b without undertakings	Freight forwarding
M.4047	Aviva/Ark Life	20.01.06	—	—	Clearance Art.6(1)b without undertakings	Life insurance
M.4048	Sonae Industria/Tarkett/JV	12.06.06	—	—	Art.6(1)(b)	Veneer sheets
M.4049	Novartis/Chiron	06.02.06	—	—	Clearance Art.6(1)b without undertakings	Vaccines, biopharmaceuticals, blood testing
M.4050	Goldman Sachs/Civen/Ahlsell	06.01.05	—	—	Clearance Art.6(1)b without undertakings	Distribution of installation products

MERGER No.	NAME	DATE	O.J.	C.M.L.R.	TYPE OF DECISION	PRODUCT SECTOR
M.4054	Koch Industries/Georgia-Pacific	19.12.05	—	—	Clearance Art.6(1)b without undertakings	Pulp, Tissue products
M.4055	Talanx/Gerling	05.04.06	—	4 [2006] IS82	Clearance Art.6(1)b with undertakings	Insurance
M.4057	Korsnäs/AD Cartonboard	12.05.06	—	—	Clearance Art.6(1)b without undertakings	Carton packaging board
M.4059	Swiss re/General Electric Insurance Solutions	24.04.06	—	—	Clearance Art.6(1)b without undertakings	Reinsurance
M.4062	SKF/SNFA	02.06.06	—	—	Art.6(1)(b)	Bearings
M.4063	Cisco/Scientific Atlanta	22.02.06	—	—	Clearance Art.6(1)b without undertakings	Broadband communication equipment
M.4066	CVC/Slec	20.03.06	—	4 [2006] IS58	Clearance Art.6(1)b with undertakings	Promotion of motor sport activities
M.4071	Apollo/Akzo Nobel IAR	29.05.06	—	—	Clearance Art.6(1)b without undertakings	Resins
M.4076	Boston Scientific/Guidant	11.04.06	—	4 [2006] IS83	Clearance Art.6(1)b with undertakings	Vascular medical devices
M.4082	Cargill/Pagnan II	06.02.06	—	—	Clearance Art.6(1)b without undertakings	Transport of agricultural commodities
M.4083	ABN Amro Capital France/L Capital/ Sanutri	31.01.06	—	—	Clearance Art.6(1)b without undertakings	Dietetic food
M.4085	Arcelor/Oyak/Erdemir	13.02.06	—	—	Clearance Art.6(1)b without undertakings	Steel products
M.4087	Eiffage/Macquarie/APRR	15.02.06	—	—	Clearance Art.6(1)b without undertakings	Motorway concessions and operations
M.4089	Gilde/Heiploeg	31.01.06	—	—	Clearance Art.6(1)b without undertakings	Wholesale of shrimps, distribution of fresh food
M.4091	Linde/Spectra	20.09.06	—	—	Art.6(1)(b)	Manufacture of gas; distribution of gaseous fuels through mains
M.4092	Andrizt/Küsters	19.04.06	—	—	Clearance Art.6(1)b without undertakings	Paper producing machinery
M.4094	Neos/BP Dormagen	10.08.06	[2006] C025	—	Art.8(1)	Refined petroleum products

Table 5

MERGER No.	NAME	DATE	O.J.	C.M.L.R.	TYPE OF DECISION	PRODUCT SECTOR
M.4096	Carrefour/Hyparlo	04.05.06	—	—	Clearance Art.6(1)b without undertakings	Supermarkets/ hypermarkets
M.4100	Seagate/Maxtor	27.04.06	—	—	Clearance Art.6(1)b without undertakings	Hard disc drives
M.4102	BASF/Engelhard	23.02.06	—	—	Clearance Art.6(1)b without undertakings	Specialty chemicals
M.4104	Aker Yards/Chantiers de l'Atlantique	27.03.06	—	—	Clearance Art.6(1)b without undertakings	Building and repairing of ships
M.4106	Isola/Polyclad	12.04.06	—	—	Clearance Art.6(1)b without undertakings	Copper-clad glass fibre laminates
M.4108	T-Systems/Gedas	27.02.06	—	—	Clearance Art.6(1)b without undertakings	IT Services
M.4110	E.On/Endesa	25.04.06	—	4 [2006] IS11	Clearance Art.6(1)b without undertakings	Electricity, gas
M.4114	Lottomatica/GTECH	19.05.06	—	—	Clearance Art.6(1)b without undertakings	Lotteries and gambling activities
M.4135	Lactalis/Galbani	24.04.06	—	—	Clearance Art.6(1)b without undertakings	Italian-type cheeses
M.4137	Mittal/Arcelor	02.06.06	—	5 [2006] IS4	Art.6(1)(b)	Iron & steel
M.4139	Sony/Nec/JV	31.03.06	—	—	Clearance Art.6(1)b without undertakings	Optical data-storage disk drive
M.4141	Linde/BOC	06.06.06	—	5 [2006] IS5	Art.6(1)(b) with conditions and obligations	Manufacture of gas
M.4146	GE/Bayer/OSi Europe Business	05.05.06	—	—	Clearance Art.6(1)b without undertakings	Silicone business
M.4150	Abbot/Guidant	11.04.06	—	4 [2006] IS83	Clearance Art.6(1)b with undertakings	Vascular medical devices
M.4151	Orica/Dyno	23.05.06	—	5 [2006] IS3	Clearance Art.6(1)b with undertakings	Explosives
M.4153	Toshiba/Westinghouse	19.09.06	—	—	Art.6(1)(b) with conditions and obligations	Machinery

MERGER No.	NAME	DATE	O.J.	C.M.L.R.	TYPE OF DECISION	PRODUCT SECTOR
M.4154	Degussa/Dow (superabsorbent polymers)	20.06.06	—	—	Art.6(1)(b)	Chemicals
M.4155	BNP Paribas/BNL	28.03.06	—	—	Clearance Art.6(1)b without undertakings	Bank, insurance
M.4157	Wendel/Materis	30.03.06	—	—	Clearance Art.6(1)b without undertakings	Building materials
M.4160	Thyssenkrupp/EADS/Atlas	10.05.06	—	—	Clearance Art.6(1)b without undertakings	Naval electronics
M.4161	SEI/VWBN	30.03.06	—	—	Clearance Art.6(1)b without undertakings	Electronic-electrical distribution systems
M.4164	Ferrovial/Quebec/GIC/BAA	23.05.06	—	—	Clearance Art.6(1)b without undertakings	Provision of airport infrastructure services
M.4165	Sonae Industria/Hornitex	28.01.06	—	—	Art.6(1)(b)	Veneer sheets
M.4170	LSG Lufthansa Service Holding/Gate Gourmet Switzerland	19.07.06	—	—	Art.6(1)(b)	Catering
M.4174	TCCC/CCHBC/Traficante	12.04.06	—	—	Art.9, total referral	Beverages
M.4173	Nippon Sheet Glas/Pilkington	07.06.06	—	—	Art.6(1)(b)	Flat glass
M.4177	BASF/Degussa Construction Chemicals	24.05.06	—	—	Clearance Art.6(1)b without undertakings	Construction chemicals
M.4178	MAN Ferrostaal/Eurotecnica GROUP	31.01.07	—	—	Art.6(1)(b)	Chemicals
M.4179	Huntsman/CIBA Te Business	30.06.06	—	—	Art.6(1)(b	Chemicals
M.4180	Gaz de France/Suez	14.11.06	[2006] C117	5 [2006] IS25	Art.8(2) with conditions and obligations	Electricity
M.4184	Boeing/Carmen	06.06.06	—	—	Art.6(1)(b)	Air transport
M.4187	Metso/Aker Kvaerner	12.12.06	[2006] C153	5 [2006] IS21	Art.8 (2) with conditions and obligations	Paper machinery
M.4191	Thales/DCN	19.03.07	—	—	Art.6(1)(b)	Ships and boats
M.4193	L'Oreal/The Body Shop	31.05.06	—	—	Clearance Art.6(1)b without undertakings	Cosmetics
M.4198	Bayer/Schering	24.05.06	—	—	Clearance Art.6(1)b without undertakings	Pharmaceuticals
M.4199	De Lage Landen/Athlon	12.06.06	—	—	Art.6(1)(b)	Finance
M.4202	Charterhouse/Elior	19.05.06	—	—	Clearance Art.6(1)b without undertakings	Food services

MERGER No.	NAME	DATE	O.J.	C.M.L.R.	TYPE OF DECISION	PRODUCT SECTOR
M.4204	Cinven/UPC France	13.07.06	—	—	Art.6(1)(b)	Telecommunications
M.4206	Veolia Transport-BCP/SNCM	29.05.06	—	—	Clearance Art.6(1)b without undertakings	Sea transport of passengers and freight
M.4207	Ccampina/Fonterra Co-operative GROUP/JV	02.06.06	—	—	Art.6(1)(b)	Dairy products
M.4208	Petroplus/European Petroleum Holdings	29.05.06	—	—	Clearance Art.6(1)b without undertakings	Petroleum products
M.4211	Schmolz + Bickenbach/Ugitech	03.07.06	—	—	Art.6(1)(b)	Iron & steel
M.4213	CAG/Motorola	23.06.06	—	—	Art.6(1)(b)	Parts and accessories for motor vehicles
M.4214	Alcatel/Lucent Technologies	24.07.06	—	—	Art.6(1)(b)	Telecommunications
M.4215	Glatfelter/Crompton Assets	20.12.06	[2006] C198	—	Art.8(1)	Paper products
M.4216	CVC/Bocchi/De Weide Blik	30.05.06	—	—	Clearance Art.6(1)b without undertakings	Production and sale of fruits and vegetables
M.4217	Providence/Carlyle/UPC Sweden	02.06.06	—	—	Art.6(1)(b)	Telecommunications
M.4220	Food Service Project/Tele Pizza	06.06.06	—	—	Art.6(1)(b)	Restaurants
M.4225	Celsa/Fundia	28.07.06	—	—	Art.6(1)(b)	Iron and steel
M.4226	DSGI/Fotovista	29.01.06	—	—	Art.6(1)(b	Retailing
M.4229	APHL/L&R/Netcare/General Healthcare Group	25.07.06	—	—	Art.6(1)(b)	Regulatory
M.4232	Scottish & Newcastle/Kuehne + Nagel/JV	28.01.06	—	—	Art.6(1)(b)	Supporting transport
M.4234	Carlson/One Equity Partners/Carlson Wagonlit	03.07.06	—	—	Art.6(1)(b)	Travel agencies
M.4238	E.ON/Prazská Plynárenská	11.07.06	—	—	Art.6(1)(b)	Electricity
M.4239	Plastic Omnium/Inopart	27.10.06	—	—	Art.6(1)(b)	Motor vehicles
M.4241	Boeing/Aviall	18.08.06	—	—	Art.6(1)(b)	Aerospace
M.4242	Thermo Electron/Fisher Scientific	09.11.06	—	5 [2006] IS38	Art.6(1)(b) with conditions and obligations	Measuring instruments
M.4249	Abertis/Autostrade	22.09.06	—	5 [2006] IS39	Art.6(1)(b)	Transport activities
M.4256	Xstrata/Falconbridge	13.07.06	—	—	Art.6(1)(b)	Mining
M.4257	Smithfield/Oaktree/Sara Lee Foods Europe	00.00.00	—	—	Art.6(1)(b)	Preservation of meat

MERGER No.	NAME	DATE	O.J.	C.M.L.R.	TYPE OF DECISION	PRODUCT SECTOR
M.4265	Philips/Avent	28.08.06	—	—	Art.6(1)(b)	Electrical machinery
M.4271	Daikin/OYL	02.10.06	—	—	Art.6(1)(b)	Electric appliances
M.4284	AXA/Winterthur	28.08.06	—	—	Art.6(1)(b)	Insurance
M.4288	Saab/EMW	31.08.06	—	—	Art.6(1)(b)	Weapons and ammunition
M.4291	Voestalpine/Profilafroid/Sap	19.09.06	—	—	Art.6(1)(b)	Iron and steel
M.4293	Nordic Capital Fund Vi/Ica Meny	08.09.06	—	—	Art.6(1)(b)	Manufacture of cocoa
M.4294	Arcelor/SNCFL/CFL Cargo	09.10.06	—	—	Art.6(1)(b)	Transport
M.4297	Nokia/Siemens	13.11.06	—	—	Art.6(1)(b)	Telecommunications
M.4298	Aggregate Industries/Foster Yeoman	06.09.06	—	5 [2006] IS23	Art.6(1)(b) and 9(3)	Quarrying of stone
M.4300	Philips/Intermagnetics	07.11.06	—	—	Art.6(1)(b)	Medical equipment
M.4301	Alliance Boots/Cardinal Health	22.09.06	—	—	Art.6(1)(b)	Pharmaceutical goods
M.4314	Johnson & Johnson/Pfizer Consumer Healthcare	11.12.06	—	—	Art.6(2) with conditions and obligations	Pharmaceutical products
M.4316	ATOS Origin/Banksys/BCC	29.09.06	—	—	Art.6(1)(b)	Finance
M.4318	Veolia/Cleanaway	21.09.06	—	—	Art.6(1)(b) with conditions and obligations	Waste
M.4319	Mondi/Schleipen & Erkens	24.10.06	—	—	Art.6(1)(b)	Manufacture of paper
M.4321	Siemens/Bayer Diagnostics	31.10.06	—	—	Art.6(1)(b)	Medical equipment
M.4323	Arla/Ingman Foods	15.01.07	—	—	Art.6(1)(b)	Food products
M.4336	MAN/Scania	20.12.06	—	—	Art.6(1)(b)	Motor vehicles
M.4337	Thales/Alcatel Divisions Transport et Systemes	07.11.06	—	—	Art.6(1)(b)	Transport
M.4338	Cinven/Warburg Pincus/Casema/ Multikabel	06.09.06	—	—	Art.6(1)(b)	Courier activities
M.4344	Lactalis/Nestle/JV (II)	19.09.06	—	—	Art.6(1)(b)	Dairies and cheese making
M.4346	NTN/SNR	27.03.07	—	—	Art.6(1)(b)	Driving elements
M.4348	PKN/Mazeikiu	07.11.06	—	—	Art.6(1)(b)	Petroleum products
M.4350	Hewlett Packard/Mercury Interactive	20.10.06	—	—	Art.6(1)(b)	Computers
M.4351	Wolseley/DT Group	06.09.06	—	—	Art.6(1)(b)	Household articles
M.4353	Permira/All3Media Group	22.09.06	—	—	Art.6(1)(b)	Publishing

MERGER No.	NAME	DATE	O.J.	C.M.L.R.	TYPE OF DECISION	PRODUCT SECTOR
M.4356	Deutsche Bank/Berliner Bank	15.12.06	—	—	Art.6(1)(b)	Finance
M.4367	APW/APSA/Nordic Capital/Capio	16.03.07	—	—	Art.6(1)(b) with conditions and obligations	Hospital activities
M.4368	Edison/Eneco Energia	19.10.06	—	—	Art.6(1)(b)	Electricity
M.4370	EBN/Cogas Energy	28.09.06	—	—	Art.6(1)(b)	Manufacture of gas
M.4381	JCI/Fiamm	12.02.07	[2006] C268	—	Art.8(2) with conditions and obligations	Electrical equipment
M.4384	Hombergh/de Pundert/PIB/Ovako	10.11.06	—	—	Art.6(1)(b)	Iron & steel
M.4389	WLR/BST	05.12.06	—	—	Art.6(1)(b)	Textiles and motor vehicles
M.4392	DSGI/FR-Invest/F-Group JV	30.11.06	—	—	Art.6(1)(b)	Real estate
M.4395	Boeing/C-Map	16.01.07	—	—	Art.6(1)(b)	Software consultancy
M.4401	Basell/Münchsmünster Cracker and Associated Assets	20.12.06	—	—	Art.6(1)(b)	Chemicals
M.4402	UCB/Schwarz Pharma	21.11.06	—	—	Art.6(1)(b)	Pharmaceuticals
M.4403	Thales/Finmeccanica/AAS/Telespazio	04.04.07	—	—	Art.8(1)	Aerospace
M.4404	Universal Music Group/BMG Music Publishing	08.12.06	—	5 [2006] IS29	Art.6(1)(c)	Entertainment activities
M.4408	Tata/Corus	21.12.06	—	—	Art.6(1)(b)	Iron & steel
M.4413	Appolo Group/GE Advanced Materials	30.11.06	—	—	Art.6(1)(b)	Chemical products
M.4415	Motorola/Symbol	08.01.07	—	—	Art.6(1)(b)	Computers
M.4417	Telecom Italia/AOL German Access Business	28.11.06	—	—	Art.6(1)(b)	Telecommunications
M.4418	Nycomed Group/Altana Pharma	13.12.06	—	—	Art.6(1)(b)	Pharmaceuticals
M.4420	Credit Agricole/Fiat Auto/Fafs	05.12.06	—	—	Art.6(1)(b)	Finance
M.4424	JT/Gallaher	21.02.07	—	—	Art.6(1)(b)	Tobacco products
M.4426	Sabic/Huntsman Petrochemicals UK	20.12.06	—	—	Art.6(1)(b)	Chemicals
M.4432	Oerlikon/Saurer	22.11.06	—	—	Art.6(1)(b)	Paints, motor vehicles accessories
M.4434	Ricoh/Danka	08.12.06	—	—	Art.6(1)(b)	Office appliances
M.4441	EN+/Glencore/Sual/UC Rusal	01.02.07	—	—	Art.6(1)(b)	Other mining and quarrying; Aluminium production

MERGER No.	NAME	DATE	O.J.	C.M.L.R.	TYPE OF DECISION	PRODUCT SECTOR
M.4442	Carphone Warehouse/AOL UK	07.12.06	—	—	Art.6(1)(b)	Telecommunications
M.4450	Umicore/Zinifex/Neptune	26.02.07	—	—	Art.6(1)(b)	Non-ferrous minig
M.4456	Mahle/Dana EPG	06.03.07	—	—	Art.6(1)(b)	Motor vehicles
M.4465	Thrane & Thrane/Nera	21.03.07	—	—	Art.6(1)(b)	Measuring appliances
M.4468	Candover Partners/Hilding Anders	15.11.06	—	—	Art.6(1)(b)	Furniture
M.4469	Scholz/Voestalpine/Scholz Austria	22.03.07	—	—	Art.6(1)(b)	Recycling
M.4475	Schneider Electric/APC	08.02.07	—	—	Art.6(1)(b) with conditions and obligations	Power supply devices
M.4476	Norilsk Nickel/OMG Nickel	06.02.07	—	—	Art.6(1)(b)	Metal production
M.4478	KKR/Goldman Sachs/Kion	20.12.06	—	—	Art.6(1)(b)	Lifting and handling equipment
M.4484	Danske Bank/Sampo Bank	30.01.07	—	—	Art.6(1)(b)	Finance
M.4494	Evraz/Highveld	20.02.07	—	—	Art.6(1)(b) with conditions and obligations	Non-ferrous metal production
M.4495	Alfa Acciai/Cronimet/Remondis/TSR Group	06.02.07	—	—	Art.6(1)(b) and 9(3)	Recycling
M.4500	Nemak/TK Aluminium "A"	03.04.07	—	—	Art.6(1)(b)	Casting of steel
M.4501	HAL/Energia/NB	09.01.07	—	—	Art.6(1)(b)	Life insurance
M.4502	Lite-on/PBDS	16.02.07	—	—	Art.6(1)(b)	Computers
M.4503	PBDS/Philips APM	16.02.07	—	—	Art.6(1)(b)	Computers
M.4504	SFR/Tele 2	19.03.07	—	—	Art.6(1)(c)	Telecommunications
M.4505	Freeport-McMoran Copper & Gold/ Phelps Dodge Corporation	20.02.07	—	—	Art.6(1)(b)	Copper production
M.4507	Givaudan/Quest International	21.02.07	—	—	Art.6(1)(b)	Detergents
M.4508	Alstom UK/Balfour Beatty/JV	30.03.07	—	—	Art.6(1)(b)	Special purpose machinery
M.4509	Philips/PLI	29.01.07	—	—	Art.6(1)(b)	Electrical appliances
M.4515	CSN/Corus	29.01.07	—	—	Art.6(1)(b)	Iron & steel
M.4517	Iberdrola/Scottish Power	26.03.07	—	—	Art.6(1)(b)	Electricity and gas
M.4518	Alcoa/Orkla/Soft Alloy Extrusion JV	19.04.07	—	—	Art.6(1)(b)	Metals
M.4519	Lagardere/Sportfive	18.01.07	—	—	Art.6(1)(b)	Publishing

MERGER No.	NAME	DATE	O.J.	C.M.L.R.	TYPE OF DECISION	PRODUCT SECTOR
M.4521	LGI/Telenet	26.02.07	—	—	Art.6(1)(b)	Telecommunications
M.4524	Nemak/Hydro Castings	23.02.07	—	—	Art.6(1)(b)	Casting of steel
M.4532	Lukoil/Conocophillips	21.02.07	—	—	Art.6(1)(b)	Motor vehicles
M.4536	Magneti Marelli/Concordia	25.04.07	—	—	Art.6(1)(b)	Electrical equipment
M.4547	KKR/Permira/Prosiebensat.1	22.02.07	—	—	Art.6(1)(b)	Telecommunications
M.4561	GE/Smiths Aerospace	23.04.07	—	—	Art.6(1)(b)	Electricity
M.4562	S&B/Halliburton/Cebo JV	18.04.07	—	—	Art.6(1)(b)	Non-metallic mineral products
M.4569	GE/Abbott Diagnostics Division	24.04.07	—	—	Art.6(1)(b)	Medical and surgical equipment
M.4576	AVR/VAN Gansewinkel	03.04.07	—	—	Art.6(1)(b)	Treatment of waste
M.4579	Investor/Morgan Stanley/Mölnlycke	27.03.07	—	—	Art.6(1)(b)	Pharmaceutical
M.4588	Petroplus/Coryton Refinery Business	26.04.07	—	—	Art.6(1)(b)	Natural gas
M.4590	Rewe/Delvita	25.04.07	—	—	Art.6(1)(b)	Retail sale
M.4591	Weather Investments/Hellas Telecommunications	04.04.07	—	—	Art.6(1)(b)	Telecommunications
M.4608	Siemens/UGS Corporation	27.04.07	—	—	Art.6(1)(b)	Publishing of software
M.4613	Eurazeo SA/Apcoa Parking Holdings GmbH	20.04.07	—	—	Art.6(1)(b)	Land transports
M.4615	Merlin/Tussauds	26.04.07	—	—	Art.6(1)(b)	Amusement park activities
M.4624	EQT/Scandic	25.04.07	—	—	Art.6(1)(b)	Hotels

TABLE 6

CHRONOLOGICAL LIST OF MERGER DECISIONS (EC)—SIMPLIFIED PROCEDURE

NAME	DATE
BHP/Mitsubishi/QCT	28.09.00
HVB/Commerzbank/DB/Dresdner/JV	04.10.00
SHV/NPM Capital	04.10.00
Thyssen Krupp Werkstoffe/Röhm	09.10.00
Atos/Origin	09.10.00
NCR/4Front	12.10.00
Mopla/Deutsche Bank/Trevira	12.10.00
Tietoenator/EDB Business Partner/JV	16.10.00
Banco Commercial Portugues/Banco de Sabadell/Ibersecurities	18.10.00
France Telecom/Schmid/Mobilcom	24.10.00
Ergo/BBV Italia	24.10.00
Apollo Group/Shell Resin Business	27.10.00
Skanska/Kvaerner Construction	27.10.00
Gruner+Jahr/Publigroupe/G+J Medien	27.10.00
RWE/Thames Water	27.10.00
ABB/Avireal/JV	08.11.00
Kohlberg Kravis Roberts/Laporte	13.11.00
BT/Amadeus/JV	13.11.00
Citigroup/Associates	14.11.00
Achmea/BCP/Eureko	17.11.00
Telefonica/Sonera/German UMTS/JV	17.11.00
Minority Equity Investments/UBF	17.11.00
CCF Loxxia/Crédit Lyonnais – Slibail/JV	21.11.00
Reuters/Verlagsgruppe Handelsblatt/Meteor	22.11.00
Techint/Stella/James Jones/Sirti JV	22.11.00
Fiat/Unicredito Banca Mobiliare/JV	27.11.00
SJPC/SC De Milo/De Milo	30.11.00
ISP/ESPN/Globosat JV	04.12.00
Liverpool Victoria Friendly Society/AC Ventures/JV	06.12.00
Endesa/Telecom Italia/Union Fenosa/Auna	06.12.00
Ratos/Quality Laboratories	07.12.00
Celestica/NEC Technologies UK	13.12.00
SHFCLP (La Poste)/Mayne Nickless Europe	13.12.00
NEC/Schott Glass/NEC Schott JV	14.12.00
Edizione Holding/NHS/Comune di Parma/AMPS	14.12.00
AGF/Zwolsche Algemeene	18.12.00
Solectron/Natsteel Electronics	19.12.00
AOL/Banco Santander	19.12.00
Marinopoulos Abette/Sephora Holding/JV	20.12.00
Du Pont/Sabanci Holdings/JV	22.12.00

Table 6

NAME	DATE
CVC/Advent/Carlyle/Lafarge	05.01.01
Telefonica Intercontinental/Sonera 3G Holding/Consortium IPSE 2000	09.01.01
Sofinim/KBC Invest/Mercator & Noordsta/VIV/Tourneoleon/De Clerck/FOC	11.01.01
Kuoni/TRX/E-TRX/TRX Central Europe JV	17.01.01
Terra/Amadeus/1Travel Com	17.01.01
Industri Kapital/Fives-Lille	17.01.01
Babcock Borsig/MG Technologies/SAP Markets/Deutsche Bank/Va Tech/ ec4ec	22.01.01
CU Italia/Banca Popolare di Lodi/JV	24.01.01
CSC Ploenzke/Dachser/E-Chain Logistics	26.01.01
Lafarge/Blue Circle/JV	29.01.01
ENI/Lasmo	01.02.01
Schroder Ventures Ltd/Homebase	05.02.01
Rewe/BML/Standa Commerciale	08.02.01
ABN Amro/Perkins Food	08.02.01
Océ-Technologies/Real Software/Océ Real Business Solutions	12.02.01
E.On Energie/enregie Oberösterreich/JCE+JME	12.02.01
Hutchison/Investor/HI3G	19.02.01
SFK99 Rahasto/Fortum/Naps Systems	22.02.01
AEA Investors/DLJMB Funding III/BF Goodrich Performance Materials	22.02.01
Berkshire Hathaway/Johns Manville	22.02.01
BASF/Bertschi/Hoyer/Vlag/JV	23.02.01
Sanmina Corporation/AB Segerström & Svensson	23.02.01
Thomson Multimedia/Technicolor	28.02.01
Ericsson/Skandia/Alleato JV	08.03.01
Banco Popolare Espanol/Fortior Holding	12.03.01
Hermes/Codan/JV	12.03.01
Telefonica/Portugal Telecom/Brazilian JV	13.03.01
Vattenfall/Hamburger Electrizitätswerke/Nordic Powerhouse	13.03.01
Gilde/Capvis/Soudronic	16.03.01
Siemens/Janet/JV	19.03.01
Deutsche Bank/Banque Worms	19.03.01
Sydkraft/ABB/German Power Trading JV	21.03.01
Marconi/RTS/JV	23.03.01
Xchange/BAE Systems/JV	23.03.01
HSBC CCF/Banque Hervet	27.03.01
Conforama/Salzam Mercatone	27.03.01
Enichem/Polimeri	06.04.01
SGS/R&S/Freeglass JV	06.04.01
VNU/RCS Editori	06.04.01
Endesa/CDF/SNET	17.04.01
Mannesmann Arcor/Netcom Kassel	17.04.01
Shell/Beacon/3i/Twister	19.04.01
Nortel/Mundinteractivos/Broad Media/JV	25.04.01
SCI SY Systems/Nokia Networks	25.04.01

NAME	DATE
Vattenfall/Hew	02.05.01
Morgan/Grenfell/Whitbread	08.05.01
Dow Chemical/Ascot	11.05.01
Bertelsmann/RTL Group	11.05.01
Apax/Schering/Metagen	14.05.01
Société Générale/Deufin	17.05.01
Techint/VAI/JV	17.05.01
Cepsa Gas Comercializadora/Total Fina Elf Gas & Power Espana	17.05.01
Rail Gourmet Holding/Narvesen	17.05.01
Ineos/Phenolchemie	17.05.01
Barclays Bank/Minimax	21.05.01
NIB Capital/Internatio-Müller Chemical Distribution	21.05.01
International Fuel Cells (UTC)/SOPC (Shell)/JV	29.05.01
Tyco/CIT	29.05.01
Nobia/Magnet	29.05.01
Rewe Com/Henkel/Ten UK/Ten DE	31.05.01
Bertelsmann/VVC/JV	06.06.01
Schroder Ventures/Grammer	13.06.01
Ciaoweb/We Cube	14.06.01
Dexia/Banco Sabadell/Dexia Banco Local	19.06.01
Goldman Sachs/SJPC/SCP De Milo/Nascent	19.06.01
CDC/Charterhouse/Alstom Contracting	19.06.01
Knorr-Bremse SFS/Webasto Thermosysteme/JV	26.06.01
Infineon/Cryptomathic JV	27.06.01
Debitel/Debitel Nederland	29.06.01
Nomura International/Le Méridien Hotels	03.07.01
Belgacom/Bas Holding/Securitas	05.07.01
Blue Circle/Michelin/JV	05.07.01
GKN/Brambles	12.07.01
Eureko/Interamerican	16.07.01
Borg Warner/Hitachi	17.07.01
EQT Northern Europe/Electrolux	20.07.01
Thomson/Carlton/JV	26.07.01
SWB/Stadtwerke Bielefeld/JV	27.07.01
GFE/Shell Hydrogen/HQC	02.08.01
RPBE/Britax	06.08.01
Sara Lee/Earthgrains	06.08.01
SCI Systems/Nokia Networks	06.08.01
Autostrade/Saba	10.08.01
Fortum/OM/JV	10.08.01
RZB/Centrobank	21.08.01
Cinven/Castrol	23.08.01
EQT Northern Europe/Duni	27.08.01
Dow Reichhold/JV	28.08.01

Table 6

NAME	DATE
3 i/WM-Data/Atea	30.08.01
EDF/Fenice	30.08.01
Liberty Mutual/Grupo RSA España	31.08.01
Endesa/Enel-Elettrogen	04.09.01
Huk Coburg/Wiener Städtische/HMA	04.09.01
NSYS/Hunting Engineering	07.09.01
Shell-Cinergy/EDA/EPA JV	13.09.01
Itochu/Marubeni/JV	14.09.01
Apax/MP	14.09.01
Collins & Aikman Product/Textron Automotive Trim	14.09.01
RWA/Verbund/JV	17.09.01
Rabobank/Autoplastics	19.09.01
Sanmina/SCI Systems	20.09.01
IF Holding/FCI/JV	20.09.01
Johnson Controls/Sagem	20.09.01
Telenor East/Eco Telecom/Vimpel-Communications	21.09.01
Ericsson/Sony/JV	27.09.01
GE Insurance Holding/National Mutual Life	27.09.01
USG/Deutsche Perlite	27.09.01
Eads/Nortel	01.10.01
Stora Enso/Stora Enso Timber	04.10.01
Degussa/Ausimont	08.10.01
3 i/Eqvitec/Pohjola/Suomi/Ion Blast	11.10.01
3 i/Oko Bank/Uniglass Engineering	11.10.01
Xchange/Bae Systems/Procur	15.10.01
Maersk It/LM Ericsson/Wac	15.10.01
Bertelsmann/France Loisirs	17.10.01
Atle/Pricerunner	23.10.01
Solectron/C-Mac	23.10.01
Alcoa/Bhp Billiton/JV	23.10.01
Merloni/FosterWheeler Italiana	23.10.01
Prudential/BPB	06.11.01
ABN AMRO/Finaref-PPR/JV	06.11.01
Thyssenkrupp/Camon/Eurig	07.11.01
Mead/Westvaco	12.11.01
BRFKredit/Codan/Boligtorvet JV	21.11.01
Skanska/Sita	21.11.01
Siemens/AEM/E-Utile	23.11.01
Posten/DSV	26.11.01
Deutsche Bank/TDC/JV	27.11.01
Siemens/Wiener Stadtwerke/Master Talk	28.11.01
Nutricia/Baxter/2.HSC	06.12.01
Rhenus/Via Verkehr Holding (SNCF)/Rhenus-Keolis	07.12.01
Cinven/Klöckner Pentaplast	07.12.01
NPM/ABN AMRO/Norit Personal Care Holding	10.12.01

NAME	DATE
Iveco/Irisbus	11.12.01
Winterthur/Prudential Assurance	12.12.01
AT&T/Concert	17.12.01
Voestalpine/Polynorm	19.12.01
Anglogold/Normandy	19.12.01
CU Vita/Risparmio Vita Assicurazioni	20.12.01
Sonae/CNP-Assurances/LL Porto Retail JV	20.12.01
Sonae/CNP-Assurances/Inparsa JV	20.12.01
Utilicorp/DB Australia/Midlands Electricity/JV	03.01.02
Crédit Suisse/Belgacom/T-Mobile/Ben Nederland	17.01.02
Berkshire Hathaway/Fruit of the Loom	23.01.02
Endesa Energia/Spinveste/Ecocicloendesa-Energia	24.01.02
PGA Motors/Jardine Motors	25.01.02
Dansk Kapitalanlaeg/Ibsen	31.01.02
DMData/Stralfors/JV	07.02.02
B.Braun/Acordis/MAT	11.02.02
E.ON/Oberösterreichische Ferngas/Jihoceska	18.02.02
ING/Dibal	22.02.02
PTT/Hermes Versand	25.02.02
Swerock/Jehander/Aros	04.03.02
ECYR/Spinveste	12.03.02
3 i/Capman/Pretax	18.03.02
Sanmina-SCI/Alcatel	21.03.02
Zürich/Deutsche Bank Insurance Business	26.03.02
Mitsubishi/MMC Auto Deutschland	26.03.02
BC Partners/Galbani	27.03.02
Société Générale/Fiditalia	04.04.02
OBI/Unicoop/JV	09.04.02
Electrabel/TotalFinaElf/Photovoltech	18.04.02
Saubermacher/Lafarge Perlmooser/JV	23.04.02
Swiss Life/Fortis France	23.04.02
First Aqua Holding Ltd/Southern Water PLC	23.04.02
ABB/Promotion Capital/Single Source	24.04.02
Hochtief/Essen and Volkswagen/JV	24.04.02
Jabil/Alcatel	24.04.02
Industri Kapital/Gardena	26.04.02
RWE Power/Lucchini/Elettra GLL JV	26.04.02
CVC/Massive	30.04.02
Post Office Limited/First Rate Enterprises Limited/JV	02.05.02
Edeka/ADEG	02.05.02
ING Groep/Piraeus Bank	02.05.02
Norddeutsche Mischwerke/Haniel Baustoff – Industrie Zuschlagstoffe/JV	03.05.02
Brack Capital/Haslemere	03.05.02
B.Braun/Acordis/MAT	11.02.02
E.ON/Oberösterreichische Ferngas/Jihoceska	18.02.02

Table 6

NAME	DATE
ING/Dibal	22.02.02
PTT/Hermes Versand	25.02.02
Swerock/Jehander/Aros	04.03.02
ECYR/Spinveste	12.03.02
3 i/Capman/Pretax	18.03.02
Sanmina-SCI/Alcatel	21.03.02
Zürich/Deutsche Bank Insurance Business	26.03.02
Mitsubishi/MMC Auto Deutschland	26.03.02
BC Partners/Galbani	27.03.02
Société Générale/Fiditalia	04.04.02
OBI/Unicoop/JV	09.04.02
Saubermacher/Lafarge Perlmooser/JV	23.04.02
Swiss Life/Fortis France	23.04.02
First Aqua Holding Ltd/Southern Water PLC	23.04.02
ABB/Promotion Capital/Single Source	24.04.02
Hochtief/Essen and Volkswagen/JV	24.04.02
Jabil/Alcatel	24.04.02
Industri Kapital/Gardena	26.04.02
RWE Power/Lucchini/Elettra GLL JV	26.04.02
CVC/Massive	30.04.02
Post Office Limited/First Rate Enterprises Limited/JV	02.05.02
Edeka/ADEG	02.05.02
ING Groep/Piraeus Bank	02.05.02
Norddeutsche Mischwerke/Haniel Baustoff – Industrie Zuschlagstoffe/JV	03.05.02
Brack Capital/Haslemere	03.05.02
Volkswagen/Svenska Volkswagen	30.05.02
New Holding for Tourism BV/Preussag AG/Neos JV	30.05.02
Cinven/Carlyle/VUP	11.06.02
Nok/Watt	13.06.02
Siemens/First Sensor Technology	14.06.02
Casino/Laurus	14.06.02
Achmea/Royal & Sun Alliance Benelux	19.06.02
Volkswagen/Din Bil	21.06.02
TXU/Braunschweiger Versorgungs AG	26.06.02
Doughty Hanson/ATU Group	15.07.02
Lehman Brothers/Haslemere	17.07.02
CVC/Six Vendex KBB	18.07.02
Kone/Partek	01.08.02
BLSI/Geopost	02.08.02
Klepierre/Finiper/IGC	05.08.02
Axa Private Equity/Bonna Sabla	05.08.02
Kingfisher/Castorama Dubois	06.08.02
Logista/Gestcamp/Logesta	07.08.02
Outokumpu OYJ/Avestapolarit OYJ	07.08.02
Corus/Redrow/JV	09.08.02

NAME	DATE
Outokumpu/Lennox	22.08.02
Vivendi Environment/Southern Water UK	23.08.02
ATG/Wallenius Wilhelmsen Lines/ATN Autoterminal Neuss	27.08.02
Electrabel S.A./ACEA S.P.A.	27.08.02
CVC/Halfords	27.08.02
Dexia/Banco Popular Espanol/Fortior	29.08.02
Dresdner Bank/Commerzbank/Montrada JV	02.09.02
Groupama Seguros y Reaseguros/Plus Ultra Seguros y Reaseguros	02.09.02
ING/Sonae/Filo JV	02.09.02
Accor/Interepargne/JV Servepar	05.09.02
DLJ Capital Funding INC/Hamsard – Bowater	05.09.02
Toyota/Toyota España	09.09.02
Hermes/OEKB/Prisma	10.09.02
TMI/Darfon/JV	10.09.02
Banco de Sabadell/Banco Comercial Portugues/Activobank JV	12.09.02
Cinven/National Car Parks	13.09.02
Prudential Financial/Sal Oppenheim/JV	13.09.02
Questor Bermuda/Teksid	13.09.02
Vestar Capital Partners/Cardo Rail	13.09.02
Macquarie Airports Luxembourg/Aeroporti di Roma	20.09.02
Toshiba/Mitsubishi/JV	20.09.02
Deutsche Telekom/Ben	20.09.02
Bayerische Landesbank/J.P. Morgan Chase/Lehman Brothers/Formula one Group	26.09.02
Rheinmetall/Diehl/Dynitec	27.09.02
Zeta 4/Monte Dei Paschi/Banca Intesa/Gori Zucchi	10.10.02
RWE Solutions/Schott Glaskontor/RWE Schott Solar	17.10.02
ABN AMRO Private Equity (UK)/Jessops	21.10.02
Deutsche Post/Wegener/Interlanden	25.10.02
Sofinco/Commercial Bank of Greece/JV	28.10.02
DMData/Kommunedata/Post Danmark/E-Boks JV	30.10.02
Finmeccanica/Telespazio	30.10.02
Sumitomo/Takeda/JV	30.10.02
Dixon/Unieuro	08.11.02
Mitsubishi/Nissho IWAI/JV	15.11.02
ACEA Distribuzione/Bticino/Siemens	19.11.02
AON Jauch & Hübener/Siemens/JV	26.11.02
Hitachi/Mitsubishi/JV	26.11.02
Credit Suisse/Blackstone/Nycomed	26.11.02
AVH/CNP/GIB JV	06.12.02
DZ-Bank/ÖVAG/VB-Leasing	09.12.02
AEGON/La Mondiale	13.12.02
Knauf/Alcopor	13.12.02
Mediatrade/Endemol/JV	16.12.02
Daimler Chrysler/Hyundai Motor Company/JV	18.12.02

Table 6

NAME	DATE
Candover/Cinven/Kap	18.12.02
Candover Investments/Ontex	19.12.02
CVC Group/El Arbol	19.12.02
Nestlé/Fonterra/JV	20.12.02
Apax/Duke/Focus Wickes /JV	14.01.03
Capvis/Quadriga/Zellweger Uster	14.01.03
Global Crossing/Hutchison/St Telemedia	16.01.03
Tebodin/Lockwood Greene/JV	16.01.03
DMData/WM-Data/JV	17.01.03
Credit Suisse/Safilo	17.01.03
Amec/FS	21.01.03
Rautakirja/Hachette Distribution Services/JV	29.01.03
Schroder Ventures Ltd/Compass	30.01.03
Aldeasa/Compass/Foodlasa	30.01.03
Emerson/Dana/JV	31.01.03
Future Capital/CDPQ/Sam Holding/Zipperling/Ormecon	03.02.03
Blackstone Group/TRW Automotive	04.02.03
Acea/BTicino/Siemens Metering/JV	10.02.03
Schroders Ventures Limited/Premiere	13.02.03
Penske/DaimlerChrystler/VM Motori	13.02.03
Burda/HDP/Catherine Nemo	21.02.03
Bain Fund Group/Sigmakalon Group	24.02.03
Apax Europe v/Goldman Sachs/Providence/Telekom Cable/JV	28.02.03
Nuon Deutschland/Stadtwerke Leipzig/Stadtlicht	14.03.03
Aeroports de Paris/Aelia	17.03.03
Duferco/Sorral/Beautor	20.03.03
Dupont Statoil/JV	25.03.03
Axa Private Equity/Tokheim International	25.03.03
ABN Amro Capital/PizzaExpress	27.03.03
Nissho Iwai/Nichimen	28.03.03
Mediaset/Telecinco/Publiespana	28.03.03
Deutsche Bahn/Westlb/Aurelis/JV	28.03.03
Carlyle/Breed Technologies	10.04.03
SGAM4D/Guggenhein/IES	16.04.03
Hamburgische Landesbank/Landesbank Schleswig Holstein	25.04.03
Delta Lloyd/ABN AMRO/JV	30.04.03
Thomesto/SCA Holz JV	05.05.03
Compass/Cremonini/JV	06.05.03
Sika/Buzzi/JV	08.05.03
Süd-Chemie/Sabic/Scientific Design JV	12.05.03
Cinven/Fitness First	15.05.03
Xstrata/MIM	19.05.03
Union Fenosa/ENI/Union Fenosa Gas	21.05.03
Wienenberger/Koramic Building Products/JV	23.05.03
ING/Sonae/Ascendente JV	27.05.03

NAME	DATE
CVC Funds/Viterra	27.05.03
P&O Ports/CMA-CGM/Egis Ports	28.05.03
ING/Entrium	12.06.03
Barclays Bank/Banco Zaragozano	12.06.03
Great-West Lifeco/Canada Life Financial	17.06.03
De Agostini Invest/Toro Assicurazioni	17.06.03
Scottish & Newcastle/Parfil	18.06.03
Victor Rijssen/Kon. Volker Wessels Stevin	18.06.03
Ente Vasco de la Energia/Hidrocantabrico/Naturcorp	19.06.03
Holtzbrink Networxs/Weltbild/1-Online Venture/Bertelsmann Online	25.06.03
Hearst/De Telegraaf Tijdschriften/JV	01.07.03
Diaego/Heineken/Olfiltra/JV	10.07.03
Investcorp Financial Services/Minimax	10.07.03
Schroder Ventures Limited/Rodenstock	14.07.03
Montagu Private Equity/Actaris	15.07.03
Total/Samsung Chemicals/JV	17.07.03
United Technologies/Chubb	18.07.03
BP/Alfa Group/Access/Renova/TNK-BP	25.07.03
GDF/Italcogim/JV	25.07.03
Allianz/Sole/Zanussi Elettromeccanica	30.07.03
Montagu Private Equity/Linpac	04.08.03
Onex/Kieft/Neue Filmpalast	04.08.03
MTU/Friedrichshafen/RWE Fuel Cells/JV	20.08.03
Bank One Corporation/Quintiles	20.08.03
Nortel/NNG-NNF	21.08.03
Rewe/Bon Appetit	22.08.03
EADS/EADS Telecom	22.08.03
REWE Bon Appetit	22.08.03
Liberty Media/QVC	25.08.03
PAI Partners/Grandvision	29.08.03
Liberty Insurance/Metlife Iberia	03.09.03
Apollo/Soros/Goldman Sachs/Cablecom	04.09.03
3i Group/Refresco	04.09.03
Permira III/Goldman Sachs Group/Blackstone Group/Debenhams	09.09.03
Sasol/Mitsubishi Chemical/JV	11.09.03
ACH/ACC	11.09.03
Toshiba/Mitsubishi Electric/JV	17.09.03
American Express Financial Corporation/Threadneedle	19.09.03
Vestar Capital Partners/FL Selenia	19.09.03
Amcor/Amcor Flexibles Europe	25.09.03
Arla/Nordzucker/JV	30.09.03
Phoenix/Tamro	30.09.03
Carlyle/Saint-Gobain Terreal	10.10.03
VW/Pon/Pon Financial Services	15.10.03
Generali/Continent Holding	15.10.03

Table 6

NAME	DATE
Advent International Moeller Holding	20.10.03
Cerberus/ANC Rental	21.10.03
UFG/Enel/UFEE/JV	21.10.03
CVC/TPG/Debenhams	05.11.03
Thyssenkrupp/Mercedes Lenkungen	10.11.03
Atos Origin/Sema Group	10.11.03
Generali/Zurich Financial Services	13.11.02
Karolin Machine Tool/ABB I-R Waterjet Systems	13.11.03
Ferroser/Teris/Ecocat JV	19.11.03
Cap Gemini/Transiciel	24.11.03
ABN Amro/Global Garden Products	26.11.03
San Paolo Imi/Santander Group/Allfunds JV	28.11.03
General Electric/Sophia	01.12.03
Ratos/Lehmann Brothers/Fastighetstornet	01.12.03
Royal Bank of Scotland Group/First Active PLC	03.12.03
Electra Partners/Azelis	08.12.03
Götz/Schwenk/Strabag/BFU JV	09.12.03
Nestle/Colgate-Palmolive JV	10.12.03
Doughty Hanson/Saft	12.12.03
Cardinal Health /Intercare Group	16.12.03
KKR/MTU	16.12.03
Nestlé/Ingman Foods	17.12.03
Investcorp Group/Hilding Anders AB	17.12.03
TPG/JPMP/Kraton	18.12.03
GE/Vivendi Universal Entertainment	19.12.03
Salzgitter/Volkswagen/JV	15.01.04
Blackstone/Apax/Sulo	15.01.04
Platinum/Hays Logistics	23.01.04
Anglogold/Ashanti	29.01.04
Hogg Robinson/Kuoni	29.01.04
Norsk Hydro/Wingas/Hydrowingas JV	02.02.04
Anglo American/Bauernfeind	04.02.04
RBS/BSCH/Britax	04.02.04
Santander/Doncasters	04.02.04
Telenor/Sonofon	05.02.04
Banque Populaire/DZ Bank/VR Factorem	06.02.04
Candover/JPMP/3i/ABB	20.02.04
Morgan Stanley/Glick/Canary Wharf	20.02.04
Vestar Capital/OGF	20.02.04
Matsushita Electric Industrial/Matsushita Electric Works	03.03.04
Eurailco/Transregio	10.03.04
Blackstone/Celanese	10.03.04
Metro/Adler	16.03.04
Apax/Permira/New Look	19.03.04
PPM Ventures/Triton/Pharmacia Diagnostics	23.03.04

NAME	DATE
General Electric Consumer France/Abbey National	27.03.04
SEI/Fujitsu/FQD	29.03.04
CD&R Fund/VWR	01.04.04
Geso/Zweckverband/Gaso	07.04.04
TPG Group/Francisco Partners/Smart JV	14.04.04
Fortis/SG/Secfinex JV	15.04.04
Endesa/Snet	20.04.04
Aegon/Cam/JV Mediterraneo Vida	22.04.04
Xchanging/Deutsche Bank/ETB JV	28.04.04
Westlb/Klöckner	05.05.04
JP Morgan/Bank One	10.05.04
Nordic capital/Trenor	10.05.04
JP Morgan/Bridgepoint/Siutsa	18.05.04
Carlyle/Saprogal	25.05.04
Glaxosmithkline/Sanofi-Synthelabo (Assets)	25.05.04
Advent/Sportfive	27.05.04
UTC/EADS Revima	03.06.04
CTS/HGK/Knapsack/JV	03.06.04
Total Lubrifiants/Endel/Daenerys JV	03.06.04
NYK Reefers/Lauritzen Cool/LCL JV	07.06.04
BBVA/BNL/JV	07.06.04
Thales/Diehl/Diehl Luftfahrt Elektronik	08.06.04
Goldman Sachs/Titan	16.06.04
Charterhouse/Autobar	17.06.04
UBS/Motor Columbus	21.06.04
Nokia/Metso/Avantone	25.06.04
Apax/PCM Uitgevers	25.06.04
Deutsche BP/Oktan/Aral Wärme Service	28.06.04
Dow Chemicals/Pic/Planet JV	28.06.04
Investcorp/Apcoa	28.06.04
Electra/Englefield/GSL JV	28.06.04
First Reserve/Blackstone/Rag American Coal	29.06.04
Apax/Capman/Solid	01.07.04
3i/Keolis	02.07.04
TPG/DLJ/CSBF/Grohe	07.07.04
Putnam/Union Investment/Union Panagora	09.07.04
TCL/Alcatel	16.07.04
Platinum/Dystar	20.07.04
PGA/GGBA	20.07.04
Goldman Sachs/Cerberus/GWS Berlin	22.07.04
Sita/Sol/Jäteässät/Hyötykeskus JV	26.07.04
Land NRW/NRW Bank	27.07.04
Siemens/3i/Aguth/Xtramind	28.07.04
Reliance/Trevira	29.07.04
Pfizer/Campto	29.07.04

Table 6

NAME	DATE
UTC/IHI	29.07.04
Doughty Hanson/Balta	29.07.04
Bridgepoint/Pets at Home Group	09.08.04
Allianz/Four Seasons	09.08.04
Barclays Private Equity France/Fives-Lille	10.08.04
KKR/Auto-Teile-Unger	12.08.04
Alpinvest/3i/CID/JV	18.08.04
Hutchison Whampoa/Rossmann Beteiligung/Dirk Rossmann	20.08.04
Shell/Saudi Aramco/Showa Shell	20.08.04
Caterpillar/Xpart	20.08.04
Swiss Re/LAHC	20.08.04
Siemens/BBC Technology	20.08.04
BBVA/BNL	20.08.04
Asquith/ISIS/JVCO	24.08.04
Helsingin/Vantaan/E.ON Finland/Lahti/Seu	24.08.04
Lactalis/Grupo Prado Cervera/Central Lechera Vallisotelana	25.08.04
Dixons Group/Kotsovolos	25.08.04
Cerberus/GDX	27.08.04
CVC/FP/Hynix System IC Business (JV)	31.08.04
RIVR/Petroplus	01.09.04
SEB Trygg Liv/Codan Pension	01.09.04
PPR/FNAC/Marinopoulos/JV	02.09.04
Rewe/ASP	03.09.04
Goldman Sachs/QMH	07.09.04
Uniqua/Claris Vita	13.09.04
KBC/Rabobank/JV	14.09.04
TGP Post/Essent Retail/Cendris-BSC JV	15.09.04
CD&R Fund VI/Culligan	15.09.04
KKR/DLJ/Jostens - Von Hoffmann - Arcade	16.09.04
Finmeccanica/Augusta-Westland	20.09.04
Deutsche Post/Guipuzcoana	24.09.04
IPR/Mitsui/Mec	07.10.04
Talanx/Neue Leben	15.10.04
Accor/Club Méditerranée	19.10.04
JPMP/Apollo Group/AMC	25.10.04
CVC/BASF Printing Inks	28.10.04
T-Mobile/Polska Telefonia Cyfrowa	28.10.04
Ripplewood/Honsel	28.10.04
Sportfive/HSG/JV	04.11.04
Conoco/Lukoil/NMN/JV	05.11.04
Cinven/CBR	05.11.04
Apax/Vista Desarrollo/Itevelesa	10.11.04
Outokumpu Wasacopper/Aurajoki/Cupru JV	12.11.04
Jabil/Philips Consumer Electronics Poland	17.11.04
Apax/Cinven/World Directories	18.11.04

NAME	DATE
Rabobank/BGZ	19.11.04
3i/Skanska FM	19.11.04
Repsol/Borealis Polímeros	19.11.04
Sabanci/Dupontsa	22.11.04
BC Partners/Picard	25.11.04
Mannesmann/Fuchs	26.11.04
Permira/Ahold	26.11.04
Siemens/Bonus Energy	29.11.04
Friends Provident/Lombard/IDH	30.11.04
Europcar/Tui/JV	06.12.04
Techint/Stella/James Jones/Investindustrial/Clessidra/Sirti	07.12.04
BP/HDPE JV	07.12.04
Auchan/La Rinascente	14.12.04
Blackstone/Gerresheimer	14.12.04
Industri Kapital/Idex	15.12.04
Cerberus/Peguform	16.12.04
Borgwarner/Beru	17.12.04
Permira/Private Equity Partners/Marazzi	17.12.04
Veolia/BVAG	17.12.04
Viterra/Deutschbau	17.12.04
Mabsa/Belgian State/BIAC/JV	17.12.04
Bridgepoint/SEA	20.12.04
APAX/Cinven/CBR Group	20.12.04
Alcadis/Isuzu/Mitsubishi/Isuzu Benelux JV	21.12.04
Isuzu/Berge/Mitsubishi/JV	21.12.04
Charterhouse/TDF	21.12.04
Codan ET AL/Nai JV	22.12.04
CDP/STMicroelectronics	22.12.04
Société Générale/Otto/Hanseatic Bank/JV	23.12.04
KKR/DSD	07.01.05
Dresdner Bank/Cetelem/JV	07.01.05
Apax/ACP/Eve JV	13.01.05
RBI/Hawker Pacific/JV	14.01.05
De Raekt/ING	21.01.05
Xstrata/WMC Resources	24.01.05
Warburg/Providence/Telcordia	25.01.05
WESTLB/DAL	27.01.05
Electra/Thyssenkrupp Fahrzeuggus	28.01.05
BT/Albacom	31.01.05
Nordic Capital/Plastal Holding	02.02.05
DIFA/Investkredit/JV	03.02.05
AXA/Camaieu	10.02.05
Citigroup/Baltisches Haus/UAB Palink/JV	11.02.05
Petronas/Sasol/Uhambo JV	14.02.05
Danske Bank/National Europe Holdings/Northern Bank Insurance Services	14.02.05

Table 6

NAME	DATE
Rabobank/IHC	14.02.05
CNP/Capitalia/Fineco Vita	14.02.05
Gilde/Bekaert	16.02.05
Intek/Gim	16.02.05
KKR/Masonite	17.02.05
CVC/CSM	18.02.05
Achmea/Athlon/Partsplan JV	23.02.05
Hochtief/ABB/JV	24.02.05
3M/Magna/I & T/JV	28.02.05
LGB/Klöckner	28.02.05
EQT/ISS/Healthcare/Carepartner JV	03.03.05
Orkla/Elkem	04.03.05
Bridgepoint/Attendo	08.03.05
CVC/Mivisa	09.03.05
Hutchinson Whampoa/North DN	10.03.05
Finmeccanica/AMS	14.03.05
BC Partners/Civen/Amadeus	16.03.05
Banca Intesa/Ifil/Marcegaglia/SIT	21.03.05
Kodak/KPG	21.03.05
Apollo/DirectTV/Hughes Network Systems	23.03.05
3i/Berkenhoff	23.03.05
Goldman Sachs/Cerberus/TET	23.03.05
Alcoa/AFL	23.03.05
EQT/Sanitec	01.04.05
EDP/Logicacmg/Edinfor	01.04.05
Severstal/Lucchini	11.04.05
Axa Private Equity/Larivière	11.04.05
DuPont/DDE	12.04.05
ÖVAG/Investkredit	15.04.05
3i/Providence/Crown Entertainment	15.04.05
The Coca-Cola Company/Coca-Cola Hellenic Bottling Company/Multon	15.04.05
Nordic Capital/Nycomed	19.04.05
Mitsubishi Tokyo/UFJ	21.04.05
Nordic Capital/Leaf INT	21.04.05
Stora Enso/Corenso	24.05.05
Dansk Supermarked/Netto	25.04.05
Sabanci/DUSA	25.04.05
ABN Amro/Banca Autonveneta	27.04.05
BBVA/BNL	27.04.05
Pirelli/DB Realestate/Investitori Associati/La Rinascente-UPIM	27.04.05
EQT/GSCP/ISS/JV	03.05.05
Lehman Brothers/Europe Reality/IHG Portofolip	10.05.05
PAI/Coin	12.05.05
PAI/FTE	19.05.05
TPG/APAX/TIM Hellas	26.05.05

NAME	DATE
Nordic Capital/Outokumpu Copper Products	30.05.05
Investcorp/Polyconcept	30.05.05
Barclays/Iveco/JV	31.05.05
CVC/Gilde/Bekaert Fencing	31.05.05
BC Partners/Dometic	01.06.05
Goldman Sachs/Euramax	06.06.05
Gluma Holdings/Glud & Marstrand	09.06.05
Siemens/Hyundai/JV	13.06.05
Gilde/DSM Bakery Ingredients	13.06.05
EQT IV/Brandtex	14.06.05
CGE/AMGA/SMAT/SAP	15.06.05
RR Donnelley/Astron	15.06.05
Thiel Logistik/Mondi/Proxar	16.06.05
3i Group/Carema	16.06.05
Trimoteur/Nibcapital/Fortis/Sandd	21.06.05
EHA/Rewe Austria/JV	27.06.05
Oranje-Nassau Group/SHV Holding/Edinburgh Oil & Gas	27.06.05
IBM/Global value	28.06.05
CVC/Cortefiel	30.06.05
Macquairie/CDPQ/Yellow Brick Road	01.07.05
Matlinpatterson LP/Matussière & Forest	04.07.05
Access Industries/Basell	04.07.05
Hyundai Motor Company/Hyundai Car UK	06.07.05
3i SGR/Giochi Preziozi	06.07.05
Ipr/Mitsui/Calpine Uk	07.07.05
Carlsberg/DLG/Sejet JV	07.07.05
Valoriza Gestion/Aguas de las palmas	22.07.05
Bilfinger Berger/WIB/JVC	26.07. 05
Sita/Flughafen Dusseldorf/FDITG	29.07.05
Goldman Sachs/Treofan	29.07.05
G+J/Styria Medien/JV	29.07.05
IPIC/OMV/JV	01.08.05
DAIG/Viterra	03.08.05
Dexia/Kommunalkredit/JV	04.08.05
Carlyle/Otor	09.08.05
Phoenix/A&C Adivar-Comfar	09.08.05
PHL/PEL	16.08.05
PAI Partners SAS/Kwik-Fit	16.08. 05
Danaher/Leica MS	22.08.05
Bertelsmann/Channel 5	26.08.05
CVC/Wavin	30.08.05
3i Group/PIHL	30.08.05
Bidvest/Deli XL	31.08.05
ABN Amro/IMCD	31.08.05
Webasto/Starck/Staxera	01.09.05

Table 6

NAME	DATE
3i/Aviapartner	02.09.05
Cleric Medical/MLP Life	05.09.05
Doughty Hanson/Moeller	05.09.05
West LB/Nord LB/Shinsei/Flowers/SGK	05.09.05
Barclays Private Equity/Neuwayer	05.09.05
Spohn Cement/HeidelbergCement	06.09.05
Apax/Versatel	06.09.05
CRH/Quester	15.09.05
Goldman Sachs a.o./CMP Fonds	15.09.05
System Capital Management-Metinvest/Leman Commodities	19.09.05
Apax/Panrico	19.09.05
Advent/Herlitz	19.09.05
Industri Kapital/Bonna Sabla	20.09.05
Advent/CCS	26.09.05
Barclays/Alstom Power Conversion	26.09.05
ML Global/BACP/N&W Global Vending	27.09.05
PAI Partners/Crown Holding GPC	27.09.05
Nomura/Kamps Food Retail Investments/Nordsee	28.09.05
AP Moller-Maersk/Kerr-McGee (North Sea Business)	28.09.05
LBO/Terreal	28.09.05
Transgourmet/Prodirest	28.09.05
CVC/Minit Group	03.10.05
Corman/Glanbia Consumer Foods/JV	04.10.05
Bayerische Landesbank/Speed	06.10.05
Permira-KKR/SBS Broadcasting	07.10.05
Deutsche Bank/Hardt/Trafalgar/Kunert	17.10.05
Tridonicatco/Toyoda Gosei/LED JV	19.10.05
Berkshire Hathaway/MEHC	20.10.05
Bain Fund Group/FCI	25.10.05
BC Funds/Fitness Frist	27.10.05
Svitzer/Wilhelmsen Offshore/JV	28.10.05
Pirelli RE/Banca Intesa/Ifil/Marcegaglia/SI/IT	28.10.05
Goldman Sachs/IHR Platz	09.11.05
Thyssen Krupp/Hellenic Shipyards	10.11.05
Johnson Controls/York	10.11.05
Apax/Barclays/Tchenguiz/Sommerfield/JV	18.11.05
Canon/Canon Espana	18.11.05
Gazprom/Sibneft	18.11.05
Mobilkom Austria/One/Paybox	21.11.05
Shell/Erg/Ionio Gas/JV	24.11.05
Philips/Lumileds	24.11.05
Polestar/Prisa/Ibersuizas/Iberian Capital/Dedalo	30.11.05
CRH/Baudedarf Lehmann/Dieter Niederste-Hollenberg/Bauking	01.12.05
Sun Capital/Sara Lee	05.12.05
Cinven/Frans Bonhomme	05.12.05

NAME	DATE
Macquarie Airports/Copenhagen/Copenhagen Airports	05.12.05
Industri Kapital/Gus Holland Holding	07.12.05
RBC/Dexia/JV	07.12.05
Credit Agricole/Banca Intesa/Nextra Investment Management	14.12.05
Arrow/DNS	14.12.05
PAI/SSK (Specialty Chemicals)	15.12.05
Gerdau/Grupo Santander/Bogey/Sidenor	16.12.05
Logista/Editorial Planeta/JV	16.12.05
Logista/Planeta De Agostani/JV	16.12.05
Gerdau/Grupo Santander/Bogey/Sidenor	16.12.05
Industri Capital/Kwintet	16.12.05
Belgian State/CVC/Post Danmark/De Post-La Poste	19.12.05
Technip/Subsea 7/Asia Pacific JV	19.12.05
JCI/SAFT/JV	19.12.05
ED & F Man/Safic Alcan	19.12.05
KKR/FL Selenia	19.12.05
VSE/Cegedel/JV	20.12.05
Fraport/Deutsche Bank/Budapest Airport	21.12.05
Hochtief Airport/CDPQ/Budapest Airport	21.12.05
Kuehne + Nagel/ACR Logistics	21.12.05
Endesa/Zedo	09.01.06
Morgan Stanley/AM Development	12.01.06
BAM/AM	12.01.06
Kalyani Brakes/Brembo/JV	13.01.06
GLB/Luminar/JV	18.01.06
SFC/SAG Gest/JV	24.01.06
Providence Carlyle/Com Hem	25.01.06
BS Investimenti/MCC Sofipa/IP Cleaning	26.01.06
Blackstone/Lion Capital/CSEB	30.01.06
Saab/Tietoenator/Tietosaab Systems JV	30.01.06
Charterhouse/Nocibé	30.01.06
Magna/CTS	31.01.06
Conoco Philips/Louis Dreyfus Refining & Marketing/Louis Dreyfus Energy Holding	31.01.06
Cognis/Golden Hope Plantations BHD/JV	01.02.06
G+J/Sanoma/JV	02.02.06
West LB/Odewald/Ash	07.02.06
Heinemann/HDS Retail/JV	08.02.06
Tessenderlo/Siemens/Advanced Power/JV	09.02.06
Investcorp/Autodistribution Group	09.02.06
Matlin Patterson/Deutsche Bank/Michel Thierry	10.02.06
Montagu/BSN Medical	10.02.06
GIB/Groupe FLO	15.02.06
BC Partners/Hyatt Regency Hotels & Tourism Hellas	17.02.06
Banca Intesa/NH Hoteles/NH Italia	17.02.06
CVC/KKR/AVR	24.02.06

Table 6

NAME	DATE
DSV/Frans Maas	24.02.06
Atel/Eosh	24.02.06
Goldman Sachs/Daiwa/SMBC/Sanyo	24.02.06
Apax/Tommy Hilfiger Corporation	28.02.06
Cerberus/Goldman Sachs/Wittur	28.02.06
EQT IV/Daimler Chrysler Off-Highway	01.03.06
Adecco/Deutscher Industrie Service	03.03.06
Lehman Brothers/Heinz European Seafood	08.03.06
AACF/Astorg/OFIC	08.03.06
Fujitsu Siemens Computer Holding/Siemens Business Services	09.03.06
TCCC/CCHBC/Fresh	09.03.06
Toyota Tsusho/Tomen	10.03.06
Mitsui/Evraz/Deniskovkaya Coal Mine JV	13.03.06
NEC/Philips Business Communications	13.03.06
Deutsche Post/Williams Lea	14.03.06
DZ Equity/L-Bank/Hornschuch	16.03.06
Bain/Texas Intruments	17.03.06
LBO France/Cegelec Holdings	20.03.06
Time Warner/CBS/JV	22.03.06
Allianz Group/Sonifim/United Broadcast Facilities	22.03.06
EnBW/SWD	22.03.06
Deutsche Telekom/Corpus/Morgan Stanley/Sireo	23.03.06
ENI/Grupo Amorim/CGD/Galp	24.03.06
Virgin/CPW/JV	29.03.06
Barclays/Tuja	30.03.06
Bosch/Mann+Hummel/Arvinmeritor Purolator	30.03.06
Nouveaux Constructeurs/Goldman Sachs Group/Deutsche Bank/Lone Star/Zapf	30.03.06
Mellon/Westlb/JV	30.03.06
Wiener Städtische/TBIH	31.03.06
Imperial Holdings/Lex Commercials/Lex Multipart	03.04.06
Jacobs Holding/Adecco	10.04.06
Blacskstone/Center Parks (UK) Group	18.04.06
Autostrade/SIAS/Costanera	18.04.06
Aegon/Caja Navarra/Seguros Navarra JV	21.04.06
Foodco Pastries/Tele Pizza	21.04.06
TowerBrook Investors/GSE	21.04.06
Wingas/ZGHG/JV	21.04.06
Burda/Hachette/JV	26.04.06
Gilde/Heiploeg/Nautica Nova	04.05.06
Deutsche Bank/Lone Star/Vivanco Gruppe	04.05.06
Costa Crociere/Royal Caribbean/Marinvest/RCT JV	04.05.06
Deutsche Bank et al/Deutsche Steinzeug Cremer & Breuer	10.05.06
Agravis/Baywa/Dr. Graüb	19.05.06
Bayerngas/Deutsche Esssent/Novogate JV	23.05.06
Investcorp/Orefi Participation	31.05.06

Chronological List of Merger Decisions (EC)—Simplified Procedure

NAME	DATE
ABN Amro/Nextiraone Europe	12.06.06
Inchcape/Lind	14.06.06
Mitsui/Vopak	14.06.06
Aleris International/Corus Group	16.06.06
Crédit Agricole/TV-ESS	16.06.06
	19.06.06
Wendel-Carlyle/Stahl	
CVCI/Amber Trust II/AB Sanitas	20.06.06
Umicore/Solvay/Solvicore/JV	20.06.06
Bouygues/Alstom	20.06.06
Arcelor/Mitsui/AMSA JV	22.06.06
	23.06.06
KPN/Heineken/ON	
Industri Kapital/Minimax	26.06.06
Merrill Lynch/Farallon/Barcelo/Playa	27.06.06
Berkshire/Iscar Metalworking Companies	30.06.06
Nordic Capital Fund VI/Dangaard	03.07.06
	07.07.06
Teck Cominco/INCO	
BP France/Vitogaz/Energaz JV	10.07.06
International Automotive Components Group/Lear Corporation	13.07.06
Fortress/Telent	14.07.06
Bridgepoint/Limoni	14.07.06
	14.07.06
Allianz Capital Partners/MAN Roland	
Advent/RWE/RWE Industrial Solutions	17.07.06
Advent/RWE Solutions	17.07.06
SCA Forest/Jämtlamell Industri	18.07.06
Carlyle/Vista/Turmed	20.07.06
	20.07.06
PAI Partners SAS/AMEC Spie SA	
Charterhouse/Fives-Lille	20.07.06
ABP/Europe Realty/Host/HHR Euro CV — HHR TRS CV	26.07.06
Goldman Sachs/Borealis/Associated British Ports	26.07.06
AXA Reim/Area/RDC/Newco	28.07.06
	28.07.06
GIMA/Synbra Group	
GDF/Camfin/Energia Investimenti JV	28.07.06
Investindustrial/Stroili ORO	28.07.06
Platinum Equity/Textron Fastening Systems	31.07.06
Ravago/Muehlstein	31.07.06
	01.08.06
Philips/BENQ/PBDS	
BC Partners/Médica	01.08.06
3i/ABX	01.08.06
Goldman Sachs/Borealis/GICSI/Associated British Ports (II)	04.08.06
Iveco/Afin	11.08.06
	11.08.06
Credit Agricole/Emporiki	
Endesa/Foster Wheeler/JV	16.08.06
Mondadori/EMAP France	17.08.06
Evraz/Strategic Minerals	17.08.06
Mibau Holding/Foster Yeoman Baumineralien/Figdor Baustoffhandel JV	17.08.06

Table 6

NAME	**DATE**
Atel Energia/Azienda Energetica-Etschwerke/Energ.IT	17.08.06
Fogeca/Mapfre/JV	18.08.06
Blackstone/Travelport	22.08.06
Nokia Corporation/Giesecke & Devrient JV	23.08.06
Macquarie/South East London & Kent Bus Company/East London Bus & Coach Company	23.08.06
	24.08.06
ALSO/GNT	
Kraft Foods/United Biscuits	25.08.06
NIBC/NPM/Deli Universal	30.08.06
BC Partners/Brenntag	31.08.06
Edison/EDF Energia Italia	31.08.06
	06.09.06
Morgan Stanley/IHG/Portfolio Hotels	
GE/CS/GIMP/JV	06.09.06
Yum/Pizza Hut	06.09.06
Toyota Tsusho/T.T. Holding/JV	06.09.06
Scor/Revios	06.09.06
	06.09.06
Phelps Dodge/Inco	
Egis/Alpine/Hochtief/Austrian Highway A5	08.09.06
Arcelor/Bamesa/Bamesa Otel	08.09.06
Aviva/De Agostini/Sopaf/Bipielle Net	08.09.06
Metro/Geant Polska	11.09.06
	12.09.06
Macquarie/Corona	
Shell/Saint-Gobain/Avancis JV	13.09.06
FCC/WRG	15.09.06
Doughty Hanson/Caudwell Group Mobile Distribution Business	18.09.06
Providence/Caudwell Group	18.09.06
	18.09.06
BC Partners/Buziol/Fashion Box	
KKR/Pages Jaunes	22.09.06
Hörmann/MN/ACP JV	25.09.06
Reof/Borletti/Printemps	25.09.06
Voestalpine/K+N/Euroshipping	26.09.06
Est/Dalmine	29.09.06
	03.10.06
MEAS/DSPL/Sadoport	
CVRD/INCO	05.10.06
TPG/Aleris	06.10.06
Cinven/Aero Invest	06.10.06
Bridgepoint/Dorna	06.10.06
	09.10.06
APHL/Permira/Clessidra/Sisal	
Goldman Sachs/Matlinpatterson/Securlog	11.10.06
Total/Cepsa	13.10.06
FCC/Alpine	16.10.06
LBO France/Vinci Airport Services	16.10.06
	17.10.06
Walter Frey Holding/Mitsubishi Motors Europe	
Cerberus/GMAC	19.10.06
PHL/IBFF	20.10.06
Apollo Group/TNT Logistics	24.10.06
HSBC/Lamda/Olympia Village	27.10.06

NAME	DATE
Deutsche Bank/AIG/Pokrovsky Hills	30.10.06
Diehl/Thales/JV	03.11.06
Fleetcor/CCS	06.11.06
Otto/CDiscount/JV	07.11.06
Permira Holdings/Borsodchem	08.11.06
	09.11.06
Veolia Cargo/Rail Link/JV	
AXA IMD/Investkredit/Europolis	14.11.06
AXA/Gerflor	15.11.06
Onex Corporation/Aon Warranty Group	17.11.06
OJSC Novolipetsk Steel/Duferco/JV	20.11.06
	21.11.06
Istithmar/Mubadala/DAE/SR Technics	
AIG/GIP/Stratfield	23.11.06
Macquairie/Thames Water	28.11.06
Schmolz + Bickenbach/Swiss Steel	29.11.06
Bertelsmann/Vodafone/Moconta	30.11.06
	30.11.06
Merril Lynch/Irish Life & Permanent	
Sun Group/Autobar Packaging	01.12.06
TPG/Telediffusion de France	04.12.06
Cinven/Gondola	04.12.06
Swiss RE/GE Life	06.12.06
	07.12.06
Alcatel/Nortel Networks	
KKR/SIF (Tarkett)	07.12.06
GE/Banque Artesia Nederland	07.12.06
Doosan/Mitsui Babcock	11.12.06
Rreef/Peel Ports Holdings/Peel Ports	11.12.06
	11.12.06
ICA Baltic/Rimi Baltic	
Österreichische Post/Trans-o-flex	12.12.06
GE/Disko/ASL	12.12.06
Blackstone/PAI/United Biscuits	12.12.06
Merck/Serono	15.12.06
	15.12.06
Goldman Sachs/Cerberus/Harpen	
Petroplus/Exxonmobil	15.12.06
SHV/Mammoet	18.12.06
HTA/CDPQ/BAA Budapest Airport	18.12.06
William Hill/Codere/JV	18.12.06
	18.12.06
MLCP/CIR/Oakwood	
Avnet/Access	19.12.06
MEIF II/Techem	19.12.06
Arrow Electronics/In Technology	19.12.06
Dresdner Bank/Gazprombank/JV	19.12.06
	20.12.06
Candover/Ferretti	
Rettig Capital/Ahlström Capital/Nordkalk	21.12.06
ONEX Corporation/Sitel Corporation	21.12.06
Arcadis/Dura Vermeer/Imtech/Asset Rail/JV	22.12.06
BC Partners/Techem	22.12.06
News Corporation/Jamba/OJOM	22.12.06
DHC/KP1	22.12.06

Table 6

NAME	DATE
Accor Services France/Groupe Caisse d'Epargne/ACE	11.01.07
An Post/Fortis/JV	12.01.07
Apollo Group/Jacuzzi Brands	17.01.07
	23.01.07
Industri Kapital/Attendo	
Advent/Carlyle/H.C. Starck	24.01.07
CVC/Fraikin	30.01.07
BG Group/Serene	01.02.07
Sun Capital/Golden Gate/Bauer	02.02.07
	06.02.07
Voestalpine/Stamptec	
L Capital 2/Calligaris	12.02.07
PAI/Lafarge	15.02.07
LBO France/Consolis	16.02.07
CNP Assurances/Skandia Vida	16.02.07
	19.02.07
3i Group/Azelis	
Advent/Oxo Group	20.02.07
ABN AMRO/Carlson/T.G.I. Friday's	21.02.07
Goldman Sachs/Onex/RAC	22.02.07
Alpha Private Equity Funds/Non Ferrous International Group	22.02.07
	22.02.07
Carrefour-Marinopoulos/Credicom/CMCC	
Charterhouse/Vivarte	26.02.07
Credit Agricole/Cariparma/Friuladria	27.02.07
Cerberus/Bawag	28.02.07
Areva/Repower	02.03.07
	02.03.07
TPG/Silver Lake/Sabre	
Bridgepoint/Rodenstock	06.03.07
ABN-AMRO/Allianz/SDU	07.03.07
LBO France/Sante Partenaires	08.03.07
Candover/Parques Reunidos	12.03.07
	12.03.07
Balfour Beatty/Galaxy/Exeter Airport	
GSW/MVV/JV	13.03.07
HTA/CDPQ/GICSI/Budapest Airport	15.03.07
Rank/Sig	15.03.07
Onex/Eastman Kodak Health Group	15.03.07
	19.03.07
Swiss Life/Capitalleben	
Holding Gonvarri/Assc/Assc Slovakia	19.03.07
Berkshire Hathaway/TTI	21.03.07
Nutrilux/Provimi	21.03.07
Delta Lloyd/Erasmus Groep	23.03.07
	23.03.07
BMW Intec/Dekra Südleasing Services	
OEP/Dailycer	26.03.07
Karstadtquelle/Thomas Cook	26.03.07
Groupe Arnault/Go Voyages	26.03.07
Vestar/Carlyle/AZ	27.03.07
	27.03.07
Sagard/Cognetas/Groupe Saint-Gobain Desjoncqueres	
NPM Capital/Desseaux	28.03.07
Shell/Coller Capital/STV	29.03.07

NAME	DATE
Citibank/Egg Bank	30.03.07
Blackstone/Cardinal Health (PTS Division)	03.04.07
TPG V/Apollo/Harrah's	04.04.07
Ricoh/IBM	04.04.07
OEP/Arvinmeritor Emissions Technologies Business	10.04.07
Deutsche Post/Metro/GS1 Germany/JV	10.04.07
INM/Providence/CAP II/APN	12.04.07
Accor/Dorint	13.04.07
EQT/CBR	13.04.07
Home Retail/Durinicum/Ogalas	13.04.07
Scor/Converium	20.04.07
China Shipbuilding/Mitsubishi/Wärtsilä/JV	23.04.07
Hanjin/Saudi Aramco/S-oil	24.04.07
ED&F MAN/Bromacom	25.04.07
3i/Enterprise	26.04.07

TABLE 7

LIST OF JOINT VENTURE DECISIONS

No.	NAME	DATE	C.M.L.R.[1]
JV1	Telia/Telenor/Schibsted	27.05.98	4 [1999] 216 (D)
JV2	ENEL/FT/DT	22.06.98	5 [1998] 152 (IP)
JV3	BT/Airtel	08.07.98	5 [1998] 294 (IP)
JV4	VIAG/Orange UK	11.08.98	5 [1998] 463 (IP)
JV5	Cegetel/Canal+/AOL/Bertelsmann	04.08.98	5 [1998] 302 (IP)
JV6	Ericsson/Nokia/Psion	11.08.98	5 [1998] 464 (IP)
JV7	Telia/Sonera/Lithuanian Telecommunications	14.08.98	5 [1998] 467 (IP)
JV8	Deutsche Telekom/Springer/Holtzbrink/Infoseek	28.09.98	5 [1998] 878 (IP)
JV9	Telia/Sonera/Motorola/Omnitel	18.08.98	5 [1998] 467 (IP)
JV11	@ Home Benelux B.V.	15.09.98	5 [1998] 661 (IP)
JV12	Ericsson/Nokia/Psion/Motorola	22.12.98	4 [1998] 183 (IP)
JV13	Wintershall/ENBW/MVV/WV/DEO	11.12.98	—
JV14	Panagora/DG Bank	26.11.98	4 [1999] 24 (IP)
JV15	BT/AT&T	30.03.99	—
JV16	Bertesmann/Viag/Game Channel	05.05.99	4 [1999] 1188 (IP)
JV17	Mannesmann/Bell Atlantic/Omnitel	21.05.99	5 [1999] 15 (IP)
JV18	Chronopost España	01.06.99	5 [1999] 19 (IP)
JV19	KLM/Alitalia	11.08.99	5 [1999] 759 (IP)
JV21	Skandia/Storebrand/Pohjola	17.08.99	5 [1999] 761 (IP)
JV22	Fujitsu/Siemens	30.09.99	5 [1999] 962 (IP)
JV23	Telefonica/Portugal Telecom/Medi Telecom	17.12.99	4 [2000] 228 (IP)
JV24	Bertelsmann/Planeta/Bol Spain	03.12.99	4 [2000] 222 (IP)
JV25	Sony/Time Warner/CDNow	21.12.99	—
JV26	Freecom/Dangaard	01.12.99	4 [2000] 217 (IP)

[1] Common Market Law Reports.

No.	NAME	DATE	C.M.L.R.
JV28	Sydkraft/Hew/Hansa Energy Trading	30.11.99	4 [2000] 217 (IP)
JV29	Lafarge/Readymix	20.12.99	4 [2000] 233 (IP)
JV30	BVI Television (Europe)/SPE Euromovies Investments/Europe Movieco Partners	03.02.00	—
JV31	HMI International Holdings/Arnoldo Mondadori Editore	15.12.99	4 [2000] 225 (IP)
JV32	Granaria/Ultje/Intersnack/May Holding	28.02.00	4 [2000] 651 (IP)
JV33	Hearst/VNU	15.12.99	4 [2000] 226 (IP)
JV34	BT/Autostrade/Blu	04.01.00	4 [2000] 240 (IP)
JV35	Beiselen/Bay Wa/MG Chemag	01.02.00	4 [2000] 428 (IP)
JV36	TXU Europe/EDF-London Investments	03.02.00	4 [2000] 432 (IP)
JV37	BSkyB/Kirch Pay-Tv	21.03.00	4 [2000] 818 (IP)
JV38	KPN/Bellsouth/E-plus	18.02.00	4 [2000] 648 (IP)
JV39	Bertelsmann/Planeta/Web	28.02.00	4 [2000] 677 (IP)
JV40	Canal+/Lagardere/Liberty Media/Multithematique Canal+/Lagardere/Canalsatellite	22.06.00	5 [2000] 182 (IP)
JV42	Asahi Glass/Mitsubishi/F2 Chemicals	21.03.00	4 [2000] 822 (IP)
JV44	Hitachi/NEC–Dram/JV	03.05.00	4 [2000] 1062 (IP)
JV45	Bertelsmann/Kooperativa Förbundet/Bol Nordic	12.05.00	5 [2000] 14 (IP)
JV46	Blackstone/CDPQ/Kabel Nordrhein – Westfalen	19.06.00	5 [2000] 402 (IP)
JV48	Vodafone/Vivendi/Canal+	20.07.00	5 [2000] 404 (IP)
JV50	Blackstone/CDPQ/Kabel Baden — Württemberg	01.08.00	5 [2000] 402 (IP)
JV51	Bertelsmann/Mondadori/Bol Italia	01.09.00	5 [2000] 592 (IP)
JV54	Smith & Nephew/Beiersdorf/JV	30.01.01	4 [2001] 596 (IP)
JV55	Hutchison/RCPM/ECT	03.07.01	5 [2001] 218 (IP)
JV56	Hutchison/ECT	29.11.01	4 [2002] IS24
JV57	TPS	30.04.02	4 [2002] IS146

TABLE 8

LIST OF CFI AND COURT OF JUSTICE JUDGMENTS (MERGER REGULATION)

CASE No.[1]	NAME	DATE	E.C.R.[2]	C.M.L.R.[3]	SUBJECT	RESULT
T–83/92	Zunis	28.10.93	[1994] II–1169	—	Admissibility	Inadmissible
T–96/92	Société Générale des Grandes Sources	27.04.95	[1995] II–1213	—	Admissibility, Rights of Workers	Inadmissible
T–2/93	Air France	19.05.94	[1994] II–323	—	Admissibility Relevant Market Definition	Admissible
T–3/93	Air France (DAN AIR)	24.03.94	[1994] II–121	—	Admissibility Meaning of Decision	Admissible
T–12/93 R	Comité Centrale Vittel	06.07.93	[1993] II–449	5 [1994] 154	Interim Measures of CFI	Rejected
T–12/93 R	Vittel and Pierval	06.07.93	[1993] II–0785	—	Interim Measures of CFI	Rejected
T–12/93	Vittel	27.04.95	[1995] II–1247	—	Admissibility, Rights of Workers	Inadmissible
C–480/93P	Zunis/Finan/Massinvest	11.01.96	[1996] I–1	5 [1996] 219	Admissibility	Inadmissible
C–68/94, C–30/95	France	31.03.98	[1998] I–1375	4 [1998] 829	Joint Dominance	Annulled
T–88/94 R	SCPA	10.05.94	[1994] II–263	—	Interim Measures	Holding judgment
T–88/94 R	SCPA	15.06.94	[1994] II–401	—	Interim Measures	Granted

[1] "T" indicates Court of First Instance Judgment; "C" indicates Court of Justice Judgment.
[2] European Court Reports.
[3] Common Market Law Reports.

Table 8

CASE No.[1]	NAME	DATE	E.C.R.[2]	C.M.L.R.[3]	SUBJECT	RESULT
T–290/94	Kayserberg SA	27.11.97	[1997] II–2137	4 [1998] 336	Procedure, Remedies Dominance	Upheld
T–322/94 R	Union Carbide	02.12.94	[1994] II–1159	—	Interim Measures	Rejected
T–221/95	Endemol	28.04.99	[1999] II–1299	5 [1999] 611	Referral to the Commission, Rights of Defense	Upheld
T–52/96 R	Sogecable SA	12.07.96	[1996] I–797	5 [1996] 570	Interim Measures	Rejected
T–87/96	Assicurazioni Generali	04.03.99	[1999] II–203	5 [2000] 312	Full Function JV	Upheld
T–102/96	Gencor	25.03.99	[1999] II–753	5 [1999] 971	Joint Dominance, Remedies	Upheld
T–22/97	Kesko Oy	15.12.99	[1999] II–3775	4 [2000] 335	Referral to the Commission, Dominance, Effect on Trade	Upheld
T–125/97	The Coca-Cola Company & Coca-Cola Enterprises	22.03.00	[2000] II–1733	5 [2000] 467	Impact of Dominance	Upheld
T–156/98	RJB Mining	31.01.01	[2001] II–337	3 [2001] 15	Merger and State Aids	Annulled
T–342/99	Airtours	06.06.02	[2002] II–2585	5 [2002] 7	Joint Dominance	Annulled
T–158/00	ARD	30.04.03	5 [2004] 14	—	Remedies	Upheld
T–251/00	Lagardère & Canal+	20.11.02	[2002] II–4825	4 [2003] 20	Ancillary Restraints	Annulled
T–310/00	MCI	28.09.04	—	5 [2004] 26	Concentration Aborted	Decision annulled
T–342/00 R	Petrolessence SG2R	17.01.01	[2001] II–67	5 [2003] 8	Implementing of Undertaking	Rejected
T–342/00	Petrolessence	03.04.03	[2003] II–1161	5 [2003] 9	Purchase of Business to be Divested	Rejected
T–374/00	Verband der freien Rohrwerke	08.07.03	5 [2004] 13	—	Substantive Assessment	Upheld
C–42/01	Portuguese Republic	22.06.04		5 [2002] 9	Concept of Member States' Legitimate Interests (Art. 21(4))	Rejected

CASE No.[1]	NAME	DATE	E.C.R.[2]	C.M.L.R.[3]	SUBJECT	RESULT
T–209/01	Honeywell	14.12.05	—	5 [2006] 14	Application for joinder with case T–210/01 Conglomerate Issues	Rejected
T–210/01	General Electric	14.12.05	—	5 [2006] 15	Vertical and Conglomerate Issues	Rejected
T–310/01	Schneider	22.10.02	[2002] II–4071	4 [2003] 17	Assessment of Dominance	Annulled
T–3/02	Schlüsselverlag	11.03.02	[2002] II–1473	4 [2004] 29	Action for Failure to act, Admissibility	Inadmissible
T–5/02	Tetra Laval	25.10.02	[2002] II–4381	5 [2002] 28	Assessment of Dominance. Conglomerate merger	Annulled
T–77/02	Schneider	22.10.02	[2002] II–4201		Art. 8(4) Decision	Annulled
T–80/02	Tetra Laval	25.10.02	[2002] II–4519	5 [2002] 29	Art. 8(4) Decision	Annulled
T–114/02	Babyliss	03.04.03	[2003] II–1279	5 [2004] 1	Remedies	Partially annulled
T–119/02	Royal Philips	03.04.03	[2003] II–1433	5 [2003] 2	Remedies, Referral to Member States	Upheld
C–170/02P	Schlüsselverlag	25.04.03		4 [2004] 27	Action for Failure to Act, Admissibility	Appeal rejected
T–282/02	Cementbouw Handel	23.02.06	—	5 [2006] 26	Interdependant Transactions	Rejected
T–346 & 347/02	Cableuropa	30.04.03	5 [2004] 25	—	Referral to Member States	Upheld
T–350/03	Wirschaftskammer Karnten and best connect Ampere Strompool GmbH	18.09.06	—	—	Third party action	Inadmissible
C–12/03P	Commission v Tetra Laval	15.02.05	—	5 [2005] 8	Conglomerate Merger	Rejected
T–48/03	Schneider Electric	31.01.06	—	—	Procedural Issues	Inadmissible
T–177/04	easyJet Airline	04.07.06	—	—	Third party actions	Rejected
T–464/04	Impala	13.07.06	—	—	Third party actions	Annulled
T–87/05	EDP	21.09.05	—	5 [2005] 23	Remedies	Rejected
T–417/05 R	Endesa	01.02.06	—	—	Interim Measures	Rejected
C–188/06 P	Schneider Electric	09.03.07	—	—	Third party actions	Rejected

TABLE 9

CHRONOLOGICAL LIST OF COMMISSION DECISIONS (ECSC)

No.	NAME	DATE	O.J.[1]	C.M.L.R.[2]	TYPE OF DECISION	PRODUCT	SUBJECT
CS1	Scrap Fund I	26.03.55	55/685	—	Authorisation	Scrap	Equalisation
CS2	COBECHAR I	03.10.56	56/295	—	Authorisation	Coal	Joint Sales
CS3	Scrap Fund II	26.01.57	57/61	—	Authorisation	Scrap	Equalisation
CS4	OKB I	26.07.57	57/352	—	Authorisation	Coal	Joint Buying
CS5	Union Charbonnière	04.11.59	59/1147	—	Authorisation	Coal	Joint Sales
CS6	OKB II	28.03.62	62/873	—	Authorisation	Coal	Joint Buying
CS7	COBECHAR II	16.01.63	63/162	—	Authorisation	Coal	Joint Sales
CS8	Präsident I	20.03.63	63/1191	—	Authorisation	Coal	Joint Sales
CS9	Geitling I	20.03.63	63/1173	—	Authorisation	Coal	Joint Sales
CS10	Geitling II	27.06.63	63/1838	—	Modification	Coal	Joint Sales
CS11	SOREMA	15.07.64	64/1969	—	Revocation	Coal	Joint Buying
CS12	Geitling III	15.12.65	65/3249	—	Authorisation	Coal	Joint Sales
CS13	Präsident II	15.12.65	65/3255	—	Authorisation	Coal	Joint Sales
CS14	COBECHAR III	27.01.66	66/309	—	Authorisation	Coal	Joint Sales
CS15	OKB III	23.11.66	66/3796	—	Authorisation	Coal	Joint Buying
CS16	Walzstahlkontor I	15.03.67	67/1373	—	Authorisation	Steel	Joint Sales
CS17	Stahlring I	14.06.67	67/2517	—	Authorisation	Steel	Joint Buying
CS18	Geitling IV	22.06.67	67/1	—	Authorisation	Coal	Joint Sales
CS19	Präsident III	22.06.67	67/4	—	Authorisation	Coal	Joint Sales
CS20	Kempense	19.12.67	67/10	—	Authorisation	Coal	Joint Sales

[1] Official Journal of the European Communities
[2] Common Market Law Reports.

Table 9

No.	NAME	DATE	O.J.	C.M.L.R.	TYPE OF DECISION	PRODUCT	SUBJECT
CS21	Falck/Redaelli I	21.12.67	[1968] L24/16	[1968] 91	Authorisation	Steel	Specialisation
CS22	Walzstahlkontor II	19.06.68	[1968] L218/6	—	Authorisation	Steel	Joint Sales
CS23	Creusot/Loire	09.07.68	[1968] L164/17	—	Authorisation	Steel	Specialisation
CS24	Saarlor I	19.12.68	[1969] L7/1	—	Authorisation	Coal	Joint Sales
CS25	Geitling V	27.11.69	[1969] L69/11	—	Revocation	Coal	Joint Sales
CS26	Präsident IV	27.11.69	[1969] L304/12	—	Revocation	Coal	Joint Sales
CS27	COBECHAR IV	22.12.69	[1970] L10/16	—	Authorisation	Coal	Joint Sales
CS28	German Scrap Cartel	21.01.70	[1970] L29/30	[1970] 503	Prohibition	Scrap	Cartel 1–291
CS29	Thyssen/Krupp/Wuppermann	27.07.71	[1971] L201/1	—	Authorisation	Steel	Specialisation
CS30	Hoesch/Rheinstahl	27.07.71	[1971] L201/12	—	Authorisation	Steel	Specialisation
CS31	Maxhütte/Klöckner I	27.07.71	[1971] L201/19	—	Authorisation	Steel	Specialisation
CS32	Dillinger/Arbed I	27.07.71	[1971] L201/27	—	Authorisation	Steel	Specialisation
CS33	Stahlring II	22.03.72	[1972] L85/17	—	Authorisation	Steel	Joint Buying
CS34	OKB IV	21.04.72	[1972] L112/22	[1972] D110	Authorisation	Coal	Joint Buying
CS35	Hoesch/Benteler	09.11.72	[1972] L283/17	[1973] D121	Authorisation	Steel	Specialisation
CS36	COBECHAR V	20.03.73	[1973] L102/19	[1973] D197	Authorisation	Coal	Joint Sales
CS37	Ruhrkohle	21.12.72	[1973] L120/14	[1973] D199	Authorisation	Coal	Article 66
CS38	Thyssen/Rheinstahl	20.12.73	[1974] L84/36	2 [1974] D1	Authorisation	Iron	Article 66
CS39	Danish Steel Distributors	21.12.73	[1974] L30/29	2 [1974] D43	Authorisation	Steel	Joint Buying
CS40	Steelmaking Supplies	22.01.74	[1974] L52/22	2 [1974] D37	Authorisation	Scrap	Joint Buying
CS41	GKN/Miles Druce	14.03.74	[1974] L132/28	2 [1974] D17	Authorisation	Steel	Article 66
CS42	Saarlor II	04.04.74	[1974] L113/18	2 [1974] D48	Authorisation	Coal	Joint Sales
CS43	BSC/Lye Trading	14.10.74	[1975] L13/45	[1975] D38	Authorisation	Steel	Article 66
CS44	Thyssen/SOLMER	20.11.74	[1975] L49/13	—	Authorisation	Iron	Article 66
CS45	Gelsenberg	16.12.74	[1975] L65/16	—	Authorisation	Coal	Article 66
CS46	Ruhrkohle	19.12.74	[1975] L21/19	1 [1975] D42	Authorisation	Coal	Article 66
CS47	Marcoke	24.01.75	[1975] L65/19	—	Authorisation	Coke	Article 66
CS48	CLIF/Marine-Firminy	05.03.75	[1975] L196/27	—	Authorisation	Steel	Article 66
CS49	Krupp/Stahlwerke	02.04.75	[1975] L130/13	—	Authorisation	Steel	Article 66
CS50	IVECO	07.04.75	[1975] L196/41	2 [1975] D64	Authorisation	Steel	Article 66

No.	NAME	DATE	O.J.	C.M.L.R.	TYPE OF DECISION	PRODUCT	SUBJECT
CS51	Minerais Préréduits	03.07.75	[1975] L249/22	—	Authorisation	Iron	Joint Buying
CS52	EGAM/Vetrocoke	11.07.75	[1976] L7/13	1 [1976] D90	Authorisation	Coke	Article 66
CS53	Maxhütte/Klöckner II	13.02.76	[1976] L95/21	—	Authorisation	Steel	Article 66
CS54	Dillinger/Arbed II	13.02.76	[1976] L95/23	—	Authorisation	Steel	Article 66
CS55	COBECHAR VI	18.02.76	[1976] L95/25	—	Authorisation	Coal	Joint Sales
CS56	Saarlor III	12.03.76	[1976] L78/18	1 [1976] D96	Authorisation	Coal	Joint Sales
CS57	BSC/Walter Blume	30.03.76	[1976] L94/44	—	Authorisation	Steel	Article 66
CS58	Walker/Champion	20.05.76	[1976] L198/6	1 [1977] D4	Authorisation	Steel	Joint Buying
CS59	Maxhütte/Klockner III	28.07.76	[1976] L270/31	—	Authorisation	Steel	Article 66
CS60	Dillinger/Arbed III	28.07.76	[1976] L270/33	—	Authorisation	Steel	Article 66
CS61	Rötzel/Krupp	20.12.76	[1976] L45/25	1 [1977] D97	Authorisation	Steel	Specialisation
CS62	Arbed	20.12.76	[1977] L45/32	1 [1977] D108	Authorisation	Steel	Article 66
CS63	Klöckner/Maxhütte IV	22.12.76	[1977] L43/32	—	Authorisation	Steel	Article 66
CS64	Saarlor IV	04.03.77	[1977] L78/20	—	Authorisation	Coal	Joint Sales
CS65	Stahlring III	05.04.77	[1977] L97/33	—	Authorisation	Steel	Joint Buying
CS66	British steel producers	17.06.77	[1977] L173/19	2 [1977] D58	Authorisation	Scrap	Joint Buying
CS67	Maier/Röchling	12.07.77	[1977] L217/11	[1977] D63	Authorisation	Coal	Joint Buying
CS68	Röchling-Burbach	27.07.77	[1977] L243/20	2 [1977] D25	Inspection	Steel	Article 47
CS69	COIMPRE	14.11.77	[1977] L309/18	1 [1978] D1	Authorisation	Iron	Joint Buying
CS70	Framtek	23.11.77	[1977] L320/52	1 [1978] D17	Authorisation	Steel	Article 66
CS71	Arbed/Rodange	06.06.78	[1978] L164/14	2 [1978] 767	Authorisation	Steel	Article 66
CS72	Ruhrkohle/Brennstoffhandel	07.06.78	[1978] L191/38	3 [1978] 40	Authorisation	Coal	Article 66
CS73	Creusot-Loire/Ugine	20.07.78	[1978] L242/10	1 [1979] 349	Authorisation	Steel	Specialisation
CS74	VCRO	28.07.78	[1978] L238/28	1 [1979] 527	Authorisation	Steel	Joint Sales
CS75	Falck/Redaelli II	20.10.78	[1978] L324/26	1 [1979] 357	Authorisation	Steel	Joint Buying
CS76	COBECHAR VII	16.11.78	[1978] L329/37	1 [1979] 462	Authorisation	Coal	Joint Sales
CS77	Cockerill/Klöckner	12.01.79	[1979] L19/37	2 [1979] 236	Authorisation	Steel	Specialisation
CS78	Cockerill/Estel	12.01.79	[1979] L19/41	2 [1979] 243	Authorisation	Steel	Specialisation
CS79	Lange/Stinnes	15.01.79	[1979] L19/44	2 [1979] 207	Authorisation	Coal	Article 66
CS80	Irish Steel/Dunkerque	27.03.79	[1979] L103/27	2 [1979] 527	Authorisation	Steel	Specialisation

Table 9

No.	NAME	DATE	O.J.	C.M.L.R.	TYPE OF DECISION	PRODUCT	SUBJECT
CS81	BSC/Dunlop & Ranken	26.07.79	[1979] L245/30	3 [1979] 631	Authorisation	Steel	Article 66
CS82	Saarlor V	06.11.79	[1979] L295/24	2 [1980) 161	Authorisation	Coal	Joint Sales
CS83	Manganese	20.12.79	[1980] L24/43	3 [1980] 762	Authorisation	Manganese	Joint Sales
CS84	German Rolled Steel	08.02.80	[1980] L62/28	3 [1980] 193	Prohibition	Steel	Trade Association
CS85	Hoogovens/Ijzerhandel	14.03.80	[1980] L85/47	2 [1980] 605	Authorisation	Scrap	Article 66
CS86	Chamber of Coal Traders	19.12.80	[1980] L374/34	2 [1982] 730	Authorisation	Coal	Equalisation
CS87	Boël/Clabercq	31.03.81	[1981] L167/1	1 [1983] 226	Authorisation	Steel	Joint Sales
CS88	Rogesa	18.06.81	[1981] L189/54	3 [1982] 438	Authorisation	Iron	Article 66
CS89	Eurocoal	14.09.81	[1981] L290/21	2 [1982] 659	Authorisation	Coal	Article 66
CS90	Zentralkokerei	30.11.81	[1981] L364/39	3 [1982] 41	Authorisation	Coke	Article 66
CS91	Chamber of Coal Traders II	10.12.81	[1981] L8/21	—	Authorisation	Coal	Equalisation
CS92	Usinor/Sacilor/Normandie	02.04.82	[1982] L139/1	2 [1983] 462	Authorisation	Steel	Article 66
CS93	Stahlring IV	26.07.82	[1982] L237/34	2 [1983] 307	Authorisation	Steel	Joint Buying
CS94	UNICO	24.04.84	[1984] L139/37	—	Authorisation	Coal	Article 66
CS95	Arbed/Cockerill-Sambre	28.05.84	[1984] L163/37	2 [1985] 83	Authorisation	Steel	Specialisation
CS96	Steelmaking Supplies II	21.09.84	[1984] L268/35	1 [1985] 801	Authorisation	Steel	Joint Buying
CS97	Manganese II	24.04.85	[1985] L119/42	—	Authorisation	Manganese	Joint Sales
CS98	Röchling-Posserl	05.02.86	[1986] L39/57	4 [1988] 213	Authorisation	Steel	Article 66
CS99	NICIA	21.03.86	[1986] L115/19	—	Authorisation	Coal	Joint Buying
CS100	Saarlor VI	12.12.86	[1987] L20/37	—	Authorisation	Coal	Joint Sales
CS101	British Fuel	09.07.87	[1987] L224/16	—	Authorisation	Coal	Article 66
CS102	Arbed/Unimetal	14.07.88	[1988] L223/39	4 [1989] 74	Authorisation	Steel	Specialisation
CS103	Eschweiler/Ruhrkohle	19.12.88	[1989] L14/37	4 [1990] 968	Authorisation	Coal	Article 66
CS104	Ruhrkohle	30.03.89	[1989] L101/35	4 [1990] 527	Authorisation	Coal	Joint Buying
CS105	British Steel/Walker	08.05.90	[1990] L131/27	—	Authorisation	Steel	Article 66
CS106	Stainless Steel Cartel	18.07.90	[1990] L220/17	4 [1990] 670	Prohibition	Steel	Cartel
CS107	Arbed/Usinor-Sacilor	09.09.91	[1991] L281/17	—	Authorisation	Steel	Joint Sales
CS108	Ensidesa S.A./Aristrain	14.12.92	[1993] L48/54	—	Authorisation	Steel	Joint Sales
CS109	Jahrhundertvertrag	22.12.92	[1993] L50/14	—	—	Coal	Specialisation

No.	NAME	DATE	O.J.	C.M.L.R.	TYPE OF DECISION	PRODUCT	SUBJECT
CS110	Steel Beam Cartel	16.02.94	[1994] L116/1	5 [1994] 353	Prohibition	Steel	Cartel
CS111	Ruhrkohle/Raab	28.02.96	[1996] L193/42	—	Authorisation	Coal	Article 66
CS112	Wirtschaftsvereinigung Stahl	26.11.97	[1998] L1/10	4 [1998] 450	Prohibition	Steel	Information Exchange
CS113	Alloy Surcharge	21.01.98	[1998] L100/55	4 [1998] 973	Prohibition	Steel	Concerted Practice
CS114	British Steel/Sogerail	02.08.99	[1999] C193/4	5 [1999] 769	Authorisation	Steel	
CS115	Usinor/Arbed/Aceralia	21.11.01	[2003] L88/1	4 [2002] IS17	Authorisation with conditions and obligations	Steel	

TABLE 10

CHRONOLOGICAL LIST OF EUROPEAN COURT JUDGMENTS (ECSC)

Case No.	NAME	DATE	E.C.R.[1]	C.M.L.R.[2]	ART.	SUBJECT	RESULT	PRODUCT
1/54	*France v HA*	21.12.54	[1954–56] 1	—	33	Prices	Annulled in part	—
2/54	*Italy v HA*	21.12.54	[1954–56] 37	—	33	Prices	Annulled in part	—
6/54	*Netherlands v HA*	21.03.55	[1954–56] 103	—	33	Prices	Dismissed	Article 66
2/56	*Geitling v HA*	20.03.57	[1957–58] 3	—	33	Joint Sales	Dismissed	Coal
13/57	*Eisen und Stahlindustrie v HA*	21.06.58	[1957–58] 265	—	33	Equalisation	Dismissed	Scrap
12/57	*Centre-Midi v HA*	26.06.58	[1957–58] 375	—	33	Equalisation	Dismissed	Scrap
18/57 R	*Nold v HA*	04.12.57	[1957–58] 121	—	33	Joint Buying	Dismissed	Coal
18/57	*Nold v HA*	20.03.59	[1959] 41	—	33	Joint Buying	Dismissed	Coal
1/58	*Stork v HA*	04.02.59	[1959] 17	—	33	Distribution	Dismissed	Coal
15/59	*Knutange v HA*	12.02.60	[1960] 1	—	33	Joint Buying	Dismissed	Scrap
16/59	*Geitling v HA*	12.02.60	[1960] 17	—	33	Joint Sales	Inadmissible	Coal
19/59 R	*Geitling v HA*	12.05.59	[1960] 34	—	39	Joint Sales	Dismissed	Coal
36/59	*Präsident v HA*	15.07.60	[1960] 423	—	33	Joint Sales	Annulled in part	Coal
(Opi. 1/61)	Opinion: Amendment to Article 65	13.12.61	[1961] 243	—	95	—	Incompatibility	—
13/60	*Geitling v HA*	18.05.62	[1962] 83	[1962] 113	35	Joint Sales	Dismissed	Coal
18/60	*Worms v HA*	12.07.62	[1962] 195	[1962] 1	40	Equalisation	Dismissed	Scrap
12/63	*Schlieker v HA*	04.07.63	[1963] 85	[1963] 281	35	Concentration	Dismissed	Steel
67/63	*SOREMA v HA*	19.03.64	[1964] 151	[1964] 350	33	Joint Buying	Annulled	Coal
66/63	*Netherlands v HA*	15.07.64	[1964] 533	[1964] 522	33	Joint Sales	Annulled in part	Coal

[1] European Court Reports.
[2] Common Market Law Reports.

Table 10

CASE No.	NAME	DATE	E.C.R.	C.M.L.R.	ART.	SUBJECT	RESULT	PRODUCT
36/64	*SOREMA v HA*	02.06.65	[1965] 329	[1966] 28	33 & 39	Joint Buying	Dismissed	Coal
4/73	*Nold*	14.05.74	[1974] 491	2 [1974] 338	—	—	—	—
160–161/73 R	*Miles Druce I*	11.10.73	[1973] 1049	1 [1974] 224	39	Concentration	Dismissed	Steel
160–161 & 170/73 R	*Miles Druce II*	16.03.74	[1974] 281	2 [1974] D22	—	—	—	—
T–57/91	*Naloo*	24.09.96	[1996] II–1019	5 [1996] 672	33	Licence Agreements	Dismissed	Coal
C–128/92	*Banks v British Coal*	13.04.94	[1994] I–1209	5 [1994] 30	41	Mining Licence	Interpretation	Coal
C–18/94	*Hopkins v British Coal*	02.05.96	—	4 [1996] 745	41	Prices	Interpretation	Coal
T–134/94; T–136/94; T–137/94; T–138/94; T–141/94; T–145/94; T–147/94; T–148/94; T–151/94; T–157/94	*NMH*	19.06.96	—	5 [1997] 227	23	Access to File	Order	Steel
T–156/94 R	*Aristrain*	25.08.94	[1994] II–715	—	39	Steel Cartel	Suspension	Steel
T–134/94, T–136/94, T–138/94, T–141/94, T–145/94, T–147/94, T–148/94, T–151/94, T–156/94, T–157/94	*NMH Stahlwerke II*	10.12.97	—	—	23	Steel Cartel	Production documents	Steel
T–134/94, T–136/94, T–138/94, T–141/94, T–145/94, T–147/94, T–148/94, T–151/94, T–156/94, T–157/94	*NMH Stahlwerke III*	16.02.98	—	4 [1998] 426	23	Steel Cartel	Production documents	Steel
T–141/94	*Thyssen Stahl*	11.03.99	[1999] II—347	4 [1998] 810	33	Steel Cartel	Annulled in part	Steel
T–134/94	*NMH*	11.03.99	[1999] II—239	—	33	Cartel	Upheld	Steel
T–136/94	*Eurofer*	11.03.99	[1999] II—263	—	33	Cartel	Partial annulment	Steel
T–137/94	*Arbed*	11.03.99	[1999] II—303	—	33	Cartel	Partial annulment	Steel
T–138/94	*Cockerill*	11.03.99	[1999] II—333	—	33	Cartel	Partial annulment	Steel
T–145/94	*Unimetal*	11.03.99	[1999] II—585	—	33	Cartel	Partial annulment	Steel
T–147/94	*Krupp*	11.03.99	[1999] II—603	—	33	Cartel	Partial annulment	Steel
T–148/94	*Preussag*	11.03.99	[1999] II—613	—	33	Cartel	Partial annulment	Steel
T–151/94	*British Steel*	11.03.99	[1999] II—629	—	33	Cartel	Partial annulment	Steel
T–156/94	*Siderurgica*	11.03.99	[1999] II—645	—	33	Cartel	Partial annulment	Steel

CASE No.	NAME	DATE	E.C.R.	C.M.L.R.	ART.	SUBJECT	RESULT	PRODUCT
T–157/94	*Eusidera*	11.03.99	[1999] II—707	—	33	Cartel	Partial annulment	Steel
T–156/98	*RJB Mining*	21.01.01	[2000] II—337	3 [2001] 308	33	Concentration	Annulment	Coal

TABLE 11

TABLE OF FINES

1. PROCEDURAL FINES

All fines are denominated in Euros

A. ARTICLE 11 REGULATION 17: SUPPLYING INCORRECT INFORMATION

COMMISSION		COURT OF FIRST INSTANCE/ COURT OF JUSTICE	
111. Theal/Watts	5 000		
168. Comptoir d'Importation	5 000		
171. Telos	5 000		
175. National Panasonic Belgium	5 000		
180. National Panasonic France	5 000		
251. Peugeot	4 000		
329a. Secrétama (maritime transport)	5 000		

B. ARTICLE 14 REGULATION 17: PRODUCTION OF INCOMPLETE DOCUMENTS OR REFUSAL TO CO-OPERATE

COMMISSION		COURT OF FIRST INSTANCE/ COURT OF JUSTICE	
153. Fabbrica Pisana	5 000		
154. Fabbrica Lastre	5 000		
183. Fédération Chaussure de France	5 000		
354. UKWAL	5 000		
359. CSM	3 000		
360. MEWAC	4 000		
391. AKZO	5 000		

C. ARTICLE 16 REGULATION 17: PERIODIC PENALTY CLAUSES

COMMISSION		COURT OF FIRST INSTANCE/ COURT OF JUSTICE	
64. Zoju IKSC–ICI	1 000		
101. Chiquita	1 000		
105. CSV	1 000		
121. Hugin/Liptons	1 000		
158. IMA Rules	100–300		
173. Hasselblad	500–1 000		
182. Ford Werke-Interim Measures	1 000	Annulled	123. Ford
197. ECS/AKZO	1 000		
273. Boosey & Hawkes	1 000		
408. Adalat	1 000	Annulled	
410. Irish Sugar	1 000		
429. VW–Audi	1 000		

Table 11

COMMISSION		COURT OF FIRST INSTANCE/ COURT OF JUSTICE	
2. FINES FOR SUBSTANTIVE INFRINGEMENTS			
24. Quinine		14. ACF Chemiefarma	
ACF Chemiefarma	210 000		200 000
Boehringer	190 000	16. Boehringer	180 000
Buchler	65 000	15. Buchler & Co.	55 000
Pointet	12 500	No Appeal	
Nogentaise	12 500	No Appeal	
Pharmacie Centrale	10 000	No Appeal	
Total	500 000	Total	435 000
27. Dyestuffs			
ICI	50 000	23. ICI	50 000
BASF	50 000	24. BASF	50 000
Bayer	50 000	25. Bayer	50 000
Geigy	50 000	26. Geigy	50 000
Sandoz	50 000	27. Sandoz	50 000
Francolor	50 000	28. Francolor	50 000
Cassella	50 000	29. Cassella	50 000
Hoechst	50 000	30. Hoechst	50 000
ACNA	40 000	31. ACNA	30 000
Ciba	50 000	No Appeal	
Total	490 000	Total	430 000
63. Pittsburgh Corning	100 000	No Appeal	
64. Zoja/CSC-ICI	200 000	37. ICI & CSC	100 000
68. WEA/Filipacchi Music S.A.	60 000	No Appeal	
69. European Sugar Industry		48. Suiker Unie	
Tirlemontoise	1 500 000	Tirlemontoise	600 000
SAY	500 000	SAY	80 000
Bégin	700 000	Bégin	100 000
Générale Sucrière	400 000	Générale Sucrière	80 000
Eridania	1 000 000	Eridania	Quashed
Societa Generale	300 000	Societa Generale	Quashed
Cavarzere	200 000	Cavarzere	Quashed
AIE	100 000	AIE	Quashed
Volano	100 000	Volano	Quashed
SADAM	100 000	SADAM	Quashed
CVS	800 000	Suiker Unie	200 000
CSM	600 000	CSM	150 000
Pfeifer	800 000	Pfeifer	240 000
Süd Deutsche	700 000	Süd Deutsche	Quashed
Süd Zucker	200 000	Süd Zucker	40 000
Total	9 000 000	Total	1 590 000
73. Deutsche Philips	60 000	No Appeal	

COMMISSION		COURT OF FIRST INSTANCE/ COURT OF JUSTICE	
78. Belgian Wallpaper		47. Papiers Peints	
Brepols	67 500	Brepols	Quashed
Genval	120 000	Genval	Quashed
Peters	135 000	Peters	Quashed
Van der Borght	36 000	Van der Borght	Quashed
Total	358 500		
84. General Motors	100 000	46. General Motors	Quashed
88. Tinned Mushrooms		No Appeal	
Blanchoud	32 000		
Champex	8 000		
Champifrance	26 000		
Euroconserves	32 000		
Faval	2 000		
Total	100 000		
101. Chiquita	1 000 000	62. United Brands	850 000
104. Hoffmann-La Roche	300 000	67. Hoffmann-La Roche	200 000
108. Miller International	70 000	61. Miller	70 000
110. Theal Watts		64. Tepea	
Tepea	10 000	Tepea	10 000
Watts	10 000	Watts	10 000
121. Hugin Liptons	50 000	68. Hugin	Quashed
126. BMW Belgium		69. BMW Belgium	
BMW Belgium	150 000		Fines Upheld
5 Dealers	each 2 000		
3 Dealers	each 1 500		
39 Dealers	each 1 000		
Total	203 500		

Table 11

COMMISSION		COURT OF FIRST INSTANCE/ COURT OF JUSTICE	
129. Vegetable Parchment		No Appeal	
Dalle	25 000		
Feldmuehle	15 000		
Nicolaus	25 000		
Rube	10 000		
Schbeipen	25 000		
Serlachius	15 000		
Total	115 000		
141. Kawasaki	100 000	No Appeal	
148. Floral	85 000	No Appeal	
152. Pioneer		98. Pioneer	
MDF	850 000	MDF	600 000
Pioneer Europe BV	4 350 000	Pioneer Europe BV	2 000 000
C.Melchers & Co.	1 450 000	C.Melchers & Co.	400 000
Pioneer High Fidelity	300 000	Pioneer High Fidelity	200 000
Total	6 950 000	Total	3 200 000
160. Johnson & Johnson	200 000	No Appeal	
165. Michelin	680 000	102. Michelin	300 000
172. Moët et Chandon (London) Ltd	1 100 000	No Appeal	
173. Hasselblad		107. Hasselblad	
Victor Hasselblad Sweden	560 000	Victor Hasselblad Sweden	560 000
Hasselblad U.K.	165 000	Hasselblad U.K.	80 000
Ilford	10 000	Ilford	10 000
Telos	10 000	Telos	10 000
Prolux	10 000	Prolux	10 000
Total	755 000	Total	670 000
178. NAVEWA-ANSEAU		101. Navewa	
7 machine producers	each 76 500		Fines Upheld
9 machine producers	each 38 500		
6 machine producers	each 9 500		
Total	939 000		
179. AEG Telefunken	1 000 000	100. *AEG*	1 000 000

COMMISSION		COURT OF FIRST INSTANCE/ COURT OF JUSTICE	
181. SSI		127. *SSI*	
		128. *NSO*	
Lourens	425 000	Lourens	425 000
BAT	350 000	BAT	350 000
Turmac	325 000	Turmac	325 000
Reynolds	150 000	Reynolds	100 000
Philip Morris	125 000	Philip Morris	125 000
Niemeyer	100 000	Niemeyer	100 000
Total	1 475 000	Total	1 425 000
186. National Panasonic	450 000	No Appeal	
189. Zinc		109. Zinc Producers	
CRAM	400 000	CRAM	Quashed
RZ	500 000	RZ	Quashed
Total	900 000		
190. AROW/BNIC	160 000	No Appeal	
191. Toltecs/Dorcet	50 000	116. *BAT*	Quashed
194. Windsurfing International		130. Windsurfing	
Windsurfing International	50 000	Windsurfing International	25 000
Ostermann	15 000	No Appeal	
Akutec	10 000	No Appeal	
Klepper	10 000	No Appeal	
Shark	5 000	No Appeal	
VWSC	5 000	No Appeal	
Total	95 000		70 000
198. Cast-iron & steel rolls		No Appeal	
Griffin	45 000		
Marichal	80 000		
SAFAK	75 000		
Achenbach	27 000		
E.Breitenbach	16 000		
L.Breitenbach	17 000		
Buch	65 000		
Gontermann	26 000		
Walzen	72 000		
Krupp	9 000		
Roland	21 000		
Thyssen	42 000		
Chambre Syndicale	29 000		
Chavanne	40 000		
	+25 000		
Berlaimont	86 000		
	+25 000		

Table 11

COMMISSION		COURT OF FIRST INSTANCE/ COURT OF JUSTICE	
Gorcy	13 000		
	+ 12 500		
Usinor	24 000		
	+ 12 500		
Innocenti	111 000		
Agostino	14 000		
Gregorio	10 000		
Zeno	8 000		
Davy Roll	85 000		
Midlang	63 000		
Tennent	26 000		
Sulzau	71 000		
Bofors	100 000		
Total	1 175 000		
	+ 75 000		
202. IPTC Belgium	5 000	No Appeal	
211. Polistil/Arbois	30 000	No Appeal	
212. British Leyland		136. British Leyland	
	350 000		350 000
216. Flat Glass (Benelux)		No Appeal	
BSN	935 000		
Glaverbel	850 000		
St. Gobain	1 450 000		
St. Roch	765 000		
Total	4 000 000		
217. Zinc Producer Group		No Appeal	
Billiton	350 000		
Metallgeselleschaft	500 000		
Penarroya	500 000		
Preussag	500 000		
RTZ	500 000		
Union Minière	950 000		
Total	3 300 000		
218. Peroxide Products		No Appeal	
Solvay	3 000 000		
Laporte	2 000 000		
Dagussa	3 000 000		
Air Liquide	500 000		
Atochem	500 000		
Total	9 000 000		
226. John Deere	2 000 000	No Appeal	

COMMISSION		COURT OF FIRST INSTANCE/ COURT OF JUSTICE	
227. Woodpulp		202. Woodpulp	
British Columbia	100 000	Annulled	
Canadian Forest	125 000		20 000
MacMillan	150 000		20 000
St Anne	200 000		20 000
Weldwood	50 000	Annulled	
Westar	150 000		20 000
Bowater	500 000	Annulled	
Chesapeake	50 000	Annulled	
Crown Zellerbach	50 000	Annulled	
Federal Paper Company	100 000	Annulled	
Georgia Pacific	150 000	Annulled	
International Pulp Sales	250 000	Annulled	
Mead	50 000	Appeal withdrawn	
Scott Paper	50 000	Annulled	
Weyerhauser	50 000	Annulled	
Pulp, Paper, Paper Board (KEA)	50 000	Annulled	
Åhlström	50 000	Annulled	
Enso Gutzeit	200 000	Annulled	
Joutseno Pulp	50 000	Annulled	
Kaukas	100 000	Annulled	
Kemi	50 000	Annulled	
Metsä Botnia	100,000	No Appeal	
Oulu	100 000	Annulled	
Schaumann	100 000	Annulled	
Veitsiluoto	150 000	Annulled	100 000
Finncell	100 000		
Billerud	50 000	No Appeal	
Iggesunds Bruk	50 000	No Appeal	
Koppafors	50 000	No Appeal	
Kornäs	50 000	No Appeal	
MoDoCell	150 000	No Appeal	
Norrlands	150 000	No Appeal	
Södra	200 000	No Appeal	
Stora	150 000	No Appeal	
Svenska Cellulosa	150 000	No Appeal	
Svenska Cellulosa–och Papperbruks	50 000	No Appeal	
Total	4 125 000	Total	1 380 000
242. ECS/AKZO	10 000 000	186. *AKZO*	7 500 000
245. Sperry New Holland	750 000	No Appeal	
246. Siemens/Fanuc		No Appeal	
Siemens	1 000 000		
Fanuc	1 000 000		
Total	2 000 000		

Table 11

COMMISSION		COURT OF FIRST INSTANCE		COURT OF JUSTICE	
247. Polypropylene					
Anic	750 000	T–6/89 Enichem	450 000	326. Anic	Fine Upheld
Atochem	1 750 000	T–3/89 Atochem	Fine Upheld	No Appeal No appeal	
BASF	2 500 000	T–4/89 BASF	2 125 000		
DSM	2 750 000	T–8/89 DSM	Fine Upheld	334. DSM	Fine Upheld
Hercules	2 750 000	T–7/89 Hercules	Fine Upheld	327. Hercules	Fine Upheld
Hoechst	9 000 000	T–10/89 Hoechst	Fine Upheld	330. Hoechst	Fine Upheld
Hüls	2 750 000	T–9/89 Hüls	2 337 000	328. Hüls	Fine Upheld
ICI	10 000 000	T–13/89 ICI	9 000 000	329. ICI	Fine Upheld
Linz	1 000 000	T–15/89 Linz	Fine Upheld	333. Chemie Linz	Fine Upheld
Montedipe	11 000 000	T–14/89 Montedipe	Fine Upheld	332. Montecatini	Fine Upheld
Petrofina	600 000	T–2/89 Petrofina	300 000	No appeal	
Rhône Poulenc	500 000	T–1/89 Rhône Poulenc	Fine Upheld	No appeal	
Shell	9 000 000	T–11/89 Shell	8 100 000	332. Shell	Fine Upheld
Solvay	2 500 000	T–12/89 Solvay	Fine Upheld	No appeal	
Statoil	1 000 000	No appeal		No appeal	
Total	57 850 000	Total	54 562 500	Total	54 562 500
248. Roofing Felt			166. Belasco		
Antwerps Teer	420 000				Fines Upheld
Compagnie Générale	150 000				
Lummerzheim	200 000				
Limburgse Asfalt	30 000				
Kempische Asfalt	75 000				
De Boer	75 000				
Vlaams Asfalt	50 000				
Belgisch Asfalt	15 000				
Total	985 000				
250. Peugeot	50 000		No Appeal		
253. Meldoc			No Appeal		
Coberco	1 360 000				
Campina	1 020 000				
Menken	425 000				
Melk Unie	3 150 000				
DOMO	600 000				
Total	6 550 000				

COMMISSION		COURT OF FIRST INSTANCE/ COURT OF JUSTICE	
254. Fatty Acids		No Appeal	
Unilever	50 000		
Henkel	50 000		
Oliofina	50 000		
Total	150 000		
269. Tipp-Ex		175. Tipp-Ex	
Gott	400 000		Fines Upheld
Beiersdorf	10 000		
Total	410 000		
272. Sandoz	800 000	174. Sandoz	500 000
275. Fisher Price	300 000		
277. Konica	150 000		
282. Hilti	6 000 000	T–30/89 Hilti	Fine Upheld
		222. Hilti	Confirmed
285. British Dental Trade Association	100 000	No Appeal	
286. British Sugar	3 000 000	No Appeal	
294. Hudson Bay	500 000	T–61/89 Danish Fur Breeders	300 000
295. Sabena	100 000	No Appeal	
299. British Plaster Board		T–65/89 British Gypsum	
British Gypsum	3 000 000		Fines Upheld
British Plasterboard	150 000		
Total	3 150 000		
300. Flat Glass		T–68/89 Flat Glass	
Fabrica Pisana	7 000 000	Fabrica Pisana	1 000 000
Societa Italiana	4 700 000	Società Italiana	671 428
Vernante	1 700 000	Vernante	Quashed
Total	13 400 000	Total	1 671 428

Table 11

COMMISSION		COURT OF FIRST INSTANCE		COURT OF JUSTICE	
305. PVC		T–79/89 PVC Non-existence		231. PVC	Annulled
Atochem	3 200 000				
Basf	1 500 000				
DSM	600 000				
Enichem	2 500 000				
Hoechst	1 500 000				
Huels	2 000 000				
ICI	2 500 000				
LVM	750 000				
Montedison	1 750 000				
Shell	850 000				
SAV	400 000				
Wacker	1 500 000				
Total	19 050 000				
Norsk Hydro	750 000	T–106/89, Norsk Hydro			
Solvay	3 500 000	T–196/89 Rev	Inadmissible		
		No appeal			
Total	23 500 000	Total	4 250 000	Total	4 250 000
306. LdPE		T–80/89 LdPE	Annulled		
Atochem	3 600 000				
BASF	5 500 000				
Bayer	2 500 000				
BP	750 000				
CdF	5 000 000				
DOW	2 250 000				
DSM	3 300 000				
Enichem	4 000 000				
Hoechst	1 000 000				
ICI	3 500 000				
Linz	500 000				
Monsanto	150 000				
Montedison	2 500 000				
Neste Oy	1 000 000				
Repsol	100 000				
Shell	850 000				
Statoil	500 000				
Total	37 000 000				

COMMISSION		COURT OF FIRST INSTANCE		COURT OF JUSTICE	
311. Welded Steel Mesh					
Tréfil Union	1 375 000	T–148/89 Tréfilunion			
SMN	50 000		1 235 000		
STPS	150 000	T–147/89 SMN	Fine Upheld		
Sotralentz	228 000	T–151/89 STPS	Fine Upheld		
Tréfilarbed	1 143 000	T–149/89 Sotralentz	57 000		
		T–141/89 Tréfileurope			
Steelinter	315 000		Fine Upheld		
Usines Gustave Boël		T–144/89 Cockerill	252 000		
	550 000	T–142/89 Boël			
Thibo Bouwstaal	420 000		440 000		
Van Merksteijn Bouwstaal		No Appeal			
	375 000				
2nd Bouwstaal	42 000	No Appeal			
Baustahlgewebe		No Appeal			
	4 500 000	317 Baustahlgewebe			
ILRO	13 000		2 950 000		
Ferriere Nord		T–152/89 Ilro	Fine Upheld		
	320 000	T–143/89 Ferriere Nord			
Martinelli	20 000		Fine Upheld		
		T–150/89 Martinelli	Fine		
Total	9 501 000	Upheld			
		Total	7 467 000		
313. Bayonox	500 000	T–12/90 Bayer	Inadmissible		
		242 Bayer	Confirmed		
330. Solvay/ICI					
Solvay	7 000 000	T–30/91 Solvay	Annulled		
ICI	7 000 000	T–36/91 ICI	Annulled		
Total	14 000 000				
331. Solvay/CFK					
Solvay	3 000 000	T–31/91 Solvay	Annulled	347. Solvay	
CFK	1 000 000	No Appeal			CFI Judgment Upheld
Total	4 000 000	Total	1 000 000		1 000 000
332. Solvay	20 000 000	T–32/91 Solvay	Quashed	347. Solvay	
					CFI Judgment Upheld
333. ICI	10 000 000	T–37/91 ICI	Quashed	346. ICI	
					CFI Judgment Upheld
340. Gosme/Martell					
Martell	300 000				
DMP	50 000				
Total	350 000				
341. Viho/Toshiba			No Appeal		
Toshiba	2 000 000				
348. Tetra Pak II		T–83/91 Tetra Pak		276. Tetra Pak	
	75 000 000		Fine Upheld		Dismissed
349. Dutch Building Cartel		T–29/92 SPO	Fine Upheld		
28 local building associations	22 250 000				

Table 11

COMMISSION		COURT OF FIRST INSTANCE		COURT OF JUSTICE
350. British Midland				
Aer Lingus	750 000			
351. Newitt/Dunlop				
Dunlop	5 000 000	T–43/92 Dunlop	3 000 000	
All Weather Sports	150 000	T–38/92 All Weather Sports	Quashed	
Total	5 150 000	Total	3 000 000	
352. Eurocheques		T–39/92 Europay		
Groupement de Cartes Bancaires	5 000 000		2 000 000	
Eurocheque	1 000 000		Quashed	
Total	6 000 000	Total	2 000 000	
353. French African Shipping		No Appeal		
1. Delmas	11 628 000			
2. Hoegh	651 000			
3. RMS Afrika	2 400			
4. UWAS	56 000			
5. Splosna Plovba	2 800			
6. Deep Sea Shipping	3 400			
7. East Asiatic WAS	55 800			
8. I. Messina	4 600			
9. Lloyd Triestino	32 000			
10. Transmare	12 800			
11. Van Uden	10 100			
12. Nedlloyd	25 800			
13. CMB	96 000			
19. Mac Lines	10 100			
15. Soc. Navale de L'Orient	1 751 000			
16. Soc. Navale Caennaise	970 000			
17. Deutsche Afrika Linien Woermann	93 200			
Total	15 306 200			
355. VIHO/Parker Pen				
Parker Pen	700 000	T–77/92 Parker Pen	500 000	
Herlitz	40 000	T–66/92 Herlitz	Fine Upheld	
Total	740 000	Total	540 000	

COMMISSION		COURT OF FIRST INSTANCE		COURT OF JUSTICE		
371. CEWAL		T–24/93 CMB a.o.		343 CMB		
CMB	9 600 000		8 640 000		Annulled	
Dafra Lines	200 000		180 000		Annulled	
Nedlloyd	100 000		90 000		No appeal	
Deutsche Afrika	200 000		180 000		No appeal	
Total	10 100 000	Total	9 090 000	Total	270 000	
381. HOV SVZ/MCN						
Deutsche Bahn	11 000 000					
385. Carton Board						
Buchmann	2 200 000	T–295/94 Buchmann	2 150 000	No appeal		
Europa Carton	2 000 000	T–304/94 Europa Carton	Fine Upheld			
Cascades	16 200 000	T–308/94 Cascades	Fine Upheld	351. Cascades	Referred to CFI	T–308/94 Cascades II 13 538 000
Enso-Gutzeit	3 250 000	T–337/94 Enso-Gutzeit	1 200 000	No appeal		
Finboard	20 000 000	T–338/94 Finnish Board Mills	Fine Upheld	357. Metsa Serlä		
Fiskeby Board	1 000 000	T–319/94 Fiskeby Board	Fine Upheld	No appeal		
Gruber & Weber	1 000 000	T–310/94 Gruber & Weber	730 000	No appeal		
'De Eendracht'	1 750 000	T–311/94 BPB de Eendracht	750 000	No appeal		
KNP	3 000 000	T–309/94 Koninklijke KNP	2 700 000	350. KNP	2 600 000	
Laakmann	2 200 000		No appeal	No appeal		
Mayr-Melnhof	21 000 000	T–347/94 Mayr-Melnkof	17 000 000			
Mo och Domsjö	22 750 000	T–352/94 Mo och Domsjö	Fine Upheld	354. Mo och Domsjö	Fine Upheld	
Papeteries de Lancey	1 500 000		No appeal			
Metsä-Serla	700 000	T–339/94 Metsä-Serla	Fine Upheld	358. Metsa Serlä Oyj	Fine Upheld	
Rena Kartonfabrik	200 000		No appeal			
Sarrió	15 500 000	T–334/94 Sarrió	14 000 000	356. Sarrió	13 750 000	
SCA Holding Ltd	2 200 000	T–327/94 SCA Holding	Fine Upheld	359. SCA Holding	Fine Upheld	
Stora	11 250 000	T–354/94 Stora Kopparbergs Bergslags	Fine Upheld	353. Stora Kopparbergs	Referred to CFI	T–354/94 Stora Kopparbergs Bergslags II 4 670 000
Enso Española	1 750 000	T–348/94 Enso Española	1 200 000	353. Enso Española	Fine Upheld	
Moritz & Weig	3 000 000	T–317/94 Moritz J. Weig	2 500 000	351. Moritz Weig	1 900 000	
Total	138 750 000	Total	128 330 000	Total	127 580 000	Total 118 338 000

Table 11

COMMISSION		COURT OF FIRST INSTANCE	COURT OF JUSTICE
389. PVC II		T–305e.s./94 PVC	375. PVC II
		Fine Upheld	Fines Upheld
Atochem	1 500 000	2 600 000	
BASF	1 500 000	1 500 000	
DSM	600 000	600 000	
Enichem	2 500 000	2 500 000	
Hoechst	1 500 000	1 500 000	
Huels	2 200 000	2 000 000	
ICI	2 500 000	1 550 000	
LVM	750 000	750 000	
Montedison	1 750 000	1 750 000	
SAV	400 000	135 000	
Shell	850 000	850 000	
Wacker	1 500 000	1 500 000	
Total	19 050 000	17 235 000	17 235 000
394. Cement		T–25/95 Cement	
1. Cembureau-Association Européenne du Ciment	100 000	0	
2. Holderbank Financière Glaris S.A.	5 331 000	1 918 000	
3. AKER A/S	40 000	14 000	
4. EUROC AB	40 000	14 000	
5. Bundesverband de Deutschen Zementindustrie	100 000	0	
6. Alsen-Breitenburg Zement-und Kalkwerke GmbH	3 841 000	0	
7. Dyckerhoff AG	12 296 000	8 043 000	
8. Heidelberger Zement AG	15 652 000	7 056 000	
9. Nordcement AG	1 850 000	0	
10. Fédération de l'Industrie Cimentière	100 000	0	
11. S.A. Cimenteries CBR	8 032 000	2 547 000	
12. Aalborg Portland A/S	4 008 000	2 349 000	
13. Agrapación de Fabricantes de Cementos de Espãna-Oficemen	70 000	0	
14. Asland S.A.	5 337 000	740 000	
15. Hispacement S.A.	102 000	No Appeal	

COMMISSION		COURT OF FIRST INSTANCE	COURT OF JUSTICE
16. Hornos Ibericos Alba S.A.	1 784 000	836 000	
17. Corporación Uniland S.A.	1 971 000	592 000	
18. Compañia Valenciana de Cementos Portland S.A.	1 866 000	638 000	
19. Syndicat Français de l'Industrie Cimentière	100 000	0	
20. Cedest S.A.	2 522 000	0	
21. Société des Ciments Français S.A.	25 768 000	13 570 000	
22. Lafarge Coppée S.A.	23 900 000	15 276 000	
23. Vicat S.A.	8 272 000	2 407 000	
24. Association of the Greek Cement Industry	100 000	0	
25. Halkis Cement Company S.A.	1 856 000	510 000	
26. Heracles General Cement Company	5 758 000	0	
27. Titian Cement Company S.A.	5 625 000	0	
28. Irish Cement Ltd	3 524 000	2 065 000	
29. F.lli Buzzi S.p.A.	3 652 000	0	
30. Cementir-Cementerie del Tirreto S.p.A.	8 248 000	7 471 000	
31. Italcementi-Fabbriche Riunite Cemento S.p.A.	33 580 000	26 789 000	
32. Unicem S.p.A.	11 652 000	6 399 000	
33. S.A. des Ciments Luxembourgeois	1 052 000	617 000	
34. Vereniging Nederlandse Cement-Industrie	100 000	0	
35. Eerste Nederlandse Cement Industrie N.V.	7 316 000	0	

Table 11

COMMISSION		COURT OF FIRST INSTANCE		COURT OF JUSTICE
36. ATIC-Associação Técnica da Industria do Cimento	70 000		0	
37. Cimpor-Cimentos de Portugal S.A.	9 324 000		4 312 000	
38. SECIL-Companhia Geral de Cal e Cimento S.A.	3 017 000		1 395 000	
39. British Cement Association	100 000		0	
40. Blue Circle Industries Plc	15 824 000		7 717 000	
41. Castle Cement Ltd	7 964 000		0	
42. The Rugby Group Plc	5 144 000		0	
Total	247 966 000	Total	113 275 000	
399. Far Eastern Freight Compagnie Générale Maritime	10 000	T–86/95 Far Eastern Freight Conference	Fines Annulled	
Hapag-Lloyd Aktiengesellschaft	10 000			
Kawasaki Kisen Kaisha Limited	10 000			
Lloyd Triestino di Navigazione SpA	10 000			
A.P. Møller-Maersk Line	10 000			
Malaysian International Shipping Corporation Berhad	10 000			
Mitsui OSK Lines Ltd	10 000			
Nedlloyd Lijnen BV	10 000			
Neptune Orient Lines Ltd	10 000			
Nippon Yusen Kabushiki Kaisha	10 000			
Orient Overseas Container Line	10 000			
P&O Containers Ltd	10 000			
Croatia Line	10 000	No Appeal		
Total	130 000		10 000	

TABLE 11

COMMISSION		COURT OF FIRST INSTANCE		COURT OF JUSTICE	
401. Tretorn		T–49/95 Van Megen Sport	Fine Upheld		
Tretorn	600 000				
Formuca Sport	10 000				
Fabra Sport	10 000				
Zürcher	10 000				
Van Megen	10 000				
Total	640 000				
405. BASF/Accinauto		T–175/95 BASF	Fine Upheld		
BASF	2 700 000				
Accinauto	100 000	T–176/95 Accinauto	Fine Upheld		
Total	2 800 000				
407. Dutch Cranes		T–213/95 Dutch Cranes	Fines upheld		
FNK	11 500 000				
SCK	300 000				
Total	11 800 000				
408. Adalat		T–41/96 Adalat	Annulled	383. Bayer	CFI judgment Upheld
Bayer	3 000 000				
409a. Fenex	1 000	No Appeal No Appeal			
413. Ferry Services					
P&O	400 000				
Stena Sealink	100 000				
Sea France	60 000				
Britanny Ferries	60 000				
North Sea Ferries	25 000				
Total	645 000				
418. Irish Sugar	8 800 000	T–228/97 Irish Sugar	7 883 326	Appeal declared inadmissible by order	
429. VW-Audi	102 000 000	T–62/98 Volkswagen	90 000 000	381. Volkswagen	90 000 000
430. Alloy Surcharge					
Acerinox	3 530 000	T–48/98 Acerinox	3 136 000	398. Acerinox	Upheld
ALZ	4 540 000	No Appeal			
Acciai Speciali Termi	4 540 000	T–19/91 R Krupp Thyssen Stainless	4 032 000	399. ThyssenKrupp	Upheld
Avesta Sheffield	2 810 000	No Appeal			
Krupp Thyssen Nirasta	8 100 000	T–45/98 Krupp Thyssen	4 032 000		
Usinor	3 860 000	No Appeal			
Total	27 380 000		22 410 000		

Table 11

COMMISSION		COURT OF FIRST INSTANCE		COURT OF JUSTICE	
434. British Sugar II		T–202/98 Tate & Lyle		387. British Sugar	
British Sugar	39 600 000		39 600 000		39 600 000
Tate & Lyle	7 000 000		5 500 000		7 000 000
Napier Brown	1 800 000		1 800 000		1 800 000
James Budgett	1 800 000		No Appeal		No Appeal
Total	50 200 000		46 900 000		48 700 000
435. Pre-Insulated Pipe Cartel				397 Dansk Rørindustri	CFI Judgment Upheld
ABB Asea Brown Boveri	70 000 000	T–31/99 ABB	65 000 000		
Brugg Rohrysteme	925 000	T–15/99 Brugg Rohrsysteme	Upheld		
Dansk Rørindustri	1 475 000	T–21/99 Dansk Rørindustri	Upheld		
Henss/Isoplus	4 950 000	T–9/99 HFB et al.	Upheld		
Ke-Kelit Kunststoffwerk	360 000	T–17/99 Ke Kelit	Upheld		
Oy KWH Tech	700 000	No Appeal			
Løgstør Rør	8 900 000	T–23/99 LR AF 1998	Upheld		
Pan-Isovit	1 500 000	T–16/99 Lögstör Rör (Deutschland)	Upheld		
Sigma Tecnologie	400 000	T–28/99 Sigma Tecnologie	300 000		
Tarco Energi	3 000 000	No Appeal			
Total	92 210 000		87 110 000		
441. *TACA*		T–191e.a./98 Atlantic Container Line and Others			
Maersk	27 500 000				
Atlantic Container	6 880 000		Fines Annulled		
Hapag Lloyd	20 630 000				
P&O Nedlloyd	41 260 000				
Sea-Land Service	27 500 000				
Mediterranean Shipping	13 750 000				
Orient Overseas Container	20 630 000				
Polish Ocean Lines	6 880 000				
DSRI Senator Lines	13 750 000				
Cho Yang Shipping	13 750 000				
Neptune Orient Lines	13 750 000				
Nippon Yusen Kaisma	20 630 000				
Transportación Maritima Mericana	6 880 000				
Hanjin Shipping	20 630 000				
Hyundai Merchant Marine	18 560 000				
Total	272 980 000				

COMMISSION	COURT OF FIRST INSTANCE	COURT OF JUSTICE
443. Greek Ferries		
Strintzis Lines 1 500 000	T–65/99 Strintzis 1 010 000	404. Strintzis CFI judgment upheld
Minoan Lines 3 260 000	T–66/99 Minoan Lines 3 260 000	402. Minoan Lines CFI judgment upheld
Anek Lines 1 110 000	No Appeal	N/A
Marlines SA 260 000	T–56/99 Marlines 260 000	401. Marlines CFI judgment upheld
Karageorgis Lines 1 000 000	No Appeal	N/A
Ventouris 1 010 000	T–59/99 Ventouris 252 500	No Appeal
Adriatica 980 000	T–61/99 Adriatica 245 000	403. Adriatica CFI judgment upheld
Total 9 120 000	7 137 500	7 137 500
455. Football tickets CFO 1 000 000		
456. Virgin/BA BA 6 800 000	T–219/99 British Airways 6 800 000 Upheld	428. British Airways Upheld
457. FEG & TU	T5 & 6/00 VEG & TU	
FEG 4 400 000	4 400 000	415. FEG CFI judgment upheld
TU 2 150 000	2 150 000	416. Technische Uni CFI judgment upheld
Total 6 550 000	6 550 000	
464. FETTCSA	T–213/00 FETTCSA Fines Annulled	394. CMA CGM CFI judgment upheld
CMACGMSA 134 000		
Hapag-Lloyd Container Linie GmbH 368 000		
Kawasaki Kisen Kaisha Limited 620 000		
A.P. Møller Maersk Sealand 838 000		
Malaysia International Shipping Corporation Berhad 134 000		
Misui O.S.K. Lines Ltd 620 000		
Neptune Orient Lines Ltd 368 000		
Nippon Yusen Kaisha 620 000		
Orient Overseas Container Line Ltd 134 000		
P&O Nedlloyd Container Line Ltd 1 240 000		
Cho Yang Shipping Co., Ltd 134 000		
DSR-Senator Lines GmbH 368 000		
Evergreen Marine Corp. (Taiwan) Ltd 368 000		
Hanjin Shipping Co., Ltd 620 000		
Yangming Marine Transport Corp. 368 000		
Total 6 932 000		

Table 11

COMMISSION	COURT OF FIRST INSTANCE	COURT OF JUSTICE
465. Amino Acids		
ADM 47 300 000	T–224/00 ADM & ADM Ingredients 43 875 000	406. Archer Daniels Midland CFI judgment upheld
Ajinomoto 28 300 000	No Appeal	
Kyowa Hakko 13 200 000	T–223/00 Kyowa Hakko Kogyo 13 200 000	No Appeal
Daesang/Sewon 8 900 000	T–230/00 Daesang & Sewon Europe 7 128 400	No Appeal
Cheil Jedang 12 200 000	T–220/00 Cheil Jedang 10 080 000	No Appeal
Total 109 900 000	102 583 240	102 583 240
466. Nathan Bricolux		
Nathan 60 000		
Bricalux 1 000		
Total 61 000		
467. Opel	T–368/00 GM & Opel Netherlands	405. General Motors CFI judgment upheld
Opel Nederland BV & General Motors Nederland BV, jointly or severally liable 43 000 000	35 475 000	
474. Volkswagen	T–208/01 Volkswagen II	411. Volkswagen
Volkswagen 30 960	Annulled	CFI judgment upheld
475. SAS/Maersk Air	T–241/01 SAS	
SAS 39 375 000	Upheld	
Maersk Air 13 125 000		
Total 52 500 000		
479. JCB	T–67/01 JCB Service	417. JCB Service
JCB Service 39 614 000	30 000 000	30 864 000
481. Michelin	T–203/01 Michelin	
Michelin 19 760 000	19 760 000	
482. Graphite Electrodes	T–236e.s./01 Tokai Carbon	
SGL 80 200 000	69 114 000	407. Graphite Electrodes & 408. SGL Carbon 75 700 000
UCAR 50 400 000	42 050 000	
Tokai 24 500 000	12 276 000	
SDK 17 400 000	10 440 000	409. Showa Denko CFI judgment upheld
C/G 10 300 000	6 480 000	
Nippon 12 200 000	6 274 400	
SEC 12 200 000	6 138 000	
VAW 11 600 000	No Appeal	
Total 218 800 000	164 372 000	

COMMISSION		COURT OF FIRST INSTANCE		COURT OF JUSTICE
483. DPAG		No Appeal		
Cross- border mail				
Deutsche Post	1 000			
486. De Post/La Poste		No Appeal		
De Post/La Poste				
	2 500 000			
487. Soda Ash		No Appeal		
Solvay	3 000 000			
488. Soda Ash (Solvay)		No Appeal		
Solvay	20 000 000			
489. Soda Ash (ICI)		No Appeal		
ICI	10 000 000			
490. Mercedes Benz		T–325/01 DaimlerChrysler		
DaimlerChrysler				
	71 825 000		9 800 000	
491. Vitamins				
Hoffman-La Roche		No Appeal		
	462 000 000			
BASF	296 160 000	T–15/02 BASF	47 975 000	
Aventis	5 040 000	No Appeal		
Takeda	37 060 000	No Appeal		
Solvay	9 100 000	No Appeal		
Merck	9 240 000	No Appeal		
Daiichi	23 400 000	T–26/02 Daiichi	18 000 000	
Eisai	13 230 000	No Appeal		
Total	855 230 000		601 645 000	
492. Citric Acid		T–59/02 Archer Daniels		
ADM	39 690 000	Midland	Fine upheld	
Cerestar	170 000	No Appeal		
Hoffman-La Roche		No Appeal		
	63 500 000			
Haarmann & Reimer		No Appeal		
	14 220 000			
Jungbunzlauer		T–43/02 Jungbunzler		
	17 640 000		Upheld	
Total	135 220 000			
493. Luxembourg Brewers		T–49e.s./02 Brewers	Luxembourg	
Bofferding	400 000		Upheld	
Wiltz	24 000			
Battin	24 000			
Total	448 000			

Table 11

COMMISSION		COURT OF FIRST INSTANCE		COURT OF JUSTICE
494. German Bank Charges				
Commerzbank	28 000 000	T–61/02 Commerzbank	Annulled	
Dresdner Bank	28 900 000	T–44/02 Dresdner Bank	Annulled	
Bayerische Hypo	28 000 000	T–56/02 Bayerische Hypo- und Vereinsbank	Annulled	
Deutsche Verkehrs-Bank	14 000 000	T–60/02 Deutsche Verkehrsbank	Annulled	
Vereins- und Westbank	2 800 000	T–54/02 Vereins- und Westbank	Annulled	
Total	108 000 000	See T–44/02 Dresdner Bank: application to set aside default judgment dismissed		
497. Industrial Gases (after erratum)		Appeal Pending		
AGA	4 150 000	No Appeal		
Air Liquide	3 640 000	No Appeal		
Air Products Nederland	2 730 000	No Appeal		
BOC Group	1 170 000	No Appeal		
Messer Nederland	1 000 000	No Appeal		
Hoek Loos	12 600 000	T–304/02	Upheld	
Westfalen Gassen	410 000	T–303/02	Upheld	
Total	25 700 000			
499. Seamless Steel Tubes				
Mannesmannröhren-Werke	13 500 000	T–44/00 Mannesmannröhren-Werke	12 600 000	423. Salgitter Mannesmann CFI judgment upheld
Vallourec	8 100 000	No Appeal		
British Steel	12 600 000	T–67e.s./00 JFE Engineering	11 700 000	
Dalmine	10 800 000	T–50/00 Dalmine	10 800 000	425. Dalmine CFI judgment upheld
Sumitomo	13 500 000	T–48/00 Corus	10 935 000	424. Sumitomo & Nippon Steel CFI judgment upheld
Nippon Steel	13 500 000		10 935 000	424. Sumitomo & Nippon Steel CFI judgment upheld
Kawasaki Steel	13 500 000		10 935 000	
NKK	13 500 000		10 935 000	
Total	99 000 000		86 940 000	
500. Interbrew & Alken Maes				
Interbrew	46 487 000	No Appeal		
Danone	44 043 000	T–30/02 Danone	43 224 500[1]	427. Danone CFI judgment upheld
Alken Maes	585 000	No Appeal		
Haacht	270 000	T–48/02 Brouwerij Haacht	Upheld	
Martens	270 000	No Appeal		
Total	91 655 000		90 836 500	

[1] This is not the amount given in the operative part of the judgment. However, Danone's appeal related to only one of two fines imposed by the Commission. The figure quoted here is the sum of the first fine (as reduced by the CFI) and the second fine (which was not the subject of the appeal).

COMMISSION		COURT OF FIRST INSTANCE		COURT OF JUSTICE
501. Zinc Phosphate				
Britannia	3 370 000	T–33/02 Britannia Alloys	Upheld	431. Britannia Aloys CFI judgment upheld
Hans Heubach	3 780 000	T–64/02 Heubach	Upheld	
James M. Brown	940 000	No Appeal		
SNCZ	1 530 000	T–52/02 SNCZ	Upheld	
Trident	1 980 000	No Appeal		
Waardals	350 000	T–62/02 Union Pigments	Upheld	
Total	11 950 000			
502. Carbonless Paper		T–109/02		
Arjo Wiggins	184 270 000		141 750 000	
Bolloré	22 680 000		Upheld	
Carrs	1 570 000	(Carrs: Case T–123/02—no need to adjudicate)		
Distribuidora Vizcaína	1 750 000		Upheld	
Mitsubishi	21 240 000		Upheld	
Guipuscoana	1 540 000		1 309 000	
Mougeot	3 640 000		Upheld	
Koehler	33 070 000		Upheld	
Sappi	0			
Torraspapel	14 170 000		Upheld	
Zanders Feinpapiere	29 760 000		Upheld	
Total	313 690 000		270 939 000	
503. Austrian Banks		T–259/02		
Erste Bank	37 690 000		Upheld	
Raiffeisen Zentralbank	30 380 000		Upheld	
Bank Austria	30 380 000		Upheld	
BAWAG	7 590 000		Upheld	
Öst. Postsparkasse	7 590 000		Upheld	
Öst. Volksbanken	7 590 000		Upheld	
NÖHypo	1 520 000		Upheld	
Raiffeisenlandesbank	1 520 000		Upheld	
Total	124 260 000		120 465 000	
504. Methionine				
Degussa	118 125 000	T–279/02 Degussa	91 125 000	
Nippon Soda	9 000 000	No Appeal		
Aventis	0	No Appeal		
Total	127 125 000		100 125 000	

Table 11

COMMISSION		COURT OF FIRST INSTANCE		COURT OF JUSTICE
505. Nintendo		Appeal Pending		
Nintendo	149 128 000			
John Menzies	8 640 000			
Concentra	825 000			
Linea	1 500 000			
Nortec	1 000 000			
Bergsala	1 250 000			
Itochu	4 500 000			
CD-Contact Data	1 000 000			
Total	167 843 000			
506. Christie's/Sotheby's		No Appeal		
Christie's	0			
Sotheby's	20 400 000			
Total	20 400 000			
508. Methylglucamine		No Appeal		
Rhône Poulenc	2 850 000			
Merck	0			
Total	2 850 000			
509. Food Flavour Enhancers		No Appeal		
Takeda	0			
Ajinomoto	15 540 000			
Daesang	2 280 000			
Cheil	2 736 000			
Total	20 556 000			
510. Specialty Graphite		T–71e.s./03 Specialty Graphite		
GrafTech	0	No Appeal		430. SGL Carbon
SGL Carbon				CFI judgment upheld
	27 750 000		18 451 970	
LCL	6 970 000	No Appeal		
Ibiden	3 580 000	No Appeal		
Tokai Carbon	6 970 000		Upheld	
Toyo Tanso	10 790 000	Appeal Pending		
Nippon Steel & NSCC, jointly and severally	3 580 000	No Appeal		
Intech EDM BV & Intech EDM AG, jontly and severally	980 000		Upheld[1]	
	60 620 000			

[1] Intech EDM AG's joint and several liability was reduced to 430 000, the fine imposed on Intech EDM BV was upheld.

TABLE 11

COMMISSION		COURT OF FIRST INSTANCE		COURT OF JUSTICE
512. Concrete reinforcing bars		T–71e.s./03 Specialty Graphite Appeal Pending		
UCAR	0			
SGL	27 750 000	Upheld		
LCL	6 970 000	No Appeal		
Ibiden	3 580 000	No Appeal		
Tokai	6 970 000	Upheld		
TT	10 790 000	No Appeal		
NCS & NSCC	3 580 000	No Appeal		
Intech	980 000	Upheld		
Total	60 620 000			
513. French Beef		T–217/03		
FNSEA	12 000 000		9 000 000	
FNB	1 440 000		1 080 000	
JA	600 000		450 000	
FNPL	1 440 000		1 080 000	
FNICGV	720 000	(T–252/03—inadmissible)		
FNCBV	480 000		360 000	
Total	16 680 000		12 690 000	
515. Deutsche Telekom		Appeal Pending		
Deutsche Telekom	12 600 000			
516. Wanadoo	10 350 000	T–340/03 France Télécom	Upheld	
517. Yamaha		Appeal Pending		
Yamaha	2 560 000			
524. Organic Peroxides				
Akzo Nobel	0	No Appeal		
Atofin	43 470 000	No Appeal		
Peroxid Chemie	8 830 000	T–104/04 Degussa removed from the register		
Peroxid Chemie & Degussa	16 730 000	No Appeal		
AC Treuhand	1000	Appeal Pending		
Peroxidos Organicos	500 000			
Total	69 531 000			
528. Microsoft		Appeal Pending		
Microsoft	497 196 304			
530. Topps				
Topps	1 590 000			
535. Belgian Architects				
Belgian Architects' Association	100 000			

Table 11

COMMISSION		COURT OF FIRST INSTANCE	COURT OF JUSTICE
538. Copper Tubes			
Boliden	32 600 000		
Buntmetall	669 500		
Halcor	9 160 000		
HME	4 490 000		
IMI	44 980 000		
KME	32 750 000		
KM Europa	17 960 000		
Europa Metalli	16 370 000		
Mueller	0		
Outokumpu	36 140 000		
Wieland	2 430 000		
Wieland Werke	24 741 600		
Total	222 291 100		
539. French Brewers			
Danone & Kronenbourg	1 500 000		
Heineken	1 000 000		
540. Spanish Raw Tobacco		Appeal Pending	
Deltafina	11 880 000		
Cetarsa	4 631 500		
WWTE	1 822 500		
Agroexpansion	2 592 000		
Taes	108 000		
ASAJA	1000		
UPA	1000		
COAG	1000		
CCAE	1000		
Total	21 038 000		
542. Needles		Appeal Pending	
Prym	30 000 000		
Coats	30 000 000		
Total	60 000 000		
543. Choline Chloride		Appeal Pending	
AKZO Nobel	20 990 000		
BASF	34 970 000		
UCB	10 380 000		
Total	66 340 000		
545. AstraZeneca		Appeal Pending	
AstraZeneca	60 000 000		
549. Peugeot		Appeal Pending	
Peugeot	49 500 000		

COMMISSION	COURT OF FIRST INSTANCE	COURT OF JUSTICE
550. Italian Raw Tobacco Deltafina & Universal, joint and severally liable 30 000 000 Mindo & Alliance One (Mindo partly jointly and severally liable 10 000 000 Transcatab & Alliance One jointly and severally liable 14 000 000 Romana Tabacchi 2 050 000 APTI 1 000 UNITAB 1 000 Total 56 052 000	Appeal Pending	
554. Methacrylates Degussa 0 Arkema 219 131 250 ICI 91 406 250 Lucite 25 025 000 Quinn 9 000 000 Total 344 562 500		
556. Dutch Bitumen Ballast Nedam 4 650 000 BAM NMB 13 500 000 BP 0 Dura Vermeer 5 400 000 Esha 11 500 000 HBG 7 200 000 Heijmans 17 100 000 Klöckner 10 000 000 Kuwait Petroleum 16 632 000 KWS 27 360 000 Nynäs 13 500 000 Shell 108 000 000 Total 20 250 000 Wintershall 11 625 000 Total 266 717 000		

TABLE 11

Table 11

COMMISSION		COURT OF FIRST INSTANCE		COURT OF JUSTICE
558. Gas Insulated Switchgear				
ABB	0			
Alstom	11 475 000			
Alstom & Areva	53 550 000			
jointly & severally				
Fuji	2 400 000			
Hitachi	50 400 000			
JAEPS & Fuji	1 350 000			
jointly & severally				
Mitsubishi	113 925 000			
Mitsubishi & Toshiba jointly & severally	4 650 000			
Toshiba	86 250 000			
Schneider	3 600 000			
Schneider & Siemens T&D jointly & severally	4 500 000			
Siemens T&D	22 050 000			
Siemens	396 562 500			
Total	750 712 000			
559. Dutch Brewers				
Heineken	219 275 000			
Grolsch	31 658 000			
Bavaria	22 850 000			
Total	273 783 000			
Sodium Gluconate (not yet published)				
Akzo Nobel	9 000 000	T–44/02 Akzo Nobel	Upheld	
ADM	10 130 000	T–329/01 Archer Daniels Midland	Upheld	
Avebe	3 600 000	T–314/01 Avebe	Upheld	
Fujisawa	3 600 000	No appeal		
Jungbunzlauer	20 400 000	No appeal		
Roquette	10 800 000	T–322/01 Roquette Frères	8 105 000	
Total	57 530 000		54 835 00	

TABLE 12

LIST OF LEGISLATION AND DOCUMENTS

(All reproduced Legislation appears in Book Four at the end of the Handbook — all page references refer to Book Four)

A. COUNCIL REGULATIONS

11. **Regulation 1534/91** [1991] O.J. L143/1 470

    On the application of Article 85(3) of the Treaty to certain categories of agreements, decisions and concerted practices in the insurance sector (as amended by Regulation 1/2003 [2003] O.J. L1/1)

12. **Regulation 479/92** [1992] O.J. L55/3 473

    On the application of Article 85(3) of the Treaty to certain categories of agreements, decisions and concerted practices between liner shipping companies (consortia) (as amended by Regulation 1/2003 [2003] O.J. L1/1)

13. **Regulation 4064/89** [1997] O.J. L180/1

    On the control of concentrations between undertakings (with amendments introduced by Council Regulation 1310/97) **(Not included)**

14. **Regulation 1/2003** [2003] O.J. L1/1 475

    On the interpretation of the rules on competition laid down in Articles 81 and 82 of the Treaty (as amended by Regulation 411/2004 [2004] O.J. L68/1)

15. **Regulation 139/2004** [2004] O.J. L24/1 496

    On the control of concentrations between undertakings (the EC Merger Regulation)

16. **Regulation 411/2004** [2004] O.J. L68/1

    Repealing Regulation 3975/87 and amending Regulations 3976/87 and 1/2003, in connection with air transport between the Community and third countries **(Not included)**

17. **Regulation 463/2004** [2004] O.J. L77/23

    Amending Regulation 823/2000 on the application of Art.81(3) EC to certain categories of agreements, decisions and concerted practices between liner shipping companies (consortia) **(Not included)**

B. COMMISSION REGULATIONS, DIRECTIVES AND DECISIONS

1. **Decision No. 25–67** [1952–67] O.J. Spec. Ed. 186 521

   Laying down in implementation of Article 66(3) of the Treaty a regulation concerning exemption from prior authorisation (as amended by [1978] O.J. L300/21 and [1991] O.J. L348/12) (no longer in force)

2. **Regulation 27/62** J.O. 1118/62; [1962] O.J. Spec. Ed. 132

   Form, content and other details concerning applications and notifications (with annex and complementary note) as amended by Regulation 2526/85 [1985] O.J. L240/1 and Regulation 3666/93 [1993] O.J. L336/1 **(Not included)**

3. **Regulation 99/63** J.O. 2263/63; [1963] O.J. Spec. Ed. 47

   On the hearings provided for in Article 19(1) and (2) of Council Regulation No. 17 **(Not included)**

4. **Regulation 67/67** [1967] O.J. L57/849; [1967] O.J. Spec. Ed. 10

   On the application of Article 85(3) of the Treaty to certain categories of exclusive dealing agreements **(Not included)**

5. **Regulation 1629/69** [1969] O.J. L209/1; [1969] O.J. Spec. Ed. II 371

   On the form, content and other details of complaints pursuant to Article 10, applications pursuant to Article 12 and notifications pursuant to Article 14(1) of Council Regulation 1017/68 as amended by Regulation 3666/93 [1993] O.J. L336/1 **(Not included)**

6. **Regulation 1630/69** [1969] O.J. L209/11; [1969] O.J. Spec. Ed. 381
Concerning hearings pursuant to Article 26 paragraphs 1 and 2 of Council Regulation 1017/68 **(Not included)**

7. **Regulation 2779/72** [1972] O.J. L292/23 **(Not included)**

8. **Regulation 3604/82** [1982] O.J. L376/33 **(Not included)**

9. **Regulation 1983/83** [1983] O.J. L173/1, Corrigendum in [1983] O.J. L281/24
On the application of Article 85(3) of the Treaty to categories of exclusive distribution agreements **(Not included)**

10. **Regulation 1984/83** [1983] O.J. L173/5, Corrigendum in [1983] O.J. L281/24
On the application of Article 85(3) of the Treaty to categories of Exclusive purchasing agreements **(Not included)**

11. **Regulation 2349/84** [1984] O.J. L219/15, Corrigendum in [1985] O.J. L113/34
On the application of Article 85(3) of the Treaty to certain categories of patent licensing agreements **(Not included)**

12. **Regulation 123/85** [1985] O.J. L17/3
On the application of Article 85(3) of the Treaty to certain categories of motor vehicle distribution and servicing agreements **(Not included)**

13. **Regulation 417/85** [1985] O.J. L53/1
On the application of Article 85(3) of the Treaty to categories of specialization agreements **(Not included)**

14. **Regulation 418/85** [1985] O.J. L53/5
On the application of Article 85(3) of the Treaty to categories of research and development agreement **(Not included)**

15. **Directive 88/301** [1988] O.J. L131/73
On competition in the markets in telecommunications terminal equipment **(Not included)**

16. **Regulation 2671/88** [1988] O.J. L239/9
On the application of Article 85(3) of the Treaty to certain categories of agreements between undertakings, decisions of associations of undertakings and concerted practices concerning joint planning and co-ordination of capacity, sharing of revenue and consultations on tariffs on scheduled air services and slot allocation at airports **(Not included)**

17. **Regulation 2672/88** [1988] O.J. L239/13
On the application of Article 85(3) of the Treaty to certain categories of agreements between undertakings relating to computer reservation systems for air transport services **(Not included)**

18. **Regulation 2673/88** [1988] O.J. L239/17
On the application of Article 85(3) of the Treaty to certain categories of agreements between undertakings decisions of associations of undertakings and concerted practices concerning ground handling services **(Not included)**

19. **Regulation 4087/88** [1988] O.J. L359/46
On the application of Article 85(3) of the Treaty to categories of franchise agreements **(Not included)**

20. **Regulation 4260/88** [1988] O.J. L376/1
On the communications, complaints and the hearings provided for in Regulation 4056/86 laying down detailed rules for the application of Articles 85 and 86 of the Treaty to maritime transport as amended by Regulation 3666/93 [1993] O.J. L336/1 **(Not included)**

21. **Regulation 4261/88** [1988] O.J. L376/10

On the complaints, applications and hearings provided for in Regulation 3975/87 laying down the procedure for the application of the rules on competition to undertakings in the air transport sector as amended by Regulation 3666/93 [1993] O.J. L336/1 **(Not included)**

22. **Regulation 556/89** [1989] O.J. L61/1

On the application of Article 85(3) of the Treaty to certain categories of knowhow licensing agreements **(Not included)**

23. **Directive 90/388** [1988] O.J. L192/10

On competition in the markets for telecommunications services **(Not included)**

24. **Regulation 2367/90** [1990] O.J. L219/5

On the notification time-limits and hearings provided for in Council Regulation 4064/89 as amended by Regulation 3666/93 [1993] O.J. L336/1 **(Not included)**

25. **Regulation 82/91** [1991] O.J. L10/7

On the application of Article 85(3) of the Treaty to certain categories of agreements and concerted practices concerning ground handling services **(Not included)**

26. **Regulation 83/91** [1991] O.J. L10/9

On the application of Article 85(3) of the Treaty to certain categories of agreements between undertakings relating to computer reservation systems for air transport services **(Not included)**

27. **Regulation 84/91** [1991] O.J. L10/14

On the application of Article 85(3) of the Treaty to certain categories of agreements, decision and concerted practices concerning joint planning and conciliation of capacity consultations on passenger and cargo tariff rates on scheduled air services and slot allocation at airports **(Not included)**

28. **Regulation 3932/92** [1992] O.J. L398/7

On the application of Article 85(3) of the Treaty to certain categories of agreements, decisions and concerted practices in the insurance sector **(Not included)**

29. **Regulation 151/93** [1993] O.J. L21/8

Amending Regulations 417/85, 418/85, 2349/89 and 556/89 on the application of Article 85(3) of the Treaty to certain categories of specialisation agreements, research and development agreements, patent licensing agreements and know-how licensing agreements **(Not included)**

30. **Regulation 1617/93** [1993] O.J. L155/18 526

On the application of Article 85(3) of the Treaty to certain categories of agreements, and concerted practices concerning joint planning and co-ordination of schedules, joint operations, consultations on passenger and cargo tariffs on scheduled air services and slot allocation at airports (as amended by Regulation 1523/96 [1996] O.J. L190/11, Regulation 1083/1999 [1999] O.J. L131/27, Regulation 1324/2001 [2001] O.J. L177/56 and the Act of Accession of Austria, Sweden and Finland [1994] O.J. C241/21 (adapted by Council Decision 95/1/EC, Euraton, ECSC [1995] O.J. L1/1), corrigendum in [1994] O.J. L15/20)

31. **Regulation 3652/93** [1993] O.J. L333/37

On the application of Article 85(3) of the Treaty to certain categories of agreements relating to computer reservation systems for air transport services **(Not included)**

32. **Regulation 3666/93** [1993] O.J. L336/1 531

Amending Regulation 27, Regulations 1629/69, 4260/88, 4261/88 and 2367/90 with a view to implementing the competition provision laid down in the Agreement on the European Economic Area

33. **Decision 94/810/EC, ECSC** [1994] O.J. L330/67

On the terms of reference of hearing officers in competition procedures before the Commission **(Not included)**

34. **Directive 94/46** [1994] O.J. L268/15

Amending Directive 88/301 and Directive 90/388 in particular with regard to satellite communications **(Not included)**

35. **Regulation 3385/94** [1994] O.J. L377/28

On the form, content and other details of application and notifications provided for in Council Regulation No. 17 **(Not included)**

36. **Decision 95/145/EC, ECSC** [1995] O.J. L95/45, [1995] O.J. L131/38 534

Concerning the conclusion of the Agreement between the European Communities and the Government of the United States of America regarding the application of their competition laws

37. **Regulation 870/95** [1995] O.J. L89/7

On the application of Article 85(3) of the Treaty to certain categories of agreements, decisions and concerted practices between liner shipping companies (consortia) pursuant to Council Regulations (EEC) No. 479/92 **(Not included)**

38. **Regulation 1475/95** [1995] O.J. L145/25

On the application of Article 85(3) of the Treaty to certain categories of motor vehicle distribution and servicing agreements **(Not included)**

39. **Directive 95/51** [1995] O.J. L256/49

Amending Directive 90/388 with regard to the abolition of the restrictions on the use of cable television networks for the provision of already liberalised telecommunications services **(Not included)**

40. **Directive 96/2** [1996] O.J. L20/59

Amending Directive 90/388 with regard to mobile and personal communications **(Not included)**

41. **Regulation 240/96** [1996] O.J. L31/2

On the application of Article 85(3) of the Treaty to certain categories of technology transfer agreements **(Not included)**

42. **Directive 96/19** [1996] O.J. L74/13

Amending Directive 90/388 with regard to the implementation of full competition in the telecommunication market **(Not included)**

43. **Regulation 1523/96** [1996] O.J. L190/11

Amending Regulation 1617/93 on the application of Article 85(3) of the Treaty to certain categories of agreements and concerted practices concerning joint planning and co-ordination of schedules, joint operations, consultations on passenger and cargo tariffs on scheduled air services and slot allocation at airports **(Not included)**

44. **Regulation 447/98**

On the notifications, time limits and hearings provided for in Council Regulation 4064/89 on the control of concentrations between undertakings **(Not included)**

C. NOTICES

TABLE 12

D. OTHER DOCUMENTS

LIST OF LEGISLATION (MERGERS)

No.	NAME	O.J.[1]	C.M.L.R.[2]
1.	Council Regulation 139/2004 on the control of concentrations between undertakings	[2004] L24/1	—
2.	Commission Regulation 802/2004 implementing Regulation 139/2004	[2004] L133/1	—
3.	Commission Notice on the concept of full-function joint venture	[1998] C66/1	4 [1998] 581
4.	Commission Notice on the calculation of turnover	[1998] C66/25	4 [1998] 613
5.	Commission Notice on the concept of concentration	[1998] C66/5	4 [1998] 586
6.	Commission Notice on the concept of undertakings concerned	[1998] C66/14	4 [1998] 599
7.	Commission Notice on restrictions directly related and necessary to concentrations	[2005] C56/24	5 [2001] 19
8.	Commission Notice on the definition of the relevant market	[1997] C372/5	4 [1998] 177
9.	Commission Notice on remedies acceptable under Council Regulation 4064/89 and Commission Regulation 447/98	[2001] C68/3	5 [2003] 1
10.	Commission Notice on a simplified procedure for treatment of certain concentrations under Council Regulation 4064/89	[2005] C56/32	5 [2000] 774
11.	Commission Notice on Case Referral in respect of concentrations	[2005] C56/2	4 [2005] 15
12.	Guidelines on the assessment of horizontal mergers under the Council Regulation on the control of concentrations	[2005] C31/5	—
13.	Best practice guidelines on the conduct of EC merger control proceedings	—	—
14.	Application of the Merger Regulation: Declaration of incompleteness	—	—
15.	Best practices guidelines for divestiture commitments — Standard model for divestiture commitments — Standard model for trustee mandate	—	—

[1] Official Journal of the European Communities.
[2] Common Market Law Reports.

No.	NAME	O.J.	C.M.L.R.
16	Commission Notice on the rules for access to the Commission file in cases pursuant to Articles 81 and 82 of the EC Treaty, Articles 53, 54 and 57 of the EEA Agreement and Council Regulation (EC) No 139/2004	[2005] C325/7	4 [2006] 24
17	DG Competition Information note on Art. 6(1)c 2nd sentence of Regulation 139/2004 (abandonment of concentrations)	—	—

LEGISLATION

1. Council Regulation 139/2004 on the control of concentrations between undertakings [2004] L24/1 (reproduced in the Legislation section below)

2. Commission Regulation 802/2004 implementing Regulation 139/2004 [2004] L133/1 (reproduced in the Legislation section below)

3. Notice on the concept of full-function joint ventures [1998] O.J. C66/1 (reproduced in the Legislation section below)

4. Notice on calculation of turnover [1998] O.J. C66/25 (reproduced in the Legislation section below)

5. Notice on the concept of concentration [1998] O.J. C66/5 (reproduced in the Legislation section below)

6. Notice on the concept of undertakings concerned [1998] O.J. C66/14 (reproduced in the Legislation section below)

7. Notice regarding restrictions directly related and necessary to concentrations [2005] C56/24 (reproduced in the Legislation section below)

8. Notice on the definition of the relevant market [1997] O.J. C372/5 (reproduced in the Legislation section below)

9. Notice on remedies acceptable under Council Regulation [4064/89] and under Commission Regulation [447/98] [2001] O.J. C68/3 (reproduced in the Legislation section below)

10. Notice on a simplified procedure for treatment of certain concentrations under Council Regulation 139/2004 [2005] C56/32 (reproduced in the Legislation section below)

11. Commission Notice on Case Referral in respect of concentrations [2005] C56/2

12. Best practice guidelines on the conduct of EC merger control proceedings (reproduced in the Legislation section below)

13. Application of the Merger Regulation: Declaration of incompleteness (reproduced in the Legislation section below)

14. Best practice guidelines for divestiture commitments (reproduced in the Legislation section below)
    - Standard model for divestiture commitments (reproduced in the Legislation section below)
    - Standard model for trustee mandate (reproduced in the Legislation section below)

15. Guidelines on the assessment of horizontal mergers [2004] O.J. C31/5 (reproduced in the Legislation section below)

16. Commission Consolidated Jurisdictional Notice [2007] under Council Regulation (EC) No.139/2004 on the control of concentrations between undertakings. (Not published yet.)

CHRONOLOGICAL LIST OF ECSC LEGISLATION

1. **High Authority Decision No. 24–54** of May 6, 1954 laying down in implementation of Article 66(1) of the Treaty a regulation on what constitutes control of an undertaking. ([1954] J.O. 345; [1952–58] O.J. Spec. Ed. 16)

2. **High Authority Decision No. 26–54** of May 6, 1954 laying down in implementation of Article 66(4) of the Treaty a regulation concerning information to be furnished ([1954] J.O. 350; [1952–58] O.J. Spec. Ed. 17)

3. **High Authority Decision No. 14–64** of July 8, 1964 on business books and accounting documents which undertakings must produce for inspection by officials or agents of the High Authority carrying out checks or verifications as regards prices. ([1964] O.J. 120/1967)

4. **High Authority Decision No. 1–65** of February 3, 1965 concerning notification of decisions on information to be obtained from checks to be made on associations of undertakings for the purposes of application of Article 65 of the Treaty. ([1965] O.J. 27/438).

5. **High Authority Decision No. 25–67** of June 22, 1967 laying down in implementation of Article 66(3) of the Treaty a Regulation concerning exemption from prior authorisation, ([1967] O.J. 154/11; [1967] O.J. Spec. Ed. 186).

    as amended by Commission Decision No. 2495/78/ECSC ([1978] O.J. L300/21). Text of Decision No. 25–67 as amended: ([1978] O.J. C255/2).

    and by Commission Decision No. 3654/91/ECSC ([1991] O.J. L348/12).

6. **Commission Decision No. 715/78/ECSC** of April 6, 1978 concerning limitation periods in proceedings and the enforcement of sanctions under the Treaty establishing the European Coal and Steel Community ([1978] O.J. L94/22).

7. **Commission Decision No. 379/84/ECSC** of February 15, 1984 defining the powers of officials and agents of the Commission instructed to carry out the checks provided for in the ECSC Treaty and the decisions taken in application thereof ([1984] O.J. L46/23).

8. **Communication on co-operation** ([1968] O.J. C75/3; as modified by [1968] O.J. C84/17).

9. **Guidelines** on the method of setting fines imposed pursuant to Article 15(2) of Regulation No.17 and Article 65(5) of the ECSC Treaty ([1998] O.J. C9/3).

10. **Commission Notice** concerning alignment of procedures for processing mergers under the ECSC and E.C. Treaties ([1998] O.J. C66/36).

TABLE 13

ALPHABETICAL LIST OF COMMISSION DECISIONS

[This list does not contain those merger decisions issued by simplified procedure, which can be found in Table 6.]
"M" denotes Mergers and Acquisition. See Book Two for references
"CS" denotes Coal and Steel. See Book Three for references
For all other Decisions, see Book One for references

TABLE 13

TABLE 13

Table 13

TABLE 13

TABLE 13

TABLE 13

TABLE 13

TABLE 14

ALPHABETICAL LIST OF CFI JUDGMENTS

See Books One and Two for references

TABLE 15

ALPHABETICAL LIST OF EUROPEAN COURT JUDGMENTS

'CS' denotes Coal and Steel cases. See Book Three for references
For all other cases, see Book One for references

TABLE 15

TABLE 16

LIST OF NATIONAL DECISIONS: ANTITRUST

BELGIUM (BE):

No.	NAME AND CASE NUMBER	DATE	SOURCE	AUTHORITY AND TYPE OF DECISION	SECTOR
BE1	Cools/CM Antwerpen	25.01.05	Revue de la concurrence belge 2006, 54	Brussels Court of Appeal Restrictive agreement	Healthcare insurance
BE2	Emond v Brasserie Haacht	23.06.05	Revue de la concurrence belge 2006, 107	Brussels Court of Appeal Restrictive agreement	Beer
BE3	SABAM v Production & Marketing	03.11.05	Revue de la Concurrence belge 2006 319	Brussels Court of Appeal Abuse of dominance	Collecting society
BE4	Thiry v. ASAF CONC-P/K–00/0011	21.12.05	*http://mineco.fgov.be/organization_market/competition/competition_council/competition_nl_007_bis.htm*	NCA Abuse of dominance	Tyres
BE5	International Gemmological Institute v Hoge Raad voor Diamant	31.01.06	Revue de la concurrence belge 2006, 154	Brussels Court of Appeal	Diamonds
BE6	TELE2 v Belgacom MEDE-V/M–05/0043	01.09.06	*http://mineco.fgov.be/organization_market/competition/competition_council/competition_nl_007_bis.htm*	NCA Abuse of dominance	Telecoms
BE7	Computer Resource Management MEDE-V/M–03/0060	14.02.07	*http://mineco.fgov.be/organization_market/competition/competition_council/competition_nl_007_bis.htm*	NCA Abuse of dominance	Software

BULGARIA (BG):

No.	NAME AND CASE NUMBER	DATE	SOURCE	AUTHORITY AND TYPE OF DECISION	SECTOR
BG1	SAC Decision No.1700/2006	15.02.06	*http://www.sac.government.bg/court22.nsf/d6397429a99ee2afc225661e00383a86/c7278d2ac4467406c2257113003eb9c1?opendocument*	SAC, 1st Grand Chamber, Cassation	Insurance
BG2	CPC Decision No.136/2006	22.06.06	*http://www.cpc.bg/system/storage/136–06–chl9.doc*	NCA	Beverages
BG3	CPC Decision No.174/2006	20.07.06	*http://www.cpc.bg/system/storage/174–%202006.doc*	NCA	Construction Materials
BG4	CPC Decision No.163/2006	11.07.06	*http://www.cpc.bg/system/storage/163–2006.doc*	NCA	Pharmaceuticals
BG5	SAC Decision No.1402/2007	09.02.07	*http://www.sac.government.bg/court22.nsf/d6397429a99ee2afc225661e00383a86/e8a73044d4ac80ebc225727800433fd2?opendocument*	SAC, 2nd Grand Chamber, Cassation	Waste Management
BG6	CPC Decision No.331/2006	28.12.06	*http://www.cpc.bg/system/storage/resh–331.doc*	NCA	Entertainment

CYPRUS (CY):

No.	NAME AND CASE NUMBER	DATE	SOURCE	AUTHORITY AND TYPE OF DECISION	SECTOR
CY1	Cyprus Telecommunications Authority/Lumiere TV Public Co. Ltd. Case1	21.08.06	*http://www.competition.gov.cy*	NCA, Abuse of Dominance	Television Broadcasting
CY2	NCA/ Cyprus Telecommunications Authority Case 2	26.09.06	*http://www.competition.gov.cy*	NCA, Abuse of Dominance	Telecommunications

No.	NAME AND CASE NUMBER	DATE	SOURCE	AUTHORITY AND TYPE OF DECISION	SECTOR
CY3	Golden Telemedia Ltd./ Cyprus Telecommunications Authority Case3	11.04.07	*http://www.competition.gov.cy*	NCA, Abuse of Dominance	Mobile Services
CY4	Mr. Alexis Philippides/ Cyprus Telecommunications Authority Case 4	28.11.06	*http://www.competition.gov.cy*	NCA, Abuse of Dominance	Internet service provision
CY5	NCA/ Major Cement Competitors, Case 5	4.04.06	*http://www.competition.gov.cy*	NCA, Abuse of Dominance	Cement Market
CY6	Cyprus Footballer's Union, Costas Malekos, Angelos Efthimiou/ Cyprus Football Federation. Case 6	19.10.06	*http://www.competition.gov.cy*	NCA, Review of legislation	Football transfer contracts

THE CZECH REPUBLIC (CZ):

No.	NAME AND CASE NUMBER	DATE	SOURCE	AUTHORITY AND TYPE OF DECISION	SECTOR
CZ1	Linde Technoplyn	04.10.04	*http://www.compet.cz/en/competition/decisions*	NCA, abuse of dominance	Energy
CZ2	RWE Transgas a.s.	13.03.07	*http://www.compet.cz/en/competition/decisions*	NCA, abuse of dominance	Energy
CZ3	Tupperware	14.12.06	*http://www.compet.cz/en/competition/decisions*	NCA, cartel agreement	Retail
CZ4	ČESKÝ TELECOM	01.10.05	*http://ns.compet.cz*	NCA, abuse of dominance	Telecom
CZ5	ČEZ, a.s	27.02.04	*http://ns.compet.cz*	NCA, reimport ban agreements	Energy
CZ6	Producers of gas-insulated switchgear	26.04.07	*http://www.compet.cz/en/competition/decisions*	NCA, bid-rigging	Construction
CZ7	ČEZ, a.s	23.10.01	*http://www.compet.cz/en/competition/decisions*	High Court decision	Energy
CZ8	Constitutional Court	29.05.97	*http://www.judikatura.cz*	Constitutional court decision,	EU law, principles application in pre-accession period

DENMARK (DK):

No.	NAME AND CASE NUMBER	DATE	SOURCE	AUTHORITY AND TYPE OF DECISION	SECTOR
DK1	Mazda Motor	26.10.06	*http://www.ks.dk/english/competition/national/2005/mazda/*	NCA, first phase	Motor vehicles
DK2	TDC—margin squeeze	10.02.06	*http://www.ks.dk/english/competition/national/2004/song/*	NCA, second phase	Professionel service
DK3	Arla—rebates and marketing contributions	10.02.06	*http://www.ks.dk/konkurrence/afgoerelser/2005/r3003/arla*	NCA, first phase	Consumer goods
DK4	Insolvency agreement in the pharmaceutical sector	20.11.05	*http://www.ks.dk/konkurrence/afgoerelser/2005/r3011/insolvens/*	NCA, first phase	Pharmaceuticals

ESTONIA (EST):

No.	NAME AND CASE NUMBER	DATE	SOURCE	AUTHORITY AND TYPE OF DECISION	SECTOR
EST1	Tallinna Sadam 31–L	07.06.02	*http://www.konkurentsiamet.ee*	NCA, abuse of dominant position	Transport
EST2	Eesti Telefon 3–3–1–66–02	18.12.02	*http://www.nc.ee*	Supreme Court, abuse of dominant position	Telecom
EST3	Tallinna Sadam 39–L	29.11.04	*http://www.konkurentsiamet.ee*	NCA, termination of tproceeding	Transport
EST4	Eesti Pandipakend 7–L	16.02.07	*http://www.konkurentsiamet.ee*	NCA, termination of proceeding	Recycling
EST5	Eesti Põlevkivi 40–L	25.08.06	*http://www.konkurentsiamet.ee*	NCA, sectoral analysis	Energy

FRANCE (F):

No.	NAME AND CASE NUMBER	DATE	SOURCE	AUTHORITY AND TYPE OF DECISION	SECTOR
F1	05–D–64 Parisian luxury hotels	25.11.05	*http://www.conseil-concurrence.fr*	NCA	Parisian luxury hotels

No.	NAME AND CASE NUMBER	DATE	SOURCE	AUTHORITY AND TYPE OF DECISION	SECTOR
F2	05–D–65	30.11.05	*http://www.conseil-concurrence.fr*	NCA	Mobile telephone
F3	06–D–03 bis	09.03.06	*http://www.conseil-concurrence.fr*	NCA	Heaters, devices of plumbing and air conditioning
F4	Parisian luxury hotels c/05–D–64	26.09.06	*http://www.conseil-concurrence.fr*	Paris Court of Appeal	Parisian luxury hotels
F5	Bouygues, SFR, Orange c/05–D–65	12.12.06	*http://www.conseil-concurrence.fr*	Paris Court of Appeal	Mobile telephones
F6	Bouygues, SFR, Orang c/ CA 07–10.303	29.06.07	*http://www.legifrance.com*	French Supreme Court	Mobile telephones
F7	06–D–18	28.06.06	*http://www.conseil-concurrence.fr*	NCA	Film advertising
F8	Royal Canin c/ 05–D–32	04.04.06	*http://www.conseil-concurrence.fr*	Paris Court of Appeal	Food for dogs
F9	04–D–48	14.10.04	*http://www.conseil-concurrence.fr*	NCA	Telecommunications
F10	DBS c/ 05–D–51	23.05.06	*http://www.legifrance.com*	Paris Court of Appeal	Procurement contract
F11	STAL c/ 04–D–39	05.10.04	*http://www.finances.gouv.fr*	Paris Court of Appeal (Order)	Slaughter and sale of animals of butcher's shop

GERMANY (DE):

No.	NAME AND CASE NUMBER	DATE	SOURCE	AUTHORITY AND TYPE OF DECISION	SECTOR
DE1	Vitaminpreise 12 HK O 56/02 Kart	15.01.04	*http://www.justiz.rlp.de*	Regional Court of Mainz, denial of cartel damages	Vitamins
DE2	Vitaminpreise 6 U 183/03	28.01.04	NJW 2004, 2243	Higher Regional Court of Karlsruhe, confirmation of decision of lower court denying cartel damages	Vitamins
DE3	Vitaminpreise Dortmund 13 O 55/02 Kart	01.04.04	*http://www.justiz.nrw.de*	Regional Court of Dortmund, granting of cartel damages for the first time in the Vitamins cases	Vitamins
DE4	Tschechisches Bier VI–U (Kart) 29/04	23.06.04	*http://www.justiz.nrw.de*	Higher Regional Court of Düsseldorf, partly annulment of interim injunction of lower court	Beer
DE5	Citroen KZR 10/03	13.07.04	*http://www.bundesgerichtshof.de*	Federal Court of Justice, interpretation of Art.81(3) EC Treaty, German provisions of the control of general terms and conditions and EC regulation 1400/2002	Automotive

DE6	Regenerative Wärmeaustauscher VI–Sch (Kart) 1/02	21.07.04	*http://www.justiz.nrw.de*	Higher Regional Court of Düsseldorf, Art.81 EC Treaty as part of the German ordre public	Heating
DE7	Bezugsbindung KZR 28/03	22.02.05	*http://www.bundesgerichtshof.de*	Federal Court of Justice, decision on selective distribution system with sales targets and obligation to purchase	Automotive
DE8	Selbstdurchschreibe-papier 22 O 74/04 Kart	29.04.05	Not published	Regional Court of Mannheim, denial of cartel damages	Paper
DE9	Filigranbetondecken VI–2 (Kart) 12/04 (V)	10.06.05	*http://www.justiz.nrw.de*	Higher Regional Court of Düsseldorf, rejection of decision of the FCO defining effect on trade between Member States very broadly	Construction Materials
DE10	Qualitative Selektion KZR 26/04	28.06.05	*http://www.bundesgerichtshof.de*	Federal Court of Justice, rejection of contractual duty for the car manufacturer to contract with anyone fulfilling the relevant qualifications under EC regulation 1400/2002	Automotive
DE11	Kfz-Vertragshändler II KZR 14/04	26.07.05	*http://www.bundesgerichtshof.de*	Federal court of Justice, referral to the ECJ because of interpretation of extraordinary right to terminate existing contracts because of the coming into force of EC regulation 1400/2002	Automotive
DE12	E.ON/Ruhrgas VI–2 (Kart) 1/06 (V)	20.01.06	*http://www.justiz.nrw.de*	Higher Regional Court of Düsseldorf, confirmation of FCO's decision on long-term gas supply contracts	Energy
DE13	Soda-Club B3–39/03	09.02.06	*http://www.bundeskartellamt.de*	FCO, abuse of dominance because of additional costs when changing supplier	Consumer Goods
DE14	Nord-KS/Xella B1–116/04	09.08.06	*http://www.bundeskartellamt.de*	FCO, decision about information rights in joint venture	Construction Materials
DE15	5–Sterne-Premium-Paket VI–U (Kart) 15/06	20.09.06	*http://www.justiz.nrw.de*	Higher Regional Court of Düsseldorf,	Automotive
DE16	Deutscher Lotto- und Totoblock KVR 31/06 (not yet published)	08.05.07	*http://www.bundesgerichtshof.de*	Federal Court of Justice confirmation	Gambling

HUNGARY (H):

No.	NAME AND CASE NUMBER	DATE	SOURCE	AUTHORITY AND TYPE OF DECISION	SECTOR
H1	Vj-57/1998 Henkel and others	09.9.98	*http://www.gvh.hu*	NCA	Paper (retail)
H2	Vj-126/2000 UPC Magyarország	23.01.01	*http://www.gvh.hu*	NCA	Telecommunications
H3	Vj-73/2001 Holcim Hungária	08.10.02	*http://www.gvh.hu*	NCA	Construction
H4	Vj-105/2001 Wrigley Hungária	05.03.02	*http://www.gvh.hu*	NCA	Food
H5	Vj-41/2002 Nemzeti Autópálya Rt.	02.06.03	*http://www.gvh.hu*	NCA	Construction
H6	Vj-100/2002 Magyar Távközlési Rt	22.01.04	*http://www.gvh.hu*	NCA	Telecommunications
H7	Vj-138/2002 Alterra Kft. and others	18.03.04	*http://www.gvh.hu*	NCA	Construction
H8	Vj-149/2003 AB Aegon and others	29.04.04	*http://www.gvh.hu*	NCA	Insurance
H9	Vj-56/2004 Adeptus Rt. and others	22.09.05	*http://www.gvh.hu*	NCA	Construction
H10	Vj-162/2004 SAP and others	15.06.06	*http://www.gvh.hu*	NCA	IT
H11	Vj-22/2005 MÁV Rt.	10.07.06	*http://www.gvh.hu*	NCA	Transport

IRELAND (IE):

No.	NAME AND CASE NUMBER	DATE	SOURCE	AUTHORITY AND TYPE OF DECISION	SECTOR
IE1	Competition Authority v	22.10.04	*http://www.bailii.org/ie/ cases/ IEHC/2004/330.html*	High Court Art.81 (infringement found) Art.82 (tying) (infringement found)	Credit Union Representation Services and Savings Protection
IE2	O'Regan & ors [2007] IESC 22	11.04.06	*http://www.bailii.org.ie/ cases/IEHC/2006/ H187.html*	High Court Infringement 81 Concept of undertaking (no infringement found)	Medical Services

No.	NAME AND CASE NUMBER	DATE	SOURCE	AUTHORITY AND TYPE OF DECISION	SECTOR
IE3	Competition Authority v Beef Industry Development Society Limited and Barry Bros (Carrigmore) Meats Limited [2006] IEHC 294	27.07.06	*http://www.bailii.org.ie/ cases/IEHC/2006/ H294.html*	High Court Infringement 81 (no infringement found)	Meat Processing
IE4	Competition Authority v O'Regan & ors [2007] IESC 22	08.05.07	*http://www.bailii.org.ie*	Supreme Court Appeal Art.81 (overturning infringement finding in High Court (IE 1)) Art.82 (tying) (overturning infringement finding in High Court (IE 1))	Credit Union Representation Services and Savings

ITALY (I):

No.	NAME AND CASE NUMBER	DATE	SOURCE	AUTHORITY AND TYPE OF DECISION	SECTOR
I1	Rifornimenti aeroportuali	14.06.06	*http://www.agcm.it*	NCA(AGCM), Decision: ex Art.81 EC Treaty, violation—fines—TAR Decision.	Jet Fuel
I2	Prezzi del latte per l'infanzia	12.10.05	*http://www.agcm.it*	NCA(AGCM), Decision: ex Art.81 EC Treaty, violation—fines	Milk industry
I3	Pannelli truciolati in legno	17.05.07	*http://www.agcm.it*	NCA(AGCM), Decision: ex Art.81 EC Treaty, violation—Fines	Wood industry
I4	Consorzio industrie fiammiferi	13.07.00	*http://www.agcm.it*	NCA(AGCM), Decision: ex Art.81 EC Treaty, violation	Match industry
I5	Merck—principi attivi	21.03.07	*http://www.agcm.it*	NCA(AGCM), Decision: Ex Art.82, EC Treaty violation—commitments accepted	Pharmaceuticals
I6	Glaxo—principi attivi	08.02.06	*http://www.agcm.it*	NCA(AGCM), Decision: Ex Art.82, EC Treaty violation	Pharmaceuticals

No.	NAME AND CASE NUMBER	DATE	SOURCE	AUTHORITY AND TYPE OF DECISION	SECTOR
I7	Gestione ed utilizzo della Capacità di rigassificazione	06.03.07	*http://www.agcm.it*	NCA(AGCM), Decision: Ex Art.82, EC Treaty violation commitments accepted	Gas
I8	Enel Trade/Clienti idonei	27.11.03	*http://www.agcm.it*	NCA(AGCM), Decision: Ex Art.82, EC Treaty violation—fines	Energy
I9	Comportamenti abusivi Telecom Italia	16.11.04	*http://www.agcm.it*	NCA(AGCM), Decision: Ex Art.3, National Antitrust law violation—fines	Telecomunications
I10	Comportamenti restrittivi sulla Borsa elettrica	20.12.06	*http://www.agcm.it*	NCA(AGCM), Decision: Ex Art.82, EC Treaty violation—commitments accepted	Energy
I11	ENI/Trans Tunisian Pipeline	15.02.06	*http://www.agcm.it*	NCA(AGCM), Decision: Ex Art.82, EC Treaty violation—fines	Gas

LATVIA (LV):

No.	NAME AND CASE NUMBER	DATE	SOURCE	AUTHORITY AND TYPE OF DECISION	SECTOR
LV1	Eggs case P 03/06/6	20.12.04	*http://www.competition.lv*	NCA, first phase	Food
LV2	Hanzas maiznicas P 05/06/2	29.03.06	*http://www.competition.lv*	NCA, first phase	Food
LV3	Advertising agencies P 05/906/3	08.05.06	*http://www.competition.lv*	NCE, first phase	Services

LUXEMBOURG:

No.	NAME AND CASE NUMBER	DATE	SOURCE	AUTHORITY AND TYPE OF DECISION	SECTOR
L1	Wintergarten Feddersen 37.928	09.03.90	Greffe	Trib. Arr. Luxembourg	Construction

No.	NAME AND CASE NUMBER	DATE	SOURCE	AUTHORITY AND TYPE OF DECISION	SECTOR
L2	Univers du Cuir 40.112	26.04.91	Greffe	Trib. Arr. Luxembourg	Retail
L3	Coditel 8.992–9.015	18.11.94	Greffe	Conseil d'État	Media
L4	Aral—Koepfler 48.053–49.567	24.03.00	Greffe	Trib. Arr. Luxembourg	Energy
L5	Lamesch—Oeko-Services 9.760	13.11.02	Pasicrisie administrative	Tribunal Administratif	Waste
L6	ICS Renting—Étoile 29.724	30.03.06	E-competitions	Cour d'Appel Luxembourg	Motor vehicle
L7	X—Inspection de la concurrence	05.03.07	*http://www.ja.etat.lu*	Tribunal Administratif	Construction
L8	X	30.04.07	Conseil de la concurrence	Conseil de la concurrence	Construction
L9	Rock—Tanklux 2007–FO–01	23.04.07	Conseil de la concurrence	Conseil de la concurrence	Energy

THE NETHERLANDS (NL):

No.	NAME AND CASE NUMBER	DATE	SOURCE	AUTHORITY AND TYPE OF DECISION	SECTOR
NL1	Heineken—out of home agreements 2036	28.05.02	*http://www.nmanet.nl*	NCA, exemption	Beer
NL2	Superunie v Interpay 2978	28.03.03	*http://www.nmanet.nl*	NCA, rejection of complaint (art 82), objective justification	Banking
NL3	North Sea Shrimps 2269	28.12.04	*http://www.nmanet.nl*	NCA, fines	Shrimps
NL4	Texaco petrol stations LJN: AT8817	23.06.05	*http://www.rechtspraak.nl*	Lower Court, imposition of fines(cartel)	Gas stations
NL5	Bicycle Producers 1615	24.11.05	*http://www.nmanet.nl*	NCA, decision after objection, relationship EC and national law	Bicycles
NL6	Secon Group/G-Star LJN: AU8309	07.12.05	*http://www.rechtspraak.nl*	Trade and Industry Appeals Tribunal, imposition of fines (cartel)	Retail
NL7	ModintLJN: AU5316	28.10.05	*http://www.rechtspraak.nl*	Trade and Industry Appeals Tribunal, imposition of fines (cartel)	Retail
NL8	Interpay NL 2910	21.12.05	*http://www.nmanet.nl*	NCA, decision after objection	Banking

No.	NAME AND CASE NUMBER	DATE	SOURCE	AUTHORITY AND TYPE OF DECISION	SECTOR
NL9	Mobile operators LJN: AY4035	13.07.06	*http://www.rechtspraak.nl*	Lower Court, imposition of fines (cartel)	Mobile operators

SLOVAKIA (SK):

No.	NAME AND CASE NUMBER	DATE	SOURCE	AUTHORITY AND TYPE OF DECISION	SECTOR
SK1	General health insurance company 2002/DZ/0/1/061	09.04.02	*http://www.antimon.gov.sk*	NCA, Abuse of dominance	Social security
SK2	Airport Bratislava 2005/DZ/2/1/127	30.11.05	*http://www.antimon.gov.sk*	NCA, Abuse of dominance	Transportation
SK3	Slovak Telecom 2005/DZ/2/1/133	14.12.05	*http://www.antimon.gov.sk*	NCA, Abuse of dominance	Telecommunication
SK4	Railway company 2005/65/R/1/093	09.09.05	*http://www.antimon.gov.sk*	NCA, Abuse of dominance	Transportation
SK5	Slovak Telekom 2005/DZ/R/2/143	21.12.05	*http://www.antimon.gov.sk*	NCA, Abuse of dominance	Telecommunication
SK6	Highways 2005/KH/1/1/137	23.12.05	*http://www.antimon.gov.sk*	NCA, Cartel agreement	Transportation

SPAIN (ES):

No.	NAME AND CASE NUMBER	DATE	SOURCE	AUTHORITY AND TYPE OF DECISION	SECTOR
ES1	Cajas Rurales Jalón Zaragoza A249/98	15.11.99	*http://www.tdcompetencia.es*	TDC, Authorisation of a minor agreement	Financial Services
ES2	Hardi International 457/99	27.03.00	*http://www.tdcompetencia.es*	TDC, Non competence clause, Limitation period	Farm machinery
ES3	CEPSA 493/00	30.05.01	*http://www.tdcompetencia.es*	TDC, Fuel exclusive distribution	Energy
ES4	Hidroeléctrica de l'Emporda 495/01	16.04.02		Audiencia Provincial of Gerona, Damages	Energy

No.	NAME AND CASE NUMBER	DATE	SOURCE	AUTHORITY AND TYPE OF DECISION	SECTOR
ES5	Pepsi-Cola/Coca-Cola r 508/02v	22.07.02	*http://www.tdcompetencia..es*	TDC, Legal privilege	Food
ES6	Telefónica/3c 9710/97	06.03.03	*http://www.poderjudicial.es*	TS, Refusal to supply	Telecommunications
ES7	Autoescuelas Alcalá 525/00	11.04.03	N/A	AN, Imposition fines	Driving school
ES8	Tabacos Canarias 915/02	13.12.04	*http://www.poderjudicial.es*	TS, Predatory pricing	Tobacco
ES9	Expertos inmobiliarios 3895/02	09.03.05	*http://www.poderjudicial.es*	TS, Attenuatting circumstances	Property
ES10	BT/Telefónica 4777/03	23.03.05	*http://www.poderjudicial.es*	TS, Repeated infringement	Telecommunications
ES11	Retevisión/Telefónica 9174/2003	20.06.06	*http://www.poderjudicial.es*	TS, Abuse of dominance	Telecommunications
ES12	Astel/Telefónica 162/2004	31.01.07	N/A	AN, Abuse of dominance, fines	Telecommunications

SWEDEN (SE):

No.	NAME AND CASE NUMBER	DATE	SOURCE	AUTHORITY AND TYPE OF DECISION	SECTOR
SE1	NCC AB and others v SCA Dnr A 1/04, MD 2004:21	07.09.04	*http://www.marknadsdomstolen.se/avgoranden2004/Dom04-21.pdf*	Administrative Supreme Court, interlocutory judgment	Road construction
SE2	Boliden Mineral AB v Fortum, Värme T 2280–02	23.12.04	N/A	Supreme Court, civil litigation	Energy
SE3	VVS-Installatörerna v SCA, Dnr A 3/04, MD 2005:5	09.02.05	*http://www.marknadsdomstolen.se/avgoranden2005/Dom05-05.pdf*	Administrative Supreme Court, imposition of fines (price agreement)	Construction sector
SE4	Norsk Hydro Olje AB and others, v SCA Dnr A, 2/03, MD 2005:7	22.02.05	*http://www.marknadsdomstolen.se/avgoranden2005/Dom05-07.pdf*	Administrative Supreme Court, imposition of fines (cartel)	Motor fuels
SE5	Keyvent AB and others v SCA, T 11660–03	14.03.05	N/A	Lower Court, imposition of fines (cartel)	Ventilation
SE6	Banverket Dnr 485/2005	06.10.05		NCA, abuse of dominant position	Railway transportation

No.	NAME AND CASE NUMBER	DATE	SOURCE	AUTHORITY AND TYPE OF DECISION	SECTOR
SE7	B2 Bredband Holding/ Telia, Sonera AB Dnr A 7/04, MD 2005:29	01.11.05	*http://www.marknadsdomstolen.se/ avgoranden2005/Dom05-29.pdf*	Administrative Supreme Court, abuse of dominant position	Telecom
SE8	Aktiebolaget Bil-Bengtsson and others v SCA T 4231–04	07.06.06	N/A	Lower Court, imposition of fines (cartel)	Motor vehicle retail sales
SE9	Assistancekåren Sverige AB and others v SCA T 15163–04	01.09.06	N/A	Lower Court, imposition of fines (cartel)	Towing
SE10	Biljett Direkt Ticnet Dnr 444/2005	07.03.07	*http://www.kkv.se*	NCA, abuse of dominant position	Event ticketing retail sales

PORTUGAL (PT):

No.	NAME AND CASE NUMBER	DATE	SOURCE	AUTHORITY AND TYPE OF DECISION	SECTOR
PT1	Portuguese Veterinary Medical Association 28/04	19.05.05	*http://www.autoridadeda concorrencia.pt/ Download/ comunicado2005_7.pdf*	Portuguese Competition Authority, Decision relating to a proceeding pursuant to Art.4 of the Law No. 18/2003, of 11 June, and Art.81 of the EC Treaty	Fixing of fees by a professional association
PT2	Portuguese Veterinary Medical Association 1302/058.5TYLSB	12.01.06	3rd Division of the Lisbon Court of Commerce	Lisbon Court of Commerce, Portuguese Veterinary Medical Association v PCA	Fixing of fees by a professional association
PT3	Portuguese Veterinary Medical Association 8638/06	None		Lisbon Court of Appeal, none (case pending)	Fixing of fees by a professional association
PT4	Portuguese Veterinary Medical Association	19.07.05	*http://www.autoridadeda concorrencia.pt/Download/ comunicado2005_7.pdf*	Portuguese Competition Authority, Decision relating to a proceeding pursuant to Art.46 of the Law No.18/2003, of June 11 (periodic penalty payment)	Fixing of fees by a professional association

No.	NAME AND CASE NUMBER	DATE	SOURCE	AUTHORITY AND TYPE OF DECISION	SECTOR
PT5	Portuguese Veterinary Medical Association 1371/05.5TYLSB	09.03.06	3rd Division of the Lisbon Court of Commerce	Lisbon Court of Commerce, Portuguese Veterinary Medical Association v PCA	Fixing of fees by a professional association
PT6	Portuguese Medical Association 7/2005	26.05.06	*http://www.autoridadedaconcorrencia.pt/Download/comunicado2006_14.pdf*	Portuguese Competition Authority, Decision relating to a proceeding pursuant to Article 4 (1a) of the Law No. 18/2003, of 11 June, and Article 81 (1a) of the EC Treaty	Fixing of fees by a professional association
PT7	Portuguese Medical Association 851/06.2TYLSB	18.01.07	3rd Division of the Lisbon Court of Commerce	Lisbon Court of Commerce, Portuguese Medical Association v PCA	Fixing of fees by a professional association
PT8	Portuguese Medical Association 5.352/07	Case pending	9thDivision of the Lisbon Court of Appeal	Lisbon Court of Appeal	Fixing of fees by a professional association
PT9	Nestlé 31/04	20.04.06	*http://www.autoridadedaconcorrencia.pt/Download/comunicado2006_9.pdf*	Portuguese Competition Authority, Decision relating to a proceeding pursuant to Art.4 (1) of the Law No.18/2003, of June 11, pursuant to Art.43 (1a) of Law No.18/2003, of 11 June	Market of roasted coffee and high roasted coffee
PT10	Nestlé 766/06.4TYLSB	15.02.07	2nd Division of the Lisbon Court of Commerce	Lisbon Court of Commerce, Nestlé Portugal, S.A. v PCA	Market of roasted coffee and high roasted coffee
PT11	GESTIRETALHO	Not available (2003)		Portuguese Competition Authority, Decision relating to a proceeding pursuant to Art.3 (1) of the Law No.370/93, of October 29, pursuant Art.5 (2) of the Law No.370/93, of October 29	Sale of consumer goods in a commercial establishment
PT12	GESTIRETALHO 662/03.7TYLSB	18.01.06	1st Division of the Lisbon Court of Commerce	Lisbon Court of Commerce, Gestiretalho—Gestão e Consultoria para a Distribuição a Retalho, S.A. v PCA	Sale of consumer goods in a commercial establishment

No.	NAME AND CASE NUMBER	DATE	SOURCE	AUTHORITY AND TYPE OF DECISION	SECTOR
PT13	Johnson & Johnson, Abbott, Bayer, Menarini, and Roche (pharmaceutical companies' cartel) 4/2005	28.12.04/ 06.10.05	*http://www.autoridadedaconcorrencia.pt/Download/comunicado2005_1.pdf* *http://www.autoridadedaconcorrencia.pt/Download/comunicado2005_10.pdf* *http://www.autoridadedaconcorrencia.pt/Download/comunicado2005_10.pdf*	Portuguese Competition Authority, Decision relating to a proceeding pursuant to Art.4 of the Law No.18/2003, of June 11	Pharmaceuticals; public tender; reactive product to determine the amount of blood sugar
PT14	Johnson & Johnson, Abbott, Bayer, Menarini, and Roche (pharmaceutical companies' cartel) 1697/05.0TYLSB	26.04.07	1st Division of the Lisbon Court of Commerce	Lisbon Court of Commerce, Johnson & Johnson, Lda., Abbott Laboratórios, Lda., Bayer Diagnostics Europe, Ltd., Menarini Diagnósticos, Lda., and Bayer Portugal, S.A. v PCA	Pharmaceuticals; public tender; reactive product to determine the amount of blood sugar

UNITED KINGDOM (UK):

No.	NAME AND CASE NUMBER	DATE	SOURCE	AUTHORITY AND TYPE OF DECISION	SECTOR
CAT decisions on liability					
UK1	Albion Water Limited v Director General of Water Services (1) [2006] CAT 36	19.01.07	*http://www.cattribunal.org.uk*	NCA, appeal discontinued	Water
UK2	Floe Telecom Limited (in Administration) v Ofcom [2006] CAT 17	31.08.06	*http://www.cattribunal.org.uk*	NCA, appeal discontinued	Telecommunications
UK3	London Metal Exchange V OFT [1062/1/1/06	15.05.06	*http://www.cattribunal.org.uk*	NCA, appeal dismissed	Electronic Trading Platforms
UK4	Mastercard UK Members Forum Limited v OFT [2006] CAT 14	10.07.06	*http://www.cattribunal.org.uk*	NCA, annulment	Banking

No.	NAME AND CASE NUMBER	DATE	SOURCE	AUTHORITY AND TYPE OF DECISION	SECTOR
UK5	Genzyme v OFT [2004] CAT 29	11.03.04	*http://www.cattribunal.org.uk*	NCA, appeal dismissed	Pharmaceuticals
UK6	JJ Burgess and Sons v OFT [2005 CAT 25	06.07.05	*http://www.cattribunal.org.uk*	NCA, annulment	Funeral services
UK7	JJB Sports plc v OFT [2004] CAT 17	01.10.04	*http://www.cattribunal.org.uk*	NCA, partially annulled	Replica football kits
UK8	Argos v OFT [2004] CAT 24	14.11.04	*http://www.cattribunal.org.uk*	NCA, appeal dismissed	Supply of toys
UK9	Apex Asphalt and Paving Co OFT [2005] CAT 4	24.02.05	*http://www.cattribunal.org.uk*	NCA, appeal dismissed	Construction
UK10	Pernod Ricard/Campbell Distillers Ltd v OFT [2004] CAT 10	10.06.04	*http://www.cattribunal.org.uk*	NCA, appeal discontinued	White Rum
UK11	Association of British Insurers v OFT [1036/1/1/04]	30.07.04	*http://www.cattribunal.org.uk*	NCA, appeal not contested	Insurance
UK12	Aberdeen Journals v Director General Of Fair Trading [2003] CAT 11	23.06.03	*http://www.cattribunal.org.uk*	NCA, appeal dismissed	Advertising
UK13	BetterCare Group Ltd v Director General of Fair Trading [2002] CAT 7	01.08.02	*http://www.cattribunal.org.uk*	NCA, annulment	Nursing home care
UK14	Institute of Independent Insurance Brokers and Association of British Travel Agents v Director General of Fair Trading [1002/2/1/01]	17.09.01	*http://www.cattribunal.org.uk*	NCA, annulment	Insurance
UK15	Napp Pharmaceuticals Holdings Limited v Director General ofFair Trading [1001/1/1/01]	15.01.02	*http://www.cattribunal.org.uk*	NCA, appeal dismissed	Pharmaceuticals

No.	NAME AND CASE NUMBER	DATE	SOURCE	AUTHORITY AND TYPE OF DECISION	SECTOR
OFT and Other Regulatory Decisions under CA98					
UK16	Associated Newspapers Ltd	02.03.06	*http://www.oft.gov.uk*	NCA, Exclusive arrangements	Newspapers
UK17	TV Eye	24.04.05	*http://www.oft.gov.uk*	NCA, Collective agreements	Telecommunications
UK18	Association of British Insurers	22.04.04	*http://www.oft.gov.uk*	NCA, Industry wide termsInsurance	
UK19	Pool Reinsurance Company Ltd	15.04.04	*http://www.oft.gov.uk*	NCA, Industry wide terms	Insurance
UK20	Lladro Commercial Agreements	31.03.03	*http://www.oft.gov.uk*	NCA, Resale price maintenance	Supply of porcelain
UK21	Bacardi exclusive distribution Agreements	30.01.03	*http://www.oft.gov.uk*	NCA, Abuse of dominance	Alcoholic beverages
UK22	General Insurance Standards Code	13.11.02	*http://www.oft.gov.uk*	NCA, Industry code	Insurance
UK23	The Society of Film Distributors	01.02.02	*http://www.oft.gov.uk*	NCA, Industry conditions	Film
UK24	Memorandum of Understanding On supply of oil in emergencies	26.10.01	*http://www.oft.gov.uk*	NCA, Exemption	Energy
UK25	Link ATM rules	16.10.01	*http://www.oft.gov.uk*	NCA, Exemption	Banking
UK26	Schools: exchange of information On future fees	20.11.06	*http://www.oft.gov.uk*	NCA, exchange of price	School fees
National Court Decisions					
UK27	James E McCabe Ltd v Scottish Courage Ltd [2006] EWHC 538	28.03.06	*http://www.bailii.org/*	Lower Court	Beer
UK28	Adidas-Salomon AG v Drape & Others [2006] EWHC 1318	07.06.06	*http://www.bailii.org/*	Lower Court	Sports sponsorship

No.	NAME AND CASE NUMBER	DATE	SOURCE	AUTHORITY AND TYPE OF DECISION	SECTOR
UK29	Provimi v Aventis [2003] EWHC 961	02.05.03	*http://www.bailii.org/*	Lower Court	Vitamins
UK30	Courage v Crehan [2006] UKHL 38	19.07.06	*http://www.bailii.org/*	Supreme Court	Beer
UK31	Attheraces v British Horseracing Board [2007] EWCA Civ 38	02.02.07	*http://www.bailii.org/*	Supreme Court	Telecommunications
UK32	English Welsh & Scottish Railways Ltd v E.On UK Ltd and Office of Rail Regulation [2007] EWHC 599 (Comm)	23.03.07	*http://www.bailii.org/*	Lower Court	Railways
UK33	Argos v OFT and JJB Sports V OFT [2006] EWCA Civ 1318	19.10.06	*http://www.cat.org.uk*	Supreme Court	Toys/Football kits

TABLE 17

LIST OF NATIONAL DECISIONS: MERGERS

BELGIUM (BE):

No.	NAME AND CASE NUMBER	DATE	SOURCE	AUTHORITY AND TYPE OF DECISION	SECTOR
BE M2	Belgacom—Vodafone Belgium—Belgacom Mobile CONC-C/C–06/0036	30.10.06	*http://mineco.fgov.be/organization_market/competition/competition_council/competition_nl_007_bis.htm*	NCA, first phase	Telecoms
BE M1	Kinepolis Remedies	16.04.07	*http://mineco.fgov.be/organization_market/competition/competition_council/competition_nl_007_bis.htm*	NCA, remedies revocation	Cinemas

BULGARIA (BG):

No.	NAME AND CASE NUMBER	DATE	SOURCE	AUTHORITY AND TYPE OF DECISION	SECTOR
BG M1	CPC Decision No.08/2005	22.12.05	*http://www.cpc.bg/system/storage/resh–308.doc*	NCA, first phase	Telecommunications
BG M2	CPC Decision No.141/2005	19.05.05	*http://www.cpc.bg/system/storage/resh–141.doc*	NCA, first phase	Beer Production

CYPRUS (CY):

No.	NAME AND CASE NUMBER	DATE	SOURCE	AUTHORITY AND TYPE OF DECISION	SECTOR
CY M1	Ansaldo Engineering S.p.A/Thomassen Turbine Systems BV, CaseM1	11.01.07	*http://competition.gov.cy*	NCA, Delay in notification	Energy
CY M2	Lanitis Bros Public Ltd./ Coca Cola Hellenic Bottling Co. S.A, Case M2	13.03.06	*http://competition.gov.cy*	NCA, Cooperation Agreements	Soft drinks
CY M3	Darbo S.A.S./Sonae Industria, SGPS S.A., Case M3	17.10.06	*http://competition.gov.cy*	NCA, First phase	Timber production
CY M4	MTN International (Mauritius) Investcom/ Areeba Limited, Case M4	17.10.06	*http://competition.gov.cy*	NCA, Delay in notification	Telecommunications

DENMARK (DK):

No.	NAME AND CASE NUMBER	DATE	SOURCE	AUTHORITY AND TYPE OF DECISION	SECTOR
DK M1	Post Danmark	30.08.06	*http://www.ks.dk/english/competition/ national/2006/postdanmark_/*	NCA, first phase	Mail
DK M2	TV2 Sport	11.04.07	*http://www.ks.dk/konkurrence/ afgoerelser/2007/r1104/tv2sport/ (Danish version only)*	NCA, first phase	Television and Media

ESTONIA (EST):

No.	NAME AND CASE NUMBER	DATE	SOURCE	AUTHORITY AND TYPE OF DECISION	SECTOR
EST M1	VP Market/Soldino Kaubandus	01.12.06	*http://www.konkurentsiamet.ee*	NCA, first phase approval	Food

EST M2	Philip Morris/Amer	25.08.04	*http://www.konkurentsiamet.ee*	NCA, second phase approval	Tobacco
EST M3	A.Le Coq/Finelin	11.11.03	*http://www.konkurentsiamet.ee*	NCA, second phase approval	Beverages

No.	NAME AND CASE NUMBER	DATE	SOURCE	AUTHORITY AND TYPE OF DECISION	SECTOR
EST M4	A.Le Coq/Finelin	24.08.04	*http://www.konkurentsiamet.ee*	NCA, second phase approval	Beverages
EST M5	Wōro Kommerts/Oskar LT	27.11.06	*http://www.konkurentsiamet.ee*	NCA, first phase approval	Food
EST M6	Elion Ettevõtted/ MicroLink	21.10.05	*http://www.konkurentsiamet.ee*	NCA, second phase approval	Telecom
EST M7	Akos Apteek—Konkurentsiamet	14.06.05	*http://www.kola.just.ee*	Lower Court, finding of illegality	Pharmac.

FRANCE (FM):

No.	NAME AND CASE NUMBER	DATE	SOURCE	AUTHORITY AND TYPE OF DECISION	SECTOR
F M1	France Antilles	31.01.07	*http://www.conseil-etat.fr*	French Administrative Supreme Court[1] Annulment of the decision of the FME	Press
F M2	TPS / CanalSat C.06–02	30.08.06	*http://www.art-telecom.com*	FME, 2nd phase, Remedies	Pay channel
F M3	Cegid/CCMX, C 2004–122	19.10.04	*http://www.minefi.gouv.fr*	FME, 1st phase	Softwares
F M4	Fiducial (Cegid), 279180	20.07.05	*http://www.u-paris2.fr*	FASC, order an opinion from the FCC	Softwares
F M5	Cegid/CCMX, 05–A–24	14.12.05	*http://www.conseil-concurrence.fr*	French competition council's[2] opinion	Softwares
F M6	Fiducial (Cegid), 279180	13.02.06	*http://listes.cru.fr*	FASC, clearance	Softwares
F M7	TPS/CanalSat, Opinion 06–A–13	13.07.06	*http://www.art-telecom.com*	Opinion	Pay channel
F M8	Seb/Moulinex, 02–A–07	15.05.02	*http://www.minefi.gouv.fr*	French competition council's opinion	Manufacturing & sale of small electrical appliances
F M9	Seb/Moulinex, C2002–2	05.07.02	*http://www.minefi.gouv.fr*	FME, 2nd phase, clearance	Manufacturing & sale of small electrical appliances

[1] French Administrative Supreme Court (*Conseil d'Etat*, hereafter "**FASC**").
2 French competition council (*Conseil de la concurrence*, hereafter "**FCC**").

No.	NAME AND CASE NUMBER	DATE	SOURCE	AUTHORITY AND TYPE OF DECISION	SECTOR
F M10	Philips (Seb/Moulinex), 249262	06.02.04	*http://www.minefi.gouv.fr*	FACS, annulment	Manufacturing & sale of small electrical appliances
F M11	Seb/Moulinex, 04–A–16	28.07.04	*http://www.minefi.gouv.fr*	French competition council's opinion	Manufacturing & sale of small electrical appliances
F M12	Seb/Moulinex, C2004–40	16.08.04	*http://www.minefi.gouv.fr*	FME, 2nd phase, clearance	Manufacturing & sale of small electrical appliances

GERMANY (DE):

No.	NAME AND CASE NUMBER	DATE	SOURCE	AUTHORITY AND TYPE OF DECISION	SECTOR
DE M1	Leggett&Platt/AGRO B5–170/03	29.09.04	*http://www.bundeskartellamt.de*	FCO, second phase annulment	Furniture
DE M2	CIE/Ish B7–38/05	21.06.05	*http://www.bundeskartellamt.de*	FCO, second phase approval	Media
DE M3	Springer/Pro7Sat1 B6–92/02	19.01.06	*http://www.bundeskartellamt.de*	FCO, second phase annulment	Media
DE M4	AKK/UKE B10–90/05	08.03.06	*http://www.bundeskartellamt.de*	FCO, second phase approval	Healthcare
DE M5	RTL/n-tv B6–142/05	11.04.06	*http://www.bundeskartellamt.de*	FCO, second phase approval	Media
DE M6	National Geographic I KVR 32/05	12.10.06	*http://www.bundesgerichtshof.de*	Federal Court of Justice, annulment of FCO's decision	Media
DE M7	Coherent/Excel B7–97/06	25.10.06	*http://www.bundeskartellamt.de*	FCO, second phase annulment*	Laser
DE M8	National Geographic II KVR 12/06	16.01.07	*http://www.bundesgerichtshof.de*	Federal Court of Justice, confirmation of FCO's annulment	Media
DE M9	Sulzer/Kemix B5–10/07	14.02.07	*http://www.bundeskartellamt.de*	FCO, annulment and demerger because of completion without clearance	Healthcare
DE M10	RWE/Saar Ferngas B8–62/06	12.03.07	*http://www.bundeskartellamt.de*	FCO, second phase annulment	Energy
DE M11	E.ON/Eschwege VI–2 Kart 7/04 (V)	06.06.07	*http://www.justiz.nrw.de*	Higher Regional Court of Düsseldorf, confirmation of FCO's annulment	Energy

HUNGARY (H):

No.	NAME AND CASE NUMBER	DATE	SOURCE	AUTHORITY AND TYPE OF DECISION	SECTOR
H M1	Csemege-Julius Meinl/ Alfa Vj-96/1999	15.11.99	*http://www.gvh.hu*	NCA, first phase	Retail (foodstuff)
H M2	Renault S.A. Vj-101/1999	31.8.99	*http://www.gvh.hu*	NCA, first phase	Motor
H M3	MOL/Slovnaft Vj-70/2000	1.9.00	*http://www.gvh.hu*	NCA, second phase	Chemicals
H M4	Holcim Vj-16/2001	9.8.01	*http://www.gvh.hu*	NCA, first phase	Construction
H M5	MOL/TVK Vj-100/2001	7.11.01	*http://www.gvh.hu*	NCA, second phase	Chemicals
H M6	Baucont Vj-80/2003	21.8.03	*http://www.gvh.hu*	NCA, first phase	Construction
H M7	B.V. Tabora/ Népszabadság/Ringier Vj-169/2004	26.4.05	*http://www.gvh.hu*	NCA, second phase	Printed media
H M8	Maspex/Apenta Vj-137/2005	29.9.05	*http://www.gvh.hu*	NCA, first phase	Food industry
H M9	Ringier/Népszabadság/ Sanoma/ F-Log Vj-116/2006	20.11.06	*http://www.gvh.hu*	NCA, second phase	Printed media

ITALY (I):

No.	NAME AND CASE NUMBER	DATE	SOURCE	AUTHORITY AND TYPE OF DECISION	SECTOR
I M1	Emilcarta/Agrifood Machinery	29.07.04	*http://www.agcm.it*	NCA(AGCM), Decision: non compliance with merger prohibition	Packaging
I M2	Radiotelevisione italiana / Rami di azienda	29.04.04	*http://www.agcm.it*	NCA(AGCM),Phase II Merger Decision: authorization without conditions	Television
I M3	Sai/La Fondiaria	12.06.03	*http://www.agcm.it*	NCA(AGCM),Phase II Merger Decision: authorization without conditions	Insurance
I M4	Koninklijke Numico/Mellin	15.06.05	*http://www.agcm.it*	NCA(AGCM), Phase II Merger Decision: authorization with conditions	Milk industry

LATVIA (LV):

No.	NAME AND CASE NUMBER	DATE	SOURCE	AUTHORITY AND TYPE OF DECISION	SECTOR
LV M1	LATTELEKOM/ MICROLINK 497/05/10/3	29.06.05	*http://www.competition.lv*	NCA, first phase	Services/Telecom
LV M2	Neste P 06/05/1	31.05.06	*http://www.competition.lv*	NCA, first phase	Goods/Oil
LV M3	LMT/ZetCOM 222/07/10/01	25.05.07	*http://www.competition.lv*	NCA, first phase	Services/Telecom

THE NETHERLANDS (NL):

No.	NAME AND CASE NUMBER	DATE	SOURCE	AUTHORITY AND TYPE OF DECISION	SECTOR
NL M1	Werner Söderström—Malmberg 4140	01.11.04	*http://www.nmanet.nl*	NCA, first phaseclearance	Magazines
NL M2	Stichting Eveab Zorg—de Weerden 4177	15.11.04	*http://www.nmanet.nl*	NCA, firts phase clearance	Hospital
NL M3	UPC-Canal+ 4490	28.06.05	*http://www.nmanet.nl*	NCA, second phase clearance	Cable networks
NL M4	KPN—Nozema Services 5454	06.03.06	*http://www.nmanet.nl*	NCA, first phaseclearance	Television transmission
NL M5	Ziekenhuis Hilvesum—Ziekenhuis Gooi-Noord 3897	08.06.05	*http://www.nmanet.nl*	NCA, second phaseHospitalpermission services	
NL M6	HHvL—SWS 4173	16.06.06	*http://www.nmanet.nl*	NCA, second phaseSocial housing permission	
NL M7	Nuon—Reliant Energy Europe LJN:AZ3274	28.11.06	*http://www.rechtspraak.nl*	Trade and Industry Appeals Tribunal, appeal to merger decision	Energy
NL M8	Cinven/Warburg Pincus—Essent Kabelcom	02.12.06	*http://www.nmanet.nl*	NCA, first phase clearance	Cable networks, television transmission

Table 17

PORTUGAL (PT):

No.	NAME AND CASE NUMBER	DATE	SOURCE	AUTHORITY AND TYPE OF DECISION	SECTOR
PT M1	Barraqueiro/Arriva (ATMS) Ccent. N. Á 37/2004	25.11.05	*http://www.autoridadeda concorrencia.pt/Download/ communicado2005_12.pdf*	Portuguese Competition Authority, Decision to oppose the concentration	Roadway and railway public transports None
PT M2	Via Oeste (Brisa)—Auto-estradas do Oeste/Auto-estradas do Atlântico Ccent. N. Á 22/2005	07.04.06	*http://www.autoridadeda concorrencia.pt/Download/ 2005_22_final_net.pdf*	Portuguese Competition Authority, Decision to oppose the concentration	Transports/Highways
	Via Oeste (Brisa)—Auto-estradas do Oeste/Auto-estradas do Atlântico Ccent. N. Á 22/2005	07.06.06	*http://www.reckon.co.uk/temp/ i005815.pdfMinister of the Economy and Innovation, Decision to authorize the concentrationTransports/HighwaysNone*		
PT M3	Sonaecom/PT AC—I—08/2006	22.12.06	*http://www.autoridadeda concorrencia.pt/Download/ 2006_08_final_net.pdf*	Portuguese Competition Authority, Decision to authorise the concentration	Telecommunications

SLOVAKIA (SK):

No.	NAME AND CASE NUMBER	DATE	SOURCE	AUTHORITY AND TYPE OF DECISION	SECTOR
SK M1	Tesco, 2006/FH/3/1/146	29.12.06	*http://www.antimon.gov.sk*	NCA, first phase	Retail

SPAIN (ES):

No.	NAME AND CASE NUMBER	DATE	SOURCE	AUTHORITY AND TYPE OF DECISION	SECTOR
ES M1	Unión Radio/Antena 3 Radio 533/1994	09.06.00	*http://www.poderjudicial.es*	TS	Media /publicity
ES M2	Salcai/Utinsa 1602/2000	01.04.02	*http://www.poderjudicial.es*	TS	Transport of persons
ES M3	Prosegur/Blindados del Norte 1585/2000	02.04.02	*http://www.poderjudicial.es*	TS	Vigilance services

SWEDEN (SE):

No.	NAME AND CASE NUMBER	DATE	SOURCE	AUTHORITY AND TYPE OF DECISION	SECTOR
SE M1	DONG Naturgas A/S/ Nova Supply AB Dnr 556/2004	06.10.04	Dnr 556/2004	NCA, second phase approval (without undertakings)	Energy
SE M2	Swedish Meats ek. för./ SLP Pärsons AB Dnr 123/2006	10.05.06	Dnr 123/2006	NCA, first phase approval (without undertakings)	Food-stuffs
SE M3	Posten AB/Strålfors AB Dnr 251/2006	12.05.06	Dnr 251/2006	NCA, first phase approval (with undertakings)	Postal

UNITED KINGDOM (UK):

Appeals of merger decisions

No.	NAME AND CASE NUMBER	DATE	SOURCE	AUTHORITY AND TYPE OF DECISION	SECTOR
UK M1	Stericycle v Competition Commission	23.03.07	*http://www.cat.org.uk*	CAT, appeal Healthcare	
UK M2	Stericycle and STG v Competition Commission	19.09.06	*http://www.cat.org.uk*	CAT, appeal of interim remedies	Healthcare
UK M3	Celesio AG v OFT	09.05.06	*http://www.cat.org.uk*	CAT, appeal	Retail pharmacy (NB costs)
UK M4	Somerfield v Competition Commission	13.02.06	*http://www.cat.org.uk*	CAT, appeal	Grocery market
UK M5	Unichem v OFT	01.04.05	*http://www.cat.org.uk*	CAT, appeal	Pharmaceuticals (NB costs)
UK M6	OFT and Others v IBA Health	19.02.04	*http://www.cat.org.uk*	Supreme Court, appeal dismissed	Healthcare

No.	NAME AND CASE NUMBER	DATE	SOURCE	AUTHORITY AND TYPE OF DECISION	SECTOR
Second Phase decisions under the Enterprise Act 2002					
UK M7	(Waterstone's/Ottakar's)	12.05.06	*http://www.competition-commission.org.uk/*	CC, second phase	Sale of retail books to consumers
UK M8	Somerfield/115 Morrison stores	02.09.05	*http://www.competition-commission.org.uk/*	CC, second phase	Grocery market
UK M9	Corus UK Limited's hot—rolled Steel sheet piling business/Arcelor SpA	10.02.05	*http://www.competition-commission.org.uk/*	CC, second phase	Steel
First phase approval decisions on acceptance of undertakings in lieu of a reference					
UK M10	Aggregate Industries/ Foster Yeoman	29.11.06	*http://www.oft.gov.uk/*	OFT, first phase, undertakings	Aggregates and asphalt

INDEX

(all references are to page number)